UTTARAKHAND

Concepts in Communication Informatics & Librarianship
(CICIL)

For a list of titles in the series,
see pp. 517-520 at the end of the book

About the Authors

J. C. Aggarwal (*b.* 1928), former Deputy Director of Education/Executive Director of Delhi Bureau of Textbooks, Delhi Administration has a varied experience in the field of education. He has singly/jointly authored about 150 books on Education, Social Sciences and Current Problems. In collaboration with S.P. Agrawal, he has written *Modern History of Kashmir, Modern History of Punjab, Documentation Encyclopaedia of UNESCO and Education* (in two Parts); *Women's Education in India; National Policy on Education: Agenda for India 2001; Indian Writings on Education, 1979 to 1986,* and *Vocational Education in India.*

His other recent publications include: *Essentials of Educational Psychology; Teacher Functions and Education in a Developing Society, Eighth Five Year Plan, Learning without Burden, Education Policy 1992, Vedas for the Young, etc.*

S.P. Agrawal (*b.* 1929) was Director, National Social Science Documentation Centre, (ICSSR) Government of India and Member Secretary, Indian Association of Social Science Institutions. He was also the Vice-Chairman of the Asia and Pacific Information Network in Social Sciences (APINESS). In 1988 he was awarded the degree of Doctor of Philosophy in Education *(Honoris Causa)* by International University Foundation. Presently, he is Member, Round Table on Research in Reading, IFLA, and Member, International Committee for Social Science Information and Documention. He is also Member of Board of Studies of National Archives of India and Hindi Advisory Committee, Ministry of Coal, Government of India. Born and brought up in the cradle of freedom movement which he joined at the tender age of twelve, he gained an insight into political problems and developed a sense of responsibility which bore fruit as an information scientist committed to Gandhiji's philosophy and action-plan in the field and its social concept. He has written extensively on various aspects of education, Indian Polity and library and information science.

Concept in Communication
Informatics & Librarianship-69

General Editor: **S. P. Agrawal**

UTTARAKHAND

Past, Present and Future

Specifically written Chapters by
Dr. Shanti S. Gupta
Vice-chancellor, Agra University

J. C. Aggarwal
S.P. Agrawal

CONCEPT PUBLISHING COMPANY, NEW DELHI - 110059

ISBN 81-7022-572-8

First Published 1995

Published and Printed by
Ashok Kumar Mittal
Concept Publishing Company
A/15-16, Commercial Block, Mohan Garden
NEW DELHI - 110059 (India)

General Editor's Introduction

Lack of Accessibility and Accountability, Pandora's Box theory for justification of Inaction, and Power-Intoxicated Blindness—are the different dimensions of the present problems of once spiritually illustrious and magnificent Uttarakhand of Uttar Pradesh.

Jallianwallabagh outrage in 1919 (for the then power-less Indians) *or* no-Jallianwallabagh—but simply a measure to contain anti-administration activities (for powerfull Britishers-in-power), Save (!) Ayodhya (for *Maulana* Mulayam Singh Yadav—as nicknamed thus) *or* Save-Our-souls on the crowd by government forces), Welfare of OBCs (for delusioned V.P. Singh as called then, by killing the very virtues of welfare) *or* no-Welfare sacrifices to Save-Our-Society (for non-reservationist students), and now in 1994, Allahabad High Court Violence by never-before-heard Government call and Muzaffarnagar killings of unoffending processionists and rapes of women participants—an act of unprovoked savagery by those who claim to be Saviours, under the very nose of Union Government of India, headed by P.V. Narasimha Rao....

Oh! Traders of Power and Crusaders of Justice! Wake up to the Reality!

Looking at the scene presented in contemporary reactions and responses by a cross-section of society, included in this CICIL title, one may not be tempted to end up with the remark: "Situation normal, all fouled up!"

But Quiet flows the Ganges....

S. P. AGRAWAL

PREFACE

Why back in 1953, the grievances of the hill people of Uttar Pradesh found an outlet in the demand for statehood floated by P.C. Joshi, the then General Secretary of the Communist Party of India. The previously sporadic demand for the creation of a hill state gained momentum after the election of Kashi Singh Aeri, President of the Uttarakhand Kranti Dal (UKD), as MLA from Pithoragarh in 1985. Popular support for this long-standing demand stems primarily from the lopsided development of the hill district by successive governments. Local resentment had been brewing because of the indifferent treatment to the region and poor political representation in the State Assembly and the Lok Sabha.

The B.J.P. Government (1991-1992) in Uttar Pradesh passed a resolution for the creation of Uttaranchal State consisting of hill districts.

The movement got intensified in 1994 on the implementation of the 27 per cent reservation policy for OBCs in Uttar Pradesh by the SP-BSP combined Government under the Chief Ministership of Mulayam Singh Yadav.

There is already 23 per cent reservation in Government services and educational institutions for STs and SCs of this region. The OBCs form only 2.5 per cent of the total population of the hill origin. With the implementation of 27 per cent reservations for OBCs, other sections of the population of Uttarakhand are most likely to be hit hard. It is also feared that there will be infiltration of OBCs from other areas of Uttar Pradesh State to Uttarakhand for getting the benefit of reservation. This is the prime reason for the present agitation.

In this book, an attempt is made to study the issue in historical perspective, i.e., the integration of princely States with the Indian Dominion, the reorganisation of States, the reservation policy, and the backwardness and unwieldly nature of the State of Uttar Pradesh and consequent neglect of the hill areas. Altogether 6 Chapters are devoted to these issues.

Chapter one provides an overview of the size, population, educational facilities and political representation of the proposed State of Uttarakhand/ Uttaranchal.

The remaining Chapters deal with the history, geography, economy and culture, etc., of the hill districts.

Matter in the book is freely drawn from the Gazetteers published by the Government of Uttar Pradesh.

It is hoped that the book will serve as a handy reference source book for all those interested in the subject—political and social field workers, administrators, advisers, historians and research scholars, etc., The authors express their gratefulness to all the publishers and writers, whose books they have consulted for incorporating the material in this book, and to Dr. Shanti S. Gupta and Shri Anil Bhat, who responded to our request to write specific chapters for this volume.

J.C. AGGARWAL
S.P. AGRAWAL

CONTENTS

Section-V

CONTEMPORARY REACTIONS AND RESPONES WITH CHRONOLOGY OF SIGNIFICANT EVENTS.

Appendices

SECTION-I

PRFFATORY OVERVIEW

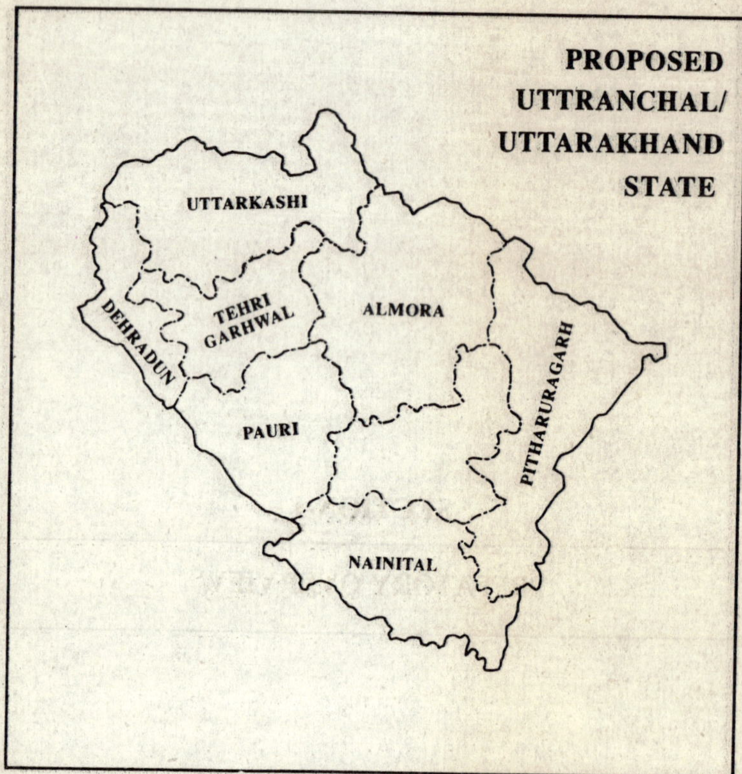

Source: Organiser, New De   Vol. XLVI, No. 7

1

UTTARAKHAND : A PROFILE

S. S. Gupta, D. Litt.

Uttarakhand of Uttar Pradesh is different than Uttarakhand of India except that both are hilly areas with strategic importance. Uttarakhand of Uttar Pradesh is surrounded by Himachal Pradesh on its North-West, Tibet (i.e., now China) on its North-East and Nepal on its West. It is the abode of gods—Brahma, Vishnu, Shiva including Kuber, Yakshas, Gandharvas, etc.; most sacred and important rivers—Jamuna, Ganga, Alaknand, Sarda and Ghaghara, with their tributaries originating from this area, most important pilagrimage centres—Badrinath, Kedarnath, Gangotri, Yamunotri, Hemkund, etc., are located here, and it has any number of natural beauty spots like—Mussoorie, Nainital, Ranikhet, Dehradun, Gaumukh, Besukital (the Exquisite Lake), the Valley of Flowers, Shri Hem Kund Sahib (The lake of Guru Govind Singh), Roop Kund (the Mystery Lake), Bugyals (Beautiful High-Altitude Meadows), Khatling Glacier, Dodital (The Angler's Paradise), Pindari Glacier, Hot Water Springs, etc. This heaven on earth is habitated by a population of simple, god-fearing, honest and poor people.

Administrative and Political Set-up

This hilly area has only eight districts, divided into two commissionaries. Nainital, Almorah and Pithoragarh are under Kumaon Commissionary and Dehradun, Tehri Garhwal, Uttar Kashi, Garhwal and Chamoli are under Garhwal Commissinary. It is both surprising and painful that most

Vice-Chancellor, Agra University.

of the Garhwal Commissionary offices function from Dehradun. Even a cursory look at the Table 1.1 will show that politically this hill area seems to have been discriminated by the Central Government—probably because, unlike other hill areas, it has predominently a Hindu population. This discrimination becomes pronounced when the basis of number of M.L.A./ M.P. is population. It may be called an exercise in secularism and democracy.

TABLE 1.1 : Peoples' Representatives

Sl. No.	Hill State	Area 000 km²	Population Lakhs	No. of Peoples's Represen-tatives M.L.A.	M.P.
1.	Mizoram	21.9	6.9	30	1
2.	Manipur	22.5	18.4	60	2
3.	Meghalaya	22.5	17.7	60	2
4.	Arunachal	83.5	8.6	30	2
5.	Nagaland	16.5	12.1	60	2
6.	Himachal	55.7	51.7	68	4
7.	Uttarakhand of U.P.	51.1	58.7	19	4

Physiographic Regions

The whole of hilly area of Uttarakhand can be divided, on the basis of height of mountains and slopes, in three parts.

1. *North Area*—It comprises of the districts of Uttarkashi, Chamoli and Pithoragarh having a height ranging between 3000 metres and more. This area has very steep slopes which are more than 600 metres per km.
2. *Middle Area*—It consists of the districts of Tehri-Garhwal, lower part of Chamoli and Pithoragarh Districts and upper part of Almora. The height of this middle area is between 2000 to 3000 metres. It has a steep slope of 300 to 600 metres per km.
3. *Lowest Part*—It comprises of the districts of Dehradun, Garhwal and lower part of Almora and Nainital district. The height of this part is between 600 to 2000 metres. It has a slope of 150 to 300 metres per km.

POPULATION

Population, Rate of Growth and Densities

All economic activity starts with man and ends with man. So, study of population of Uttarakhand assumes importance.

Table 1.2 gives the idea of population of Uttarakhand.

The Table 1.2 shows:

1. That the total area of Uttarakhand is 51,125 km^2. It is almost 17.3 per cent of the land area of U.P.
2. That the total population of Uttarakhand was 48.31 Lakh in 1981, i.e., 4.3 per cent of the population of U.P. That means that the area of Uttarakhand has relatively more land and less population as compared to whole of U.P. This is borne out by the arithmetic density of population. In Uttarakhand, density of population in 1981 was 94.4 as against 377 for whole of U.P.
3. That the physiological density, rural density and agricultural density of Uttarakhand were also lower than the whole State of U.P.
4. That the physiological density of population gives the relationship between total population and arable land. This density is vary high as compared to Arithmetic density. This shows that agricultural land in this area is very little. Further, the agricultural land, obviously, is much lesser in the three nothern districts, which have high mountains.
5. Rural density and arithmetic density are almost the same. This reveals that urban population is not much.
6. Agricultural density gives the relationship between total agricultural population with the total arable land. This is high because most of the population depends on agriculture and arable land is less.
7. That inspite of density of population of Uttarakhand being lesser than whole of U.P., the people of Uttarakhand are the poorest in the State because their agriculture is poor and they have not many other gainful sources of employment.
8. That the population of Uttarakhand is increasing at the rate of 2.14 per cent per year when the population of U.P. is rising at the rate of 2.51 per cent per year. It will be worth while to analyse the causes of this lower rate of increase of population. This case-analysis assumes greater importance because the maxim is that greater the poverty, higher the percentage increase of population. One of the reasons may be that quite an appreciable number of male population

TABLE 1.2 : Population of Uttarakhand

Sl.	District	Area km²	Population		Percentage increase	Rate of Development	Density of Population (Persons per Km²) 1981			
			1981 Lakh	1991 Lakh	1981-91	1981-91	Arithmetic	Physiological*	Rural	Agricultural+
1.	Uttarkashi	8016	1.90	2.37	24.74	24.52	24	568	22	471
2.	Chamoli	9125	3.64	4.41	21.15	18.22	40	775	38	667
3.	Pithoragarh	8856	4.89	5.57	13.91	13.87	55	693	52	569
4.	Tehri Garhwal	4421	4.97	5.75	15.69	15.60	113	558	108	583
5.	Almora	5385	7.57	8.24	8.85	8.81	141	667	132	535
6.	Dehradun	3088	7.61	10.14	33.24	33.22	247	1351	126	871
7.	Garhwal	5440	6.37	6.64	4.24	5.97	117	623	106	892
8.	Nainital	6794	11.36	15.57	37.06	37.03	167	554	121	443
	Total	51125	48.31	58.69	21.49		94.4			
	U.P. State (whole) (Whole)	294413 Sq km	1108.62	1387.60	25.16		377	643.75	309	555

* Physiological density co-relates the total population with its arable land.

+ Agricultural density co-ralates the total agricultural population with its total arable land.

leave their homes in search of employment.

It is worth noting here that the rate of increase of population of this area was between 4.24 per cent to 37.06 per cent when the rate of economic development (1981-89) was lesser than this. It means that more people will go below poverty line.

9. That the districts of Uttarkashi, Chamoli and Pithoragarh have very high mountains. Table 1.2 shows that the land area of these three districts is larger than the rest of the five districts. Again, the population of these districts is lesser than the rest of the districts of Uttarakhand. Consequently all type of densities of population are lesser. Inspite of this, it is widely known that the people of these three districts are the poorest amongst the people of Uttarakhand.

To sum up, this Table reveals that most of the people of this area depend upon agriculture, that they are poor as agriculture is not developed, that they have not many alternative sources of employment and that quite an appreciable male population are compelled to leave their homes in search of jobs.

Sex-Ratio

Idea of sex-ratio can be had from the Table 1.3.

Table 1.3 clearly demonstrates that the number of females per 1000 males is higher in this hilly area, except the districts of Dehradun and

TABLE 1.3: Sex-Ratio

Sl. No.	District	Population in Lakh (1191)	Sex-Ratio (per 1000 Males)
1.	Uttarkashi	2.37	928
2.	Chamoli	4.41	1059
3.	Pithoragarh	5.57	1031
4.	Tehri Garhwal	5.75	1073
5.	Almora	8.24	1106
6.	Dehradun	10.14	851
7.	Garhwal	6.64	1112
8.	Nainital	15.57	874
	Total	56.69	—
	U.P. State (whole)	1387.60	892

Nainital. The reason is clear. Most of the males, because of non-availability of gainful employments, go to plains for earning bread. Certainly this is not good for the people of the area. It will adversely effect their social, political and economic life.

Rural-Urban Ratio

Table 1.4 gives the idea of Rural-Urban population and its rate of growth.

Following inferences can be drawn from Table 1.4.

TABLE 1.4 : Rural-Urban Population

S. No.	District	Population in Lakh 1981	% Rate increase of population Total	Rural	Urban
1.	Uttarkashi	1.90	29.19	25.31	120.47
2.	Chamoli	3.64	24.53	26.68	139.01
3.	Pithoragarh	4.89	15.35	12.23	126.54
4.	Tehri Garwal	4.97	25.25	23.34	95.25
5.	Almora	7.57	18.41	18.20	21.69
6.	Dehradun	7.61	31.93	27.49	36.93
7.	Garhwal	6.37	15.35	11.00	79.84
8.	Nainital	11.36	43.45	33.95	78.66
	Total	48.31	(+) 43.45	(+) 33.95	(+) 139.01
		Max.			
		Min.	(+) 15.35	(+) 11.00	(+) 21.69
	U.P. State (whole)	1108.62	(+) 25.49	(+) 19.70	(+) 61.22

1. That about 80 per cent of population resides in villages. This is too big a pressure of population on agriculture which it can only ill afford.
2. That in this area, not only the number of cities is less but comparatively their population is also lesser with the result that the percentage of urban population of this area is lesser than the all India figure.
3. That migration from outside areas to urban areas is taking place in a big way. That alone can explain the phenomenal rise in urban population in districts like, Chamoli (139.01), Pithoragarh (126.54), Tehri Garhwal (95.25), etc. This may be because "outsiders" are trying to drain out the forest, mineral and other wealth of the area.
4. That the rate of increase of rural population of this area is lower in three districts mainly because the male population goes out of the

area in search of jobs.

S.C., S.T. and Other Backward Classes (OBC)

Uttarakhand, it appears, is in flames due to the reservation policy declared by Mulayam Singh Yadav Government in 1994 (back dated to 1993). The policy gives reservation to Scheduled Castes, Schedulted Tribes and Other Backward Classes, both in admissions and jobs. The percentage of reservation is 21.00 per cent, 2.0 per cent and 27.0 per cent respectively. It is, therefore, desirable to understand the view point of the people of Uttarakhand.

Table 1.5 gives the division of population.

TABLE 1.5 : S.C., S.T. and Other Backward Classes (OBC)

Sl.	District	Population 1991 in lakh	% of Population 1991			% Increase of Population (1971-81)	
			S.C.	S.T.	OBC	S.C.	S.T. OBC
1.	Uttarkashi	1.90	21.93	0.95		22.48	544.33
2.	Chamoli	3.64	17.26	2.52	between	28.08	12.37
3.	Pithoragarh	4.89	19.45	3.54	0.25 %	14.98	12.88
4.	Tehri Garhwal	4.97	12.77	0.01	to 2 %	21.83	84.37
5.	Almora	7.57	20.56	0.28		21.45	15.20
6.	Dehradun	7.61	11.93	9.99		35.08	23.37
7.	Garhwal	6.37	11.74	0.11		28.33	168.22
8.	Nainital	11.36	16.47	6.51		32.57	40.79
	State Average		21.16	0.21		26.44	17.19

Table 1.5 shows :

1. That when the U.P. State average of S.C. and S.T. is 21.16 per cent and 0.21 per cent of population respectively in Uttarakhand, their average ranges between 11.74 per cent to 19.45 per cent and 0.01 to 9.99 per cent respectively. The reservation of these two communities to the tune of 23 per cent, therefore, may not be very wrong, although it is slightly on the higher side.
2. That when the U.P. State average of OBC is about 27 per cent, in Uttarakhand it is below 2 per cent. So, to reserve 27 per cent seats for the OBC in Uttarakhand, both in admissions to educational institutions and services, is highly unjustifiable. It will simply mean

that beckward people of plains will get the benefit of this reservation at the cost of people of Uttarakhand who are already poor. This is more unfair because as per Government's own statistics, more than 80 per cent of population of this area is below the poverty line.

It will not be out of place to have a little indepth study of the problem. Indian Law, as existing today, defines the three words, Scheduled Castes, Scheduled Tribes and Other Backward Classes as below:

1. 'Scheduled Castes' means such castes, races or tribes or parts of or groups within such castes, races or tribes as are deemed under Article 341 to be Scheduled Castes for the purposes of this Constitution" [Article 366 (24) of the Constitution]. And, Article 341 says :
"The President may with respect to any State (or Union Territory) and where it is a State..., after consultation with the Governor. . . thereof by public notification specify the castes, races or tribes or parts of or groups within castes, races or tribes which shall for the purposes of this Constitution be deemed to be Scheduled Castes in relation to that State (or Union Territory as the case may be).
Thus the whole concept depends upon the sweetwill of the politicians.
2. 'Scheduled Tribes' means such tribes or tribal communities or part of or groups within such tribes or tribal communities as are deemed under Article 342 to be Scheduled Tribes for the purpose of this Constitution. [Article 366 (25) of the Constitution]. Article 342 is almost a repetition of Article 341 except in place of castes it uses the word tribes.
3. Article 340 only says that the President may appoint a Commission to investigate the conditions of socially and educationally backward classes. . . So, like Scheduled Castes and Scheduled Tribes. This concept is also vague.

In Vedas, we do not find any mention of S.C., S.T. or Backward Classes. Only one verse of *Rig Veda* (x, 90, 12) uses the word Shudra. It appears that this word is an interpolation. In Vedas, we find mention of *Daas* (Slaves) or *Daitya* (Bad and Cruel Persons), but not of Shudras or Backward Classes.

A close look at the Indian society, before the advent of Mugal or Muslim rulers will show that villages were self-sufficient and almost a Republic. In those days, crafts, trade and professions were prosperous. It might be revealing to know that most of the present day Scheduled Castes, or Backward Classes were associated with crafts, trades or professions. For example—

Obviously, in this situation, the concept of untouchability or higher and lower or discrimination could not and did not arise. It was a later

TABLE 1.6 : Castes and Professions, Trades and Crafts

Scheduled Castes	Profession	Trade	Crafts
1. Valmiki	Cleanliness	Pig Breading,	—
2. Dhobi	Washing of Clothes	—	—
3. Chamar	—	—	Leather Industry
4. Kanjaar	—	Repairing of Leather Goods	Rope Making, Bamboo and Grass Goods
5. Kori	—	—	Textile
Backward Classes			
1. Yadav	—	Dairy Industry and Road Transport	—
2. Lodha	Agricultural Labour	—	—
3. Kahar	Water Lifting Domestic Service	—	—
4. Lohar	—	—	Blacksmithy Metal Casting Armoury
5. Badahi	—	—	Carpentry, Wood-work, Armoury.
6. Kewat	—	Water Transport and Fishing,	Boat and Ship-making
7. Darji (Tailor)	—	—	Garment Industry
8. Gadaria	—	Animal Husbandry	—
9. Kumhar	—	—	Earthen Pot Industry
10. Teli	—	—	Oil Industry, Perfumery
11. Nai	Hair Cutting Massage, Beauty-Parlour, Match-Making		
12. Swarnkar	—	—	Ornaments of Bullions

development.

Before the advent of Muslim rulers in India, due to failure of social leaders to understand the structure and dynamism of Hindu society, and probably some selfish motives of some people, the rigidities and deformatories started creeping into the Hindu society. This slow movement got a fillip when Muslim rulers are said to have started forcibly killing or converting innocent Hindus. To save Hindus and to indirectly force them to stick to their religion, these rigidities and consequently deformatories became more pronounced. And whatever little was left was completed by shrewd Britishers, who wanted to destroy self-sufficient village economy so as to serve their own trade and colonial interests, and therefore ruthlessly destroyed village crafts, trades and professions and reduced these self-employed, self-contained and happy people to the mercy of others. Thus, the Hindu society was, under the scheme of 'Divide and Rule', given the names of Upper-Castes, Scheduled Castes and Backward Castes.

If the present reservation policy is viewed in the light of this historical truth, then one will unhesitatingly reach to the inevitable conclusion that our political parties are pursuing the same British Policy of 'Divide and Rule' for vote catching and keeping themselves in power. This is neither going to make villages self-sufficient, nor check mass migration of population to cities, nor improve the socio-politico-economic condition of these poor people—Scheduled Castes, Scheduled Tribes and Other Backward Classes.

Physical Fitness

Physical fitness of the people depends upon the quality of food they get and eat, body exersion they undertake and the treatment that is ready at hand when they fall ill. An attempt was made to know the facilities of treatment that people of Uttarakhand have. Table 1.7 gives an idea.

Table 1.7 clearly shows that the facilities of medical aid are more than the facilities available in whole of U.P. The reasons of this are not clear, more so when this area has an healthy environment and everyone, willy-nilly, has to take physical exercise.

Statistics of the various diseases reveal:

1. That the hyper endemic malariometric region roughly coincides with the Terai belt, i.e., Dehradun, Garhwal and Nainital.
2. That the Uttarakhand region has very low floria endemic rate (less

TABLE 1.7 : Medical and Health Services

(Per Lakh Population)

S. No.	District	No. of Allopathic Hospitals and Primary Health Centres	No. of Homoeopathic Dispensaries	No. of Welfare Centres
1.	Uttarkashi	12.57	1.05	2.10
2.	Chamoli	12.36	0.28	2.48
3.	Pithoragarh	10.43	0.41	2.46
4.	Tehri Garhwal	8.64	0.81	2.01
5.	Almora	10.30	0.53	1.99
6.	Dehradun	11.03	0.40	0.79
7.	Garhwal	11.45	0.48	2.36
8.	Nainital	7.57	0.27	1.15
	U.P. State (whole)	2.71	0.27	0.94

than one).

3. That the goitre is found in high concentration in the Uttarakhand region, i.e., Nainital, Uttarkashi, Almora, Pithoragarh, Garhwal, Tehri-Garhwal and Dehradun. In the district of Chamoli the concentration is less than 148.
4. That the Uttarakhand area is almost free from anaemia.

Intellectual Fitness

Intellectual development mainly depends upon the educational facilities available, their quality, teacher-pupil ratio, etc. An idea of these educational facilities of the region can be had from Table 1.8

It is very clear from Table 1.8 that all the districts of Uttarakhand are better placed in matter of educational facilities than the rest of U.P. It has even three Universities one at Garhwal and two at Nainital. There is also a Forest Research Institute at Dehradun. But the unfortunate part is that it has no Engineering College, Agricultural College or Medical College. Further, it has been reported that most of the Schools and Colleges have sanctioned post of teachers, specially of Science subjects, but quite a few of them are lying vacant.

The result of this good infra structure is that percentage of literacy is quite high in this hilly area as is clear from Table 1.9.

The percentage of literacy in Uttarakhand is higher than that of

TABLE 1. 8: Educational Facilities

(Per Lakh of Population)

S. No.	District	Junior Basic School		Senior Basic School		No. of School		No. of Colleges		Universities
		1	2	1	2	1	2	1	2	Deemed Universities
1.	Uttarkashi	224.14	56	30.8	25	14.14	25	0.52	14.8	—
2.	Chamoli	194.3	39	34.5	26	18.93	23	0.82	14.8	—
3.	Pithoragarh	178.4	34	29.84	24	17.70	27	0.82	15.9	—
4.	Tehri-Garhwal	172.3	38	37.5	23	15.87	24	0.20	9.3	—
5.	Almora	162.67	32	27.7	20	18.35	26	0.66	12.5	—
6.	Dehradun	99.2	45	29.9	19	11.42	24	0.92	23.9	1
7.	Garhwal	196.6	41	34.8	20	24.1	26	0.63	12.8	1
8.	Nainital	99.8	37	22.1	20	9.59	24	0.35	26.4	2
	U.P. State (whole)	65.1	42	12.6	17	1.9	23	0.10	12.5	—

Note : There is no Engineering College, no Medical College, Technical school in this area
(ii) 1 = Number; 2 = Teacher-People Ratio

TABLE 1.9 : Literacy Pattern

S. No.	District	% of Literacy	% of Growth of Literacy 1971-81	% of Literacy of Rural Area 1981	% of Female Literacy 1981
1.	Uttarkashi	28.92	6.88	26.21	9.17
2.	Chamoli	37.46	8.79	35.16	18.34
3.	Pithoragarh	39.08	7.21	37.37	20.30
4.	Tehri Garhwal	27.89	8.60	26.20	9.42
5.	Almora	37.76	9.68	35.21	20.27
6.	Dehradun	52.58	8.84	38.84	42.03
7.	Garhwal	41.06	9.06	38.46	27.13
8.	Nainital	37.81	5.87	33.24	27.10
	U.P. State (whole)	27.16	5.48	23.06	14.04

whole of U.P. It is also higher in rural areas as also in females. In the light of this fact, the reservation policy in admissions, specially of backward classes, recently introduced in U.P. assumes great importance which makes the agitation justifiable.

Working Force

It will be in the fitness of things to know how the working force of Uttarakhand is employed. Table 1.10 gives the idea.

TABLE 1.10 : Working Force (1981)

S. No.	District	% of total main workers in total population	% of marginal workers to total workers	% of cultivators to total main workers	% of agricultural labourers to total main workers
1.	Uttarkashi	52.12	11.53	78.71	0.57
2.	Chamoli	44.74	6.24	80.93	0.33
3.	Pithoragarh	38.33	16.96	78.11	0.65
4.	Tehri Garhwal	44.69	5.74	85.11	0.28
5.	Almora	31.51	20.63	73.26	1.57
6.	Dehradun	32.56	4.81	27.94	7.94
7.	Garhwal	36.21	16.68	71.45	0.82
8.	Nainital	31.68	12.10	44.70	19.09
	U.P. State (whole)	29.22	4.46	58.57	15.98

As per Census definition the 'main workers' are those who are engaged in work for at least 183 days in a year, and 'marginal workers' are those who have worked any time during the preceding year but for less than 183 days.

Several interesting facts emerge from Table 1.10

1. That in Uttarakhand area percentage of total main workers to total population is the highest in the northern districts which have the highest mountains of the area and is lowest in the district of the south, which has the lowest heights of the mountains of the area. Further, this percentage is higher than that for whole of U.P.
2. That the percentage of marginal workers to total workers is appreciable and this is also higher than that of U.P. average.
3. That the major portion of work force is employed in agriculture.
4. That the percentage of agricultural workers is quite low. This average is much lower than that of U.P.
5. That the work force employed in industry, transport, etc., is negligible as its percentage has not been mentioned in the *Planning Atlas of U.P.*

WATER RESOURCES

Water is one of the most important necessities for man. It quenches his thirst, helps in cleaning things, is an essentiality for growing crops and helps in generating hydro-power. So, it is desirable to know water-resources of Uttarakhand.

Water Table

The ground water resources are of immense value for the economy. Hence their scientific evaluation, managment and planning are pre-requisites afor their judicious utilisation and conservation. The net available ground water resources of Uttarakhand are as given in Table 1.11.

Table 1.11 : Net Availability of Ground Water Resources (as on 3-12-83)

(Million Cubic Meters)

S. No.	District	Net availability	Net Draft	Utilisation of Under Ground Water Resources (per cent)
1.	Uttarkashi	—	—	—
2.	Chamoli	—	—	—
3.	Pithoragarh	—	—	—
4.	Tehri Garhwal	—	—	—
5.	Almora	—	—	—
6.	Dehradun	554	17	3
7.	Garhwal	—	—	—
8.	Nainital	692	218	32
	U.P. State (whole)	77833	23755	31

In Uttarakhand availability of water in six districts out of eight has not been recorded simply because it may be too deep. In the rest of the districts—Dehradun and Nainital—which have a height of 600-2000 metres, the water table is quite poor—it being 554 and 692 respectively when in most of the districts of U.P., it has been ranging between 1042 to 3025. Consequently, its utilisation is almost negligible.

Rivers

Uttarakhand is an area from where the most important rivers of U.P. originate and have a network of their tributaries. The famous rivers are Tons, Yamuna, Ganga, Alaknanda, Mandakni, Sarda, etc. These rivers are perennial.

Rainfall

Rainfall in this area ranges between 240 cm to less than 60 cm per year. A peculiar phenomana is that rainfall decreases as the height of mountains increases.

Irrigation and Drinking Water

The idea of irrigation and drinking water can be had from Table 1.12.

It is a pity that our own Government, which calls itself democratic and socialistic, have failed to provide even drinking water to the poor villagers in spite of forty years of planning.

Table 1.12 shows that the percentage of irrigated area to net sown area in Uttarakhand, except in the districts of Nainital and Dehradun is very low, and that understandably tubewell irrigation has not much role

TABLE 1.12 : Irrigation

Sl. No.	District	% of Villages provided with piped drinking water	% of net irrigatied area to net sown area	%of Irrigated Area to net Irrigated Area			% of growth in net irrigated area (1950-51 to 1980-81)
				Tube-well	Canal	Other Sources	
1.	Uttarkashi	47.4	14.92	—	22.16	77.84	—
2.	Chamoli	46.2	5.37	—	34.59	65.41	—
3.	Pithoragarh	48.1	8.76	—	8.27	91.73	—
4.	Tehri Garhwal	25.6	14.31	—	14.93	85.07	—
5.	Almora	30.9	9.58	—	26.60	73.40	—
6.	Dehradun	62.0	42.03	7.47	58.43	34.10	64.2
7.	Garhwal	22.2	8.40	2.68	40.17	57.15	—
8.	Nainital	70.4	65.27	39.45	53.92	6.63	372.4
	U.P.		54.89	53.45	33.67	12.93	

to play in this hilly area but it is a pity that even the canal irrigation is not well developed when most of the dams are located in this area and the people of this area had to surrender their limitted land. Further, the main sources of irrigation appears to be traditional ones which are costly, inefficient and labour intensive. It is obvious that due to poor political importance, this hilly area has been neglected by the successive Governments.

MINERALS

Uttarakhand is deficient in mineral wealth. It is more deficient in metallic minerals. An idea of minerals found in Uttarakhand can be had from Table 1.13.

TABLE 1.13 : Minerals

S. No.	District	Minerals: Metalic	Minerals: Non-Metalic
1.	Uttarkashi	Zink	Lead, Kyanite
2.	Chamoli	Zink, Lead, Copper Iron, Magnesite, Dolmite	Asbestos, Stib-nite, Talc, Soapstone
3.	Pithoragarh	Copper, Magnesite	Phosphorite, Talc, Soapstone, Graphite, Kyanite, Sulphur, Limestone
4.	Tehri-Garhwal	Zinc, Copper, Iron, Dolmite,	Rock Phosphate, Gypsum, Limestone
5.	Almora,	Zinc, Copper, Iron Tungstone, Magnesite	Graphite, Talc, Building-Stone, Soapstone
6.	Dehradun	Zinc, Dolmite,	Building-Stone, Marble, Morrum, Gypsum, Limestone, Phosphorite
7.	Garhwal	Copper, Iron, Gold,	Mica, Limestone, Gypsum, Borytes, Graphite
8.	Nainital	Iron, Gold, Dolmite,	Gypsum, Gravel, Limestone, Building Stone

The Table 1.13 clearly demonstrates that Uttarakhand is more poor in metallic minerals than non-metallic minerals. It reveals that the metal based industries have hardly any future in this area.

FOREST WEALTH

Forests play an important role in the life of a country. Table 1.14 gives us an idea of the forest wealth of Uttarakhand.

TABLE 1.14 : Forests

S. No.	District	% of under Forest (in hectares)	Per Capita Forest Area (in hectares)	Per Capita Production of Timber (In Cubic Metre)	Per Capita Production of Fuelwood (In Cubic Metre)
1.	Uttarkashi	88.38	3.64	0.23	0.004
2.	Chamoli	61.24	1.01	0.14	1.49
3.	Pithoragarh	53.39	0.28	0.09	0.07
4.	Tehri Garhwal	69.14	0.54	0.04	0.01
5.	Almora	54.31	0.19	0.04	0.14
6.	Dehradun	68.93	0.20	0.02	0.01
7.	Garhwal	63.23	6.38	0.04	0.01
8.	Nainital	63.23	6.38	0.04	0.01
	U.P. State (whole)	17.41	0.03	0.005	0.015

Thus, Table 1.14 reveals:

1. That all the districts of Uttarakhand have more than 50 per cent area under forests when the whole of U.P. average is less than 18 per cent. This percentage is quite high than the ideal prescribed percentage of 33.
2. That per capita area under forests is also appreciable, except that in district of Chamoli.
3. That per capita production of timber and fuel are also good.

The forests of this area consist of Moist Temperate Forests, Subtropical Lime Forests, Sub Alpine and Moist Alpine Forests, Dry Alpine Scrul and Moist Deciduous.

The Forest wealth of this area consists of :

1. *Lisa*—2 lakh quintal per year. It gives a revenue of 5.5 crore rupees.
2. *Bhavar Grass*—10 lakh quintal per year. It is used for manufacturing paper.
3. *Medicinal Plants*
4. *Timber*—It is used for manufacturing furniture, plywood, hard board, games material, match box sticks.
5. *Bomboo* and *Cane.*
6. *Silk*
7. *Colours*

8. *Insence*, etc. (dhoop-batti, agar-batti)

It is unfortunate that the forests are being cut on a large scale and the day is not far off when the area under forests will become negligible. It will have far reaching consequences on environment, rainfall, soil erosion, agriculture, industry, etc.

It is a sad aspect that most of the forest wealth is taken away from this hilly area and is used by the people of the plains. The poor people of the area are drained for no fault of theirs.

POWER

Power—Hydro-electric, Thermal, Wood, Oil, Wind, etc.—is a necessity of life. Without it neither the food can be cooked nor the wheels of machines, big or small, can move. It is, therefore, essential to know how Uttarakhand is placed in matter of power.

The only data available for Uttarakhand is of electricity. This data, it appears, is only of Hydro-electricity and not of Thermal or Nuclear.

In this hilly area of Uttarakhand, a number of river vally projects have been completed. Some more are under construction or at the envisaged stage. Thus, Uttarakhand is made to lose substantial portion of its valuable land. And in exchange, it has also not got the benefits of these schemes because the canal network and also electricity generated are mainly used to develop the rest of Uttar Pradesh. This bears testimony to the Drain Theory.

The position of Hydro-electric Project, as on 1984 was as given in Table 1.15.

TABLE 1.15 : Hydro-electric Projects

S.No.	Completed		Approved		Proposed
1.	Chibro	1.	Vyas	1.	Loharinagpala
2.	Khodri	2.	Lakhwar	2.	Palamaneri
3.	Dhakrani	3.	Maneribhali-I	3.	Koteshwar
4.	Dhalipur	4.	Maneribhali-II	4.	Tanakpur
5.	Kulhal	5.	Tehri	5.	Khare
6.	Chilla	6.	Vishnuprayag	6.	Srinagar
7.	Kalagarh				
8.	Khatima				

Table 1.16 shows energy consumption of Uttarakhand.

TABLE 1.16 : Energy Consumption

S. No.	District	Per Capita Consumption (1980) KwH	Growth of per Capita consumption 1970-71 to 1982-83	% of Electrified villages 1982-83
1.	Uttarkashi	10	754.5	44.22
2.	Chamoli	10	N.A.	31.24
3.	Pithoragarh	20	3642.9	20.69
4.	Tehri Garhwal	10	800.0	24.06
5.	Almora	20	445.0	40.00
6.	Dehradun	300	151.3	57.63
7.	Garhwal	10	420.0	24.27
8.	Nainital	100	146.9	76.17
	India (whole)			145.95
	U.P. State (whole)			105.12

Thus, Table 1.16 reveals some very interesting facts—

1. That except Dehradun and Nainital, which were famous hill stations even in British days, the per capita consumption in rest of the six districts, even after 30 years of independence, was very low. It means that the electricity, even in 1980 was mainly confined to urban areas and there too, only to a few selected people. This also indirectly reveals almost a complete lack of industrial consumption.
2. That in 12 years (1970-71 to 1982-83), per capita consumption substantially increased. The range of increase is 151.3 to 3642.9 per capita. This rise needs explanation, specially in case of Pithoragarh which is located at the North end and has high mountains.
3. That except Nainital and Dehradun, the percentage of electrified villages in 1982-83 was less than half.

This area has no Thermal Generation or Nuclear Energy Generation Centres. And probably, these two types of energies are also not made available to the poor people of this area.

LIVE-STOCK

Live-stock plays a key role in the agricultural economy more so in hilly areas. From this point of view the present study of live-stock of Uttarakhand becomes more important.

When we talk of live stock for U.P. we mainly take into account cows, bulls, bullocks, he and she-buffaloes, sheep, goat, horses, ponies, mules, donkeys, camels and pigs.

The position of live-stock in Uttarakhand is depicted in Table 1.17

Knowledgeable persons tell that Uttarakhand has a very little number of camels, pigs, donkeys and mules.

TABLE 1.17 : Live-stock (1978)

S. No.	District	No. of Live-stock per 100 hectare of land	No. of Live-stock per 1000 population	No. of Milch Cattle per 1000 population	No. of Male cattle per 1000 of plough
1.	Uttarkashi	40	1888	300	1654
2.	Chamoli	58	1516	310	1586
3.	Pithoragarh	101	1747	270	1562
4.	Tehri Garhwal	80	975	170	1463
5.	Almora	100	851	120	1460
6.	Dehradun	109	486	490	1826
7.	Garhwal	92	1097	120	1558
8.	Nainital	71	491	400	1527
	U.P. State (whole)	176	517	140	1552

Number of live-stock for whole of Uttarakhand is appreciably low as compared to whole of U.P. This is not a good position. The position is worse in case of northern districts of Uttarkashi, Chamoli and Pithoragarh which have very high mountains. The position is slightly better in the southern part of Uttarakhand which has mountains of least height of the area.

Except for the district of Nainital, number of live-stock per 1000 population is very high as compared to figures of whole of U.P. This is mainly because this whole area had low density of population.

Similarly, number of milch cattle per 1000 population for Uttarakhand is quite high as compared to whole of U.P. However, one or two things are worth noting here. First, the yield per cattle is quite low as compared to rest of U.P. Second, the number of goats and sheep is more and the number of cows and buffaloes is less.

Number of male cattle per 100 of plough is higher in case of districts of Uttarkashi, Chamoli, Pithoragarh (north part), Dehradun and Garhwal than whole of U.P. This data loses all relevance when we do not know how much area is under 1000 plough in these districts and rest of U.P.

TRANSPORT

Developed transport system is pre-requisite of economic and social development as it integrates the functions of production, marketing and consumption, and interlinks people and places. It also helps in generating more employment opportunities. By transport system we mean road, rail, water and air transport. All these four types should not only be developed but must have a coordinated development so that unnecessary competition between them may not exist.

Following is the relative position of these four types of transport available in Uttarakhand.

Air-Transport

There is not a single aerodrome in this hilly area because of terrain. So, there is no air traffic in Uttarakhand.

Water Transport

It is not possible to have water transport in this area because of high mountains and steep slopes. However, wood logs are thrown in the rivers and carried down stream. This is the only water transport available.

Railways

The Himalayan Region, because of terrain difficulties, has remained inaccessible for rail transport; it is only at the foot-hills that there are a few rail-heads, which were established by the British Rulers. (Table 1.18)

Obviously, rail transport is not contributing much for the economic development of the area.

TABLE 1.18: Rail-Heads

Place	Gauge	Line
Tanakpur	Meter	Single
Kathgodown	Braod	Single
Ram Nagar	Braod	Single
Kotdwara	Braod	Double
Rishikesh	Braod	Single
Dehradun	Braod	Single

Road Transport

An idea of roads and consequently road transport can be had from Table 1.19.

In Uttarakhand, there is not a single National Highway. It has only "other roads". This negligence assumes extra significance when we know that this area has China on North-East and Nepal on East.

TABLE 1.19: Roads

S. No.	District	Surfaced Road per 1000 of sq. km. area	Surfaced Road per 1 lakh population	% of village linked	Index Accessibility
1.	Uttarkashi	33.0 km	154.7 km	5.5	0.2
2.	Chamoli	27.1 km	75.5 km	8.5	0.4
3.	Pithoragarh	41.7 km	76.8 km	7.9	0.5
4.	Tehri Garhwal	65.6 km	65.9 km	5.6	1.0
5.	Almora	121.8 km	89.3 km	9.9	1.4
6.	Dehradun	139.4 km	58.8 km	18.6	2.4
7.	Garhwal	114.9 km	101.5 km	11.2	1.1
8.	Nainital	109.5 km	73.1 km	26.0	1.5
	U.P. State (whole)	143.9 km	41.6 km	14.2	3.5

The northern part of Uttarakhand, which has high mountains, has almost no roads except upto Gainchvan, Uttarkashi, Trijugi Narayan, Badrinath and Shama. And these roads were constructed because of tourist and religious traffic and not from defence point of view.

Thus, Table 1.19 clearly shows :

1. That surfaced roads per 1000 sq km are much less in all the eight districts of Uttarakhand as compared to U.P.'s average of 143.9 km. It also shows that the surfaced roads are relatively more in southern part of Uttarakhand and these go on decreasing as we go towards north and the height of the area goes an increasing with slopes.
2. That the surfaced roads for 1 lakh population is much higher in Uttarakhand as compared to U.P. This may be because here the density of population is quite low.
3. That there are practically no roads connecting villages with towns as the percentage of villages linked with roads is very low except that of Nainital and Dehradun.

4. That Index Accessibility shows the relationship between surfaced roads per 1000 km^2 area and surfaced roads per 1 lakh population. This relationship gives an idea of road development. Obviously, in Uttarakhand road development is quite poor.

These facts show that Uttarakhand is quite undeveloped in matter of transport, both for men and material. With these poor transport facilities the economic development and social awakening cannot be of proper degree.

COMMUNICATION

Communication facilities mainly consists of Post-Offices, Telephones, Television and Radio Centres. Amongst these four, from industry, commence and trade point of view, only Post-Offices and Telephones are important.

Eight districts of Uttarakhand are not badly placed as far as Post-Offices are concerned. Table 1.20 gives the idea—

From the Table 1.20, it is evident that Uttarakhand, from both parameters—population and area—is well served by Post Offices.

TABLE 1.20 : Post-Offices

S. No	District	No. of Post-Offices per Lakh Population	No. of Post Offices per 100 sq. km
1.	Uttarkashi	40 — 78	2 — 1.2
2.	Chamoli	40 — 78	2 — 4
3.	Pithoragarh	40 — 78	2 — 4
4.	Tehri Garhwal	40 — 78	4 — 6
5.	Almora	40 — 78	6 — 8
6.	Dehradun	30 — 40	6 — 8
7.	Garhwal	40 — 78	6 — 8
8.	Nainital	20 — 30	2 — 4
	U.P. State (whole)	10 — 20	4 — 6

The position of Telephones is also not bad as is evident from Table 1.21.

Mussorrie has High Power Television Transmitters. Nainital, Pauri and Bageshwar have Television Centres and Almora has a Radio Station.

TABLE 1.21 : Telephones

S. No.	District	No. of Telephones per Lakh Population
1.	Uttarkashi	100—200
2.	Chamoli	100 -200
3.	Pithoragarh	50 —100
4.	Tehri Garhwal	5—50
5.	Almora	100—200
6.	Dehradun	400—816
7.	Garhwal	100—200
8.	Nainital	200—400
	U.P. State (whole)	100—200

AGRICULTURE

India is primarily an agricultural country. Hence, its economy, more so in case of Uttarakhand, depends upon its agriculture and forests. If agriculture is in poor health, its people will also be poor. The following description gives a glimpse of the condition of agriculture.

Land Utilisation (1981-82)

Table 1.22 gives the idea of land utilisation of these eight districts.

It shows:

1. That out of 53.17 lakh sq km area only 6.96 sq km, i.e., 13.09 per cent is available for agriculture.
2. That 3.11 lakh sq km of land, i.e., 5.84 per cent can also be brought under cultivation as it is cultivable waste.
3. That rest of the area, i.e., 43.10 sq km (81.06%) is either under Forest or Pastures or not cultivable.

Variation in Land Utilisation

Table 1.23 shows the variation in land utilisation during a period of 12 years, i.e., 1969-70 to 1980-81.

It is surprising that out of eight districts of the region, data for six district is not available.

In case of Dehradun district, the area under forest, cultivable waste,

TABLE 1.22 : Land Utilisation (1981-82)

(In lakh sq km)

Sl. No.	District	Reported Area	Net area sown	Current Fallow Land	Other Fallow Land	Culti-vable Waste	Usar and Uncult-ivable land	Non-Agricul-tural land	Groves and Trees	Forest	Pasture and other land	Grazing
1.	Uttarkashi	8.01	0.30	0.10	0.01	0.24	0.06	0.04	0.02	0.71	0.19	
2.	Chamoli	8.58	0.44	0.005	0.01	0.20	1.77	0.18	0.41	0.52	0.26	
3.	Pithoragarh	6.21	0.73	0.02	0.07	0.59	0.29	0.12	0.33	0.33	0.72	
4.	Tehri-Garhwal	5.73	0.74	0.28	0.02	0.64	0.08	0.08	0.06	0.39	0.14	
5.	Almora	7.23	1.10	0.01	0.06	0.69	0.53	0.15	0.39	0.39	0.50	
6.	Dehradun	3.20	0.56	0.03	0.03	0.11	0.01	0.16	0.04	0.22	0.00009	
7.	Garhwal	7.21	1.03	0.03	0.06	0.34	0.25	0.25	0.13	0.46	0.45	0.31
8.	Nainital	7.00	2.06	0.55	0.03	0.06	0.30	0.15	0.40	0.01		
	Total	53.17	6.96	1.025	0.34	3.11	3.05	1.16	1.806	3.41	2.13009	

TABLE 1.23 : Variation in Land Utilisation

Sl. No.	District	Forest	Usar and uncultivable waste	Non-Agri-culturable	Cultivable	Other cultivable Crops and Groves	Current Fallow	Other Fallow	Net Area Sown
1.	Uttarkashi	NA	NA	NA	NA	NA	NA	NA	NA
2.	Chamoli	NA	NA	NA	NA	NA	NA	NA	NA
3.	Pithoragarh	NA	NA	NA	NA	NA	NA	NA	NA
4.	Tehri Garhwal	NA	NA	NA	NA	NA	NA	NA	NA
5.	Almora	NA	NA	NA	NA	NA	NA	NA	NA
6.	Dehradun	+ 35.2	–83.9	–3.8,	+11.4.3	–87.4	+ 18.1	+ 31.0	+ 24.5
7.	Garhwal	NA	NA	NA	NA	NA	NA	NA	NA
8.	Nainital	–0.7	+ 129.5	+ 75.0	–63.1	+ 5.1	–61.0	–44.0	+ 162.5

current fallow, other fallow and net area sown have increased and under *usar* and uncultivable waste, non-agriculture and other cultivable crops and grores/groves have decreased. One fails to understand how area under *usar* and uncultivable waste can decrease.

In case of Nainital district the areas under forest, cultivable waste, current fallow and other fallow have decreased and in other cases it have increased. Here the pattern of variation is quite different than that of Dehradun

However, it is good that in case of both the districts of Dehradun and Nainital, the net area sown has increased.

Soil Group

All the eight districts of Uttarakhand have Brown Hill soil. Some parts of the districts of Nainital, Garhwal and Dehradun have Bhabar soil and the lower part of Nainital has also Tarai Soil.

Size of Holdings

The idea of the size of holdings can be had from Table 1.24.

Table 1.24 clearly shows—

TABLE 1.24 : Size of Holding (1976-77)

S. No.	District	Average size of holding in hectare	Average size of Marginal Holding in hectare	% of Small and Marginal Holdings to Total Holdings	% of Area under Small and Marginal Holdings to Total area under holdings
1.	Uttarkashi	0.89	0.26	85.15	44.95
2.	Chamoli	0.94	0.36	87.03	58.22
3.	Pithoragarh	0.54	0.28	95.34	70.66
4.	Tehri Garhwal	0.90	0.39	88.61	67.65
5.	Almora	0.52	0.30	96.44	78.91
6.	Dehradun	1.09	0.34	84.03	41.62
7.	Garhwal	1.30	0.32	78.57	35.31
8.	Nainital	2.03	0.35	66.20	20.71
	U.P. State (whole)	1.18	0.36	85.77	45.56

1. That the average size of holdings in five districts of Uttarkashi, Chamoli, Pithoragarh, Tehri-Garhwal and Almora is less than the average of U.P. In these districts it ranges between 0.52 hectare to 0.94 hectare. And in the rest of the three districts of Dehradun, Garhwal and Nainital, it is higher than the whole of U.P. It appears that height of mountains and the size of land holdings are inversely related.
2. That the average size of marginal holdings in these eight districts ranges between 0.26 hectare to 0.39 hectare which is almost equal to the average of U.P.

Chemical Fertilizers Used (1980-81)

Table 1.25 gives the idea of Chemical Fertilizers used in the eight districts of Uttarakhand.

Fertility of soil decreases after each crop. So, it is to be recouped. Even in this hilly area fertilizers have come in vogue.

TABLE 1.25 : Chemical Fertilizers

(kg. per hectare)

S.No.	District	Nitrogen	Phosphorus	Potash	N P K
1.	Uttarkashi	<15	8 - 12	< 2	< 20
2.	Chamoli	< 15	< 4	< 2	< 20
3.	Pithoragarh	< 15	< 4	< 2	< 20
4.	Tehri Garhwal	< 15	<4	< 2	< 20
5.	Almora	< 15	< 4	< 2	< 20
6.	Dehradun	< 15	< 4	< 2	< 20
7.	Garhwal	< 15	< 4	< 2	< 20
8.	Nainital	60—81	> 16	> 8	> 80

Most of U.P. soils are deficient in nitrogen. The average consumption of nitrogen for whole of U.P. is 35.42 kg per hectare. In seven districts of Uttarakhand, nitrogen consumption is quite low—it is less than 15 kg per hectare.

Six districts of Uttarakhand, except Nainital and Uttarkashi, consume less that 4 kg per hectare of Phosphorus. This consumption is lower that that of U.P.

In the consumption of Potash also, the intake of the eight districts of Uttarakhand is less than the average of U.P.

In case of NPK also, the consumption is less than the average of U.P.

So, it can be concluded that if yield per hectare is to be increased, the use of chemical fertilizers will have to be increased.

Principal Crops

The idea of principal crops grown in Uttarakhand and their relative importance can be had from Table 1.26.

The Table 1.26 reveals—

1. That important crops are—wheat, peddy and millet.
2. That in cash crops—sugar cane is grown sparingly.

The data of yield per hectare could not be secured.

This clearly demonstrates that Uttarakhand is neither self-sufficient in food crops nor in cash crops.

INDUSTRIES

It is a well established fact that even a prosperous agricultural country cannot provide people sufficient employment opportunities and a comfortable life. For this, agriculture must be supplemented with various types of industries—agro-based, engineering, mechanical, electronic, etc. They must be, as per need, of various sizes—cottage, small and large

It is unfortunate that the Government of Uttar Pradesh during the last 40 years has not provided sufficient infra-structure to develop this hilly area of Uttarakhand with the result that more than 80 per cent of people of this area are below the poverty line.

The idea of the industrial development of the area can be had from the following facts.

Industrial Estates

The industrial estates have been established for balanced industrial development for promoting small sector units which help in generating more employment opportunities.

The Government of Uttar Pradesh has established the following Industrial Estates.

1. *Urban Industrial Estates* — Dehradun and Almora.
2. *Semi-Urban Industrial Estates* — Kotdwara and Bhimtal.

TABLE 1.26 : Per cent Share of Principal Crops in Total Croped Area

Sl. No.	District	Wheat	Paddy	Maize	Gram	Barley	Bajra	Jwar	Arhar	Sugar-cane	Patato	Groun-dnut	Must-ard seed	All Food Crops	Non-Food Crops	Cer-eals	Pulses
1.	Uttarkashi	31.5	20.4	1.0	0.01	1.7	—	—	0.08	—	1.3	0.0	0.59	82.1	17.9	80.6	1.5
2.	Chamoli	32.1	26.3	0.4	—	3.1	—	—	0.6	—	0.9	0.0	0.25	91.1	8.9	90.8	0.3
3.	Pithoragrh	33.1	26.3	3.5	0.32	6.7	—	—	0.03	0.1	0.7	0.0	0.02	93.9	6.1	89.5	4.3
4.	Tehri-Garhwal	33.1	14.5	1.5	0.01	4.3	—	—	0.58	—	0.5	—	0.26	94.7	5.3	93.3	1.5
5.	Almora	33.6	20.7	1.3	0.0	4.9	—	—	0.02	—	0.5	0.0	0.05	95.9	4.1	94.8	1.1
6.	Dehradun	31.4	19.4	12.7	1.6	2.7	—	—	0.13	6.6	1.1	0.3	1.97	79.9	22.1	73.8	4.1
7.	Garhwal	28.0	18.9	1.5	0.07	6.2	—	—	0.19	0.0	0.1	0.0	0.54	97.9	2.1	97.1	0.9
8.	Nainital	33.9	32.1	4.2	2.02	0.7	—	—	0.22	10.0	0.6	0.0	4.90	77.6	22.4	73.6	3.9
	State Average	32.1	21.6	4.9	9.07	3.1	4.1	2.8	3.03	6.0	1.1	1.0	1.82	82.8	17.2	70.7	11.7

3. *Rural Industrial Estates* — Vikasnagar
4. *New Industrial Estates* — Srikot and Balbhdrapur.

These four industrial estates are almost an apology for this big area. Further details are not available about the number of functional units, the types of units, the quantum of production, the employment they provide, etc.

Industrial Complexes

An industrial complex comprises industries which are inter-related in so far as they make complementary demands and enjoy spatial proximity which ensures the benefits of agglomeration economies under a package programme, such a clustering of inter-related industries is relevant for regional development.

Uttarakhand has six industrial complexes. They are—

1. *Dehradun*—Electronic (10 Units), Hoisery and Ready Made Garments (5 Units)
2. *Kashipur*— Hoisery (20 Units)
3. *Rudrapur*—Forest Based Industries (10 Units)
4. *Mohan*—Forest Based Industries (20 Units)
5. *Bhimtal*—Electronic Compex (10 Units)
6. *Almora*—Electronic Complex (10 Units)

Engineering Industries

Uttarakhand has the following Engineering Units—

1. *Cement*—Pithoragarh and Mandarsu
2. *Chemical*—Rishikesh (Drugs & Pharmaceuticals) and Almora.
3. *Mechanical (HMT)*—Kathgodam
4. *Electronics and Electricals*—Haridwar (Bharat Heavy Electronic Ltd.), Bhimtal and Bhowali.

Agro-Based Industries

1. Sugar—Doidwala, Kichha, Bazpur, Sitarganj, Majhola
— (4 in Nainital District and 1 in Dehradun District)
2. Paper — Kichha (Nainital)
3. Textile — Jaspur, Kashipur

A study of level of development of this area was undertaken by Economic and Statistics Directorate, Government of Uttar Pradesh. The

TABLE 1.27 : Level of Development (1980-81) : Rank Scores

S. No.	District	Agricultural Development	Infra-Structural Development	Industrial Development	Total Development
1.	Uttarkashi	215 (L)	202 (VL)	198 (VL)	843 (UD)
2.	Chamoli	206 (L)	211 (VL)	158 (VL)	745 (UD)
3.	Pithoragarh	195 (L)	212 (VL)	132 (VL)	681 (UD)
4.	Tehri Garhwal	246 (VL)	179 (VL)	198 (VL)	858 (UD)
5.	Almora	225 (VL)	135 (H)	127 (L)	603 (D)
6.	Dehradun	189 (M)	45 (VH)	106 (M)	360 (D)
7.	Garhwal	283 (VL)	159 (L)	203 (VL)	737 (UD)
8.	Nainital	62 (VH)	49 (VH)	123 (M)	275 (D)

D = Developing; DD = Developed; H = High; L = Low; M = Medium;

UD = Under Developed; VH = Very High; VL = Very Low;

results of this study are presented in Table 1.27

This factual study reveals that out of eight districts of Uttarakhand, five districts are under-developed, one is developing and only two are somewhat developed.

Future Possibilities

A. Industries

This hilly area provides an ideal condition for the development of electronic industries, silk industry, woolen industry, forest based industries—sports goods, paper, furniture, animal based industries like skins and hides, horns, etc., cottage goods industry, dairy industry etc. When Switzerland can become an industrial country, why not Uttarakhand!

B. Tourism

This hilly area has innumerable natural beauty spots which can be developed. If proper efforts are made, it may attract tourists from world over and become a great foreign currency earner.

REFERENCE SOURCES

1. Survey of India Maps.
2. Census of India.
3. Board of Revenue, Government of Uttar Pradesh.
4. Directorate of Agriculture, Government of Uttar Pradesh.
5. Chief Conservator of Forests, Government of Uttar Pradesh.
6. State Planning Institute, Government of Uttar Pradesh.
7. Economics and Statistics Directorate, Government of Uttar Pradesh.
8. U.P. History Congress, Proceedings of Session II, Kumaun University, Nainital, 1986.
9. *Geography of Uttar Pradesh*, by A.R. Tiwan, National Book Trust, New Delhi, 1971.
10. Uttar Pradesh 1978.
11. *Uttarakhand, Garhwal Himalayas,* by K.S. Ferria, *Aisan Journals,* Dehradun.
12. *Panchjanya Weekly,* Delhi.
13. *Uttaranchal Pradesh Kyoan : Aik Vivechan,* Uttaranchal Uttlan Parishad, Laxmi Printers, Mathura, 1988.

SECTION-II

BACKGROUNDERS TO THE DEMAND FOR THE FORMATION OF UTTARAKHAND/UTTRANCHAL STATE

2

INTEGRATION OF PRINCELY STATES WITH THE INDIAN UNION

2.1 Background

Before we discuss the problem of formation and reorganisation of States and Union Territories in independent India, it is proper to refer to the policy of the Indian National Congress before 1947. In 1938 at the Haripura session of the Congress, the following resolution was passed:

> "The Congress stands for the same political, social and economic freedom in the States as in the rest of India and considers the States as integral parts of India which cannot be separated. The *Purna Swaraj* or Complete Independence, which is the objective of the Congress, is for the whole of India inclucive of the States, for the integrity and unity of India must be maintained in freedom as it has been maintained in subjection. The only kind of Federation that can be acceptable to the Congress is one in which the States participate as free units enjoying the same measure of democratic freedom as the rest of India. The Congress, therefore, stands for full responsible Government and the guarantee of civil liberty in the States and deplores the present backward conditions and utter lack of freedom and suppression of civil liberties in many of these States."

On June 15, 1947, the All India Congress Committee (AICC) laid down its policy towards the Indian States. The Congress Resolution Stated:

"The A.I.C.C. cannot admit the right of any State in India to declare its independence and to live in isolation from the rest of India. That would be a denial of the course of Indian history and the objectives of the Indian people today."

"The A.I.C.C. trusts that the rulers of the States will appreciate fully the situation as it exists today and will in full co-operation with their people enter as democratic units in the Indian Union, thereby serving the cause of their own people as well as of India as a whole.

"The Committee does not agree with the theory of paramountcy as enunciated and interpreted by the British Government, but even if that is accepted the consequences that follow from the lapse of that paramountcy are limited in extent. The privileges and obligations as well as the subsisting rights as between the States and the Government of India cannot be adversely affected by the lapse of paramountcy. The rights and obligations have to be considered separately and renewed or changed by mutual agreement. The relationship between the Government of India and the States would not be exhausted by the lapse of paramountcy. The lapse does not lead to the independence of the States. Both from the point of view of the spirit underlying the Memorandom of May 12, and the Statement of 16 May, 1946, as well as the acknowledged rights of the people all over the world today, it is clear that the people of the States must have a dominating voice in any decision regarding them. Sovereignty, it is admitted, resides with the people and if paramountcy lapses resulting in the ending of the relationship of the States to the Crown, the inherent rights of the people are not affected thereby for the worse."

Jawaharlal Nehru pointed out on that occasion that the claim of the States to independence could not be sustained as independence did not depend on a mere declaring by a State but rested fundamentally on recognition by other States. The lapse of paramountcy of the British Crown did not make the Indian States independent. He said :

"There is certain inherent paramountcy in the Government of India, which cannot lapse—inherent paramountcy in the dominant State in India must remain because of the very reasons of geography, history, defence, etc., which gave rise to it when the British became the dominant power in India."

Nehru also pointed out that there were only two alternatives before the States. Either they were to join the Indian Union and become equal and autonomous partners in it or accept the paramountcy of the Indian Union as they could not live in a void. "There was no third way out of the situation—third way meaning independence or social relation to a Foreign Power." Nehru made it clear that the Indian Union did not desire any paramountcy or suzerainty but it was not prepared to allow the Indian States to have their agreements with any Foreign Power. "We cannot permit anything to happen in India in any State which affects fundamentally the security of India either in relation to defence arrangements or in relation to contact with Foreign Powers." Nehru concluded with the following warning:

> "I should like to say and other countries to know that we shall not recognize the independence of any State in India, further that any recognition of any such independence by any foreign power will be considered an unfriendly act."

Clement Richard Attlee, Prime Minister of England, also observed thus:

> "A feature running through our relations is that they (the States) have received no international recognition of independence of India as a whole. With the ending of these treaties and agreements, the States regain their independence. But they are part of geographical India and their Rulers and people are imbued with a patriotism no less great than that of their fellow Indians in British India. It would be, I think, unfortunate if owing to the severance of their paramountcy relations with the Crown they were to become islands cut off from the rest of India. The termination of their existing relationship need have no such consequences. In fact, already a number of States have declared their willingness to enter into relationship with the new Dominions and some have been represented in the Constituent Assembly of India. It is the hope of His Majesty's Government that all the States will in due course find their appropriate place with one or the other Dominion within the British Commonwealth."

2.2 Indian Independence Act, 1947

Indian Independence Act was introduced in the British Parliament on July 4, 1947 and the same was passed on July 18, 1947. The main provisions of the Act were as follows:

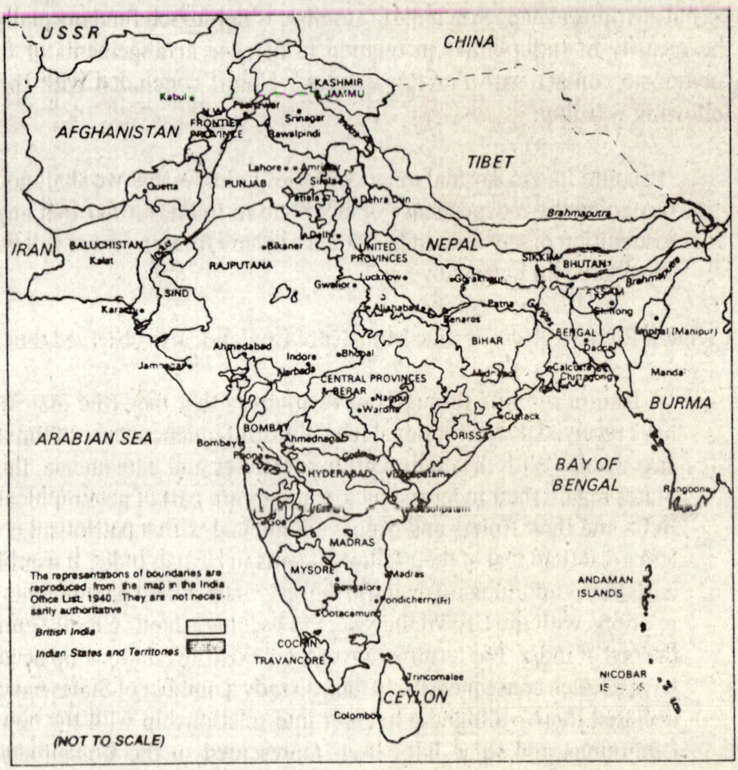

Map 2.1: India before Partition

Source : *Transfer of Power 1942-47*, Vol. XII, Her Majesty's Stationery Office London, 1983.

1. Two separate Dominions of India and Pakistan would be brought into existence on August 15, 1947 and all the powers which were previously exercised by the British Parliament would be transferred to them.
2. Territories of the two Dominions were to be defined.
3. Each Dominion would have its own Governor-General, though one person could act for both in dual capacity.
4. The Constitutent Assemblies of the two dominions were to act as constitution making bodies as well as legislative bodies in their respective Dominions.
5. All laws in force in the two Dominions on August 15, 1947, would be applicable until amended by the Legislative bodies of these Dominions.
6. The members of civil and military services would continue enjoying their existing rights and privileges and would have a continuity of service.
7. The Act of 1935 and the orders-in-council accompanying it would remain in force as they were until amended or replaced by a new Constitution in each dominion.
8. The reserved and the discretionary powers of the Governor-General under the Act of 1935 were however abolished.
9. The British paramountcy on the Indian States would lapse and these States would be able to join India or Pakistan or to remain independent.
10. There was to be an omission of the words "Emperor of India" from the Royal Style and Titles.
11. The office of the Secretary of State for India was abolished and his work was taken over by the Secretary for Commonwealth Affairs.

According to the Instrument of Accession, Indian States were required to hand over to the Indian Union only the subjects of defence, foreign relations and communications. In other matters, their autonomy was to be scrupulously respected. Sardar Patel made it clear to the Princes that it was not the desire of the Congress "to interfere in any manner in the domestic affairs of the States." He also appealed to the patriotism of Indian Princes thus:

> "We are at a momentous stage in the history of India. By common endeavour we can raise the country to a new greatness while lack of unity will expose us to fresh calamities. I hope the Indian States will bear in mind that the alternative to cooperation in the general interest is anarchy and chaos which will overwhelm great and small alike in

common ruin if we are unable to act together in the minimum of common tasks. Let not the future generations curse us for having had the opportunity but failed to turn it to our mutual advantage. Instead let it to be our proud privilege to leave a legacy of mutually beneficial relationship which would raise this Sacred Land to its proper place among the nations of the world and turn in into an abode of peace and prosperity.".

Addressing the Chamber of Princes on July 20, 1947, Louis Mountbatten also endorsed the appeal of Sardar Patel and advised the Indian States to accede to one or the other of the Dominions before August 15, 1947. He pointed out that if nothing was put in the place of co-ordinated administration that had grown up under the British rule, only chaos would result and that was bound to hurt the State most. No State could live in isolation.

Mountbatten also stressed the factors that were to be taken into consideration by the States while acceding to any Dominion: "There are certain geographical compulsions which cannot be evaded." "The vast majority of States were irretrievably linked up with India." He concluded his address thus:

> "I am not asking any State to make intolerable sacrifice of either its internal autonomy or independence. My scheme leaves you with all the practical independence that you cannot possibly use and makes you free of all those subjects which you cannot possibly manage of your own. You cannot run away from the Dominion Government which is your neighbour any more than you can run away from the subjects for whose welfare you are responsible."

The net result of all the efforts was that by August 15, 1947, with the exception of Junagadh, Hyderabad and Kashmir, more than 500 States acceded to the Indian Union. On August 15, Mountbatten paid the following tribute to Sardar Patel:

> "Thanks to that far-sighted Statesman, Sardar Vallabhbhai Patel, Minister in-charge of the States Department, a scheme was produced which appeared to me to be equally in the interests of the States as of the Dominion of India. It is a great triumph for the realism and sense of responsibility of the rulers and the governments of the States as well as for the Government of India that it was possible to produce an Instrument of Accession, which was equally acceptable to both

sides, and one moreover so simple and straightforward that within less than 3 weeks, practically all the States concerned had signed the Instrument of Accession."

2.3 Integration of States

The accession of States was only a partial solution of the problem of the States. The administration of the Indian States required to be modernised. The work of integration, democratisation and modernisation of the Indian States was done simultaneously. Integration involved the elimination of the small States by their merger with the neighbouring Provinces or States, or their consolidation into larger political units by means of the Unions of the States. Integration also involved the establishment of "a common Centre in the whole of India, able to function efficiently in the Provinces and States alike in matters requiring all-India action." In the terms of the White Paper on the States, "The aim was the integration of all elements in the country in a free, united and democratic India."

Orissa and Chattisgarh States were the first to be merged. These States were 39 in number and had a population of 70 lakhs and an area of 56,000 sq miles. Individually those States were too small for a modern system of administration. Their mergers were negotiated by Sardar Patel on 14th and 15th December, 1947. According to the Merger Agreements, the ruling Princes surrendered to the Dominion Government "full and exclusive authority, jurisdiction and power for and in relation to governance" of their States and agreed to transfer their administration on January 1, 1948. On January 1, 1948, these States became parts of Orissa and Central Provinces. On December 16, 1947, Sardar Patel observed :

> "It should be obvious to everyone, however, that even democracy and democratic institutions can function efficiently only where the units to which these are applied can subsist in a fairly autonomous existence. Where, on account of smallness of its size, isolation of its situation, the inseparable link with a neighbouring autonomous territory, be it a Province or a bigger State, in practically all economic matters of everyday life, the adequacy of the resources to open up its economic potentialities, the backwardness of its people and sheer incapacity to shoulder a self-contained administration, a State is unable to afford a modern system of Government, both democratisation and integration are clearly and unmistakably indicated."

The next merger was that of the Deccan States numbering 17. They were merged with Bombay in March 1948. Kolhapur was merged later on. In June, 1948, the Gujarat States numbering 289 were merged in Bombay Presidency. In May, 1949, Baroda was merged in Bombay Presidency. A few small States in the Punjab, the States of Banganapalli, Pudukotto and Sandur in Madras, Cooch-Behar in West Bengal, the Khasi Hills States in Assam and Tehri-Garhwal, Banaras and Rampur in U.P. were merged in the surrounding Provinces in 1948 and 1949.

The Merger Agreements of practically all the States were in identical terms. The merged States became part and parcel of the Provinces into which they were included. The people of the merged States were given representation in the Provincial Legislatures. The Government of India Act, 1935, as amended was applied to them in the same way as was done to other Provinces of India.

Another form of integration of States was the consolidation of States into Centrally administered areas. This was done in the case of Himachal Pradesh, Vindhya Pradesh, Kutch, Bilaspur, Bhopal, Tripura and Manipur. 21 States in East Punjab were consolidated into the Union of Himachal Pradesh. This Union was inaugurated on April 15, 1948. Vindhya Pradesh was created by consolidating the Bundelkhand and Baghelkhand States numbering 35. Vindhya Pradesh was created into a States Union in April, 1948 with a responsible ministry but later on its Government was taken over by the Government of India on January 1, 1950. Kutch was made a Chief Commissioner's Province in May 1948. The State of Bilaspur in the Punjab was taken over by the Government of India on October 12, 1948, the State of Bhopal on June 1, 1949, and the State of Tripura on October, 15, 1949.

Another form of integration of States was the formation of the States Unions. These Unions were created "with due regards to geographical, linguistic, social and cultural affinities" of the people living in the States. Their rulers came to be known as Rajpramukhs.

On February 15, 1948, the United States of Kathiawar (Saurashtra) was inaugurated with 222 States, estates and talukas. The important States of the Union were Nawanagar and Bhavanagar.

On March 18, 1948 was created the United States of Matsya consisting of Alwar, Bharatpur, etc. The Union of Vindhya Pradesh was created on April, 1948. The United States of Gwalior, Indore and Malwa or Madhya Bharat was inaugurated on May 28, 1948. The Patiala and East Punjab States Union (PEPSU) consisting of 7 big States such as Patiala, Nabha, Kapurthala, etc., was inaugurated on August 20, 1948.

The United States of Rajasthan was created in three stages. The first

United States of Rajasthan consisting of Mewar and nine other small Rajputana States was inaugurated on April 13, 1948. The State was reconstituted to include Jaipur, Jodhpur, Jaisalmer and Bikaner. On May 15, 1949, the United States of Matsya was incorporated into Rajasthan. The United State of Travancore-Cochin came into being on July 1, 1949.

When the Unions of the States were created, full-fledged responsible government was established in them. It is true that the people living within the Centrally-administered areas were not given full control over their administration, but the people of other Indian States were given responsible government. Legislatures were set up in the States and the Ministries were made responsible to them. The Rajpramukhs were made constitutional heads.

3

FORMATION AND REORGANISATION OF STATES AND UNION TERRITORIES: Constitutional Provisions

PART I

The Union and its Territory

1. *Name and territory of the Union*—(1) India, that is Bharat, shall be a Union of States.

[1] [(2) The States and the territories thereof shall be as specified in the first Schedule.]

(3) The territory of India shall comprise—

(a) the territories of the States;

[2] [(b) The union territories specified in the First Schedule; and]

(c) such other territories as may be acquired.

2. *Admission or establishment of new States*—Parliament may by law admit into the Union, or establish, new States on such terms and conditions as it thinks fit.

[3] 2A. [*Sikkim to be associated with the Union*]—*Rep. by the Constitution (Thirty Sixth Amendment) Act,* 1975, s.5 (w.e.f. 26-4-1975).

3. *Formation of New States and Alteration of Areas, Boundaries or names of Existing States—Parliament may by law—*

(a) form a new State by separation of territory from any State or by uniting two or more States or parts of States or by uniting any territory to a part of any State;

(b) increase the area of any State;

(c) diminish the area of any State;

(d) alter the boundaries of any State; and

(e) alter the name of any State.

[4] [Provided that no Bill for the purpose shall be introduced in either House of Parliament except on the recommendation of the President and unless, where the proposal contained in the Bill affects the area, boundaries or name of any of the States[5] ***, the Bill has been referred by the President to the Legislature of that State for expressing its views thereon within such period as may be specified in the reference or within such further period as the President may allow and the period so specified or allowed has expired.]

[6][*Explanation I*—In this article, in clauses (a) to (e), "State" includes a Union Territory, but in the proviso, "State" does not include a Union Territory.

Explanation II—The power conferred on Parliament by clause (a) includes the power to form a new State or Union Territory by uniting a part of any State or Union Territory to any other State or Union Territory.]

4. *Laws made under articles 2 and 3 to provide for the amendment of the First and the Fourth Schedules and supplemental, incidental and consequential matters* — (1) Any law referred to in article 2 or article 3 shall contain such provisions for the amendment of the First Schedule and the Fourth Schedule as may be necessary to give effect to the provisions of the law and may also contain such supplemental, incidental and consequential provisions (including provisions as to representation in Parliament and in the Legislature or Legislatures of the State or States affected by such law) as Parliament may deem necessary.

(2) No such law as aforesaid shall be deemed to be an amendment of this Constitution for the purposes of Article 368.

FIRST SCHEDULE

(Articles 1 and 4)

I. The States

	Name	Territories
1.	Andhra Pradesh	[8][The territories specified in sub-section (1) of

		section 3 of the Andhra State Act, 1953, sub-section (1) of section 3 of the States Reorganisation Act, 1956; the First Schedule to the Andhra Pradesh and Madras (Alteration of Boundaries) Act, 1959, and the Schedule to the Andhra Pradesh and Mysore (Transfer of Territory) Act, 1968, but excluding the territories specified in the Second Schedule to the Andhra Pradesh and Madras (Alteration of Boundaries) Act, 1959.]
2.	Assam	The territories which immediately before the commencement of this Constitution were comprised in the Province of Assam, the Khasi States and the Assam Tribal Areas, but excluding the territories specified in the Schedule to the Assam (Alteration of Boundaries) Act, 1951[9][and the territories specified in sub-section (1) of section 3 of the State of Nagaland Act, 1962][10][and the territories specified in sections 5, 6 and 7 of the North-Eastern Areas (Reorganisation) Act, 1971].
3.	Bihar	[11] [The territories which immediately before the commencement of this Constitution were either comprised in the Province of Bihar or were being administered as if they formed part of that Province and the territories specified in clause (a) of sub-section (1) of section 3 of the Bihar and Uttar Pradesh (Alteration of Boundaries) Act, 1968, but excluding the territories specified in sub-section (1) of section 3 of the Bihar and West Bengal (Transfer of Territories) Act, 1956, and the territories specified in clause (b) of sub-section (1) of section 3 of the first mentioned Act.)
[12] [4.	Gujarat	The territories referred to in sub-section (1) of section 3 of the Bombay Reorganisation Act, 1960.]
5.	Kerala	The territories specified in sub-section (1) of section 5 of the States Reorganisation Act, 1956.

6.	Madhya Pradesh	The territories specfied in sub-section (1) of section 9 of the States Reorganisation Act, 1956 [13][and the First Schedule to the Rajasthan and Madhya Pradesh (Transfer of Territories) Act, 1959].
[14][7.	Tamil Nadu	The territories which immediately before the commencement of this Constitution were either comprised in the Province of Madras or were being administered as if they formed part of that Province and the territories specified in section 4 of the States Reorganisation Act, 1956. [15][and the Second Schedule to the Andhra Pradesh and Madras (Alteration of Boundaries) Act, 1959,] but excluding the territories specified in sub-section (1) of section 3 and sub-section (1) of section 4 of the Andhra State Act, 1953 and [16][the territories specified in clause (b) of sub-section (1) of section 5, section 6 and clause (d) of sub-section (1) of section 7 of the States Reorganisation Act, 1956 and the territories specified in the First Schedule to the Andhra Pradesh and Madras (Alteration of Boundaries) Act, 1959].
[17][8.	Maharashtra	The territories specified in sub-section (1) of section 8 of the States Reorganisation Act, 1956, but excluding the territories referred to in sub-section (1) of section 3 of the Bombay Reorganisation Act, 1960.]
[18][9.	Karnataka]	The territories specified in sub-section (1) of section 7 of the States Reorganisation Act, 1956 [19][but excluding the territory specified in the Schedule to the Andhra Pradesh and Mysore (Transfer of Territory) Act, 1968].
[20][10.]	Orissa	The territories which immediately before the commencement of this Constitution were either comprised in the Province of Orissa or were being administered as if they formed part of that Province.
[20][11.]	Punjab	The territories specified in section 11 of the States Reorganisation Act, 1956 [21][and the territories referred to in Part II of the First

Schedule to the Acquired Territories (Merger) Act, 1960] [22][but excluding the territories referred to in Part II of the First Schedule to the Constitution (Ninth Amendment) Act, 1960] [23][and the territories specified in sub-section (1) of section 3, section 4 and sub-section (1) of section 5 of the Punjab Reorganisation Act, 1966].

[20] [12.] Rajasthan	The territories specified in section 10 of the States Reorganisation Act, 1956 [24][but excluding the territories specified in the First Schedule to the Rajasthan and Madhya Pradesh (Transfer of Territories) Act, 1959].
[20] [13.] Uttar Pradesh	[25] [The territories which immediately before the commencement of this Constitution were either comprised in the Province known as the United Provinces or were being administered as if they formed part of that Province, the territories specified in clause (b) of sub-section (1) of section 3 of the Bihar and Uttar Pradesh (Alteration of Boundaries) Act. 1968 and the territories specified in clause (b) of sub-section (1) of section 4 of the Haryana and Uttar Pradesh (Alteration of Boundaries) Act, 1979, but excluding the territories specified in clause (a) of sub-section (1) of section 3 of the Bihar and Uttar Pradesh (Alteration of Boundaries) Act, 1968, and the territories specified in clause (a) of sub section (1) of section 4 of the Haryana and Uttar Pradesh (Alteration of Boundaries) Act. 1979.]
[20] [14.] West Bengal	The territories which immediately before the commencement of this Constitution were either comprised in the Province of West Bengal or were being administered as if they formed part of that Province and the territory of Chandernagore as defined in clause (c) of section 2 of the Chandernagore (Merger) Act, 1954 and also the territories specified in sub-section (1) of section 3 of the Bihar and West Bengal (Transfer of Territories) Act, 1956.

[20] [15]. Jammu and Kashmir	The territory which immediately before the commencement of this Constitution was comprised in the Indian State of Jammu and Kashmir.
[26] [16. Nagaland	The territories specified in sub-section (1) of section 3 of the State of Nagaland Act, 1962.]
[27] [17. Haryana	[28] [The territories specified in sub section (1) of section 3 of the Punjab Reorganisation Act, 1966 and the territories specified in clause (a) of sub-section (1) of section 4 of the Haryana and Uttar Pradesh (Alteration of Boundaries) Act, 1979, but excluding the territories specified in clause (b) of sub-section (1) of section 4 of that Act.]]
[29] [18. Himachal Pradesh	The territories which immediately before the commencement of this Constitution were being administered as if they were Chief Commissioner's' Provinces under the names of Himachal Pradesh and Bilaspur and the territories specified in sub-section (1) of section 5 of the Punjab Reorganisation Act, 1966.]
[30] [19. Manipur	The territory which immediately before the commencement of this Constitution was being administered as if it were a Chief Commissioner's Province under the name of Manipur.]
20. Tripura	The territory which immediately before the commencement of this Consitution was being administered as if it were a Chief Commissioner's Province under the name of Tripura.
21. Meghalaya	The territories specified in section 5 of the North-Eastern Areas (Reorganisation) Act. 1971.]
[31] [22. Sikkim	The territories which immediately before the commencement of the Constitution (Thirty-sixth Amendment) Act, 1975, were comprised in Sikkim.]
[32] [23. Mizoram	The territories specified in section 6 of the North-Eastern Areas (Reorganisation) Act, 1971.]
[33] [24. Arunachal Pradesh	The territories specified in Section 7 of the North-Eastern Areas (Reorganisation) Act,

		1971.]
[34][25. Goa		The territories specified in section 3 of the Goa, Daman and Diu Reorganisation Act, 1987.]

II. The Union Territories

1.	Delhi	The territory which immediately before the commencement of this Constitution was comprised in the Chief Commissioner's Province of Delhi
	[35] *	* * * *
	[36] *	* * * *
[37] [2].	The Andaman and Nicobar Islands	The territory which immediately before the commencement of this Constitution was comprised in the Chief Commissioner's Province of the Andaman and Nicobar Islands.
[37] [3.]	[38][Lakshadweep	The territory specified in section 6 of the States Reorganisation Act, 1956.
[39] [[37] [4.]	Dadra and Nagar Haveli	The Territory which immediately before the eleventh day of August, 1961 was comprised in Free Dadra and Nagar Haveli.
[40][[41][[38] [5.]	Daman and Diu	The territories specified in Section 4 of the Goa, Daman and Diu Reorganisation Act, 1987.
[43][[38] [6.]	Pondicherry	The territories which immediately before the sixteenth day of August, 1962, were comprised in the French Establishments in India known as Pondicherry, Karikal, Mahe and Yanam.
[44][[38][7.]	Chandigarh	The territories specified in Section 4 of the Punjab Reorganisation Act. 1966.
	[44][*	* * * * *
	[45][*	* * * * *

The State Legislature

Article **168,** Constitution of Legislatures in states (1) For every State there shall be a Legislature which shall consist of the Governor, and —

(a) in the States of [46] ***, Bihar [47] ***[48, 49] ***, [50] [Maharashtra], [51] [Karnataka], [52] *** [53] [and Uttar Pradesh], two Houses;

(b) in other States, one House.

(2) Where there are two Houses of the Legislature of a State, one shall be known as the Legislative Council and the other as the Legislative Assembly, and where there is only one House, it shall be known as the Legislative Assembly.

169. *Abolition or Creation of Legislative Councils in States*—(1) Notwithstanding anything in Article 168, Parliament may by law provide for the abolition of the Legislative Council of a State having such a Council or for the creation of such a Council in a State having no such Council, if the Legislative Assembly of the State passes a resolution to that effect by a majority of the total membership of the Assembly and by a majority of not less than two-thirds of the members of the Assembly present and voting.

(2) Any law referred to in clause (1) shall contain such provision for the amendment of this Constitution as may be necessary to give effect to the provisions of the law and may also contain such supplemental, incidental and consequential provisions as Parliament may deem necessary.

(3) No such law as aforesaid shall be deemed to be an amendment of this Constitution for the purpose of article 368.

[54][**170.** *Composition of the Legislative Assemblies*—(1) Subject to the provisions of Article 333; the Legislative Assembly of each State shall consist of not more than five hundred, and not less than sixty members chosen by direct election from territorial constituencies in the State.

(2) For the purpose of clause (1) each State shall be divided into territorial constituencies in such manner that the ratio between the population of each constituency and the number of seats allotted to it shall, so far as practicable, be the same throughout the State.

[55] [*Explanation* — In this clause, the expression "population" means the population as ascertained at the last preceding census of which the relevant figures have been published:

Provided that the reference in this Explanation to the last preceding census of which the relevant figures have been published shall, until the relevant figures for the first census taken after the year 2000 have been published, be construed as a reference to the 1971 census.]

(3) Upon the completion of each census, the total number of seats in the Legislative Assembly of each State and the division of each State into territorial constituencies shall be readjusted by such authority and in such manner as Parliament may by law determine.

Provided that such readjustment shall not affect representation in the Legislative Assembly until the dissolution of the then existing Assembly:]

[56][Provided further that such readjustment shall take effect from such date as the President may, by order, specify and until such readjustment

takes effect, any election to the Legislative Assembly may be held on the basis of the territorial constituencies existing before such readjustment:

Provided also that until the relevant figures for the first census taken after the year 2000 have been published, it shall not be necessary to readjust the total number of seats in the Legislative Assembly of each State and the division of such State into territorial constituencies under this clause.]

171. *Composition of the Legislative Councils*—(1) The total number of members in the Legislative Council of a State having such a Council shall not exceed one third of the total number of members in the Legislative Assembly of that State.

Provided that the total number of members in the Legislative Council of a State shall in no case be less than forty.

(2) Until Parliament by law otherwise provides, the composition of the Legislative Council of a State shall be as provided in clause (3).

(3) Of the total number of members of the Legislative Council of a State—

(a) as nearly as may be, one-third shall be elected by electorates consisting of members of municipalities, district boards and such other local authorities in the State as Parliament may by law specify;

(b) as nearly as may be, one-twelfth shall be elected by electorates consisting of persons residing in the State who have been for at least three years graduates of any university in the territory of India or have been for at least three years in possession of qualifications prescribed by or under any law made by Parliament as equivalent to that of a graduate of any such university;

(c) as nearly as may be, one-twelfth shall be elected by electorates consisting of persons who have been for at least three years engaged in teaching in such educational institutions within the State, not lower in standard than that of a secondary school, as may be prescribed by or under any law made by Parliament;

(d) as nearly as may be, one-third shall be elected by the members of the Legislative Assembly of the State from amongst persons who are not members of the Assembly;

(e) the remainder shall be nominated by the Governor in accordance with the provisions of clause (5).

(4) The members to be elected under sub-clauses (a), (b) and (c) of clause (3) shall be chosen in such territorial constituencies as may be prescribed by or under any law made by Parliament, and the elections under the said sub-clauses and under sub-clause (d) of the said clause shall be held in accordance with the system of proportional representation by

means of the single transferable vote.

(5) The members to be nominated by the Governor under sub-clause (e) of clause (3) shall consist of persons having special knowledge or practical experience in respect of such matters as the following, namely:—

Literature, science, art, co-operative movement and social service.

172. *Duration of State Legislatures*—(1) Every Legislative Assembly of every State, unless sooner dissolved, shall continue for [58][five years] from the date appointed for its first meeting and no longer and the expiration of the said period of [58][five years] shall operate as a dissolution of the Assembly:

Provided that the said period may, while a Proclamation of Emergency is in operation, be extended by Parliament by law for a period not exceeding one year at a time and not extending in any case beyond a period of six months after the Proclamation has ceased to operate.

(2) The Legislative Council of a State shall not be subject to dissolution, but as nearly as possible one-third of the members thereof shall retire as soon as may be on the expiration of every second year in accordance with the provisions made in that behalf by Parliament by law.

NOTES

1. Subs. by the Constitution (Seventh Amendment) Act, 1956, s. 2, for ci. (2)
2. Subs. by s. 2 *ibid,* for sub-clause (b)
3. Ins. by the Constitution (Thirty-fifth Amendment) Act, 1974; s. 2 (w.e.f. 1-3-1975)
4. Subs. by the Constitution (Fifth Amendment) Act, 1955, s. 2 for the proviso.
5. The words and letters "specified in Part A or Part B of the First Schedule" omitted by the Constitution (Seventh Amendment) Act. 1956 s. 29 and Sch.
6. Ins. by the Constitution (Eighteenth Amendment) Act. 1966, s. 2.
7. Subs. by the Constitution (Seventh Amendment) Act. 1956, s. 2, for the First Sch.
8. Subs. by the Andhra Pradesh and Mysore (Transfer of Territory) Act. 1968 (36 of 1968) s. 4 for the former entry (w.e.f. 1-10-1968).
9. Added by the State of Nagaland Act. 1962 (27 of 1962). s. 4 (w.e.f. 1-12-1963).
10. Added by the North-Eastern Areas (Reorganisation) Act, 1971 (81 of 1971) s. 9 (w.e.f 21-1-1972).
11. Subs. by the Bihar and Uttar Pradesh (Alteration of Boundaries) Act. 1968 (24 of 1968), s. 4 for the former entry (w.e.f. 10-6-1970).
12. Subs. by the Bombay Reorganisation Act, 1960 (11 of 1960), s. 4 for entry 4 (w.e.f. 1-5-1960).
13. Ins. by the Rajasthan and Madhya Pradesh (Transfer of Territories) Act. 1959) s. 4 (w.e.f. 1-10-1959).
14. Subs. by the Madras State (Alteration of Name) Act, 1968 (53 of 1968) s. 5 for "7 Madras" (w.e.f. 1-10-1969).
15. Ins. by the Andhra Pradesh and Madras (Alteration of Boundaries) Act. 1959 (56 of 1959) s. 6 (w.e.f. 1-4-1960).

16. Subs. by s. 6 *ibid.*, for certain words (w.e.f. 1-4-1960).
17. Ins. by the Bombay Reorganisation Act. 1960 (11 of 1960) s. 4 (w.e.f. 1-5-1960).
18. Subs. by the Mysore State (Alteration of Name) Act., 1973 (31 of 1973), s. 5 for "9 Mysore" (w.e.f. 1-11-1973).
19. Ins. by the Andhra Pradesh and Mysore (Transfer of Territory) Act. 1968 (36 of 1968, s. 4 (w.e.f. 1-10-1968).
20. Entries 8 to 14 renumbered as entries 9 to 15 by the Bombay Reorganisation Act., 1960 (11 of 1960), s. 4 (w.e.f 1-5-1960).
21. Ins. by the Acquired Territories (Merger) Act. 1960 (64 of 1960), s. 4 (w.e.f. 17-1-1961).
22. Added by the Constitution (Ninth Amendment) Act. 1960, s. 3 (w.e.f. 17-1-1961).
23. Ins. by the Punjab Reorganisation Act. 1966 (31 of 1966) s. 7 (w.e.f. 1-11-1966).
24. Ins. by the Rajasthan and Madhya Pradesh (Transfer of Territories) Act, 1959 (47 of 1959) s. 4 (w.e.f. 1-10-1959).
25. Subs, by the Haryana and Uttar Pradesh (Alteration of Boundaries) Act. 1979 (31 of 1979), s. 5 for the former entry (w.e.f 15-9-1983).
26. Ins. by the State of Nagaland Act, 1962, (27 of 1962), s. 4 (w.e.f. 1-12-1963)
27. Ins. by the Punjab Reorganisation Act. 1966 (31 of 1966), s. 7 (w.e.f. 1-11-1966)
28. Subs. by the Haryana and Uttar Pradesh (Alteration of Boundaries) Act. 1979 (31 of 1979), s. 5 for the former entry (w.e.f 15-9-1983).
29. Ins by the State of Himachal Pradesh Act. 1970 (53 of 1970). s. 4 (w.e.f. 25-1-1971)
30. Ins. by the North-Eastern Areas (Reorganisation) Act, 1971 (81 of 1971) s. 9 (w.e.f. 21-1-1972).
31. Ins. by the Constitution (Thirty-sixth Amendment) Act. 1975, s. 2 (w.e.f. 26-4-1975)
32. Ins. by the State of Mizoram Act. 1986 (34 of 1986), s. 4 (w.e.f. 20-2-1987)
33. Ins. by the State of Arunachal Pradesh Act, 1986 (69 of 1986, s. 4 (w.e.f. 20-2-1987)
34. Ins. by the Goa, Daman and Diu Reorganisation Act, 1987 (18 of 1987), s. 5 (w.e.f. 30-5-1987).
35. Entry 2 relating to "Himachal Pradesh" omitted by the State of Himachal Pradesh Act, 1970 (53 of 1970), s. 4 (w.e.f. 25-1-1971).
36. Entries relating to Manipur and Tripura omitted by the North-Eastern Areas (Reorganisation) Act. 1971 (81 of 1971), s. 9 (w.e.f 21-1-1972).
37. Entires 4 to 9 renumbered as entires 2 to 7 by s. 9 ibid. (w.e.f. 21-1-1972)
38. Subs. by the Laccadive, Minicoy and Amindivi Islands (Alteration of Name) Act. 1973 (34 of 1973), s. 5 for "the Laccadive, Minicoy and Amindivi Islands." (w.e.f. 1-11-1973).
39. Ins. by the Constitution (Tenth Amendment) Act, 1961, s. 2.
40. Subs. by the Goa. Daman and Diu Reorganisation Act., 1987 (18 of 1987), s. 5 for entry 5 (w.e.f. 30-5-1987).
41. Ins. by the Constitution (Twelfth Amendment) Act, 1962, s. 2.
42. Ins. by the Constitution (Fourteenth Amendment) Act, 1962, ss. 3 and 7 (w.e.f. 16-8-1962).
43. Ins. by the Punjab Reorganisation Act, 1966 (31 of 1966), s. 7 (w.e.f. 1-11-1966),
44. Entry 8 omitted and entry 9 renumbered as entry 8 by the State of Mizoram Act. 1986 (34 of 1986) s. 4 (w.e.f. 20-2-1987).
45. Omitted by the State of Arunachal Pradesh Act., 1986 (69 of 1986) s. 4 (w.e.f. 20-2-1987).
46. The words "Andhra Pradesh," omitted by the Andhra Pradesh Legislative Council (Abolition) Act, 1985 (34 of 1985), s. 4 (w.e.f. 1-6-1985).
47. The word "Bombay" omitted by the Bombay Reorganisation Act. 1960 (11 of 1960), s. 20 (w.e.f. 1-5-1960).
48. No date has been appointed under s. 8 (2) of the Constitution (Seventh Amendment) Act. 1956 for the insertion of the words "Madhya Pradesh" in this sub-clause.

49. The words "Tamil Nadu" omitted by the Tamil Nadu Legislative Council (Abolition) Act, 1986 (40 of 1986) s. 4 (w.e.f. 1-11-1986).
50. Ins. by the Bombay Reorganisation Act, 1960 (11 of 1960), s. 20 (w.e.f. 1-5-1960).
51. Subs. by the Mysore State (Alteration of Name) Act. 1973, s. 4 for "Mysore" (w.e.f. 1-11-1973), which was inserted by the Constitution (Seventh Amendment) Act, 1956, s. 8 (1).
52. The word, "Punjab", omitted by the Punjab Legislative Council (Abolition) Act, 1969 (46 of 1969), s. 4 (w.e.f. 7-1-1970).
53. Subs. by the West Bengal Legislative Council (Abolition) Act. 1969 (20 of 1969), s. 4 for "Uttar Pradesh and West Bengal" (w.e.f. 1-8-1969).
54. Subs. by the Constitution (Seventh Amendment) Act, 1956 s. 9 for art. 170.
55. Subs. by the Constitution (Forty-second Amendment) Act, 1976, s. 29 for the Explanation (w.e.f. 31-1-1977).
56. Ins. by s. 29 ibid. (w.e.f. 3-1-1977)
57. Subs. by the Constitution (Seventh Amendment) Act. 1956, s. 10 for "one fourth".
58. Subs. by the Constitution (Forty-fourth Amendment) Act, 1978, s. 24, for "six years" (w.e.f. 6-9-1979). The words "six years" were subs. for the original words "five years" by the Constitution (Forty-second Amendment) Act, 1976 s. 30 (w.e.f. 3-1-1977).

Appointment

The State Reorganization Commission was constituted under the Ministry of Home Affairs vide their Resolution No. 53/69/53-Public dated December 29, 1953.

Terms of Reference

The Commission will investigate the conditions of the problem, the historical background, the existing situation and the bearing of all important and relevant factors thereon.

Contents

Introductory; *Part I:* The Problem; State of the Indian Union; Rationale of Reorganization; Time for Reorganization; *Part II:* Factors Bearing on Reorganization: Cost of Change; Unity and Security of India; Language and Culture; Financial Viability; Requirements of National Development Plans; Regional Planning and a Balanced Economy; Smaller vs. Larger States; Some other Factors; *Part III:* Proposals for Reorganisation: Basic Pattern of the Component Units; Madras; Kerala; Karnataka; Hyderabad; Andhra; Bombay; Vidarbha; Madhya Pradesh; Rajasthan; The Punjab; Delhi; Uttar Pradesh, Bihar; West Bengal; Assam; Manipur; Orissa; The Reorganized Units; *Part IV:* Administrative and Allied Matters; Safeguards for Linguistic Groups; The Integration of Services; Financial and other Administrative Measures; The Unity of India; Notes and summary; Note on Himachal Pradesh; Note on Uttar Pradesh; Summary of Conclusions and Recommendations; Appendices I and II.

Recommendations

The problem of the reorganization of States is urgent as with large-scale planning the country has to think in terms of enduring political units. The integration of States has removed the main hurdle in the way of rationalization of the existing units. Further deferment of a general reorganization will cause dissatisfaction and disappointment.

In proposing any changes in the existing structure, due consideration should be given to the unsettling consequences of reorganization. The changes proposed should be such as would compensate, in terms of the welfare of the people, for the administrative dislocation and the heavy burden on the administrative and financial resources of the country which they entail.

In the interests of the national unity, it is necessary that the administrative and political structure of the country should be based on the primacy of the nation.

The administrative set-up in strategic area should be determined primarily by considerations of national security. Where border areas are not under the direct control of the centre, it would be safer to have relatively large and resourceful States.

It is neither possible nor desirable to reorganize States on the basis of a single test of either language or culture; a balanced approach, which takes all relavant factors into account, is necessary.

Financial viability has an important bearing on reorganization proposals, but it has to be considered along with other relevant factors.

Some degree of dislocation in the working of the next plan is likely to be caused by any scheme of reorganization; this dislocation, however, should be considered along with the possible advantages of reorganization. Steps should also be taken to minimize the unsettling effects of reorganization.

The States cannot be so reorganized as to conform to economic regions. Nor can the principle of economic self-sufficieny within an administrative unit be regarded as a clear criterion. Consistently with these principles it would be desirable to avoid as far as possible wide disparities in resources between the various States.

The wishes of the people should be regarded as an important factor bearing on reorganization but they have to be considered along with other relevant factors.

The facts of the existing situation are more important than the previous historical associations of different areas. Undue importance cannot be attached, therefore to historical arguments.

Geographical contiguity of the units is important from the point of view of administrative convenience. Other geographical factors have to be regarded as secondary.

The existing constitutional disparity between the different constituent units of the Indian Union should disappear as a necessary consequence of reorganization.

In respect of three of the Part C States, namely, Himachal Pradesh, Kutch and Tripura, the Central Government should retain supervisory powers for a specified period to maintain their present pace of development.

Such of the existing Part C States as cannot be merged in the adjoining areas for security and other imperative consideration should be administered by the Centre as “territories”.

The component units of the Indian Union should thus consist of two categories;

(a) "States" forming primary federating units of the Indian Union; and
(b) "Territories" which are Centrally-administered.

Madras

This State should include the existing territories subject to the following adjustments, namely:

(i) The five taluks of Agastheeswaram, Thovala, Kalkulam, Vilavancode and Shencotta, now forming part of Travancore-Cochin, should be transferred to the State of Madras; and
(ii) The districts of Malabar and South Kanara and Kollegal Taluk of Coimbatore District should be detached from Madras.

Kerala

The State of Kerala should be formed, which should consist of the following areas:

(a) The State of Travancore-Cochin minus the five taluks proposed to be transferred to Madras;
(b) Malabar District (including Fort Cochin and the Laccadive Islands), Kasaragod Taluk of South Kanara District and the Amindive Islands.

Karnataka

The State of Karnataka should be created consisting of the following areas:

(a) The present State of Mysore, excluding Siruguppa Taluk, Bellary Taluk, Hospet Taluk and a small portion of Mallapuram Sub-Taluk of Bellary District;
(b) The four Kannada-speaking districts of Bombay, namely, Dharwar, Bijapur, North Kanara and Belgaum (except Chandgad Taluk of Belgaum District);

(c) The districts of Raichur and Gulbarga from Hyderabad;
(d) South Kanara District of Madras minus Kasaragod Taluk;
(e) Kollegal Taluk of Coimbatore District of Madras; and
(f) Coorg.

Hyderabad

Apart from the districts of Raichur and Gulbarga, the Marathwada districts should also be detached from Hyderabad State. The residuary State which should continue to be known as Hyderabad should consist of the Telugu-speaking districts of the present State of Hyderabad, namely, Mahbubnagar, Nalgonda, Warangal (including Khammam), Karimnagar, Adilabad, Nizamabad, Hyderabad and Medak, along with Bidar District, and Munagala Enclave in Nalgonda District belonging to Krishna District of Andhra.

The residuary State of Hyderabad might unite with Andhra after the General Elections likely to be held in or about 1961, if by a two-thirds majority the Legislature of Hyderabad State expresses itself in favour of such unification.

The future of the remaining areas of Hyderabad, consisting of the districts known as Marathwada, is dealt with later on under Bombay.

Andhra

Andhra State should for the time being continue as it is, subject to certain minor adjustments which are mentioned below:

The talukas of Siruguppa, Bellary and Hospet and a portion of Mallapuram Sub-Taluk of Bellary District should be transferred to Andhra.

Munagala Enclave of Krishna District, as has already been Stated, should be transferred to Hyderabad.

There should be no change in the present position regarding Madras city and its future should be regarded as finally settled.

Bombay

The State of Bombay should be reconstituted so as to include the existing Bombay State minus Abu Road Taluk of Banaskantha District and the Kannada speaking districts of Dharwar, Bijapur, North Kanara and Belgaum (excluding Chandgad Taluk), plus the following areas;

(a) The marathi-speaking districts of Hyderabad namely, Osmanabad, Bhir, Aurangabad, Parbhani and Nanded;
(b) Saurashtra; and
(c) Kutch.

Vidarbha

A new State to be known as Vidarbha should be created, consisting of the following Marathi-speaking districts of Madhya Pradesh, namely, Buldana, Akola, Amaravati, Yeotmal, Wardha, Nagpur, Bhandara and Chanda.

Madhya Pradesh

After the separation of Vidarbha, a new State, which may be known as Madhya Pradesh, should be created consisting of:

(i) The 14 districts of the residuary Madhya Pradesh;
(ii) The whole of Bhopal and the whole of Vindhya Pradesh;
(iii) Madhya Bharat except Sunel Enclave of Mandsaur District; and
(iv) Sironj Sub-Division of Kotah District of Rajasthan.

Rajasthan

After the proposed merger of Sironj in the new Madhya Pradesh State, Rajasthan should continue in its present form subject to the addition of territories mentioned below;

(i) Ajmer; and
(ii) Abu Road Taluk of Banaskantha District of Bombay, Sunel Enclave of Mandsaur District of Madhya Bharat and Loharu Sub-Tehsil of Hissar District of the Punjab.

The Punjab

There is no case for dividing the present Punjab State. Pepsu and Himachal Pradesh should, however, be merged in the Punjab.

Loharu Sub-Tehsil of Hissar District, as already stated, should be transferred to Rajasthan. Apart from the safeguards referred to in Paragraph 24 of this Summary, Himachal Pradesh should be represented in the Punjab Cabinet by at least one member.

Uttar Pradesh

There is no case for dividng Uttar Pradesh, and this State should continue in its existing form.

Bihar

It does not seem to be either necessary or desirable to create a Jharkhand State in South Bihar, the special needs of this area should, however, be recognized. Seraikella and Kharsawan should continue to be part of Bihar. Some adjustments in the two eastern districts be longing to Bihar are indicated under West Bengal.

West Bengal

A portion of Purnea District east of the river Mahananda and Purulia Sub-District of Manbhum District minus the Chas Thana should be transferred from Bihar to West Bengal.

Subject to the recommendations summarized in the immediately preceding paragraph, no boundary adjustments seem to be called for in order to satisfy claims and counter-claims in respect of the border areas of Bihar, West Bengal, Assam and Orissa.

Assam

Assam should continue as it is subject to the changes mentioned below.

The demand for the creation of a Hill State in Assam is impracticable and there is also no reason, having regard to the peculiar features and circumstances of Assam, why a separate Hill State should be created; Special attention should, however, be paid to the development of the hill districts and an enquiry into the working of the autonomous bodies created under the sixth Schedule to the Constitution should be undertaken.

Tripura should be merged in Assam. The present arrangements with regard to the North-East Frontier Agency should continue.

Orissa

No changes are called for in the boundaries of Orissa which were fixed in 1936 after a prolonged and detailed examination.

Jammu & Kashmir

No recommendation are made in regard to Jammu and Kashmir. The units or area which have not been dealt with so far will be directly administered by the Centre and will be known as territories.

Delhi

Delhi should be constituted into such a Centrally-administered territory; the question of creating a Municipal Corporation with substantial powers should be considered.

Manipur

Manipur should be a Centrally-administered territory for the time being. The ultimate merger of this State in Assam should be kept in view.

Andaman and Nicobar Islands

The *status que* in the Andaman and Nicobar Islands should continue. The arrangement in regard to areas which have been or may be brought under Central administration in future, either before or after becoming *de jure* part of the territory of India, must be flexible, until the position is finally clarified.

Constitutional recognition should be given to the right of linguistic minorities to have instruction in their mother tongues at the primary school stage subject to a sufficient number of students being available. The Central Government should acquire powers to enforce this right on the lines of the provisions contained in Article 347 of the Constitution.

The Government of India should adopt, in consultation with the State Governments, a clear code to govern the use of different languages at different levels of State administration and take steps, under Article 347, to ensure that this code is followed.

The domicile tests in force in certain States operate to the disadvantage of minority groups. The Government of India should, therefore, undertake legislation under Article 16 (3) of the Constitution in order to simplify and liberalize the requirements as to residence.

In examinations regulating entry into the Public Service of the States, a candidate should have the option to elect as the medium, apart from the main language of the State, the Union language, namely, English or Hindi, or the language of a minority constituting about 15 to 20 per cent or more of the population of the State.

As far as possible, Public Service Commissions should be constituted to serve more than one State. Appointments to Public Service Commissions serving even single States should be made by the President as in the case of appointments to joint Public Service Commission.

The reconstitution of the sanctioned State Cadres and the integration of Services should be accorded very high priority, and must be decided on the basis of certain general principles, due regard being paid to the option of the employees, the need for a mixed element in the services, *inter se* seniority in the State of origin, etc., and also the needs of the new States. The body constituted to integrate the service personnel of different States should be one that inspires confidence, and only one appeal against decisions regarding integration should be permitted.

After the scheme of reorganization has been given effect to, it may be necessary for some of the new administrations to review the number and territorial extent of the existing districts as well as Commissioners charges and the rationalization of the administrative structure. Decisions on the reorganization proposals should, if possible, be taken before the next Finance Commission commences its enquiries. If may be necessary to grant ways and means advances to newly-constituted units in order to help them to tide over temporary difficulties. Pending a comprehensive review, grants-in-aid on Revenue or Capital account as well as long-term loans should be made available to the new units as nearly as possible on the existing basis. The Government of India should fix the existing statutory and development grants and long-term loans with reference to the principles on which such grants or loans have been sanctioned.

Payments under Articles 278 of the Constitution may be continued and apportioned population-wise among new units until such time as the position is reviewed by the Finance Commission.

Pending the amendment of Article 264 (b) of the Constitution, appropriate portions of the divisible pools pertaining to Part C States, which are now retained by the Centre, may be distributed among the new units, where necessary, in proportion to their population. Assets and liabilities should be divided on the basis of principles which should, as far as practicable, be of general application. Financial settlements in the case of Part C States need not be elaborate, but may be based on a review of the position as it exists today and the needs of these areas. The question of setting up some special machinery to expedite the final settlements regarding assets and liabilities should be considdered.

It will be necessary to adapt current inter-State agreement regarding water rights, etc., with due regard to the broad basis on which they may have been drawn up, and this question should be taken up as soon as possible after decisions regarding reorganization have been reached. The creation of Special Development Boards for certain areas which are underdeveloped should be considered. A permanent body, in which members of the Planning Commission may be included, should be set up in order to examine the grievances, if any, on the score of the alleged neglect of certain areas.

The Government of India should consider the question of formulating an Industrial Location Policy for the whole of India, in order to ensure an equitable distribution of development expenditure. As a general rule, 50 per cent of the new entrants in the All-India Services should be from outside the State concerned, this computation being made after deducting the number of posts in any State which are to be filled by promotion. Certain All-India Services, namely, the Indian Service of Engineers, the Indian Forest Service and the Indian Medical and Health Service, should be constituted. Regular transfers to and from the Centre and the States in respect of personnel belonging to the All India Services should, as far as possible be arranged. The curriculum of studies for the new entrants to the All-India and Central Services should include such basic and essential subjects as Indian history, geography, religions, customs and manners.

In formulating a policy regarding the recognition of Hindi in Competitive Examinations for the All-India and other services, the need for encouraging the study of other Indian languages, and particularly of the South Indian language, should be kept in view.

At least one-third of the number of Judges in the High Court of a State should consist of persons who are recruited from outside that State.

For some time to come, English should continue to occupy an important place in our universities and institutions of higher learning even after the adoption of Hindi and the regional languages for official and educational purposes. Osmania University should be placed under the Central Government and the medium of instruction in this University should be Hindi. One more Central University should be established further South and arrangements should be made for the study of South Indian languages in the North.

Reorganization has a legitimate place in this country, but its limitations must be recognized. If the supremacy of the Union not merely in the political but also in the economic thinking of the country is fully realized, the issues arising out of the reorganization of States should not assume the proportions of major political controversies.

4.3 Bombay City

The Maharashtrians raised a lot of hue and cry over the city of Bombay. The Congress High Command declared that it was willing to make alterations in the recommendations of the Commission if all the interested parties agreed upon any alternative. Prolonged negotiations were held and many changes were made in the recommendations of the Commission but the problem of Bombay City gave headache to all. It was decided to create the bilingual State of Bombay containing all the territories of Maharashtra and Saurashtra with Bombay as capital. The Bill was passed by the Lok Sabha and Rajya Sabha and received the assent of President on August 31, 1956.

4.4 The States Reorganisation Act, 1956

The States Reorganisation Act provided for the creation of the new State of Andhra Pradesh by adding certain territories to the existing State of Andhra Most of the territories were to be taken from the State of Hyderabad. Certain territories were added to the State of Madras. Provision was made for the creation of the new State of Kerala comprising the territories of the existing State of Travancore-Cochin. A new Part 'C' State known as Laccadive, Minicoy and Aminidivi Islands was created. To the existing State of Mysore, certain territories taken from Hyderabad, Madras, Bombay and Coorg were added. A new State of Bombay consisting of certain territories taken from the States of Hyderabad and Madhya Pradesh and the territories of the existing States of Bombay, Saurashtra and Kutch was to be created. A new State of Madhya Pradesh comprising the territories of the existing State of Madhya Pradesh, Vindhya Pradesh, Bhopal and certain territories of Rajasthan was to be created. Patiala and East Punjab States Union was added to the State of Rajasthan was tobe created. Patiala and East Punjab States Union was added to the State of Punjab. The first Schedule to the Constitution of India was amended. There were to be 13 Part 'A' States of Andhra Pradesh, Assam, Bihar, Bombay, Kerala, Madhya Pradesh, Madras, Mysore, Orissa, Punjab, Rajasthan, Uttar Pradesh and West Bengal, one Part 'B' State and five Union Territories of Delhi, Himachal Pradesh, Manipur, Tripura, and the Laccadive, Minicoy and Amindivi Islands.

With effect from January 20, 1957, the State of Jammu & Kashmir was declared to be an integral part of India. The Constituent Assembly dissolved itself after framing a new Constitution for the State.

After the establishment of the composite State of Bombay under the

States Reorganisation Act, 1956, there was a lot of agitation for the separation of Maharashtra from Gujarat. For a long time the Government of India resisted the demand. This led to riots on a large scale and ultimately the Government of India was forced to enact the Bombay Reorganisation Act, 1960. It received the assent of the President on April 25, 1960. It provided for the creation of two separate States of Maharashtra and Gujarat. The capital of Maharashtra was to be Bombay and that of Gujarat was to be at some other place. The Legislative Assembly of Gujarat was to consist of 132 and that of Maharashtra 264 members. There was to be no Legislative Council for Gujarat, but the Legislative Council of Maharashtra was to consist of 78 members. Provision was also made for the division of the assets of the former State of Bombay between Maharashtra and Gujarat.

In July 1960, the Government of India decided to set up the new State of Nagaland with Kohima as its capital. This was done to statisfy the discontented elements in that region. An Act was passed in 1962 to implement that decision. In April 1970 was created the new State of Meghalaya.

4.5 Punjab Boundary Commission 1966

Terms of Reference

On 23 April, 1966 a three member Punjab Boundary Commission (*Chairman:* Justice Jayantilal Chhotalal Shah, *Members:* S. Dutt, and M.M. Philip) was set up to recommended:

(i) The adjustment of the existing boundaries of the Hindi and Punjabi regions of the present State (Punjab) to secure linguistic homogeneity and also;

(ii) To indicate boundaries of the Hill areas of the present State which were contiguous to Himachal Pradesh and had cultural and lingustic affinities.

The Commission was required to apply the linguistic principle with regard to the census figure of 1961 and other relevant considerations. The Commissions was asked to take into consideration other factors, namely:

1. Administrative convenience.
2. Economic well-being.
3. Geographical contiguity; and

4. Facility of Communication.

The Commission submitted its report on 31 May, 1966.

Background to Recommendations

In recommending adjustment of the boundary, due consideration must undoubtedly be given to the effective maintenance of irrigation and power distribution systems. The proposed division of the State of Punjab necessitates division of the irrigation and power distribution systems, and that must be done keeping in mind the paramount purpose of ensuring linguistic homogeneity. The points of division suggested by the Chief Engineer (Projects) which may avoid serious dislocation of the irrigation system is to fix the boundary line of certain points indicated by him but acceptance of the scheme would completely upset the principle of linguistic homogeneity. Another Engineer suggested that the canal systems should be located intact, canal by canal, in the State they serve and not cut, particularly not towards or near the tail ends, for the effect of such cutting on the inhabitants depending on canal irrigation in the tail and areas of another State may result in serious consequences. He said that if it is not at all practicable to leave the whole canal system in one State, the division should be at only those points from below which fairly high discharge still flows, so that satisfactory distribution of water to cultivators served by the irrigation canals beyond these points may be ensured. He then suggested that in respect of the Upper Bari Doab Canal from Ravi river, the Eastern Canal from Beas River and Sirhand Canal no division was necessary. He suggested that division of the Bhakra Main branch, should be made at certain points near Tohana. About Narwana Branch, he suggested that a suitable point for division could be at Tangri south of Ambala. He also said that electric power supply Grids should be cut, if necessary, at certain fixed points to ensure that to untoward result would ensure therefrom, and since there were two Grids in Punjab (i) 132000 Volts Jogindernagar, Amritsar, Ludhiana, Ropar and Bhakra Grid and (ii) 22000- Volts Bhakra, Ganguwal, Kotla, Dhulkot, Panipat and Delhi Grid, to ensure effective supplies to consumers it would be advisable to retain the first Gird in one State as a whole and to divide the second Grid at any of the sub-stations Ganguwal, Kotla, Dhulkot or Panipat. He suggested that division at any other point will greatly complicate the supplies of power to the State for which the control of the Grid line is a other hands. These suggestions which contain several alternatives may also seriously upset the linguistic principle.

The Chief Engineer, Electricity Board, was of the view that the proposed reorganisation of the present State of Punjab was likely to create serious impact on the future set up of the Punjab State Electricity Board, and recommended that Joint Electricity Board with separate Chief Engineers for Distribution System for the consuming States and a common organisation for planning, execution and operation of major works, (not covered by distribution system) should be constituted. In his opinion, broadly speaking, there should be a common Board with subjects like generation, transmission works, their planning, design, procurement, execution, research and operation etc. under Central Agencies, and distribution workers and their operation should be dealt with by respective Chief Engineers who would be *ex officio* members of the Board, but responsible to the respective States for carrying out the works according to the budget requirements. The Joint Board as proposed, in the view of the Chief Engineer, would meet all the technical requirements of the Region and be in the interest of coordinated power development and power consumption, and meet the regional interests of the respective States.

The sources of water supply and power lie in a majority of cases within the hilly areas of Himachal Pradesh, and the beneficiaries of water and power will hereafter in respect of some channels of supply, be the Punjabi-speaking, the Hindi-speacking States, Delhi and Rajasthan. Though Himachal Pradesh derives no direct irrigation benefit from the waters of the rivers having their sources in its territory, its claim to have a voice in the maintenance of reservoirs, disposal of waters and distributors of power cannot be ignored.

A legalistic approach to a complex problem on the just solution of which depends the prosperity of many territorial units, would be impermissible. Having carefully considered the problem, we are of the view that constitution of Joint Boards, one for Irrigation and another for power, of the beneficiary States and the State which is the source of supply of water and power, having authority to lay down policies and execute them, consistently with the legitimate need of the State concerned, under the supervision of the Central Government may be a practical solution of the problem raised by the division of the territory into separate units in which the canal and power supply lines are situated.

Recommendations

We recommend that:

1. (i) The District Simla, Kulu, Kangra, Lahaul-Spiti;

(ii) Development Blocks Gagret, Amb and Una (excluding the village Kherabagh, Samipur, Dhabhaur and Kalseh and village Kosri from Tehsil Una (District Hoshiarpur);

(iii) Tehsil Nalagarh (District Ambala); and

(iv) Enclaves Dalhousie, Balun and Bukloh in Chamba District which are hill areas and have cultural affinity with the people of Himachal Pradesh;

should be merged with Himachal Pradesh.

2. That districts Gurdaspur (excluding Dalhousie, Balun and Bukloh), Amritsar, Kapurthala, Jullundur, Ferozepore, Bhatinda, Patiala, Ludhiana, and Tehsils Barnala, Malerkotla and Sangrur (District Sangrur), Tehsil Ropar (Distrct Ambala), Tehsils Dasuya, Hoshiarpur and Garhshankar, and Development Blocks Anandpur, Nurpurbedi and villages Kherabagh, Samipur, Bhabhaur and Kalseh from Una Block and village Kosri in Una Tehsil will form the Punjabi-speaking State; and

3. That District Hissar, Mohindergarh, Gurgaon, Rohtak and Karnal, and Tehsils Narwana and Jind (District Sangrur) and Tehsil Kharar (including Chandigarh Capital Project), Naraingarh Ambala, and Jagadhri will form the Hindi-speaking State.

Adjustments of the boundaries of the three States should be made on the division territory as set out.

In conclusion we would like to make a few general observations.

Agitation for setting up separate linguistic States in the territory of Punjab raised its head more than 18 years ago. It is unfortunate that strong passions have been aroused on that problem. The Punjab has been at the forefront among the States of India in war and peace. It has been the sword arm of the country in times of war; and in times of peace it has led all other States in agricultural production, and parts of the State are humming with small scale industry. We fervently hope that after the dust of conflict has settled, the people of Punjab to whichever State they belong will in healthy rivalry achieve higher targets of production, agricultural and industrial, and bring about all-round prosperity and contribute to a higher standard of living for all our people. The people of Punjab share the common aspirations and ideals with the rest of our people, and we trust that nothing will be done in either State to prejudice the linguistic preferences of the minorities residing within their territory. It is on the cultivation of a tolerant attitude towards the claims of others within the constitutional framework that democracy flourishes, and we share the optimism with many others that the people of Punjab will maintain the democratic ideal.

The Commission signed the Report on May 31, 1966 with a note on Kharar—Chandigarh by S. Dutt

I regret that I am unable to agree with the recommendations which my colleagues propose to make about Kharar tehsil including Chandigarh. In my view, Kharar tehsil as a whole, with the exception of Kalka Police Station, should be merged with the proposed Punjabi State; the area of Kalka Police Station should be merged with Himachal Pradesh. I give my reasons below:

2. Kharar is a tehsil of Ambala district with a total population of 332.361 according to the 1961 Census, of whom 183,452 (55.2 per cent) are Hindi-speaking. The total rural population of the tehsil is 200,425 of whom 112,723 (56.2 per cent) are Punjabi-speaking and 86,777 (43.3 per cent) are Hindi-speaking. The urban population totals 131,936 — 15.1 per cent Punjabi-speaking and 73.3 per cent Hindi-speaking. The majority of the urban population belong to Chandigarh Capital Project area (89,000). The other three towns are Kharar with a population of 8,216, Kurali (6,390), Manimajra (9,901) and Kalka (18,668). It will thus be seen that while in the whole of Kharar tehsil the Hindi-speaking people are in a majority (55.2 per cent) in the rural areas the Punjabi-speaking people hold the majority (56.2 per cent)

3. Under the Sachar Formula of 1949 Kharar tehsil was placed in the Punjabi region. It did not then include Pinjore Police Station which in 1961 had a population of 28,635, Pinjore, which formerly formed part of the Pepsu, was included in the Kharar tehsil after Pepsu's merger with the Punjab. Under the Punjab Regional Committees Order, 1957, Chandigarh was made bilingual and therefore it was not included either in the Punjabi-speaking or in the Hindi-speaking region. The rest of the Kharar tehsil in Punjab which was divided between the Hindi and the Punjabi regions under the Regional Committee Order. The Hindi areas of tehsil Kharar consist of 17 villages in Zail Mubarakpur and the areas of the Pinjore Police Station and Kalka Police Station; the rest of the tehsil exclusive of the Chandigarh Capital Project area forms part of the Punjabi-speaking region. Both the language areas of the tehsil are contiguous with the Chandigarh capital, but it appears that the latter is surrounded on three sides by the areas included in the Punjabi region and on the remaining side on the south-east by the area included in the Hindi region. A further point need to be mentioned. Although Chandigarh Capital Project is bilingual for the purpose of election of the Legislative Assembly it forms part of the Chandigarh Assembly Constituency. This Constituency includes, besides Chandigarh, the area of the Kharar tehsil also.

4.6 President's Assent to the Punjab Reorganisation Bill

The recommendations of the Punjab Boundary Commission with some modifications were incorporated into the Punjab Reorganization Bill, which was duly approved by both Houses of Parliament. The President gave his assent on 18th September, 1966. As per recommendations of the Boundary Commission, the Punjabi-speaking areas that went to Punjab were—Districts of Gurdaspur (excluding Dalhousie, Balum and Bukloh), Amritsar, Kapurthala, Jullundur, Ferozepur, Bhatinda, Patiala, Ludhiana and Tehsil Barnala, Malerkotla and Sangrur (Distrct Sangrur), Tehsil Ropar (Distrct Ambala), Tehsils Dasuya, Hoshiarpur and Garhshankar and Development Blocks Anandpur, and villages, Kherabagh, Samipur, Bhabhaur and Kalseh from Una Block and village Kosri.

The Hindi-speaking areas that went to Haryana were—district Hissar, Mohindergarh, Gurgaon, Rohtak and Karnal and Tehsils Narwana and Jind (District Sangrur) and Tehsil Kherar (including Chandigarh Capital Project) Naraingarh, Ambala and Jagadhri.

The Hilly areas were given to Himachal Pradesh. These were:

(i) District Shimla, Kulu, Kangra, Lahaul Spiti;
(ii) The Development Blocks Gagret, Amb and Una (excluding the villages Kherabagh, Samipur, Bhabhaur and Kalseh) and village Kosri from Tehsil Una (District Hoshiarpur);
(iii) Tehsil Nalagarh (District Ambala); and
(iv) Enclaves—Dalhousie, Balum and Bukloh in Chamba District which are hill area and have cultural affinity with the people of Himachal Pradesh.

The rest of the territory of Punjab was to belong to Punjab. Provision, was made for the allocation of seats in the Council of States. House of the People, and Legislative Assemblies. There was to be a common High court for the States of Punjab and Haryana and the Union Territory of Chandigarh. Provision was also made for the distribution of assets, etc. among the States.

4.7 Reaction to Commission's Report and Follow-up

The Punjab Reorganisation Act, 1960 did not satisfy the aspirations of the Sikhs and they were particularly sore about Chandigarh. The Sikhs started agitation once again and Sant Fateh Singh went on fast unto death and fixed a date for burning himself alive unless Chandigarh was given to Punjab. There were negotiations at the eleventh hour and ultimately it was agreed to refer the disputes between the States of Punjab and Haryana to the arbitration of Indira Gandhi, the then Prime Minister of India. On account of certain circumstances, the decision was not given by Indira Gandhi. The result was that tension began to grow between the two States. Shri Pheruman went on fast unto death to get Chandigarh for Punjab. Sant Fateh Singh once again declared that he would go on fast on January 26, 1970, and immolate himself on February 1, 1970, if Chandigarh was not given to Punjab. He actually went on fast on January 26. The situation became tense. It was under these circumstances that Indira Gandhi announced on January 29, 1970 that Chandigarh will be merged in Punjab and Haryana will be compensated by the transfer of 114 Hindi-speaking villages of Fazilka Tehsil including Fazilka and Abohar towns and 6 villages from the Chandigarh Union Territory. In addition, Haryana was to get from the Government of India Rs. 20 crores, half of which was to be in the form of a grant and the rest as loan to build a new capital. Chandigarh was to remain a Union Territory for the maximum period of five years as joint capital of both Punjab and Haryana, after which it was to be transferred to Punjab. It was also announced that the remaining territorial disputes between the two States be referred to a Commission which was to be required to submit its report within a short time. The matter still remains unresolved.

4.8 Formation of other States

In April 1970 was created the new State of Meghalaya. In the beginning of 1971, Union Territory of Himachal Pradesh was re-organised as a State. The North-Eastern Areas (Reorganisation) Act, 1971 gave Manipur, Tripura and Meghalaya the status of States. Union Territories were created out of Mizoram and Arunachal Pradesh by reorganising the State of Assam.

Sikkim joined the Indian Union in 1975.

The States of Arunachal Pradesh, Goa and Mizoram were created in 1987.

From all accounts, it appears that the creation of the Uttarakhand State merits immediate consideration. Past history of creating some States in the wake of widespread disturbances, hunger strike and self-immolation need not to be repeated. Shall we be wise from our past experience!

4.9 Formation/Reorganisaton of States and Union Territories at a Glance

Sl. No.	State	Formation of Year	Remarks
1	Andhra Pradesh	November 1, 1956	Telugu-speaking areas were separated from the composite Madras State and a new Andhra State came into being in October 1953. With the passage of the State Reorganisation Act, 1956, the Andhra and the Telangana areas were amalgamated and the Andhra Pradesh came into being on November 1, 1956.
2.	Arunachal Pradesh	February 20, 1987	After Independence it was a part of North East Frontier Agency and later on made a Union Territory and thereafter full-fledged State.
3.	Goa	May 30, 1987	Goa was liberated from the Portuguese on December 19, 1961. On May 30, 1987, Goa was conferred Statehood and Daman and Diu made a separate Union Territory.
4.	Gujarat	May 1, 1960	With the reorganisation of State of Saurashtra and the Union Territory of Kachch along with the former British Gujarat became a part of the bigger bilingual State of Bombay. Present State of Gujarat came into being on May 1, 1960.
5.	Haryana	November 1, 1966	Earlier it was a part of the Punjab State.
6.	Himachal Pradesh	April 15, 1948	After Independence 30 States of the area were united. With the reorganisation of Punjab, on November 1, 1966, certain areas,

			belonging to it were includid in Himachal Pradesh, On January 25, 1971, it became a full-fledged State.
7.	Karnataka	November 1, 1973	After Independence the United Mysore state was created in 1956 and renamed Karnataka in 1973.
8.	Madhya Pradesh	November 1, 1956	The State of Madhya Pradesh was formed on November 1, 1956, under the provisions of the States Reorganisation Act, 1956. If consists of 17 Hindi speacking destricts former State of Madhya Bharat (except Sunel enclave of Mandsaur district), former Vindhya Pradesh, state of Bhopal and Sironj sub-division by Kotah district, which was earlier an envlave of Rajasthan in Madhya Pradesh
9.	Maharashtra	May 1, 1960	Reorganisation of States brought for the first time all Maratha-speaking regions in one state of Maharashtra first by breaking up of the old Central Provinces and Hyderabad, and finally the bilingual Bombay State.
10.	Manipur	January 21, 1972	After integration with the Indian Union in 1949, it was made a Part 'C' State. After the State Reorganisation Act, 1956, it became a Union Territory. In 1972, Manipur was made a full-fledged State.
11.	Meghalaya	January 21, 1972	Meghalaya was created as an autonomous State within the state of Assam on April 2, 1970. As a full-fledged State, Meghalaya came into existence on January 21, 1972.

12. Mizoram	February 20, 1987	It was one of the districts of Assam till 1972 when it became a Union Territory.
13. Nagaland	December 1, 1963	In 1957, this territory was made a centrally, administered area, to be administered by the Government of Assam. It was known as Naga Hills district of Assam. In January 1961, it was renamed as Nagaland and given the status of the State of the Indian Union. It was formally inaugurated in 1963.
14. Punjab (Reorganised)	November 1, 1966	After Independence, Punjab was divided into East Punjab (India) and West Punjab (Pakistan). Eight princely States of East Punjab were grouped together to form one single State called PEPSU—Patiala and the East Punjab States Union—with Patiala as its capital. PEPSU State was merged with Punjab in 1956. The reorganised Punjab came into being in 1966.
15. Rajasthan	November 1, 1956	The process of uniting scattered States commenced from 1948 to 1956 when the states Reorganisation Act was promulgated. First came Matsya Union (1948) consisting of a few States, gradually other States merged with this Union. By 1949, major states like Bikaner, Jaipur, Jodhpur and Jaisalmer joined this Union, making it United States of Greater Rajasthan. Ultimately by 1956, present State of Rajasthan formally came into being with Ajmer State, Abu Road Taluka and Sunel Tappa joining it.

16.	Sikkim	April 26, 1975	It is commonly believed that in 17th century Phuntsog Namgyal became the first ruler of Namgyal dynasty which was ruling till Sikkim joined the Indian Union in 1975.
17.	Tamil Nadu	January 14, 1956	The State is the successor to the old Madras Presidency which in 1901 covered the bulk of the Southern Peninsula. The composite Madras State was later reorganised and the present Tamil Nadu was formed in 1969.
18.	Tripura	January 21, 1972	Tripura was annexed to Indian Union in 1947. It became a in part 'C' State and with the reorganisation of states in 1966, it became a Centrally Administered Territory. It became a full-fledged State in 1972.
19.	Uttar Pradesh	January 1, 1950	The British combined Agra and Oudh into one Province and called it United Provinces of Agra and Oudh. The name was shortened to the United Provinces in 1935. In January, 1950, after Independent United Provinces was renamed as Uttar Pradesh.
20.	West Bengal	1947	At the time of Independence Bengal was divided into two provinces:—East Bengal (Pakistan) and West Bengal (India)
21.	Chandigarh (Union Territory)	November 1, 1966	It was constituted as a Union Territory on November 1, 1966. It serves as the joint capital of both Punjab and Haryana.
22.	Dadra and Haveli (Union Territory)	August 11, 1961	It was liberated from the Portuguese rulers by people themeselves on August 2, 1954. After liberation of this territory,

			it was administered by the people themselves. The territory was merged with the Indian Union on August, 11, 1961 and administered as a Union Territory.
23.	Daman and Diu (Union Territory)	May 1, 1987	Daman and Diu along with Goa was a colony held by the Portuguese even after Independence. In 1961, it was made an integral part of India. It was part of the erstwhile Union Territory of Goa, Daman and Diu was made a separate Union Territory on May 1987 when statehood was conferred on Goa.
24.	Delhi (Restricted Powers)	1994	It was made a Union Territory on November 1, 1956. Its set up and status has undergone several changes. In December, 1991 Parliament passed Constitution (74th Amendment) Bill providing National Capital Territory of Delhi, a Legislative Assembly with a Chief Minister. It acquired the status of a State. (with limited powers) in 1993. On November 1, 1956 Union Territory was formed.
25.	Lakshadweep (Union Territory)	1973	The Laccadives, Minicoy and Amindivi Group of Island were renamed as Lakshadweep in 1973.
26.	Pondicherry (Union Territory)	1954	It was once the original headquarters of the French in India.

Note: India comprises 26 States and 6 Union Territories. Names of Assam, Bihar, Jammu and Kashmir, Kerala, Orissa, Uttar Pradesh and Andaman and Nicobar have remained unchanged.

5

RESERVATION POLICY AND AGITATION FOR UTTARAKHAND

5.1 Introduction

Among other considerations leading to the demand for the creation of the Uttarakhand State, is the issue of reservation. Uttarakhand, the land of peace, has become a land of unrest on account of the announcement of 27 per cent reservation for OBCs who form a negligible two per cent in Uttarakhand. It will, therefore, be appropriate first to go into the rationale of reservation.

5.2 Reservations: Constitutional Provisions

PART XVI

Special Provisions Relating to Certain Classes

330. *Reservation of Seats for Scheduled Castes and Scheduled Tribes in the House of the People*—(1) Seats shall be reserved in the House of the People for—

(a) the Scheduled Castes;
[1][(b) the Scheduled Tribes except the Scheduled Tribes in the autonomous districts of Assam; and]
(c) the Scheduled Tribes in the autonomous districts of Assam.

(2) The number of seats reserved in any States [2][or Union territory] for the Scheduled Castes or the Scheduled Tribes under clause (1) shall

bear, as nearly as may be, the same proportion to the total number of seats allotted to that State [2][or Union territory] in the House of the People as the population of the Scheduled Castes in the State [2][or Union territory] or of the Scheduled Tribes in the State [2][or Union territory] or part of the State [2][Union territory as the case may be, in respect of which seats are so reserved, bears to the total population of the State [2][or Union territory].

[3][(3) Notwithstanding anything, contained in clause (2), the number of seats reserved in the House of the People for the Scheduled Tribes in the autonomous districts of Assam shall bear to the total number of seats allotted to that State a proportion not less than the population of the Scheduled Tribes in the said autonomous district bears to the total population of the State.]

[4] *[Explanation* — In this Article and in Article 332, the expression "population" means the population as ascertained at the last preceding census of which the relevant figures have been published.

Provided that the reference in this Explanation to the last preceding census of which the relevant figures have been published shall, until the relevant figures for the census taken after the year 2000 have been published, be construed as a reference to the 1971 census.]

331. *Representation of the Anglo-Indian community in the House of the People*—Notwithstanding anything in Article 81, the President may, if he is of opinion that the Anglo-Indian community is not adequately represented in the House of the People, nominate not more than two members of that community to the House of the People.

332. *Reservation of Seats for Scheduled Castes and Scheduled Tribes in the Legislative Assemblies of the States*—(1) Seats shall be reserved for the Scheduled Castes and the Scheduled Tribes[5][[6][except the Scheduled Tribes in the autonomous districts of Assam], in the Legislative Assembly of every State.[7]***

(2) Seats shall be reserved also for the autonomous districts in the Legislative Assembly of the State of Assam.

(3) The number of seats reserved for the Scheduled Castes or the Scheduled Tribes in the Legislative Assembly of any State under clause (1) shall bear, as nearly as may be, the same proportion to the total number of seats in the Assembly as the population of the Scheduled Castes in the State or the Scheduled Tribes in the State or part of the State, as the case may be, in respect of which seats are so reserved, bears to the total population of the State.

[8][(3A) Notwithstanding anything contained in clause (3), until the taking effect, under Article 170, of the re-adjustment, on the basis of the first census after the year 2000, of the number of seats in the Legislative

Assemblies of the States of Arunachal Pradesh, Meghalaya, Mizoram and Nagaland, the seats which shall be reserved for the Scheduled Tribes in the Legislative Assembly of any such State shall be,

(a) if all the seats in the Legislative Assembly of such State in existence on the date of coming into force of the Constituion (Fifty-seventh Amendment) Act, 1987 (hereafter in this clause referred to as the existing Assembly) are held by members of the Scheduled Tribes, all the seats except one;

(b) in any other case, such number of seats as bears to the total number of seats, a proportion not less than the number (as on the said date) of members belonging to the Scheduled Tribes in the existing Assembly bears to the total number of seats in the existing Assembly].

(4) The number of seats reserved for an autonomous district in the Legislative Assembly of the State of Assam shall bear to the total number of seats in that Assembly a proportion not less than the population of the district bears to the total population of the State.

(5) The constituencies for the seats reserved for any autonomous district of Assam shall not comprise any area outside that district.[9]

(6) No person who is not a member of a Scheduled Tribe of any autonomous district of the State of Assam shall be eligible for election to the Legislative Assembly of the State from any constituency of that distrct.[9***]

333. *Representation of the Anglo-Indian community in the Legislative Assemblies of the States*—Notwithstanding anything in Article 170, the Governor[10***] of a State may, if he is of opinion that the Anglo-Indian community needs representation in the Legislative Assembly of the State and is not adequately represented therein,[11] [nominate one member of that community to the Assembly.]

334. *Reservation of seats and special representation to cease after* [12][*fifty years*][12]—Notwithstanding anything in the foregoing provisions of this part, the provisions of this Constitution relating to—

(a) the reservation of seats for the Scheduled Castes and the Scheduled Tribes in the House of the People and in the Legislative Assembly of the States; and

(b) the representation of the Anglo-Indian community in the House of the People and in the Legislative Assemblies of the States by nomination.

shall cease to have effect on the expiration of a period of[12] [fifty years] from the commencement of this Constitution:

Provided that nothing in this article shall affect any representation in the House of the People or in the Legislative Assembly of a State until the dissolution of the then existing House or Assembly, as the case may be.

335. *Claims of Scheduled Castes and Scheduled Tribes to services and posts*—The claims of the members of the Scheduled Castes and the Scheduled Tribes shall be taken into consideration, consistently with the maintenance of efficiency of administration, in the making of appointment to services and posts in connection with the affairs of the Union or of a State.

336. *Special provision for Anglo-Indian community in certain services*—(1) During the first two years after the commencement of this Constitution, appointmens of members of the Anglo-Indian community to posts in the railway, customs, postal and telegraph services of the Union shall be made on the same basis as immediately before the fifteenth day of August, 1947.

During every succeeding period of two years, the number of posts reserved for the members of the said community in the said services shall, as nearly as possible, be less by ten per cent than the numbers so reserved during the immediately preceding period of two years:

Provided that at the end of ten years from the commencement of this Constitution all such reservation shall cease.

(2) Nothing in clause (1) shall bar the appointment of members of the Anglo-Indian community to posts other than, or in addition to, those reserved for the community under that clause if such members are found qualified for appointment on merit as compared with the members of other communities.

337. *Special provision with respect to educational grants for the benefit of Anglo-Indian community*—During the first three financial years after the commencement of this Constitution, the same grants, if any, shall be made by the Union and by each State[13]*** for the benefit of the Anglo-Indian community in respect of education as were made in the financial year ending on the thirty-first day of March, 1948.

During every succeeding period of three years the grants may be less by ten per cent, than those for the immediately preceding period of three years.

Provided that at the end of ten years from the commencement of this Constituiton such grants, to the extent to which they are a special concession to the Anglo-Indian community, shall cease:

Provided further that no educational institution shall be entitled to receive any grant under this article unless at least forty per cent of the annual admissions therein are made available to members of communities other than the Anglo-Indian community.

338. *Special Officer for Scheduled Castes, Scheduled Tribes etc.* — (1) There shall be a Special Officer for the Scheduled Castes and Scheduled Tribes to be appointed by the President.

(2) It shall be the duty of the special officer to investigate all matters relating to the safeguards provided for the Scheduled Castes and Scheduled Tribes under this Constitution and report to the President upon the working of those safeguards at such intervals as the President may direct, and the President shall cause all such reports to be laid before each House of Parliament.

(3) In this article, references to the Scheduled Castes and Scheduled Tribes shall be construed as including references to such other backward classes as the President may, on receipt of the report of a Commission appointed under clause (1) of article 340 by order specify and also to the Anglo-Indian community.

339. *Control of the Union over the administration of Scheduled Areas and the welfare of Scheduled Tribes*—(1) The President may at any time and shall, at the expiration of ten years from the commencement of this Constitution by order appoint a Commission to report on the administration of the Scheduled Areas and the welfare of the Scheduled Tribes in the States.[13]***

The order may define the composition, powers and procedure of the Commission and may contain such incidental or ancillary provisions as the President may consider necessary or desirable.

(2) The executive power of the Union shall extend to the giving of directions to[14] [a State] as to the drawing up and execution of schemes specified in the direction to be essential for the welfare of the Scheduled Tribes in the State.

340. *Appointment of a Commission to investigate the conditions of backward classes*—(1) The President may by order appoint a Commission consisting of such persons as the thinks fit to investigate the conditions of socially and educationally backward classes within the territory of India and the difficulties under which they labour and to make recommendations as to the steps that should be taken by the Union or any State to remove such difficulties and to improve their condition and as to the grants that should be made for the purpose by the Union or any State and the conditions subject to which such grants should be made, and the order appointing such Commission shall define the procedure to be followed by the Commission.

(2) A Commission so appointed shall investigate the matters referred to them and present to the President a report setting out the facts as found by them and making such recommendations as they think proper

(3) The President shall cause a copy of the report so presented together with a memorandum explaining the action taken thereon to be laid before each House of Parliament.

341. *Scheduled Castes*—(1) The President [15][may with respect to any State [16][or Union Territory] and where it is a State[17]*** after consultation with the Governor[18]*** thereof] by public notification[19] specify the castes, races or tribes or parts of or groups within castes, races or tribes which shall for the purposes of this Constitution be deemed to be Scheduled Castes in relation to that State [16][or Union territory] as the case may be.]

(2) Parliament may be law include in or exclude from the list of Scheduled Castes specified in a notification issued under clause (1) any caste, race or tribe or part of or group within any caste, race or tribe, but save as aforesaid a notification issued under the said clause shall not be varied by any subsequent notification.

342. *Scheduled Tribes*—(1) The President[20] [may with respect to any State [16][or Union territory], and where it is a State[17]*** after consultation with the Governor[18]*** thereof], by public notification[21] specify the tribes or tribal communities or parts of or groups within tribes or tribal communities which shall for the purposes of this Constitution be deemed to be Scheduled Tribes in relation to that State [16][or Union territory], as the case may be.]

(2) Parliament may be law include in or exclude from the list of Scheduled Tribes specified in a notification issued under clause (1) any tribe or tribal community or part of or group within any tribe or tribal community, but save as aforesaid a notification issued under the said clause shall not be varied by any subsequent notification.

5.3 The First Backward Classes Commission, 1953-55

The First Backward Classes Commission, set up by a Presidential Order under Article 340 of the Constitution of India on January 29, 1953, submitted its report on March 30, 1955.

Composition

Chairman

1. Shri Kakasaheb Kalelkar, M.P.

Members

2. Shri Narrayan Sadoba Kajrolkar, M.P.
3. Shri Bheekha Bhai, M.P.
4. Shri Shivdayal Singh Chaurasia
5. Shri Rajeshwar Patel, M.P.
6. Shri Abdul Qaiyum Ansari, M.L.A. (Bihar)
7. Shri T. Mariappa, M.L.A. (Mysore)
8. Lala Jagannath
9. Shri Atma Singh Namdhari, M.P.
10. Shri N.R.M. Swamy, M.P.
11. Shri Arunangshu De, Member-Secretary

Terms of Reference

The Backward Classes Commission shall—

(a) determine the criteria to be adopted in considering whether any sections of the people in the territory of India (in addition to the Scheduled Castes and Scheduled Tribes specified by notifications issued under Articles 341 and 342 of the Constitution) should be treated as socially and educationally backward classes; and in accordance with such criteria, prepare a list of such classes setting out also their approximate numbers and their territorial distribution.

(b) investigate the conditions of all such socially and educationally backward classes and the difficulties under which they labour;

and make recommendation.

(i) as to the steps that should be taken by the Union or any State to remove such difficulties or to improve their condition; and

(ii) as to the grants that should be made for the purpose by the Union or any State and the conditions subject to which such grants should be made;

(c) investigate such other matters as the President may hereafter refer to them; and

(d) present to the President a report setting out the facts as found by them and making such recommendations as they think proper.

The Commission may—

(a) obtain such information as they may consider necessary or relevant for their purpose in such form and such manner as they may think appropriate, from the Central Government, the State Governments and such other authorities, organizations or individuals as may, in the opinion of the commission, be of assistance to them;

(b) hold their sittings or the sittings of such sub-committees as they may appoint from amongst their own members at such authority of the Chairman; and

(c) visit or depute a sub-committee of their to visit such parts of the territory of India as they consider necessary or convenient.

Methodology Followed

The Commission issued a Questionnaire comprising 182 questions for eliciting the views of the Governments and the general public on various aspects of its inquiry. It also undertook extensive tour of the country to collect on the spot evidence.

After sifting and sorting the facts collected, the Commission formulated the following criteria identifying socially and educationally backward classes.

(i) Low social position in the traditional caste hierarchy of Hindu society;

(ii) Lack of general educational advancement among the major section of a caste or community;

(iii) Inadequate or no representation in Government service; and

(iv) Inadequate representation in the field of trade, commerce and industry.

The Commission also prepared a list of 2399 backward castes or communities for the entire country and 837 of these were classified as 'most backward'. The Registrar General and Census Commissioner of India assisted the Commission in making population projections of 930 backward castes or communities.

Major Recommendations

The recommendations of the Commission for upliftment of the backward classes are extremely wide-ranging and comprehensive. They cover such fields as Extensive Land Reforms, Reorganisation of Village Economy, Bhoodan Movement, Development of Livestock, Dairy Farming, Cattle Insurance, Bee-keeping, Piggery, Fisheries, Development of Small and

Cottage Industries, Rural Housing, Public Health and Rural Water Supply, Adult Literacy, University Education, Representation of Backward Classes in Government service, etc. Some of the noteworthy recommendations of the Commission are:

(i) Undertaking caste-wise enumeration of population in the Census of 1961;
(ii) Relating Social backwardness of a class to its low position in the traditional caste hierarchy of Hindu society;
(iii) Treating all women as a class as "backward";
(iv) Reservation of 70 per cent seats in all technical and professional institutions for qualified students of backward classes; and
(v) Minimum reservation of vacancies in all Government services and local bodies for other Backward Classes on the following scale:

Class I	25%
Class II	33.1/3%
Class III & IV	40%

Dissenting Views on Linking Caste with Backwardness

It is of interest to note the Commission could not present a unanimous report. Five of its Members recorded minutes of dissent. Dr. Anup Singh, Shri Arunangshu De and Shri P. G. Shah were opposed to the view of linking caste with backwardness. They were also opposed to the reservation of posts on the basis of caste. On the other hand, Shri S. D. S. Chaurasia strongly advocated the acceptance of caste as the criterion for backwardness in his 67-page minute of dissent. Shri T. Mariappa's minute of dissent was concerned only with the inclusion of a couple of castes in the list of Other Backward Classes.

Shri Kaka Kalelkar, the Chairman, took a rather equivocal stand on this issue. Though he did not record a formal minute of dissent in his forwarding letter to the President he opposed the acceptance of caste as the basis for backwardness. He also expressed his reservations regarding several other important recommendations made by the Commission.

Government Action on the Report

After a detailed examination of the Commission's Report, the Government laid its copy together with a Memorandum of action taken before each

House of the Parliament on September 3, 1956 in compliance with Article 340(3) of the Constitution. In this Memorandum it was observed, "For the purpose of the enquiry specifically contemplated in Article 340 of the Constitution it was necessary to consider whether these other backward sections could be properly classified, and the Commission had to find objective tests and criteria by which such classifications were to be made; they had to find indisputable yardsticks by which social and educational backwardness could be measured. The report of the Commission has not been unanimous on this point, in fact, it reveals considerable divergence of opinion." It was further Stated, "The Commission's list contains as many as 2399 communities out of which 930 alone account for an estimated population of 11.5 crores; Scheduled Castes and Tribes will make up another 7 crores" (on the basis of 1951 Census). Regarding the acceptance of caste as criterion for backwardness, it was Stated, "It cannot be dinied that the caste system is the greatest hindrance in the way of our progress towards an egalitarian society, and the recognition of the specified castes as backward may serve to maintain and even perpetuate the existing on the basis of caste."

Regarding the recognition of a large number of castes and communities as backward, it was pointed out, "If the entire community, barring a few exceptions has thus to be regarded as backward, the really needy would be swamped by the multitude and hardly receive any special attention of adequate assistance, nor would such dispensation fulfil the conditions laid down in Article 340 of the Constitution."

In view of the above, the Government considered it necessary that "some positive and workable criteria should be devised for the specification of the socially and educationally backward classes" and to undertake further investigation "so that dificiencies that have been noticed in the findings of the Commission are made good........ It was also pointed out in the Memorandum that the Planning Commission had already formulated the development programmes for the removal of backwardness and "the main point to be stressed was whether the special needs of the backward classes could be intensively and effectively served by appropriate shifts of emphasis or by re-arrangement of priorities within the framework of the existing programmes or whether additional programmes needed to be drawn up".

No Discussion in the Parliament

Incidentally, the Commission's report was not discussed by the Parliament.

After presenting the Memorandum to the Parliament, the Government made efforts "to discover some criteria other than caste which could be of practical application in determining the backward classes." The Deputy Registrar General was asked to conduct a pilot survey to see if backwardness could be linked to occupational communities instead of caste. Such a survey was undertaken by it failed to throw up the desired criteria. The matter was also discussed at a conference of State representives on 7-4-1959 and subsequently reviewed at a meeting of State officers convened by the Ministry of Home Affairs, but no consensus emerged as a result of these efforts.

5.4. Second Backward Classes Commission, 1978-80

Appointment Commission (Mandal Commission)

In exercise of the powers conferred by Article 340 of the Constitution, President appointed a Backward Classes Commission to investigate the conditions of socially and educationally backward classes within the territory of India. The composition of the Commission was as follows:

Composition

1. Shri B.P. Mandal (ex-M.P.) (*Chairman)*
2. Shri R. R. Bhole M.P.
3. Shri Dewan Mohan Lal
4. Shri L.R. Naik* (ex-M.P.)
5. Shri K. Subramaniam
6. Shri S. S. Gill (*Secretary)*

Terms of Reference

(i) to determine the criteria for defining the socially and educationally backward classes;

(ii) to recommend steps to be taken for the advancement for the socially and educationally backward classes of citizens so identified;

(iii) to examine the desirability or otherwise of making provision for the reservation of appointment or posts in favour of such backward classes of citizens which are not adequately represented

---

* Shri L. R. Naik was appointed in place of Shri Dina Bandhu Sahu, who resigned from membership of the Commission on November 5, 1979 on health grounds.

in public services and posts in connection with the affairs of the Union or of any State; and

(iv) present to the President a report setting out of the facts as found by them and making such recommendation as they think proper.

In this connection, the Commission may also examine the recommendations of the Backward Classes Commission appointed earlier and the consideration which stood in the way of the acceptance of its recommendations by Government.

Recommendations

Reservation of SCs and STs is in proportion to their population, i.e., 22.5 per cent. But as there is a legal obligation to keep reservations under Articles 15(4) and 16(4) of the Constitution below 50 per cent, the Commission recommends a reservation of 27 per cent for OBCs. This reservation should apply to all Government services as well as technical and professional institutions, both in the Centre and the States.

Special educational facilities designed at upgrading the cultural environment of the students should be created in a phased manner in selected areas containing high concentration of OBCs. Special emphasis should be placed on vocational training. Separate coaching facilities should be provided in technical and professional institutions to OBC students to enable them to catch up with students from open quota.

Special programmes for upgrading the skills of village artisians should be prepared and subsidised loans from financial institutions granted to them for setting up small scale industries. To promote the participation of OBCs in the industrial and business life of the country. a separate network of financial and technical institutions should be created by all State Governments.

Under the existing scheme of production-relations, Backward Classes comprising mainly small land-holders, tenants, agricultural labour, village artisans, etc., are heavily dependent on the rich peasantry for their sustenance. In view of this, OBCs continue to remain in mental and material bondage of the dominant castes and classes. Unless these production-relations are radically altered through structural changes and progressive land reforms implemented rigorously all over the country, OBCs will never become truely independent. In view of this, highest priority should be given to radical land reforms by all the States.

At present no central assistance is available to any State for implementing any welfare measures for other Backward Classes. Several

State Governments expressed their helplessness in undertaking more purposeful development programmes for backward classes in view of lack of resources. It is, therefore, recommended that welfare programmes specially designed for OBC should be financed by the Central Government in the same manner and to the same extent as done in the case of SCs and STs.

5.5. Supreme Court Judgement, November 1992

Following were the chief features of the Supreme Court Judgement on the reservation issue:

1. The Constitution allows reservations for any backward class which is not adequately represented in services.
2. Caste is an index for identifying the "Other Backward Classes" mentioned in the Constitution.
3. The OBCs are entitled to a 27 per cent quota because the total reservations would still be within the 50 per cent limit.
4. Reservations will be extended only to those OBCs common to the Mandal and State lists.
5. The creamy layer class was excluded from the perview of the reservations.

Key Statements from the Judgement

"If some members are too advanced socially, the link between them and the rest of the class snaps. The creamy layer would be a misfit in the class."

"There should be a periodic revision of the OBC lists to exclude those who have ceased to be backward or for the inclusion of new classes."

"Once they enter the service, efficiency of administration demands that these people earn promotions like all others."

5.6. Mandal Report and the Judgement

1. Mandal Report recommended 27 per cent reservation for Socially and Economically Backward Classes in government jobs.

   The court has removed the military and several sensitive civil posts from the ambit of quotas.
2. Mandal identified 3,743 OBCs.

The court has almost halved this by upholding the State lists instead. Castes adequately represented in government are also to be removed.

3. Mandal wanted all OBCs to be treated equally.

   The court has ordered the removal of the creamy layer and made a distinction between the Backward and the More Backward.

4. Mandal wanted unfilled vacancies carried forward.

   The court says they can be dereserved. It has also said that there has to be a 'minimum standard' to qualify for even the reserved posts.

5. Mandal wanted reservation to apply to promotions.

   The court has ruled that they be restricted to the original appointments only.

6. The Rao Government wanted to reserve 10 per cent of the posts for the weaker sections among the forward castes.

   The court has said this in unconstitutional.

5.7. Uttarakhand and Reservations

Reservation Policy announced by Chief Minister Mulayam Singh Yadav in the month of September 1994 led to spontaneous Uttarakhand agitation. As observed in *India Today* (September 13, 1994), "What angers the hill residents is that the 27 per cent quota is being enforced in the hills although the OBCs constitute less than 2 per cent of the population there. With the backward region dubbed a 'money-order economy', which subsists on money sent home by migrant workers the protester are demanding development of the whole area."

Observer feel that the Uttarakhand agitation in connection with anti-reservation movement in the hill districts was a "resounding success."

Even a senior official admitted: "We never expected such a show of strength." "In fact the stir is already causing unrest in the army which draws heavily from the hill regions for the personnel. The Chief of Army Staff General B. C. Joshi met Mulayam Singh Yadav recently to inform him about the effect of the agitation on the forces", as stated *India Today* in its special report. The special report further added, 'But Mulayam remains strangely unmoved. He has variously dismissed it as a 'BJP conspiracy' and even tried to play off the hill folk against the people in the plains. At a recent press conference, he said the stir could boomerang if the people in the plains decided to target the hill folk working there. This provoked angry protests in the hills and moved an agitationist to ask: 'Is

Mulayam the Chief Minister of the State or only of the plains.'

"Mulayam has also tried to use the situation to embarrass his political foes. Of the 19 MLAs from the hill, only one is from the SP, while the rest are from the BJP. the Congress (I) and the Uttarakhand Kranti Dal (UKD) or are Independents. If the BJP or the Congress (I) do not support the stir, they stand to lose clout in the hills and, if they do, they will antagonise the OBCs in the plains."

The ruling party pro-reservation bandh on September 13, 1994 led to several ugly incidents as well as deaths. The Allahabad High Court premises witnessed so much violence that it referred the case to the Supreme Court which ordered a CBI inquiry.

NOTES

1. Subs. by the Constitution (Fifty-first Amendment) Act, 1984, s. 2 for Sub-clause (b) (w.e.f 16-6-1986).
2. Ins. by the Constitution (Seventh Amendment) Act, 1956, s. 29 and Sch.
3. Ins. by the Constitution (Thirty-first Amendment) Act. 1973, s. 3.
4 Ins. by the Constitution (Forty-second Amendment) Act., 1976, s. 47 (w.e.f. 3-1-1977).
5. Subs. by the Constitution (Fifty-frist Amendment) Act, 1984, s. 3 for certain words (w.e.f. 16-6-1986).
6. Subs. by the Constitution (Thirty-first Amendment) Act, 1973, s. 4 for certain words.
7. The words and letters "specified in Part A or Part B of the First Schedule" omitted by the Constitution (Seventh Amendment) Act., 1956, s. 29 and Sch.
8. Ins. by the Constitution (Fifty-seventh Amendment) Act, 1987, s. 2 (w.e.f 21-9-1987).
9. Certain words omitted by the North-Eastern Areas (Reorganisation) Act. 1971, s. 71 (w.e.f. 21-1-1972).
10. The words "or Rajpramukh" omitted by the Constitution (Seventh Amendment) Act, 1956, s. 29 and Sch.
11. Subs. by the Constitution (Twenty-third Amendment) Act. 1969 s. 4 for "nominate such number of members of the community to the Assembly as he considers appropriate."
12. Subs. by the Constitution (Sixty-second Amendment) Act, 1989, s. for "forty years" (w.e.f. 20-12-1989).
13. The words and letters "specified in Part A or Part B of the First Schedule" omitted by the Constitution (Seventh Amendment) Act, 1956, s. 29 and Sch.
14. Subs. by s. 29 and Sch., *ibid.*, for "any such State".
15. Subs. by the Constitution (First Amendment) Act, 1951, s. 10, for "may, after consultation with the Governor or Rajpramukh of a state."
16. Ins. by the Constitution (Seventh Amendment) Act, 1956, s. 29 and Sch.
17. The words and letters "specified in Part A or Part B of the First Schedule" omitted by s. 29 and Sch., *ibid.*
18. The words "or Rajpramukh" omitted by s. 29 and Sch., ibid.
19. See the Constitution (Scheduled Castes) Order, 1950 (C.O. 19), the Constitution (Scheduled Castes) (Union Territories) Order, 1951, (C.O. 32), the Constitution (Jammu and Kashmir) Scheduled Castes Order, 1956 (C.O. 52), the Constitution (Dadra and Nagar Haveli) Scheduled Castes Order, (C.O. 64), the Constitution (Pondicherry)

Scheduled Castes Order, 1964 (C.O. 68), the Constitution (Goa, Daman and Diu) Scheduled Castes Order, 1968 (C.O. 81) and the Constitution (Sikkim) Scheduled Castes Order, 1978 (C.O. 110)

20. Subs. by the Constitution (First Amendment) Act, 1951, s. 11 for "may, after consultation with the Governor or Rajpramukh of a state."

21. See the Constitution (Scheduled Tribes) Order, 1950 (C.O. 22), the Constitution (Scheduled Tribes) (Union Territories) Order, 1951 (C.O. 33), the Constitution (Andaman and Nicobar Islands) Scheduled Tribes Order, 1959 (C.O. 58), the Constitution (Dadra and Nagar Haveli) Scheduled Tribes Order, 1962 (C.O. 65), the Constitution (Scheduled Tribes) (Uttar Pradesh) Order, 1967 (C.O. 78) the Constitution (Goa, Daman and Diu) Scheduled Tribes Order, 1968 (C.O. 82), the Constitution (Nagaland) Scheduled Tribes Order, 1970 (C.O. 88) and the Constitution (Sikkim) Scheduled Tribes Order, 1978, (C.O. 111).

6

UTTARAKHAND IN 1991 ELECTION MANIFESTOES

6.1 Bharatiya Janata Party

The BJP recognises that regional imbalances have developed in some States because of their size. The party would appoint a Commission to report on formation of smaller States which are economically and democratically viable. Initially BJP will have Uttarakhand, Vanachal and Union Territory of Delhi as three new States of the Indian Union.

6.2 Communist Party of India

Action plan to resolve the Jharkhand, Uttarakhand, Bastar, Bodo and other similar tribal and ethnic problems in accordance with the democratic aspirations of the people and the requirements of Indian Unity and democracy.

6.3 National Front

The existing special reservations for the people of the Hill areas of U.P. Shall continue. The National Front shall try to evolve a consensus on their demand for a Uttarakhand State.

7

UTTAR PRADESH: Land of Indian Prime Ministers and Yet Backward and Unwieldy

7.1 Prime Ministers of India

Of the nine Prime Ministers of India, since independence, seven have hailed from Uttar Pradesh. Out of about 47 years, they have dominated the scene for about 42 years.

1.	Jawaharlal Nehru (1889-1964)	August 15, 1947 to May 27,1964
2.	Lal Bahadur Shastri (1904-1966)	June 9, 1964 to January 11, 1966
3.	Indira Gandhi (1917-1984)	January 24, 1966 to March 24, 1977
4.	Morarji Desai (1896-)	March 24, 1977 to July 28, 1979
5.	Charan Singh (1902-1987)	July 28, 1979 to January 14, 1980
6.	Indira Gandhi (1917-1984)	January 14, 1980 to October 31, 1984
7.	Rajiv Gandhi (1944-1991)	October, 31, 1984 to December 1, 1989

Notes: Gulzari Lal Nanda acted as Prime Minister during the period May 27, 1964 to June 9, 1964 and January 11, 1966 to January 24, 1966.

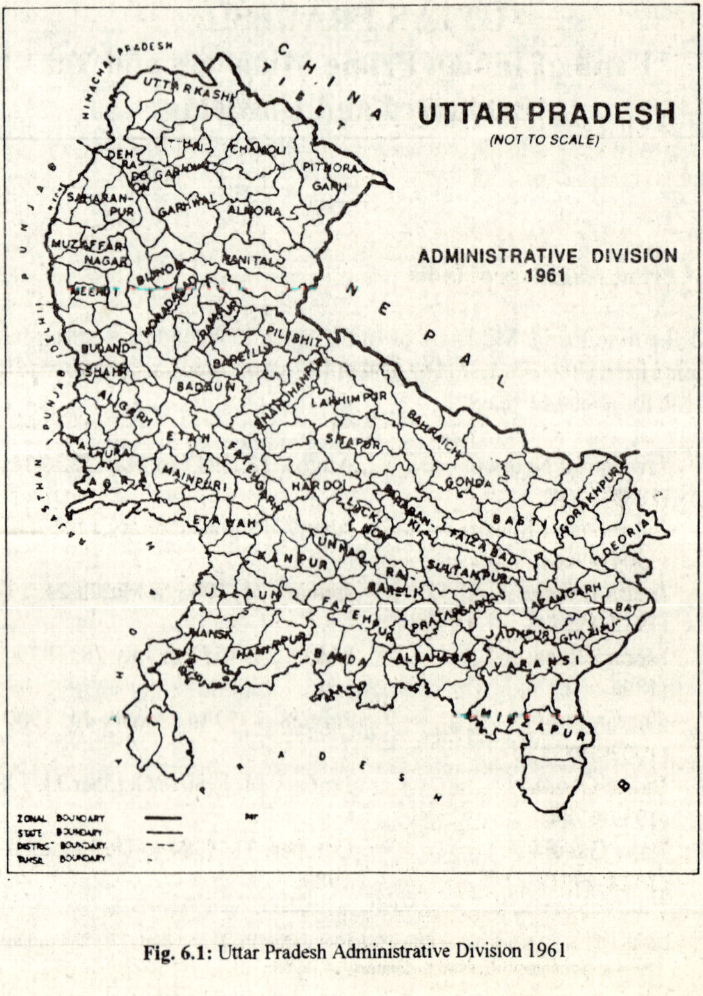

Fig. 6.1: Uttar Pradesh Administrative Division 1961

8.	Viswanath Pratap Singh (1931-)	December 2, 1989 to November 10, 1990
9.	Chandra Shekhar (1927-)	November 10, 1990 to June 21, 1991
10.	P.V. Narasimha Rao (1921-)	June 21, 1991 — till date

7.2 Uttar Pradesh: Basic Data at a Glance

Area: 2,94,411 sq. km	Population : 13,91,12,287
Capital: Lucknow	Principal Languages: Hindi and Urdu

7.3 History and Geography

History of Uttar Pradesh is very ancient and interesting. It is recognised in the later Vedic Age as *Brahmarshi Desa* or *Madhya Desa.* Many great sages of the Vedic times like Bharadwaja, Yagyavalkya, Vasishta, Vishwamitra and Valmiki appear to have flourished in Uttar Pradesh. Several sacred books of the Aryans were also composed here. Two great epics of India, *Ramayana* and *Mahabharata* appear to have been inspired by Uttar Pradesh. *Ramayana* features the royal family of Kosala and *Mahabharata* centres around the royal family at Hastinapur both in Uttar Pradesh.

In the sixth century BC, Uttar Pradesh was associated with two new religions, Jainism and Buddhism. Mahavira, founder of Jainism is said to have breathed his last at Doora in Uttar Pradesh. It was as Saranath that Buddha preached his first sermon and laid the foundations of his order. In the post Buddhist period, several centres in Uttar Pradesh like Ayodhya, Prayag, Varanasi and Mathura became reputed centres of learning. Sri Sankaracharya, the great Hindu reformer, established one of his *ashramas* at Badrinath in Uttar Pradesh. In the medieval period, Uttar Pradesh passed under Muslim rule and led the way to a new synthesis of Hindu and Islamic cultures. Ramananda and his Muslim disciple Kabir, Tulsidas, Birbal and many other intellectuals contributed to the growth of Hindi and Urdu languages.

Uttar Pradesh preserved its intellectual leadership even under the British administration. The British combined Agra and Oudh into one province and called it United Provinces of Agra and Oudh. The name was shortened to the United Provinces in 1955. After Independence, in January 1950, United Provinces was renamed as Uttar Pradesh. Uttar Pradesh is bounded by Tibet and Nepal in north, Himachal Pradesh in north-west, Haryana in west, Rajasthan in south-west. Madhya Pradesh in south and Bihar in east. Uttar Pradesh can be divided into three distinct regions (1) northern mountains, (ii) southern hills plateau, and (iii) Gangetic plain.

7.4 Agriculture

Agriculture is the main occupation of almost 78 per cent of the population. Uttar Pradesh is the largest producer of foodgrains, sugarcane and oilseeds. During 1992-93, wheat production was 199.07 lakh mt, rice 96.09 lakh mt, oilseeds 13.65 lakh mt, jute 0.01 lakh mt, pulses 24.81 lakh mt, patato 59.08 lakh mt, cane 1,066.77 lakh mt, fish 12.14 lakh mt, and apple 2.12 lakh mt. The State is India's 'sugarcane bowl' producing 25.55 lakh mt. There are 1,796 veterinary hospitals for cattle.

7.5 Industry and Minerals

By February 1993, medium and large industrial undertakings cumulated to 1,311 with an investment of Rs. 9,739.51 crore and small scale industries (SSI) units numbered more than three lakh having an investment of Rs. 1,801 crore. After the introduction of liberalised Industrial Policy wherein people are free to choose any location by just filing an Industrial Enterpreneurs Memorandum with the Secretariat of Industrial Approval in the Government of India, 13.46 per cent entrepreneurs have opted for Uttar Pradesh. Presently, 262 medium and large industries are under implementation, besides 29 new projects have been taken up in 1992-93.

There are 7,44,850 artisans in the State. Hand knitted woollen carpets of Varanasi and Mirzapur, *chikan* of Lucknow, terracota of Gorakhpur, wood carving of Saharanpur, brass and EPNs wares of Moradabad and hand printing of Farrukhabad have excelled in their craftsmanship and vividness of colours and designs. In the total export of woollen carpets, 75 per cent is contributed by Uttar Pradesh alone. During 1991-92 about 15 million tonnes of major minerals and 58 million cubic meters of minor minerals were produced in the State which valued at over Rs. 554 crore. Important mineral based industries include large cement plants in Senbhadra, mini cement plants in Lucknow. Dehradun and Almora, dead burnt magnesite plants in Almora and Pithoragarh, calcium carbide plant in Dehradun and synthetic emery plant in Banda, silica-sand beneficiation plant in Allahabad, and elemental phosphorus plant in Lalitpur. The mineral industry is labour intensive and provides employment to about one lakh persons.

7.6 Forests

Uttar Pradesh Forest Department has geared itself to increase the forest covers of the State from present 17.4 per cent (51,502 km) to 33 per cent as required by National Forest Policy 1988. During 1992-93, the following specific schemes were implemented to improve the quality and productivity of the existing forest and to increase the tree wealth of the State: (i) Social Forestry Programme; (ii) Industrial and Pulpwood Plantation; (iii) Fuelwood and Fodder Scheme; (iv) Energy Plantation Scheme; (v) Soil Conservation works in civil and Soyam Forest; (vi) Soil Conservation and Afforestation Scheme in Tehri Dam Catchment Area; (vii) Ramganga Project; (viii) Matatila Project; (ix) Integrated Wasteland Project; (x) Poverty Alleviation and Welfare Schemes, and (xi) World Food Programme.

7.7 Irrigation and Power

By the end of Seventh Plan irrigation facility in a total area of 104.35 lakh hectare was available through 69.150 km of canals and 26.985 government tube-wells which increased to 73,070 and 28,109 as on, 1992. Irrigation potential in an area of about 1.05 lakh hectare was created through large, medium and minor irrigation projects. Major irrigation projects under construction include Lakhwar Vyasi, eastern Ganga canal, modernisation of Upper Ganga canal, Maudaha Dam, Sarda Sahayak, Saryu canal and Urmil dam. An outlay of Rs. 362.87 crore for major and medium schemes was earmarked for this purpose during 1992-93.

Uttar Pradesh has some of the oldest power houses to supply electricity throughout the State. The U.P. State Electricity Board, which generates, transmits and distributes power in whole of the State, was established on April 1, 1959. At that time, the total generating capacity of hydro, thermal and diesel power houses was 263.5 MW which has now been raised to 4,643.75 MW. Important power projects implemented since 1947 are hydro electric—Mohammadpur (1950-54), Khatima (1954-56), Pathri (1955-56), Rihand (1961-62), Matatila (1964-66), Dhakrani (1965-66) Dhalipur (1965-66), Obra (1970-72), Chibre (1974-76), Kulhal (1974-76), Ramganga (1975-77), Chilla (1980-81), Khodri (1983-84), Maheri-Bhali (1984-85), and Khara (1992-93); thermal projects-Harduaganj 'A' (1962-65), Harduaganj 'B' (1967-73), Harduaganj 'C' (1976-78), Panki (1967-68), Panki Extension (1976-77), Obra (1967-72), Obra Extension (1973-82), Parichha (1983-85), Anpara 'A' (1985-88), and Tanda (1987-90). All thermal projects except Harduaganj 'A' are in operation. As on January 31, 1993, 83,781 villages and 51,837 Harijan Bastis have been electrified. Besides 6,60,216 private tube-wells and 31,226 State tube-wells have been energised.

7.8 Transport

Roads

Roads in Uttar Pradesh was categorised as under (i) PWD upto 31 March 1992—Black Top 60,065 km, Water Bound Macadam 15,329 km. Brick Soling 14,555 km. Eastern Roads 9,765 km, (ii) roads maintained by other departments—(a) black top 7,028 km, (b) Water Bound Macadam 3,072 km, (c) Brick Soling 19,168 km, (d) Earthen Roads 43,319 km. Number of on-road vehicles in Uttar Pradesh was 2,39,159 upto March 1993.

Railways

Important railway junctions are Agra, Kanpur, Allahabad, Mughalsarai, Tundla, Gorakhpur, Gonda and Lucknow.

7.9 Festivals

The biggest congregation perhaps of the world, *Kumbh Mela* is held at Allahabad every twelfth year. Apart from Allahabad it is also held at Haridwar every sixth year. In Allahabad, there is a *Magh Mela* every winter in January when people come and settle there for a month to have a dip in Sangam every morning. Among other fairs is *Jhoola* fair of Mathura, Vrindavan and Ayodhya that last a fortnight when idols are placed in gold and silver *Jhoolas* or cradles. A dip in the Ganga or *Kartik Poornamasi* is supposed to be the holiest and there are big congregation at Garhmukteswar, Soran Rajghat, Kakora, Bithur, Kanpur, Allahabad, Varanasi, Ayodhya and Haridwar. A very famous cattle fair is held at Bateswar in Agra district. Deva in Bara Banki district has become famous because of Muslim saint Warish Shah. Beside, important festivals of Hindus, Muslims, etc., are widely celebrate in the State.

7.10 Tourist Centres

Uttar Pradesh has varied attractions for all kinds of tourists. Besides ancient places of pilgrimage, like Varanasi, Vindhyachal, Ayodhya,

Chitrakoot, Prayag, Bageshwar, Jageshwar, Pauri, Naimishranya, Mathura, Vrindavan, Haridwar, Rishikesh, Badrinath, Kedarnath, Gangotri, Yamnotri, Nanakmatta, Hemkund Sahib, Deva Sharief of Pearanklar, Dargah of Sheikh Saleem Chishti in Fatehpur, Sarnath, Sharvasti, Kushinagar Sankisa, Kampil, Piprahva and Kaushambi. Places like Agra, Ayodhya, Sarnath, Varanasi, Lucknow, Mathura, Prayag, Jhansi, Gorakhpur, Jaunpur, Kanauj, Mahoba, Devgarh, Bithur and Vindhyachai have rich treasures of Hindu and Islamic architecture and culture. Uttar Pradesh has a treasure of magnificent scenic beauty spots like Sangam in Allahabad, Hindon (Ghaziabad) and Tanda Waterfall in Faizabad, Okhla, Dehradun, Musoorie, Chakrata, Nainital, Ranikhet, Almora, Kausani, Pindari, Galcier, Corbett National Park and Dudhwa Sanctuary.

TABLE 7.1 : Area, Population and Headquarters of Districts.

Districts	Area sq km.	Population	Headquarters
1. Agra	4,027	27,51,021	Agra
2. Aligarh	5,019	32,95,982	Aligargh
3. Allahabad	7,261	49,21,313	Allahabad
4. Almora	5,385	8,36,613	Almora
5. Azamgarh	4,234	31,53,885	Azamgarh
6. Baharaich	6,877	27,63,750	Baharich
7. Ballia	2,981	22,62,273	Ballia
8. Banda	7,624	18,62,139	Banda
9. Bara Banki	4,402	24,23,136	Barabanki
10. Barelli	4,120	28,34,616	Bareilli
11. Basti	3,735	27,38,522	Basti
12. Bijnor	4,561	24,54,521	Bijnor
13. Budaun	5,168	24,48,338	Budaun
14. Bulandshar	4,352	28,44,859	Bulandshar
15. Chamoli	9,126	4,54,871	Chamoli
16. Dehra Doon	3,088	10,25,679	Dehra Doon
17. Deoria	5,445	44,40,024	Deoria
18. Etah	4,446	22,44,998	Etah
19. Etawah	4,326	21,24,655	Etawah
20. Faizabad	4,511	29,78,484	Faizabad
21. Farrukhabad	4,274	24,40,266	Fatehgarh
22. Fatehpur	4,152	18,99,241	Fatehpur
23. Garhwal	2,590	6,82,535	Pauri

24. Ghaziabad	2,590	27,03,933	Ghaziabad
25. Ghazipur	3,377	24,16,617	Ghazipur
26. Gonda	7,352	35,73,075	Gonda
27. Gorakhpur	6,272	30,66,002	Gorakhpur
28. Hamirpur	7,166	14,66,491	Hamirpur
29. Hardoi	5,986	27,47,082	Hardoi
30. Jalaun	4,565	12,19,377	Orai
31. Jaunpur	4,038	32,14,636	Jaunpur
32. Jhansi	5,024	14,29,698	Jhansi
33. Kanpur (Dehat)	5,111	21,38,317	Kanpur (Rural)
34. Kanpur (Nagar)	1,065	24,18,487	Kanpur
35. Kheri	7,680	24,19,234	Kheri
36. Lalitpur	5,039	7,52,043	Lalitpur
37. Lucknow	2,528	27,62,801	Lucknow
38. Mainpuri	2,760	13,16,746	Mainpuri
39. Mathura	3,811	19,31,186	Mathura
40. Meerut	3,911	34,47,912	Meerut
41. Mirzapur	4,522	16,57,139	Mirzapur
42. Moradabad	5,967	41,21,035	Moradabad
43. Muzaffarnagar	4,008	28,42,543	Muzaffarnagar
44. Nainital	6,794	15,40,174	Nainital
45. Pilibhit	3,499	12,83,103	Pilibhit
46. Pithoragarh	8,856	5,66,408	Pithoragarh
47. Pratapgarh	3,717	22,10,700	Pratapgarh
48. Rae Bareli	4,609	23,22,810	Rae Bareli
49. Rampur	2,367	15,02,141	Rampur
50. Saharanpur	3,689	23,09,029	Saharanpur
51. Shahjahanpur	4,575	19,87,395	Shahjahanpur
52. Sitapur	5,743	28,57,009	Sitapur
53. Sultanpur	4,436	25,58,970	Sultanpur
54. Tehri Garhwal	4,421	5,80,153	Narendranagar
55. Unnao	4,558	22,00,397	Unnao
56. Uttarkashi	8,016	2,39,709	Uttarkashi
57. Varanasi	5,092	48,60,582	Varanasi
58. Haridwar	2,360	11,24,488	Haridwar
59. Maiu	1,713	14,45,782	Maiu
60. Sidharthnagar	3,495	17,07,885	Navgarh
61. Firozabad	2,361	15,33,054	Firozabad
62. Maharajganj	N.R.	16,76,378	Maharajganj
63. Sonbhadra	6,788	10,75,041	Roberts Ganj

Source : India 1993, Publication Division, Government of India, 1994.)

TABLE 7.2: Human Development : U.P. vis-a-vis Other States

Items	All India	U.P.	Rank	Bihar	Rank
1. Per capita net State Domestic Product at current prices (new series) (1990-91)	N.A.	Rs. 3072	18 out of 20 States for which data available	Rs. 2122	20
2. Per capita Expenditure at 1982-83 prices (1990-91)	Rs. 41.58	Rs. 29.39	14 out of 15 States	24.34	15 at the bottom
3. Literacy Rate 1992-93					
(a) Total	52.11	41.06	27	38.48	31 (last)
(b) Males	64.13	55.73	26	52.59	25
(c) Females	39.29	25.31	2.9	22.89	30
Total No of States & UTs-31)					
4. Crude Birth Rate (1991 Census)	29.3	35.1	Heighest next only to Madhya Pradesh	30.5	Among the 8 highest
5. Crude Death Rate (1991 Census)	9.8	11.1	Among 5 highest	9.8	Among the 6 highest
6. Infant Mortality Rate (1991 Census)	80	93	Among the 3 highest	69	Normal
7. Life Expectancy					
(a) Male	55.9	52.3 years	At the bottom	54.9	Almost at the bottom
(b) Female (1991 Census)	55.9	49.6	at the bottom	52.3	Almost at the bottom
8. Enrolment Ratio (1992-93)					
(a) Classes I-V	105.7	88.6	Almost at the bottom	81.4	Almost at the bottom
(b) Classes VI-VII	67.5	55.6	Almost at bottom	37.1	At the bottom

TABLE 7.3: Real per Capita Expenditure of Major States (At 1982-83 Prices)*

(Rupees)

States	RTE		RSE		REDN		RMPH	
	1975-76	1990-91	1975-76	1990-91	1975-76	1990-91	1975-76	1990-91
Andhra Pradesh	247.90	505.74	73.67	175.94	37.70	82.71	18.41	33.68
	(9)	(10)	(11)	(10)	(12)	(11)	(10)	(13)
Assam	229.43	609.86	73.89	184.53	43.88	106.46	17.59	45.96
	(12)	(5)	(10)	(8)	(8)	(7)	(11)	(6)
Bihar	161.30	356.08	41.99	119.02	23.41	72.20	9.79	24.34
	(15)	(15)	(15)	(15)	(15)	(14)	(15)	(15)
Gujarat	320.94	699.89	110.71	215.23	52.96	113.89	22.19	42.53
	(4)	(4)	(3)	(6)	(3)	(4)	(8)	(8)
Haryana	409.00	755.38	90.79	218.23	49.89	106.56	22.74	43.49
	(2)	(2)	(6)	(4)	(5)	(6)	(7)	(7)
Karnataka	293.56	576.85	82.20	188.33	44.74	94.12	20.83	37.27
	(6)	(8)	(9)	(7)	(7)	(9)	(9)	(9)
Kerala	305.93	594.39	132.71	227.23	85.11	131.27	31.55	49.08
	(5)	(7)	(1)	(3)	(1)	(2)	(1)	(4)
Madhya Pradesh	222.74	447.71	68.09	151.37	33.69	70.95	16.81	34.61
	(13)	(12)	(13)	(13)	(13)	(15)	(12)	(11)
Maharashtra	365.64	702.09	98.42	216.62	51.71	117.08	25.31	45.37
	(3)	(3)	(4)	(5)	(4)	(3)	(4)	(5)
Orissa	242.82	489.54	73.08	156.55	37.73	78.86	16.40	33.74
	(10)	(11)	(12)	(12)	(11)	(12)	(13)	(12)
Punjab	451.96	943.52	132.70	250.27	66.21	144.01	27.57	57.64
	(1)	(1)	(2)	(1)	(2)	(1)	(2)	(2)
Rajasthan	264.91	539.24	82.26	181.59	41.06	94.18	26.32	60.04
	(8)	(9)	(8)	(9)	(9)	(8)	(3)	(1)
Tamil Nadu	267.93	594.83	95.78	234.30	45.11	112.72	22.80	50.29
	(7)	(6)	(5)	(2)	(6)	(5)	(6)	(3)
Uttar Pradesh	206.41	428.53	48.98	125.32	30.78	74.68	10.62	29.39
	(14)	(14)	(14)	(14)	(14)	(13)	(14)	(14)
West Bengal	230.66	430.90	85.44	166.09	38.43	92.05	22.82	36.32
	(11)	(13)	(7)	(11)	(10)	(10)	(5)	(10)
Mean	281.41	578.30	86.05	187.37	45.49	99.45	20.78	41.58
Standard Deviation	75.99	146.43	24.99	38.06	14.49	21.26	5.79	9.78
Coefficient of Variation(%)	27.00	25.32	29.04	20.31	31.85	21.37	27.84	23.51

* Figures relate to three year averages centered on the years shown.

Note: Figures in parentheses are ranks.

RTE : Real per capita total expenditure

RSE : Real per capita social expenditure

REDN : Real per capita educational expenditure

RMPH : Real per capita medical, public health, family welfare and water supply and sanitation expenditure

Source : Reserve Bank of India. Development Research Group Study 6, Social Sector Expenditure and Human Development 1993. University News, March 14, 1994).

TABLE 7.4: Indicators of Human Development (other than per Capita Income and Product)

States	Sex Ratio per 1000 Males	Literacy Rate			Work Participation Rate (Total workers as perce-ntages of total Population)			C.B.R. (Crude Birth Rate)	C.D.R. (Crude Death Rate)	Natural Increase (CBR CDR)	I.M.R. (Infant Mort-ality Rate)	Male life expect-ancy of birth (1981 -88)	Female life expe-ctancy of birth (1981-88)
		Persons	Males	Females	Persons	Males	Females						
	1	2	3	4	5	6	7	8	9	10	11	12	13
India	927	52.21	64.13	39.29	37.46	51.55	22.25	29.3	9.8	19.5	80.0	55.9	55.9
Andhra Pradesh	972	44.09	55.13	32.72	45.05	55.48	34.32	26.0	9.7	16.3	73.0	57.3	60.3
Arunachal Pradesh	859	41.59	51.45	29.69	46.24	53.76	37.49	30.9	13.5	17.4	N.A	N.A	N.A
Assam	923	52.89	61.87	43.03	36.09	49.45	21.61	30.9	11.5	19.4	81.0	52.4	52.5
Bihar	911	38.48	52.49	22.89	32.16	47.92	14.86	30.5	9.8	20.7	69.0	54.9	52.3
Goa	967	75.51	83.64	67.09	35.28	49.56	20.52	16.8	7.5	9.3	N.A	N.A	N.A
Gujarat	934	61.29	73.13	48.64	40.23	53.57	25.96	27.5	8.5	19.0	69.0	55.9	57.9
Haryana	865	55.85	69.10	40.47	31.00	48.51	10.76	33.1	8.2	24.9	68.0	61.5	59.5
Himachal	976	63.86	75.36	52.13	42.82	50.64	34.82	28.4	8.9	19.5	75.0	58.5*	62.9*
J&K	—	—	—	—	—	—	—	—	—	—	—	60.2*	60.7*
Karnataka	960	56.04	67.26	44.34	41.99	54.09	29.39	26.8	90.0	17.8	77.0	59.8	62.4
Kerala	1,036	89.79	93.62	89.13	31.43	47.58	15.85	18.1	6.0	12.1	17.0	65.9	72.2
Madhya Pradesh	931	44.20	58.42	28.85	42.82	52.26	32.68	35.8	13.8	22.0	122.0	50.5	51.8
Mahara-shtra	934	64.87	76.56	52.32	42.96	52.16	33.11	26.2	8.2	18.0	60.0	60.1	62.8
Manipur	958	59.89	71.63	47.60	42.18	45.27	38.96	19.6	5.5	14.1	N.A	N.A	N.A
Megha-laya	955	49.10	53.12	44.85	42.67	50.07	34.93	32.4	8.8	23.6	N.A	N.A	N.A
Mizoram	921	82.27	85.61	78.60	48.91	53.87	43.52	N.A	N.A	N.A	N.A	N.A	N.A
Nagaland	886	61.65	57.62	54.75	42.68	46.86	37.96	18.5	3.3	15.2	N.A	N.A	N.A
Orissa	971	49.09	63.09	34.68	37.53	53.79	20.79	28.8	12.7	16.1	126.0	53.6	53.1
Punjab	882	58.51	65.66	50.41	30.87	54.22	4.40	28.6	8.0	20.6	53.0	63.0	64.7
Rajasthan	910	38.55	54.99	20.44	38.87	49.30	27.40	34.3	9.8	24.5	77.0	53.5	54.3
Sikkim	878	56.94	65.74	46.69	41.51	51.26	30.41	26.5	8.8	17.7	N.A	N.A	N.A
Tamil Nadu	974	62.66	73.75	51.33	43.31	56.39	29.89	20.7	8.8	11.9	57.0	57.4	58.5
Tripura	945	60.44	70.58	49.65	31.14	47.55	13.76	24.4	7.6	16.8	N.A	N.A	N.A
Uttar Pardesh	879	41.06	55.73	25.31	32.20	49.68	12.32	35.1	11.1	24.0	93.0	52.3	49.6
West Bengal	917	57.70	67.81	46.56	32.19	51.41	11.25	26.7	8.1	18.6	70.0	57.9	59.1

Union Territories													
Andman & Nicobar	818	73.02	78.99	65.46	35.24	53.32	13.13	19.9	5.7	14.2	N.A	N.A	N.A
Chandigarh	790	77.81	82.04	72.34	34.94	54.33	10.33	14.1	4.0	10.1	N.A	N.A	N.A
Dadra & Nagar Haveli	952	40.71	53.56	26.98	53.25	57.50	48.79	30.4	11.4	19.0	N.A	N.A	N.A
Daman & Diu	969	71.20	82.66	59.40	37.63	51.63	23.17	27.8	9.0	18.8	N.A	N.A	N.A
Delhi	827	75.29	82.01	66.99	31.64	51.72	7.36	24.1	6.0	18.1	N.A	N.A	N.A
Laksha-dweep	943	81.78	90.18	72.89	26.43	44.17	7.60	27.1	4.7	22.4	N.A	N.A	N.A
Pondichery	979	74.74	83.68	65.63	33.08	50.55	15.24	18.9	6.4	12.5	N.A	N.A	N.A

Note: 1. In cols 12-13 the life expectancy at birth is based on the Age specific Death Rates averaged over 1981-88 as estimated by Sample Registration System (SRS)

2. N.A Stands for Not Available.

3. Figures and Proportion in Columns 1 to 7 are based on final population totals of 1991 census, while columns 8 to 10 are based on Sample Registration System (SRS) estimates of 1991.

* Relates to the period 1981-85

Source : Registrar General and Census Commissioner, India, *University News*, January 1994.

TABLE 7.5 Enrolement Ratio in Classes-I-V and VI-VIII of Schools for General Education

State/Union Territory	Classes 1-5 (5-11 years)			Classes 6-8 (11-14 Years)		
	Boys	Girls	Total	Boys	Girls	Total
1	2	3	4	5	6	7
Andhra Pradesh	121.5	96.6	109.2	68.6	43.0	55.9
Arunachal Pradesh	129.9	93.4	111.5	59.4	39.8	49.7
Assam	115.5	107.3	111.5	69.3	54.3	62.1
Bihar	105.8	56.2	81.4	51.5	22.0	37.1
Goa	105.2	95.9	100.5	107.4	91.4	99.4
Gujarat	145.0	114.0	129.8	87.9	57.5	73.0
Haryana	92.5	81.1	87.0	73.2	51.8	63.0
Himachal Pradesh	125.5	110.5	110.0	123.9	97.6	110.8
Jammu & Kashmir	104.1	72.6	88.7	80.1	49.2	65.1
Karnataka	119.4	110.4	115.0	69.6	52.0	61.0
Kerala	98.4	96.5	97.5	106.0	104.1	105.0
Madhya Pradesh	117.7	87.7	103.2	89.1	53.5	71.9
Maharashtra	142.9	129.4	136.3	92.1	70.8	81.8

Manipur	115.1	105.6	110.5	64.5	57.1	60.9
Meghalaya	78.4	72.1	75.2	42.8	37.5	40.1
Mizoram	137.8	133.0	135.5	75.3	70.7	73.0
Nagaland	109.9	101.3	105.7	69.7	68.8	69.3
Orissa	120.7	89.2	105.4	75.7	44.1	60.2
Punjab	103.4	96.6	100.1	79.7	67.8	74.0
Rajasthan	115.2	57.5	87.1	77.5	27.6	53.3
Sikkim	124.0	111.9	118.0	55.1	53.0	54.1
Tamil Nadu	143.4	129.2	136.5	110.9	88.8	100.1
Tripura	143.3	119.7	131.7	94.5	73.4	84.2
Uttar Pradesh	103.7	72.0	88.6	73.4	35.7	55.6
West bengal	137.9	130.2	134.1	114.0	99.6	106.9
A & N Island	101.0	86.1	93.3	82.7	72.8	77.9
D&N Haveli	116.3	83.6	100.8	57.5	37.3	47.8
Daman & Diu	—	—	—	—	—	—
Delhi	84.0	85.5	84.7	80.5	76.2	78.5
Lakshadweep	158.7	133.6	146.2	133.0	102.9	118.4
Pondicherry	148.0	136.2	142.2	137.6	124.6	131.2
India	118.0	92.7	105.7	80.5	53.8	67.5

Conclusions

Almost in every aspect, U.P. and Bihar are the most backward States economically and educationally. Incidentally they happen to be the two populous States with 13,91,12,287 (16.44 per cent of country's total 8,63,74,465 (10.21% of country's total population, accounting for 26.65 per cent population of India. Perhaps the backwardness of India can be ascribed to the backwardness of there two, States. There seems to be a serious defect in the system of organisation. It is all the more serious in the case of State of Uttar Pradesh which has given seven Prime Ministers as already Stated. May be, backwardness is due to the unwiedly nature of this State. This perhaps points out to the need of the bifurcation of the State.

SECTION-III

VIABILITY OF PROPOSED UTTARAKHAND STATE

8

UTTARAKHAND:
Basic Data Including Comparative Study of other Smaller States and Union Territories Having Population Less than One Crore

8.1 Introduction

Tables 8.1 to 8.5 provide data on population, area, headquarters and literacy rates, etc.

TABLE 8.1: Area, Population and Headquarters of District in Uttarakhand

	District	Area sq km	Population 1981	Population 1991	Headquarters
1.	Almorah	5,385	7,57,373	8,36,613	Almora
2.	Chamoli	9,126	3,64,346	454,871	Chamoli
3.	Dehradun	3,088	7,61,668	10,25,679	Dehradun
4.	Garhwal	5438	6,37,877	6,82,535	Pauri
5.	Nainital	6,794	11,36,523	15,40,174	Nainital
6.	Pithoragarh	8,856	4,89,267	5,66,408	Pithoragarh
7.	Tehri Garhwal	4,421	4,97,709	5,80,153	Narendranagar
8.	Uttarkashi	8,016	1,90,948	2,39,709	Uttarkashi
	Total	51,124	48,35,711	55,26,142	

Note: Final figures as per 1991 Census.

TABLE 8.2: Sex-wise Population and Literacy (1991)

Sl. No.	District	Female	Male	Literacy Female	Rate Male
1.	Almorah	4,32,889	3,92,245	33.40	62.00
2.	Chamoli	2,27,135	2,14,532	34.22	63.78
3.	Dehradun	4,66,519	5,48,17	49.77	66.02
4.	Garhwal	3,50,738	3,15,427	41.99	66.80
5.	Nainital	7,26,342	8,31,073	35.14	54.40
6.	Pithoragarh	2,82,874	2,74,274	31.98	63.48
7.	Tehri Garhwal	2,97,805	2,77,547	21.93	57.47
8.	Uttarkashi	1,14,444	1,23,328	19.12	55.17

Note : Provisional figures as per 1991 Census. Final sex-wise figures not available.

TABLE 8.3: Sex-wise Literacy Rate All India and Uttar Pradesh

	Total	Female	Male
All India	52.11	39.42	63.86
Uttar Pradesh	41.71	26.02	55.35

TABLE 8.4: Districtwise Density of Population and Females per Thousand

Sl. No.	District	Density of Population per sq km	Females per 1000 Males
1.	Almorah	153	1,106
2.	Chamoli	48	1,059
3.	Dehradun	329	851
4.	Garhwal	123	1,112
5.	Nainital	229	874
6.	Pithoragarh	63	1,031
7.	Tehri Garhwal	130	1,073
8.	Uttarkashi	30	928
	Uttar Pradesh	471	892

TABLE 8.5: Diverse Data of Garhwal Mandal (1991 Census)

	Item	Dehradun	Garhwal	Chamoli	Tehri	Uttarkashi
1.	Area sq km	3,088	5,438	9,126	4,421	8,016
2.	Rural Population	51%	90%	92%	96%	93%
3.	Urban Population	49%	10%	08%	047%	07%
4.	Agriculturists	36%	72%	81%	85%	79%
5.	Other Enterprises	64%	28%	19%	15%	21%
6.	Villages	743	3237	1516	1953	669
7.	Availability of water in villages	88%	66%	94%	82%	95%
8.	Electricity Consumption	90%	50%	66%	59%	83%
9.	Utilisation of Electricity	79%	05%	01%	06%	09%
10.	Nationalised Banks	112	56	26	39	18
11.	Per Capita Loan Distribution	Rs. 1468	Rs. 385	Rs. 288	Rs. 308	Rs. 485
12.	Factories (Under 1948 Act)	106	09	00	07	00
13.	Small Scale Units	1,748	928	151	1,324	1,420
14.	Post offices	249	416	320	257	116
15.	Telegram offices	34	59	60	42	15
16.	Telephones	8,834	1,167	541	510	430
17.	Allopthic hospitals	94	95	52	45	28
18.	Ayurvedic hospitals	35	38	59	56	39
19.	Homeopathic hospitals	08	06	06	07	04
20.	Primary Schools	855	1285	817	967	452
21.	High Schools	197	231	169	221	126
22.	Inter College	82	182	91	106	37
23.	Colleges	07	05	03	02	02

Source: Panchyanja, September 18, 1994.

TABLE 8.6: Political Representation of Uttarakhand and others Hill States

	State	Area in Thousand km	Population in Lakh	MLAs	MPs
1.	Arunachal Pradesh	83.7	8.6	30	2
2.	Himachal Pradesh	55.7	51.7	68	4
3.	Manipur	22.3	18.3	60	2
4.	Meghalaya	22.4	17.7	60	2
5.	Mizoram	21	6.9	30	1
6.	Nagaland	16.6	12.1	60	1
7.	Uttarakhand	51.6	59.3	19	4

TABLE 8.7:Population and Area of Smaller States/Union Territories Uttraranchal/ Uttarakhand

S.No.	State/Union Territory	Area sq km	Population	Per cent of Total Population of India	No. of Dists.
1	2	3	4	5	6
1.	Delhi	1,483	93,70,475	1.11	NA
2.	Jammu and Kashmir	22,2,236	77,18,700	0.91	14
3.	Himachal Pradesh	55,673	51,11,079	0.61	12
4.	Tripura	10,491	27,44,827	0.32	3
5.	Manipur	22,327	18,26,714	0.22	08
6.	Meghalaya	22,429	17,60,626	0.21	NA
7.	Nagaland	16,579	12,15,575	0.14	07
8.	Goa	3,702	11,68,622	0.14	02
9.	Arunachal Pradesh	83,743	8,58,392	0.10	11
10.	Pondicherry	492	8,07,045	0.09	04
11.	Mizoram	21,081	6,86,217	0.08	03
12.	Chandigarh	114	6,40,725	0.08	NA
13.	Sikkim	7,096	4,05,505	0.05	04
14.	Andaman and Nicobar Islands	8,249	2,79,111	0.05	03
15.	Dadar and Nagar Haveli	491	1,38,401	0.01	NA
16.	Daman and Diu	112	1,01,439	0.01	02
17.	Lakshadweep	32	51,681	0.01	NA
18.	Uttarakhand (Proposed)	51,124	59,26,142	0.69	08

Source: 1. Census 1991
2. India 1995 (for Number of Districts)

8.3 Uttarakhand: Case for Statehood

'Other things being equal, Uttarakhand compares, favourably with the smaller States and Union Territories with a population of less than one crore. Here a comparison on thee indicators, i.e, area population, percentage to total population of India and the number of districts is made in respect of 17 States and Union Territories. It may be recalled that at present there are 26 States and 6 Union Territories.

Following points emerge from the comparative data in Table 8.7

1. In area, out of 18 States and Union Territories (Including Uttarakhand), Uttarakhand ranks third.
2. In terms of population also its rank is 3.
3. As regards percentage to total population of India, its position is again at number 3.
4. Compared with the number of districts, its position is quite viable. Of the 14 States and Union Territories for which data is available, its rank is 4.

Other considerations relating to the formation of a State as contained in para 7 of the Resolution setting up the States Reorganisation Commission 1953-55 are: Common language and culture of the area, pattern of living, preservation and strengthening of the unity and security of India, financial, economic and administrative matters. By and large, Uttarakhand satisfies these requirements.

9

ECONOMIC VIABILITY OF UTTARAKHAND STATE (PROPOSED): Some Question and Answers

Following facts deserve careful consideration regards the viability of the Uttarakhand State.

1. Uttarakhand is self-sufficient in the production of foodgrains. It is estimated that as against the requirement of about 10,22,000 m. tonnes of foodgrains for the population, about 15,28,000 m. tonnes were available in 1989-90. (latest year for which figures are readily available).

2. According to the recommendations of the Indian Council of Medical Research (1984), average dietary per capita requirement of cereals for an India is 432 gm per day, i.e., 158 kg per capita per year. It is estimated that in 1988-89, there was a surplus of 27 kg. per capita; of course in the area of pulses there was a shortage. On the whole taking cereals and pulses together situation was quite satisfactory.

3. Production of fruit and vegetable is not only sufficient but also surplus. Production of vegetables in 1989-90 was 5.4 lakh m. tonnes as against the requirement of 4.13 lakh m. tonnes, thus showing a surplus of 1.30 lakh m. tonnes. Vegetable production was 5.43 m. tonnes as against the requirement of 4.13 m. tonnes, resulting a surplus of 1.20 m. tonnes. The surplus quantity of fruits and vegetables can be either marketed or preserved for commercial purposes.

4. Forests, which can be of prime source of revenue of this region have been indiscriminately cut for the last many decades. There has been hardly any modern scientific afforestation in this region. This needs to be done for bringing in regular inflow of revenue and steady source of employment for the people of this region.

5. The hydro-electric potential of the two big perenial rivers and their numerous tributaries is immense. These rivers could generate enough power to make the region self-sufficient in power.

The river system of Kumaon region may be categorised under three principal systems: (1) The Ganga System (2) The Kali System and (3) The Ramganga System. Kali has several tributaries, the principle ones being the Kuthi, bangti, Dhauli, Gori and Sarju. The Ramganga system includes rivers Girthi and Pinder, which are tributaries of Alaknanda and have major courses in Garhwal. Principal tributaries of Ramganga are Gagas, Nail and Deogarh. Alaknanda is the biggest river of Garhwal Himalayas. Its main tributries are Vishnuganga, Birahi, Nandakini, Pinder and Mandakini. Bhagirithi, the second largest river of Garhwal takes its origin at Gaumukh glacier near Tibet border. It slopes down through Gangotri and Uttarkashi and receives Bhilanganga river at Tehri. The Bhagirithi and Alaknanda confluence at Deoprayag to form the Ganga.

The Kumaon region abounds in natural lakes of varying dimensions. According to reports, there are in the Kumaon and Garhwal waters 30 and about 70 species of fish respectively.

The aquatic system of the region has high potential of fish production if harnessed properly and scientifically.

6. *Minerals*—The region is rich in non-metallic mineral deposits. Kumaon region has India's largest known deposits of magnestice Dolomite is found in abundance in the region. Limestone one of the most industrial minerals is available in large quantity. There are definite indications of the existence of uranium and graphite. Indications are that there is a vast reserve of building stones, Dehradun is known for the large limestone deposits in India. Uttarakhand has sufficient amount of minerals and their proper exploitation will go a long way in the development of its economy.

7. At present only about 14 per cent total geographical area is being used for agriculture. Agriculture can be suitably combined with horticulture and vegetable growing. Animal husbandry could be properly combined with poultry farming. Medicinal plants can be grown at high altitude.

8. There is great scope for industrial development in the area. incentive schemes like special State capital subsidy and special transport subsidy for the hill areas need to be strengthened.

9. It is observed that both lotic as well as lentic water systems in Uttarakhand have enormous potential for fish production. By adopting scientific management techniques, conservation of sustained yield and improvement, the potential fish production can be easily realised which would greatly contribute to the growth of the economy of this region.

As observed by V.V. Giri "The prime requisite is the establishment of a sound, solid and broadbased economy and adequate training to the population to make full use of the resources of modern science and technology. In undertaking this delicate task under the hazardous and inhospitable condition of the unapproachable terrain of the Himalaya, those in change of a social welfare work in the border area will have to make a determined effort and utilize all the resourcefulness at their command. Any change that we contemplate should come about through the volition of the beneficiaries, as a result of their experience and self realization".

It is also to be remembered that more than economics other factors like cultural, linguistic, political and social factors play a vital role in determining the formation of a State. Economic viability is not a critical criterion. All States are dependent on sharing central resources to a lesser or a greater extent. Uttarakhand has great potential of development in three area of power, tourism and horticulture. A good deal of sustained research is needed in different fields. Industrial potential of hill districts in the field of electronics, instrumentation, cement, photo-film, paper, rayon, canning, food processing, dairy farming and milk products, etc., needs to be harnessed.

Question-Answers on Uttarakhand State

Q. Will the state be a viable unit?

A. Yes, Past lessons are, obvious for us. The creation of Gujarat out of the Greater Maharashtra led to the prosperity of the people of Gujarat region—perhaps even more prosperity than the separate state of Maharashtra as it exists to-day. Doubts regarding the viability of the Haryana State proved to be baseless. In fact, this State became the first in the country to electrify almost all its villages. People of Himachal Pradesh also prospered.

There are vast untapped mineral resources in Uttarakhand and if exploited properly could bring about industrialisation and economic prosperity.

Q. Are not the employment avenues limited and restricted? Will there be more employment opportunities?

A. No. There is a great scope for the creation of employment opportunities. With the scientific harnessing of natural resources like, water, forest and land, employment opportunities on a large scale would be available. Agriculture has to be made modern and scientific. With 27 per cent reservations on their heads, employment opportunities for them, if the present policy is followed, will decrease by 25 per cent (OBCs are only about 2 per cent)

Q. Will there be proportionate reduction in the political elout and power?

Ans. Perhaps not! Notwithstanding the fact that the hill areas have given three popular and strong Chief Ministers to Uttar Pradesh, it has remained a backward area. This is not to minimise the important role played by them in enabling the people of hill areas to get jobs and other employment opportunities in the large cities including Delhi. The new opportunities will enable them to gain more power on their own strength.

Q. Will the creation of a hill State lead to the slowing down the process of development?

Ans. No. In fact the situation is otherway round. The demand for a hill State has gained momentum on account of the non-development and backwardness of the area.

SECTION IV

REGIONAL AND DISTRICT PROFILE

10

KUMAON REGION

Ancient History: An Overview*

The great mass of the population in Kumaon and Garhwal profess a belief little differing from the orthodox Hinduism of the plains. The existing inhabitants belong to the Khasa or Khasiya race and speak a dialect of Hindi akin to the language of the Hindus of Rajputana. All their feelings and prejudices are so strongly imbued with the peculiar spirit of Hinduism that although their social habits and religious belief are often repugnant to those who strictly observe the orthodox ceremonial usages of Hinduism, it is impossible for any one that knows them to consider the Khasas to be other than Hindus. There are several facts connected with their history that show, whatever their origin may have been, that the Khasas have for centuries been under the influence of the Brahmanical priesthood. The shrines of Kedar and Badari are both within Garhwal and from time immemorial have been visited by crowds of pilgrims from all parts of India, whose enthusiasm for Hinduism must have acted on the hill men brought into connection with them as guides and purveyors. Again, many of these pilgrims took up their residence in the hills and leavened the manners and observances of the rough indigenous population. Many other immigrants arrived to take service amongst the petty princes of the hills or to receive their daughters in marriage, and thus we find a considerable sprinkling of families all through these hills who consider themselves one with the various castes in the plains whose tribal name they bear. To the

* At several places the description/analyses seems to be coloured. It may be recalled that these Gazetters were prepared during British rule in India.

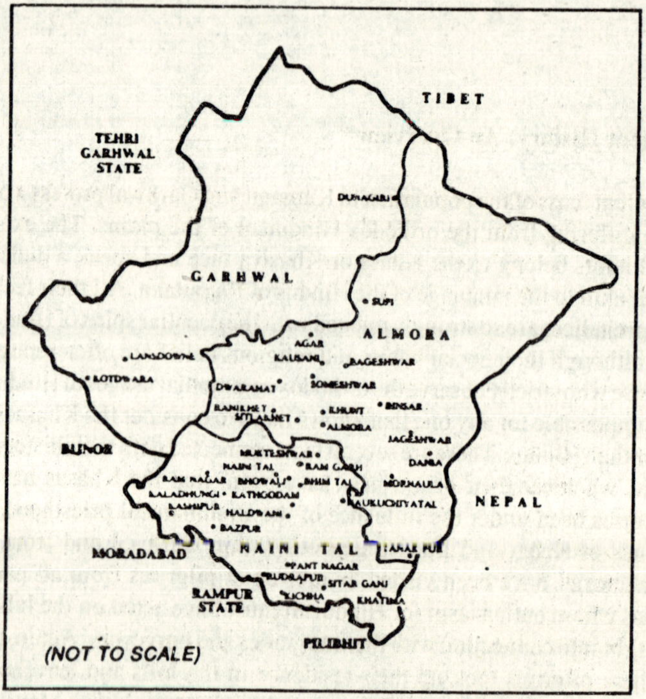

MAP 10.1 : Kumaon Before 1947

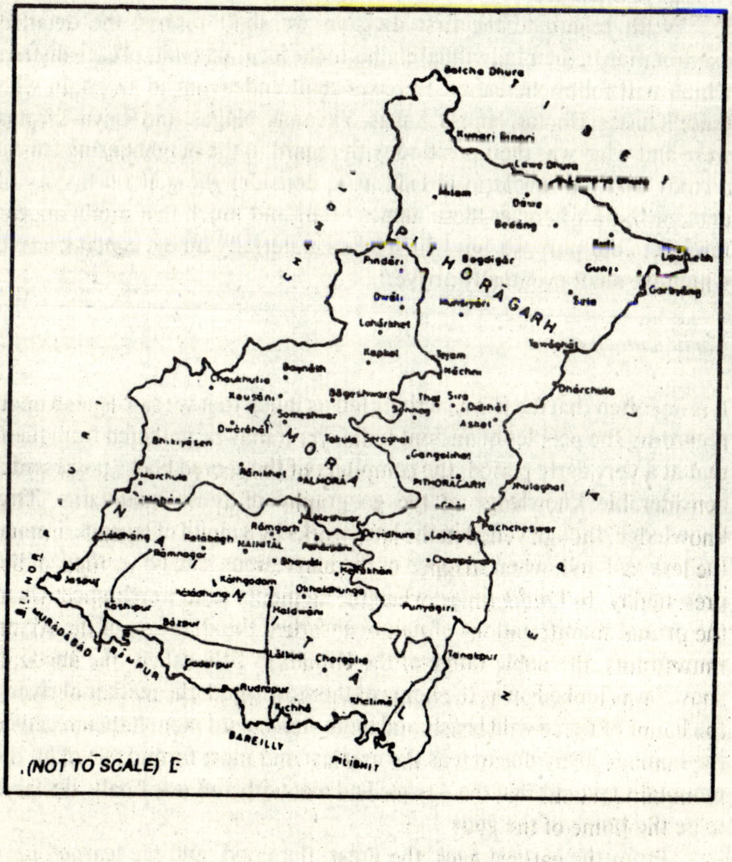

MAP 10.2 : Kumaon

north in the inter-alpine valleys of Bhot, we have a tribe of decided Tibetan origin and whose affinities are found in the trans-Himalayan tribes of Hundes. They are known as Bhotiyas by the people of the lower hills, who in turn are designated Khasiyas by the Bhotiyas, whilst the people of the adjoining portion of Tibet are knwon as Hunas or Huniyas. In addition to the tribes already enumerated there are the Rajis or Rajyas, the modern representatives of the Rajya-Kiratas and the Tharus and Bhuksas of the Tarai lowlands and traces of the Nagas and Sakas, whilst others contend that we have here also old Baktrian (Yavana) colonies. For our present purpose it is only necessary to observe that there are, at the present day, three great divisions of the population, the immigrants from the plains, the Khasas and Bhotas.

With regard to the first division we shall reserve the detailed examination of their individual claims to the local accounts of each district which will follow hereafter. Here we shall endeavour to ascertain who these Khasas, Bhotas, Hunas, Sakas, Yavanas, Nagas, and Rajya-Kiratas were and what was their position with regard to the neighbouring tribes, a study that will necessarily lead us to consider the general history of ancient India wherever these names occur and much that might appear foreign to our purpose, but which bears materially on the conclusions to which we shall eventually arrive.

Early Knowledge

It is not often that the Hindu writers tell us much that we can depend upon regarding the peoples of ancient India, yet it may be gathered from them that at a very early period, the compilers of the sacred books possessed a considerable knowledge of the geography of these mountains. This knowledge, though veiled in the later works by a cloud of legends, is none the less real and, when stripped of the marvellous, can be verified, at the present day. In *Vaidik* times, when the elements were worshipped, when the primal manifestations of nature absorbed the devotion of the Aryan immigrants, the noble range of the Himalaya fitly called 'the abode of snow,' was looked on as the home of the storm-god, the mother of rivers, the haunt of fierce wild beasts and more fierce wild men. It then received the homage justly due to it as the greatest and most formidable of all the mountain systems that the Aryans had met with and was finally declared to be the home of the gods.

From the earliest ages, the great, the good, and the learned have sought its peaceful valleys to enjoy nearer communion with the deity. In the manuals of the later *Pauranik* records we find almost every hill and river reverently and lovingly described and dedicated to some one or other of the members of the great pantheon. Legands of the gods and saints and holy men adorn the story of each peak and pool and waterfall and give that realistic turn to the teaching of the earlier priesthood which appears to have been peculiarly adapted to the Hindu mind. "He who thinks[1] of Himachal, though he should not behold him, is greater than he who performs all worhip in Kashi. In a hundred ages of the gods I could not tell thee of the glories of Himachal. As the dew is dried up by the morning sun, so are the sins of mankind by the sight of Himachal."

Sources of Information

The sources of our information may be thus briefly indicated. First the *Vaidik* records. Max Muller assigns a date between 1200 and 1000 BC to the older hymns of the Rig-Veda;[2] Haug places their composition between 2400 and 2000 BC; and Duncker states that the immigration of the Aryas took place about 2000 BC, and the origin of the oldest songs of the *Veda* cannot, therefore, be considered earlier than the sixteenth century before Christ. For the songs of the *Mantra* period containing the later hymns, Max Muller gives 1000 and 800 BC as the date of their composition, whilst Haug and others place them between 2000 and 1400 BC. The works of Muller's *Brahmana* period include the *Brahmanas, Upanishads, Aranyakas,* and similar writings chiefly expository of those of the preceding period which are included in the *Sanhitas* or collections of the four Vedas. To the *Sutra* period are assigned the six *Vedangas* or branches of *Vaidik* exegesis and the Sutras or redactions of the ancient *Sakhas* containing aphorisms relating to sacrificial and domestic duties and the like. These last belong to the *Smriti* or traditional class. The epic poems or Itihasas form the secomd division and are represented by the *Mahabharata*[3] and the *Ramayana*. To the third division and latest in point of time belong the *Puranas* and their continuations to the present day, including the local collections of legends regarding the lives of the saints, the holy places and the miracles performed there.... Aryas came from Central Asia and established themselves on either bank of the Indus. The greater number of the hymns of the *Rig-Veda* refer to this period of the Aryan history and distinguish between the immigrants and the aborigines. To the latter they give the generic name of Dasyu, which subsequently included the non-Aryana tribes as well as those of Aryan descent who separated from Aryan practices in matters of religion and polity. The later Vaidik records indicate the gradual advances of the Aryas to the south-east until we find them in the *Itihasa* or epic period occupying the whole of the upper Duab.

Vaidik Geography

The geographical indications in the *Rig-Veda* are of the meagre description and consist of the enumeration of certain rivers in the celebrated 'hymn to the rivers', and the names of a few tribes and countries.[4] The rivers named show that the Aryas were then living in the tract between the Indus and the Satlaj and were not well acquainted with the region between the latter river and the Ganges. The rivers Ganges and Drishadvati or Kaggar are named but once, the Sarasvati and Jumna are only mentioned a few times, but the Sindhu or Indus is frequently referred to and to it as 'the most copious of streams' the river-hymn is the passed. In one verse, the other rivers are asked to receive this hymn: "Receive my humn, O Ganga, Yamuna, Sarasvati, Sutudri, along with the Parushni: listen, O Marudvriha along with the Asikni and Vitasta; O Arjikiya along with the Sushoma." In the succeeding verse the Rasa, Sveti, Kubha, Gomati, and Krumu are mentioned as tributaries of the Indus. The Sutudri is the Satlaj; the Parushni is the Iravati or Ravi; the Marudvrilla is the Chinab after its confluence with the Jhelam; the Asikni is the Acesines of Chinab; and the Vitasta is the Hydaspes or Jhelam. The names Arjikiya and Sushoma signify, according to Lassen, vessels used in the preparation of the Soma juice and are not the names of rivers. The Kubha is the Kophenes or Kabul river, the Krumu and Gomati being the Kurum and Gomal rivers. The Sveti is the Swat river and the Rasa appears to be some other affluent of the Kabul river. The earliest seat of the Aryas in India is therefore the lower Kabul valley and the adjoining tract along the Indus, a place of which we shall have much to say hereafter. The knowledge of the Himalaya is confined to certain allusions to winter; thus in the *Rig-Veda* we have[5] the prayer: "May we rejoice living a hundred winter *(satahimah)* with vigorous offspring." In the *Atharva-Veda* the following passages occur: "He whose greateness these snowy mountains *(himavanto)* and the sea with the aerial river declare." "May thy mountains be snowy *(himavanto)*, O earth, and thy wilderness beautiful." Again in the same work the medicinal plant *kushtha* is said to be produced to the north of the Himavat and to be carried thence to the east. In the *Aitareya-Brahmana* the Uttara Kurus are referred to thus: "Wherefore in this northern region all the people who dwell beyond the Himavat (called) the Uttara Kurus and the Uttara Madras are consecrated to glorious rule." In a passage of the *Kaushitaki-Brahmana*[6] it is written: "Pathya Svasti (a goddess) knew the northern region. Now Pathya Svasti is Vach (the goddess of speech).

Hence in the northern region speech is better known and better spoken and it is to the north that men go to learn each; men listen to the instructions of any one who comes from that quarter, saying, "he says (so and so), for that is renowned as the region of speech." On this the commentator remarks: "Language is better understood and spoken'; for Sarasvati is spoken of (as having her abode) in Kashmir, and in the hermitage of Badarika (Badrinath in Garhwal) the sound of the Vedas is heard." So also Lassen: "An account is to be found in an ancient record, according to which the Sanskrit had been preserved in greater purity in the northern countries than elsewhere, and Kashmir and Badari, at the sources of the Ganges, are specified by the commentator as such regions. This is, however, not sufficient to prove that in the different provinces of India there were then fundamental differences in the sacred language." The medical treatise of Charaka makes the physician Bharadvaja a disciple of Indra and assigns to the neighbourhood of the Himalaya that gathering of sages out of which came the instruction of Bharadvaja by Indra. The treatise referred to has, according to Weber,[7] "rather high pretensions to antiquity; its prose here and there reminds us of the style of the Srauta-sutras." From the later Vaidik records, therefore, we learn that as early as several centuries before the Christian era the shrine of Badari was celebrated as a seat of learning and as the abode of holy men.

Vaidik Ethnography

We next turn to the names of the peoples known to the Vaidik writers. In a verse of the *Rig-Veda,* Visvamitra asks: "What are thy cows doing amongst the Kikatas? They yield no milk for oblations and they heat no fire," implying that they were a people who knew not Aryan rites. Again in the *Atharva-Veda,* in an invocation to Takman, the personification of itch, as Chachak Devi is now of small-pox, it is said that his abode was among the Mujavats and Mahavrishas. As soon as born, he sojourned amongst the Bahilkas, and he is here desired to depart to the Gandharis, Mujavates, Angas, and Magadhas. The Kikatas are elsewhere explained to be one with the Magadhas or people of Behar. The Bahlikas are the people of Balkh; Gandhara is the tract around Peshawar, and the Mujavats are elsewhere explained[8] to be a mountain tribe of the north-west frontier. In the Brahmanas, the name 'Bahika' is applied to the tribes of the Panjab generally, and it would appear that they as well as the Kambojas, a frontier tribe to the north-west, spoke a dialect of Sanskrit, for Panini, in his grammar, explains the dialectic difference between the speech of the Aryas and that of the Bahikas and Yaska, those between the Aryan speech and the language of the Kambojas. There is also evidence[9] to show that the people of Gandhara were in the habit of holding intercourse and contracting alliances with the Aryas.

From these indications Muir argues that: "Although in individual passages of the *Mahabharata* hatred and contempt are expressed in reference to the tribes living along the Indus and its five great tributaries, yet there is no trace of these tribes being regarded as of non-Indian origin.".... "The Indians distinguish not expressly, but by implication, the nations dwelling between the Indus and the Hindu Kush into two classes—first those to the eastward of the Indus, and some of those immediately to the westward of that river, as the Gandharas, are in their estimation Indians; .... but with the exception of the Kashmiras and some less known races these Indians are not of the genuine sort; the general freedom of their customs is regarded as a lawless condition." And Weber[10] similarly remarks: "The north-western tribes retained their ancient customs which the other tribes who migrated to the east had at one time shared. The former kept themselves free from the influence of hierarchy and of caste which arose amongst the latter as a consequence of their residence amongst people of alien origin (the aborigines). But the later orthodox feelings of the more eastern Aryas obliterated the recollection of their own earlier freedom and caused them to detest the kindred tribes to the westward as renegades, instead of looking on themselves as men who had abandoned their own original institutions." Thus we have three classes of inhabitants in Upper India, that branch of the Aryas to whom the composition of the *Vedas* is to be attributed; their brethren in race and language who did not follow them in the development of their religious system and the aboriginal tribes.[11]

Aryas and Dasyus

The question remains as to who were Aryas and who were Dasyus. The primitive meaning of the word 'Arya' is still a subject of discussion, some trace it throughout the Indo-European region in the 'Airya' of the ancient books of Persia[12]; in the name 'Ariana' applied to the tract comprising Herat, Afghanistan, Khorasan, and Biluchistan; in the name 'Aryaka' (Irak); in the word 'Ariya' in the inscriptions of the Achaemenides; in the name 'Iran' in those of the Sassanides; in the 'Arioi' (Ossetes) of the Caucasus; in 'Argeia,' an old name of Greece; in the name 'Hermann' (Arminius) in Germany; and even in 'Erin,' the old name of Ireland. The meaning attached to the word in the earlier hymns of the *Rig-Veda* appears, however, to be 'light-coloured,' 'pale,' 'white,' as compared with the Dasyus or black Antocthones. Gradually as the Aryan forces advanced the word carries with it the meaning of free, noble, brave, masterful, wise, as opposed to the enslaved, debased, and ignorant Dasyus, and here we find the white-faced immigrants[13] called collectively the Aryan 'varna,' or 'colour', a word which is to-day translated by caste *(baran)*. The Greeks also knew of this contrast between the dark and light coloured races of India, for Ktesias records[14] that the Indians were white and black, and that he himself had seen several of the fairer race. The Dasyus are described as a black-skinned race who despised the rites and ceremonies of the Aryas, and again as goblins and demons inhabiting the forests and mountains of the frontier countries.

In the *Rig-Veda* it is recorded[15] that Indra, "armed with the lightning and trusting in his strength, moved about shattering the cities of the Dasyus," and the gods are prayed to "distinguish between the Aryas and those who are Dasyus": "By these (succours) subdue to the Aryas all the hostile Dasa people everywhere, O Indra, whether it be kinsmen or strangers who have approached and injuriously assailed us, do thou enfeeble and destroy their power and vigour and put them to flight."... "who delivered (us) from the destroyer, from calamity; who, O powerful (god), didst avert the bolt of the Dasa from the Arya in (the land of) the seven streams."... "He who swept away the low Dasa colour" *varnam* "scattered the servile hosts of black descent"... "conquered the black-skin." Again Manu writes that those tribes which are without the pale of the castes, whether they speak the language of the Mlechchhas or of the Aryas, are called Dasyus[16], and there is not wanting evidence to show that some of the opponents of the orthodox immigrants to whom we owe the Vedas were of their own colour or caste. In the hymns of the *Rig-Veda* we have addresses to Indra implying the existence of Aryan foes as well as Dasyus: "Do thou, heroic Indra, destroy both these our foes (our) Dasa and our Arya enemies"... "May we, associated with thee, the mighty one, overcome both Dasa and Arya through thy effectual energy"... "Whatever ungodly person, Dasa or Arya, designs to fight against us, let these enemies be easily subdued by us." The Aryan tribes, we further learn, were divided into clans, each under its own Raja, and the newcomers pressed on the old settlers and fought with them. A formidable coalition of the Bharatas and others whose family priest was Visvamitra attacked the Tritsus on the Sarasvati, whose spiritual guides belonged to the family of Vasishtha, and we have the prayers of both priests invoking the aid of Indra in the coming battle.

The Bharatas were defeated and the song of victory of Vasishtha shows us that the enemies against which his side fought were Aryas. In the *Aitariya-Brahmans,* the author, after quoting a saying of Visvamitra, adds: "Most of the Dasyus are descended from Visvamitra." Thus we see how certain Aryas who did not follow the orthodox guides became classed with the aborigines, and thus arises one source of the great confusion observed in the later ethnology. The system existing on earth was also transferred to the sphere of the gods, and here we find the Dasyu race represented by the Rakshasas, Danavas and Daityas, sometimes the rebellious subjects, and sometimes the slaves[17] of the deities. It is in the later records that most details are given, but before proceeding further we will note the route by which the Aryas passed into Upper India. So late as 1840, Professor Benfey argued that most probably the Aryas dwelt for some time in little Tibet, near the sources of the Indus, before passing into India, and that the route adopted by them was through the passes along the Kumaon and Garhwal frontier to Indraprastha. In this view he was supported by Professor Weber as the only one consistent with the material at their disposal. On reading through the *Rig-Veda,* however, both these eminent scholars abandoned this position and agreed in the result now generally accepted, that the Aryan tribes moved from Baktria into India by the Hindu Kush through the Kabul valley and across the Indus[18] to the Sarasvati, the route that has been taken in every successive great invasion of India.

Itihasa Period

From the Sarasvati, the Aryas pressed on and occupied the upper Duab, and it is here we find them in the Itihasa period, when the *Mahabharata* was written. The Uttara Kurus are now mentioned as living in Hari Varsha, as a people whom no one attempts to conquer and their country as the home of primitive customs. In describing the condition of the southern Kurus it is said that "they vied in happiness with the northern Kurus." In the *Ramayana,* it is recorded that the Uttara Kurus are liberal, prosperous, perpetually happy and undecaying. In their country there is neither cold nor heat, nor decrepitude, not disease, nor grief, nor fear, nor rain, nor sun, a description which has been localised in Kumaon, but here agrees better with the tract to the north of the Kashmir valley. Lassen remarks that though the country of Harivarsha belongs to the region of mythical geography, the existence of the Uttara Kurus has a basis of geographical fact from (1) the way the country is mentioned in the *Vedas;* (2) its existence in historical times[19] as a real country: and (3) it being referred to as the home of primitive customs.

As regards the frontier tribes, the *Mahabharata* mentions the conquest by the Pandavas of "the Utsavasankatas, seven tribes of Dasyus, inhabiting the mountains." Again, "Pikasasani conquered the Daradas with the Kambojas and the Dasyus who dwell in the north-east region, as well as the inhabitants of the forest, with the Lohas, the farthest Kambojas and the northern Rishikas." Moreover, Saineya, the charioteer of Krishna, is said to have "made the beautiful earth a mass of mud with the flesh and blood of thousands of Kambojas, Sakas, Savaras, Kiratas, Varvaras, destroying thy host. The earth was covered with the helmets and shaven and bearded heads of the Dasyus," clearly intimating that the word 'Dasyu' is here a generic term denoting the whole of the tribes who are previously mentioned in this passage. The same record affirms their connection with the Aryas in the verses: "These tribes of Kshattriyas, viz., Sakas, Yavanas, Kambojas, Druviras, & c., have become Vrishalas from seeing no Brahmans." This statement is repeated subsequently with the addition of the Mekalas, Latas, Konvasiras, Saundikas, Darvas, Chauras, Savaras, Bardbaras and Kiratas. Again the Yavanas are said to be descendants of Turvasu, the Vaibhojas to be sprung from Druhyu, and the Mlechchha tribes from Anu. The *Mahabharata* thus not only uses the world 'Dasyu' as a generic term for the border tribes, but also makes these tribes to belong to the Kshattriya or warrior race. How it came to pass that these Kashattriyas lost their Aryan status is thus related: "Satyavrata was degraded to the condition of a Chandala or outcast and called Trisanku on account of three sins *(tri-sanku)* of (1) killing a cow, (2) displeasing his father, and (3) eating flesh not properly consecrated. But on his repentance and feeding the family of Visvamitra during a twelve years' drought, he was transported to heaven. His descendant Bahu was vanquished by the tribes of Haihayas and Talajhangas[20] and died in exile. To him a posthumous son named Sagara was born, who nearly exterminated the Haihayas and would have also destroyed the Sakas, Yavanas, Kambojas, Paradas and Pahalavas, had they not applied to their family-priest, Vasishtha, for protection. The priest desired Sagara to refrain from the slaughter of those who were as good as dead, for he had compelled the tribes to abandon the duties of their caste and all association with the twice-born, and Sagara thereon imposed on them peculiar distinguishing marks. He made the Yavanas shave their heads entirely, the Sakas to shave the upper half of their heads, the Paradas to wear their hair long, and the Pahlavas to let their beards grow. He deprived them of all religious rites and thus abandoned by Brahmans, they becames Milechchhas."[21] This instructive legend shows us that the writers of the Itihasa and early Pauranik periods believed that these tribes had a common origin with themselves, though, as Muir[22] shows, "they, at the same time, erroneously imagined that these tribes had fallen away from Brahmanical institutions: thus assigning to their own polity an antiquity to which it could in reality lay no claim." In another passage of the *Mahabharata* we have the statement that "in the region where these five rivers (Panchnad, Panjab) flow after issuing from the mountains dwell the Buhikas called Arattas.... The names of the country is Aratta; the water of it is called Bahika, there dwell degarded Brahmans, contemporary with Prajapati. They have no Veda, no Vedic ceremony, not any sacrifice. The gods do not eat the food offered by servile *(dasamiyanam)* Vratyas. The Prasthalas, Madras, Gandharas, Arattas, Khasas, Vasatis and Sindhusauviras are nearly all very contemptible." Here we have the Khasas associated with the tribes of the Panjab, which would show a more westerly location than Kumaon.

Nagas on the Jumna

The same record shows us that around Hastinapur,[23] the seat of the Pandu raj, were Dasyus variously known as Asuras, Daityas, Bhillas, Rakshasas and Nagas. The great Khandava forest in the valley of the Jumna near Indraprastha or old Delhi was occupied by the Nagas under their king Takshaka, who were expelled by fire and driven to take refuge in the hills. The Aryas continued their progress and preceded by *Agni,* (the god of fire), occupied the whole country as far as the Sadanira or Gandak. We also read that Arjuna during his exile visited the holy places and at Hardwar met Ulupi, the daughter of the Naga Raja Vasuki, whom he espoused. The same record gives a brilliant description of the city of the Naga Raja, that it "contained two thousand krores of serpent inhabitants; and the wives of all those serpents were of consummate beauty. And the city contained more jewels than any person in the world has ever seen, and there was a lake there which contained the water of life and in which all the serpents used to bathe." Throughout the *Mahabharata* the Himalaya is considered holy ground, the well-loved home of the gods, where there were many places of *pilgrimage (tirthas).*

Pandavas Retire to the Himalaya

After the destruction of Dwaraka, when the Pandavas were told by Vyasa that their power had departed and that they should now think of heaven alone, it was to the Himalaya that they retired. Placing Parikshit on the throne of Hastinapur and Yuyutsau in Indraprastha, "Yudhishthira then took off his earrings and necklace and all the jewels from his fingers and arms and all his royal raiment; and he and his brethren, and their wife

Draupadi, clothed themselves after the manner of devotees in vestments made of the bark of trees. And the five brethren threw the fire of their domestic sacrifices and cookery into the Ganges and went forth from the city following each other. First walked Yudhisthira, then Bhima, then Arjuna, then Nakula, then Sahdeva, then Draupadi, and then a dog. And they went through the country of Banga toward the rising of the sun; and after passing through many lands they reached the Himalaya mountain, and there they died one after the other and were transported to the heaven of Indra." From Kurmachal in the extreme east near the Kali to Jamnotri and the Dun, the wanderings of the Pandavas are noted by some rock or stream commemorating some exploit or calling to mind some scene in the story of their travels. At Deo Dhura, the grey granite boulders near the crest of the ridge are said to have been thrown there in sport by the Pandavas.

Close to the temple of Devi in the same place are two large boulders, the uppermost of which, called 'Ran-sila,' is cleft right through the centre by a deep fresh-looking fissure, at right angles to which there is a similar rift in the lower rock. A smaller boulder on the top is said to have been the weapon by which Bhima Sena produced these fissures and the print of his five fingers is still pointed out. Ran-sila itself is marked with the lines for carrying on the gambling game of *pachisi* which even in their wanderings the Pandavas could not abandon. They are also the reputed founders of the five temples to Siva as Kedareswar and did penance at Pandukeswar close to Badarinath. All along the course of the sacred river are pools and streams, temples and rocks, sacred to the Pandavas and across the Ganges in Tihri, the course of the Jumna is in a lesser degree conscreated to their memory. At Bhimghora above Hardwar the priests show the imprint of the hoofs of Bhima's horse, and they say that Drona, the preceptor of the Pandavas, resided in the eastern portion of the valley of Dehra Dun, the Drona-kas-asrams of the Kedara-Khanda.

Manu

The law-book of the Manavas is clearly in its present form the outcome of many hands at various times, but will be more conveniently referred to under the received title 'Manu'. It is still the great authority on the systematic ethnography and cosmogony of the Hindus, and affords us further evidence of the existence of the belief that the majority of the border tribes were regarded as of the same stock as the Aryas, but degraded members of it. It tells us that the references made in the Shastras to castes other than the four is merely "for the sake of convenicnce and conformity to common usage." Even the very lowest classes, such as the Nishadas and Chandalas, are derived from the miscegenation of the four castes. Like the authors of the *Mahabharata*, Manu affirms that the Kshattriya tribes of Paundrakas, Odras, Draviras, Kambojas, Yavansa, Sakas, Paradas, Pahlavas, Chinas, Kiratas, Daradas, and Khasas, became Vrishalas or outcasts from the extinction of sacred rites and from having no intercourse with Brahmans. Further, as already noticed, he declares that "all the tribes which by loss of sacred rites and the like have become outcasts from the pale of the four castes, whether they speak the language of the Mlechchhas or of the Aryas, are called Dasyus." Here we have again the connecting link between the earlier and the later records and the natural explanation of the entire phenomena. As in Africa, at the present day, the tribes converted to Islam, leaving behind them their heathen practices, look with contempt and even hatred on their brethren in race who adhere to paganism, so the Aryas despised those of their race who remained content with the primitive belief which was once their common property and refused to accept the sacerdotal innovations, or who being of non-Aryan descent declined to accept the Brahmanical creed. The terms of abuse used towards these tribes by the priestly writers prove nothing more than the existence of the *odium theologicum* which has burned fiercely in all climes and countries from the earliest dawn of history to the present day. The preceding extracts show that even in the most orthodox writings the Khasas are looked on more as heretical members of the great Aryan family than as outcast aborigines, and that from a very early period they have been recognised as an important tribe in Upper India.

Allusions to Badari

According to the *Mahabharata*, Krishna visited the hermitage of Upamanyu in the Himalaya, where "the mongoose sports in a friendly fashion with snakes and tigers with deer." He also visited the Pandavas in their exile and is said to have himself, in company with Arjuna, lived a considerable time in Badari. Arjuna as Nara and Krishna as Narayana "mounted on the chariot of righteousness, performed an undecaying penance on the mountain Gandhamadana," There they were visited by the sage Narada, who "descended rapidly from the sky to the spacious Badari. There he saw the ancient gods, the two most excellent Rishis," and there he remained with them for a thousand years. Again it is said that the Chakravarti Raja Dambhodbhava, having an overweening conceit of his own prowess, visited Gandhamadana (Badari group of peaks) with his army and resolved to overthrow the Rishis. They tried to put him off by saying that they were divested of all earthly passions and lived in an atmosphere of peace. Dambhodbhava, however, resolved to attack them, when Nara took a handful of straws and scattering them to the winds so whitened the air and so filled the eyes, ears, and noses of the men of Dambhodbhava's army that they fell at Nara's feet and sued for peace; referring doubtless to a snow-storm encountered by the invaders. In another part of the same record Krishna is thus addressed: "Formerly Krishna, thou didst roam for ten thousand years on Gandhamadana, where the Muni Sayangriha was... Thou didst stand on the spacious Badari, a hundred years with thy arms aloft, on one foot, subsisting on air, with thy outer garments thrown off, emaciated, with thy veins swollen." Badari is also called Siddhasrawa, 'the hermitage of the perfect', "where the illustrious Vishnu was perfected when performing a great act of austerity in the form of a dwarf, when the empire of the three worlds had been taken away from Indra by Bali." Tradition states that Rama performed austerities at Rikhikes, and his brother Lachhman at Tapuban, in order to wipe away the sin of slaying Ravana. The grammarian Vararuchi also visited the Himalaya and by propitiating Mahadeva obtained from him the materials for his Paniniya grammar.[24] When near his death Vararuchi again retired to Badari, and "throwing off this mortal coil, resumed as Pushpadanta[25] his seat amont the brilliant spirits of heaven." Gunadhya, brother of Pushpadanta, followed his example and worhsipped 'the crescent-crested deity' in his mountain home. It was here, too, that Sahasranika, raja of Kausambhi, when wearied with the toils of state, spent his declining years in solitude and devotion.[26]

Pauranik Period

We now come to the Pauranik period and find that the legends concerning the Himalaya have grown with the people, and that in the later development of Hindu mythology they occupy a much more important place. There is little doubt that the story of Mount Meru, the Olympus of the Indian gods, was suggested by the sight of the lofty summits of the Himalaya crowned with perpetual snow. In the geographical notices contained in the *Puranas,* we have the traditional distribution of the countries and peoples then known to the compilers, and to their pages ....we must look for the little further aid to our researches that can be derived from indigenous sources. Lassen[27] writes: "It is true that we might be tempted to discover in the superior sacredness which they (the Aryas) ascribe to the north, a reference, unintelligible to themselves, to a closer connexion which they had formerly with the northern countries; for the abodes of most of the gods are placed to the north in and beyond the Hiamalaya and the holy and wonderful mountain of Meru is situated in the remotest regions in the same direction. A more exact examination will, however, lead to the conviction that the conception to which we have referred has been developed in India itself and is to be derived from the peculiar character of the northern mountain-range. The daily prospect of the snowy summit of the Himalaya glittering far and wide over the plains and in the strictest sense insurmountable, and the knowledge which they had of the entirely different character of the table-land beyond, with its extensive and tranquil domains, its clear and cloudless sky and peculiar natural productions, would necessarily designate the north as the abode of the gods and the theatre of wonders; while its holiness is explicable from the irresistible impression produced upon the mind by surrounding nature. Uttara Kuru, the Elysium in the remotest north, may be most properly regarded as an ideal picture, created by the imagination of a life of tranquil felicity, and not as a recollection of any early residence of the Kurus in the north. Such at least is true of the representation which we have of this country in the epic poems. It is, however, probable that originally, and as late as the Vaidik era, a recollection of this sort attached itself to that country, though in later times no trace of it has been preserved."

Discovery of Kailas

It is not difficult, therefore, to picture the Aryan immigrants arriving at the Ganges and sending some adventurous spirits to explore its sources. After traversing the difficult passes across the snowy range and the inclement table-land of Tibet, they discovered the group of mountains called Kailas[28] and the lakes from which flowed forth the great rivers to water and give life to the whole earth. The rugged grandeur of the scene, the awful solitude and the trials and dangers of the way itself naturally suggested to an imaginative and simple people that they had at length rediscovered the golden land[29] the true homes of their gods whom they had worshipped when appearing under milder forms as storm and fire and rain in the plains below.

In the course of time, Brahmanical innovations caused the worship of Agni, Vayu or Indra, Surya and the other Vaidik gods to give place to a system where the intervention of a sacerdotal caste between the worshipper and his creator was essential. The transfer to the new system of the localities already held sacred soon followed, and Brahma, Vishnu, and Siva, the triad of the new revelation, took possession of the Himalaya. In place of domestic worship offered by individuals for individual good and addressed to unreal presence, a highly ornate ritual was introduced, administered by a consecrated class and addressed to visible types. It is in this later stage that we find Hinduism as described in the *Puranas,* so late indeed that the worship of Brahma had already almost become obsolete. In the Vedas,[30] "the one universal Being is of a higher order than a personification of attributes or elements and however imperfectly conceived, or unworthily described is God. In the Puranas, the only Supreme Being is supposed to be manifest in the person of Siva or Vishnu either in the way of illusion or in sport; and one or other of these divinities is therefore also the cause of all that is,— is, himself, all that exists." The Puranas exhibit a sectarial fervour and exclusiveness not found in the *Ramayana* and only to a qualified extent in the *Mahabharata.* "The are no longer," says Professor Wilson, "authorities for the Hindu belief as a whole; they are special guides for separate and sometimes, conflicting branches of it; compiled for the evident purpose of promoting preferential or, in some cases, the sole worship of Vishnu or Siva."

The Puranas

Before proceeding further with our subject, it will be convenient succinctly to describe here the *Puranas* which form the class of writings that give us the greatest details concerning the Himalaya. There are eighteen *Puranas* compiled at various times by different hands.[31] The *Vishnu Purana,* which has been translated by Professor H.H. Wilson and edited by Dr. F. Hall, is the principal, and next to the *Bhagavata* is still regarded as the great authority on matters connected with their religion by large sections of the Hindu community. Both are compiled in the form of a dialogue in which some person relates the contents in reply to the inquiries of another. In the extracts hereafter given from the *Skanda Purana,* the narrator is Suta[32] .... Each Purana is divided into *khandas* or books, which are again subdivided into chapters which often consist of *mahatmyas* or collections of local legends like the Manasa-khanda and Kedara-khanda of the *Skanda Purana* noticed hereafter. Regarding this latter work, professor Wilson writes: "It is uniformly agreed that the Skanda Purana, in a collective form, has no existence and the fragments in the shape of *samhitas, khandas* and *mahatmyas,* which are affirmed in various parts of India to be portions of the Purana, present a much more formidable mass of stanzas than even the immense number (81,100) of which it is said to consist." The more celebrated of these portions are the *Kashi-khanda,* giving a description of Benares, and the *Utkala-khanda*, giving an account of the holy places in Orissa. Besides these, there are a *Himavat-khanda* devoted to Nepal, a *Rewa-khanda,* a *Brahmottara-khanda* and others. There are also several separate samhitas or collections. The *mahatmyas* are, however, the most numerous, and even Colonel Vans Kennedy thinks that they "have rather a questionable appearance." Many of the *khandas,* such as the *Kashi-khanda,* are quite as local as the *mahatmyas,* "being legendary stories relating to the erection of certain temples or groups of temples and to certain *lings;* the interested origin of which renders them, very reasonably, objects of suspicion." Professor Wilson adds: "In the present state of our acquaintance with the reputed portions of the *Skanda Purana,* my own views of their authenticity are so opposed to those entertained by Colonel Vans Kenndey, that instead of admitting all the *samhitas* and *khandas* to be genuine, I doubt if any one of them was ever a part of the *Skanda Purana"* ... "There are in all parts of India various compilations ascribed to the Puranas which never formed any portion of their contents and which, although offering, sometimes, useful local information and valuable as preserving local popular traditions, are not, in justice, to be confounded with the Puranas so as to cause them to be charged with even more serious errors and anachronisms than those of which they are guilty." The *Skanda* and *Brahmanda*[33] Puranas are those to which the majority of the modern fabrications have been attributed by their authors who have "grafted personages and fictions of their own invention on a few hints from older authorities." They retain the form of the genuine Purana, the dialogue and many of the stories giving them the local colouring necessary for the particular object in view. "Still," as I have elsewhere said, ... disfiguired by... interpolations of later times, the Puranas with the great epic poems, are the chief amongst the few historical records we possess of any antiquity to assist us in compiling an account of the heroic age."

The Fashioning of the Earth

We shall now briefly refer to the geography of the Puranas which.... is... closely connected with the geography of northern Kumanon and the adjoining part of Tibet. One account of the creation of the earth relates how Vishnu, in his boar incarnation, supported the earth on his tusks[35] as it was about to sink into the waters and then fixed it on the thousand heads of the king Ananta; whilst another likens the earth to a lotus, the stalk of which springs from the navel of Vishnu as he lies asleep at the bottom of the ocean. The world was then in chaos and Brahma arose and formed the seven great island continents: Jambu, Plaksha, Salmali, Kusa, Krauncha, Saka and Pushkara, separated from each other by the seas.[36] Jambu-dwipa is again divided into nine *varshas* or regions and in the centre of all is the glorious mountain of Meru, of various colours[37]; on the east it is white like a Brahman; on the south it is yellow like a Vaisya; on the north it is red like the dawning morn or a Kashattriya; and on the west it is dark like the dry leaves or a Sudra. Meru is circular in shape and forms the germ of the lotus.[38] It stands on the most elevated portion of the central division of Jambu known as Ilavrita. South of Meru the Nishadha mountains separate lavrita from Harivarsha; south of the latter, the Hemakuta divides it from Kimpurusha; and further south the third or Himavat range forms the boundary between Kimpurusha and Bharata. Similarly three ranges of mountains form the boundaries of countries on the north. First come the Nila range between Ilavrita and Ramyaka on the north; then the Sweta mountains bordering the country of Hiranmaya where there is much gold; and again the Sringin range separating Hiranmaya from the country of the Uttara Kurus. All these names would lead us to believe that the writers had the country to the north of the Kashmir valley in view, though the names subsequently mentioned are clearly connected with upper Garhwal and Kumaon. To the east of Ilavrita lies the country of Bhadrasva and to the west the country of Ketumala. Four mountains form buttresses to Meru—on the east is Mandara; on the south Gandhamadana or Merumandara; on the west Vipula or Kumuds, and on the north Suparswa. On each of these stands severally a *kadam*-tree *(Anthocephalus cadamba), a jambu*-tree *(Eugenia Jambolana),* a *pipal*-tree *(Ficus religiosa),* and a *nyargrodha*-tree *(Ficus indica).* There are also four great forests and four great lakes[39] the waters of which are partaken of by the gods and which are called Arunoda, Mahabhadra, Asitoda, and Manasa.

Source : E.T. Atkinson; *Kumaon,* reprint, Cosmos Publications Delhi, 1974

Contemporary Economy

Kumaon has a complex and varied economic set up. In the past, the people were solely dependant on agriculture. Now this trend is slowly changing even though agriculture and allied activities continue to be the mainstay of the economy.

Agriculture is by far the main source of livelihood for the people of Kumaon with nearly 70 per cent of the total population dependent on agriculture, horticulture and animal husbandry.

Land Use

Kumaon has a total land area of about 21, 743 sq km of which 20.1 per cent is under agriculture. Table 10.1 shows the land use pattern in Kumaon *(U.P. Government Statistics, 1985):*

TABLE 10.1: Land Use

	Particulars	Area (In hectares)	% of total
1.	Forest area	1127492	54.35
2.	Cultivable wasteland	159559	07.69
3.	Non-cultivable wasteland	70925	03.42
4.	Current fallow	8676	00.42
5.	Other fallow	17671	00.85
6.	Land use for other than agricultural use	59310	02.86
7.	Grasslands	124641	06.01
8.	Land under orchards	88759	04.28
9.	Net sown area	417343	20.12
10.	Total	2074376	100.00

Table 10.2 gives the net sown area in different parts of Kumaon. It shows that the percentage of the net sown area to, the total geographical area is very high in the plains (*U.P. Government Statistics,* 1981):

TABLE 10.2: Net Sown Area in Different parts of Kumaon

District	Sub-division/Tehsil	Net Sown area as % of geographical area
Pithoragarh	Champawat	12.92
	Didihat	23.96
	Dharchula	03.83
	Munsiari	03.86
	Pithoragarh	22.67
	District average	11.54
Almora	Almora	16.19
	Bageshwar	10.70
	Ranikhet	36.01
	District average	19.42
Nainital	Nainital	08.07
	Haldwani (plain)	21.32
	Kashipur (plain)	29.56

Kichha (plain)	79.50
Khatima (plain)	63.59
District average	29.34

Land Capabilities

Precise and detailed land capability studies for different parts of Kumaon have not been carried out. In general, arable land in Kumaon may be grouped into the following:

1. *High grade land:* This is extremely good agricultural land that is irrigated.
2. *Medium grade land:* This is a fairly good agricultural land which is unirrigated.
3. *Low grade land:* This is a poor quality agricultural land which is used for raising coarse kharif crops.

Agricultural Workers

In the absence of alternate sources of employment, agriculture is the main sector in which a large proportion of the working force of Kumaon is engaged.

REFERENCES

1. From the Manasa-Khanda of the *Skanda Purana* in Sir John Strachey's notes to which also I am indebted for a paraphrase of a portion
2. See Hist. Anc. Sans, Lit. : Duncker, *Hist. Ant.* IV, 30
3. As to the date of this work, see Gazetteer, II., 60, note. That the principal part of the *Mahabharata* belongs to a period previous to the political ascendancy of Buddhism had been proved by Professor Lassen; Muller's History above quoted, p. 62. The archaic portions of the *Mahabharata* may be earlier than some of the works of the Smriti class and the older portions of the *Vishnu Purana* may be earlier than portions of the *Ramayana,* but still the general statement given above is correct.
4. Etude sur is geographie et les populations primitives du nordouest de I'Inde d'apres les Hymnes Vediques, by M.V. de Saint-Martin, Paris, 1850, Muir's Sansk, Texts, II., 341, 353.
5. *Ibid,* p. 323,
6. Written by Sankhayana for members of the Kanshitak Sikha: see Muller, *Arc. Sansk, Lit.,* 180, 346: Weber, *Hist, Ind. Lit.,* p. 50.
7. *Ibid.,* p. 368.
8. In the Mahabharata.
9. *Muir,* II., 353.
10. Quoted from *ibid.,* 354.

11. It may be well to notice here in what respect the tribes not belonging to the four classes, such as the Bhaikas and Khasas, offended the prejudices of the twice-born. One of the charges brought against them is the boldness and unchastity of their women, "who sang and danced in public, drunk and undressed, wearing garlands and perfumed with unguents." Another charge is that they had no Veda, no Vailik ceremony and no sacrifice. Again, a Brahman then becomes a Kshatriya, a Vaisya or a Sudra, and eventually a barber. The aboriginal tribes would also seem to have been in the habit of burying their dead. *Muir,* II., 412, 482.
12. Van den Gheyn. Le nom primitif dos Aryas. Precis Historiques, 1880.
13. Muir, Sans, Texts, II. 360, 'hatvi dasyun pra dryum varnam avat;' slaying the Dasyus he protected the Aryan colour.'
14. M'Crindle's Ktesias, p. 13.
15. *Muir,* l.c., 358.
16. The Dasyus had chiefs over each tribe, several of whom are named. They lived incities, were intelligent and knew the law, but did not adopt the Brahmanic ritual, especially the complicated system of sacrifice requiring the aid and presence of several priests. See *Muir,* II., passim.
17. Dasyu is connected with dasa in the sense of 'slave'; *Muir,* II., 367.
18. *Ibid.,* 309, 337. Larsen writes: "The diffusion of the Aryas towards the south, points to the conclusion that they came from the north-west from the country north of the Vindhyas, probably from the reg on bordering on the Jamuna and the eastern part of the Panjab. Their extension to the east between the Himalaya and the Vindhya also indicates the same countries as their earlier seats. We find, moreover, evident traces of the Aryas in their advance from the north-west, having severed asunder the earlier population of Hindustan and driven one portion of it towards the northern and another portion towards the souther hills. Further, we cannot assume that the Aryas themselves were the earlier inhabitants who were pushed aside: for the inhabitants of the Dakhin, like those of the Vindhyan range, appear always as the weaker or retiring party, who were driven back by the Aryas. We cannot ascribe to the non-Aryan tribes the power of having forced themselves forward through the midst of an earlier Aryan population to the seats which they eventually occupied in the centre of the country; but, on the contrary, everything speaks in favour of their having been originally settled in those tracts where we find them at a later period and of their having once occupied an extensive territory." Again, he writes: "There is only one route by which we can imagine the Aryan Indians to have immigrated into India: they must have come through the Panjab and they must have reached the Panjab through western Kabulistan. The road leading from the country on the Oxus into eastern Kabulistan and the valley of the Panjkora or into the upper valley of the Indus, or from Gilgit over the lofty plateau of Deotsu down on Kashmir, roa is now known to us as the roughest and most difficult that exist and do not appear to have been ever much or frequently used as lines of communication. We can only imagine the small tribes of the Daradas to have come by the second route from the northern side of the Hindu Kush into their elevated valleys, but we cannot suppose the mass of the Aryas to have reached India by this road. All the important expeditions of nations or armies which are known to us have proceeded through the western passes of the Hindu Kush, and if we suppose the Aryan Indians to have come into India from Baktria, this is the only route by which we can assume them to have arrived.
19. Ptolemy describes Serika or China as surrounded by mountain ranges, the Annibian, Auxacian, Asmiraean, Kasian, Thagurian, Emodus and another called Ottorokorrae, an 1 pieces the Ottorokorrae southernmost of all near the Emodian and Serikan mountains. It was doubtless from the ancient legend quoted in the text that the Greeks derived their idea of the Hyperboreans, the people who lived a thousand years, a long and happy life,

free from disease and care in the land all paradise: see McCrindle's *Aucient India,* 24, 77.

20. Assited by the Sakas, Yavanas, Kabojas, Paradas and Pahiavas, according to the *Vayu Purana,* Wilson, VIII, 290.
21. Wilson, VIII., 294, who notes that the Greeks commonly shaved a portion of the head; but it is doubtful whether they ever shaved the head completely. The Skythians shave the fore part of the head, gathering the hair at the back into a long tail, as do the Chinese. The mountaineers of the Himalaya shave the crown of the head, as do the people of Kafristan, with the exception of a single tuft. It is doubtful who the Paralas are, except the ancestors of the Brahuis may be assigned to them, and then the Paidavas will be the Parthians.
22. I., 488.
23. In the Meerut district.
24. Wilson, III, 174.
25. *Ibid.,* 184: Badari is mentioned in the *Padma Puranas* as one of the celebrated Vaishnava tirthas where bathing is particularly enjoined. Pushpadanta was born as Devadatta and from worshipping Mathadeo was through his favour united with Jaya, daughter of Raja Susarma, and retired in his old age of Badari. So also in the *Vamana Purana* the sacred character of the lings at Kedar and Badari is extolled: *Ibid.,* VI., Ixxv.
26. *Ibid,* III. 196.
27. *Muir,* II., 337.
28. The name Kailas seems to be of Tibetan origia, which would apparently show that the Hindus discovered the country around Manasarovar after it had already been occupied by a Tibetan race.
29. Hiran maya, Suvarna-bhumi.
30. Wilson's works, VI., xiii: Gazetteer, II., 61.
31. They are the (1) Brahma (2) Padma, (3) Vaishnava, (4) Shaiva, (5) Bhagavata, (6) Naradiya, (7) Markandeya, (8) Agneya, (9) Bhavishya, (10) Brahma Vaivarta, (11) Lainga, (12) Varaha, (13) Skanda, (14) Vamana, (15) Kaurma, (16) Matsya, (17) Garuda, and (18) Brahmanda.
32. Wilson's Works, VI., xviii.
33. Colonel Wilford in exposing the forgeries of his own pandit who had fabricated a khanda for each of these *Puranas* calls the Skanda, Brahmanda and Padma Puranas the "Puranas of thieves and impostors." *As. Res.,* VIII., 252.,
34. Gazetteer, II., 61.
35. Compare Ward, I., 3; 3; Wilson, VI, 39. To the present day the local theory regarding earthquakes is that they are due to Vishnu changing his burthen from one tusk to another.
36. It is said that all the islands except Jambu have perished. Between Jambu and Plaksha is the salt sea; between the latter and Salmali, a sea of sugarcane juice and then a sea of wine, of clarified butter, of curds, of milk and of fresh water.
37. Compare the existing Tibetan appellations: Gyanak, the great black or China; Gya-gar, the great white or India; and Gya-ser, the great yellow or Russia.
38. In the shape like an inverted cone.
39. For a long description of each lake from the Vayu Purana see Wilford in As. Res., VIII., 326. According to him the Puranas place a great lake called Bindu-sarovara to the north of Manasarovara, and but for its distance it might be identified with the Rawan Hrad or Rakhas Tal, the Cho Lagan of the Tibetans which adjoins and is connected with Cho Mapan. On the Chinese map of India O-neou-tchi is given as the name of lake Mana and the Gangri range has the same name. In the Ceylonese books it is called Anotatte. The Arunoda lake or 'lake of the dawn,' which is said to lie east of Mana, may be the Cho Konkyu or Gungyut-cho, smaller but similar to the others, which lies near the source of the Brahmaputra. To the west of Mana is the Sitoda lake, from which issues the Apara Gandaki or 'western Gandak,' identified by Wilford with the Chakshu or Oxus: so that this

lake must be the lake of the Pamir, but is more probably the Cho Moriri, the source of the Western Satlaj. The Mahabhadra lake in the north may be identified with one of the lakes of the table-land. There appears to be a mingling of facts true of the country to the north of Kashmir with facts true of the country north of Kumaon in these accounts. In some Meru clearly indicates the group of mountains to the north and west of Kashmir, and in others those in the neighbourhood of lake Mana.

11

ALMORA DISTRICT

Origin of Name

The district is named after the headquarters town of Almora, situated in its southern part. According to a local tradition the earliest grantees of Almora were a family of Tiwaris who are required to supply sorrels daily for cleansing the vessels of the Sun temple at Katarmal. Sorrel is locally called *lamora* (Sanskrit *amla*) which, in course of time, got corrupted into almora and gave its name to the Khagmara hill on which it is grown. There is an interesting anecdote as to how the Khagmara hill, now known as Almora, came to be chosen as the capital of the Chand rajas.

It is said that once when Balo Kalyan Chand (1560-65) was hunting in the forests around the Khagmara hill, a hare appeared before him. Followed by the king it reached the top of the hill, assumed the form of a tiger and disappeared. The raja consulted his diviners about the occurrence and was told that his enemies would find that they had tigers to deal with, and was advised to establish his capital on the hill where the tiger had vanished. The king ordered the construction of a palace for himself and as a preliminary step a large crowbar was driven into the ground. It pierced so deep into the earth that the diviners announced that it had gone right through the back of the Sesha Naga, the serpent god, believed to support the earth, presaging that the king's dynasty would endure for ever. At the behest of the incredulous king, who desired to verify the statement, the crowbar was taken out of the ground and its point was found stained with blood. The diviners then gave out that as a punishment for the raja's presumption and disbelief, the rule of his descendants would last only a few generations. However, the king made, the place his capital which came to be called Almora.

Ancient History: An Overview

The area covered by the district of Almora lies in that part of the central Himalayas, which, in the Manasa-khanda section of the *Skanda Purana,* is designated the Manasa-khanda, one of the five divisions of the Himalayan region, and is said to have extended from the Mansarowar lake in the north to the Bhabar and Tarai in the South.[1] This region has also been known in different times by the names of Kiratamandala, Khasadesha, Kulindavishaya, Kurmachala, Kurmavana, Kurmaprastha and Kumaon, and has been traditionally described as the land of gods and demons and a place of penance for the rishis. Numerous legends are associated with different places, mountains, rivers and forests of the district. It is believed that in order to save the earth, Vishnu, in his second incarnation, assumed the form of a *kurma* (tortoise) and remained standing for three years at a particular spot which is identified with the Kanadeo hill in the eastern Gagar range, near Chhinapani, in *patti* Charl of tahsil Champawat of this district. The specific rock on which the god stood came to be known as the Kurmashila, the entire hill as the Kurmachala and the surrounding forest as the Kurmavana.[2] It is from these terms that the name Kumaon is supposed to have been derived. For a long time the name, in the form of Kali Kumaon, that is Kumaon on the river Kali, remained confined to the small tract round about that hill, now roughly covered by the Champawat tahsil, but during the mediaeval period, when the power of the Chand rajas of Champawat expanded rapidly, the name, Kumaon, gradually came to denote the entire region extending from the snow ranges in the north to the Tarai in the south.[3]

Another legend connects the district with Siva. It is said that after avenging himself on Daksha, his father-in-law, for his spouse *Sati's* self-immolation by fire, Siva besmeared his own body with her ashes and came to what is known as the mountain of Jageshwar (Jogeshwar), the Tankara hill in *patti* Darun of tehsil Almora. The place was full of beautiful plants and deodar trees and, seating himself on a rock, identified with the Iswardhar hill, he took to the performance of severe austerities to propitiate the eternal Brahma. The sage Vasishtha and many other rishis resided on this mountain with their wives. One day these holy women chanced to go where Siva sat lost in contemplation. They were so struck with his charms that they were rooted to the ground, spell-bound. Their husbands, worried at their long absence from home, went out searching from them and finding them thus bewitched, blamed and cursed Siva. He returned their curses and they were transformed into the seven stars of the Saptarshi constellation (Ursa Major). As a result of the sages' curse the lingam of Siva broke and fell down on the ground. It was worshipped by all the gods as Yogishvara. Vishnu then cut up the lingam with his discus into several pieces, called the Jyotirlingas, which were scattered throughout the world for being worshipped. The smaller fragments were preserved at Jogeshwar where a temple was erected to enshrine them.[4] Vaidyanatha (Baijnath in patti Katyur of tehsil Almora) is said to be the place where Siva was resting when Himachala (the Himalayas personified), Parvati's father, at the instance of Brahma, came to invite Siva to his house in order to give his daughter in marriage to him.[5] Bageshwar, also in tahsil Almora, is supposed to be the place where, after their marriage, Siva and Parvati rested and were worshipped by the gods who gave Siva the name Vagishvara (lord of speech).[6] Again, it was here that Siva is said to have assumed the form of a tiger *(vyaghra)* in order to dupe the rishi Markandeya and make him allow the Saryu (Sarju) to flow on. Siva was also, therefore, called Vyaghreshvara, corrupted into Bagehwar.[7]

The district seems to have been inhabited since pre-historic times, its early inhabitants being probably the Yakshas, Asuras, Rakshasas, Daityas or Danavas and Nagas.[8] Who appear to have been supplanted, in the course of time, by the Kiratas, Khasas and Kunldas.[9] There are still about a dozen villages in the district which bear the name Jakh (a corruption of Yakshi), Jakhani, Jakhera, Jakhnaula, Jakhola and Jakhsaurh. All these names point to the association of the Yakshas with this district. The Asura (Daitya or Danava) king Hiranyakashipu and his successors down to Banasura are said to have ruled over these Himalayan regions in early times. The Danpur tract in the district is said to owe its name to the Danavas; Kotalgarh, in tahsil Champawat, is the oldest fort in the district and is said to have been originally built by the Asura king, Banasura, and the original name of Sui, in the same tahsil, is said to have been Shronitapura which was his capital.[10] One legend has it that the several head of Kumbhakarna, the brother of the Rakshasa king Ravana of Lanka, was thrown by Rama into Kurmachala because the Rakshasas already resided in these parts.[11]

These Asuras, Daityas, etc., do not seem to have been confined to the hills and were probably the people referred to int he Vedic literature as Dasas or Dasyus. They are described as the chief enemies the early Aryans had to encounter in their expansion in northern India. When the Aryans were firmly entrenched in the plains, some of their kings, such as, Mandhatri, Yayati, Kartavirya Arjuna, Sagara, Raghu and Bharata, appear to have attempted to conquer the Himalayan country. In particular, Divodasa and Sudasa, the Tritsu kings of Panchala, are said to have waged a prolonged war against the Asura king. Shambara, who is reputed to have possessed 90 or 99 strong forts in and near these hills, which his enemies tried repeatedly to destroy.[12]

The Kauravas and Pandavas of the Hastinapur royal family were the next important princes from the plains who are said to have effected the conquest of these parts. Among those who brought presents, including gold dust and sheep-wool blankets, to the Pandava king. Yudhishthir, on the occasion of his Rajasuya sacrifice, in token of their allegiance, were the Kunindas, Khasas, Kiratas, Tanganas and Paratanganas, who probably belonged to different parts of the Kumaon-Garhwal Himalayas.[13] After the Pandava brothers, had gambled away their kingdom they passed a part of the period of their exile in these hills, and Lakhanpur in tahsil Ranikhet is supposed to be the site of the Vairatapattana where they passed the last year of their banishment incognitio.[14] Arjuna is said to have married a Naga princess of the hills[15] and to have fought with Siva disguised as a Kirata in the Darukavana, the forest near Jogeshwar.[16] Bhima is said to have married a Rakshasa maiden, Hidimba. Their son, Ghatotkacha, was an important Rakshasa chief of what is now the Kali Kumaon tract of the district, where the Ghatku temple, named after him, still stands on the Kanadeo hill.[17] Subahu, the ruler of Kulindavishaya a region which probably included the western and souther parts of this district, was a friend of the Pandavas and had accorded them warm hospitality during their exile.[18] Certain parts of the district also appear to have been conquered by Dushasana, a brother of the Kaurava King. Duryodhana.[19] Thus in the Mahabharata War while Subahu, the Kuninda, and Ghatotkacha, the Rakshasa, fought on the side of the Pandavas, some of the Kiratas, Khasas and Hunas, probably also of this region, are said to have sided with the Kauravas.[20]

After the Mahabharata War the district seems to have remained for some time under the sway of the kings of Hastinapur whose authority was, perhaps, never more than nominal. The actual rulers were the local chiefs of whom the Kulindas (or Kunindas) were probably strong in the southern and western parts of the district. The Nagas appear to have held dominion over what are now *pattis* Danpur, Salam and Nakuri of tahsil Almora. Nakuri, the original form of which is said to have been Nagpur, was, perhaps, their chief stronghold. There is a temple dedicated to Vasuki Naga in Danpur and another dedicated to Nagdeo Padamgir in Salam. They were, perhaps, important Naga chiefs of ancient times who are still worshipped in the district as serpent gods.[21] Several place names like Nag, Nagargaon, Nagarjan, Nagar Kotia, Nagar Seem, Nagchula and Nagtalia are also reminiscent of the hold the Nagas once exercised over the district. The Kiratas of the district probably belonged to that group of the four mentioned in the *Mahabharata,* which hailed from the northern slopes of the Himalayas, wore skins and lived on tubers and fruits. They were once powerful enough to give the region the name Kiratamandala, but their chief stronghold appears to have been the north-eastern part of the district where the present day Rajis (Rajyakiratas or Rawats) of Askot, who are supposed to be descended from them, still reside.[22] The Khasas were another ancient people who probably belonged to an early Aryan stock and were widely scattered even in those times. There is little doubt that the regions they inhabited included the mid-Himalayas where this district lies. The epithet *ekasana* used for them in the *Mahabharata* is supposed to mean that they were even then a settled people as opposed to other wandering tribes. They gave this region the name Khasadesha or Khasamandala and their descendants, the present-day Khasas, still form the bulk of the population.

Location, Boundaries, Area and Population[23]

Location and Boundaries

The district occupies the middle portion of the Kumaon Division and lies between Lat. 29° 3' and 30° 19' N. and Long 79° 21' and 80° E. It is bounded on the north by district Chamoli, on the west by district Garhwal, on the south by district Nainital and on the east by district Pithoragarh and the territory of Nepal which is separated from it by the Kali river.

Area

The area of the district as given by the Central Statistical Organisation, is 7,004 sq km but, according to the settlement report of 1965, it is 4,365 sq. km, which figure, however, does not include areas under the snowy ranges and the glaciers in the northern part of the district and the reserved forests. It is the twelfth biggest district in the State of Uttar Pradesh.

Population

According to the census of 1961, the population of the district, is 6,33,407 (females 3,28,948). The rural population is 6,06,163 (females

3,18,780) and the urban 27,244 (females 10,168). The district stands 46th in the state in respect of population. Its population in 1961 was higher by 3,10,312 persons, or 96.05 per cent, than what it was 60 years earlier.

History of District as Administrative Unit

In its earliest use, Kumaon signified the tract of country called Kali Kumaon, lying to the right of the Kali. It was not till after the Chands had established their capital at Almora, about AD 1563 that the name, Kumaon, was applied to the area now covered by the Pithoragarh, Almora and Nainital districts. During the reign of Kolyan Chand, the portion of Tarai now forming part of the Nainital district was annexed by the nawab of Avadh. Towards the end of the 18th century, Kumaon was invaded and captured by the Gorkhas. It passed into the hands of the British in 1815, and remained as a district of the same name till 1891.

The district of Almora came into existence on October 13, 1891, when the hill *pattis* surrounding Nainital and the Nainital Bhabar were constituted into the district of Nainital, and the remaining areas of the erstwhile Kumaon district into the district of Almora. This change was effected as the district of Kumaon was too big to be satisfactorily controlled by the district officer.

The parganas transferred to the district of Nainital were Chhakhta, Kota, Dhaniyakot, Ramgarh, Kutauli, Mahruri and Dhyanirau which however, were not all transferred in their entirety. *Patti* Mahruri Dolphar, in pargana Mahruri, and 11 villages of *patti* Mahruri Malli and *patti* Talli Rau in pargana Dhyanirau came to district Almora. At the same time *pattis* Kosian Malla and Kosian Talla were added to pargana Dhaniyakot and *pattis* Talla Bisand and Bichla, Bisaud were transferred to pargana Kutauli from pargana Narahmandal. As jointly recommended by the assistant commissioner of Almora and the deputy collector of Nainital in 1893, the exchange of several villages between the two districts was sanctioned to make the southern boundary of the district more natural. As a result, three villages of *patti* Mahruri Malli (district Nainital) were added to *patti* Malla Bisaud of this districtl village Nayeli was separated from *patti* Malla Bisaud and added to *patti* Mahruri Bichli. Village Lanki was separated from *patti* Salam Talla and village Wara from *patti* Chalai and both the villages were added to *patti* Chaubhainsi of district Nainital. These exchanges increased the area of the district by 46 sq km. The eastern portion of the Bhabar, known as Tallades or Tanakpur circle, which had been transferred from this district to Nainital in 1891, was given back to the district in 1896, because, being cut off from the rest of the Bhabar in district Nainital by some 48 sq km of dense forests, it was more easily accessible from Champawat, in district Almora, than from Haldwani, in district Nainital, and also as the transfer enabled the cultivators of pargana Kali Kumaon of district Almora, who migrated to this tract during the winters, to remain in district Almora throughout the year. At the time of the transfer, the Jugbura river was accepted as the natural boundary of the district in the south and in consequence a small triangular strip, measuring 4,313 acres (1,745 hectares) of pargana Bilheri of district Nainital, was also added to this district. Later, it was found uneconomical to maintain a separate establishment under the Deputy Commissioner, Almora, to supervise the comparatively small area of the government estates transferred to the district. Accordingly, in 1910, Tanakpur Bhabar or Tallades, with an area of 16,318 acres (6,604 hectares) was again transferred to district Nainital which had a superintendent for the Tarai and Bhabar government estates. The district then contained 12 parganas and 101 *pattis*. The parganas of Johar, Danpur, Barahmanda, Pali Pachhaon Phaldakot, Chaugarkha and Gangoli formed tahsil Almora while those of Darma, Askot, Sira, Shor and Kali Kumaon made up tahsil Champawat. In 1913, pargana Chaugarkha was abolished and the *pattis* comprised in it were divided between parganas Barahmandal and Gangoli. About this time a reframing of parganas and *pattis* was undertaken, some new *pattis* were created and the district was divided into four subdivisions or tahsils: Almora, Pali, Kali Kumaon and Pithoragarh, of which the constitution by parganas is given below, the number of *pattis* in each pargana being given in brackets against its name:

Sub-divisional Tahsil	Parganas	
Almora	1.	Barahmandal (20)
	2.	Danpur (8)
Pali	1.	Pali Pachhaon (25)
	2.	Phaldakot (4)
Kali Kumaon (Champawat)	1.	Pali Kumaon (15)
	2.	Gangoli (4)
Pithoragarh	1.	Shor (11)
	2.	Sira (5)
	3.	Askot (2)
	4.	Darma (4)
	5.	Zohar (3)

Pattis Bel and Berang of pargana Gangoli were transferred to tahsil Pithoragarh in 1947. The remaining two pattis of the same pargana, Athigaon Palla and Athigaon Walla, were transferred to tahsil Almora in 1948. On February 24, 1960, tahsil Pithoragarh, comprising 30 *pattis*, and *pattis* Athigaon Palla and Athigaon Walla of tahsil Almora were separated from the district to form the district of Pithoragarh.

Sub-divisions, Tahsils and Thanas

The district has now three subdivisions, Barahmandal, Pali and Lohaghat, each consisting of a single tahsil, viz., Almora, Ranikhet and Champawat respectively.

The Barahmandal subdivision, with headquarters at Almora, comprising the north-eastern part of the district, is the largest subdivision. It is bounded on the north by district Chamoli, on the east by district Pithoragarh, on the south by tahsil Champawat and district Nainital and on the west by tahsil Ranikhet. It consists of parganas Danpur and Barahmanda, 30 *pattis* and 1,851 inhabited and 219 uninhabited villages and Almora town. The total population is 3,06,594 (females 1,56,594), the rural population being 2,89,992 (females 1,49,663) and the urban 16,602 (females 6,931). The tahsil Almora has been divided into eight development blocks, viz., Lamgara, Dhaula Devi, Bhainsia Chhan, Takula, Bagheshwar (Kanda), Kapkot, Garur (Baijnath) and Hawalbagh.

The Pali sub-division, with headquarters at Ranikhet, lies in the north-western portion of the district and is bounded on the north by district Chamoli, on the east by tahsil Almora, on the south by district Nainital and on the west by district Garhwal. It consists of parganas Pali Pachhaon and Phaldakot, 29 *pattis* and 1,293 inhabited and 91 unibhabited villages and Ranikhet town. The total population is 2,46,249 (females 1,31,906), the rural population being 2,35,607 (females 1,28,669) and the urban 10,642 (females 3,237). The tahsil Ranikhet is divided into six development blocks viz., Tarikhet, Dwarahat, Chaukhutia, Syaldey, Salt and Bhikia Sain.

The Lohaghat sub-division, with headquarters at Lohaghat, comprises the southern part of the district. It is bounded on the north by tahsil Almora and district Pithoragarh, the latter being separated from it by the river Sarju. On the east lies Nepal which is separated from it by the river Kali. Towards the south and west the boundary is formed by district Nainital. The subdivision consists of pargana Kali Kumaon, 15 *pattis* and 733 inhabited and 138 uninbahited villages. The population is 80,564 (females 40,448). The tahsil Champawat has been divided into three development blocks, Barkot, Champawat and Lohaghat.

Thanas

For purposes of police administration there are three thanas (police-stations), Almora, Ranikhet and Bageshwar. In areas situated beyond the jurisdictions of the thanas, police duties are performed by the revenue police.

TOPOGRAPHY

The district lies in the Himalayas and consists of a series of riders and valleys. The snow-clad peaks and glaciers lie in the extreme north of Tahsil Almora, and the ranges diverging from the Nanda Devi group of mountain extend to the southern and south-eastern parts of the district. Its elevation rises from 300 m. in the extreme south-east, on the bank of the Kali, to 7,526.5 m. at the Nanda Khat peak near the northern boundary of the district in tahsil Almora. The mountains and ridges are separated from one another by a large number of river valleys. The greater part of tahsil Champawat has the appearance of a plateau, or an upland consisting of undulating downs. The district may thus be divided into three main natural regions-the mountains and ridges, the river valley and the upland.

Mountains and Ridges

The ridges, diverging southward from the mountain mass of Nanda Devi, extend in the northern part of the district to the right of the Pindar river. A ridge of Nanda Devi runs south-westward along the northern boundary of the district to the Nanda Khat (6,611 m.), Panwali Doar (6,663 m.), Maiktoli (6,803 m.) and Mrigthuni (6,855 m.) peaks and goes on to the Trisul, a peak of the Nanda Devi group. A ridge, descending southward from the Panwali Doar, separates the valley of the Sundardhunga from that of the Pindar and, ending near the confluence of the two streams, is known as the Mairal Chuting Dhar. The remaining boundary of the district to the north of the Pindar river is formed by another ridge, descending southward from the Trisul peak and comprising the peaks of Tharkot (6,099 m.) Baroltoli (6,275 m.), Dhak (4,268 m.) and Chovelia (3,699 m.). A minor ridge running south-eastward from the Tharkot peak separates the valley of the Sundarbhunga from that of the Baur Gad. Another minor ridge, known as the Manglachaur Dhar, takes off from the Chovelia peak and runs to the right bank of the Pindar, separating this district from that of Chamoli.

The most important spur in the district is that which, proceeding from the Nanda Kot peak on the eastern border of the district, runs down the left bank of the Pindar through tahsil Almora in a south-westerly direction and comprises the peaks of Nandakhani (6,029 m.) Laspa Dhura (5,913 m.) Dangthal (6,050 m.), Salgawar (4,533 m.) Nand Kund (4,113.5m.), Dhakuri (3,213 m.) and Sahinkhani (3,069 m.) and, separating the district of Almora from that the Chamoli, goes on to the Dudatoli range in the latter district. It is one of the main watersheds of Kumaon and separates the Sarju, the most westerly of all the streams that consitutes the Kali or the Sarda drainage system, from the rivers Pindar and Ramganga which ultimately find their way into the Ganga. The Debra is the chief peak in this part of the spur and is connected by a minor ridge with the Bhatkot peak.

Excluding the snowy peaks and the spur adjoining them, the Bhatkot, in conjunction with the mountains of the Pinath and the Gopalkot, is the biggest mountainous mass in the district and forms a portion of another main watershed in the Kumaon Himalayas. It divides the valley of the Ramganga to the west from that of the Gomati in the east. From the Bhatkot, a fine ridge containing the peaks of Kausani (1,888 m). Akwa (2,15 m.) and Binsar (2,411 m.) runs eastward to Bageshwar. It separates the valley of the Kosi from that of the Gomati and is particulary notable for its fertile slopes covered with pasture lands and forests. East of the Sarju, at Bageshwar, a fine range of hills rises to a height of about 1,980 m. and runs eastward to the Kalinag peak in district Pithoragarh. From the Binsar hill a ridge runs south-eastward to the Garanath (2,117 m.) and Almora-Binsar (2,296 m.) mountains. A range running from the latter towards the north expands into a mountain-knot, known as the Wallapani (1,902 m.). From there, another chain runs south-eastward down to the junction of the Jaingan and Sarju rivers. Another range, running south-east, contains the Jogeshwar peak (2,346 m.) and ends beyond the dak bungalow in village Naini where the road to Pithoragarh drops down to the Sarju. Yet another range running south-west terminates beyond the town of Almora at the junction of the Sual and Kosi rivers. One of its offshoots, which takes off at Dinapani, runs along the Petsal stream up to its junction with the Sual, about 8 km. from the town of Almora. From there mounts a spur from the Lamgara and Bandani Devi ridges and turns southwards encircling *patti* Mahruri Malli and the headwaters of the Busauri and the Sakuni rivers, which meet the Kali Rau stream under Mukteshwar. From Jogeshwar a minor range strikes off to the south and bending east concludes an irregular course in the farther corner of *patti* Rangor, just above the junction of the Panar and Sarju rivers. The ridge along with its numerous offshoots given the *patti* a most rugged appearance and makes the interior of the *patti* very difficult of access. Another fine range containing the Jalna and Mornaula peaks runs to Devidhura. These ranges are well wooded and are covered with pine on their lower slopes while the loftier summits are crowned with the oak and rhododendron.

In the north western part of the district the hills are, as a rule, low and the slopes easy, but chains of greater elevation mark the boundaries. Here the Bhatkot range is broken by the Ramganga, west of which another high chain runs into district Chamoli. The Jaurasi ridge, a spur of this chain, runs down south-eastwards, separating the valley of the Ramganga from that of the Binau. The Bhatkot range runs through tahsil Ranikhet and falls through Dunagiri and Dwarahat into the low bare hills of the three Dora pattis which lie between the river Gangas and Ramganga.

From Pandwakhal, at the head of the Khetsar glen, a fine range sweeps round the north-west corner of tahsil Ranikhet as far as Sarainkhet where it divides into two lofty ridges which enclose the tract of Chaukot, know as Lokhora, and unite at Khamlekhgarhi. At Jairaj, a few kilometres east of Khamlekhgarhi, it again bifurcates, one spur, known as Manila, running down to Bhikia Sain at the junction of the Nair and the Ramganga, and the other, enclosing the Nair on the west and terminating at the junction of the Ramganga and the Deota near Jharigaon.

A ridge, running southward from the Bhatkot mountain, separates the valley of the Gagas from that of the Kosi. Near Ranikhet it takes a westerly bend and runs past Sauni and Gajarghati to Mohan in district Nainital. A spur, called Sher Danda, diverges from the ridge at Ranikhet and descends to Khairna in district Nainital. From Gujarghati a spur runs to the junction of the Naurar and Ramganga rivers below Bhikia Sain. Another spur, called the Bellekh, runs from Sauni towards the south, separating this district from district Nainital. All these ridges and spurs are well wooded, chiefly with the pine, oak and rhododendron but the Sher Danda ridge is somewhat barren. A chain of hills which descends precipitously to the Bhabar in district Nainital marks the southern boundary of tahsil Champawat.

River Valleys

The rivers Pindar, Ramganga and Kali, along with their tributaries and subtributaries, provide the district with numerous valleys which play an important role in separating the mountain masses from one another and in discharging the surplus moisture of the surrounding tracts.

The valleys of the Pindar and its tributaries, the Kaphni, the Sundar-dhunga, the Sorag and the Baur are covered with forests of rhododenron varied by oak, sypress and fir trees. The tract occupied by these valleys is separated from the rest of the district by a ridge, 3,048 m. high. The soil is stony and of inferior quality. The gently sloping hill-sides have been cleared of forests and brought under the plough. The staple crops grown here are *chuwa, phaphar* and *mandua* in Kharif and barley in Rabi.

The valleys of the Sarju, the eastern Ramganga and the Gomati occupy the tract lying to the south of the spur bordering the Pindar valley on the left in pargana Danpur and the eastern part of pargana Barahmandal and comprise the bigger part of tahsil Almora. They are separated from one another by lines of hills converging upon the mighty mass of snowy mountains which culminate in the Nanda Devi Peak, north of the Pindar glacier. The valley of the Sarju in its upper part, is well wooded.

The valley of the eastern Ramganga contains parts of the *pattis* of Danpur Malla and Danpur Bichla. It is fertile though somewhat thickly wooded. The main Kharif crop is mandua and a little rice is also grown. Some of the villages produce only one crop in the year. In these parts agriculture is a somewhat precarious pursuit, the proximity to the snowy ranges and the glaciers rendering the crop liable to damage from sudden hailstorms.

The valley of the Gomati, also known as the Katyur valley, opens into the valley of the Sarju near Bageshwar and occupies the *pattis* of Katyur Malla and Katyur Talla. In the valley of the Garur which opens into the Gomati valley, south of Baijnath, lies the *patti* of Katyur Bichla. About a century ago, the low rich valleys of Katyur Malla and Katyur Bichla suffered from very bad climate due to thick forests which then covered them. These jungles were also infested by a variety of wild beasts. Conditions in Katyur Talla were comparatively better, as the area under cultivation there had increased which improved the climate. The valleys, however, are generally very fertile, both owing to the quality of the soil and the existence of ample sources of irrigation. In addition to the usual crops, turmeric, ginger and chilli are also produced here.

The valley of the Kali occupies a narrow strip in tahsil Champawat. It is characterised by the existence in it of abrupt precipices of great height, broken by small and steep ravines. The valley of the Lohaghat also known as the Lohawati, which runs through the upland, and that of the Ladhiya, which forms the southern boundary of that tract, also open into the Kali valley. The valleys of the Ladhiya and its tributaries yield rice of excellent quality. Chilli and turmeric are also grown here. The people here do not, as a rule, migrate but they have two distinct blocks of cultivation, one in the lowland along the river bed where they live during the winter and the other in the upland.

The valleys of the Ramganga, the Gagas and the Kosi rivers along with those of their tributaries, cover almost the entire tahsil of Ranikhet. The valley of the Kosi also occupies the western part of pargana Barahmadal in tahsil Almora. In all these valleys, except that of the Gagas, cultivation is both careful and efficient and in certain areas the entire hill side is covered with terraced fields. The rivers are utilised to the fullest extent. The *seras* that line the Ramganga from Ganai to Masi, the valley of the Binau and the fine irrigated villages in the Kathlar glen of *patti* Giwar Walla and of the Khetsar glen in *patti* Giwar Palla, offer a picture of agricultural prosperity hardly equalled elsewhere in the district. Except in the vicinity of the Silor Mahadeo range, the Gagas river is little used for irrigation, its course lying between overhanging precipices with no cultivation at their base. All the usual crops are raised in these valleys. The irrigated land produce wheat and the finest rice. Turmeric and chilli are grown in the valleys of the Ramganga and the Gagas and of their tributaries, particularly in the Salt *pattis*. These tracts also produce ugal, a superior sort of buck-wheat, in favour with the Hindus on fasting days. Fruits are grown nearly in all the villages, the Chaubattia garden near Ranikhet being famous for its fruits.

The valleys of the Kosi and its tributaries in tahsil Almora contain fertile land. The valleys of the Kali Gad and Kuch Gad rivers open into the Kosi valley in tahsil Raniket. Here the soil is on the whole fertile and crops like wheat, barley, *mandua, jhangora,* rice and pulses, are grown. There are some good seras in the valley of the Kuch Gad but the Kali Gad is too narrow to be used for irrigation.

Upland

The upland or plateau is an elevated stretch of undulating downs. It extends from Assi on the west to Gumdes on the east. From the north the ascent to this plateau is fairly gradual through irregular ridges running up from the Panar river in *patti* Chalsi. On the south it is bounded by a ridge which separates it from the valley of the Ladhiya river. This ridge abounds in oak and rhodedendron forests. In the northern parts the deodar woods are a most striking feature of the landscape. They have been planted, in most cases, around temples and in some instances can be almost described as extensive forests. The plateau has tracts of good loam, free from stone, with gentle slopes and ample sources of irrigation, yet the standard of cultivation is low and the quality of the crops raised is rauch inferior to that of the less favoured *pattis.* In *patti* Sui Bisung, however, such is the natural fertility of the soil, that even neglect does not prevent the crops from being excellent.

RIVER SYSTEM AND WATER RESOURCES

The distrct is drained by three distinct river systems, the Pindar in the north, the Ramganga in the West and the Kali in the east. The other rivers and streams of the district either join the main rivers or their tributaries. A description of the rivers and their tributaries and subtributaries is given below:

Pindar and its Tributaries

Pindar

This river rises from the Pindari, glacier, lying between the Nanda Kot and Nanda Devi mountains, at an elevation of 3,816 m. above sea-level, in the northern part of tahsil Almora, It runs southward past Phurkia and Dugli to Dwali where it is joined by the Kaphni on the left bank. It then bends south-westward and runs past Khati to Wachham near which it receives the Sundarbhuga on its right bank. Flowing a few kilometers further in the same direction, it takes a westerly course near Letauli and is joined on the right by the Sorag Gad near the village of Sorag, and later by the Baur, also on the right, to the south-cast of Kunwari, where it leaves the district to enter district Chamoli.

The Pindari glacier occupies about two-third of the whole breadth of the head of this valley. A description of the glacier, in the words of R. Strachey who visited at about the middle of the last century, is given below:

> "It seems to be a vast rounded mass of rocks and ground utterly devoid of any sign of vegetation, standing up out of a grassy valley. From the foot of its nearer extremity the river, even here unfordable, rushes in a turbid torrent out of a sort of cave, the top of which is but a few feet above the surface of the water. The end, immediately over the source of the river, is very steep and

of dull black clour. It is considerably fissured, the rents appearing to arise from the lower parts, tearing themselves from the upper by their own weight. On a closer examination this abrupt end proves to be a surface of ice covered with sand and gravel and curiously striped by the channels made by the water that runs down it as it melts. Behind this the glacier rises less steeply, like a bare gravel hill to its full height, which is about 500 feet above the water of the river when it leaves the cave. In some places, however, are seen great fissures both vertical and horizontal, the latter evidently made by the separation of regularly stratified layers."

The glacier is formed by the meeting, about 3 km. above the source of the river, of two ice-streams, one coming from the north-west and the other nearly from the east. The feeder from the north-west is larger than that from the east, and its surface is at a considerably higher level for some 90 m. below their first junction. It descends with a great inclination, entirely filling the gorge down which it comes in a cascade of ice. It assumes the general appearance of a confused mass of irregular steps which are again broken up transversely into peaks of every shape. The west part of this cascade continues nearly in its original direction after having passed the point below which the glacier bends sharply to the south-west, thus completely crossing the glacier. The steps in which in falls, however, also gradually change their direction so as to remain nearly perpendicular to the general current of ice. The transition to the regular level ice is very sudden and begins much higher up on the west than on the east side. A small tributary, also descending in a cliff of ice, meets the main glacier from a ravine on the east, not far above where it takes the sudden bend. The feeder from the east is formed by the union of two smaller glacier, one from the north-east and the other from the south-east, which is the larger of the two. Another small glacier meets the main one from the north-west, a short distance below the point where it bends southwards. Its inclination is very great, but it perfectly maintains its continuity of structure to the bottoms.[24]

The description of the glacier as given by Major Madden is also worth recording.

The moraine is constituted of gravel, mud, and blocks of stone embedded in ice; the stones are very small. There is a very steep descent to where the river issues from a cave in the face of the glacier, about 20 feet high, by perhaps 90 feet wide; the impending roof is riven into four or five successive thick ribs of ice. The recent heavy rains had thoroughly washed the Pindari glacier, and its surface exhibited a sheet of the purest ice, except on and near the terminal esarpment, which being covered with rubble, resembles, at a short distance, a steep bank of mud, and such is said to be the appearance in May and June of the Milam glacier. But to make quite sure fragments have frequently been broken off which everywhere were perfect ice, the only difference perceptible, between this and the Alpine ice, being a coarse granular structure here ... That the mass is moving downwards seems confirmed by the form of snow at its head, viz., a succession of terraces, with steep wales.[25]

Kaphni

This stream, a feeder of the Pindar, rises in the Kaphni Gal glacier and runs in a southerly direction past Baialigair to Khatia Kharak. Just before it reaches the latter place, it takes a westerly direction to join the Pindar from the left below the dak bungalow at Dwali. During the rains the water of the united stream at the confluence is of a milky colour. It is separated from the Pindar river by a ridge culminating in a peak, 5,652 m. high. The left bank of the river is formed by the Kotela ridge.

The Kaphni glacier also was visited by R. Strachey who describes the valley for two or three kilometers below the end of the glacier as being generally similar to the Pindar valley, but somewhat more rugged and desolate in appearance. The glacier begins, about 3 km. above the source of the valley which is nearly a kilometer broad in its upper part, in a precipitous fall of ice, some 18 m. to 22 m. high, exhibiting a ribbon—like structure. From the foot of the fall the slope is still considerable, yet the surface is very even. The glacier is poined by two small tributaries on the east and one on the west, which bring down considerable quantities of debris as their beds slope sharply. The moraines are confined to the tide of the glacier though small stones may be seen scattered all over the ice. The crevasses are most strongly marked near the sides and are inclined at an angle of about 45o from the longitudinal axis downwards.

Sundardhunga

The stream, which is a considerable feeder of the Pindar, is formed by the union of the Maiktoli and Sukhram streams near the village of Sundardhunga, in *patti* Danpur Malla of tahsil Almora. The Maiktoli, rising from the Burhtgal glacier runs southwards for about 5 km. to unite with Sukhram which, having emerged from the Mrighthumi glacier, runs eastward to the village of Sundardhunga. The Sundhardhunga river throughout its course runs in a southerly direction and joins the Pindar from the right near the village of Wachham.

Sorag

This stream, a small tributary of the Pindar, rises from the Punli Dhar range and running southward for about 8 km. joins the Pindar from the right near the village of Sorag.

Baur

This stream, an affluent of the Pindar, is formed by the union or the Tatoni and Chakalbagar stream at Samdar in *patti* Danpur Malla of tahsil Almora. The Tatoni, rising from the eastern slope of the Baroltoli peak, runs south-eastward to join the Chakalbagar which emerges from the southern slope of the Bhanoti peak and flows south-westward to Samdar. Thence onwards the stream is called the Baur and runs southward to meet the Pindar from the right to the south-east of Kunwari.

Ramganga and its Tributaries

Ramganga

Rising in district, Chamoli, this river enters the district near Chulera Sim in *patti* Giwar Palla of tahsil Ranikhet and runs south-ward to the village of Punabagar where it is joined by the Bimoli Gandhera stream from the left. It then runs south-west and near Amsari is joined on the left by the Tarag Gadhera river. Flowing in the same direction, it is fed by the Kuthrar Gad from the left and the Khastari Gadhera, Nagar and Kalron streams from the right, all joining it near Ganai. Further down, it is fed by numerous hill torrents from either side. From Ganai the river runs south-westward till it is joined by the Binau from the right, near Chachroti. It then flows southwards to Bhikia Sain where it is joined by the Gagas from the left. It again flows south-westward in a very tortuous course as far as Banasi and separating this district from district Garhwal, meets the Pandali Rao Stream from the left, at a place where the boundaries of the Almora. Nainital and Garhwal districts coverage. The river leaves the district at Chaknakal.

Gagas

This stream rises in *patti* Kairarau of tahsil Ranikhet to the west of the

Bhatkot range near Dunagiri, and runs due south through the tahsil. It then takes a south-westerly course through Athaguli. From this point it takes a westerly direction and after receiving the Khirau, Riskan and Khor tributaries from the right, respectively at Baret, Kotli Godholia and Dharpeti, and the Jam, Kanari and Naurar streams from the left, respectively at Sangura, Naugaon and Dhura, it joins the Ramganga near the village of Bhikia Sain. The river is utilised for irrigation in its upper reaches but, for the last 16 km., when it flows through a deep gorge, there is no cultivation near its banks. It is locally associated with the sage Garga.

Kosi

This stream, an important tributary of the Ramganga, is also known as the Kosila or Kaushalya in *patti* Katyur Bichla of tahsil Almora. It is fed from the high chain of hills comprising the Birchulakot (2,456 m.). Gopalkot (2,758 m.). Bhatkot (2,769 m.) and Pinath peaks and the northern declinity of the Milkali peak (2,279 m.). On the east a mountain range forms the watershed between the Kosi and Gomati rivers. The latter is a tributary of the Sarju while the Kosi joins the Ramganga. Flowing southward through the tahsil of Almora it forms a considerable stream near Someshwar, at an elevation of about 1,384m. above sea-level, where it is fed by some streams from the southern declivitices of the Bhatkot and the Milkali peaks on the right and by a stream from the left. It then flows south-eastward as far as Gagil in *patti* Syunara Talla, and then taking a southerly course runs to Hawalbagh. In its course it receives the waters of numerous mountain torrents on either side and has a fall of about 300 m. To the soutch of Halwalbagh it is joined by the Nana Kosi river. It is joined by the Sual river from the left near Chaunsali. From Chaunsali it runs westward forming the boundary between this district and district Nainital. Near Naugaon, in *patti* Kandarkhua of tahsil Ranikhet, it bends sharply southward to leave the district near Bujan, 865 m. above sea-level, in the same tahsil. Here it is joined by the Kali Gad and the Kuch Gad streams, respectively at Kakrighat and Bujan. It again appears on the southern boundary of the district and, once more separating it from district Nainital, flows westward to leave the district opposite Mohan in district Nainital.

Sual

This stream, a chief tributary of the Kosi, rises near the village of Bhaspar in *patti* Lakhanpur Malla of tehsil Almora. Running westward it traverses the *patti* and runs to Almora, separating *pattis* Lakhanput Talla and Khas Parja on the north from *patti* Uchyur on the south, and runs to Chaunsali where it joins the Kosi.

Kali and its Tributaries

Kali

This river, which rises in the Kala Pani springs in district Pithoragarh, touches the Almora district at its confluence with the Sarju, to the north-east of the Kalimat hill, and runs southwards separating this district from Nepal. It leaves the district to the north-west of Barmdeo in district Nainital. In its course through the district, the river is joined by a number of streams and hill torrents, the chief being the Ladhiya which joints it near village Shim.

Loharghat

This stream, a considerable affluent of the Kali, rises in *patti* Gangol of tahsil Champawat and runs south eastward in a sinuous course past Lohaghat up to Chala, after which it assumes the form of a considerable stream and takes a north-easterly direction to join the Kali near seam. It is locally known as the Lohawati river. A local legend has it that Lohawati is a corrupted form of 'Lohabatti', meaning an iron water caused the iron chains of some Brahmanas, incarcerated by a Chand raja in an old temple. to melt away as they sat warming their hand before a fire, having performed ablution in the stream.

Ladhiya

This stream enters the district from district Nainital near Borabagar in *patti* Talli Rau, tahsil Champawat, and runs south-eastward through the patti which it leaves to the east of Machiadh Bhadari. It then takes an easterly course separating *pattis* Palbelon Malla and Talla Des on the north from *patti* Palbelon Talla on the south, as far as its junction with the Kali on the right bank, near the village of Shim. Its only considerable tributaries are the Ratla, which joins it on the left near Gholiarheta in *patti* Talli Rau, and the Kwairala, which joins it on the same bank at Bilkhet in *patti* Palbelon Malla. There are, all along its course and the courses of its tributaries, considerable tracts of good irrigated land which yield rice of excellent quality.

Sarju

This stream a considerable affluent of the Kali to which it often gives its name, rises on the southern slope of a ridge in patti Danpur Malla of tahsil Almora. Running south-westward, it is separated from the sources of the eastern Ramganga on the east and from those of the Kaphni on the west by spurs emanating from the mountainous mass which culminates in the Nandakot peak. Pursuing the same direction and after receiving the waters of numerous minor streams from either side, it enters *petti* Dhampur Talla and is joined by the Kanal stream from the right. A short distance lover down and about 50 km. from its source, it receives the Pungar from the left and, a kilometre further downwords, the Lahor from the right. From this point it runs southward to Bageshwar where it is joined by the Gomati river from the right. It then runs South-eastward, separating this district from district Pithoragarh, and joins the Kali near Pacheswar in the latter district. Here it is joined by many streams, the chief being the eastern Ramganga. About 5 km. south east of Bageshwar the Panar stream joins it from the right. It is the most impetuous torrent in the district, dashing over the rocks with tremandous force, and creating a roaring sound.

Ramganga (eastern)

This stream, a considerable tributary of the Sarju, rises from a horseshoe-shapped depression on a ridge in patti Danpur Bichla of tahsil Almora. To the north the ridge culminates in a peak, 6,050 m. high, and on the east it runs south, forming the water-parting between this stream and the Goriganga in district Pithoragarh. The ridge lying to the west of the river runs in a southerly direction and separates it from the Kaphni. The river, right from its source, rushes in a southerly direction, separating district Almora from district Phithoragarh and leaves the district near village Chilkia to enter the latter district where it joins the Sarju near Rameshwar.

Gomati

This stream, which is another important tributary of the Sarju, rises on the northern border of district Almora near the Debra mountain and runs south-eastward through *patti* Katyur Malla. Reaching the neighbourhood of Baijnath, where it is joined by the Garur on its right bank it forms the boundary *between* pattis Katyur Malla and Katyar Bichla and runs in the same direction for about 8 km. to enter *patti* Katyur Talla through which it flows till its junction with the Sarju near Bageshwar.

Punger

Rising near village Sangar from a ridge on the eastern border of *patti* Nakuri in tahsil Almora, the Pungar runs south-westward through the *patti* as far as Hatsia where it forms a considerable stream. It then takes a westerly course and after reaching Mahatgaon flows through a deep gorge. Near Bugdungra it bends slightly northwards to join the Sarju from the left near Sartana. Right from its source to its confluence with the Sarju it flows in a tortuous corse, the widest section of the river lying between Hatsia and Bugdungra.

Panar

This stream, also a considerable affluent of the Sarju, rises near Mornaula in *patti* Salam Malla, tahsil Almora, near Mirtoli in *patti* Regaruban of tahsil Champawat. It drains the southern declivities of the mountain range running north-east from Jalna to the Deopar peak (2,092 m.) and thence south-east past Pali (1,527 m.) to Gauli (1,399 m.), and forming the waterparting between this river and the Sinyon Gad which joins it near Dasaula.

Lakes

There is no lake of any importance in the district except the Tarag Tal, situated in the eastern valley of *patti* Giwar Walla. Surrounded on three sides by high mountains, it is a picturesque lake formed by a natural dam made by big boulders, below which a stream gushes out. A rough path leads to this place from Ganai and continues over the Bhatkot ridge to Baijnath, but the route is very difficult and is only practicable on foot. In the neighbourhood of the lake an excellent hemp crop is raised.

GEOLOGY

Geomorphologically, the district may be divided into three major units, the Nag Tibba range, the central terrain of the Someshwar and Katyur valleys, and the Great Himalaya. The Nag Tibba range forming the southern mountain-rempart and running through Champawat, Devidhura,

Mornaula, Almora and Ranikhet to the western boundary, of the district, is formed of crystalline metamorphic and granitic rocks of great antiquity. The central terrain of the Someshwar and Katyur valleys, comparatively less rugged and mature, exposes immense piles of sedimentary rocks. The lofty Great Himalaya or Himadri range of the *patti* of Danpur Malla extends northwards and culminates in the imposing peaks of Nanda Devi and Nanda Kot in district Chamoli. This extremely rugged and very youthful terrain is made up of the crystalline metamorphis and associated granitic intrusive rocks.

Stratigraphy

Stratigraphically the different rock groups of the district are arranged below in order of increasing age:

Rock Group		Age
Berinag Quartzites	—	Devonian
Badolisera-Tejam Calc Group	—	Between Algonkiau and Early Ordobician
Lohaghat Group (Almora Crystallines)	—	Precambria
Valkrim Series	—	Archaean

Vaikrita Series

The Great Himalaya range, or Himadri, is made up of a tremendous thickness of metamorphic and granitic intrusive rocks the bridle-path to the Pindari Glarier reveals the 15,000 metre thick full scquence of the group. The lower part consists of granetiferous biotic muscovite augen gneisses and mica schists and the upper part is built up of scricite quartzites with intercalations of calc granulites (diopside-actinolite-scapolite-carbonate granulite). These metamorphic rocks are penetrated by multiple veins and dykes of tourmaline-bearing aplitic granite and pegmatite. At the top of the sequence there is a distinctive horizon of porphyroblastic biotite schists, called the Budhi schist. The age of Vaikrita Series is Archaean. The rocks are, therefore, older than 70 per cent million years. These rocks constitute the floor of the great basin in which the sediments were laid for the next five hundred and odd million years.

Lohaghat Group (Almora Crystallines)

It forms a huge synclinal structure and extends from the Kali valley in the east to the western border of the district. The metamorphic and associated granitic rocks build up the great Nag Tibba range along the southern border of the district. Working in the Lohaghat sub-division, three formations in the great pile of metamorphic and associated granitic rocks have been distinguished and collectively designated the Lohaghat group. Of these three formation (1) the lowest, Gorakhnath formation consists of (a) phyllonites chlorite-sericite-biotite-schists and gneissose quartz-porphyry, (b) garnetiferous mica schists and interbedded micaceous quarizites, and (c) para-gneisses, augen gneisses (migmatites) with mica schists, all rich in liotite. The same sequence of rocks with practically identical lithology, is exposed in the lower part of the of the northern limb of the great Lohaghat syncline and has been designed the Sarju formation, as the rocks are unfolded by the Sarju river and its tributaries. (2) The Champawat Granodiorites is a huge sill-like intrusive batholith disposed nearly concordantly with the metamorphics. The plutonic body is made up predominantly of biotite granodorites with local transitions into quartz-diorite and quartz-monzonite, all characterized by an abundance of biotite. This suits is penetrated by later dykes of tourmaline-bearing aplites granites and pegmatites (3) The uppermost Gumalikhet formation, occupying the central axial zone of the Lohaghat syncline, is constituted of spotted slates and phyllites at their contact with the granodiorites and an immense thickness of black carbonaceous slates, brown slates and feldspathic greywacks. There are a few lenticular pockets of coaly matter.

It may be noted that the Gorakhnath formation constitutes the southern, northward-dipping limb of the syncline and the Champawat Granodiorite occurs towards the top of this limb, while the Sarju formation is the representative of the Gorakhnath formation in the northern southward dipping limb. The granodiorites form a very attenuated horizon in the northern limb. The slates and quartzites of the Gumalikhet formation occupy the axial part of the syncline and are best exposed near Lohaghat in the Kali valley. The same sequence and lithological types are seen all along the Nag Tibba range from the Kali river to the western border of the district. In the Barakot-Daniya-Duram tract one more formation, the Duram Quartzites, is developed over the Gumalikhet siates. In the western part of the district, in the Ranikhet-Dwarahat area, the succession includes a prominent horizon of a variety of maggmatites.

The same group of rocks is exposed in a comparatively smaller synclinal inher along the Bageshwar-Baijnath-Gwaldam belt.

The lithology of the Lohaghat-Almora-Ranikhet group strongly resembles that of the Daling series of the Sikkim-Bhutan-Himalaya. The group is also regarded as the much metamorphosed Chandpur series of Precambrian times.

Calc Zones of Badolisera and Tejam

A group of lime slates is found extending from the south of Bageshwar to Someshwar and farther on to Lohba in the Ramganga valley in the west. A detailed study of the group in the Pithoragarh area made in 1962 revealed four constituent formations of which only two are developed in the Almora district: (1) the Gangolighat Dolomites consisting of stromatolite-bearing cherty dolomities and dolomitic limestones with spectacular lenticular deposits of crystalline magnesite and layers of soapstone and talcose phyllite, and (2) the Shor Slates, comprising olive-green, grey, dark and brown slates, interbendded with subordinate argillaceous and dolomitic limestones and intercalations of prominent fine-grained, fawn-coloured protoquartzites. Occasionally the great development of the protoquartizites overshadows the slates.

The Gangolighat Dolomites, with rich magnesite deposits, are exposed again as a result of folding in the wide belt extending from Tejam in district Pithoragarh through Kapkot in *patti* Danpur Talla to the Pindar valley, north-west of Gwaldam in district Chamoli. This zone has been called the Calc Zone of Tejam.

The Calc group has been correlated with the Deoban Series and is supposed to belong to the period between Algonkian (700 million years) and Early Ordovician (580 million years).

Berinag Quartzites

This is a group essentially of quartzites and inter-bedded metamorphosed basic lavas and intrusives. The chief rock type are: coarse-grained, current-bedded orthoquartzities sericite-quartzites quartz-sericite schists, chlorite schists and amphibolites. Many of the basic beds retain their former amydaloidal features. Towards the bottom of the sequence, quartzites are frequently pebbly and occasionally include boulder-conglomerates. The basal part of the sequence in many places comprises purple tuffaceous phyllites, interbedded with siliceus limestones. The quartzite group everywhere rests upon the carbonate rocks of the Calc Zones of Badolisera and Tejam and, therefore, constitutes as persistent a belt as the group of which it rests. There is evidence to show that the contract is a rhrust plane and the underlying dolomites are inverted. The southern belt extends from Berinag in the Pithoragarh district through the valley of the Gomati near Bageshwar, to Puniabagar in pargana Pali in the west. The northern belt forms a sort of fringe along the base of the Great Himalaya range and may be traced from Girgaon in district Pithoragarh through Loharkhet to the Nandakini valley in the Chamoli district in the west.

The Berinag quartzites have been correlated with the Nagthat series of doubtful Devonian age (400 to 350 million years.)

In the valley of the Ladhiya river and the mountain slopes descending into the valley in the extreme south-eastern part of the district, there is a group of quartzites of white, green and purple colours and interbedded chlorite schists, amphibolites and amygdaloidal lavas or sometimes diorite or even gabbro. Except for the degree of metamorphims, which is smaller in this case, there is a very close similarity between this group and the Berinag Quartzites. The Nagthat quartzites of the Nainital area extend south-eastward and constitute what has been designed the Ladhiya formation.

Structure and Tectonics

Structurally the district may be divided into four units, separated from one another by a thrust plane. The first of these units is the thrust bound synclinally folded mass of crystalline rocks of the southern mountain rampart which extends along the Champawat-Devidhura-Almora-Ranikhet-Dudatoli tract. This unit is evidently the south-eastern continuation of an uprooted, far-travelled pile of rocks which has been called the Garhwal Nappe. The southern boundary of this vast synclinal sheet is demarcated by the Ladhiya Thrust, which is the local name for the great Garhwal Thrust. In the western part of the district the same thrust was called the South Almora Thrust. The boundary of the synclinal sheet is also delimited by a thrust, called the North Almora Thrust in the eastern part. This Sarju-North-Almora. Thrust is traceable from Kanari Chhina and a little south of Someshwar of Dewalkhal in the north-west.

The second unit is the Great Himalaya or the Himadari range in the northern part of the district which is made up of a colossal pile of metamorphic and granitic rocks. A profound thrust, called the Main Central Thurst, separates this crystalline mass from the underlying quartzites of the sedimentary zone. Obviously, the crystallines have ridden over the quartzites undernath. On the whole, the startification of the crystalline rocks dip uniformly towards north-east, with no structural complications of great magnitude. It is interesting to note that nearly everywhere the thrust-contact is occupied by the basic intrusive of spilitic composition.

Between the North Almora-Sarju Thurst in the south and the Main Central Thrust in the north lies the sedimentary zone, comprising the Calc Group of Badolisera-Tejam and Berinag Quartzites and forming the third unit. These rocks are exposed thus in a tectonic window. The zone is complexly folded into anticlines and synclines and most of them are a symmetrical overturned or even reversed and cut by reverse faults along the limbs. The contact between the Calc group and the overlying quartzites represents a thrust plane.

The fourth unit is the thrust-bound synclined mass of crystalline rocks of the Bageshwar-Baijnath-Gwaldam belt and represents a detached piece of the larger thrust-sheet, the Garhwal Napple of the Lohaghat-Almora-Dudatoli belt. Thus unit is thus a techonic inlier or Klipper of crystline rocks infolded with the underlying Berinag Quartzites. The thrust that bounds this klippe is seen a little south of Kausani and Bageshwar.

Earthquakes

The district of Almora lies in the Seismic Zone III of heavy hamage The intensity of earthquake shocks is of the order of 5.3 to 6.9 (Richter Scale). The earthquake of 1959 caused some damage in *patti* Danpur Talla.

Economic Mineral Deposits

Very rich deposits of high grade crystalline magnesite occur extensively in the Calc Zones of Tejam and Badolisera, those at Dewaidhar being estimated to be about 7.9 million tons, at Girichhina 3.5 million tons, in the Punwar valley area 12.19 million tons, and in the Lahor valley area 2.54 million tons. Other important deposites are found in many places in the Pungar and Tuper valleys, at Jhiroli, Harap and Jakhera in the Lahor valley and at Chani, Nail, Tanga, Dauri, Agar-Chhahana, Ganai, Boragar, Rithal, Tachhni, Phadvari, Girichhina and Someshwar. Magnesite is mainly used in making refractory bricks for the iron and steel industry and also in the preparation of sorel cement and many magnesium salts of pharmaceutical value. As a filler it is used in the making of rubber.

Besides magnesite, the dolomites of the calc zones contain many spondic pockets and stringers and dissemination of copper minerals such a chalcopyrite, bornite, medlachite, azurite and cuprite. Lead sulphide of galena is sometimes associated with copper mineral as at Shiskhani next Dewaidhar. Copper mineralization is observed at Dhrauli. Thela and Dungri Dhar near Bageshwar.

Magnesite is associated with the pockets and lentils of talc in many localities. Talc deposits of Girichhina have been commercially exploited for years. Talc is used in the making of switch-boards, acid-proof table tops, kitchen and laboratory sinks, tubes, furnace-linings, etc. It is the base of a variety of cosmetics, such as talcum powder and face creams and many insecticides. As a filter, talc is used in the manufacture of rubber soap, linoleum and paper.

Pockets of flaky graphite in the Almora-Lohaghat crystallines have been reported from a number of localities like Diuri, Chhira, Ukkakot Kayala and Satjun. Graphite is used as a moderator in the nuclear power plants and in the manufacture of crucibles, a variety of refractory article brushes for electrical-motors, paints, pigments, foundry-facings, pencils and lubricants.

CLIMATE

This Himalayan district has a highly rugged, marked with steep and high ridges and deep and narrow valley, through which flow the Ramganga, the Kosi, the Sarju and their tributaries. The general slope is towards the south or south-east in the eastern half and towards the west or south-west in the western half. The elevation is high, ranging from about 1,500 m. to 3,000 m. above sea-level towards the north, while is the valleys in the south, elevations as low as 300 m. may be reached. The climate, therefore, depends largely on elevation and exposure to the sum and winds. The chief climatic feature of the district is its severe winter which lasts from December to March, and during which considerable precipitation occurs, often as snowfall, in association with western disturbance passing eastward across north India. The district, situated as it is on the southern slopes of the Himalayas, gets most of its rainfall from the monsoon current which penetrates through the valleys from June to September.

Rainfall

Annual precipitation is the least, 120 cm., in the Almora region. Beyond this region, precipitation increases with elevations and the increase is most marked towards the south-west where the precipitation is of the order of 200 cm. to 220 cm. near the district border and towards the north it increases to about 180 cm. beyond Kausani. Owing to the nature of the terrain, precipitation is highly variable spatially and is determined by elevation and exposure to rain-bearing winds. About 75 per cent of the annual rainfall, occurs during the monsoon months, June to September. With the onset of the summer monsoon, rainfall increases sharply in June. July is the rainiest month which, with August, accounts for about 50 per cent of the annual precipitation. In September, depressions from the Bay of Bengal occasionally reach U.P. and affect the weather in the district, when heavy rain may occur. With the withdrawal of the monsoon in September rainfall rapidly decreases, and November is practically rainless. Winter precipitation, though only about 15 per cent of the annual total, is of significant economic importance for the winter crops, and is associated with the passage of the western disturbances and is mostly in the form of snowfall over higher elevations, the snow accommulation in the valley being considerable. April, ushers is premonsoon showers, which become more frequent in May or June till the advance of the monsoon. These rains are generally associated with thunderstones. About 7 per cent of the annual precipitation occurs during these premonson months.

The rainfall is fairly variable. During the period between 1901 and 1965, annual rainfall at individual station varied between 80 per cent and 120 per cent of their respective normal rainfalls in 65 to 70 per cent of these years. Rainfall also varied from the lowest percentage of 55 of the annual normal rainfall recorded at Ranikhet on 1918, to the higher percentage of 162 of the normal rainfall at Champawat in 1914. Instances of consecutive years of low (i.e. less than 80 per cent of the normal or excessive (more than 120 per cent of the normal) rainfall are rare, Champawat alone experiencing one spell of three consecutive years (1921-23) when the rainfall in each year exceeded 120 per cent of the normal.

Temperature

Meterological data, other than those pertaining to rainfall, are not available for any place in the district. Inference about the climate has, therefore, to be drawn from altitude, topography, location etc., together with the available data for the neighbouring regions where similar climatic conditions are known to exist. Temperature, variations from place to place are considerable and depend upon factors like elevation, location and exposure to the sun. At higher elevations, as the isolation is intense temperatures in the open are considerably higher than in the shade in summer. In the valleys, pools of cold stagnant air cause considerable variations in day temperatures. January is the coldest month with the mean maximum temperature of 10°C. at altitudes of 2 km., the mean minimum temperature being about 2°C. Cold waves in the wake of the western disturbance often make the conditions more rigorous, when temperatures below freezing point are recorded. Temperatures as low as –6°C. can be expected during January or February at this elevation. Much lower temperature should be expected at higher altitudes and towards the north.

After Janauary, both day and night temperatures begin to rise. The rise, which is rapid till April, being about 4°C. per month, continues till June which is the warmest month, when the mean maximum temperature of 25°C. and the mean minimum temperature of 15°C. are attained. On individual days during the summer, the maximum temerature may rise up to 33°C. at elevations of about 2 km. With the onset of the monsoon, day temperatures fall slightly in July and remain more or less steady at 20°C. till August, while the night temperatures continue to be steady at about 15°C. The temperatures continue to fall further but after October the fall in both day and night temperatures is rapid till December when winter is fully established.

The diurnal range of temperature is generally high, between 8°C. and 10°C. except during the monsoon months of July to September, when the lower limit drops down to about 5°C.

Humidity

The relative humidity increases rapidly with the onset of the monsoon and is generally above 80 per cent during July to September. The driest part of the year is the pre-monsoon period, when the humidity may become as low as 35 per cent during the afternoon. During winter, humidity appreciably increases towards the afternoon at places situated at high levels.

Cloudiness

Skies are heavily clouded during the monsoon months and for short spells when the region is affected by western disturbances, otherwise they are generally clear or lightly covered with medium or high clouds. Usually clouding tends to increase towards the afternoon.

Winds

Owing to the nature of the terrain local effects are pronounced and, when the general prevailing winds are not too strong to mask these effects, there is a tendency for a diurnal reversal of winds blowing up the slopes during the day (anabatic flow) and the down the slopes at night (katabatic flow). The katabatic wind can blow with considerable force.

Special Weather Phenomena

Thunderstorms are rare in November and December and most frequent in the premonsoon and monsoon month of April to September, during which period more than 80 per cent of the thunder storms occur. Winter and pre-monsoon thunder storms are occasionally accompanied with hail. Hill fog is common during the monsoon. In the winter months fog may occur in the wake of western disturbances and, in the valleys morning fog is frequent.

FLORA

The total forest area, 2,117. 153 sq km, in the district under the forest department comprises 20.719 sq km of the Nainital, 599.016 sq km of the West Almora, 803.722 sq km of the East Almora, 394.536 sq km of the Pithoragarh, 256.400 sq km of the Haldwani, 22.820 sq km of the Ramnagar, and 19.940 sq km of the Kalagarh forest divisions. The civil forest of the district, which is under the control of the deputy commissioner, has an area of 1,272 sq km and the Panchayati forest occupies an area of 717.330 sq km.

The forests of the district have suffered greatly during the past. The low-lands of the river valleys, which were covered with dense jungles, have now been brought under the plough. About a century ago, the valleys of *pattis* Katyur Malla and Katyur Bichla were covered with rich forest growth infested with wild beasts like tigers, bears and leopards. In parganas Pali and Phaldakot and the western portion of pargana Barahmanda, cultivation has reached the maximum economic limits and the forest area left over is not sufficient for the needs of the agricultural population. The forests in the southern part of the district also suffered from reckless felling of trees of all species, which reached a climax between the years 1855 and 1861, when the demands of the railways for sleepers attracted numerous contractors who were at liberty to cut trees where and how they pleased. The result was that large numbers of trees were felled and large quantities of timber were left to rot in the forests for want of transport. It took several years to recover for use the timber thus left behind by the railway contractors. In 1861, the local officers, took prompt and energetic steps to stop this denudation of the area and by 1868, the forests of the district had been placed under the change of the forest department for proper management.

Taking into consideration difference in altitude and climatic conditions, the flora of the district may be divided into three main botanical divisions-the *sal,* the *chir* and the oak forests.

Sal Forests

These forests are confined to the valley of the Kali in tahsil Champawat and are found up to a height of about 1,220 m. The sal tree is rare in other parts of the district. In the hills it does not attain the height to which it grows in the plains. Other associated trees which also grow at the same elevations are the *haldu, tun, sain* and *kharik.* The *tun* and *kharik* rarely occur in the forest. The sal logs are chiefly used in buildings. The bhyunl, an extremely useful tree grows in the valleys and on the lower slopes. It is carefully protected, for its leaves afford excellent fodder for cattle and the fibres of its young shoots are made into ropes. It is usually grown on the boundaries of fields. Up to a height of about 900 m. trees which usually grow in the plains, such as the mango, pipal, banyan and sissoo, are also common.

Chir Forests

The *chir* forests are by far the most important as also the most extensive ones. The altitude range for the growth of *chir* is a wide one, extending from 790 m. to well over 2,150 m., but the limits are greatly influenced by local conditions. Thus though, as a rule, it ceases to be the dominant species at heights of about 2,075 m. on the southern aspects and of about, 1,950 m. on the northern aspects, it may be found still dominating on dry and sunny ridges at heights of 2, 150 m. to 2,195 m. The *chir* is usually found alone for it appears to have the power of driving away all other vegetation from the tract where it grows. It requires good drainage and either does not grow or languishes on poorly drained stiff soil. It can survive in very dry places, but it benefits from a good water-supply both in the atmosphere and in the soil. The best trees are, therefore, commonly found near nullahs, and their growth is often better, given suitable conditions of soil, moisture, etc., on the moisture northern slopes than on the drier southern aspects. In all *chir* forests, the pine is the dominant tree, and it is not unusual to find it the only species represented, although on northern aspects, where there is more moisture in the soil and fires are less destructive, scattered trees of other species may also occur. *Chir* forests are seldom very dense. The ground is covered with grasses, sometimes dense. There is also a discontinuous undergrowth of shrubs, often so widely distributed that even from a short distance their presence is scarcely noticeable. The chief undergrowths associated with these forests are *Glochidion velutinum, Ficus roxbughii* and *Indigofera pulchella* with the semi-shrubs, *Indigofera dosua, Inula cappa* and *Plectranthus ternifolius.* In the lower parts, *Combretum nanum* is often found and locally *Engethardtia colebrookiana, Bauhinia variegata, Aechmanthera tomentosa* and *Lespedeza stenocarpa* are the prevailing species, while *Ouercus incana, Rhododendron arboreum, Myrica rubra, Pieris ovalifolia* and *Symolocos crataegoides* often occur as single trees.

Oak Forests

These forests are generally draped in a rich epiphytic flora of mosses, ferns and lichens on account of the presence, in the soil as well as in the atmosphere, of moisture of which the percentage rises noticeably during the monsoon. The forests of the northern aspects are usually not liable to the ravages of fire, while those on the southern aspects have been considerably thinned down due to recurrent fires. All the varieties of oak provide good fodder and therefore, oak forests suffer from reckless lopping which reduces them to scrub woods. The principal varieties of oak found in the district are the banj, tilonj and kharshu, each occupying a more or less distict altitudinal zone.

Banj is the commonest species and reaches its maximum development between the altitudes of 2,075 m. and 2,290 m. but it also occupies moisture ravines, running into the chir zone where it is often found at as low an elevation as 910 m. A notable feature of this species is its capacity to establish itself on the highly unfavourable southern aspects, where, however, these forests are always very open, while those on the northern aspects are usually dense. At higher el vations, the oak is gradually replaced by other species, though sometimes it occurs even at heights of 2,900 m. on the southern aspects. With it may sometimes be found *rianj,* a local but gregarious species, which tends to occupy rather hotter and drier sites than the *banj,* mostly between elevations of 1,200 m. and 2,000 m. The best growth of bank is found in the Sual basin, specially near Binsar, and Akwabinsar. Phanyanth *(Quercus glauca)* also occurs with the bank, thriving in moist nullahs, the elevations favourable to its optimum growth being between about 1,525 m. and 1,675 m. It is rarely seen above heights of 2,075 m. Though widely distributed, it is not an abundant species. The other associated trees found in the banj forests are burans *(Rhodedendron arboreum)* and *ayar (Pieris avalifolia). Euonymus pendulus, Ilex dipyrena, Betula alnoides, Mochilus duthiei* and *Fraxinus micrantha contribute* to the tree canopy and there is commonly a dense undergrowth of *Myrsine africana, Desmodium liliaefolium, Viburnum cotinifolium, Indigofera gerardiana,* the *Rubus* species and various *Lauranceae*. The trees which accompany the *banj* in the nullahs down to the lower elevations are *Alnus nepalensis, Carpinus viminea, Carpinus faginea. Cornus macrophylla, Meliosma pungens, Accr oblongum* and *Stransiaesia glaucescens*. Epiphytic growths, mosly herbaceous (mosses, lichens, ferns, orchids, *Sedum trifidum, Rhaphidophora,* etc.), but sometimes woody *(Hymenopogan parasiticum* and various types of climbers like *Vitis Hedra, Smilex parviflia* and *Holboellia),* are characteristics of the *banj* forests.

The *tilonj* forests are found between the altitude of 2,150 m. and 2,450 m., increasingly replacing the *banj* trees with the ascent. This species forms a finer tree than *banj,* perhaps, largely because it is less accessible, but also on account of its mode of growth. In the district it is seen to the best advantage in the forest of Pinath, though it grows quite fairly in the forests of Morpateuri and Binsar. It attains its maximum development on deep moist soils, especially where there is limestone in the sub-soil. On account of the density of their growth and the moist conditions prevalent in the forests of this species of oak, fires very rarely damage them. The associated growths found in these forests are the *banj, Pyrus lanata, Meliosma, dilleniaefolia, Aesculus, Acer spp.,* and Cedreal sirrata, among trees, and the *Sachizandra grandiflora* among climbers. Silver fir is found in a restricted area near the Bhatkot mountain and in the Pindar valley.

Above the *tilonj* zone, the *kharshu,* locally known as *khaura,* becomes the dominant species. A small tract of the *kharshu* forests occurs near the Bhatkot peak and its abundant growth is confined to the Pindar watershed round the Sahikhani peak and the top of the Majkot mountains. It requires a minimum elevation of 2,450 m., to grow although, as in Dhakuri, it may sometimes be found even at levels of 2,150 m. It is found alike on the northern and southern aspects and is pre-eminently a gregrious species. It forms stands almost as pure as those of *chir* with only an occasional *pyrus* or *Meliosma*. Where the soil is extra moist and deep, a rich development of most of the *tilonj* associates as well as new forms such as the *Betula utilis, Pyrus, foliolosus* an. .he *shrubs Rhododendron barbatum* and *Lenicera may* be found in the Kharshu forests. Silver fir accompanies it throughtout its distribution and at places the yew and the box also occur in fair numbers.

The species of *Arundinaria (bamboo)* found in the district are *A. falcata* (Domingala). A *falconeri* (Deoningala). A. *spathiflora* (Jumra) and *A. journsarensis* (Tham). *A falcata,* with a wide range of altitudes to grow in, occurs chiefly in nullahs at lower elevations. This species is brittle and sparingly used. *A falconeri,* occurring higher up than *A. falcata,* is the most generally available species used for basket making. The *A. spathiflora* forms very dense clumps under the *kharshu* and is purely local to the district. It is more brittle than *A. falconeri,* but is freely used, especially for making mats. The *A. jounsarensis* which occurs near Dhakuri and Bhatkot is rare and also most valued.

Among the other species of trees found in the district, the chief are the deodar, *tun* and alder. The deodar is not indigenous to the district but grows in a few places, locally known as *banis,* having multiplied from trees planted around temples. Such *banis* are found near Someshwar. There are only a few small *banis* outside the reserve forests. The *tun* occurs at lower elevations, but, owing to the heavy demand for it in the past, it has become rare. The alder occurs in almost every watercourse and often forms fine large trees.

FAUNA

The wild life of the district has suffered greatly from reckless shooting uncontrolled felling of trees, increase in the cultivated area and development of transport facilities through the forests during the past several decades. Still, there is to be found in the district large varieties of animals, birds reptiles and fish.

Animals

The sambur, which is the most widely distributed of all the deer tribes, is found up to an altitude of about 3,050 m. It is called the *jarau,* and is a stouter and more massive beast than the sambur of the plains and has very heavy horns which are shed during May. The rutting seasons occurs in October or November. The *kankar* or barking deer is also met with up to the same height. The must-deer is found in the upper ranges at heights above 2,400 m. up to altitudes beyond which trees cease to grow. It has now become almost extinct owing to its reckless killing for the valuable musk pod. The animal is about 50 cm. in height and has a brownish grey colour with harsh and brittle hair. It is generally solitary, very active and sure-footed and prefers rocky precipitous areas. The nilgai is occasionally found at the foot of the hills and the four-horned antelope in the sal forests. The goral, or Himalayan chamois, may be found in places as high as 3,350 m. above sea-level, although its usual habitat is at heights between 900 m. and 2,750 m. Both sexes have horns, those of the male being about 15 cm. and of the female 10 cm. long. They are generally found in groups of three to four, and frequent moderately steep grassy slopes, not too thickly covered with pine. The *goral* is very tenacious of life and will often carry away a lot of load. The *thar* is found in the most precipitous area of the upper ranges between the heights of 2,100 m. and 3,700 m., according to the season. Males and females both have horns, but those of the latter are much slighter and shorter. The male is about a metre in height and carries horns about 40 cm. long. The *sarau,* which also belongs to the goral family, is nearly as large as the *thar.* It inhabits precipitous rocks clothed with dense forests and is a very shy, strange and uncouth beast. It horns are 20 cm. to 25 cm. in length. The bharal or wild blue sheep is rare in the district. It frequents the grassy slopes between altitudes of 3,000 m. and 5,000 m., below the snowline. A good ram carrier horns 60 cm. to 65. long. Its meat is found to be especially tasty in September. The tiger is generally seen in tahsil Champawat but rarely to its north. It may be found up to an altitude of 3,000 m. It is quite different from the tiger found in the plains, being of a stouter built with longer and more furry hair and a shorter and thicker tail. In the earlier part of British rule, the Katyur valley was almost deserted, being the haunt of man-eating tigers, but the animal is now rare and is only occasionally seen in the district. The *bagh* or *baghera* (panther) is exceedingly hold, often making inroads in search of prey, into the heart of a village. The snow-leopard is rare in tracts south of the snowy range, but one or two frequent the hills where the bharal is found. It is much abhorred by sportsman as a game destroyer. Its coat is of a yellowish colour with dark grey marks all over except on the stomach which is pure white.

The Himalayan black bear is common throughout the district. In the upper ranges it hibernates throughout the winter and is generally seen during the rains. It is a good tree climber and feeds on acorns and other wild fruits, but its favourite food is *mandua.* Much damage is done by it to fruit gardens of Binsar and other places. It occasionally kills cattle, sheep and goats and, like the sloth-bear, is not above eating carrion on occasion. Its sight and hearing are both keen. It is a ferocious and courageous beast and does not hesitate to attack a man if disturbed. Black bears maul many hillmen every year, the head and the face being the usual targets. The wolf is rarely seen in the hills and prefers submontane tracts. The wild dog hunts in packs, the sambur or chital being its favourite quarry. It is said that a pack hunts in relays, always driving the prey in a circle. The hind quarters and abdomen of the victim are the first to be attacked. The jackal is found up to a height of 2,150 m. Its ordinary food is carrion and vegetable matter, especially pumpkins and maize, but it kills a great many young deer and often catches birds and occasionally attacks wounded animals. Both the plains fox and the hill fox occur in the district. The fox has a fine fur, but is a poor runner on level ground, and even on open hillsides an ordinary half-bred greyhound can easily catch it. The wild pig is found throughout the district up to an altitude of 3,050 m. and chiefly prefers oak forests, living on mast. The *chatraila* (pine-marten) and the *ud* (other) are great destroyers of game and fish, respectively. The monkeys and *langurs* are found througout the district and do much damage to the crops, though the latter are often content with acorns and other wild fruits.

Birds

The district is very rich in bird life. Most of the birds of the plains occur in the hills where, in addition, there are many species peculiar to the colder regions. Birds of prey, eagles, hawks, falcons and vultures are very common. Among game birds the *lungi* pheasant is found at a height of about 3,700 m. and the monal between the altitudes of 2,400 m. and 3,700 m. the *kokla* on *pokra* is seen between the heights of 1,800 m. and 3,700 m. and the *chir* pheasant between those of 1,500 m. and 2,400 m. The *kalij,* hill partridge and block partridge frequent the thick forests up to a height of 2,400 m. among partridges the *chakor* is very common in the district, but the snow partridges are rare. The Himalayan snow cock is found at or near the snowline. The woodcock is commonly seen near Almora. Among pigeons, the wood-pigeon an the blue rock-pigeon are very common. Flocks of snow pigeons are also seen in the higher ranges. Duck and teal occasionally rest on the rivers. Among other birds found in the district are various types of turushes water-ouzels, yellow and pied wagtails, swallows, swifts, kingfishers, wood peckers, cuckoos, tree-creepers, shrikes, orioles, robins, red-starts and warblers.

Reptiles

In the district there are about 34 species of snakers, 26 being are non-poisonous. The cobra is found up to a height of 1,800 m. The krait is very common in the low hills and grows to a length of about a metre. Its colour is deep lustrous blue-black, or streaked and reticulate with, white, below it is white. The Wall's krait has a glistening black colour, marked with milky white cross formed of smallish oval or round spots above. Below it is white, mottled with slate colour towards the tail. It resembles the common krait in appearance but is larger in size. king cobra grows up a length of 2.5 m. The male cobra is jet-black in colour. The *CallophisMac Clellandi* is rarely seen in the district. Its body and tail are raddish brown in colour, with generally a black vertebral-line the nape to the top of the tail. Its had and the neck are black with a yellow bar behind the eyes and the belly is such in colour with black cross bands or quadrangular spots. A variety of *nigriventer* is also seen in the district and though venomous, its bite is not fatal. Russell's viper is common up to a height of 1,800 m. It colour above is greyish or reddish brown with three rows of blaskish brown annular ocelli, each surrounded by an inner white and an outer black ring down the back and the sides. It has broad arrow mark on the head, formed by two pale lines running from the snout over the eyes to the temporal region. The *Ancistrodon himalayanus* is the only hill snake found above the altitude of 2,500 m. In colour it is dark brown, indistinctly marked with darker spots edged with black. The belly is black marbled with yellow, a blackish band extending from the eyes to the gape. It is about 65 cm. in length and is venomous, though its bite is not fatal. The *Lachesis gramineus,* the green pitted viper, is seldom seen in the district. It grows to a length of 90 cm. to 95 cm. It is one of the handsomest of the tree snakes and its bite is not necessarily fatal.

Among the non-venomous snakes, the python is the most notable. It grows to a length of about 9 m. but specimens of over 6 m. are rare. It is seldom seen in the hills where it is called *charao.* The rat snake is also common and grows to a length of about 230 cm. The blood-sucker lizard, in spite of its name, is perfectly harmless and grows to a length of 25 cm. to 40 cm. The leech is particularly active during the rains and perfers oak forests. After a smart shower it appears in very large numbers and a barefooted way farer is soon made uncomfortably aware of its presence.

Fish

Fish abound in almost all the streams of the district. Among the larger *species*, the *mahaseer* and the *kalabans* are very common. The *gunch*, or the fresh water shark, inhabits the deeper pools of the Sarju. The trout is rare, but the *chilwa* swarms wherever there is running water. Among other species found in the district are the *asela, rohu* and *garra.* In the latter part of the hot weather, fish run up the stream to deposit the ova and return in the rainy season.

Game-laws

The game-laws obtaining in the district are governed by the Wild Birds and Animals Protection Act, 1912 (Act VIII of 1912), as amended by the Wild Birds and Animals Protection (U.P. Amendment) Act, 1934 (Act XIII of 1934) and sub-section (1) (i) of section 26 of the Indian Forest Act, 1927 (Act XVI of 1927), as amended by the Indian Forest (Uttar Pradesh Amendment) Act, 1965.

Source : Saiyid Ali Akhtar Rizve, *Almora Gazetteer*, Govt. of India Press, Lucknow, 1979.

REFERENCES

1. Atkinson, E.T., *The Himalayan Districts of the North-Western Provinces of India*, Vol. II, pp. 297-298; Dabral, S.P., *Uttarakhand Ka Itihasa*, pp. 151-152; Pande, B.D. *Kumaun Ka Itihasa*, pp. 160-162.
2. *Ibid.*, p. 1; Nautiyal, K.P.: "The Numismatic History of Kumaon"—*The Journal of the Numismatic Society of India*, Vol. XXIII (1961), p. 375; Atkinson, *op. cit.*, Vol. II pp. 299, 506.
3. *Ibid*, p. 506, Pande, *op. cit.*, p. 1: Nautiyal, *op. cit.*, p. 375.
4. Pande, *op. cit.*, pp. 164-165; Atkinson, *op. cit.*, Vol., II, pp. 301-303
5. *Ibid.*, p. 305, Footnote 4; Pande, *op. cit*, p. 164.
6. *Ibid.*, p. 172
7. *Ibid.*, p. 173; Atkinson, *op. cit.*, pp. 317-318
8. *Ibid.*, pp. 373-3761 Sankratyayana, Rahul; *Kumaon*, pp. 20, 25, 26
9. *Ibid.*, pp. 20, 25, 26 30; Berreman, G.D.: *Hindus of the Himalayan*, pp. 14-19. Nautiyal, *op. cit.*, p. 375; Atkinson, *op. cit.*, pp. 269, 282-283, 362-366, 376-380.
10. *Ibid.*, Vol. III, pp. 334-335; Pande, *op. cit.*, pp. 13-15, 108.
11. *Ibid.*, p. 13
12. Majumdar, R.C. and Pusalker, A.D. (Ed.): *The History and Culture of the Indian People*, Vol. I, pp. 249-250, 293-294; Macdonell, A.A. and Keith, A.B.: *Vedic Index of Names and Subjects*, Vol. I, pp. 198, 262, 320-323, 347, 349, 471-473; Vol. II, p. 355; Sankratyayana, *op. cit.*, p. 31; Atkinson, *op. cit.*, Vol. II, pp. 272-375-277, 279-280
13. *Mahabharata*, Sabha-parva, Ch. 48; Moti Chandra: 'Geographical and Economic Studies in the Mahabharata, Upayana parva'—*The Journal of the U.P. Historical Society*, Vol. XVII, Part I, pp. 32, 36-37, 39

14. Cunnigham, A.: *The Ancient Geography of India*, p. 229; Dabral, *op. cit.*, p. 222; Pande, *op cit.*, pp. 99, 188
15. Atkinson, *op. cit.*, Vol. II, p. 281
16. *Ibid.*, pp. 317, 777-778
17. *Ibid.*, pp. 506, 807-808; Pande, *op. cit.*, p. 13.
18. *Mahabharata*, Vana-Parva, Ch. 140; Dabral, *op. cit.*, p. 167; Moti Chandra, *op. cit.*, pp. 32-40.
19. *Mahabharata*, Sabha-parva, Ch. 28; Agrawala, V.S.: Harshacharita, p. 164; Pande *op. cit.*, pp. 169-170.
20. *Mahabharata*, Udyoga-parva, Ch., 19, 160; Drona-parva, Ch. 83, 121; Karnaparva, Ch. 85; Dabral, *op. cit.*, pp. 176-181.
21. Powell-Price J.C. : "Some Notes on the Early History of Kumaon"–*The Journal of the U.P. Historical Society*, Vol. IV, Part 2 (July, 1930), p. 6; Atkinson, *op. cit.*, Vol. II, pp. 270, 281, 318, 373-375
22. *Ibid.*, pp. 363-368, 732; Powell-Price, *op. cit.*, p. 6; Sankratyanana, *op. cit.*, pp. 20, 26; Moti Chandra, *op. cit.*, pp. 40-41
23. Figures pertaining to population relate to 1961, and those of area to 1967-68, unless otherwise indicated.
24. Atkinson, E.T.: *The Himalayan Districts of the North-Western Provinces of India*. Vol. I, pp. 182-183.
25. *Ibid.*, Vol. III, p. 659.

12

CHAMOLI DISTRICT

Origin of Name

The District of Chamoli, which was formed in 1960, consists of and takes its name from the tahsil and subdivision of Chamoli which, prior to 1960, was a part of the district of Garhwal and occupied the central part of the Uttarakhand Division till December 20, 1968, when that Division was abolished, and the district was included in the newly formed Garhwal Division.

Location, Boundaries, Area and Population

Location and Boundaries

Situated in the Himalayas, the district which is nearly half the size of its parent district, Garhwal, is broad in the north and narrows towards the south and is somewhat cupshaped, its length from north to south being about 129 km. and its breadth from west to east about 117 km. To its north lies Tibet and to the north-west the district of Uttarkashi. On the east it is bounded by the Pithoragarh, on the south and south-east by the Almora, on the south-west by the Garhwal and on the west by the Tehri Garhwal districts.

Area

The census records of 1961 give the area of the district as 9,130 sq. km. it being third in area among the districts of the state. According to the

Central Statistical Organisation, however, the area is 9,128 sq. km.

Population

According to the census of 1961, the population of the district is 2,53.137 (males 1,20,092 and females 1,33,045) all in the rural area, there being no urban area in the district. It stands 53rd in the State in respect of population. (Latest figures are given separately).

History of District as Aministrative Unit

In British times the area covered by the subdivisions or tahsil of Chamoli now the district of Chamoli, was a part of the district of British Garhwal, also called Pauri Garhwal after the name of its headquarters town Pauri. The district then formed part of the Kumaon Division. The district of Chamoli was formed in 1960 out of 28 *pattis* (of the district of Garhwal) which now constitute the tahsils or subdivision of Joshimath, Ukhi Math, Chamoli and Karnaprayag. The district was included in the Uttarakhand Division which was abolished in December, 1968, and it was included in the Garhwal Division.

Sub-divisions, Tahsils and Thanas

Each of these 4 sub-divisions–Joshimath, Ukhi Math, Chamoli and Karnaprayag, forms a tahsil of the same name; a brief account of each being given below.

The tahsil or sub-division of Joshimath is the largest tahsil of the district and is bounded on the north-west by the Uttarkashi and on the east by the Pithoragarh and Almora districts. On the west it is bounded by the tahsil of Ukhi Math, and on the south by that of Chamoli and on the south east by a narrow strip of the tahsil of Karnaprayag. It has a population of 15,207 (males 8,122 and females 7,085), and contains 77 villages.

To the west lies Ukhi Math, the smallest tahsil or sub-division of the district, bounded on the north by the Uttarkashi and on the south by the Garhwal districts and on the east by the tahsils of Joshimath and Chamoli, a high range of mountains and the Mandakini river separating it from the district of Tehri Garhwal on the west. It has a population of 57,787 (males 27,002 of female 30,785), and contain 286 villages.

The tahsil of Chamoli is a tract of very irregular outline. It comprises 7 *pattis*. On the north it is bounded by the Joshimath, on the west by the Ukhi Math, and on the south by the Karnaprayag tahsils, a narrow strip of the last named tahsil separating it from the Almora district to the east. It has a population of 72,167 (males 34,565 and females 37,602) and contains 386 villages.

The tahsil of Karnaprayag occupies the southermost portion of the district and comprises 14 *pattis.* On the east, sout-east and south it is bounded by the district of Almora. on the south-west by that of Garhwal and on the north by tahsil Chamoli excepting a narrow strip which touches tahsil Joshimath. It has a population of 1,07,976 (males 50,403 and females 57,573), and contains 780 villages.

Thanas

For purposes of police administration there are 4 thanas (police stations) in the district–each tahsil having one. During the season of pilgrimage, usually from May to mid-November, a temporary thanas also functions at Badrinath in tahsil Joshimath.

Geology

The geology of the region shows that the Himalayas are the youngest mountains in the world. During early Mesozoic times, or the secondary geological period, the land mass now covered by them was occupied by the great geosynclinal Tethys sea. The probable date of the commencement of the elevation of the Himalaya is about the close of the Mesozoic period, but the unravelling of the story of their structure has only just begun, and in many cases no dating of the rocks is yet possible, though they include ancient and relatively recent crystalline intrusives, rocks and sediments allied to the Peninsular part of India. The section of the range in the district is deeply cut into by the headwaters of the Alaknanda river, this trunk stream seeming to have reached a later stage of development than its tributaries. This much, however, is known that there has been intense metamorphosis. In some parts uplift has been considerable since the mild Pleistocene period, in others there are great stretches of high but studied topography and elsewhere there are the deepest gorges. The direction of folding in these mountain masses is generally north to south. The geological features of the district form two major divisions which lie north and south of an imaginary line extending east-south-east between the villages of Hilang in tahsil Joshimath and Loharkhet in the adjoing district of Pithoragarh. The northern division, which is occupied by higher ranges and snow-covered peaks consists entirely of medium to high grade metamorphic rocks and is intruded by later volcanic rocks. The division to the south, occupied by ranges of lower altitudes, consists essentially of sedimentary and low grade metamorphic rock also intrueded by later volcanics. Geologically very little is known of the first division which consists of rocks such as quartzites, marbles and various types of micaceous schists and gneisses with a few sporadic occurrances of garnet, graphite iron, kynite, mica and vein quartz. The division to the south of the imaginary line is better known geologically and consists of rocks such as gneisses, limestone, phyllites, quartzites, sericite-biotite schists and slates. The minerals that are found in the district are the following.

Asbestos

This is of the amosite variety and can be used for the production of asbestos, cement bricks, laboratory asbestos sheets and paper, but is not considered to be of economic importance.

Magnestic

This is of an average quality, is crystalline in nature, and is found associated with crystalline dolomites and sometimes with soapstone. The magnesium carbonate found here is also of average quality and its mineralisation has also been reported to occur in the district.

Soapstone or Steatite

This white saponaceous stone resembling pipe-clay is obtained in a lenticular body and is associated with mineral pyrites, which adds a colour to it, and in places with magnesite. It can be mined for use as a filler in soap and in the cosmetic industry. In the past various utensils were made of it which, whes polished, had the apearance of marble.

Copper

The copper mines in the district were extensive and of repute during the period of the Hindu and the Gurkha rules. All the rich mines have since been exhausted and at present they do not offer a fair field for the employment of capital. The metal occurs sporadically, encrustations of chalybite having also been observed as well as of malachite and azurite. The ore is chiefly copper pyrites and grey or vitreous copper ore, with the red oxide and green carbonate in smaller quantities, the latter being scarce.

Iron

Small and sporadic occurrences of iron are known to occur in several parts of the district but are of hardly any economic importance. from ore, rich in haematite, and magnetic ore, with haematite and siderite, also occur in the district.

Graphite

In the past this mineral, als known as plumbago, found mostly in *patti* Lohba, was used as a dye but no large deposits have been noticed for a long time.

Gold

Although no gold mine has been discovered in the district, the sands of the Alaknanda and the Pindar are said to be auriferous to a limited extent.

Gypsum

This mineral is found on the banks of some rivers and was used in the past for the manufacture of saucers and bowls. When ground to a fine powder it is known as plaster of Paris and can be used for a number of purpose.

Lead

Deposits of this metal were fairly numerous in the past but it is found in somewhat inaccessible places and has long since ceased to be worked.

Slate

This dense, fine-grained metamorphic rock, which is produced from a fine clay, can be split into thin, smooth plates and is quarried throughout the district. It is suitable for roofing purposes, the thin dark blue slates being somewhat inferior in quality.

Limestone

By burning this mineral, lime is procured which can be used as mortar. There are two distinct ranges of limestone hills in this district, the first, north of the Alaknanda in Nagpur, the second, running from Lohba *patti* to the Pindar and again to the Alaknanda in *patti* Bacchansyun in district Garhwal. Reserves of *dolomite* (magnesian lime-stone) exist in the district and tufaceous deposits are also found near several small nullahs.

Building Stone

Stone which can be used for building purposes is available in most parts of the district. Sandstone is found in abundance in the lower hills. Gneiss and chlorite schists which are available throughout the district are fequently used for building purposes.

Sulphur

This yelow mineral, also known as brimstone is found in the district as green sulphate of iron and is obtainable from iron pyrites and copper mines, its presence being characterised by a small as of rotten eggs. Sulphur spings also occur in many parts in the district.

Bitumen

The brownish-white natural sulphate of alumina known as *shilajit* is found in rocks at a fairly high altitudes and occurs in small lumps which generally have an admixture of red sand and micaceous stone embedded in them. It is used in Ayurvedic medicines and during the season when there is an influx of pilgrims, it fetches good incomes to those who deal in it.

Some other minerals found in the district are antimony, arsenic, lignite or brown marble, mica and silver.

Physiographically the district, which lies in a region of tectonic or folded and overthrust mountain chains, has strata which are structurally minded by complex folds, reverse faults, overthrusts and nappes of great dimension, all these as well as frequent earthquakes of varying intensify give reason to believe that the region is still unstable. Although any movement or tremor of the earth's crust in the district is not produced by volcanic activity, the Chaukhamba peaks appear to be the crater of an extinct volcano.

Climate

As the elevation of the district ranges from 1,200 m. to 8,000 m. above sea-level, the climate of the district very largely depends on altitude. The winter season is from about mid-November to March. As most of the region is situated on the southern slopes of the outer Himalayas, mansoon currents can enter through the valleys, the rainfall being heaviest in the monsoon from June to September.

Rainfall

Most of the rainfall occurs during the period June to September when 70 to 80 per cent of the annual precipitation is accounted for in the southern half of the district and 55 to 65 per cent in the northern half. In association with depressions from the Bay of Bengal which occasionally affect the weather in the district in September, heavy rains may occur causing floods. At time during the monsoon spurts of heavy rain cause floods in the river. Considerable precipitation also occurs during the winter months, about 15 to 30 per cent occurring in the northern half of the district and 10 to 15 per cent in the southern. About 8 per cent of the annual rainfall occurs during April and May. July and August are the rainiest months and November the month with the least rainfall. Precipitation during winter is associated with the passage of western disturbances and is mostly in the form of snow particularly at higher elevations. Premonsoon rainfall is accompanied frequently with thunderstorms. Considering the period from 1901 to 1950 the total number of years when the rainfall was less than 80 per cent of the normal was 11 at Joshimath, 8 at Bironkhal, 7 at Karnaprayag and 6 at Ukhi Math, Joshimath and Karnaprayag, a spell of 3 and one of 4 consecutive years of such low rainfall being registered at Joshimath only. The records of rainfall are more representative of the river valleys where the 7 rain-gauge stations in the district are located. The details of the rainfall up to 1963 reveal that the highest annual rainfall was in 1924, when it amounted to 198 per cent of the normal and the lowest in 1943 when it amounted to 53 per cent. The heaviest rainfall in 24 hours recorded in the district was 255.3 mm. at Bironkhal on September 29, 1924.

The rains usually break earlier than in the plains, heavy showers apparently of local origin, accompanied by northerly and westerly winds, frequently occuring about the same time as the monsoon reaches Bombay. The scouring action of these early showers on the dried up and pulverous soils very great, and the damage done by erosion, in spite of the comparative smallness of the fall, is usually much greater than at any other time of the year.

Temperature

The details of temperature recorded at the meteorological observatories in the district which are situated in the valley show that the highest temperature in the district was 32.8°C on June 15, 1958, and the lowest-16.7°C on December 31, 1962. January is the coldest month after which the temperatures begin to rise till June or July. Temperatures vary with elevation. The mean maximum and the mean minimum temperatures during the warmest months were recorded as being of the order of 27°C and 2°C respectively at an altitude of 2 km. and 9°C and -12°C at a height of 6 km. above sea-level. During the winter cold waves in the wake of western disturbances may cause temperatures to fall appreciably. Snow accumulation in valleys in considerable.

Humidity

The relative humidity is high during the monsoon season, generally exceeding 70 per cent on the average. The driest part of the year is the premonsoon period when the humidity may drop to 35 per cent during the afternoon at certain high stations. The highest and lowest percentages of humidity, based on available data up to 1963, in the district were 94 and 32 respectively.

Cloudiness

Skies are heavily clouded during the monsoon months and for short spells when the region is affected by the passage of western disturbances. During the rest of the year the skies are generally clear to lightly clouded.

Winds

Owing to the nature of terrain, local effects are pronounced and when the general prevailing winds are not too strong to mask these effects, there is a tendency for diurnal reversal of winds, the flow being anabatic during the day and katabatic at night, the latter being of considerable force.

Flora

The flora of the district mostly include the vast series found in the Himalayas and ranges from the sub-tropical pine to the Alpine pastures. The total forest area in the district under the management of the forest department in 1964-65 was 5,08,691 hectares of which an area of 2,85,392 hectares was class I forest and an area of 2,23,299 hectares was class II forest. There are some other forests which are under the management of the panchayats, but the figures of their area are not available. The forest of the district can be divided into the following botanical divisions.

Himalayan Sub-tropical Pine

These forest are found between the heights of 910 m. and 1,825 m. throughout the district. The trees which are commonly found in these forests are *Anyar, Caryotexis wallichii, Rubus ellipticus, Rhus semialata, Laptodermis lancolata* and *Desmodium* sanense on the northern aspect of the hills; *Hamiltoni suaveolens. Engelhardia calebrooki, Ficus roxburghii, Indigofera dosua, Desmondium gyrans* and *Piectranthuis terrifolius* on both the northern and southern aspects, while *aonla, dhaula, Celerodandron serrotum, Bauhinia variegata, Bohemeria nogulosa, Wendlandia exserta, Indigofera pulchella* and *Phus parviflora* are met with on the southern aspect of the hills.

Moist Temperate Seral Forests

These forests are found between the altitudes of 1,200 m. and 2,150 m. along the streams and the newly formed beds with undergrowth of *Sarcococca preuniformus* spp. *Barberis* spp. and *Ainslea aptera* specially in the western part of Joshimath and the eastern part of Karnaprayag tahsils.

Banj Oak Forests

These forests are found between the heights of 1,825 m. and 2,450 m. but at places their limits ascend up to 2,600 m. on the southern aspect and descend to 1,200 m. on the northern aspect of the hills. Trees commonly met with in these forests are *burans, anyar, Carpinus viminea* and *Ilex odorala.* In moist places the ground is covered with shrubby undergrowth of *Ainslea aptera, Barberis, Hypericum, Desmodium* and *Indigofera.* Near the habitations, *banj* suffers extensively from lopping fire occurring in its stunted growth, while burans and anyar are not so affected.

Oak Scrub Forests

These forests are found in the localities of *banj* oak forests near the habitations. Sometimes due to excessive damage, *banj* oak is replaced by scattered bushes of *Barberis Chitriya, Basiatice* and *Cretargus cronulata.*

Tilonj Forests

These forests are found between the same altitudes as those of the oak and are associated with the *Laurancea, Ilex, Betula alnoides,* etc. The shrubby undergrowth consists of *Rubus spirea, Indigofera* and *Ainslea aptera.*

Lower Blue Pine Forests

These forests are found between the heights of 1,825 m. and 2,600 m. specially in tahsil Chamoli and Karnaprayag having *Euscholtzia polistachya, Vibumum foctens, Rosa microphylla, Vibumum contonifolium, Exaecarea acerifolia,* etc. as shrubby undergrowth.

Dry Coniferous Forest

On deep soils between the altitude of 1,825 m. and 2,600 m., over a small area on all aspects except the steep southern slopes with quartizitic subsoils, mainly deodar is found associated with *Kharasu, akhrot, kharik, syan* and *maira.* The undergrowth consists of shrubs such as *Abeliatriflora, Sumiperus, Macropoda, Prunus jacqumontii, Ribes grosulaia* and *Rosa sericea,* the shrubby undergrowth consisting of *Achyranthes bidentata* and *Aralia cissifolia.*

Moist Temperate Decidous Forests

These forests are found on deep moist soils between the heights of 1,825 m. and 2,750 m. along hill streams. The top canopy consists of *pangar, kanchula, maira sour, akhrot, dalla* and *kabasi,* the shrubby undergrowth consisting of *Viburum spirea, Sorbiflora Barberis* spp. *Strobilanthas wallichii*, etc.

Cypress Forests

These forests are found between the heights of 2,125 m. and 2,600 m. on rocky slopes and precipitous ground mixed with *tilongi kali, Corpinus ninerea, Eunonimus pendulus, Ilex, Machiusduttii,* etc.

Kharasu Forests

The Kharasu forests are found between the heights of 2,450 m. and 3,500 m. mixed with *kanchula, pangar, saur* and *burans*. The shrubby undergrowth consists of *Rosa scricea, Rosa macrophylla Viburum joeten, Contoneaster ocuminate, Ribes glacraia* and *ringats.*

Western Oak Forests

These forests are commonly found on the southern aspect of the hills between the altitudes of 2,450 m. and 2,900 m mixed with *kharasu, tilonj, pangar, kanchula, kabasi,* etc. the chief under growth being *Rhamnus purpurrea, Wickstroemia cancacenda, Rosa macrophylla, Skimmia bursola, Rubus niveus.* Among creepers which are found here and *Vitis scmicrodala, Schizandras grandiflora* and *Hedera heliz.*

Dry Temperate Deciduous Forests

These forests consisting of *kabasi* trees are found between the heights of 2,450 m. and 2,750 m. in the northern part of the district, *Lonicara* supp. and *Rosa serecea* the shrubby undergrowth.

Temperature Hippophae Scrub Forests

These forests, consisting of *ames* scrubs, are found between the heights of 2,275 m. and 3,200 m. of gravel beds along the banks of the streams mixed with *gadbhains.*

Kharak Forests

The forests are found above the altitude of 2,215 mt. and have practically no tree growth except the *Rumex nepalens* undergrowth.

Ringal Forests

These occur above a height of 2,425 m. mixed with high level oak and coniferous trees.

Alpine Fir Birch Forests

These grow better between the heights of 2,900 m. and 2,500 m. in all aspects of the hills except in the moist area. The plants growing in these forests are fir, birch and Rhododendron. The undergrowth consists of *Pyrus folilosa, Cotoneaster acuminata, Rolsericea, Ribes glaciala, Ribes rubrum, Lonicera spp.* and *Smilex vagnia*

Birch-Rhododendrons Forests

These forests are found between the altitudes of 2,900 m. and 4,125 m. and in them are found the *bhuj* and Rhododendrons with *Pyrus foliolose* as 90 per cent of the under growth. Other plants which grow here are *Rubus-nivesus, Swilax vaginal Cotoneaster* spp. *Lonicera* spp. and *Pologorum vaccinifolium.*

Alpine Scrub Forests

Between the altitudes of 3,350 m. and 4,275 and with a rainfall above 1,016 mm. evergreen scrubs are found consisting of *Rhododendron asthopogeu, Junipexus recurvu, J. communis, Locera parviflora,* etc. In the dry inner ranges having a rainfall less than 255 mm grow exeophytic dwarf shrubs consisting of *Eurotia ceratoides, junipexus pseudosabina, J. communis, Caranga* spp. and *Artimisia* spp.

Alpine Pastures

Between the heights of 2,050 m. and 2,975 m. on the northern aspect of the hills and between the altitudes of 2,500 m. and 4,425 m. on the southern aspect of the hills the land is covered with shortgrasses and herbs, which are used as pasture where professional graziers bring their cattle.

Other Forests

In the warm valleys of the extreme southern part of the district some species of trees of the plains such as the mango, *Jamun, pipal,* banyan and *shisham* grow here and there up to an altitude of about 915 m. The sal, which is found up to a height of 1,220 m. is seldom seen north of the river Pindar but it is usually not allowed to stand near cultivated tracts because it is said to attract white ants. The *tun* and the *kharik*, or *kharak* are to be seen growing up to an elevation of about 1,250 m. which is also suitable for the growth of *haldu* and *dhauri.* Carefully protected by the cultivator on the *pugar* (terrace wall of a field), the leaves of the *bhyunl* tree afford excellent fodder for cattle.

In the Alaknanda valley, the bases, slopes, gorges and tops of the hills up to the height of 1,067 m. are well wooded with high trees such as catechu, *bahera, har* (or *harara*), *amaltas, bel, kachnar* and dhak. A large variety of creepers some of which have broad green leaves also thrive in the vicinity of the trees.

From about 1,220 m. to 1,829 m. *chir* abounds and above this level oak and *chimul* are found; the former being a hard wood, is used for making agricultural implements and the latter for fuel. The *chir* wood is commonly used for building purposes in the district, and its logs and sleepers are floated down the Alaknanda to the plains. *Chir* is also tapped for resin but the quantity of turpentine produced in the district is small.

Above an elevation of 3,439 m. *moru* or *tilonj* and *kharasu* grow and their timber is also used for manufacturing agricultural implements. The pangar or horse-chestnut and the maple are found up to a height of 3,048 m., especially in the Riniganga valley. The wood of the latter is used for making drinking vessels and bowls known as *lahauri-doba.*

Spruce, silver-fir, *kail* and *kharasu*, oak and some trees of small economical value are the principal trees found in the forests of the upper Himalayas (above 3,018 m.). Fine forests of silver-fir, kail and pine occupy the slopes on the left bank of the Alaknanda from Pipalkoti to Joshimath. The *Surai* of Himalaya sypress and the Himalayan cedar forests which lie along the Alaknanda in *patti* Talla Painkhanda and the Neoza pine forests near Tapoban along the Dhauli, are fairly extensive and have trees of *thuner* (yew), *papari* (boxwood), *Kharasu* and deodar. The birch grows up to an elevation of about 3,658 m. above which lies an expanse covered with bush and grass variegated in summer by Alpine flowers of many colours. The places of the richest vegetation are between the elevations of 2,134 m. and 3,658 m. where the epiphytic form of flora, ferns, mosses, creepers and many varieties of flowers make the region beautiful especially after the rainy season. *Colquhounia* is abundant on the main Badrinath and Trisul ranges and *ringals* from the undergrowth of the forests up to an altitude of 2,286 m.

Many medicinal blooms, herbs and plants, greatly valued in Ayurveda grow in the district. Most of the flowers and plants come up during the rains but wither away from October to May, imparting the characteristic brown colour to the countryside during the winter. In there parts *Senecio rufinervis*, a perennial herb forms a dense undergrowth to the exclusion of most other plants. Aromatic plants are also found in abundance at higher altitudes. The groves in the district covering an area of 430.72 hectares are mostly in the warm deep southern valleys and consist chiefly of mango, guava, banana, papaya and jackfruit trees, but apple, pear, peach, plum, apricot, cherry, chestnut, mulberry, strawberry, litchi and loquat also florish. Other cultivated trees of the district include species of citron of which the chief are malta, orange, lime, sweet-lime, and orange which, though thriving in the warm valleys, can also be grown up to a height of about 1,677 m. The vine is raised in groves where the rains are not to heavy.

The chief varieties of timber trees found in the groves of the district are pine, tun, deodar and many varieties of walnut. The timber of the deodar trees is considered to be sacred and is noted for durability and resisting insect pests and dry rot. It is in great demand for making doors and roofs of temples. In the past a very fine grove of the deodars surrounded the Binsar temple in the south-western extremity of tahsil Karnaprayag.

Fauna

The district is rich in fauna and has been the habitat, from time immemorial, of a large variety of mammals, various species of birds, reptiles and fish. In the *Mahabharata* there is mention of deer-hunting in this area by Pandu, the father of the Pandavas, who is said to have taken up his abode at Pandukeshwar. During the Muslim times some Muslims were settled in this area by the local rulers as royal *shikaris*. They prepared food for his distinguished Muslim guests. About the middle of the nineteenth century many villages were deserted because of the dread of wild animals including tigers and leopards for whose destruction the government offered rewards. Tigers are found up to an elevation of about 3,048 m. and in the past haunted the big forests of Chandpur and Dudhatoli, occasionally reaching the thick forests of Vasuki and Tungnath and were seen even near the snow range of Kedarnath. Leopards have been shot in large numbers for decades in many parts of the district. The number of wild animals has considerably decreased on account of their destruction and the thinning of the forests which are being cleared for cultivation and other purpose such as schemes of development.

Among the animals of the district are the tiger, leopard, panther, snowleopard, Himalayan black bear, brown bear, wild dog, *chutraila* or pine marten and Himalaya weasel. The first is found throughout the district and is extremely dangerous when it becomes a man-eater. The snow leopard which is met with at higher altitudes above the tree line, some 3,658 m to 3.963 m above sea-level, hunts at night, preying on wild sheep and goats, musk-deer and marmots. Like other beasts of prey its movements are regulated by those of its prey. It is hunted for its valuable fur. The black Himalayan bear is common in the district and is found up to a height of 915 m. It frequently plunders wild beehives, for their honey and is a serious menance to the crops particularly at the time of harvest and occasionally becomes carnivorous killing goats and sheep and even cattle. It is fond of *mandua,* the local variety of millets, and fruit and in consequence causes serious damage to fields and orchards. The brown bear is rare and is known to live on the bare open peaks high above the tree line in the watershed of the Mandakini and Kailganga. Fearing and avoiding human beings it does not become a man-eater but often becomes a terror to live-stock. Myopic and hard of hearing but possessing a keen sense of smell like all bears, the black type is likely to be surprised at close quarters. Taken unawares, it rushes to furious attack in self-defence and is very dangerous, several cases of its having maulled people have been reported. Wild does are generally seen in the forests of the Pindar valley and Dudhatoli. The *otter (ud)* is found in the waters of the Pindar. Caps are made of its skin and its fur, worn round the neck, is considered to be efficacious in curing goitre. Other wild animals to be seen in the district are the hyaena, jungle cat, wolf, jackal, porcupine and mountain fox. The wild-bear is widely distributed in the district and is found up to a height of 2,743 m., chiefly in the oak forests. Living on crops, roots, insects, offal and carrior it is highly prolific and is most destructive to agricultural cropes, orchards and forest plantations. The goral or Himalayan chamois, serow and that are widely distributed between the elevation of 2,131 m. and 3,658 m. The flesh of the animals which have horns, specially that of the male, is valued by the hill people. The bharal which lives on grassy slopes between the heights of 3,048 m. and 4,572 m. is prized for its skin. The Himalayan marmot of the seiuriod family (order *rodentia*) is one of the mammals that lives at the highest altitudes usually favouring an elevation between 3,963 m. and 5,487 m. and is valued for its fur. Among the deer tribe the sambar or *jarao, kakar* (barking deer) and *kastura* (musk-deer) are the only members of the *cervidae* family which are represented in the district. The first, a massive beast living in the dense forests of the district, does a great deal of damage to cereal crops, particularly during winter in high altitudes up to 3,048 m., and the second, which derives its name from its cry, which is like the bark of a dog and is usually heard in the mornings and evenings, is a graceful animal and is harmless. Both these have food value. The *kastura,* which is a protected animal through-out the state and is seldom found below 2,439 m. is the rarest animal of the district. It occurs in the difficult and inaccessible areas of tahsils Ukhi Math and Joshimath and in the catchment area of the Kailganga in tahsil Karnaprayag. The male musk-deer yields musk which is a valuable article of commercial importance.

Birds

The district is particularly rich in avifauna and the birds found here are mostly of the same kinds as those occurring throughout the Himalayan region. Birds of prey such as eagles, falcons, hawks and vultures and very common. Formerly hunters living in the neighbourhood of Joshimath earned considerable amounts from the sale of hawks captured in their aeries and *baz-bina* (hawk's musk) was a regular item of revenue taken in kind under the Hindu rulers and the Gurkhas. Among the game birds, the most common are the *ban titar, Kala titar* (black partridge) and *chakor,* the last named being found right up to the snowline (above Niti). The *junguria* or *karmonal* (snow partridge), which is found above the tree line and below the snowline on steep and rocky ground breeds throughout the altitudes it inhabits between 3,048 m. to 4,572 m. above sea-level. It is reported to be the finest game bird for the table. The horned pheasant, which is really more a partridge than a pheasant, is represented by the *lungi* or *lunji* and the *jawar*. Both the species which breed in May and June at elevations between 2,439 m. and 3,353 m., have maginificent males with beautiful plumage. Other important birds of this family are the *chir* or Chir pheasant, *pukras, pokras* or *koklas* (Kokla pheasant) locally called *kaleej* or *murga* (white-crested Kalij) The last, occurring up to an altitude of abour 2,439 m., is the commonest of all and an excellent game bird. The *monal* is found in forests between 2,439 m. and 3,658m. in height particularly where there are birch trees. The cock is valued for its brilliant and attractive plumage while the young bird is considered good for the table but is one of the protected species in the state. All the interesting members of this family *(Phasianidae)* found in the district except the peafowl are some of the prettiest birds of India.

Among the protected non-game birds, the chief are the common king fisher. White-breasted king-fisher, pied king-fisher, blue-jay or Indian roller, black-headed oriole, small cuckoo, Indian cuckoo and Eurpoean cuckoo. The Indian scarlet minivet which is an unprotected non-game bird belonging to the *pericrocotidar* family looks very beautiful when on the wing. A rare member of the *phononodidae* family, seen near Amsor in tahsil Karnaprayag in February, 1966, was perhaps a white bulbul, the most attractive among the bulbul species and, perhaps, a migratory bird. Other birds which are commonly found in the district are the common swallow, pied wagtail, ashy wren-warbler, Indian wren-warbler, Alpine swift, house swift, parakeet, rock-pigeon and Himalayan woodpecker.

Reptiles

Snakes are somewhat rare in the district but the cobra and the Russel's viper or necklace snake are common and they may be found up to a height of 1,829 m., the latter being viviparous and nocturnal in its habits. The only hill snake found above 2,439 m. is *Ancistrodoń Himalayans* which attains a length of about 62 cm., and is venomous though its bite is not fatal. Among the non-venomous snakes the *charao* (rock-snake) which may grow to a length, of about 9 m. although specimens over 6 m. in length are rare, is occasionally seen on the rocky slopes of the lower hills. The python, a protected species, has been found as far up as the slopes below the Tungnath range in tahsil Ukhi Math. The rat-snake which attains a length of about 3 m., is common it does not bite but strikes its victim with its tail, the flesh of the part so struck decaying. Non-poisonous snakes also sometimes occur in the tanks near the temple of Trijugi Narain and to be touched by them is considered auspicious by Hindu pilgrims who bathe in these tanks. About 10 species of lizards inhabit this region and can be seen basking in the sun on rocks. Of these the blood-sucker (which grows to a length of about 35 cm.) is harmless in spite of its name. The bull-frog and common toad, both amphibians, are met with throughout the district.

Large and varied groups of insects are found in the district and some, such as the snow-fly, thrive in the glaciers. The leech, which is particularly active during the rains, is of common occurrence in oak forests. In May and June swarms of flies are to be seen all along the route up to Gulabkoti, the *mora,* a small stinging fly, is also found in the district and causes small painful sores.

Fish

Fish abound in almost all streams of the district and riparian villagers find in it an important supplement to their ordinary food. The common species found here are *asela* or *saul, mahasher, kalabans* or *karanuch* and *fucta* or *phar kata.* Other species found in the district include *gadara, gadiyal* or *guluwa, tarra, symplu* and *nama, nawoo* or *japa,* The *Cyprinus carpio var specularis* variety of the mirror carp has been introduced into the Diuri Tal in tahsil Ukhi Math.

Game-laws

Shooting is prohibited in the religious centres of the district. The general rules regulating hunting, shooting, and fishing in the reserved forests of the district are governed by the Indian Forest Act, 1927, Indian Forest (U.P. Amendment) Act, 1951 and The Wild Birds and Animals Protection Act, 1912 as amended by the U.P. Act XIII of 1934.

SUPPLEMENTARY INFORMATION
1971 CENSUS

Area	9,125 sq. km.
Population	
Total	2,92,571
Males	1,41,962
Females	1,50,609
Percentage of population in rural area – 95.8	
Position in the State – 53rd.	
Sub-divisions, Tahsils and Thanas	
Joshimath	
Total Population	22,196
Males	13,484
Females	8,712
Number of villages	93
Number of towns	2
Ukhi Math	
Total Population	64,757
Males	30,886
Females	33,871
Number of villages	327
Chamoli	
Total Population	83,802
Males	40,740
Females	43,062
Number of villages	417
Number of towns	1
Karnaprayag	
Total Population	1,21,816
Males	56,852
Females	61,964
Number of villages	812

History

The region covered by the district of Chamoli formed part of the district of Pauri Garhwal of the Kumaon Division till 1960. It occupies the north-eastern corner of the Garhwal tract and lies in the central or mid-Himalayas in the very heart of the snowy range described in ancient books as Bahirgiri, one of the three divisions of the Himalayan mountains,[1] The region lay in the Udichya-dishi (northern quarters) of Bharatavarsh (India)[2] and was included in Aryavarta and Brahmarshidesha.[3] Tehri Garhwar, Garhwal and Almora have been celebrated in ancient Indian literature as Kedar Kshetra and Hindu kingdoms of Brahmapura, Kumaon and Garhwal flourished here. According to another tradition the Himalayan country is said to be made up of five divisions one of which is Kedar-Khanda, which has been specifically dealt with in the Kedara-Khanda section of the *Skanda Purana,*[4] where it is said, 'it surpassed all the tirthas and it is a land where nature stands personified. It is the sum total of all the *tirthas* on earth. There is no place on this fair earth which can compare to this holy land.' The district lies in this division, which is further divided into Kedara-kshetra and Badri-kshetra, known after their presiding deities, Kedarnath and Badrinath, respectively.[5] The area covered by the district has formed part of what was known at different times as Kuninda-vishaya, Kiratamandala, Khasamandala, Baoni, Garhvana, Garhpal or Garhwal.[6]

No palaeolithic finds have been obtained from the district but the existence of some burial mounds of a peculiar type containing pieces of early painted pottery like dishes and bowls has been reported from the neighbourhood of the village of Malari in the Dhauli valley, pargana Painkhanda.[7] The copper implements associated with the earlier inhabitants of the upper Ganga-Yamuna doab, whom the Aryans encountered on their arrival,[8] may have been made of copper obtained from the mines in this district. Among the archaeological remains may be mentioned the celebrated old temples of Badrinath and Kedarnath; the ruins of sixteen old temples at Adibadri, and of the fort of Chandpurgarhi with two flights of steps each formed of one solid block of stone built by the early rajas of Garhwarl; the fine old temple repaired and restored about the beginning of the 19th century at Gopeshwar with an iron trident (about 5 m high.) bearing an old inscription, standing in its courtyards; a collection of temples bearing marks of great antiquity at Joshimath with religious sculptures, some of a superior style of workmanship, and some said to be the hand-work of Bactrian-Greek artists; the ruins of temples at Karnaprayag on both the sides of the confluence there and at the nearby village of Simali; the four copper-plate grants of the ancient Katyurirajas preserved till recently in the old temple at Pandukeshwar; and a number of shrines, caves and rocks pointed out as being associated with ancient sages, heroes or mythological personages mentioned in the *Puranas*.[9]

Legends and folk tales and names of certain places such as Jakh, Jakhu and Jakhini, probably derived from the terms Yaksha,[10] point to the association of this region with the legendary Yakshas. Other legends connect the region with the Asuras. They were the Dasas or Dasyur of Vedic literature who came in conflict with the Aryans in the course of letter's expansion in norther India.[11] The Nagas were yet another early people who inhabitated parts of the district, particularly the Alaknanda valley which was probably known in their times as Nagaloka. Places like Nagpur, Nagnath and Urgam, from *uraga*, a variety of snake, the celebrated Naga shrines such as those of Sheshanaga in Pandukeshwar Takshaka naga in Dasoli, Vasuki and Pushkar Nagas in Nagpur, Worchanaga in Urgam and Lohandianaga in Jelam, and the Nagaraja-tok (a non-descript) Naga shrine found in or near many villages are reminiscent of the Nagas.[12] The Kulindas and Kiratas are also reported to have been inhabitants of this region.[13] The Tanganas, whose memory is preserved in the name of the *chatti* (halting place) known as Tangani, between Chamoli and Joshimath, and in the term *tanghana* used for sturdy hill ponies, were probably a branch of the Khasas by whom they were subsequently absorbed.[14] The Khasasa are by far the most important of the old inhabitants of the district,[15] their servitors or menials coming to be known as Doms, now usually given the more honourable appellation Shilpkar of artisan.[16] In the early centuries of the Christian era a branch of the Sakas is alleged to have come to the district where it settled down ultimately fusing with the Khasa.[17] The Hunas seem to have infiltrated into the district from Tibet which is still called Hunadesha and its inhabitants Huniyas, by the people of the district. From about this time the Rajputs, Brahmanas, Vaishs and Shudras from the plains also began to immigrate to and settle down in the district.

The Indo-Aryan race learned to look up to these Himalayan heights with an extraordinary awe and reverence almost from the earliest times in their history. Ancient Indian literature (Brahmanical, Jain and Buddhist) has depicted the Kumaon-Garhwal Himalayas in general and the region covered by the present district of Chamoli in particular as the vertiable abode of devas and rishis, the holiest of the holy regions and a paradise on earth.[18] Most of the principal gods and goddesses of the Hindu patheon, a majority of the incarnations of Vishnu, all the greater rishis, some of the *tirthankaras* and some of the Buddhas and a number of great emperors, heroes, learned men and celebrated devotes are in some way associated with this region about which there is no dearth of legends and traditions and which has ever had a powerful human appeal. Brahma, Vishnu and

Siva (The Hindu trinity) are intimately connected with this area. Brahma is said to have started the process of creation here and to have resided on Mount Meru, variously identified with the Satopanth, Chaukhambha or Gandhmadan massifs of the district. Vishnu is believed to have had his foremost abode *(dhama)* at Badrikashrama (Vishalapuri) in the middle of the forest, Badri-vana, where he is worshipped under the name of Badrinath, Badrinarayana or Badrivishala, the valley of the Alaknanda from Satopanth, about 24 km. beyond Badrinath, up to Nand Prayag in the south being known specifically as the Badri-kshetra in which lie the Pancha-badri, the five places sacred to Badri or Vishnu-Adbadri near Karnaprayag, Vridhabadri at Animath, between Pipalkoti and Joshimath, Bhavishyabadri at Subhain, beyond Tapoban, Yogabadri at Pandukeshwar and Vishalabadri at Badrinath.[19] Of the incarnations of Vishnu, the fish, the tortoise, the bear, Narayana, Narsimha, Vamana, Parashurama, Rama and Krishna are associated with this region. Siva is by far the most preferred and perhaps the oldest deity of the district. His original local name seems to have been Kedar. The term Siva is also said to have originated in this region which contains more Saiva emblems and shrines than Vaishnava.[20] Siva's many connections with these hills as set out in the Puranas–such as his permanent abode in Mount Meru or in Kailas, his consort Parvati being the daughter of Himachala (personification of the snow range), his sons Karttikeya and Ganesa having been born and nurtured here and his most famous temple (one of the twelve Jyotirlingas) being Kedarnath–make him virtually the god of the people of these parts.[21] The entire Garhwal region being known as Kedar-Khanda after him and a portion, roughly the western half of the Chamoli district, being known as Kedar-kshetra or Kedar-mandala which has within its bounds the Panch-kedar, the five spots or shrines sacred to him, Kedarnath, Tungnath, Rudranath, Madhyamaheshwar and Kalpeshwar.[22]

Vishnu, in the form of the divine fish is said to have steered to safety Manu's ship with the seven great rishis and other surviving creatures aboard to a spot called Naubandhana on the Mana ridge in the extreme north of the district which with the Mana village is believed to have been named after Manu.[23] Narayana, the fist human avatar of Vishnu is also believed to have been born, with his twin-brother Nara, to Kashyapa's son Dharma and Daksha's daughter Matamurti at what is now called Badrinath which is for this reason also called Narayana-kshetra, the two peaks on either side of Badrinath still being called the Nara and Narayana peaks. Narada, the divine ministrel, bard and sage, was a great devotee of Narayana and made this region his permanent abode by reason of which it is also called Narada-kshetra, a tank called Narada-kunda and a rock in its vicinity called Narada-shila also being located near Badrinath.[24]

Rishabhadev or Adinatha, the first *tirthankara* of the Jain tradition. who is believed by the Jains to have been the harbinger of human civilization and the first to preach dharma to mankind, is said to have come to these parts with many of his disciples, to have practised austerities here and to have moved on to Kailas where he attained nirvana. Bharata his son, who is said to have been the first paramount sovereign of the earth, came here to pay homage to him and to celebrate the occasion of his training nirvana.[25] The Jains believe that the principal idol in the Badrinath temple was originally that of a *tirthankara* and they come to this place on pilgrimage. The Buddhists also visit the temple assuming the image to be that of the Buddha. Several peaks and rivers of the district are as much celebrated in the Jain and Buddhist traditions as in the Hindu.[26]

According to Hindu tradition the earliest king of the district seems to have been Kubera, the lord of the Yakshas, who ruled from the beautiful city of Alakapuri which is supposed to have been located in the north of the district on the glacier of the same name from which the Alaknanda takes its rise. Ancient Indian literature, both religious and classical, has numerous reference to him, his Yakshas, Kinnarasa, Gandharvas and Apsaras, his Alakapuri, his pleasure-garden, the Nandan-kanana, identified by some with the famous valley of flowers' of the district and his fabulous wealth.[27]

The Yakshas appear to have been superseded by the Asuras some of whose earlier chiefs were Sahasrakavacha, Raktabija and Mahishasura. According to local tradition the Rakshasa King Ravana alias Dashamauli (ten-headed) is said to have resided for some time at Dasoli, which is supposed to be named after him and to have practised penance at Tungnath.[28] Local tradition also has it that Shambara, the powerful Asura king who was a formidable opponent of the early Aryans and possessed 90 or 99 strong forts or fortified cities, belonged to the Garhwal-Kumaon Himalayas. He fought against Divodasa and Sudasa, the Tritsu (or Bharata) kings of Panchala, for 40 years, the fact being alluded to at a number of places in the Rigveda.[29] Banasura was another powerful Asura chief who seems to have principally ruled over what is now the pargana of Nagpur in tahsil Ukhi Math, Bamsu being said to be named after him, Lamgodi being supposed to mark the site of his capital Shonitapura and Ukhi Math being said to be the place of residence of his daughter, Usha. Usha's love affair with Aniruddha, Krishna's grandson, led to a fierce fight between Krishna and Banasura in which the latter was killed,[30] the dynasty probably coming to an end with him.

REFERENCES

1. *Mahabharata,* Sabha-parva, ch. 27, v. 3; Bhishma-parva, ch. 9, vv. 49-50; Datar, B.N.: *Himalayan Pilgrimage,* pp. 7-8.
2. Majumdar, R.C. and Pusalker, A.D. (Ed.): *The History and Culture of the Indian People,* Vol. 1, p. 252
3. *Ibid;* Avasthi, G.C: *Veda-dharatala,* pp. 50, 53, Macdonell, A.A. and Keith, A.B. : *Vedic Index of Names and Subjects,* Vol. II, pp. 125-126.
4. Raturi, H.K. *Garhwal-ka-Itihasa,* p. 1; Bahadur, Raj P.R. : *Garhwal Ancient and Modern,* p. 14; Atkinson, E.T.: *The Himalayan Districts of the North-Western Provinces of India,* Vol. II, pp. 323-350
5. Nautiyal, G.P.: *Gall of Badrinath,* (1962), p. Bahadur, *op. cit.,* pp. 12-13
6. *Ibid.,* pp. 13, 188; Datar, *op. cit.,* p. 12; Nautiyal, *op. cit.,* p. 4
7. Dabral, S.P.: *Uttarakhand-ka-Itihasa,* Vol. II, pp. 24, 70-80, 98; Ancient India, *(Bulletin of the ASI),* pp. 9, p. 54
8. *Ibid,* pp. 71, 91-93
9. Further, A.: *Monumental Antiquities and Inscriptions in the North-Western Provinces and Oudh,* pp. 44-46; *Indian Archaecology, 1956-57—A Review,* p. 63: Atkinson, op. cit., Vol. III, pp. 1, 23, 25, 167-168, 325, 372-373, 394, 556, 651-652: District Statistics to Vol. XXXVI—*Garhwal District,* C. Vol. (1925), p. 14; Dabral, *op cit.,* pp. 293-307.
10. *Ibid.,* pp. 109-110; Atkinson, op. cit., vol. II, pp. 297, 299-300, 348, 376, Sankratyayana, Rahul: *Kumaon,* pp. 20, 25
11. *Ibid.,* p. 31; Atkinson, *op. cit.,* Vol. II pp. 272, 280; Bahadur, *op. cit.,* pp. 71-74, 172
12. *Ibid.,* p. 71; Painuli, P.N.: *A Torist's View of the Valley of Gods,* pp. 31-32; Sankratyayana, *op. cit.,* pp. 25-26.
13. *Ibid.,* p. 26
14. *Ibid.,* pp. 26, 20-29
15. *Ibid.,* pp. 20, 26-30: Berreman, G.D.: *Hindus of the Himalayas,* pp. 14-19; Atkinson, *op. cit.,* Vol. II., pp. 269, 283, 362, 375-382
16. *Ibid.,* pp. 370-371: Berronan, *op. cit.,* pp. 20-21., Sankratyayana, *op. cit.,* p. 30
17. *Ibid.,* pp. 32-34
18. *Ibid.,* Vol. 11, p. 271: Oakley, E.S. : *Holy Himalaya,* pp. 130-131: Mukerjee, Padhar Kamal: *A History of Indian Civilization:* Vol. 1, p. 67
19. *Ibid.,*pp. 25-28; Atkinsep, *op. cit.,* Vol. II. pp. 284, 231; Nautiyal, *op. cit.,* pp. 4, 8-9
20. *Ibid.,* pp. 13-15; Bahadur, *op. cit.,* pp. 74, 169; Rerreman, *op. cit.,* pp. 104-107; Atkinson, *op. cit.,* Vol. II. pp. 301-307, 701, 720-722, 739-741
21. *Ibid.*
22. *Ibid.,* Vol. III, pp. 556-557; Nautiyal, *op. cit.,* pp. 13-14; Painuli, *op. cit.,* pp. 80-84
23. *Mahabharata,* Vana-parva, Ch. 187, v. 50; Avasthi, *op. cit.,* pp. 558-559; Munshi, K.M.: *To Badrinath,* p. 32.
24. *Ibid.,* pp. 26, 31, 32-33; Painuli, *op. cit.,* p. 115.
25. *Ibid.,* p. 133; Jinasena: *Adi Purana,* Parvas 33 and 47, Vol. II, pp. 132-137, 507-508; Datar, *op. cit.,* p. 50
26. *Ibid.,* pp. ix, 4, 12; Munshi, *op. cit.,* pp. 28-29; Nautiyal, *op. cit.,* p. 5; Painuli, *op. cit.,* p. 115: Bahadur, *op. cit.,* p. 10
27. Ibid., p. 46; Datar, *op. cit.,* pp. 13, 30; Nautiyal, *op. cit.,* pp. 11, 67-69; Munshi, *op. cit.,* pp. 8, 39; Painuli, *op. cit,* pp. 105, 128.
28. Bahadur, *op. cit.,* pp. 71, 73
29. Ibid., pp. 12, 71, 171-172; Sankratyayana, *op. cit.,* p. 31; Macdonell and Keith, *op. cit.,* Vol. I, p. 363: Vol. II, p. 354
30. Painuli, *op. cit.,* p. 79; Bahadur, *op. cit.,* p. 72

13

DEHRADUN DISTRICT

Origin of Name

The district is named after the headquarters town Dehra Dun. "Dehra" appears to be a corruption of *dera* signifying a temporary abode or camp. Ram Rai, guru of the Udasi Sikhs, on being ordered by Aurangzeb to retire to the wilderness of the Dun, had pitched his tents here in what is now the Khurbur locality of the town, and had also built a temple nearby Dhamawala. Around these two sites grew up the town popularly known as Dehra. The term *dun* or *doon* means the low-lands at the foot of a mountain range, and as the bulk of the district lies in such a tract, it justifies the *dun* part of the name. Another derivation of the term dun is stated to be from Dronashram, hermitage of *guru* Drona of the Kauravas and Pandavas of Mahabharata time, who sojourned for a season in the village of Dwara, six kos east of Dehra to perform his devotions at a lonely spot.

Location, Boundaries, Area and Population

Location and Boundaries

The district is situated in the north-western region of the state. It is bounded on the north by the Uttarkashi district, in the east by the districts of Uttarkhashi and Tehri Garhwal and in the south by the district of Saharanpur, at its extreme southern tip touching the boundary of district Bijnor. The eastern boundary of the district underwent a slight change in 1956 because of the transfer of two villages Tapoban and Dhalwala to the district of Tehri Garhwal. The western boundary of the district adjoining the Sirmur district of Himachal Pradesh with the rivers Tons and Yamuna separating the two.

Area

According to the surveyor general of India the area of the district was 3,106 sq. km. in 1961. According to the Central Statistical Organisation the district had an area of 3,088 sq. km. in 1971 and occupied 52nd position in the state in regards to size. For land utilisation purposes the area of the district, however, stood at 2,627.3 sq. km.

Population

According to census 1971 the district had a population of 5,77,306 (females 2,51,198), the rural population being 3,05,529 (females 1,36,840) and the urban 2,71,777 (females 1,14,358). The district stood 49th in the state in respect of population.

History of District as Administrative Unit

Originally the Dun formed part of the region mentioned as Kedar-khand in the *Skanda Purana.* By the 3rd century B.C. it was included in the kingdom of Asoka. The recorded history reveals that for centuries the tract formed a portion of the Garhwal kingdom with some interruptions from Rohillas and was under the occupation of the Gurkhas for about two decades, till 1815, when the entire territory between the Kali and the Satlaj, was annexed by the British. In that year the tract now comprising tahsil Dehra Dun was added to district Saharanpur. In 1825, however, it was transferred to the Kumaon Division. Up to this time the pargana of Janunsar Bawar was under the charge of the British resident at Delhi. In 1828, Dehra Dun and Jaunsar Bawar were placed under the charge of a separate Deputy Commissioner and in 1829, the Dehra Dun district was transferred from the Kumaon Division to the Meerut Division. Since then Jaunsar Bawar also seems to have been treated as an integral part of the Dehra Dun. In 1842 a resolution of government annexed the Dun to Saharanpur district and placed it in the charge of an officer, subordinate to the collector and magistrate of that district, with the title of Superintendent but since 1871 it is being administered as a separate district. No change of any importance appears to have occurred in the administrative history of the district till 1956 when the villages of Tapoban and Dhalwala of this district were transferred to district Tehri Garhwal. The district was included in the Meerut Division till 1968 when it was transferred to the Garhwal Division.

Sub-division, Tahsils and Thanas

Unlike other districts of the State the number of sub-division exceeds that of tahsils, the number of the former being three and that of the latter two. The tahsil of Chakrata is coterminous with the sub-division of the same name. The tahsil of Dehra Dun on the other hand, because of its two distinct topographics, has been split into the sub-divisions of Dehra Dun and Mussoorie, the former comprising the plains or the valley parts of the tahsil, and the latter the mountaneous ones.

According to the census of 1971 the tahsil of Dehra Dun covers an area of 2,363.4 sq. km and is divided into two sub-division called the Eastern Dun and the Western Dun. It includes the whole of the valley from the Yamuna to the Ganga, stretching southwards up to the crest of the Siwaliks and northwards to the outer ranges of the Himalayas. It is bounded on the east by the districts of Tehri Garhwal and Garhwal, on the south-west by the district of Saharanpur, on the north-west by Himachal Pradesh, on the north by tahsil Chakrata and part of district Tehri Garhwal. At its extreme southern tip it touches the boundary of district Bijnor. The population of the tahsil in 1971 was 4,98,178 (females 2,10,303).

Chakrata, the northern tahsil and subdivision of the district, is formed by the hill pargana of Jaunsar Bawar and is roughly an elliptical mass of mountains, stretching due north from the outer ranges of the Himalayas. The southern half of the tahsil is encircled by the Tons in the west and the Yamuna in the east and south. It covers an area of 263.9 sq. km. and is bounded on the north by the district of Uttarkashi, on the east by the districts of Uttarkashi and Tehri Garhwal, on the west by Himachal Pradesh and on the south it adjoins the Dehra Dun tahsil. The population of the tahsil in 1971 was 79,128 (females 31,875). The tahsil contains only one town namely Chakrata.

Thanas

For purposes of police administration, there are 9 police-stations in the district of which tahsil Dehra Dun has eight, and Chakrata one.

Topography

The district comprises two distinct tracts, themontane, which includes the

Chakrata tahsil, and the submontane, which includes the Dehra Dun tahsil.

Montane Tract

The tract consists entirely of a succession of mountains and gorges and comprises Jaunsar Bawar, the hilly pargana of the district with which it has physically and historically no connection. It is in shape roughly an oval with its major axis lying north and south. The great physical feature of the tract is the ridge separating the drainage area of the Tons from that of the Yamuna. It has several high peaks, and gives off several ridges on either side towards the great rivers. Even in the hills, Jaunsar Bawar has the character of being one of the wildest and most rugged tracts, affording naturally very little level ground, and that only in small patches. The mountains are peculiarly rough and precipitous and there is much eliff and rock and few village, so that cultivation is necessarily small and very labourious. The whole rock, almost, is limestone which no doubt gives a massy, irregular character to the mountains. The ravines are, as a rule, deep and sudden in their descent, often ending in dark chasms, sometimes wooded, but as often, exhibiting bare faces of preciptous rock, covered here and there with a finy wiry grass.

Sub-montane Tract

Below this montane tract lies the Dun proper, which is an open valley bounded by the Siwalik hills in the south, and the outer scarp of the Himalayas in the north.

The Dun is an irregular parallelogram in shape with its longer axis lying almost due north-west and south-east: and its existence as such is due to the presence of the Siwalik hills, as a well-marked range extending along the entire south-western border of the Dun. To the south they present a steep face scarred by frequent precipices. On the north a long gentle declivity slopes inwards and forms a longitudinal shallow valley terminated by the outer range of the Himalayas. The Siwaliks are in fact the obstacle which confines the detritus swept down by torrents from the greater mountains on the north, so that the resultant valley is considerably raised above the level of the great plains to the south. It is to this elevation of the land at their northern base that the Siwaliks owe their tame and insignificant appearance when viewed from a point within the Dun.

The drainage of the valley is borne by two rivers rising at no great elevation, a few kilometres south of Dehra, and flowing east into the

Ganga and west into the Yamuna respectively. The drainage fall is, therefore, not so abrupt as in similar formations where it is carried steeply through a break in the Siwaliks direct to the plains. The surface of the Dun undergoes constant changes. A multitude of torrents pours down from the Himalayan hills during the rainy season. They carry with them an immense volume of water, which continuously undermines their containing banks and thus the stream beds widen until they cover a very large space. The following year the torrent will select for its main channel a new portion of its wide bed, and the process of erosion will be carried on in a new direction.

The most striking physical features of the valley are the marvellous natural boundaries within which it is enclosed the Himalaya mountains, the Siwalik hills, and the rivers Ganga and Yamuna. The Himalayas and Siwaliks are always in view and can never be forgotten by the most casual visitor. The Ganga and Yamuna are not such conspicuous features in the landscape, and their rushing streams may only impress a close observer from their banks. But their names are as well known as the mountains from which they rise, and are inseparably connected with the history and religion of the peoples of India from the remotest times up to now. Of no other district in India can it be more truly said that the names of its boundaries are better known than the names of the district itself.

The Dun is apparently a single valley but in reality it belongs to two great river systems, those of the Ganga and the Yamuna. The water parting runs up to Majra and from therein an almost straight line through Dehra to Rajpur and Landour. Owing to the great amount of debris brought down from the incomparably greater drainage area of the Himalayas, the main drainage line is much nearer to the Siwaliks than the Himalayas. Therefore, the torrents from the latter range are more important than those from the former.

The Dun is well wooded and its surface is pleasantly diversified. The exception are the Nagsidh and Kalanga hills, both near Dehra. The beauty of the scenery has aroused the enthusiasm of many visitors. "The scenery of these mountain dales," writes the author of the Imperial Gazetteer, "can hardly be surpassed for picturesque beauty even among the lovely slopes of the massive chain to which they belong. The perenial streams nourish a fresh and luxuriant vegetation, whilst the romantic hills to the south and the sterner mountains on the north give an exquisite variety to the landscape". To quote the words of Baker, a former superintendent; "The general aspect of the Dun is perhaps better known than that of any other district in these provinces, and hence its beauties have attained a celebrity second only to Kashmir itself."

Eastern Dun

The Himalayas here rise abruptly from the valley and consequently there are fewer of the long sloping plateaux that form such a marked characteristic of the western sub-division. The surface of the centre of the valley is diversified by two isolated hills—Nagsidh, an off-shoot of the Siwaliks and Kalanga, an outlier of the lower Himalayas. Both these hills are divided from the parent ranges by river, the Nagsidh by the Suswa and the Kalanga hill by the Song.

Western Dun

The lower slopes of the Himalayas here rise at a more gentle gradient. The Asan drains the whole of the valley except the small portion to the extreme east which lies within the basin of Suswa. The Western Dun contains four well-defined tracts. The first, which may be called the river tract, comprises the land to the east of the Dehra-Asarori road lying round the source of the Suswa, and the shelving land on both sides of the Asan from its source to its confluence with the Yamuna. The second tract consists of the uplands on the crest of the ridge where the town of Dehra Dun stands—a fine, well irrigated and very fertile plateau defined by the Tons river on the west, the Asan and Suswa on the south and the Rispana on the east. The third is a similar triangle of rich land at the north-western extremity of the district watered by the Katapathar canal. Between these two and the north of riverain land fringing the Asan is the submontane tract. This consists of a striking series of parallel plateaux bounded on east and west by hill torrents. To the south, these plateaux slope gently down towards the Asan. The summits are occupied by village sites and stony unirrigated fields.

Mountains

The mountains of the district are the Himalaya and Siwalik ranges. These titles are misnomers. The term, 'Himalaya', is properly applied only to the highest range covered with eternal snow, while Indian writers have used the word Siwalik to designate the outer and lower ranges of the Himalayas as well as the quite distinct chain to which modern custom has limited the use of that name. The word Siwalik was formerly explained as being equivalent to 'Sawalakh', that is to say the range of 1,25,000 peaks. But it is now recognized as a derivation from the name of the god Siva, the presiding deity of the region. Simiarly, parts of the Dun are said to lie in the region particularly scared to that god, and known after his famous temple at Kedarnath as Kedarkhand.

The Siwaliks

The Siwaliks (to adopt the modern limited use of the name) extend along the entire southern border of the district, from the Yamuna to the Ganga, running parallel to the Himalayas. Some of the peaks even display in miniature all the features of the grandest mountains. In passing through them from the south one beholds an endless succession of sharp, towering peaks, nearly perpendicular precipices and a maze of little valleys. From the drainage line of the Asan and the Song-Suswan, the ground rises southward by uniformly easy slopes, when alone the gradient becomes steep. At the extreme south-east corner of the district where the range is pierced by the Ganga it expands into a mountain not known as the Motichur hill.

The Siwaliks nowhere present a well-defined single ridge. Numerous long and high subordinate ridges run out in every direction, very often sweeping suddenly round and assuming a direction parallel to the main ridge and by their size obscuring it, so that the chain of the Siwaliks at first sight appears to be an inextricably confused mass of ridges, spure and peaks. This peculiar conformation is most conspicuously developed in the western portion of the range.

The Siwalik range is quite distinct from the Himalayan system. Though its upheaval was accompanied by movements of the Himalayan mountain themeselves and probably by increase in the latter's elevation, yet the Siwalik range is of more recent formation and is perhaps the most recently formed range of similar magnitude on the earth. It is still in the first stage of growth, and it may be expected in the future to rise in altitude and expand in width.

Himalayas

On the north, and north-east the horizon is bounded by the Mussoorie range, which opposite the town of Dehra Dun bends back and encloses a portion of the valley in an immense amphitheatre. This range forms here the outer scarp of the Himalayan system and eulminates in the Landour peak and Top Tibba. To the south, a number of minro ridges run towards the Dun.

River System and Water Resources

The chief rivers of the district are the Ganga, Asan, Suswa, Yamuna and Tons.

Ganga

The Ganga touches the district at Rishikesh, near which it receives the Chandna Rao (Chandrabhaga Nadi). About 10 km. lower, it receives the waters of the Song and the Suswa, the two main rivers of the Eastern Dun. Thence, distributing its waters into several streams encircling wooded islands, it leaves the district near Hardwar after forming the boundary between the Dun and Garhwal.

Asan

The Asan river rises in a clayey dip to the west of the Asarori-Dehra road, and after a north-westerly course of about 42 km. falls into the Yamuna. It drains the whole of the Western Dun and receives on either bank mountain torrents, which rise in the Siwaliks or the Himalayas. The chief of its tributaries is the eastern Tone rising in the hill below Mussoorie.

Suswa

The Suswa river rises in a clayey depression near the source of the Asan but to the east of the Asarori-Dehra road. It flows south-east, draining the Eastern Dun and receiving, like the Asan, the minor streams rising in the hills to the north and south. The first affluents of any importance to join the Suswa are the Rispana Rao and the Bindal. Later the Suswa receives the waters of the song.

Song

This river rises in Tehri Garhwal and after running parallel to the Dun for some kilometres in a north-west direction unites with the Bindal. Here it breaks, in a wide gorge, through the last line of the outer scarp of the Himalayas and receives the Baldi river near village Dwara. Thence the combined waters flow in a south-easterly direction until they meet the Suswa. About two or three kilometres below the junction of the Song and the Suswa, a third torrent of importance, the Jakhan Rao, is received. The Suswa maintains a parallel course at short distances. The portions of the

Eastern Dun north of these rivers to the east of the Tirsal forest, and the khadar of these rivers themselves, present a network of streams, and it is often difficult to distinguish the main rivers from their tributaries.

Yamuna

The Yamuna rises in the Uttarkashi district in the mass of peaks known as Bandarpunch or Yamnotri. Its basin is separated from that of the Ganga by a great ridge having its origin in the Mussoorie range. It enters the district at a point in *khat* Bondar, about 20 km. due east of Deoban, these receiving the small stream called the Riknar Gad. A few kilometre lower down in receives another similar stream, the Khutnu Gad, and is joined by the Amlawa, a stream which rises at the southern base of the Deoban mountain. About 3 km. further to the west below the iron suspension bridge on the Chakrata road, it also receives the waters of the western Tons. Thence entering the valley of the Dun, about 175 km. from its source, the Yamuna receives near Rampur Mandi the water of the Asan.

Tons

This river is the chief affluent of the Yamuna in the district. It rises north of the Yamnotri peak in the Harki Dun and first issues as a stream called the Supin. Later it receives the waters of the Rupin and from this point the united stream is called the Tons. About thirty kilometres lower down, it is joined by the Pabar. A smaller tributary, the Kunigadh, rising at the north-east corner of *khat* Bawar then joins the Tons. It then forms to a little distance the boundary between the district and the district of Sirmur (in Himachal Pradesh) as far as Kalsi, where it joins, and merges into the smaller but more illustrious Yamuna.

Geology

The first reference to the geology of the Dehra Dun district was made by Fisher in 1882 in an article entitled *Geological Sketch of Musuri and Landour*, in which he mentioned the existence of limestone and quatzite around Mussoorrie.

Slates and quartzites with red and mottled beds occurring in the Chakrata-Kailane region north of Sindhil and Seligad are the oldest rocks of the district which have been correlated with the Simla slates. They are separated from the Jaunsars by Tons thrust.

The rocks of the Jaunsar series forming a syncline have the widest distribution in Dehra Dun district and are divided into Maudhalis, Chandpurs and Nagthats. The Mandhalis consist of a complex association of limestone, quartzites, grits, slates phyllites and boulder beds whereas the Chandpurs are composed of banded quartzites and boulder buds whereas the Chanpurs are composed of banded quartzites and phyllites with occasional lava flows. Intrusions of dolerite are common in the Chandpurs. The Nagthats are essentially made up of quartzites, sandstones, conglomerates and phyllites of purple and greenish colours. The understood. The Chandpurs seem to have been thrust upon the Mandhalis and are overlain by Nagthats with unconformity.

The rocks of Nagthats stage are overlain by Blaini-Infra Krol-Krol-Tal succession which form a synclinal basin occupying the Mugsioni ridge. The Blainis consisting of boulder beds, slates and limestones are overlain by bleached black carbonaceous and pyritie slates of Infra Krols, The Krols are essentially made up of calcareous slates, impure limestones, red shales and massive dolomitic rocks with occasional bands of crypto-crystalline high grade limestone between Sidoli and Cloud End, south of Mussoorie. They are overlain by Tals which are well developed in the Mussoorie syncline. The lower Tal is characterised by black cherty beds with dark micaceous shales and slates and the upper Tal by ferruginous quartzites and grits, sandstones, green, red and purple silty material with shelly limestone at the top. Current beddings and ripple marks are common in the upper Tals.

The Jaunsars along with Blaini-Krol succession are thrust over the autochthonous Tertiaries on the south by Krol thrust. The distribution of Dagshai rocks comprising purple sandstones and red shales is quite sporadie. Exposures are seen in the Tons and Amalava rivers near Kalsi and also, as a narrow indefinite outcrop, below the Krol thrust. Some patches of Dagshai-Subathu rocks are also seen on the Simla slates near about Debra in the Chakrata region indicating that Tertiary sedimentation may have occurred in the region in Dagshai times. The Siwaliks are conspicuous in the southern parts of Dehra Dun. The lower and Middle Siwalik stages, comprising soft greenish sandstones interbedded with chocolate and greenish concretionary clays with lenticles of coal and massive sandstones with calcareous concretions inter-bedded with bright clays, are seen south-west of Siwalik range and north-west of Dehra Dun forming high hills. The upper Siwaliks constituting conglomerates inter-bedded with loose brown and rocks crop out in the Siwalik range as a narrow intermittent strip along the Krol thrust.

Minerals

Limestone

Associated with the upper Krol dolomitic limestones in the Dehra Dun district occurs a belt of limestone. The limestone occurs more or less at the boundary of the upper Krols and red shales.

Gypsum

Gypsum is associated with the upper Krol dolomites. It occurs as lenticular masses of varying sizes running along the beeding direction of the dolomites and appears to be a replacement of upper-krol dolomites.

Tufa

Large masses of cale-tufa occur on a flat plain, within an area of 1,000 metres by 3,000 metres. The material appears to be suitable for the manufacture of good class lime which can be utilized in several chemical industries.

Copper

A copper mine exists on the bank of the Amlava river near kalsi. Another copper locality is Punaha in the Jaunsar Bawar area close to *kalsi.*

Lead

Several old lead mines are situated in the Tona Valley. The lead which occurs in the shattered limestone and slate was worked to a certain depth after which it was abandoned. It may either be due to impoverishment of the ore or to difficulties of mining with increasing depth. The ore also contains a small percentage of silver.

Gold

Gold washing has been carried out at several places from the sands of the Yamuna river. The return, however, is barely remunerative.

Phosphorite

The occurrence of phosphate in Mussoorie was first reported in 1885 during the course of a search for fossils in the area.

The phosphorite varies in physical, chemical and mineralogical characteristics, with shule, chert or carbonate base.

Marble

A continuous band of white to greyish white, eryptocrystalline, closely joined marble occurs in the district.

Climate

The district has within its limits lofty peaks of the outer Himalayan as well as the Dun with climatic conditions nearly similar to those in the plains. The temperature of any given locality in the district depends very largely on the elevation. In general, the climate is temperate. The year may be divided into four seasons. The period from about the middle of November to February is the cold season. The hot season which follows continues up to about the end of June. The monsoon season is from July to about the third week of September. The following period, till the middle of November, is the post-monsson or transition season.

Rainfall

Records of rainfall in the district are available for one hill station and six other stations at lower altitudes for periods ranging from 70 to 101 years. The average annual rainfall in the district, excluding Mussoorie, is 2,281.7 mm. while in general the rainfall increases as one proceeds from the south-west towards the north-east, the region around Rajpur gets the maximum rainfall, while the areas around Ambari and to the north get the least rainfall in the district. About 87 per cent of the annual rainfall in the district is received during the months from June to September, July and August being the rainiest. The variation in rainfall from year to year in the district is appreciable. In the period of 50 years from 1900, the highest annual rainfall, which was 147 per cent of the normal, occurred in 1917, while the lowest forming only 58 per cent of the normal was recorded in 1907 and 1918. During the period, the annual rainfall in the district was less than 80 per cent of the normal in 8 years, two of them being consecutive. Considering the rainfall at individual stations, two consecutive years of such low rainfall occurred thrice at Dehra Dun, twice at Bhogpur and once each at Rajpur and Mussoorie. The annual rainfall in the district was between 1,900 and 2,500 mm. in 26 years cut of 50.

The frequency of annual rainfall in the district between 1901-1950 is given in Table 13.1.

TABLE 13.1: Annual Rainfall Frequency: 1901-1950

Range in mm.	No. of years
1301-1500	2
1501-1700	2
1701-1900	6
1901-2100	11
2101-2300	9
2301-2500	6
2501-2700	2
2701-2900	4
2901-3100	6
3101-3300	1
3301-3500	1

On an average there are 79 rainy days (i.e., days with rainfall of 2.5 mm or more) in a year in the district. This number varies from 72 at Ambari to 96 at Mussoorie.

The heaviest rainfall in 24 hours recorded at any station in the district was 440.4 mm. at Rajpur on August 25, 1954.

In winter the higher peaks are under snow-on a north aspect-until April. Local tradition says that the winter rains do not finally clear until snow falls on Bhadraj, rising immediately above the Dun valley to the west of Mussoorie. Being situated at a higher altitude the winter rains are aften accompanied with snowfall at places like Mussoorie. After heavy fall of snow the view of Mussoorie from Dehra Dun is pieturesque. Except on the tops of the hills, however, the snow soon melts and disappears in two or three days.

Temperature

There are two meteorological observatories in the district, one at Mussoorie and the other at Dehra Dun. The district being hilly, temperature variations due to difference in elevation are considerable. However, the records of Dehra Dun may be taken as representative of the conditions in the Dun, and those of Mussoorie as broadly representative of the hilly regions. After February both day and night temperatures begin to increase rapidly. Generally May and the early part of June constitute the hottest parts of the year, the highest maximum temperature in May at Dehra Dun so far being 36.2°C. and that at Mussoorie 24.8°C. On individual days, the maximum temperature rises to over 42°C at Dehra Dun, while at Mussoorie the maximum does not exceed 32°C. In the hilly regions, the summer is pleasant, but in the Dun the heat is often intense, although not as intense as in the plains of the adjoining districts. Afternoon thundershowers which occur on some days bring welcome relief from the heat. With the onset of the south-west monsoon over the district, by about the last week of June, there is an appreciable drop in the day temperatures, but the nights are nearly as warm as during summer. With the withdrawal of the monsoon by about the third week of September, temperatures begin to decrease, the drop in night temperatures being now more rapid. January is generally the coldest month, the mean daily maximum temperature being 19.1°C at Dehra Dun and 10.2°C at Mussoorie. The means daily minimum temperature in January is 6.1°C at Dehra Dun and 2.5°C at Mussoorie. During the cold season cold waves affect the district in the rear of passing western disturbances, the minimum temperature sometimes falling down to about a degree below the freezing point of water at places like Dehra Dun, and at places such as Mussoorie, it drops to about -6°C or -7°C when snowfalls occur.

The highest maximum temperature recorded at Dehra Dun was 48.9°C on June 4, 1902, and that at Mussoorie was 34.4°C. on May 24, 1949. The lowest minimum temperature at Dehra Dun was −1.1°C on February 1, 1905 and January 11, 1945, while at Mussoorie it was −6.7°C. on February 10, 1950.

Humidity

The relative humidity is high during the south-west monsoon season, generally exceeding 70 per cent on the average. The morning are comparatively more humid than the afternoon. It is less during the rest of the year, the driest part of the year being the summer season with the relative humidity in the afternoons becoming less than 45 per cent.

Cloudiness

During the south-west monsoon season and the short spells of a day or two in the cold season, in association with passing western disturbances, skies are generally heavily-clouded or overcast. The hills are often seen enveloped in clouds. During the rest of the year it is usually lightly clouded or clear.

Winds

Winds are generally light. In the Dun, winds in the post-monsoon and in the mornings in the rest of the year, are variable in direction though northerly to north-easterly winds are sometimes experienced during post-monsoon and winter mornings. In the afternoons winds are mostly from directions between south-west and north-west throughout the year, except in October and November. In the hilly regions, in the period from May to September, winds blow from directions between south-west and south-east. In the post-monsoon and cold seasons these winds continue to be most common, but on many days in the mornings northerly to north-easterly winds also blow. In March and April, morning winds are northerly to north-easterly and afternoon winds south-easterly to south-westerly.

The Table 13.2 gives the month-wise mean wind speed and the annual mean wind speed for Dehra Dun and Mussoorie:

TABLE 13.2: Wind Speed for Dehra Dun and Mussoorie

Months	Mean wind speed in km per hour	
	Dehra Dun	Mussoorie
January	2.6	6.7
February	3.1	7.4
March	3.6	7.9
April	4.2	7.9
May	4.1	8.4
June	8.6	7.8
July	2.7	5.6
August	2.5	4.7
September	2.8	5.4
October	2.3	6.1
November	3.0	6.8
December	2.6	6.8
Annual	3.2	6.7

Special Weather Phenomena

During the cold season, passing western disturbances affect the weather over the district, causing occasional thunder-stormes, some of which are accompanied with hail. Thunder-storms occur during the summer and monsoon season also. Fog occurs occasionally during the cold season.

The frequency of special weather phenomena for Dehra Dun and Mussoorie is given in Table 13.3.

TABLE 13.3: Weather Phenomena for Dehra Dun and Mussoorie

Months	Mean number of days with									
	Thunder		Hall		Dust-storm		Squall		Fog	
	D	M	D	M	D	M	D	M	D	M
1	2	3	4	5	6	7	8	9	10	11
January	3.0	1.6	0.2	2.0	0.0	0.0	0.0	0.3	0.2	3.0
February	2.0	1.6	0.1	1.7	0.0	0.0	0.1	0.3	0.3	1.6
March	5.0	4.0	0.8	1.8	0.0	0.0	0.4	0.5	0.0	0.7
April	4.0	5.0	0.2	1.2	0.0	0.0	0.3	0.5	0.0	0.4
May	8.0	8.0	0.2	0.8	0.2	0.2	0.1	0.8	0.0	0.5
June	10.0	9.0	0.5	0.2	0.1	0.1	0.1	0.3	0.2	6.0
July	12.0	9.0	0.0	0.0	0.0	0.0	0.0	0.0	1.1	19.0
August	12.0	0.0	0.0	0.1	0.0	0.0	0.0	0.0	0.8	17.0
September	10.0	9.0	0.0	0.1	0.0	0.0	0.0	0.3	0.6	13.0
October	3.0	2.0	0.1	0.1	0.0	0.0	0.0	0.0	0.0	3.0
November	0.5	0.5	0.0	0.1	0.0	0.0	0.0	0.0	0.1	1.0
December	0.7	1.4	0.0	0.7	0.0	0.0	0.0	0.1	0.1	2.0
Annual	70.0	60.0	1.6	9.0	0.3	0.3	1.0	3.0	3.0	67.0

D = Dehra Dun; M = Mussoorie

FLORA

Forests

The Garhwal rajas derived a considerable revenue from the Dun forests in pre-British days, mainly through excise collected at posts created at the passes of the Siwaliks. In the early years of the British rule no attempt was made at forest conservation, confusion prevailed, and the forests were auctioned and leased experimentally while valuable sal forests were being recklessly denuded. The absence of conservancy was absolute. The district abounded in fine trees 100 or 200 years old and upwards. Most of these fell before the axe and probably the rest would have gone with them had the roads been little better. Since 1844 the British authorities, stopped to leasing the forests and kept the collection of dues in their own hand till the establishment of forest department in 1855, which also concentrated its energies on the collection of revenue at first without making any attempt at systematic conservancy. It was not until 1877 that the forest, measuring about 777 sq. km were properly demarcated. The village forests included those not reserved by the department and those found within the boundaries of large waste land grants. They were declared to be the property of the zamindars of the villages.

In 1864 regular forest operations were commended under the commissioner of Meerut Division, but it took 13 years to properly demarcate the forests, to make roads and to lay down the rights of the government and the people. Although in 1878 the Forest Act had become law, it was not till 1887 that the first working plan for the forests of tahsil Dehra Dun could be prepared and the scientific management of forests started. In the beginning of the present century consideable areas of land in the eastern Dun, mainly covered with grass or patches of inferior forests, were excluded from the original demarcation of the reserved forests as waste land blocks and portions of these were from time to time leased for cultivation.

The forests in tahsil Chakrata were until 1800 much neglected. Little or no restrictions were placed upon their utilisation by surrounding villages. In 1864 the cutting of deodar was forbidden when the proposals of commissioner, Meerut Division—who was also made conservator of forests for his division, were approved by government. Following the appointment of a conservator of Forests for the North-western Provinces in 1868 rules began to be more stringently enforced. In 1972 the demarcation of the forests into three classes was carried out. The first class, measuring about 6,360 hectares, was denominated government forest. They consisted chiefly of deodar. In these the villagers were allowed no rights whatever. The second class was open government forests. These contained mixed trees spreading over an area of 30,972 hectares. The villagers were allowed rights of fuel and grazing, and on certain conditions building timber, and cultivation. The third, class measuring about 66,005 hectares was made over entirely to the villagers for their own use, with the reservation of the government's superior right, that is to say, sale or alienation of forest land was forbidden. It included all waste land lying outside the first and second classes. The rights of the villagers were further extended in 1919.

In 1932, the government sanctioned a scheme in the district in which agriculture is allowed for four years on lease in certain areas where new forests are to be developed, and this continues to be in force here even today.

Private or village forests of tahsil Dehra Dun taken over by the Forest Department on July 1, 1952, as a consequence of the enforcement of the U.P. Zamindari Abolition and Land Reforms Act, 1950 (Act No. 1 of 1951) have also been brought under scientific management since 1955-56 when the first working plan was prepared for these forests. The recommendations of the working plan are carried out by trained forest officers and subordinate field staff. Poorly stocked forest, grassy banks and forests of low economic value are being replaced by plantation of fast growing species which are of industrial importance. The third class or the village forests of tahsil Chakrata have greatly diminished since they were made over to zamindars owing partly to the natural recklessness of the unreasoning fear of their being taken over by the forest dapartment if maintained in good condition. So far there is no working plan for this class of forest in which villagers have got unlimited rights.

In the course of different working plans prepared by the forest department for the development and scientific management of the reserved forests of the district, plantations have also been raised over grassy blanks and in open or poor types of forests. Species of plantation raised includes mulberry, *semal, tun, khair, sissoo, pulla, bahera, eucalyptus* and bamboo.

The following Table 13.4 gives the details of the forest areas in the district for the last five years ending in 1970-71:

TABLE 13.4: Forest Areas 1966-67 to 1970-71

(In hectares)

Year	Under the forest department	Private forests	Total
1966-67	1,50,517	16,500	1,67,017
1967-68	1,52,786	16,500	1,69,286
1968-69	1,53,058	16,500	1,69,558
1969-70	1,53,320	16,575	1,69,895
1970-71	1,50,803	16,575	1,67,378

Botanical Divisions

The flora of the district include a vast range varying from tropical to

Alpine species owing to the variation in altitude and aspects.

The forests in the western part of tahsil Dehra Dun may be divided into two botanical divisions, the broad leaved or the sal forests and the coniferous forests.

Sal Forests

They occur over the Dun valley up to the top of the Siwalik ridges in the south, and up to an altitude of about 1,300 metres in the north. Sal is generally pure but towards the top of the Siwalik ridges, mixture of miscellaneous species increases and , at some places, chir is found mixed with sal. Sal is the main timber species, which is converted into scantlings, railway sleepers, planks and *ballies* etc. Sal timber is also largely used for constructional purposes. The main consuming centres are Delhi, Rohtak, Meerut and Punjab. In the lower part near nullahs *jamun* is quite common. The main associates of sal are *Asna (Terminalia tomentosa) haldu (Adina cordifolia), bahera (Terminalia belerica), Sandem (Ougenia dalbergiodes), jhingan (Lonnea grandis), dhaman (Grewia clastica), pula (Kvdia calycina), kachnar(Banhine - avari -egata), semla(Bauhinea retusa), dhauri (Lagerst reemia parviflora), bakli (Anogeis-sus-latifolia), padal (Stereospermun Suavestens), semal (Salmalia malabarica), aonla (Emblica officinalis), amaltas (Cassia fistula), tun (Cedrela toona) dhanldhak (Erythrina suberoser), har(Terminalia chebula), kanju (Haloptelea integrifolia), Kharpat (Garuga pinnata), kumbhi (Carcya arborea), lisora (Cordia dichotoma), phaldu (Mitragyna parvilora),* and *kusum (Scheichera oleosa).*

In between the top of the Siwalik ridge and the lower parts generally the following species are found, the mixture varying according to aspect, altitude and soil conditions: *rohini (Mallotus philippinensis), chamror (Ehretia laevis), bhilawa (Semecarpus anacardium), maidalakri* or *chandana (Litsea chinensis or Litsea glutinosa), chilla (Casearia tomentosa), domsal (Milliusa velutina), dudhi (Wrightia tomentosa), kathbilwa (Buchnania lanzan), khaja (Bridclia rctusa), Kurkha (Holarrhena andidycenterica), tarcharbi (Sapium sebiferum).*

Among the shrubs, the following are common: *Karu (Clerodendorn infortunatum), gandela (Murraya keonigu), binbu or ban (Glycosmis pentaphylla), bansa, besinga (Adhatoda vasika),* bhang *(Connabis sativa), bhatta (Desmodim species) bhat kataiya (Solanum indicium), bindu (Golebrookia oppositifolia), chameli (Jasmin-um arborascens), chanchia (Flemingia chappar), daia (Callicarpa macrophylla), dhaula (Woodfordia floribunda), ber (Ziziphus species), khatber (Ziziphus xylophyra), marophali (Helacteris isora), simala (Vitex negundo), panwar (Cassis tora) Phalsa (Grewia sapida), satawar (Asparagus raicmosus), kuri (Lantana camera), karaunda (Carrisa opaca), kalabasinga (Pogostemon plectran thoides) bamboo (Dendrocalamus strictus).*

Among the climbers the most common are *Maljhan (Bauhinia vahili), agla (Acacia pennata), alai (Cacsal piniadeeap etala), amarbel (Coyrtia carmosa), kalidudhi (Ichmocarpus frutescens), dudhi (Vallaris haynei), gauj (Milletia auriculata), giloe (Tinaspora cordifolia), medha singhi (Cryptolepis buchanani), ramdatuan (Smilax macrophylla), roel (Combretum decandrum), tarur (Dioscoria species).*

The most common grasses which are generally found in open forests or grassy banks along streams and on hill slopes are *Baib or bhabar (Eulaliopris binata), goria* or *gorla (Chrysopogon contratus), kans (Saccharuma spantaneum), panni (Vetiveria zizanioides), marari (Inperata cylindrica), rosha (Cymbopongon martinu), muni (Saccharuma munja), pirlu (Thysamolcana agrostis), tachloor suni (Aristida cyanantha).*

Coniferous Species

Chir (Inu Eoxburghi) is the only coniferous species which is found in the old reserved forests of Dehra Dun division. A few deodar *(Cedrus deodara)* trees may also be seen. The associates of *chir are banj, oak, ayar (Pieris ovalifolia) burans (Rhododendronar-boreum), mehal (Pyrus pasha).* The undergrowth consists of *Kilmora (Berberis asiation), sakina (Indigoferapulchella), hisalu (Rubus clliplicus)* etc.

Near the streams in sheltered localities there is heavy growth of shrubs like *kilmora (Berberis asiatica) dhaula, thor (Euphorbia royliana), bhilmora (Rumex hastatus), kuri (Nyclanthes arbortristis* and *satawar.*

The drier aspects generally carry grasses, the most common of which are *goria* or *gorla (Chrysopogon montanus, kumaria (Heteropogan contortus), nakli bhabar (Ereophorum coinosum)* and *ringal (Arundinarea fulcata).*

The flora in the eastern part of tahsil Dehra Dun may be divided into fourteen Botanic divisions described below.

Moist Siwalik Sal Forests

These forests are found in the Motichur and Thana forest ranges of the East Dehra Dun forest division. The sal Trees growing here are of very low quality. The typical associates of the salara *bakli* and *sain*. The underwood is usually light consisting of *rohini amalias, rial (Buchanania lanzan)* and *aonla,* the undergrowth being *karaunda (Carissa opara), gandhela, bindu (Loleti rookia), dhaula* and *vasica (Adhatoda vasica).*

Moist Bhabar Doon Sal Forests

These forest cover a large area of about 160 sq. km. in the Thano and Barkot forest ranges. Sal is the dominant species in the overwood, forming nearly pure stands, its typical associates being *sain* and *dhauri (Lager stroenia parviflora).* The underwood consists of *sandan, dhaman (Greura Clastica), rohini, chamror (Ehretia laevis), amaltas.* In moist places *jamun, machilus, Listsea chinenss* are quite common. The underwood growth includes *karaunda, chameli (Jasminus pubescens)* and *gauj* and *(Milletia auriculata)*

West Gangetic Moist Decidous Forests

These forests are found in the Kansaro, Barkot, Motichur and Thana forest ranges. They represent closed forests of medium to good height, including a number of dominat species comprising most of the associates of the sal such as *safed siris, bahera, jhingan, kharpat,* and *dhauri.* The underwood growth is generally open and consists of *karaunda, rasica,* and *jharheri.* The grasses found here are *kans, garla* and *munj.*

Low Alluvial Savana Woodland Forests

These forests are usually found on the higher and more stable alluvial terraces in Thana, Lachhiwala, Barkot, Motichur and Kansaro forest ranges. The tree growth is generally poor and scattered consisting of *ambaro (Spondias magifera), semal, saijana (jhingan), kharpat, dhauri* and *siris.* The under-growth is sparse and consists of *vasica, jharberi* and *karaunda.*

Sub-Montane Hill Valley Forests

These forests which are found in Motichur, Barkot and Lachhiwala forest ranges, consist mainly of evergreen species able to withstand the wetness of the sites occupied. The species occurring are *gular (Ficus glomerata), gutel, jamun, tun, safed siris,* and occasionally *semal* and *khair.* The underwood consists of *kala tendu* and *Salix tetrusperma,* the undergrowth comprising cane and *Ardesia solanacca.*

Dry Siwalik Sal Forests

These forests occur on the higher slopes of Siwaliks. The sal is the predominant species in the overwood with its main associates of *sain, bakli, pipal (Buchanania lanzan), kachnar* and *guiral (Bauhinia* spp.). The underwood consists of *sandan, dhaman, chamror, harsingar (Nyctanthes arbortristis),* etc. The undergrowth comprising the *dhaula* and *Indigofera pulchela.* The common grass is *baib* and *gorla* and bamboo clumps also occur frequently.

Northern Dry Mixed Deciduous Forests

In the plains these forests consists of *semal, khair, kanju, bahera, amaltas* and *bel (Aegl marmalos).* The *gutel* occcurs near the river banks and water. The undergrowth consists of *gandhela, jharberi* and *bindu.* In the hills the common species found are *bakli, semal, jhingan, bahera, khair, rohini, genthi (Bochnaeria rugulosa), khinni (Sapium insigne), mandora (Erythrina suberosa), chamror, chilla* and *harsingar.* The undergrowth is light consisting of *basinga, bindu* and *gandhela.* Grasses like *goria kumaria (Heteropogon contortus)* and *baib* are fairly common.

Dry Deciduous Scrub Forests

These forests represent a degradation stage of the dry deciduous forests in the *Kansaro,* Barkot, Motichur and Thana forest ranges. The main species of trees found are *jhingan, khinni, mandana* and *amaltas.* Common shrubs are *harsingar, karaunda, mainphal (Heronephis spinosa), gandhela* and *bindu.* The *Euphorbia* scrub generally occurs on higher elevation with very dry, rocky and bouldery soil.

Khair-Sissoo Forests

These forests occur in *Thano*, Lachhiwala, Barkot and Motichur forest ranges on gravelly alluvium of streams and rivers. *Khair* and sissoo occur mixed but sissoo generally predominates, The undergrowth is generally thin consisting of *basingha, gandhela* and *ber.*

Sub-Tropical Siwalik Chir Forests

These forests occur in Bahera, Koelpura, Motichur and Nahi forest blocks mixed with dry mixed deciduous forests and sal forests. The pines stand singly or in groups.

Sub-Tropical Himalayan Chir Forests

These forests occur in Thano forest range between the altitudes of 1,200 m. and 2,200 m. The occurrence is, however, local and in small patches.

Himalayan Sub-Tropical Scrub Forests

These forests occur in Thano forest range on shallow and excessively dry soil in outer Himalayan chir forest zone. The tree species mostly occur along moist ravines and nullahs and consists of *Ficus roxburghii, burans (Rhododendronarboreum), ban* and *Pyrus pashia.* The shrubs usually consist of *Indigofera, Rubus ellipticus, Vibrum* and *Euphoribia* species.

Banj Forests

These forests occur almost pure forming a somewhat open canopy of sapling and poles of coppiee growth in thano forest range.

Himalayan Temperate Secondary Scrub Forests

These forests also occur in Thano forest range. They represent a degradation stage of banj forests. The common shrubs are *kilmora, Rubus ellipticus* and *surai (Eupharbiaroy leane).*

The forests in tahsil Chakrata are scattered in the north west and south and are surrounded by cultivation, but greater part of the forests form a compact belt. The forests of the tahsil have been divided into the following botanical divisions:

Dry Siwalik Sal Forests

This type of forests occur on the slopes near the junction of the Tons and the Yamuna rives in the neighbourhood of the Kalsi between the altitudes of 466 m. and 1,220 m. The forests are an admixture of *sal, bakli, sain, haldu, sandan, jhingan* and *ban (Dendrocalamus strictus),* with shrubby growth of *kurri (Nyctanthes arbortristis), karamunda (Carissa opaces), gandhela* and *dhaula* on hotter slopes and *arusa (Adhtoda yasica)* in the lowest parts. The *ruil (Combretum decandrum)* has overrun large areas in Kalsi, the climbers being *malihan (Bauhinia yehlii)* and *guai (Milletia auriculata).* The *kunaria (Heteropogon contortus), baib* and *gold (Vhrysopogon fulvus)* are the main grasses found her.

The sal growing here is of low quality and height, mixed with other species and after broken up into characteristically pure groups or mixed patches of varying extent between which its associates predominate. Regeneration of sal and its associates is deficient, very slow and difficult to obtain.

Khair-Sissoo Forests

This type which is primarily *seral* type of dry deciduous forest, occurs in a narrow belt along the Yamuna in Kalsi, Rampur Mandi, Majog, Sangred and Tiuni forest blocks and along the Tons in a narrow belt. It is a deciduous forests in which sissoo predominates. The canopy is light. *Khair* is present only in Kalsi and Rampur Mandi blocks and absent elsewhere. The characteristic grass is the *kans.*

Sub-Tropical Transition Broad leaved Forests

These forests occupy a narrow fringe below the *chir* forests in Majog. Sangred, Tiuni, Chandnigad and Anu forest blocks, which are some sort of remnants of dry tropical deciduous and moist tropical deciduous forests mixed with low level broad-leaved associates of *chir.* These are confined in a narrow belt on either side of the Tons river between Anu the junction of the Tons and Pabar and long nullahs. The species consists of *siris, sandan, semal, kachnar, kakra, mahua, kharik, rohina, puna (Ehretia acuminata)* and *jhingan*, with shrubby growth of *arusa, kandai, dais (Cellicarpa macrophylla)* and *kashmoi (Barberis lycium).* The *ari (Caesalpinia sepiaria)* a climber occurs at some places and *suina (Arundinella nepalensis)* and *mirch-gandha (Cymbopogon martinii)* are the main grasses. The forests are open, heavily grazed and burnt.

Sub-Tropical Himalayan Chir (Pine) Forests

The forests of this type are typically a pure association of *chir*, considerably influenced by the annual or periodic fires which take place. Depending on the aspect this type occupies almost the whole of the area up to an altitude of 2,100 m. No other trees occur in the top canopy except at higher altitudes and along nullahs. The *kail (Pinus-wallichiena)*, which is more mesophytic, tends to replace it at higher altitude and sheltered cooler sites.

There is practically no underwood, and shurbs are few, but where moist conditions are a little more favourable there tends to be an underwood of broad-leaved trees such as *banj, ayar* and *burans* along nullahs, The undergrowth is usually of grasses, mainly *golds, kumeria, suina, tachla (Apuldomutica aristata)* and *golringal (Arundinsria falcata)* which appears on cool and shaded aspects only. Shrubs are generally absent of very rare, the chief ones being *anwin (Glochidion velutinum)*, and *bhekoi (Prinsepia utilis)* on dry slopes, which may degenerate to *suru (Euphorbia ravleana)* and *dhaula* by continuous burning and grazing and *hinsalu (Rubus ellipticus), sinar (Delbergia siahvopleuca)* and *banwan (Myrsine africana)* in the moist places.

The quality and development of forests depends upon the locality and way they were handled in the past. Trees of very good quality are found in the lower parts of Khunigad, Sangred, Majog, Banpur and Kurog forest blocks. Often, however, there is much variation in quality in the same compartments, it decreases with increasing height.

Riverain Chir Forests

At one or two place in the Khunigad forest block small patches of sand and boulders have been sparsely colonised by chir. The forest which is bushy and poorly developed probably because of trampling by animals. The area occupied by such forests is very small.

Himalayan Sub-Tropical Scrub and Sub-tropical Euphorbia Scrub

These two types have been grouped together as they occur side by side on the exposed southern aspects in lower chir forests and are often difficult to differentiate. These occur generally below the altitude of 1,500 m. where, as a result of fire and excessive grazing, the overwood has been destroyed or has been unable to develop owing to excessively dry and shallow soil and only open scrub formations cover the ground. The former types frequent sites where some soil is left and the main species found in *ninwa (Rhus parviflora)* with little *gandhela* or *arusa.* The latter type is found on dry rocky exposed slopes devoid of soil, where only open scrub of suru is found, which is usually pure but sometimes associated with *dhaula* and *ninwa*. Ther ground cover consists of coarse grasses like *kumaria* and *mirch-gandha.* Examples of such types can be seen in Majog, Dhadu, Anu, Dharagad and Dhanras forest blocks.

Kau (Olea cuspidala) Scrub Forests

This type of forests characterised by *kau,* occupied sizeable areas on the flatter alluvial ground along the Tons river. These forests have mostly been cleared for cultivation and only remnants of this type are seen in the Anu and Dandu blocks where malformed trees of *kau* with a few *kakra* and *siris* are seen struggling for survival. There is a dense undergrowth of *ninawa* and *gandhela* and the ground cover consists of coarse grasses like *kumaria* and *mirch-gandha.*

Ban Oak Forest

Ban (Quercus incana) forests are found above chir forests upto about 2,250 m. but do not cover extensive tracts except in Ekra, Burasti, Danda and Kurog blocks, *Ban* formations come down a dump nullahs between the altitudes of 1,500 m. and 2,100 m. in chir forests zone. The forests are generally well stocked except near villages and are irregular in age. Regeneration is deficient though found at places. The main associates are *ayar, kaula (Machilus odoratissima* and *M. duthied), shurur (Litses umbrass)* and *bhadrai (Phoeba lanceolatza).* The undergrowth is fairly dense in moist places but is sparse otherwise and consists of *kakahinsar (Rubus lasiocarpus), hinsalur, taknoi (Lonicera guinouclocularis), matoi (Desmodium tiliaefloum), chambai (Wikstroemia concescens), bhakoi, kashmoi (Barberis aristata)* and *masroi (Coriaria nepalensis).* Along nullahs and moist places some *darli (Cedrela serrata)* is also found. Climbers are few, the *mithiari (Hedera helix)* and *kuioi (Rosa moscheta)* being the commonest. Mosses and lichens are found on trees and epiphytic growth of ferns takes place during monsoon season. In some places these forests are being invaded by kail and chir.

Moru Oak Forests

The *moru* forests occur only locally and are usually confined to nullahs and damper and moist sites and below temperate moist deciduous forests at an altitude of 2,250 m. These forests are rarely pure and are generally mixed with ban in the lower reaches and either with *spruce, kharsu (Quercus semicarpiiolia)* or high level moist deciduous species like *kanju (Acer pictum), kanial (Acer caesium), khaksha (Cornus marophylla), pangar (Aescuslus indica), utis (Alnus nepalensis)* and *darli* in the higher reaches. The undergrowth consists of *kalahinsar, taknoi, bhutnoi (Viburnum cotinfolium), kanderu (Ilex dipverena), thantha (Rhamnus virgata), lish (Rhamnus purpurea), chamuna (Daphne paprrecea)* and *tiliard (Sarcococea prumiformis)* with some ringals in the nullahs.

Oak Scrub Forests

Ban oak forests are exposed to damage or destruction through several agencies. Near habitations looping is extremely prevalent and combined with fuel and the heavy grazing demand oak and its associated species are reduced to low, stunted unsound trees, and but coppice burans and ayar, both being unpalatable stokc, and poor fuels, are generally left. The undergrowth consists of *kaskmal, kashmoi, bhekoi* and *gingaru (Crataegus crenulata).* This type is found in Danda, Kotha, Kua, Bandla, Korwa, Singori, Raura and Ekra forest blocks.

Moist Deodar Forests

These forests are mainly confined to Koti, Murach, Darmigad, Konaiw, Mundali, Konasar, Riknar, Kurog and Ekra blocks occupying a zone between the altitudes of 1,800 m. and 2,500 m. On dry exposed aspects this type may ascend up to 2,700 m. These forests are not pure and are mixed with varying proportions of *kail.* The proportion of *kail* is governed by the slope and the treatment the forests received in the past. Steeper areas have more deodar while in the easier slopes kail tends to invade deodar especially if the area had fellings in the past. Some spruce is also found mixed with deodar along nullahs and a mixture of fir, spruce with deodar, at higher altitudes, is also not uncommon. The *leuri (Cuperesus trulosa)* tends to mix with deodar on exposed and steep limestone rocks in Kanasar forest block. A second storey of scattered trees of *burans, mone, ayar* and occasionally maples, is also present. The ground cover consists of shrubs like *kalahinsar, kashmoi, matoi, taknoi, chambia, chamua* and *ghugtai (Deutzia staminea).* The *banapsa (Viola canescens)* is found as ground flora. The *kandar (Vilis semicordala) kaunia-bali (Clematis montana), mithiari* and *kujoi* are amongst the common climbers.

Western Mixed Coniferous Forests

This type is normally found above 2,400 m. in most of the area of tahsil Chakrata but on cool aspects and easy slopes these forests descend down into the deodar zone. The fir, spruce, deodar and *kail* are found mixed in varying proportions and varying intermixture of evergreen and deciduous broad leaved species are also found.

Amongst the evergreen broad leaved species *kharsu* associates in the higher reaches and *moru*, *ban* and *burans*, in the lower reaches. Along the nullahs deciduous species like *pangar, kanial, kanju, akhrot (Juglans regia), angau (Euonymus lacenis), hoi (Meliosma dilleniaefolia), lish, shangri (Carpinus viminca), kaint* and *khaksha* are found.

The *ban-chulu (Lonicera angustifolia), Smilax, vaginata bhutnoi, Richhoi (V. stellulatum), shunjai (Jasminum humile), bhuiroi (Deutzia corymbosa), takoi (Spiraca cencescens), matoi* and *kugoi* and are the species of shrubs found in these forests.

The ground flora consists of *banapsa, Fragaria vesca, smaiva (Valeriana willichii)* and *Polvgonum speciosum,* ferns like *Adiantum venustum* and grasses like *Bromus uniloides* and *oplsimenus undulatifolius.* Weed growth of *Impericns* spp. and *jani (Strobilcinthes gallichii)* takes place in rains, the *kauni (Clematis barbellate), bani (Schizandra grandiflora), holbali (Jasminum officinale), mithiari* and *kandar* being the climbers.

Moist Temperate Deciduous Forests

This type is found in extremely small strips along nullahs and cool moist hollows and depressions within the temperate region between 2,100 m, and 2,750 m. The main species are *pangar, kanju, kanjal, shangri, emroi (Ulmus wallichiana), akhrot, kharsu* and *bhotia-badam (Sorvlus colurns),* the shrubs being similar to those found in the mixed coniferous forests.

Himalayan, Temperate Secondary Scrub Forests

This type is found in the burnt areas within the temperate region especially in Dharmigad, Khunigad and Mundali forest blocks, the original crops have been burnt and a few trees of deodar and *kail* are found. The ground is covered mainly with *sakina (Indigofera pulchella), bhuiroi, kalahinsar* and *kujoi,* In most of these areas plantations of deodar, *kail* and other broad leaved species have been attempted with varying success.

Kharsu Forests

This type occurs in a narrow broken strip above the altitude of 2,700 m. on either side of the main ridge parting the catchment areas of the Yamuna and the Tons rivers. The *kharsu* forests generally have a good density and height varying from 12m. to 20 m. Brown moss hangs on the trees. *Kharsu* is the predominant crop but it may be mixed with a little *moru.* A scattering of conifers, mainly *mordinda* and *rai,* may be present on cooler aspects and deodar on hotter aspects.

The other species found with *kharsu* are *banbeli, iamnoi angau, bhutnoi, richhor* and *tirnoi (Viburnu foetens)*. At certain places ringals are also met with. *The polygonum speciosum, Frogaria vesco, Geranium wellichianum, Viola* spp. and *Veleriana harowickii* are the common herbs found here.

West Himalayan Upper Oak-Fir Forests

These are typically two storeyed forests with *morinda* and *rai* standing singly or in strips or groups over *kharsu, moru* and other evergreen, deciduous species like *konail, goi (Meliosma dilleniaefolia) angau* and *kabderu (Ilex dipyrena)*. The shrubs consists of *kimioi, bhera, taknoi, richhoi, Smilax yaginala, Barberis* spp. *sharnoi (Asparagus* spp.*) bashroi (Salix elegans), shunjai* and *lish*. Herbaceous growth of *Fragaria* spp., *Aisliacs sptera, Polygonum speciosm* and *banapsa* is also present. The climbers consist of *mithiari kandar,* and *kauniabali (Clematis montana)*.

Himalayan Temperate Parkland

This is a park-like land with trees of decidous or coniferous species chiefly *porinda* and rai standing over a grassy turf. These are generally found in places where the grazers keep their herds for a long time and also on easy slopes in fir, high level deciduous or fir-kharsu forests.

Stray trees of *jamnoi, kanial, pangar* and *morinda* are found in such places. The shrubby growth is characterised by browsed stray clumps of *bunchula, ruinsh, Tirnoi* and *Barberis* spp. The ground flora consists of *Primula dentculats, Fragaria indica, banapsa,* and *Rumex nepalensis.*

Himalayan Temperate Pastures

These pasture lands are derived from the park land by elimination of tree species and most of the shrubby growth. The grasses commonly inhabiting such pasture lands belong to the geners, *Festuca, Agrosis, Calamogrostis, Bromus, Danthonis* and *Dactylis*. In the lower elevation these grasses may be found mixed with *Themeda anthera, Hetropogon* spp. and *Chrysopogon* spp.

Cypress Forests

This type is confined to steep and rugged lime-stone rocks in Kanasar forest block occupying a very small area. It is an open forest of leuri occurring in patches either pure or mixed with deodar and kail, with practically no undergrowth. The forests are unworkable because of the difficult terrain of the ground.

Alder Forests

These forests occupy very small strips, of 5 m. to 15 m. width along stream and nullahs in the Khunigad, Rikhnargad and Kuroggad forest blocks. This type cuts into the subtropical zone and ascends up to 2,500 m. but appreciable areas are not found about the altitude of 1,900 m. the main species at lower heights is *Khunisand* which, at an attitude of about 1,800 m. is replaced by *utis*. These species grow mostly pure but may be mixed with a little *ban, burans* and *kaula*. The shrubby growth consists of *lakoi* and *Barberis* spp.

Low Level Blue Pine Forests

These forests are found throughout the temperate zone. At places the *kail* may descend down to the *chir* zone especially in the Kanasar forest block where protection from fire has been affected. It tries to replace deodar within deodar forests wherever there are gaps or the fellings of deodar are done as in the Dharmigad and Kanasar blocks.

Fauna

The district has been the habitat of a large variety of mammals and various species of birds, reptiles and fish.

Animals

Among the chief species of wild animals found in the district are the tiger, panther, Himalayan black bear, sambar, spotted deer, hog deer, gural, wild boar, elephant, jackal fox and poreupins *(syahi)*. A census operation carried out in 1978 for tigers revealed that there were only 11 tigers left in the district in that year. Tiger is not found in tahsil Chakrata but there are cases when a stray tiger following the herds of Gujar cattle has been sighted. Leopards are found almost everywhere in this tahsil though not in large numbers. They carry away sheep and goats and sometimes kill cattle also. There was a time when both tiger and panther were quite common in the Dun valley, but gradually their numbers have declined so much so that the tiger is today a rare sight. This is due to indiscriminate shooting reduction in the numbers of the deer family as well as continuous disturbance in their habitat due to plantation activities. All types of shooting have now been prohibited in the forests of the district since October 15, 1965, for a period of 10 years. Sambar has also declined in numbers. The Himalayan black bear is fairly common in deodar and fir forest near Molta and Chambi. It lives on roots, acorn of oaks, grains, fruits and bark of trees and also feed on carrions, eggs and birds but seldom kills for flesh though there are execptions. The wild cat is found near about the Kalsi forest block and preys on birds and poultry. The *kastura* or musk deer frequents steep hills near Mundali and is found above the altitude of 2,700 m. It has become rare due to poaching for musk supply. The barking dear or *kakar* likes thick forests preferably of oaks and avoids dry rocky area. It is found near Moltas, Ringali and Mundali, though not in large numbers. *Gural* is found in the hilly forests of the Binhar, Bakarna, Batoli and Rekholi forest blocks. Wild bear occur everywhere, but they are more numerous in the forest block of Jhajra. The elephant is the biggest representative of the non-game animals. The forests of the West Dehra Dun division along the Siwalik slopes were never visited previously by wild elephants, but for some years now herds of these have been coming from the Lansdowne side and operate mainly between Karwa Pani and Timli. Jackals are found all over the district. Melinos and Albinous of all species have been declared protected by government.

Birds

All the birds of the plains are found in the Dun valley. Among game birds may be mentioned the black *partridge (kala titar)*, grey partridge *(safed titar)*, red jungle fowl *(murgi)*, snipe, kalij pheasant, brahimint duck teal goose, spot bill duck, green pigeon *(harial)*, chakor partridge, common pochard and black bulbul. Wood-cocks are not common.

In the hills many well-known Europeans species are to be met with: thrushes, water ouzels, yellow and pied wagtails, swallows, swifts, king-fishers, wood-peckers, cuckoo, tree-creepers, shrikes, robins, red-starts and warblers of many kind. The *kalij (Lophura locomela)* is a common bird which inhabits areas below 2,600 m. and prefers heavy undergrowth of forests. The *koklas (Pucrasia macrolopha)* is found in deodar and fir forests and prefers moist wooded forests with undergrowth. The monal is sometimes seen in the *kharsu* and fir forests and is not as common as other pheasants. Among partridges the *chakor (Alectoris gracal)* is found on rocky slopes dotted with bush and grass throughout Jaunsar Bawar and is a regular visitor of cultivated fields. It is found in parties of six to twenty.

The black partridge *(Francolinus francolinus)* is sighted singly or in pairs up to the altitude of 1,800 m. in grassy scrub patches near cultivation. The *peora* or hill partridge *(Arborophila targueola)* is a dweller of *ban* forests. Among pigeons the *harial (Treron sphenurs)* is seen in flocks in summer mostly in *ban* forests and the blue-rock *(Columba livia)* is found up to an altitude of 1,800 m. and visits cultivated fields regularly. The ringed dove *(Streptopelia decaocts)* is a migratory bird which frequents wooden land and comes near cultivation or outhouses of bungalows in search of food. The *wood-cock (Scolopax rusticola)* is a dweller of moist fir forests and being mainly a nocturnal creature is seldom sighted.

Reptiles

In this district the commonest reptile is the harmless ratsnake *(dhaman)*, which grows to two metres and more while the cobra is the most poisonous one. King cobra and python also occur occasionally in these forests. Python, monitor lizard, water lizard and crocodile have also been declared protected species.

Fish

The rivers of the district abound in fish. *Mahasher* and other varieties of fish are found in the Ganga. Fishing in the Yamuna near Kulhal used to be quite popular in the past but this attraction has now ceased. About 35 varieties of fish are found in the district, the chief being *karaonch (Labeocalbasu), doongra (Labeodero) mahasher (Tortor), bhitti (Puntiustict), phaddar (Puntiussophore), singhi (Hetropneus fossilis) sua (Exenentodoncancila), bam (Macestocembalus Armatus)* and *parhan (Wallagoattu).*

Game-Laws

Till the beginning of the present century, the wild life of the district was greatly imperilled on account of indiscriminate activities of hunters and poachers. Its depletion was so rapid that certain species were threatened with extinction. In order to preserve wild life and game species from further ravages, a number of Acts such as the Wild Birds and Animals Protection Act, 1912, the Indian Forest Act, 1927, the Wild Birds and Animals Protection U.P. Amendment Act, (Act XIII of 1934), U.P. Private Forests Act, 1948, and the Indian Forest Act, 1951 were enforced in this district as elsewhere in the State.

The game-laws obtaining in the district, at present are governed by the Wild Protection Act, 1972. This Act imposes a total ban on the shooting of such species as the tiger and the leopard, which were otherwise getting close to extinction, Game rules are available from the Forest Department of the State. Facilities for big game shooting in the district (except the preserved species) are provided in the Jhabrawala and Barkot forest blocks of Dehra Dun forest division against permits obtainable from the Chief Wild Life Warden, U.P.

Source : Dangli Prasad Varun, *Dehradun Gazetteer,* Government of India Press, Lucknow, 1979.

14

GARHWAL DISTRICT

Origin of Name

Garhwal forms part of the Garhwal Division, a vast hill tract, comprising the five districts of Chamoli, Dehra Dun, Tehri Garhwal, Uttar Kashi and Garhwal. The word or name Garhwal means having or possessing *garh* (forts), Tradition has it that the tract was a "Bawani" meaning having *bawan* or 52 forts, the region at one time being occupied by 52 chiefs, each with his own fort. The name has also been interpreted to denote a country of *gads*—a *gad* being the local term for a narrow valley. The district of Garhwal as the name suggests, is like a fort, having high ridges for the ramparts, the *bhabar* for the gradient and the town known as Kotdwara (meaning *dwar* or gate of the *kot* or fort) on the left bank of the river being the entrance to the fort.

Location, Boundaries, Area and Population

Location and Boundaries

The district lies between Lat. 29° 26' and 30° N. and Long. 78° 12' and 79° 14' E. In shape it looks like an equilateral triangle with its southern apex protruding between the districts of Bijnor and Naini Tal, the western between the districts of Bijnor and Dehradun and the North-eastern between Tehri Garhwal and Chamoli. It is bounded on the north and north-west by the Alaknanda and the Ganga respectively which separate it from the districts of Tehri Garhwal and Dehra Dun. The north-eastern side is bounded by district Chamoli and the eastern by district Almora.

District Naini Tal and Bijnor lie to the south-east and south-west respectively and that of Dehra Dun to the north-west. The maximum length from east to west is 103 km. and the maximum breadth from north to south about 100 km.

Area

According to the Central Statistical Organisation of India, the district had an area of 5,440 sq. km in 1971 and stood 23rd in respect of area among the districts of Uttar Pradesh.

Population

According to the census of 1971 the population of the district was 5,53,028 (females 2,91,974), the rural population being 5,18,181 (females 2,78,344) and the urban 34,847 (females 13,630.). The district then stood 50th in respect of population in Uttar Pradesh.

History of District as Administrative Unit

Centuries ago, the entire Garhwal region was divided into a number of petty principalities, said to have been 52 in numbers, which were subsequently united under Ajaypal, 37th in the line of descent among the Panwar rulers, who had started the process of integration in A.D. 883. In 1803, the Gurkhas from Nepal invaded this region and the ruler Raja Pradyuman Sah was killed at Dehra Dun but his son Sudarshan Sah succeeded in freeing the region from them in 1815 with the help of the East India Company but the latter compelled him to cede to it a substantial area which was administered directly by the Company through a Commissioner. In 1837, Garhwal became a separate subdivision under an Assistant Commissioner and in 1891 it was constituted a district which was named British Garhwal. It was then divided into three subdivisions. Pauri, Lansdowne and Chamoli, each under the charge of a deputy collector. After Independence, in 1947, the word "British" was dropped from the name. In 1960 the sub-division or tahsil of Chamoli was separated to form the district of Chamoli. The district formed part of the Kumaon Division till 1968. when it was included in the newly created Garhwal Division.

Sub-division, Tahsils and Thanas

The district has been divided into two sub-divisions, Barahsyun and

Lansdowne, the former comprising tahsil Pauri and the latter tahsil Lansdowne.

Tahsil Pauri, comprising the north-eastern part of the district, is bounded on the north-west by the Ganga and on the north by the Alaknanda, both separating it from district Tehri Garhwal. On the north-east lies the district of Chamoli and the south-eastern boundary is formed by the district of Almora and tahsil Lansdowne, the latter forming the western boundary also. According to the census of 1971, it has a population of 2,05,163 (females 1,11,693), the rural population being 1,90,139 (females 1,05,598) and the urban 15,024 (females 6,095). The tahsil contains 1,207 inhabited and 185 uninhabited villages besides the towns of Pauri, Srinagar and Bah Bazar (Bah). For development purpose, it has been divided into six development blocks.

Tahsil Lansdowne, comprising the major portion of the district is bounded on the north-west and north by district Tehri Garhwal and tahsil Pauri respectively, the former being separated from the tahsil by the river Ganga and the latter by the river Nayar. On the east lies the Almora district and on the south-east the district of Naini Tal. The southern and the western boundaries are formed by district Bijnor and on the north-west lies the district of Dehra Dun, the Ganga flowing in between tahsil Lansdowne and district Dehra Dun. Tahsil Lansdowne, which is bigger than the Pauri tahsil in size has, according to the census of 1971, a population of 3,47,865 (females 1,80,281), the rural population being 3,28,042 (females 1,72,746) and the urban 19,823 (females 7,535). The tahsil contains 2.029 inhabited and 157 uninhabited villages besides the towns of Kotdwara. Lansdowne and Dogadda. For development purpose it has been divided into eight development blocks.

Thanas

There are four thanas in the district, one each located at Kotdwara, Lansdowne, Pauri and Srinagar, most of the police work being done by the *patwari* who has the powers of a station officer within his own *patti*. The *patwaris* are collectively known as the Garhwal revenue police. The number of police out-posts in the district is 11 of which one is located at Devaprayag (in district Tehri Garhwal)

Topography

The district is almost entirely mountanious with no level terrain except the pasture of Panai on the banks of the Alaknanda, the helm of Srinagar and the submountainous tract. It consists of a succession of steep mountain ridges divided from each other by deep valleys which are narrow and precipitous. Physiographically, it may be divided into three main parts, the mountains and ridges, the valleys and lastly, the submountainous tracts.

Mountains and Ridges

The spur which gives the key to the mountain system of Garhwal is one which proceeding from Nandakot in district Chamoli, runs down the left bank of the Pindar in a south-westerly direction in district Chamoli and afterwards in westerly direction to the Dodatoli range in this district which is the most massive range in the whole of the Garhwal Division. The main peak, Dodatoli, on the eastern border of the district, is 3,174 m. above sea-level. Spurs which preserve a mean elevation of 2,438 m. branch off from this peak in all directions. Of these the most important are the one to the north-west of the Dhanpur range, another south-west of the Devithank and Ameli group and a third, south-ward of the Khatli hills. In the Dhanpur range, once remarkable for its copper mines the precipitous black rock of the Bandhangarhi spur is observed. The range runs due east and west, preserving an altitude of over 2,740 m for 11 km. and contains several peaks over 2,950 m. in height. It continues east-ward and southward through Khirsu. Devidat (above Pauri) and Ranigarh (Adwani), all its peaks being above 2,130 m. above sea-level and only a few parts of the range being less than 1,830 m. to Byansghat, the whole thus separating the Nayar valley from the Alaknanda. The Ameli spur, which continues as far as the junction of the eastern and western Nayars and separates the valley formed by these two rivers. The Binsar spur, with its continuing ranges, froms the eastern and southern boundaries of the Nayar basin the Ranigarh forming its northern and western boundaries. The Khatli range which is joined to the Dodatoli by the Binsar spur runs east and west and continues from Khamlekgarhi on the Almora border to Rikhnikhal, a low pass between the Iriyakot and Painon *patties.* The principal peak is over 2,440 m. above sea-level, several being above 2,130 m. The ridge, continuing towards the west between Rikhnikhal and Chametakhal (above 1,200 m.) is known as the Utain range from the principal peak which is over 2,100 m. in height. The ridge thence continues in a succession of peaks, among which the Kalongarhi (Lansdowne) and the Langurgarhi are the most important and passes to Karaunnda *(Kich-ka-danda)* where the ridge splits into two which enclose the Huin) valley and separate it on the one hand from the Nayar and the Ganga and on the other from the minor streams flowing direct to the plains.

Valleys

The valleys in the district are deep depressions, from the line of drainage for all surplus water between the ranges and are the other natural and distinctive features of the district. The continuous action of water has ploughed those valleys out of the great mountain mass. The chief valleys in the district are those of the Ganga, the Alaknanda, the Ramganga and the Nayar and its two branches.

The Ganga valley, which commences almost from the confluence of the Bhagirathi and the Alaknanda near Bah comprises a narrow belt as far as Byansghat (in pargana Barhasyun) and a strip along the northern part of pargana Ganga Salan. The valley in pargana Barhasyun is comparatively wider and well cultivated. The villages are large and the population is hard working. In pargana Ganga Salan it is rocky and rugged as the river forces its way through steep precipices. Here the villages are small and poor, the population is sparse and only scattered patches of cultivated land are found here and there.

The Alaknanda valley borders the district on the north from Sivanandi to Bah and includes the Panal and Srinagar valleys. The road to Badrinath runs through it, the scenery along it being particularly striking and beautiful. Devalgarh the seat of the early rajas of Garhwal, Srinagar, the ancient capital, and the Dhanpur copper mines are located in this valley. The upper portion of the valley is covered with forests of *banj* (oak) and *chir* (pine). In the lower portions the forests have been cleared from the level ground and gently sloping hills and the tracts so cleared have been brought under the plough.

Patlidun is the name given to the grassland lying on both sides of the Ramganga. This grassland forms a valley about 20 km. long and 1.5 km. to 3 km wide. It is separated from the Kohtri and Chokham *duns* by some kilometres of precipitous and broken tract on the west. On the south two ridges of low hills separate it from the *bhabhar*. The whole country is one mass of watercourses, known locally as *sots* or *raos,* which drain the ridges on both sides of the Ramganga valley. The sal (*Shorea rubusta* forests, through which the Ramganga flows, the situated on slopes, sometimes gentle, sometimes precipitous and steep till 1858 when it was handed over to the forest department. The villagers and cultivators were removed from the area and were given lands elsewhere. Tigers and wild animals are fairly numerous in the area and owing to the broken nature of the country and unlimited water supply the tract forms a natural game preserve. The forest department has inspection bungalows every 13 to 15 km. down the Ramganga from where it enters the reserved forests to Kalagarh.

The valleys of the two branches of the Nayar drain the central part of the district. The northern and southern branches of the Western Nayar join at Paihani and from there onwards the valley assumes an average width of half to two kilometre. The valley is fertile as that of the Ganga is pargana Barahsyun. There are many villages here and people are better off than in other areas. The eastern Nayar joins the Western Nayar near Naugaon. There are duns or valleys in almost every hill *patti* through which small rivers flow, taking their rise in the low Garhwal hills, the notable ones being the Chokham and Kohtri *duns* which lie to the west of Patlidun and are much smaller in extent. Each of these duns is generally traversed by a forest road down which timber and forest produce pass to the plains and which are also used by the hill villagers for the export of grass and merchandise.

Bhabhar or Sub-mountainous Tract

This is a narrow strip of land about 95 km in length and not less than 3 km in width, stretching along the foot of the hills. This tract is waterless as the rivers disappear underground after debouching from the hills, to reappear above the surface some kilometres further south. Cultivation is carried on only by irrigation through canals which tap the river water before it sinks into the ground. At the time of the British occupation in 1815 the *bhabhar* was entirely covered with forest but the remains of a fort and a tank at Mawakot (about 8 km. west of Kotdwara) point to the fact that in the time of the Garhwal rajas, this tract was inhabited, its value apparently being in its grazing grounds and forest produce. There are a few villages just outside the hills below the Patlidun which have been under the plough since the early part of the last century but cultivation in right earnest may be said to have begun only in 1869-70. The forests, which abounded in this area were very gradually cleared and more and more land brought under the plough. Practically the whole of the cultivation in this part of the district is dependent on the canals taken from the Khoh and Malin rivers and other streams.

River System and Water Resources

The chief rivers flowing through the district are the Ganga with its tributaries, namely, the Alaknanda, the Nayar, the Huinl, the Malin; and the Ramganga with its tributary the Mandal. There are several small streams which rise in the lower hills of Garhwal and join these rivers either in the district or in district Bijnor.

Ganga

Rising in the Gaumukh glacier in district Uttar Kashi the Ganga first known as the Bhagirathi assumes the name 'Ganga' after the confluence of the Bhagirathi and the Alaknanda near Devaprayag (in district Tehri Garhwal). On the opposite side of Devaprayag is Bah where it first touches this district and flows south forming the northern and north-western boundaries of the Garhwal district which it separates from district Tehri Garhwal as far as Lakshaman Jhula. At Byansghat it is joined by the Nayar. From this point it flows almost due west as far as Lakshaman Jhula having received the Huinl river at Phulari. From Lakshaman Jhula it takes a south-westerly course to Hardwar separating the district from district Dehra Dun and then leaves the district.

Huinl

This stream, also known as the Huil or Hinuwal, rises in the ranges of *patti* Dalralyun, drains the tract to the south and west of the Nayar drainage area and, taking a north-westerly course for about 32 km. turns due west and falls into the Ganga on its left bank at Phulari about 8 km above where the Ganga debouches into the plain at Rishikesh. There is a large section of irrigated land along its banks wherever the valley widens out.

Ramganga

This river, also known as the Western Ramganga, rises in the Dodatoli and running through district Almora enters district Garhwal in the south-eastern part of tahsil Lansdowne near the Gaula where it receives the Mandal. It then flows through the tahsil in an easterly direction as far as its junction with the Palain, about 3 km. north of the Baksar rest house. Turning south-ward and flowing for some kilometers through tahsil Lansdowne, it leaves the district near Kalagarh. The river always contains water and during the rains is a seething torrent, debouching on the plains at Kalagarh.

Malin

The river, a tributary of the Ganga, bears this name when it issues from the hills at Chaukighat. In the upper reaches it is known as the Saurgadh, its source being among the ranges to the east of the Saur village in *patti* Walla Ajmer. It first runs in a westerly direction as far as the village of Ranesa, then takes a southerly direction till it leaves the district near the village of Haldu Khata. It is a river of some historical interest. It has been tentatively identified with the Erineses mentioned about 300 B.C. by the Greek ambassador, Megasthenes; some 250 years later the poet Kalidasa immortalized the stream in his famous drama, *Abhigyan Shakuntalam*. It was on the banks of the Malin that the king Dushyanta, persued an antelope to its refuge in the shrine of the rishi Kanva and it was in the forest on the river bank Dushyanta first met Shakuntala, his future queen. Canals have been taken out from the river just below the Chaukighat to irrigate the areas in the *bhabar*.

Mandal

This river, a tributary of the Ramganga, rises on the southern slope of the ranges lying in the eastern parts of *pattis* Talla Badalpur and Painon of pargana Talla Salan and has three main sources. The most westerly, rising near Maraura in Talla Badalpur, takes a south-south easterly course through Painon and passing the village of Jamri and Dabrya joins, near Jhart, the main branch which rises close by in the eastern declivities of the Dhargaon range. The third branch drains the eastern part of *patti* Painon and flowing nearly due south by Badiyargaon and Kotri joins the main stream at Raunderi. The united stream flows nearly due east through *pattis* Painon, Bunga and Bijlot with a course of about 32 km. until it joins the Ramganga on the right bank at the head of the Patlidun above Sarapdhuli. In the dry season the Mandal is a petty stream but becomes torrential during the rains. For the last 15 km of its course it has a very slight fall. Its wate is largely used for irrigation, there being many fine flat along its banks which are highly cultivated. The hills on both sides are covered with sal forests.

Alaknanda

The Alaknanda rises in district Chamoli and first touches district Garhwal near Sivanandi. It then flows almost due west for about 15 km. separating the district from district Chamoli as far as Rudraprayag. The turning south-west it flows for about 70 km. from Srinagar to Devaprayag and separates the district from district Tehri Garhwal.

Nayar

One of the main tributaries of the Ganga in this district is formed by the confluence at Batkholu (in *patti* Manyarsyum, pargana Barahsyurn) of the eastern and western branches of the Nayar. The former known as Eastern Nayar, rises in the north-western slopes of the Dodatoli range at an elevation between 2,130 m and 2,750 m. At first it follows a south-westerly course, then a southerly and then a westerly to the confluence with the Western Nayar or Chiphalghat. From there the united stream flows north-west and falls into the Ganga at Byansghat, at an elevation of about 430 m. above sea-level. From their sources to their junction both branches have a rapid fall but below the junction the river forms a succession of deep pools which have an abundance of fish.

The Eastern Nayar flows through parganas Chandpur, Malla Salan, Talla Salan and Barahsyun and for a short distance forms the boundary between Chaundkot and Malla Salan. From the junction the united streams form the boundary between parganas Ganga Salan and Barahsyun. The streams which unite to form its headwaters near Marwara in *patti* Choprakot are the Syonis, Khirganga, Landholi, Dumodhyar and Pathargadh. The principal feeders on the right bank are the Musetigadh and Machhlad, which drain the eastern *pattis* of pargana Chandkot and at their junction form the boundary between *pattis* Kalagarh and Gurarsyun. On the left the Eastern Nayar receives first the Khatalgadh which rises near Lakhora in district almora and drains *patti* Khatli and then the Maidi which drains the entire valley of Kurya and the upper portions of Sila. There are some large villages close to the banks of the Eastern Nayar among which are Marwara, Hansuri, in *patti* Choprakot, Chorpala in Walla Khatli, Kalwari in Iniyakot and Kande, Babina and Toli in Malla Badalpur.

The northern branch of the Western Nayar takes its rise near Khand in *patti* Kandarsyun of pargana Devalgarh and flowing in a south-westerly direction unites with the southern branch near Paithani in the same *patti*. The latter drains the high lands of *patti* Dhaijyuli and is the more considerable of the two, flowing about 19 km. north-west before reaching the junction. The Western Nayar receives numerous feeders draining the slopes on either side of the tract through which it flows, among them being the Pasin, Kota and Ira streams on the right bank and the Peu kul and other minor torrents on the left. Usually in August and September (a favourable time of the year) the river is blocked in many places by weirs, to which are fixed conically shaped baskets arranged to catch the fish coming down with the flood water. The inhabitants along the banks regard fish as one of their staple foods.

Geology

Geomorphologically, the district may be divided into four zones: the outermost southern belt of the Siwalik rocks forming the southern hill-rampart of the district; the mountain range of Gankia Danda-Lansodowne-Ghungti belt; the central valley of the Nayar river and its tributaries opening a belt of slate series and the northern belt of very high mountains of Golikhal-Sount-khal-Dodatoli Dharmallhori Gali, made up of immense pile of crystalline metamorphic and associated granitic rocks.

Earthquakes

The district falls in a zone liable to heavy damage by earthquakes. Being situated in the Himalayan Boundary Fault Zone of the central Himalayan thurst the district experience the effect of moderate to great earthquakes occurring there. The important earthquakes experienced in the district were the Kangra earthquake of April 4, 1905, Dharchula earthquake of August 28, 1916, Kapkote earthquake of December 28, 1958, and Kinnaur earthquake of January, 1975. In the seismic map of India (prepared under the auspices of the Indian Standards Institution) district Garhwal has been placed in zone IX, the maximum intensity actually experienced due to past earthquakes having reached VIII on the Modified Mercalli Intensity Scale—1931 (between I, meaning 'not felt' and XII, meaning 'total damage').

Economic Mineral Deposits

High grade limestone, used in the manufacture of cement, lime, sugar and paper, occurs in the upper Krol formation of the Lakshaman Jhula area and the deposits are mined extensively Upper Tal limestone, between the Bidasini and Huinl valleys to the east of the Ganga valley, has been found useful for cement making. Limestone is also used as flux in the steel and maganese industries. It is used as a filler in the making of papers, rubber and soap. Most commonly, lime is prepared from this rock.

Lenses and pockets of gypsum occur in the upper Krol lime-stones of the Lakshaman Jhula area. Dhotra, near Lakshaman Jhula is one of the main sources of gypsum in Uttar Pradesh, which is used mainly for the making of plaster of Paris.

There is a possibility of the occurrence of phosphatic deposits in the lower Tals of the Lakshaman Jhula-Huinl tract in the Ganga valley.

Small sporadic pockets of graphite have been reported from Mansari.

Climate

A fairly long and moderately severe winter is the chief characteristic of the climate of the district. Being situated on the southern slopes of the Himalayas, it gets a good rainfall from the south-west monsoon current but tropical heat may be experienced from April to May and in the first half of June in the valleys and comparatively lower elevated areas.

The rainy season generally commences from the third week of June and lasts till the end of September. The period from October to middle of November constitutes the post-monsoon season and after which the winter season sets in, which lasts till about the middle of March and is followed by the summer or pre-monsson season (middle of March to middle of June).

Rainfall

Long-term rainfall records are available for five rain-gauge stations, Pauri, Srinagar, Kotdwara, Bironkhal and Lansdowne.

Rainfall in the district has large variations, mainly due to its orography in the south-western part of the district the annual rainfall is 2,117 mm at Lansdowne, while at Srinagar in the north it is as low as 948 mm. Nearly 80 per cent of the annual rainfall is received during the monsoon months (June to September). July and August are the rainiest months when nearly 55 per cent of the annual rainfall in the district occurs. The winter precipitation, from December to February, accounts for nearly 10 per cent of the annual rainfall. There are two rainfall minima, one in April and the other in November. After April, the rainfall gradually increases till June and after that sharply during July and August. It decreases rapidly after the withdrawal of the south-west monsoon in September. During the monsoon, under favourable conditions, spurts of heavy rain may occur in the hills causing inundations of the small tributaries. Precipitation during winter months is often associated with the passage of low pressure systems from the west known western disturbances, and is sometimes in the from of snowfalls, particularly at higher elevations. Precipitation during the premonsoon months in mostly associated with thunderstorms.

The year to year variation of rainfall in the district as a whole is not very appreciable. In the fifty-year period 1991 to 1950, the district recorded the highest rainfall in 1917 and the lowest in 1918. The frequency of annual rainfall in the district in various ranges is given in Table 14.1

TABLE 14.1: Annual Rainfall Frequency

Range in mm.	No. of years	Range in mm.	No. of years
901-1000	3	1,601-1,700	6
1001-1100	2	1,701-1,800	2
1101-1200	3	1,801-1,900	1
1201-1300	8	1,901-2,000	3
1301-1400	6	2,001-2,100	2
1401-1500	10	2,101-2,200	1
1501-1600	3		

The average number of rainy days (days having rainfall of 2.5 mm. or more) varies from 59 at Srinagar to 83 at lansdowne.

The heaviest rainfall in 24 hours recorded at any station in the district was 349.0 mm. at Kotdwars on August 27,1892.

Temperature

There being no meteorological observatory in the district, the description that follows is based on records of observatory stations in the surrounding districts having similar climatic conditions.

The temperature varies considerably from place to place depending on the elevation. Generally the end of May or the beginning of June is the hottest period. The mean daily maximum temperature in the valleys (with elevation less than 1,000 m.) is around 36°C in the month of May and around 26°C at about 2,000 m. and still lower at higher altitudes. On individual days the maximum temperature may rise to over 40°C in the valleys and to about 24°C at 2,000 m. in the month of May. With the on set of the monsoon, the day temperatures fall by about 3°C to 5°C with its withdrawal by the end of September, both day and night temperatures start falling, reaching the lowest values in January. The mean daily maximum and minimum temperatures in January in the valleys at the elevation of less than 1,000 m. are of the order of 19°C and 6°C at the elevation of 2,000 m. During the winter months cold waves, associated with western disturbances many bring night temperatures down appreciably, even to below the freezing point of water on some occasions.

Humidity

Summer (March to May) is the driest part of the year with relative humidity between 30 to 40 per cent. During the monsoon season (from June to September) the humidity attains a value of about 70 to 90 per cent while it remains between 50 to 60 per cent during the remaining parts of the year.

Clouds

In the monsoon months from July to September, skies are generally heavily clouded. Heavy clouding also persists in short spells during the winter months when the district is affected by passing western disturbances.

Winds

Winds are generally light, of the order of 3 to 4 km. per hour in the valleys and 5 to 8 km. per hour at elevations about 2,000 m. above sea-level and increase in velocity in the higher altitudes. In the wake of western disturbances and in association with thunderstorms, they may become quite strong. Strong katavatic winds may also be experienced during the night as local effects produced by the nature of the terrain.

Special Weather Phenomena

Thunderstorms occur througout the year, their frequency being the least in November and December. Their activity is greatest during the period from May to September and during winter and the pre-monsoon months they are sometimes accompanied by hail. Dust-storms are rare and occur, if at all, in the valleys in summer. Fog is common during the monsoon months and it may also occur in association with western disturbances. Morning fog may occur in the valleys frequently in winter

Flora

The flora of the district includes the vast range found in the Himalayas, varying from the sub-tropical species growing in the outer range of low hills and the *bhabhar* tract, to the templerate species growing in the higher altitude in the north. Till the beginning of the last quarter of the 19th century the forest of the district had been neglected. Certaiin tracts were seriously prejudiced by the absence of adjacent forests from which people could procure wood for building, agricultural implements fuel, etc. Indiscriminate fellings in the past also resulted in denudation of hill sides and consequent land-slips. They also suffered greatly by the extension of cultivation which led to extensive deforestation. In the beginning of the present century the parganas of Chaundkot and Barahsyun were a thickly populated and intensely cultivated belt of the district but the pasture for cattle and wood for fuel and building was greatly in deficit. The Nayar valley (lying to the south of the parganas of Chaundkot and Barahsyun was covered, for the most part with a prolific bush jungle and supplied the neighbouring villages with fuel and, to a certain extent, timber. The pressure of population here found its outlet in what is known as *khatil,* an intermittent form of cultivation which consisted in roughly clearing the forests and sowing the land so exposed without terracing or otherwise protecting it and then abandoning it after a crop or two has been taken, the operation being repeated in another forest block. Thus a steep hillside is stripped of its protection against the weather, land-slips destroy the hillsides and any fertile riverain land and much useful fuel is wasted. This type of cultivation has long been prohibited in the district. Owing to the scanty population and unhealthy climate in the southern tract of the district, therewas reckless extension of cultivation into the forest areas which occurred in the northern portion of the district. Similarly the forests of the Dodatoli and Dhanpur ranges in the north of parganas Chaundkot and Barahayum remained mostly unaffected they were mostly on a higher altitude for cultivation. The southern forests were transferred to the forest department in 1878 and the remainder were left under the district administration (and were called district forests). Since the forest settlement of 1911-17, a part of the district forests was declared to the reserved forest. As a result of the Kumaon forest grievances Committee recommendations about 26,330 ha. of reserved forest ceased to be reserved in 1921. In 1964 about 35,200 ha. of district forests were vested in the forest department.

The forest area of the district comprises the whole of the Garhwal and Lansdowne forest divisions and the greater part of the Kalagarh forest division. The area of the forests in the district under the department is about 2,46,247 ha. of which an area of 69,011 ha. lies in the Garhwal forest division, 35,150 ha. in the Lansdowne forest division and 92,086 ha. in the Kalagarh forest division. The civil or district forests occur in strips around abadi sites and their exact area is not known.

The forests in the district extend from about 250 m. to over 3,000 m. above sea-level and may be divided into three main altitudinal floristic divisions, the outer foot-hill forests, the warm temperate forests and the cool temperate forest.

Outer Foot-hill Forests

These forests occur between the altitudes of 250 m. to 1,100 m. sal being the dominant species often growing by itself or with a small admixture of its common associates *asna (Terminalia altavar, T. tomentosa), haldu (Adina cardifolia)* and *dhauri (Lagersbronemia speciosa).* The extensive sal forests are interrupted by grassy patches in flat lowlying pockers, strips of as riverain forests and tracts of miscellaneous forests. These forests are of the following main types and are described briefly below.

Riverain Forests

These forests are chiefly composed of sissoo *(shisham-Dalbergia sissoo)* which occure pure or mixed with *khair (Acacia catechu), ber (Zyzyphus* spp.) *kanju, ehretia* and *semal (Salmalia malaborica).* Among grasses are *kans (Sackharump spontanum) munj (Succharum munja), sui (Aristida cyanantha), Arundodonese, fragmites* and *Tuypha elephantina.* The common shrubs growing here are *rohini, Adhatoda vasica, Murraya koenighii, Pogostemon* spp., *Lantana* spp. *(causal), Pulranjiva* spp. and *jhou* (tamarix).

Plain Miscellaneous Forests

The common species found in these forests are *khair, semal, dhak, sissoo, kanju* and *ber* at lower altitudes and *jamun (Syxzygum umini), pyaman, kaula (Macholus odoratissime), pabal, qutel (Trewia nudiflora), Jhingan (Lannea arandis), siris (Albizzia* species), *bahera (Terminalia belerica) pula, chila* and *amaltas (Cassia fistula).* The undergrowth consists of *Colebrookia murroya, Glycosmis helicters* and *Citrus medica.*

Bhabar Forests

The Common plants found in these forests are *haldu, kusum (Sohleishera oleosa), phaldu (Mytragyna parvifolia) khumbhi (Caleya urborea) dhauri, saonjna (Moringa ptery gosperma), Wrightia tomentosa* and *Litsala Polyaltha.* The under growth consists of *Milletia ansculter* and *Clerodendton infortunatum.* The common grasses are *dub (Desmostachya bipinnata) khas (Veticeria zizarioides), siru (Imperata cylinbrica)* and *Neyraundia arundinancea.*

Hill Forests

The species growing in these forests is the sal with its chief associates the *sain (Asna), dhauri, bakli, sandan (Ougenia dalbergiodes), bhalawa (Semecarpus anacardium), kathhalawa (Buchanania latifolia), harra (Terminalia chebula), cheura (Bassia butyracea)* and *Bassia latifolia, Bamboo (Dendrocalamus strictus)* is a very common undergrowth. Less common are *Bischofia javanica, Engelharevita, colerookiana, Ardisia humilis, Calicarpa mecropuylla* and *Bochmeria rugulosa.* On higher slopes *Woodjordia frutions* and *Indigofera* (species) are common. The common grasses are *baib (Eulaliopsis binata), kumeria (Heberopogen contorlus)* and *goria (Chrysopogen montana).* At its higher reaches sal is closely associated with *chir (Pinus, roxburghii)* forming two-storeyed forests with *chir* in the top canopy and sal in the lower storey. A very rare and peculiar admixture of sal and a moist temperate species, *banj (Quercus incana), Acer oblongum* and *Machilus adoratissima* occurs along with associates banj at an elevation of about 850 m. at Rathuwadhat in the Adnala range of the Kalagarh forest division in cold moist valleys on its northern slopes where the *banj* is coming up profusely in natural regeneration.

Warm Temperate Forests

Between the altitudes of 1,000 m. and 2,000 m., the dominent species is the *chir (Piuns roxburghii).* There is hardly any undergrowth except for some casual *Rubus berberis* and *indigofera* shrubs. The vast *chir* expanses are broken up by pockets of *banj* oak on the moist river banks and in the cool northern aspects. *Buruns (Rhododendron arboreum)* and *ayar (Pieris ovaliforlia)* are the two common associates of *banj* oak which descends casually even below the chir zone in moist shady localities and also extends far above the higher reaches of the *chir,* where its common associates are *hill toon (Cedrella serrata), pangar (Acsculus indica),* bird cherry walnut and *Acer* (species). At about 2,300 m. or even 2.000 m in cool aspects, *banj* occurs with moru *oak (Quercus dilatata).*

Cool Temperate Forests

Between the attitudes of 2,650 m. and 3,350 m., the oak gives place to *kharsu (Quercus semecarpifolia)* which occurs mixed with the high level pines such as silver fir and spruce. In the nullahs the common species are *alder (Alorusnitida)* and *elms (Ulmus willichiana)*

In order to replenish and even to supplement the growing stock of valuable timber, species of industrially important plantations of *khair sissoo, haldu, semal siris (Cedrela toona) toon* and *mulbery* have been raised in the *bhabar* and *walnut,* chestnut, *chir, cypress,* bird cherry, maple ash, cypress and willows in the hills. By doing silvicultural, thinnings in the commercially important species, such as sal, sissoo, *khari, chir* and firs, the natural phenomenon of the survival of the fittest is implemented in order to create optimum growing conditions. Methods of control are applied in exploiting the number of mature trees in order to ensure a sustained yield of such trees. As a measure of strict fire control, the vegetation is preserved and noteworthy feature is that the vegetation zones are ascending, sal extending higher than its original upper limits and chir, oak and their associates also doing likewise.

Fauna

From times immemorial the district has been the habitat of a large variety of materials, birds, reptiles and fish. Among animals the elephant was once found in its wild state in the Garhwal *bhabar* and formerly considerable herds of elephants used to range the *bhabar* forests, particularly near about Patilidun but the depridations of the Balrampur, *Kheddah* thinned their numbers so drastically that the practice was discontinued from 1903. As a result, the population of wild elephants has increased, especially in the Lansdowne forest division.

Tiger *(Panthera tigris)* is fairly common in the *bhabar* and is found up to about 3,000 m. The panther *(Panthera pardus),* which is common throughout the district, is very troublesome. The snow leopard *(Panthera uncia)* occurs (but rarely) in upper Garhwal. The hyaena *(Hyaena pinnacus)* is scarce and is called here *charak.* The common sloth bear *(Ursus labiatus)* is found in the *bhabar* and lower *hills.* The black Himalayan bear *(Ursus tibetanus* or *torquatus)* is very common, occurring down to about 1,000 m. and in the cold weather being found even in the *bhabar.* A good tree climber and fond of honey and the millet *(mandua)* it feeds on acorn and other jungle fruit and occasionally is even carnivorous. It is rarely seen except in the rains and not infrequently kills cattle, sheep and goats. Jungel cats of many kinds are common. The wild dog is not uncommon in the Dodatoli and some other places. The jackal *(Carris aurcus)* is found almost everywhere. The mountain fox here has a good thick fur. The *cutraila* or pine martin and od or otter cause much destruction langur *(Poesvtis antellus)* and the ordinary monkey of the plains. The blue bull *(Boselaphus tragocamelus)* is found chiefly in the *bhabar* tract.

Among the deer tribe the samber is the most widely distributed. It is found in the *bhabar* and in the hills (where it is called *jarao*) up to 3,000m. The hill sambar is much heavier than his plains counterpart and has very heavy horns. It is not very easily found as its home is in the middle of dense forests. The *chital* or spotted deer is the commonest of all its tribe and is found only in the submontane forests and occurs in herds of 60 or 80. The swamp deer *(gon)* and the hog deer *(parha)* are occasionally found by the river banks in the *bhabhar,* the formar now being almost extinct. The barking deer (kakar) is about a metre high. of a bright chestnut' colour, with forked horns rising from large pedicles. It derives its name from its cry, which is like the bark of a dog and is usually heard in the morning or the evening.

Among other wild animals are the goral *(Himalayan chamois)* found up to 3,100 m. It likes steep slopes not too thickly covered with pine. The average horn measurement is 10 to 15 cm. The *sara (Capricornis sumatralnsis)* is somewhat larger than the goral and is shy and likes dense jungles which cover precipitious rocks.

Birds

The district is rich in avifauna and in particular in pheasants, partridges, pigeons, doves and water-foul of various kinds. Birds life has a zonal distribution. Among pheasants the prized monal *Lophorphorus impeyan).* which is becoming extinct, is found above 2,700 m., the *koklas (Pucrasia macrolopha)* from 2,000 to 3,000 m. and the rather uncommon chir pheasant *(Catreus wallichii)* between 1,900-3,000 m. among partridges the well known *chakor (Alectoris gracea)* is very common; and the *peora (Arborophila torcueola)* is found occasionally in the denser forests. The black partridge *(Francolinus francolinus)* is often heard in sparsely populated areas.

The woodcock *(Scolopux rusticola)* is rare. In the *bhabar* and lower hills peafolw *(Pavo cristatus)* and red jungle fowl *(Gallus gallus)* are plentiful. Ducks occasionally rest on the rivers during their migration. among pigeons, the blue-rock *(Columba livia)* and the wood pigeon *(Columba palumbus)* are common. The ordinary birds of the plains like partridge *(Francolinus pondicerianus),* quail *(Coturniz communis)* and snipe *(Capella gallinago)* are to be found in the bhabar.

Reptiles

Snakes are not numerous but most of the species occurring in the plains are found in the district. The cobra, krait and the Russel's viper are commonly found up to 1,800 m. Among the non-venomous snakes, the python is most notable. It grows to a length of about 9 m. but specimens of over 6m though rare, are sometimes to be met with. The rat-snake and the pit viper, which attain a length of about 3 m. are also seen in the district. Among lizards the chief are the monitor lizard and the common house gecko. Several species of lizards are also frequenly seen. The crocodile and the *gharial (Gavialis gangecticus)* are found in the Ganga and the Ramganga.

Fish

Fish are found in almost all the rivers and streams of the district and in most part constitute the common food of the people. The chief species are *mahasher (Barbus tor), rohu (Labeo rohita), kali machi (Barbus chilinoides), asola (Schizothorax richardsoni, S. Plagiostomus* and *S. sinuatus), baiyan (Mastacembelus armatus), dhaur (Bareilus bendelisis,* B. *Barna,* B. *Nagra)* and *oadera (Nemacheilus bevani).*

Game Laws

Till the beginning of the last quarter of the nineteenth century, the wild life of the district was greatly imperilled on account of the wide and indiscriminate measures used by hunters and poachers. The process of depletion was so rapid that certain.

Ancient History

The early traditional history of the district of Garhwal is not without interest. It is situated in what has been described in ancient Indian literature as Upagiri, the outer ranges of the mid-Himalayan mountains, which comprises lowlying peaks rising contiguously with the plains of northern India.[1] The region of which this district forms a part has also been named Kedara Khanda, which has always been regarded by Hindus as the region of Kedarnath, that is Siva, and has been looked upon with reverence almost from the earliest times in its history.[2] Every hill river and temple of the district is reverently regarded and dedicated to one or other member of the greater Hindu pantheon. Legends of the gods, saints and holy men are associated with almost each peak, lake and waterfall.[3]

The district has also been associated with some mythological personalities mentioned in Brahmanical literature. Srinagar is associated with Satyansandha, a ruler is Satayuga, who invoked the goddess Durga to grant him power to kill the demon Kolasur. His request was granted and the place where Sriyantra the weapon used in its destruction, was lodged was called Srikshetra which gradually became Srinagar. The site where kolasur was killed is said to be the village Kulasu[4] (in tahsil Pauri). Srinagar is also believed to be the site of the disillusionment of Narada the great sage who being lured by the charm of Muni Shilanidhi's daughter had yearned to marry her his desire remaining unfulfiled.[5]

Traditional stories and names of places, sometimes corrupt in form, indicate that since primitive times the region including this district was inhabited, the earliest known inhabitants being the Yakshas. Ancient Indian literature contains numerous references to Kubera, who was their king.[6] The memory of the association of the Yakshas with this area lingers in a number of place names in the district such as Jakhan, Jakholi, Jakheti, etc. The Nagas were also connected with this region and the Alaknanda valley, the lower regions of which were most possibly known as Nagaloka.[7] The presence of Naga *toks (shrines)* and the apparent prevalence of Naga worship performed in most of the villages of the district even now are reminisent of the Naga elements in the history of the region's civilization.

The pre-Aryan people in this region were those usually known by the generic name Asuras, also referred to as Dasyus ro Dasas in Vedic literature. They opposed and gave fight to the Aryan invaders at every step. Their king, Shambara, a formidable opponent of the early Aryans, had great hold on Garhwal and Kumaon. He fought with Sudar the Bharata king of the Tritru family for about forty years, which is alluded to in a number of places in the Rigveda.[8]

The Aryans looked upon the Himalayan region with great reverence. The sanctity of this place also attracted Rama, the famous Aryan king of Kosala. It is said that he visited Srinagar for a few days and offered a thousand lotus flowers to Siva for explating his sin in killing the Rakshasa king Ravana[9] who was veteran devotee of Siva himself, at the shrine called Kamleshvara.[10]

A number of ancient Kshatriya kings of the plains seem to have tried to extend their authority over these parts. It was perhaps Arjuna, the third Pandava prince, who during the course of a Rajasuya Yajna (sacrifice) performed by his eldest brother Yudhisthira, as king of Indraprastha,[11] subjugated the hill kings and annexed the Himalayan region. The Kiratas, the Kunindas or Kulindas, etc., stated in the *Mahabharata* to have subjugated the older inhabitants and made them serfs inhabitated the Terai region. The rulers of the subjugated kingdoms are said to have presented gold dust clothes of different kinds and a conch having mystic powers of Yudhisthira in token of their alligiance to him.[12] When the Pandavas had lost their deminion by staking it in a gambling match with their cousins, the Kauravas, and were forced to go into exile for thirteen years and to spend the last year incognito[13] they had also sojourned for sometime at Sripura[14] in Garhwal which is identified with Srinagar, the capital of Subahu, the lord of Kulindavishya who accorded them a cordial welcome.[15] Even after completing the period of exile the Pandavas were not given their share in the kingdom and were supposedly forced to fight the battle of the *Mahabharata* for their claim in 1400 B.C.[16] In the war Subahu with his three sons sided with the Pandavas and helped them in achieving victory.[17] The Pandavas appear to have retained their supermacy over this area and Subahu's descendants ruled here as tributaries of the kings of Hastinapur. Janamejays, the great grandson of Arjuna, drove the Nagas out of the plains in order to avenge his father Parikshit's death which was caused by the Nagas. The Nagas took refuge in the hills and strengthened their position. It was probably at this time that the nominal sway of the Kurus ended in these parts.[18]

In course of time, in all probability, the Kulindas were replaced by the Kiratas after whom the region came to be called Kiratamandala. Another subsequently important tribe of the district was the Khasa, which originally penetrated these parts from the west, overpowered the old inhabitants in the 6th or 5th century B.C.[19] and gradually gained prominence in the district. They professed to be Rajputs who had given up their honourable position in society because they could not observe strictly the ceremonial usages of their relgion due to their living in a far off region and a different climate.[20] They established a number of petty Khasa chieftainships after which the region was called Khasamandala.[21] They adopted the Buddhist religion generally and during their reign Garhwal achieved great prosperity.[22] They apparently maintained their independence and were in power at the advent of Chandragupta Maurya (c. 321-297 B.C.)[23] whom they helped in defeating the Nandas and in ascending the throne of Patliputra.[24] During his rule over Magadha, they formed a prominent section of his army and achieved great fame in fighting,[25] an indication that this district formed part of the Mauryan empire. This fact is confirmed by the inscription on the major rock edict of Asoka at Kalsi in district Dehra Dun on the Western border of district Garhwal. A Buddhist mission was sent to propagate Buddhism in these regions during the reign of Asoka.[26]

For about a couple of centuries after the downfall of the Mauryas the district remained free from the control of any suzerain power from the plains. For sometime the Yavanas (the Greeks) exercised political influence over the region, including the area covered by this district. But they were soon driven away by Amoghbhuti, the powerful Kulinda king who had consolidated his power in the Himalayan region, as is evident from the one thousand silver coins of his reign, discovered in Sumarigaon near Srinagar and other places near this district. The abundance of coins also goes to show that there was peace and prosperity during his reign. His descendants were unable to defend their kingdom against foreign invaders.[27] In the beginning of the second quarter of the first century B.C. the Sakas, who belonged to the same stock as the Khasas and had certain affinities with them[28] invaded India from the north-west and probably penetrated the Himalayan tracts including this district and established a satrapy here. A few coins bearing the names of Haridatta, Shivpalita and Sivadatta, discovered in this region[29] and assigned to the first century A.D., establish that these rulers might have been the local Kulinda or Khasa chiefs or that the Sakas acted as satraps of the Indo-Scythian or Indo-Parthian monarchs of north-west India. In the last quarter of the first century A.D. this area, of which the district formed a part, came under the domination of the Kushanas, whose empire covered the western and central Himalayas as far as Tibet. During the reign of Kanishka (c. 78-104 A.D.) Buddhism seems to have gained a fresh impetus in the Himalayas. Foreign writers of the period like Pliny and Ptolemy mention the region under the name of Tanganoi, a term derived from the name of the Tangan tribes of this area and its inhabitants as being Khasas and Kiratas.[30]

After the disintegration of the Kushana empire in the second quarter of the third century A.D.[31] a number of Saka-Kushanas, including members of the royal family, took refuge in this area.[32] An inscription discovered at Jagatgram, on the left bank of the Yamuna opposite Kalsi, describes Shilavarman (assigned to the third century A.D.) as 'the Lord of the Mountain' it also mentions that he performed an Ashwamedha sacrifice. The greater part of the Garhwal region seems to have been under his domination.[33]

About the close of the third or the beginning of the fourth century A.D. Vasudeva, probably of Saka-Khasa descent, allegedly set up a small principality in this region.[34] According to tradition the founder of the earliest known historical dynasty of these parts was Vasudeva of the Katyuri dynasty. The connection between the Katyuris and the Sakas is evident from the use of the Saka era, the worship of the god Surya. by the Katyuris, because Kartikeya was regarded as their family deity and the commencement of the genealogical lists of the Katyuris with Salivahana, the great Saka king after whom the capital city was named Kartiykeyapura.[35] The Katyuri dynasty gradually came to be regarded as the indigenous ruling family of the region. It continued to rule over this district till subdued by the emperor Samudragupta about the middle of the fourth century A.D.[36]

The Chinese pilgrim, Huien Tsang, visited in 635, the Himalayan kingdom of the name of Brahmapura, the capital probably also having the same name. He called it Po-lo-hih-no-pu-lo and described it as having a circumference of 4,000 *li* (1,067 km.) with mountains on all sides.[37] Presumably this kingdom covered a major portion of the present Kumaon and Garhwal regions. According to one view Brahmapura lay in Garhwal[38] and possibly was the area covered by the forest near Lachhmanjhula. No ancient relices are found here but there is a mound across the Ganga where signs of an ancient habitation are found.[39]

The death of Harsha in 647 marked the beginning of a period of anarchy and unrest in the whole of northern India. The intrusions by the Tibetan kings became a recurring feature.[40] The Garhwal region was divided into a number of principalities governed by petty local chiefs. A number of fortresses or small castles are scattered all over this region. Parasugarh, Baghgarh and Devalgarh are located in this district. The chiefs used to fight among themselves and no single ruler is known to have had his seat of government within the district.[41] In the 7th and 8th centuries the Katyuri rulers had developed a powerful kingdom with its out-post at or near present Joshimath,[42] (in Chamoli district). The details of this dynasty have come to light through an inscription engraved in the southern part of a Siva temple at Bageshwar (in district Almora) which mentions three grants made by three kings in favour of the god Vyaghresvara. The defective nature of the transcript makes it difficult to be definite about the names of two kings in the first and probably the earlies charter, the first name being read as Basantadeva and the second being illegible. Basantadeva seems to be identical with Basantideva, who figures in all the existing genealogical lists of the Katyuris, the 21st in the Doti list and the 32nd in the Askot list in descent from Salivahana.[43] One of these two rulers may have founded the Joshimath branch of the Katyuris near about 650. It appears that the kingdom was split up in the time of Basantideva's son. The main line continued in the Katyuri valley in district Almora while the other ruled almost independently at the new capital of Karttikeyapura near Joshimath. The names of the kings in the second charter, who seem to have succeeded those mentioned in the first, have been read as Kharparadeva, his son, Kalyanaraja deva and the latter's son. Tribhuvanarajadeva. It is not known if Kharparadeva was a direct descendat of Basantideva or a usurper of his throne but he was one of those brave kings who inflicted a crushing defeat on the Tibetans in 704.

These three kings apparently ruled in succession during the greater part of the 8th century. The third charter (grant) refers to four generations of kings in the last decade of the 8th century—Nimbar, perhaps the founder of the line, Ishtaganadeva. Lalitansuradeva and Bhudeva, the donor of this grant.[44]

During the reign of Ishtaganadeva, Shankaracharya the famous Hindu philosopher (c. 788 to 820) and a renowened scholar of the Vedanta visited this district in the course of his pilgrimage of this region. He is said to have attained enlightenment in this region and to have brought about a change in the religious beliefs and practices of the local people as he had done elsewhere in the course of his mission for the revival of the Hindu religion as it prevailed prior to the Buddha. He is also credited with having prohibited human sacrifice at Srinagar.[45] Lalitasuradeva as also known from two copper plate grams preserved in the temple of Yogabadri at Pandukeshwar, issued in the 21st or 22nd year of his reign corresponding to 853 and 854 according to which his reign commenced in 832. Somadevi was his queen who was probably instrumental in issuing one of the grants. Both he and his father were endowed with the titles of *Paramabhattaraka, Maharajadhiraja* and *Parameshvara.*[46] Lalitasuradeva's inscription throws light on the cultural, political and economic conditions of the people of this region and their extensive cultural contacts with the neighbouring rulers. Bhudeva ruled from 954 to probably the end of the 10th century. Nothing is known about the immediate successors of Bhudeva which suggests another dynastic change after him. The founder of the new dynasty was Salonaditya, which is also confirmed by the text of the copper plate grant preserved in the temple at Baleshwar (in district Almora) which was issued from Karttikeyapura by Deshtadeva, son of Ichchhatadeva and the grandson of Salonaditya, in his 5th regnal year. Deshtadeva patronised the learned Brahmanas in his court and is described as a mighty conqueror. His son, Padmatadeva, was also a powerful king. Two copper plate grants preserved in the temple of Pandukeshwar, one issued in the 25th regnal year of Padmatadeva and the other issued in the 4th regnal year of Subhikshrajyadeva, Padmatadeva's son, who probably founded a new city known as Subhikshapura in the vicinity of the old capital or who may have simply renamed the old place.[47] Sometime in the latter half of the 12th century his successors abandoned the capital near Joshimath and moved to the Katyuri valley in the Almora district.[48]

The inscriptions of the Katyuri kings are written in the Kutila script in good Sanskrit couched in the classical eulogistic style.[49] Their text show that the Katyuri state was well-organised, powerful and flourishing. It was extensive and dominated the entire Kumaon-Garhwal region.[50] Different classes of nobles and high dignitaries and several grades of feudatories existed in the kingdom.[51] Marked similarites of language, style and content between the Katyur grants and those of several monarchs in the plains, particularly the Pala kings of Bihar, have been noticed,[52] plains did not exercise any influence over these parts, which were ruled by the Katyuri Kings who were devotees of various gods and Brahmanas and who compared themselves with Pauranic heroes like Prithu.[53]

Source : Dr. Parmanand Misra, *Garhwal Gazetter,* Superintendent Government Press, Allahabad, 1989.

REFERENCES

1. *Mahabharata,* Sabha-parva, Ch. 27/3.
2. Raturi, H.K., *Garhwal Ka Itihasa,* p. 1
3. Atkinson, E.T., *The Himalayan Districts of the North-Western province of India,* Vol. II, p. 271.
4. Bhakt Darshan, *Garhwal Ki Divangat Vibhutiyan,* p. 24
5. *Ibid.*
6. Barthwal, M.S., *Garhwal Me Kaun Kahan,* p. 10
7. Sankratyayana, R., *Kumaon,* pp. 25-26
8. Rapson, E.J., *The Cambridge History of India,* Vol., I, p. 73, Pandey, B., *Kumaon Ka Itihas,* p. 57, Macdonell, A.A. and Keith. A.B., *Vedic Index of Names and Subjects,* Vol. I, p. 363
9. Bhakt Darshan; *op. cit.,* p. 25
10. *Ibid.*
11. *Mahabharata,* Sabha-parva, Ch. 26/3
12. *Ibid.,* Ch. 25/1-7
13. Mahabharata, Sabha-parva, Ch. 76/21-24, Majumdar, R.C. and Pusalker. A.D. (Ed.), *The History and Culture of the Indian People,* Vol. I, p. 365
14. *Mahabharata,* Vana-parva, Ch. 140/24-25
15. *Ibid.*
16. Majumdar and Pusalker, *op. cit.,* Vol. I, pp. 394, 396
17. *Mahabharata,* Karna-parva, Ch. 95/4
18. Sankratyayana, *op. cit.,* pp. 25-26; Bahadur, Ral, P.R., *Garhwal Ancient and Modern,* pp. 71-72.
19. Raturi, *op. cit.,* pp. 267-68
20. Walton, H.C., *British Garhwal-A Gazetteer,* p. 112
21. Raturi, *op. cit.,* pp. 267-88
22. Ibid., p. 313; Barthwal, *op. cit.,* p. 11
23. Bahadur, *op. cit.,* p. 175
24. Sastri, K.A.N., *Age of the Nandas and Mauryas,* pp. 146-47
25. Raychaudhuri, H.C., *Political History of India,* p. 269
26. Sastri, *op. cit.,* pp. 216-17
27. Dabral S.P., *Uttarakhand Ka Itihasa,* Vol. III, pp. 169, 263
28. Sankratyana, *op. cit.,* pp. 32-34
29. Majumdar, R.C. and Pusalker, A.D. (Ed.), *The History and Culture of the Indian People,* Vol. p. 161

30. Atkinson, *op. cit.*, Vol. II, p. 352-56
31. Majumdar, R.C. and Pusalker, A.D. (Ed.), *The History of Culture of the Indian People*, Vol. III p. 54
32. Majumdar and Pusalker, *op. cit.*, Vol. II, p. 151
33. *Indian Archaeology*, 1953-54-A Review, pp. 10-11
34. Majumdar and Pusalker, *op. cit.*, Vol. II, p. 151
35. Sankaratyaya, *op. cit.*, pp. 33-34; Atkinson, *op. cit.*, pp. 383, 467-68; Tamrapatras from Pandukeshwar Temple, Raturi, *op. cit.*, pp. 288-305
36. Tripathi, R. S., *History of Ancient India*, pp, 243-244; Majumdar and Pusalker, *op. cit.*, Vol. III, pp. 8, 12
37. Watters, T., *On Yuan Chwang's Travels in India*, Vo. I, p. 329, Vol, II, p. 338
38. Cunningham, A., *The Ancient Geography of India*, p. 300
39. Raturi, *op. cit*, p. 333
40. Atkinson, *op. cit.*, p. 471; Majumdar, R.C. and Pusalker, A.D. (Ed.), *History and Culture of the Indian People*, Vol. IV, pp. 122-23.
41. Raturi, *op. cit.*, p. 332; Barthawal, *op. cit.*, p. 11; Bhakt Darshan, *op. cit.*, p. 4
42. Bahadur, *op. cit.*, p. 185
43. Bajumdar and Pusalker, *op. cit.*, Vol. p. 192
44. *Ibid.*
45. Bahadur, *op. cit.*, pp. 157-58; Pandey, *op. cit.*, pp. 160-189
46. Majumdar and Pusalker, *op. cit.*, Vol. IV, pp. 122-23.
47. Majumdar and Pusalker, *op. cit.*, Vol. IV, p. 123, Dabral, *op. cit.*, pp. 456-61
48. Atkinson, *op. cit.*, Vol. II, pp. 493-94
49. *Ibid.*, p. 470
50. Sankratyayana, *op. cit.*, pp. 27, 39
51. *Ibid.*, pp. 39-45
52. *Ibid.*, p. 43, Atkinson, *op. cit.*, Vol. II, pp. 488-492
53. Sankratyayana, *op. cit.*, pp. 39-41.

15

NAINITAL DISTRICT

General Features

Boundaries and Areas

The district of Naini Tal occupies the southern and south-eastern portion of the Kumaun division. It is of irregular shape, bounded on the north by Almora and a portion of Garhwal, on the east by a portion of the Almora district and Nepal, on the west by the Garhwal and Bijnor districts, and on the south by Pilibhit, Bareilly, the Rampur State and Moradabad.

Topography

The district is of a most heterogeneous description. the northern portion consists of hills, the outer ranges of the Himalayas, which in many places rise up steep from the gentle slopes at their feet, while elsewhere there are several series of low forest-clad hills which form as it were the outworks of main range of mountain. From the hills we pass through the curious phenomena of the Tarai to the ordinary alluvial plain that characterises the north Hindostan.

The Hills

The mountains of the outer Himalayas in this district have a general elevation of about 6,500 feet above the level of the sea while the highest summits attain to a height of over 8,000 feet. They have this peculiarity, that the outermost range is of considerably greater elevation than the intermediate chains lying between it and the outlying spurs of the great snowclad of Almora and Garhwal.

Mountain Systems

The chief mountain range of the district is the Gagra which forms the southern brow of the Himalayan system. It lies to the south of the Kosi river and extends eastwards from Mohan above Ramnagar, with an average breadth of eight or ten miles. Commencing on the east there is on the eastern boundary of patti Kosyan Talla the Saonchaliya peak attaining an elevation of 8,504 feet; to the south-east lies Badhan-dhura 8,408 feet; further east a peak, Bhurapatal, rises to 8,244 feet, and, east of this again is Badhan-tols with a height of 8,612 feet. The main ridge, still running slightly south-east, takes a sudden bend south by Binaik-dhura, the summit of which attains on elevation of 8,186 feet. Here the chain is broken by a deep valley along which runs the road from Dechauri to Ratighat following the course of the Baur southwards from the village of Pangot and the tributary of the Kosi known as the Dhaur from Pangot northwards. Beyond this valley on the east the range rises up again precipitously to China, above Naini Tal, with an elevation of 8,568 feet, and the other peaks which surround the lake and continues in a south-easterly direction to Liriya-kanta and thence eastwards to the Ninglat or Gagar ridge above Ramgarh. The Gagar range is also known as Gargachal from the legend that the Rishi, Garga, once resided near the Gagar fort.

Below the main outworks of the Himalaya there frequently occurs a lower line of hills known as the Siwalik or sub-Himalayan chain. These Siwaliks are most marked in the Dehra Dun and Saharanpur districts, and here only occur to a very modified extent. They can be seen alone at the foot of the Kotah Bhabar, but even here they present no great barrier between the plains and the uplands, and further east they are so blended with the outer range of the Himalaya that a geologist alone can trace their sequence. In the Kotah Bhabar (Katch Dun) these small hills rise abruptly from the apparently level surface of the flat country below to a height of a few hundred feet only; they are composed of sandstone and conglomerates, and the dip of the strata is usually towards the general mass of the mountains at a low angle. To the north a long gentle declivity slopes inwards, forming a longitudinal shallow valley by meeting the foot of the next line of hills. This valley is known as the Kotah Dun. It is cut through by the passage of several streams and closed to either end by the near approach to each other of the two ranges that flank it. The surface of the Dun is tolerably level, but broken up into steps or plateaux at different heights. A large portion of the area is under forest; but round the villages, and especially below Kotah and Dechauri, there are wide stretches of very fine cultivation, amply irrigated by the numerous canals.

Bhabar

Immediately below the foot of the hills there lies a narrow belt of country, usually covered with forest and remarkable for an entire absence of water—a phenomenon eminently characteristic of this tract. This belt of waterless forest land is called the Bhabar* and has a breadth of from five to fifteen miles; it lies between 28° 56' 40" and 29° 35' 22" north latitude, and between 78° 57' 40" and 80° 1'8" east longitude. In the east the Dhyanirau Bhabar is comparatively narrow, and it is not till we come to the Chhakhta Bhabar in the centre of the district that we get a breadth of eight to twelve miles, or rather more in place, that lasts as far eastwards as the Phika. Though no stream or springs exist, the Bhabar is clothed with stretches of forest, finding its nourishment in the few feet of alluvial matter that rests on the boulder and shingle deposit below, and with canal-fed cultivation. The Bhabar includes the four *pattis*, known as Chaubhainsi, Chhakhata, Kotah and Chilkia, each of which has been separately described. Formerly Tanakpur or the Tallades Bhabar also belonged to this district, but it was transferred in 1896 to Almora for administrative reasons, and the present eastern boundary is the Kamin river. In the Bhabar no water rises from the ground. Throughout its whole extent not a single spring nor any water can be seen, except occasionally where one of the larger rivers takes its course. In the rains alone torrents cut into the ground, and the channels thus formed exhibit characteristic sections of this remarkable tract. It may then be seen that there is but a thin covering of alluvial soil on a vast dry bed of boulders and shingle through which all rain that falls sinks rapidly, and which absorbs in the same way all the minor streams of the outer ranges. Instead of reeds and grasses, gigantic haldus and khairs rear their heads above a tangled undergrowth of creepers and thorns which present a barrier to progress that an elephant alone can surmount. Towards the hills we find the sal tree, and in Kotah great groves of mangoes, while large tracts of cultivation appear whereever irrigation is available. For this purpose the streams of the lower hills are turned into artificial channels before they reach the shingle deposit, and even the lakes are dammed up to retain a sufficient supply of water for the Bhabar. West of the Sawaldeh *sot,* however, there is little irrigation or

* The word is said to mean 'porous'.

cultivation, and the Bhabar there remains almost untouched by the plough. The acutal slope of the ground between the Tarai and the foot of the hills is considerable, though not apparent to the traveller, except when he observes the rapidity of the current in the irrigation channels that line the roads by which the Bhabar is crossed.

Tarai

To the south of the Bhabar lies the Tarai, which extends south-wards to the cultivated plains of Rohilkhand. It stretches from the Sarda on the east to the Kashipur parganas on the west, and lies between 28° 43' and 20° 26' north latitude, and between 78° 53' and 80° east longitude, with an average breadth of eleven miles from north to south. Its general appearance is that of a plain sloping gently towards the south-east, the average fall being twelve feet in the mile. The country in general is a tract of forest and swamps, with scattered patches of cultivation which are larger and closer in the south. The northern half chiefly consists of jungle or savannahs of grass and reeds: the country is still chiefly suitable for grazing only, although of late years there has been a marked extension of cultivation from the south to the line of springs in the north. These springs rise in a series of morasses that are formed along the southern edge of the Bhabar by syphonic influence on the sub terranean drainage, and are strongest and most numerous where the breadth of the Bhabar above them is greatest. Thus they are particularly strong to the west of the Kosi, where there is a large extent of boulder formation to the north; but further east, between the Dabka and Baur, where the Siwaliks of the Kotah Dun extend far to the south and the Bhabar is very narrow, the springs are but feeble. In the extreme east again, beyond the Nandhaur, the depth of the boulder formation is very small, and the spring-level of that part of the Bhabar is not more than eight or ten feet below the surface, so that the rainfall and drainage water flow off rapidly, instead of being absorbed; consequently there are no large spring-fed streams, as to the west of the Nandhaur, for the sources of supply are in this case wanting. From this line of springs flow sluggish streams, which carry off only a portion of the superfluous mositure; they are constantly doubling back their course and the channel is seldom well defined. The land between is slightly undulating, rising as it leaves one channel and falling as it approaches the next. The undulations to the north are small and decided, while to the south, as the distance between the rivers increases, the country is more level. The soil of the Tarai is everywhere a moist alluvial deposit, without any sign of the rock formations of the Bhabar.

Kashipur

Lastly, there is the level country in the south-west corner which comprises the subdivision of Kashipur. This calls for no detailed description; it resembles the plains of Rohilkhand, save that it is less highly cultivated and contains more open grass jungle than the southern districts. There is no clearly defined physical boundary between the plains of Kashipur and the Tarai; the northern portion of the pargana, indeed, resembles the Tarai in every respect, but the change occurs gradually as the soil loses its marshy character and a different vegetation springs up. Further south there are large open tracts slightly undulating and scored with water courses; the whole of it would be capable of cultivation were the cultivators forthcoming, although, as it is, it forms a valuable grazing-ground. The climate is far less unhealthy than that of the Tarai, but is decidely more malarious than the ordinary district of the plains.

Rivers

None of the rivers in this district have their origin in the snowy heights of the upper Himalaya. To the east there is the Sarda, indeed, but this merely touches the eastern boundary of pargana Bilheri in the Tarai, while the Ramganga lies well in the Bijnor district to the west. The Kosi alone rises to the north of the district in the hill country of Almora, and all the others spring from the lower ranges of hills both in Naini Tal and Garhwal.

Hill Rivers

The main drainage lines of the hill country of this district are the watersheds of the Kosi, Gola and Nandhaur rivers. There are one or two others of less importance, such as their affluents and the Ladhiya which drains the north-eastern corner, while numberless other rivers and torrents originate in the outer slope. The latter, however, will be dealt with separately in describing the rivers of the Bhabar.

Ladhiya River

The Ladhiya waters some small but excellent irrigated plots or *seras* in the patti of Malli Rau, but its total length within the district from Joshiura, where it first becomes useful, to Khairagaon, where it passes into the Kali Kumaun pargana of Almora and leaves the district of Naini Tal, is only six miles.

Kosi River

The Kosi rises in patti Borarau Palla of the Almora district and flows in a southerly direction to Someswar, and thence south-east to Almora, near which place it is joined by the Nana Kosi and the Sual. From its junction with the latter it forms for some distance the boundary between the districts of Almora and Naini, running in a westerly direction as far as Khairna, and receiving on its right bank the Ulabaghar and Kuchgarh streams, which flow from pargana Phaldakot, and on its left the Ramgarh *gadhera,* which rises in the Gagar range. From Khairna it ceasses to be the boundary, flowing through the northern portion of parganas Dhaniyakot, past Ratighat, where it is fed by the Dhaura, which rises on the western slopes of China, but after a course of some miles it again separates the two districts, dividing Kosyan Talla from Talla Salt. In this portion of its course it takes a north-westerly direction as far as Mohan, where it turns abruptly to the south-east and subsequently south by Dhikuli to Ramnagar, where it debouches from the hills at an elevation of 1,204 feet above the sea. Its bed is strewn with boulders and the gradient is steep. Between Khumaria and Ramnagar it is fed by numerous torrents with very steep beds down which the drainage in the rains pours with great velocity and which occasionally cause great damage. The bed is broad and full of islands which are covered with *khair* and *shisham* trees. Leaving Ramnagar it flows far about seventy miles through the plains and falls into the Ramganga. The Kosi is a most erratic and treacherous river in its behaviour, being subject to very violent floods which do an immense amount of damage to the cultivation on its banks and to the irrigation works. Large protective works have been constructed from time to time with the object of keeping the river within a defined channel, but their success has never been much more than temporary. The erosive power of the stream is enormous, as the gradient of the bed about Ramnagar is a mean slope of 38 feet to the mile. The Kosi is the only river which has a very great effect on the agriculture of the hill *pattis* of the district. Between Khairna and Ukhaldhunga its bed is wide and the fall gradual, so that much alluvial land of exceptional fertility has been formed either in its bed or on its banks. Until the disastrous floods of 1880 the villages along the Kosi had some of the finest irrigated lowlying lands in the hill portions of either the Naini Tal or Almora districts; but they suffered greatly in that year from diluvion and have not yet fully recovered.

Gola River

The Gola takes its rise on the southern slopes of the ridge to the south of

Dol in Dolphat in Almora and the extreme north of patti Chaubhainsi. It has a course generally south to Khansyun in Bisjyula, whence it turns westwards, forming the boundary of Chaugarh as far as its junction with the stream lending from Malwa Tal. It thence turns south again and afterwards north by west, taking in on its right bank the overflow of Bhim Tal which comes down by the Barakheri stream, and at Ranibagh receiving the surplus waters of Sat Tal and Naini Tal which are brought down by the Ballia. The river leaves the hills at Kathgodam and flows by Haldwani to the Tarai where it becomes known as the *Kichha,* and eventually joins the Ramganga on its left bank. Another branch of the same river becomes the Dhaura, which flows southwards through the Bhabar and Tarai to the east of the parent stream. The Gola is largely utilized for irrigation purposes and supplies water to most of the clearings round and near Haldwani in the Chhakhata Bhabar. In times of floods it becomes a violent and dangerous torrent, changing its channel through a wide bed. The upper reaches of the Gola produce a little good alluvial soil, but from Khansyun to the end of its course through the hills it is a waste of rock and pebble which continually increases by erosion from the banks.

Nandhaur River

The Nandhaur river rises on the southern slopes of the lower hills in patti Chaugarh under a high peak of over 7,000 feet in height. After a short south-easterly course it runs due, west and again south, entering the Bhabar by the pass above Chorgallia. It flows south past Chorgallia through the Bhabar and Tarai, and thence into the Pilibhit district, eventually joining the Ramganga in Shahjahanpur. Below Chorgallia it is known as the Deoha, and further south as the Garra. At Chorgallia the Nandhaur feeds a canal which irrigates the whole of the Chorgallia circle.

Dabka River

The Dabka rises on the southern declivity of the Gagar range, south of pattis Uchakot and Dhaniyakot, between the heights of Saonchaliya and Badhan-dhura. In the upper part of its course it forms the boundary between Malla and Talla Kotah, and leaves the hills just above the village of Kotah. Thence it flows in a south-westerly direction to the village of Baruading, where it passes from the hills that enclose the Kotah Dun. It receives on its right bank the Kicheri torrent, and continues in the same direction as far as the submontane road, but from that village it is known as the Gatiya for a few miles. From the road it turns south wards and assumes the name of Ghugha through the Gaibua circle of Chilkia and the north of Bazpur, but further south it is generally known as the Nihal. It is crossed by the road from Kaladhungi to Moradabad, a short distance within the borders of the Rampur State, and eventually, after a course of about ninety miles, joins the Ramganga in the Moradabad district. The Dabka is not a great river in the hills it is everywhere fordable, except after heavy and continued rainfall, and then only for a few hours, in the Kotah Dun, however, it is frequently impassable after much rain, and the size and number of the boulders in its bed confirm the popular saying that it is a good servant, but a bad master.

Bhabar River

Like the Dabka there are several other rivers which have their source on the Binaik-dhura ridge on the side towards the plains; the chief are the Baur to the west; the Nihal, which rises under Ayarpatha and flows past Kaladhungi; and the Ballia. The steepness of the descent make those rivers nothing but turbulent and destructive water-courses, until they are caught and trained by the irrigation works on the foot of the hills for use in the Bhabar. The only permanent streams of any importance in the Bhabar are the Nandbaur or Deoha, the Gola and the Kosi, each of which has been already noticed. There is besides a host of other streams which may be now briefly mentioned. Nothing can be more confusing than the nomenclature of these streams, some of which possess three or four names in a course of twenty miles; some divide or coalesce with others, and again divide accordingly as they receive a larger or smaller supply of water. One year one of a group carries the main stream and another year another. Thus in the east the Naudhaur divides into two just below the hills, the eastern branch picking up the drainage from the east as far as the Kamin and becoming the Deoha, while the western branch is known as the Kailas. West of this is the Gola, with its eastern branch the Sukhi, which is also fed from the numerous hill streams rising in the Deoguru ridge that overlooks the Bhabar. Next comes the Bhakra, which rises in the southern slopes of Chhakhata and flows past Pipalparao into the Tarai; then the Baur, and then the numerous little streams which drain the Kotah Dun; then the Dabka, and beyond this the Kosi. West of the Kosi the only river of any importance is the Dhela, which is joined by the Sawaldeh and flows through Chilkia and Kashipur; beyond this is the Pathariya, and lastly the Phika, which forms the western boundary of the district. Everyone of these rivers, as well as many of the smaller streams, are utilized for irrigation purposes and their waters drawn out to feed the numerous canals.

Tarai River

In the Tarai there are not only these streams, but a vast number of others which originate in the swamps along the northern border. They are almost all very similar in character and, with the exception of the Sarda on the extreme east, they are all tributaries of the Ramganga, which falls into the Ganges in the Hardoi district. The drainage system of the Tarai as a whole resembles the reticulations of a leaf, the streamlets on the edge of the moist country uniting to form larger channels which again feed the arterial lines of drainage and all eventually join the great midrib stream, the Ramganga. Most of these rivers are subject during the rains to heavy floods; they are nearly all used for irrigation, but none of them are navigable. "These Tarai streams are blocked in their courses with fallen trees and overhanging branches to an extent almost inconceivable to one not acquainted with them, and in high flood the velocity is greatly 'diminished by their presence. I consider it for this reason of the greatest importance that a narrow belt of trees should be maintained along the course of every stream which should never be allowed to be encroached on by cultivators."[1] So numerous are these streams and so unimportant, except as sources of irrigation, that it would be useless to attempt to describe them in detail. On the east is the Sarda, which forms the boundary of pargana Bilheri, separating it from Nepal. Continuing from east to west we have amongst others the Saniha, Chauka, Khakra, Lohiya, Jagbars and Kamin in pargana Bilheri; the Deoha and Kailas in Nanakmata; the eastern Bahgul in Kilpuri; the Dhaura, Kichha (the continuation of the Gola), Baror and the western Bahgul in Rudarpur; the Dimri, Bhakra, Nihal and Baur in Gadarpur; the Dabka, Ghuga and Naiya in Bazpur; and lastly in the Kashipur pargana, which may be here classed with the Tarai, there are the Kosi, Bahilla, Dhela and Phika, besides numerous smaller streams.

Lakes

The hill country, and especially pargana Chhakhata, which has been styled the Westmoreland of Kumaun, contains several lakes of great size and beauty. The name Chhakhata itself is said to be derived from the Sanskrit and to signify 'the sixty lakes, although it would be far from easy to identify the whole number. The chief of these lakes are Naini Tal, Bhim Tal, Malwa Tal, Sat Tal, Naukuchhiya Tal and Khurpa Tal, each of which will be separately described. Besides these there are many other smaller lakes, such as Sukha Tal, a name given to several small sheets of water which usually dry up during the summer months, Sariya Tal, near Naini

Tal on the Kaladhungi road, Khuriya Tal, and so on. These lakes form one of the most remarkable and beautiful features of the lower Himalaya in Kumaun. The manner in which some of them have been put to practical use for irrigation purposes will be described later.

Geology

Viewed geologically, the district presents as great a medley as in almost every other aspect. In the extreme south there is the Tarai, a zone of recently formed Gangetic alluvium, and above this the Bhabar, which consists of still newer deposits; a gently sloping mass of coarse gravels forming at the present day from the *debris* brought down by streams from the hills. Above that the sub-Himalayan zone, from three to eight miles wide, of low forest-covered hills, including the Kotah Dun and the valley of the Nandhaur near Aonla Khera, displays a great sequence of fresh-water deposits of the upper tertiary age, comprising chiefly the lower Siwalik Nahan sandstone, but with occasional representatives in the flatter duns of the middle and upper Siwalik sand-rock and conglomerates. All have an apparent dip towards the higher hills and are separated therefrom by the great main-boundary, reversed fault.[2] The higher hills, as far as the Almora boundary, comprise an older set of black or dark slates and fine quartzites forming many of the lower hills and valleys; a massive dark blue-grey limestone or dolomite, capping many of the ridges and well developed near Naini Tal,[3] beds of nuatzite and basic laws flows, well exposed near Bhim Tal and the neighbouring country[4] and possibly other more schistose and granitic rocks in the parts not yet geologically surveyed. No fossils have been found in any of these rocks, but they are probably very ancient. The presence of a series of hill tarns or rock basins in this part of the Himalaya is a surface only explicable on the theory of differential earth movements, complicated by faulting, and possibly in some cases by the action of once underground streams. The steep slopes of the limestone-capped slate hills combined with a heavy rainfall near the plainward edge of the hills have from time to time caused landslipe of considerable size in the neighbourhood of Naini Tal or a continuous weathering and scattering down the slopes of the greatly disintegrated and shuttered slate.[5]

Minerals

The mineral products of the district are various, but of no great value. They may be briefly dealt with under the heads of metals, stone and building materials, and others. Beginning with the second, there is an abundance of good building stone in most parts of the hills. At Naini Tal the stones chiefly used are limestone and clay schists. Limestone is found throughout the hill pattis, while sandstone is equally abundant. The most important limestone deposits are those at Chunakhan in the Kotah Bhabar and in the Timlia *sot,* about six miles east of Ramnagar. Lime is also manufactured at Naini Tal and in Dhyanirau in the hills. At Gayia both the blue limestone and the tufa lime are obtainable in some quantity, and on the Dabka, Baur and Gola rivers many limestone boulders are found and used for the manufacture of lime. The stone from the quarries at the foot of the hills yields by far the best quality of lime, while that obtained from the tufa deposits is very inferior. The former cost from Rs. 16 to Rs. 17 per 100 maunds, or from Rs. 20 to Rs. 22 when obtained from Government forests. This lime is mostly non-hydraulic and as a rule is used with one to two parts of washed sand; when mixed with *surkhi* or pounded brick it becomes slightly hydraulic and can be used for works in streams and for wet foundations. In the Tarai the only local source of lime is a deposit near Chhatarbhoj in the Dalpura forest of a kind of half formed kankar, which is, however, non-hydraulic. For works on which this cannot be used, lime is obtained from the Bhabar, or occasionally kankar lime is imported from the districts of Bareilly, Moradabad and Philibhit.

Building Materials

The cost of building materials and masonry work naturally varies with the locality. In the hills, stone is universally employed: in the Bhabar split boulders answer the purpose of bricks; and in the Tarai alone are bricks used to any extent for building purposes. Nine-inch bricks cost from Rs. 680 to Rs. 1,000 per lakh, and first class brick-work in the Tarai costs Rs. 27 per 100 cubic feet, though to this must be added a charge of 12 annas for every mile from the kiln. Rough work in bricks and mortar costs Rs. 20 per 100 cubic feet. Stone is sometimes carted to the Tarai from the foot of the hills for the better kind of work, but owing to the great expense is, as far as possible, dispensed with. Brick or stone houses are not, however common, and are mainly confined to the towns of Kashipur and Jaspur. Concrete work in Naini Tal costs about Rs. 16 per 100 cubic feet when done in lime and shingle, and Rs. 24 with the addition of pounded brick, on the cart road the costs is Rs. 10 and Rs. 15 respectively; and in the Tarai, when broken bricks are exclusively used, Rs. 16. The cost of excavation varies according to the nature of the soil; in Naini Tal it is sometimes as much as Rs. 500, while in the Tarai it is often as low as Rs.

5 per 100 cubic feet. Rubble in lime mortar ranges from Rs. 14 in Naini Tal to Rs. 12 in the Tarai; but in Portland cement it costs Rs. 50. Dry walling costs from Rs. 5 to Rs. 6-8-0 per 100 cubic feet according to quality. Roofing in the hills is usually done in slates, which are found in the neighbourhood of Naini Tal. In the Tarai brick-work roofs cost Rs. 32 per 100 cubic feet; while iron rods cost Rs. 18, and galvanized iron and planking Rs. 24; the price is somewhat higher in the hills.

Metals

The precious metals can hardly be said to occur in this district, at any rate in appreciable quantities; a small amount of gold is obtained by washing from the sands of the Dhela river, and possibly it occurs in minute quantities elsewhere; the work is solely carried on by Doms. Copper is found in places, but is no longer worked; there are formerly a good mine at Kemukhet of parganas Dhyanirau. The only metal deserving mention is iron, the ore of which is found in various parts of the hills, notably at Dechauri, Kaladhungi and the Ramgarh pargana. The workable ore, however, contains a large amount of earthy impurities, and not much more than 50 per cent of metal. That of Ramgarh is the variety known as scaly iron ore and yields very good iron; similar to this is the bed at Dhaniyakot on the Kosi. The mining of iron in this district is of great antiquity. In patti Agar there is a caste of Doms known as Agaris, whose special profession was till recently that of miners. There are several mines there that have been worked within late years, chiefly those at Lusgani, Nathuakhan, Gulla and Satbanga. In Ramgarh, too many mines were worked as late as 1884, but they are now all abandoned. The mining industry was very flourishing at the commencement of British rule, and the Ramgarh mines were leased at a nominal rent to the headman of the Agaris, who till 1826 controlled all the iron mines of Kumaon. It received its first check in 1833, when the miners emigrated from Ramgarh to Khatsari in Pali of Almora, and the business never afterwards recovered its early importance. The existence of iron soon attracted the attention of Government, and in 1856 the Directors sent out a Mr. Sowerby and a large staff of mining assistants to carry on the smelting of iron on account of Government in the interior. The fact was soon established that iron of an excellent quality could be manufactured at rates below the cost of iron imported from England, and a number of private individuals, under the style of Davis & Co., were permitted to undertake operations for the same purpose in other parts of the lower hills.

Kumaun Iron Company

The avowed object of the Government enterprise was to induce private companies to work by demonstrating the financial and physical possibility of carrying on iron works as a remunerative industry in this province. Messrs. Davis proposed to take over the tract between the Dabka and the Bhakra, and their proposals were accepted with an assurance that they might proceed in confidence to make their arrangements, as Government would grant the lease sought. They therefore took over the Khurpa Tal works in the rains of 1858, and paid their cost price in 1863. This company also erected buildings as Kaladhungi at a cost of Rs. 1,25,000. On the failure of the Government works at Dechauri Colonel Drummond offered to take them over at a valuation. These works were given over to Drummond & Co. who paid the capital under agreement into the treasury in 1861. The forest rules were relaxed in favour of both companies, so as to allow them entire control over the fuel supplies, and eventually, in November 1862, both companies were amalgamated under the title of the North of India Kumaun Iron Works Company (Limited). Soon after the formation of the Company instructions were received from the Secretary of State to construct a tramway to Khurja on the East Indian Railway, chiefly, it would appear, to afford an outlet for the iron manufactures of Kumaun. The tramway was to be laid with cast-iron rails manufactured at Dechauri, and the company lost no time in making several thousand maunds of pig iron. Before the rails were made, however, the Government announced its determination not to undertake this line itself, but to hand its construction over to the Oudh and Rohilkhand Railway. It was essential to the success of the enterprise that some such outlet should exist, and the company accordingly determined to close its works for a time and await the opening of the line.

A license was granted by Government, but unfortunately it was not executed till too late. The agreement contained several conditions binding the company to produce a specfied amount of iron each year, to reforest the area cut down for fuel, and among other stipulations to pay a fixed rent and a royalty on every ton of iron produced; the capital was to be paid up before the execution of the deed and the full value of the works at Trichuri, Ramgarh and Khurpa Tal paid in four instalments, the last falling due on the 1st of September 1865. The penalty for failure to comply with these conditions was forfeiture of the property. The purchase-money of Khurpa Tal was alone paid up, but Government suspended the forfeiture clause in 1868. The license was not sent up from Calcutta till June 1864, and in fact was not prepared for signature until after the suspension of the works by the company, and it was then never signed. The capital was expended and the concern was wound up in 1864. A later attempt was made to resuscitate the company, but without success, and the enterprise was abandoned in 1876. Government then took over the works for three years, but also failed and on the conclusion of the lease reverted to the old idea of pushing the manufacture with private capital; but this, too, was of no effect, as no one was found to take up the work of the company. Undoubtedly these works had not a fair trial—an opinion which was held by Sir Henry Ramsay, who considered that if properly started they would pay their way readily. The fuel difficulty could not have been felt for many years at Dechauri and Kaladhungi, although at Ramgarh the works necessarily failed on account of the distance of the forest and the difficulty of carrying fuel. All the works are now in ruins, and all hope of renewing the industry has been abandoned.

Other Minerals

The other minerals are of little importance or interest. Coal is absent, although indications of lignite appear near Ranibagh and in the Barakheri pass near Bhamauri. Analysis was made of a specimen from Ranibagh; but though the returns were fairly good, the deposits are far too small to be workable.[6] Similar traces have been found in the bed of the Phika stream. Sulphur occurs in small quantities; there are sulphureous springs at Naini Tal and Kathgodam, while green sulphate of iron is found in the form of iron pyrites in many parts of the hills. Alum or *phitkari* occurs in different parts of Kumaun and abundantly in the aluminous shales near the village of Jakh on the road from Naini Tal to Khairna, and also in the bed of the Kosi below Almora, where it appears as an incrustation on the rocks. Gypsum is found in pargana Chhakhata, and especially in the bed of the Nihal river on the Kaladhungi road. It has been successfully employed in the manufacture of plaster of Paris.

Forest History

From time immemorial the forests in Kumaun were considered the property of the ruling power, and as such invariably formed a source of revenue to the State. The most simple mode of realizing this revenue was that of subjecting the products of the forests to a small propreitary due in the shape of duties payable by the exporters. At the commencement of British rule these dues were leased out to the zamindars of the pargana in which the collecting depots were situated and were styled *kath-bans, kath-*

mahals and *ghikar*, from the principal items assessed in each case; the first signifying timber *(kath)* or bamboos, the second *kath* or catechu, and the third the ordinary ghi or clarified butter, the later being a grazing tax. In 1818 the revenue realized from these dues was Rs. 2,644 for Kumaun, and in 1823 had risen to Rs. 5,733. In 1824 the collections of the dues was entrusted to the authorities of the Moradabad and Bareilly districts in consequence of the difficulties regarding the boundaries that had occurred, but in 1826 the duty of collecting them was restored to the hill districts. In 1828 the forest dues were leased to the farmers of the grazing tax at the same rate, as it was found that the two could not then be usefully separated.

Grazing Dues

This grazing tax was one of the many miscellaneous items of revenue that descended to the British from former Governments. In the hills this cess was abolished at the first settlement, but in the Bhabar and Tarai it was continued under the name *gai-charai*; the cattle of the hillmen, however, were exempt, the tax being chiefly levied on the cattle of the plains villages that came into the forests during the hot weather. During the two or three years succeeding the conquest the number of cattle proceeding from the hills to the Bhabar and Tarai was not so great as to render any cess on them an object of interest to the Government; but the security afforded by the abolition of the old rural guard *(chaukidari)* system and the introduction of an efficient police led to increased report to the plains. It was therefore resolved in 1822 to subject all cattle sent to graze in the Bhabar and Tarai to a uniform tax of these annas for each female buffalo, two annas for each cow, and one anna for each bullock a year. The form of this tax for the year 1822-23 was given out in three leases, aggregating Rs. 2,077 per annum. The unsettled state of the boundaries between Kumaun and Rohilkhand became a fertile source of dispute between the farmers of this tax for the hill and plains portions of the submontane tract. Many of the hillmen having made their arrangements with the Rohilkhand farmers paid the duties to times and were again called upon to pay by the hill farmers, who claimed the right to leavy these dues in all places in which the *chaukidari* cattle dues had formerly been collected. In 1823 the cattle belonging to the kamins, sayanas and thokdars or headmen of parganas in the hills and to pardhans or headmen of villages in the Bhabar and those belonging to permanent residents were exempted from these dues. In 1826 the boundary between the hills and Rohilkhand was finally arranged and separate farms for the grazing dues were established. The principle on which the collections were made was that the farmer within whose jurisdiction the cattle-pens were situate was entitled to collect the tax. The dues were very rarely collected per head, the plan being to count in each *goth* or cattle-pen the *agalas* or *donas*, that is the wooden bars to which the cattle were tied at night. The customary rate was to consider each agalas containing eight buffaloes and eight cows liable to a tex of two rupees.

Boundary Disputes

To make this point in the history of the management of the forest more clear, it will be necessary to refer to these boundary disputes. In the earlier years there were no exports of any value from the portion of the lowland tract lying below the chain of custom posts established to levy the export duty, and it was thoughts that no difficulty could arise is regard to the collection made there, but the unsettled state of the boundary between the Bhabar and Tarai and the conflicting claims of the land holders of the frontier villages, both of the hills and of the plains, soon led to innumerable complaints in which the district authorities on both sides found themselves partizans. The records show a voluminous correspondence on this subject extending over several years. Early in 1819 Mr. Traill reported on the encroachments made by the zamindars of Bilheri on the forests lying along the foot of the hills now included in the Tallades Bhabar. This tract was valuable to the hillmen as affording them pasture for their cattle during the winter months, when the grass in the hills dried up and becames useless for fodder. During the Gurkha rule a Joint Commission had been appointed by the Nepal Government and the Nawab of Oudh to settle these disputes and the Saniha nala was fixed upon as the boundary between the two States. The hillmen had always occupied the jungle to the north of this boundary and were anxious to undertake the cultivation of the portions lying at the foot of the hills which had recently been taken possession of by the Bilheri landholders.[7] It was agreed that an attempt should be made to settle the disputed boundary on the basis of that which existed is 1801, when Rohilkhand was ceded to the British, and that advantage should be taken of this arangement to demarcate the whole line of boundary between Rudarpur and the Nepal frontier. The difficulty was much enhanced by the claims set up by Major Hearsey, who is 1814 had purchased the entire taluqa of Bilheri at auction for arrears of revenue and now demanded possession of a portion of the Kumaun Bhabar, on the plea that it belonged to the lowland pargana. A commission was appointed to investigate these matters, and it was at length decided that the Saniha nala had always been and should continue to be, the boundary between the hills and the low country.[8] The collection of all dues was handed over to the plains authorties, but in 1826 was again entrusted to the Commissioner of Kumaun.

Government Forests

The first attempt at reservation appears to have been made in 1826, when, on the recommendation of Mr. Traill, a proclamation was issued, prohibiting the cutting of sal on all the *thaplas* or flats immediately adjoining the lower ranges along the whole extent of the Bhabar. These areas, which may be considered the first reserve in Kumaun, were excluded from the leases of forest produce already mentioned. No other steps towards conservancy were, however, undertaken. The denudation of trees of all species appears to have continued steadily and reached its climax between 1855 and 1861, when the demands of the railways for sleepers attracted numerous contractors of these parts, and to them uncontrolled liberty was given to cut where and how they pleased, with the result that large numbers of trees were felled and for want of transport were left lying in the forests. To such an extent was this reckless felling carried on during this period that for several years after the control of the forests was taken in hand by the Commissioner, the energy of the officials was directed towards extracting the timber thus left by the contractors. Fortunately the gravity of the situation was realized by the Commissioner, then Major Ramsay, in 1861 and he took prompt and energetic steps to stop the further denudation of the forests and to place this valuable property on a sounder and more prominent footing. In the following year Major Ramsay was appointed Conservator in addition to his ordinary duties. The farming of leases and indiscriminate felling of trees were stopped, forest officers, were appointed, and a system of conservancy was begun under which all trees considered fit for felling were first marked by the officials, and fire conservancy was also taken in hand. The immediate result of these measures was a greatly-increased forest revenue, for whereas in 1831 the total amounted to only Rs. 2,923, and had risen in 1846 to Rs. 12,502 for Kotah and Chhakhata alone, from 1859 to 1868 the average annual surplus was nearly Rs. 70,000.

Kumaun Forest Division

In 1868 the forests were first placed under the control of the officers of the Forest Department, Major Pearson being the first Conservator; but little change was made in the working arrangements. It was not until the 5th of September. 1877 that the forests were gazetted as Government forests, and the reserves of the Kumaun forest division were formally demarcated.[9] This division, which with the other forests of this district forms part of the Central Circle, orginally included the Naini Tal Forests of the present Garhwal division, and extended from the Sarda on the east to the boundary of the Garhwal district on the west. The reserves thus constituted were subdivided into twelve blocks, consisting of the most important sal forests on lower hills and in the Bhabar, exclusive of the Iron Company's grant and some tracts containing good *khair* and shisham forests. The total area of the blocks which lie in the present Kumaun forest division was, according to the reservation of 1877, in all 674.5 square miles, of which 290.5 square miles were open to the exercise of recorded rights, leaving an unburdened area of 384 square miles of State forests. On the passing of the Indian Forest Act (VII of 1878), it was necessary to reclassify and regazette the existing state forests as "reserved" and "protected" forests. The Conservator, in consultation with the Commissioner and district officers, gave up 38.67 square miles of the original forests, and the remaining area, 638.83 square miles, were gazetted as reserved forests."[10] At the same time Colonel Garstin demarcated 290.7 square miles of these reserves, as before, for the exercise of rights. These open forests were demarcated by means of round numbered pillars, while the boundaries of the closed reserves were generally defined by means of square pillars. The villages adjoining the forests were given from liberal rights of pasturage, timber and forest produce generally.

Forest Area

The Kumaun Forest Division as at present constituted is divided into eight ranges, each consisting of several blocks. Each range is in the charge of a ranger or deputy ranger, while forest guards exercise supervision over two or more blocks. Three of these ranges, the Dogari, Sarra Nadi and Sarda ranges are situated in the Almora district and call for no further mention in this place. The present area of the division is 510 square miles of which 277.27 square miles are open to the exercise of recorded rights and 232.73 squares miles are free. Of this, 186.5 square miles belong to the Almora district. The forests are situated partly on the outer and lower slopes of the Himalayas and partly in the Bhabar and Tarai. In this district the hill area is 185.8 square miles, and that in the plains 135.3 square miles. The hill forests consist, first, of those on the lower hills up to an altitude of 3,000 feet, and contain sal trees, with an admixture of sain, haldu, rohni and others; and secondly, those at a greater elevation which contain chir, pines and oaks. The forests on the plains comprise the sal-producing areas, the shisham and khair forests on the old alluvial deposits of the Bhabar and Tarai, and the open savannahs of the eastern portion of the division.

Iron Company's Forests

The Kumaun Iron Company had a large grant of forest, extending from the Manar Gadhera, about a mile west of the Dabka, as far as the Bhakra river, about half-way between Kaladhungi and Haldwani. The grant was bounded on the north by the hills, and on the south towards the Bhabar by a line of pillars, and the area was about 350 square miles. It is difficult to say what portion of their rights Government resolved to grant to the company, for the deed was never executed, but it would appear that only fuel rights were intended and no others were expressed in the draft. After the dissolution of the Company, part of the grant, amounting to 72.48 square miles of forest and known as the Kotah, Dechauri and Fatehpur blocks, was added to the Kumaun Forest Division.[11] Of this area, 59.4 square miles were open to the exercise of recorded rights and concessions, and 13.08 square miles became the unburdened property of the State. The rights granted over these forests were revised by the Local Government and the revised list was published in the Gazette.[12] The Kotah block was then transferred to the Garhwal Division. Of the others, the Dechauri range comprises seven blocks, known as Dechauri and Deigaon, Narni and Kaladhungi, both of which are in the hills, and the plains blocks of Musabangar, Kalyanpur and Sanani, Pawalgarh, Karari and Garappu, and Chunakhan, Dhamola and Kusamrauli. It has a total area of 37,945 acres, of which 13,798 acres are in the hills. Karari, Kusamrauli and Garappu blocks were among the 15 blocks of various sizes which were reserved in 1899, when an addition was made to the sal and khair reserves.[13] Garappu is open to rights, but the others are closed. The Fatehpur range consists of four forest guards, beats and comprises the blocks known as Nihal and Mona, Bhakra and Fatehpur, Kathgodam and Beluti, and the Bhakra Khair and Chaunsila blocks. Of these Mona, Fatehpur, Kathgodam and Beluti, with an area of 15,838 acres, are in the hills and the others in the plains, the total area of the range being 28,493 acres. The Bhakra Khair block was reserved in 1899 under the same notification as Garappu. The Beluti block was added to the open reserves in 1890.[14]

Chhakhata Range

The other ranges of the division in this district are the Chhakhata, Nandhaur and Jaulasal ranges. The Chhakhata range consists of sal on the *thaplas* or terraces below the hill patti of Chhakhata and some very fine haldu below. It has an area of 39,524 acres, of which nearly half is in the hills. There are seven beats and seventeen blocks. Of these Ratighat, Gurkharak, Jampokhra, Shimlia, Patraui and Asni are in the hills, and the remainder, Dolpokhra, Lakhman Mandi, Horai, Maulani, Sila, Gola, north and south Dolpokhra, Kotkhara, Sukhi and Kailas are in the Bhabar. Dolpokhra, Sila, Maulani and Kotharra were reserved in February 1899, and Kailas, Sukhi and Gola in September of the same year.

Nandhaur Range

The Nandhaur range is wholly situated in the hills and has an area of 48,623 acres. It is divided into 22 blocks constituting eight beats. About one-third is sal forests and the remainder is chiefly khair and mixed jungle. The beats are known as Sankheri and Karakot, Bilot and north and south Selani, Ratarau and north and south Khopani, east and west Lobchula, Bulhsani and north and south Aonlakhera, Chilla and Gaunia Rau, Durgapipal and north and south Kholgarh and Kundal, Better and lower Nala.

Jaulasal Range

The Jaulasal range consists of the hill blocks of Chunagarh, Hathgarh, Chamuadhunga, Birgot and Bhargot, with an area of 21,153 acres, and Hauspur, east and west Jaulasal, Sutlimath and Kalga in the plains, with an areas of 27,700 acres.

Management

From the year 1880 to 1890 the forest revenues were collected by what was known as the *chauki* system, under which two parallel series of depots were established, at the upper of which all dues were realized and passes issued, and these latter were checked at the lower line of chaukis. During the first portion of this period, from 1880 to 1885, the felling of trees was regulated by an annual plan of operations in which were detailed the area to be worked, the number of trees to be felled, and the various works of improvement to be undertaken during the year. The first regular working-plan framed by Mr. Hearle for the Nandhaur forest came into operation in 1886 and in it fellings were prescribed for ten years. This plan however, only continued in force till 1893, for in the following year a new working-plan was prepared by Mr. Bryant for all the forests of the division, and this is still in force. According to the present working plan the forests are divided into ten working circles. In the hill circle timber is only supplied to right-holders; in the Sarkhet circle, between the Bhakra and Gola, selection fellings are made, but are limited to the supply of 200 sal trees given free yearly to His Highness the Nawab of Rampur. In the Nandhaur, Kathgodam and Kalaunia circles selection fellings are prescribed for the next 36 years, while elsewhere only improvement fellings for 20 years are to be made. Fire conservancy was first started in the Horai and Jaulasal forests in 1876, when 11,200 acres were protected. From time to time additional portions of the more valuable forests were brought under protection, till in 1902 the protected area amounted to over 65 per cent of the whole. The work is facilitated by a complete system of firelines 100 feet and 50 feet wide according to the exigencies of the case. The number of failures in this direction have been but few, and the success of fire conservancy is assured; the people do not resent it as formerly, for they have discovered from practical experience that the quality of fodder grass is improved by protection, while the other numerous forest products by which they make a living in the cold weather have greatly increased. The benefit thus afforded during the last 20 years is immense and is seen in the dense thickets of poles, saplings and seedlings which have come up in the old ruined forests. Another important branch of conservancy is climber cutting. The luxuriance of vegetable growth in the semi-tropical forests at the foot of the hills is perhaps most noticeable among the larger parasites, chief among these is the gigantic "elephant creeper" *(Bauhinia vahlii)*. To such dimensions do these vegetable pests attain, that a single elephant creeper will sometimes cover the tops of the trees over a quarter of an acre of dense forest. Suppression and extermination of these natural enemies are, therefore, among the chief factors in the future prosperity of a timber-producing area. Regular cutting operations were taken in hand in 1887 in the Nandhaur and the Kalaunia working circles, and these have been systematized and enlarged in the present working plan so as to embrace all the forests in which either selection or improvement fellings are carried on. The average revenue of the division since 1880 has been Rs. 1,59,500 and the expenditure about Rs. 60,000. The division is well supplied with rest-houses, there being 15 bungalows for the convenience of the officers on tour, while the rangers and forest guards are provided with double-storyed houses.

Garhwal Forest Division

As the forest of the Kumaun Division increased in area and became too extensive for a single charge, the portions to the west of the Dabka were transferred to the Garhwal Forest Division, and some of the hill forests west of Kathgodam were made over to the Naini Tal Division. The history of the Garhwal forests belongs to the account of that district, for with exception of the more recent additons the whole area lies within the borders of Garhwal. The blocks in this district lie on the low hills of Kotah, in the Chilkia Bhabar, and the north of Kashipur. They comprise the Kotah forest to which were added a portion of the Iron Company's grant; the Chilkia forest, a large and valuable area containing much fine sal timber; and the small Garhibulchand forest of the Chilkia Bhabar, lying between the Patharia and the western boundary of the district. In the last named the trees are chiefly sal, but the soil does not seem suited for the growth of large trees. In western Kotah, on the other hand, there is finer sal then in any other part of Kumaun. Formerly, as in the Kumaon Division the *chauki* system was in vogue here, but this has been replaced by the *"coupe"* system, as elsewhere. A "coupe" or block of forest is set apart for felling for a year, and the produce is sold by auction. The purchaser thus obtains a monopoly, but has to pay royalty on export. The felling is all done under the supervision of the forest officials, and the trees to be cut are first marked by the ranger. The headquarters of the division are at Naini Tal.

Naini Tal Forest Division

The Naini Tal Forest Division comprises two subdivisions, Naini Tal and Ranikhet, of which the latter lies in the Almora district. The forests in and around the settlement of Naini Tal were demarcated in 1865, and taken over by Government with a view to supplying the local wants. Prior to 1845 all the trees were considered to belong to the villages within whose boundaries they were situate and those within the valley were alone protected. Some years later the Commissioner took over the forests near Naini Tal, and no trees could be felled without his permission, a royalty being levied on each tree to meet the expense of conservancy. In 1879 these forests were gazetted as protected. Up to 1885 the subdivision formed a part of the Kumaun Division, but was then separated. The forests of the present Naini Tal subdivision lie on the southern and outer slopes of the Himalayas. Several other aspects, with abrupt scarps, rigid precipices and poor shales prevail, although the tract presents great varieties. The heights vary from 2,000 to 8,000 feet. The original reserved area was confined to

Ranikhet, but several subsequent alterations occurred. In 1885 part of the Iron Company's grant was reserved and given to Naini Tal. This now consists of 36 square miles. In 1890 the Gagar and Ninglat reserves were added, with an area of 19 square miles.[15] In the following year the six square miles of the Dalmar Mora forest were taken in.[16] In 1898 a further addition of 30 squares miles near Naini Tal was made,[17] and this was followed in 1899 by four other reserves at Mukhtesar, Sat Tal, Ramgarh and Harial Danda, with a total area of eight square miles; but of this Mukhtesar is under the control of the Imperial Bacteriolgist[18]. Lastly, the old cantonment of Khurpa Tal was made over to the Forest Department in 1902. Thus the total area of the Naini Tal subdivision is about 100 square miles. The dominant species are chir and oak, with a small proportion of miscellaneous forest. Altitude and local conditions define their regions. The chir usually occupies prominent ridges and spurs and hot open places, while the oak confines itself to the higher altitudes, northern slopes and cool areas. There are gregarious sal areas below 4,000 feet in which *Terminalies* and other associates species find a place; but the miscellaneous trees are of littel value. About 22 square miles are covered with chir, 46 square miles with oak and miscellaneous woods, and the rest is unproductive. There was a regular forest survey in 1878, but the subsequent additions still require to be surveyed in detail. All external boundary lines follow natural features or else are demarcated artificially. Many of the natural boundaries need more distinct definition, but this process is in gradual operation.

Management

A working-plan was framed for the Naini Tal reserves in 1888 by Mr. Fernandez and this was revised in 1896 by Mr. Hearle. The areas added subsequent to 1898 still remain to be brought under prescriptions. In addition to the conduct of these plans, the divisional officer is associated with those of the Naini Tal municipal and cantonment forests and the Mukhtesar reserve. Fire protective measures were introduced in 1876, and were extended as successive areas were brought under control. The physical and natural difficulties are almost insurmountable, yet the measure of success has undoubtedly been good: incendiarism has been responsible for the more serious failures; but the crime is not general, and free grants of grass and other privileges have enlisted the sympathies and assistance of many of the villagers. Protection costs roughly Rs. 2,500 per annum, but should be considerably increased if the fortuitous element of luck is to be eleminated. Breaches of forest law are somewhat numerous, but except in the case of fires are of a petty character and are usually compounded. Crime is not serious, considering the floating character of the population, thez traffic and the numerous patches of cultivation amid the reserves. A record of rights and privileges has been prepared for all the reserves and, since first sanctioned, there have been revisions of settlements entailing slight changes. A very liberal scale was adopted as is obvious from the fact that the limits have never been reached. These rights chiefly refer to fuel, timber for dwellings and cow-shads, and grazing. Only 32 square miles of the whole division are closed to all animals, the balance being partially opened. The forest is very heavily taxed in this direction as only the accessible blocks are utilized. The mischief is diminished by the annual migration to the Bhabar, although on the other hand the passage through the forests of sheep and goats imported by Bhotiyas, exceeding 27,000 head per annum, is a serious matter, as allotted grazing-grounds are denuded of reproduction. In this forest division the permit system is in vogue, and all the forest revenue is collected by retail sale. This method, which has taken the place of the old chauki system, is one that involves a vast amount of work for the Forest Officer. The timber trade of the Naini Tal forest is limited to the supply of timber for building at Naini Tal, Ranikhet and Almora—a constantly decreasing quantity. The chief work is that of supplying fuel and charcoal for the Naini Tal settlement—an expensive undertaking as the incidence of royalty per maund of wood is exceptionally small. The Naini Tal supply was worked at a loss for some time, and now only pays actual expenses. Since 1880 the average annual revenue from this division has been Rs. 67,400 and the expenditure nearly Rs. 55,000.

District Forests

In the beginning of 1896 the whole of the waste land in the hill *pattis* of the district was declared to be Government forest. It was styled "protected" and was placed under the control of the district authorities. The term "waste land" must be taken in its widest significance: it comprehends the whole of the lands lying outside the village boundary and exclusive only of the reserved forests. The Deputy Commissioner was placed in direct charge, and a trained ranger was lent by the Forest Department to carry on and supervise the work of conservation. By this measure a large area was taken up and saved from speedy destruction: and not a moment too soon. The question of the denudation of the hillsides had become acute. Not only had several large grants in fee-simple been lately made, but the rapid spread of potato cultivation was becoming alarming. The method adopted by the cultivators was to clear a patch of forest and then to utilize the virgin soil for growing potatoes. This patch would become exhausted in two or three years, and then the process would be repeated, so that one village would clear a whole hillside in a very short time: the more so as tehy found this occupation very lucrative compared with the results obtained from the ordinary forms of agriculture. The increase of the population in Naini Tal, the growth of Ranikhet and, above all, the opening up of the railway from Bareilly to Kathgodam had tended to create a demand for this vegetable, and the case with which it can be grown in this district made the crop a favourite one with the hill people. In the north of the district, especially towards Ranikhet, the hillsides have been laid completely bare, so that there is no hope of restoration by natural reproduction. In many places the stripping of the hillsides had resulted in the loosening of the cap-soil which fell with the next heavy downfall of rain. Hence in this district, and even more so in Almora, large areas of valuable "talaon" land have gone to utter ruin and what was once a fertile valley has now become nothing but a boulder-strewn torrent bed. The loss has been considerable, both to the villagers who had to continue to pay revenue till a temporary settlement could be made in their favour, and still more so to the State, which has thus lost the income which would have accrued from some of the richest land in the district. The results of protection have already been beneficial: the threatened shortage of the fuel supply, which constituted a real fear for the future, has been now averted; the remaining hillsides have been saved, and the standing menance to the cultivated lands from possible landslips, as far as possible, removed; and—a far more serious matter—the unfavourable effect upon the rainfall which would result from the disappearance of the forests is no more to be feared.

As was only to be expected, the villagers raised a great outcry at this measure, but the step was necessary and, moreover, they have been very generously treated. Every village has the right of free grazing in the adjoining forest, and every year they obtain a liberal grant of timber, which is almost invariably more than they actually require. If this proves insufficient for their needs, they are permitted to buy extra timber at a very greatly reduced rate. The great difference between the present and the old regime lies in the fact that all trees are now felled on a principle of selection, whereas in the past they were indiscriminately cut down as they happened to stand nearest to the village. Even under the present system control of the forests is no easy matter, and the damage done to the young trees by cattle and sheep is very large. It is not, however, possible to ensure close supervision over so large an area, and reproduction is very slow.

Steps are now being taken to put selected forests under more efficient control.

Management

The system adopted in the reserved forests is also followed here, as far as is possible under the very different conditions. No tree can be felled until it has been marked by the Ranger or his assistants the foresters, who act as Deputy Rangers. There is a regular record-of-rights for each village drawn up at the time of settlement: and the Forest Act is strictly enforced, so far as it applies to protected forests. The part of Forest Officer is taken by an officer of the district staff, who is placed in charge of the forests and deals with all offences and complaints in this connection, and is empowered to compound offences under Section 67, subject to the control of the Deputy Commissioner. The total area of protected forest in this district, at the time when the forests were first taken over in 1896, was 220,371 acres, or 344 square miles. This has been subsequently reduced, although only to an inappreciable extent, by the transfer of certain small portion to the Forest Department, referred to in the account of the Naini Tal reserves. In 1900 the remainder of the forest was divided into two ranges: The Gola range and the Kosi range, so called from the chief rivers which run through them. Each of these is in the charge of a forester under the Ranger, whose business it is to supervise their work, and to submit their reports to the officer in charge of the district forest.

Revenues

In these district forests are found all the timber trees which grow in the hills. The most valuable are *chir* and *sal,* but the large number of less useful trees classed as miscellaneous or *Kukat;* all have their use and help materially to swell the revenue derived from these forest; they are chiefly employed as fuel for lime and charcoal-burning, and, though issued free of charge to the right-holders, yet, as these works are generally carried on by contractors, they form an item of some importance. Although these forests were originally started for conservation and not for commercial reasons, yet they are self-supporting, and now show a considerable balance which ought under judicious management to increase. The income, which is credited to the Forest Department, showed a deficit of Rs. 1,130 in 1896, but for the three years ending 1902 has averaged over Rs. 3,400. The chief sources of revenue are sawn timber, charcoal, lime kilns and minor forest produce. They are mainly derived from contracts which are given out annually, the contractor in the case of sawn timber paying a royalty on each tree felled. As in the reserves, only the trees which have been marked may be cut. Right-holders obtain their timber at half rates. In all cases trees are paid for according to girth measurement and an established rate holds throughout the district. The minor forest produce, such as catechu, resin and fibre, is exported from the hills through the chaukis at Kaladhungi, Ramnagar, Kathgodam and Chorgallia, and the right to collect and sell such produc is leased annaully by auction at Haldwani through the Forest Department. The contract system is also extended to the sale of fuel and grass for fodder: the right is sold by auction for each *parao,* and the purchaser is bound to sell at a fixed rate at three annas per maund for fuel, eight annas per mound of dry grass and four annas per maund of green grass. Right-holders are allowed to graze free of charge, but a small sum is realized annually from outsiders under the head of grazing dues, when the Bhotiya traders or the inhabitants of the upper hills come and go from the Bhabar. The right-holders of every village have to submit an indent every August for the coming year. These indents must be first approved by the officer in charge and then the trees are marked by the Ranger. Chir and sal trees are given free of charge; unreserved trees may be cut by right-holders for their agricultural and domestic use without previous sanction.

At present the staff is very small and consists of a Ranger, with headquarters at Bhowali, two foresters stationed at Khairna and Bhim Tal and six forest guards, at Bhowali, and on the Managhir, Binaik-dhura, Kutauli, Dhyanirau and Chhakhata beats.

Tarai Forests

The civil forests of the Tarai and Bhabar are manged by the estate, having been removed from the control of the Forest Department in 1865. The reason for the transfer was the small value as timber-producing areas. The sal-covered patches, some of which extend for several miles into the plains, are, with the exception of Barkoli, almost worthless for timber, as the young trees generally become rotten at the core before they arrive at maturity. The trees in the Tarai are poor, but the sal of the Bhabar is of fair quality. Beyond occasional patches of khair and shisham in Bilheri, there are few trees of any commercial importance. The forest areas, however, are of great value as grazing lands and as fuel and fodder reserves. A small tax is levied on grazing and on the export of produce, and the proceeds are appropriated to the general improvement of the estates. The levying of these dues has been formally recognised and has been declared at successive settlements to be vested in Government.

Timber Trees

The timber trees and forest produce of this district differ to a considerable extent according to the altitude and locality and present many peculiar features differing from those of the forests of the plains.

Submontane Forest

In the forests below the hills and those clothing the outer spurs the most common and at the same time the most valuabel tree is the sal *(Shorea robusta),* which occurs from the Phika to the Sarda and also in the Duns. It ascends the hills in places to 3,000 feet and is found in the valleys to a great distance inland. This tree is usually characteristic of the tracts which is affects, and through other trees occur, the sal predominates. It grows as a rule to a height of 60 to 90 feet, with clear stems from 30 to 40 feet long and six to eight feet in girth. It is the most valuable and lasting building timber and also supplies the best sleepers produced in northern India. For general utility it is second only to teak. The export of sal consists of logs, beams, sleepers, rafters and smaller scantlings and planks; a considerable quantity of dry poles are also exported for the native marts. Of the indigenous building timbers, sain *(Terminalia tomentosa)* is prized next to sal, and there is a fair demand for rafters and planks of this species. It is common in the submontane tract and the Duns, attaining a height of from 80 to 100 feet, and a girth of eight or ten feet. The heart-wood is dark brown, tough, strong, elastic and very durable. It is used for indoor work, agricultural implements and boat-building. The haldu *(Adina cordifolia)* occurs abundantly in the open plains along the foot of the hills from the Sarda to the Ramganga and seconds the valleys to 3,000 feet. In the Bhabar are found trees of from 60 to 100 feet high, and with a girth of from ten to eighteen feet. The wood is yellow, smooth-fibred and fine-grained, and is fairly durable. This timber is largely exported in the form of rafters, beams and planks, chiefly to Anupshahr in the Bulandshahr district. When not exposed to the weather, haldu wood lasts well and is therefore chiefly used in the exterior of buildings. The dhauri *(Lagerstroemia parviflora)* is a handsome tree, common all over the submontane tract, where it attains a height of some 70 feet and a girth up to nine feet. There is a great demand for its timber which on account of its close resemblance to sal is styled "white sal" by the local traders, and is not unfrequently passed off as sal in the markets of the plains. The shisham *(Dalbergia sissoo)* occurs throughout the submountane tract in moist places, on the banks of streams and in islands in the rivers. The timber is of a high quality and is chiefly used in the manufacture of furniture in Bareilly. The khair *(Acacia catechu)* occurs in the submontane tract and up to 3,000 feet. As a timber tree it is not very largely employed, although the heavy, red, tough wood is of considerable value for agricultural implements and similar articles. It is chiefly preserved for the resin or catechu which will be mentioned later.

Hill Forests

In the hill forests the conifers clothe almost every ridge and valley, together with oaks, rhododendrons, maples, birches and others and afford an inexhaustible supply of every class of wood equal in quality to that procurable in Europe. On the lower slopes a great variety of timber is found. The list includes most of the trees that occur in the submontane forests and several others, few of which deserve special mention. The most valuable is the tun *(Cedrela toona)*. It is not now very common in this district, but is carefully preserved, as its wood is in great demand. It chiefly grows between 4,000 and 6,000 feet and attains a height of about 70 feet; the wood is close-grained, hard, capable of taking a high polish, and when properly seasoned makes an excellent furniture wood. The sandan *(Ougeinia dalbergioides)* is very common on the dry slopes of the outer hills, ascending to 5,000 feet and attaining a height of 50 feet; the wood is close-grained, hard, tough and durable; it is much valued for wheels, ploughs and furniture work. The har *(Terminalia chebula)* is not very common in this district, but is found on the China range above Dechauri. It grows to a height of from 60 to 80 feet. The timber is of a brownish colour, closegrained and heavy, and is used for the same purposes as sandan. The maples *(Acer pictum* and *Acer oblongum)* occur up to 7,000 feet. They are very ornamental trees, but the timber is of no great value. The Himalayan birch *(Betula acuminata)* is also common above 6,500 feet. The wood is close-grained and takes a fine satin polish: it is especially good for panels and indoor work. The rhododendron, which is very common in this district, is a less useful tree, as its timber is of a poor quality, it is chiefly employed for fuel and for inferior charcoal.

Oaks

There are four species of oak found in this district. The commonest is the banj *(Quercus incana)*, which occurs in all parts of the upper hills. The leaf is small and indented, and silvery grey underneath. The wood is used for buildings and agricultural implements and for charcoal burning, but is not of a very high quality. The karshu *(Quercus semicarpifolia)* occurs in Naini Tal and several other places in great abundance, being usually found at high elevations. It has a small, shiny, indented leaf. The wood is hard and heavy and is used for building and furniture. The tilonj *(Quercus dilatala)* is common throughout the hills. It has a much larger and less shiny leaf than the karshu and bears the closest resemblance to the English oak of all the Himalayan species. The wood is hard, durable, heavy and of a brownish colour; it is considered the best for all general purpose. Lastly, there is the rianj *(Quercus lanuginosa),* a smooth-stemmed species with a large leaf, grey underneath. It occurs near Naini Tal and at a few other places. The wood is of a greyish-brown colour, hard, and very heavy and is not easily worked.

Conifers

The conifers constitute the most valuable section of the timber trees of the hills both for quantity and quality. In many parts they occur in unbroken masses for miles and present a scene of great magnificence. The chir *(Pinus longifolia)* occurs throughout the Kumaun Division from 2,500 feet upwards. This tree appears to have the power of driving out all other vegetation from the tracts it occupies, and chir forests are interspersed only with a scanty undergrowth of the smallest shrubs. In many cases chir grows on slopes along the banks of the river and can be floated down without difficulty. One of its most valuable properties is as a turpentine producer, of which more will be said later. Of the other kinds, that known as *Pinus excelsa* alone grows in this district, but is not indigenous, as it is only to be found in the plantations on China. Next to the chir the most common of the conifers is the Himalayan cypress *(Cupresus torulosa),* called by the natives surai. This grows in great abundance at Naini Tal and other places in the district. In its general appearance it greatly resembles the silver fir of the Himalayas. The older trees in a favourable climate grow up in a slender column with a yellowish green foliage. At Naini Tal the boughs with a southern aspects are fuller and more regular, giving the tree a lop-sided appearance. The cypress has an average height from sixty to one hundred feet, while the girth varies from six to twelve feet; but these measurements vary with the position and elevation. The wood is hard, tough and of reddish colour. It was formerly used extensively for house-building in Naini Tal and is freely employed for indoor work throughout Kumaun. There are no natural groves of deodar *(Cedrus deodarus),* the

Himalayan cedar, in this district. The chief plantation is that on the China range near Naini Tal, where it has flourished greatly; nowhere do we find the magnificent groves of deodar which so often surround the temples in many parts of Almora. The only other conifers that occur here are those which have been planted experimentally on China. These include the Himalayan silver fir *(Abies webbiana),* which is common in Garhwal and the north of Almora; the Himalayan spruce *(Abies smithiana),* which grows naturally in the north of Garhwal; the Himalayan pencil cedar *(Juniperus excelsa),* which comes from the north of Almora and Nepal; and the ground cypress *(Juniperus communis),* which also comes from high altitudes in the north.

Bamboos

The other trees of the district are of little importance, and only the bamboos and the fruit trees call for any separate mention. Bomboos form the most important portion of the minor forest produce of all forest divisions and one that increases in value every year. They are of many varieties, from the small ringals which grow abundantly in the hills and are used for matting, baskets and innumerable other purposes, to the large bamboos of all kinds and sizes which grow in profusion along the foot of the hills and throughout the submontane tracts.

Minor Forest Produce

In the Naini Tal forest division one of the most important sources of income under the head of minor forest produce is turpentine. A still was established at Bhowali in 1895, and has proved a great success: in five years it had rapid all capital and maintenance charges. Operations have recently been extended, and profitable results are anticipated. In 1901 the manufacture was doubled at the cost of only half of the original outlay. The turpentine is obtained from chir, each tree yielding on an average 2.25 *sers* of rosin, although better results are expected for the future. In the Kumaun division there is a large income under the head, which includes drugs, tans, dyes, gums, reeds, fibres and grasses. The most important is catechu, an extract from the khair tree. The work is carried on by Doms from November till the rains. A considerable amount of gum is extracted from the babul *(Acacia arabica)* of the Bhabar, and in this tract, too, lac is also found and collected. The forest of the lower hills and the submountane tract yield an immense quantity of materials for ropes, cordage, twine, basket-making and matting. The *babar* grass alone is sufficient to supply all India with a valuable material for making coarse cordage and paper. The principal markets for minor forest produce are Chorgallia, Haldwani, Kaladhungi, Ramnagar and Chilkia. Good roads connect all these marts with the different lines of railway, the construction of which has considerably lines of railway, the construction of which has considerably enhanced the commercial value of forest products.

Forest Trees

The fruit trees of the district fall into two main classes, the first comprising those which grow wild, and the second those which have been introduced from Europe or elsewhere and are cultivated in gardens and orchards. Both classes contain a good number of species, but varying much in quality. Most of the European fruit trees have been introduced from the Government plantations at Ranikhet and elsewhere. The cultivation of fruit has been greatly encouraged by the growth of the settlements at Naini Tal and Ranikhet and in some instances the European planters have found it more profitable to grow fruit than maintain the old tea plantations; the fine orchards of General Wheeler at Ghorakhal and Mr. Deriaz at Ramgarh supply fruit to Naini Tal during the season and export large quantities of fruit to Calcutta and other places. Among the wild fruit trees there are the walnut, which both grows wild and is planted throughout the hills; the pomegranate, which also is found in a wild state throughout Kumaon; the wild pear and apple, uselss species, which, however, supply good stocks for grafting; the wild cherry and the jamun. The cultivated fruit trees are very numerous; the most common is the mango, which florishes exeedingly well in the Kotah Dun; while the others include apples, pears, cherries, citrons, limes, oranges, guavas, peaches, apricots and plums. Almost all of these are favourite objects of cultivation with the natives and are sold in large quantities in the Naini Tal markets.

Fauna

The zoology of Naini Tal is very varied and deserve some attention. The wide range of climate and elevation furnishes a list which comprises most of the animals of the plains as well as those of the hill tracts of these provisions.

Elephants

Wild elephants are still to be found in considerable numbers between the

Sarda and the Ganges. Their principal *habitat,* however, is the Patli Dun and the lower parts of Garhwal although fair numbers occur in the eastern half of the Kumaun forest division. In former years they were much more numerous. The common practice was to catch them in pite, but this caused such loss of cattle that it was prohibited in 1817, and thereafter all elephants found in pits were confiscated and sold on behalf of Government. The system was highly uneconomical, for fully three-fourths of the animals captured were either fatally or seriously injured. The restriction was, however, removed in 1827, and rules were framed for the digging of pits and the collection of dues on the capture of elephants. Little advantage accrued from this permission, either to the persons engaged in catching the elephants or to Government. After the mutiny a regular *kheddah* was established at the foot of the hills for the purpose of catching elephants for the public service, but this was soon abandoned, and but few operations were conducted in this district. At present no one is allowed to kill or capture an elephant without special permission of the local authorities, and this is only given in the case of solitary old males which are often very dangerous to human life.

The tiger is found here and there from the Tarai up to the highest points of the district, those which resort to the hills migrating from the Bhabar. Forty years ago tigers were very numerous in all parts, but owing to the extension of cultivation, the growth of population, and the greater use of arms of precision, their numbers have vastly diminished. In the Tarai the tiger attains a very large size, and several animals of over ten feet in length have been obtained. But the official returns, which are necessarily far from complete, show what a diminution in the number of animals there has been. From 1860 to 1880 rewards were paid in the Kumaun district for the destruction of no less than 624 tigers, and average of over 31 yearly. From 1892 to 1900 inclusive the number was 161 in all, excluding seven cubs. The total average has thus fallen to only 18 annually, while since 1897 it has been under 14. During the same period 32 persons were killed by tigers. The whole of the Tarai long held an unenviable notoriety as well for the insalubrity of its climate as for the number of tigers it harboured. The returns can only be considered as approximate, for in many cases the reward was not claimed. The panther or leopard is much more common. It occurs throughout the *Tarai* and *Bhabar*, and is frequently found at all elevations in the hills: it is a slighly-built, wiry animal with enormously powerful forelegs, and is for its size the most fearless and savage of the cat tribe, attacking an elephant without hesitation when brought to bay; it is a most destructive animal, and does immense damage to cattle, sheep and goats. The number of rewards paid for the destruction of leopards or panthers between 1860 and 1880 was 2,718 for the old district of Kumun. Between 1892 and 1901 the number of rewards paid for leopards killed was 454, including cuts, which gives an annual average of 49 animals, from which it would appear that their numbers have also diminished to a considerable extent.

Bears

The brown bear of the upper Himalayas does not occur in this district, but two other species are found in considerable numbers. The first is the Himalayas black bear *(Urses tibetanus)* which is met with throughout the hills down to 3,000 feet, but is now very rare. This animal does not hybernate in this district; it is a bold creature, doing great damage to the crops and fruit trees, and occasionally attacking sheep. The other is the ordinary sloth bear *(Ursus labiatus)* and is found occasionally in the sal forests of the lower hills and in the Tarai, where it lives in swampy ground and marshes. Its principal food is ants, beetles, fruits, roots and honey, and it rarely consumes flesh. Of both kinds, 146 were killed between 1892 and 1901, or rather rewards were given for their destruction. They seldom kills human beings, only two deaths being reported from this cause for the same period.

Deer & C

Several species of the stag and antelope tribes are found in this district. The largest and finest is the well-known sambhar or jarau as it is generally called here *(Rusa aristotelis)*. This animal is found in all the great forests, not only in the *Tarai* and *Bhabar*, but also in the hills, where it occurs up to all heights. Those that permanently frequent the hills possess more massive horns and are more robust in build than those of the *Bhabar* and *Tarai*. Sambhar are not found in any great numbers now, for the females are not so prolific as those of other stage, and the species has become somewhat scarce owing to the exertions of sportsmen and the reduction of the jungle area. The commonest of all the stag tribe is the spotted deer or chital *(Asia moutlatus)*, which is found in the forests along the foot of the hills, but never occurs beyond the second range of low hills. They are gregarious, and the herds consist of ten or twenty, but when the grass is burnt they crowd together for mutual protection. They have suffered greatly at the hands of native hunters, who have almost exterminated them in places where they were once abundant. Unlike the sambhar, who sheds his horne in May, chitas lose at irregular times from October to March, but chiefly in October and November. The stags begin to rut as soon as their new horns are perfect. The swamp deer or gond *(Rucervus duvaucelii)* was formerly plentiful all through the Tarai, but the clearing of the jungle has reduced its numbers. It seldom occurs west of the Dabka, but even to the east it is nowhere common. It chiefly affects swampy ground covered with reeds and tall grass; but it is also found at certain seasons in dry tracts where there are patches of long grass along the edge of the sal forests. The stags shed their magnificent horns in March. The hog-deer or parha *(Hyelaphs porcinus)* is found in grassy swamps and grass jungle along the banks of streams from the jungles of the Tarai to the foot of the hills. The rutting season occurs between October and February and the horne are shed in March or early April. The barking-deer or kakar *(Cervulus aureus)* is common throughout the forests from the Bhabar to the highest hills of the district. Its hard bark may be heard at all times of the day or night, but it seldom ventures out into the open. It is generally a solitary animal, except during the rutting season of October and November, when two or three may be seen feeding together. The males shed their horns in May. The nilgai *(Portax pictus)* is only found in a few patches of forest along the foot of the hills, and usually close to cultivation; it does much damage to young wheat, and no ordinary fence will keep it out. The fourhorned antelope or chausingha *(Tetraceros quadricornis)* is also found occasionally in this district, chiefly in the low plateaux and hills covered with sal forest and the dry jungle between them and the Tarai. It is generally seen alone or in pairs and is usually found in grass patches or glades in the forest. The well-known Indian antelope or blackbuck *(Antilope cervicapsa)* occurs in herds here and there in open plains or low grass jungle of the Tarai, but the horns are small and rarely exceed eighteen inches. Besides these, we have in the hills the gura or Himalayan chamois *(Antilope duvaucelii)*. This animal is found throughout the outer ranges of the Himalaya from 3,000 feet upwards. Gural generally occur in parties of three and four ; but in places where they are abundant herds of ten and twelve are met with. The female produces her young, generally one, through sometimes two, in April and May. The sarau or forest goat *(Nemorhoedus bubalina)* is a strange-looking animal found in most of the rough, rocky hill forests above 3,000 feet. It affects preciptous, densely-wooded places, is solitary in its habits, and is rarely seen in the open except at dusk and early dawn. It is very fierce when brought to bay by dogs, and can inflict sever wounds with its short sharp horns. Its flesh is very coarse, strong and unpalatable. The female, which like the gural also carries horns, produces one kid, generally in March or April.

Conidoe

The wolf is found throughout the submontane tract, but does not seem to enter the hills. Rewards are given for the destruction of this animal, but it is not very common. Far more destructive is the wild dog *(Cuon rutilans)*. These animals occur throughout the Tarai and Bhabar ; they are migratory in their habits and hunt in packs. They live chiefly on deer, and especially the sambhar, which, on account of its weight, is more easily run down, but they also kill large numbers of cattle in the forest clearings. A small pack of wild dogs seems to strike terror into jungle, which is rapidly deserted on their approach. Even the tiger is said to fear the wild dog, which is the most fearless and impudent of all Indian animals. The amount of game destroyed by them must be enormous ; especially among the chital and sambhar, far more of which must fall yearly to the red dog than to the rifle. As soon as they have thined out one jungle, they go on to the next, often boldly following the high road. A reward is given for their destruction, but the average number of payments does not exceed one yearly, and in no year have more than four claims been presented, although they have greatly increased in numbers of late years. Jackals are nowhere more common than in the Tarai and the scrub jungle along the foot of the hills. They ascend the valleys communicating with the plains, but are seldom found above 7,000 feet. Their ordinary food is as usual carrion, but they kill a great many young deer and often catch pea-fowl and are very fond of maize. They are most persistent on following a wounded deer, but they rarely venture near it until it is so exhausted as to be obliged to lie down. Jackals frequently go mad and are then more dangerous than mad dogs, as they attack all living beings they meet. Hyaenas are common in the submontane tract, but seldom enter the hills. They frequent broken raviny ground, where cover is abundant, sometimes in forest and sometimes in thorn jungle and sandy watercourses, where there is plenty of long grass. The hyaena is a skulking, cowardly animal, nocturnal in its habits; it sometimes kills dogs, sheep and goats, but generally feeds on carrion. A reward of two rupees is given for the destruction of each animal.

The common Indian monkey found all over these provinces occurs throughout the district up to heights of 7,000 feet. These animals generally establish themselves on a steep bank in a mango grove near a village or in forest or precipitous ground near outlying cultivation, whence they emerge when unobserved and do immense damage to cultivated crops. Perhaps a more common species in this district is the *langur*, large herds of which are to be met with throughout the wooded portions of the hills at all heights. They feed on fruits and flowers and on the buds and young leaves of many trees and plants, but from August to February acorns form their chief diet, and during those months they are to be found in all the oak forests. They are fond of potatoes, but seldom attack other crops. They are especially prevalent around Naini Tal and is the mixed forests of the Bhabar. The Himlayan *langur* is easily distinguished from the Bengal *langur* by its hands being concolorous with its body, and by its loud grunting note of alarm, while the hands of the latter are jet black and its voice is more of a deep bass mournful bellow.

Other Animals

The other mammalia call for no detailed mention. They include the badger, porcupine, the common Indian fox, the hill fox, the otter, black-crapped marten, the hare, wild pig, the pigmy hog of the Tarai, several species of wild cat, bats, moles, shrews, rats squirrels and the mongoose. Poroupines are very numerous both in the hills and the submontane tracts, making their own burrows in the level country, and using natural caves and crevices in the hills. Wild pig occur in large numbers at all elevations and do immense damage to potatoes and other crops. In the hills they especially frequent the oak forests, and here, as a rule, the largest boars are found. The pigmy hog *(Porculia salvania)* is rare: it occurs in the Tarai and Kashipur, and its flesh is greatly prized by the Tharus and Bhuksas.

Reptiles

There are some eight or nine species of lizard found in this district, all of them being fairly common. One of the most familiar sights to the traveller in the hills is that of the large "blood-suckers" that run in and out of the crevices in the walls at the sides of the hill roads. They grow to a length of about 15 inches and are beautiful creatures, gleaming with every colour of the rainbow. In spite of their name they are perfectly harmless. Besides these, there are the large common water-lizard, which is found as great as four feet in length and is common near water as its name implies. Then there are two or three smaller lizards whose predominating colours are green and brown and are found everywhere, and are only to be distinguished by the naturalist. Of the snakes, 23 species are recorded as being found in this district. Of these 15 are entirely harmless while the remainder are venomous in a greater on less degree. All the harmless snakes belong to the colubrine order, and are for the most part common in both the Bhabar and the hill pattis. The commonest of all is the well-known "dhaman" of the plains, that grows to a lenght of some seven feet. It is of a light brownish olive in colour, with a long pointed tail. When beet it assumes a very pugnacious attitude and strikes out in the most ferocious manner, but without doing any damage. The grass-snakes are very common on the grassy slopes of the hills at the elevations, and many may be seen by the roadside in a day;s walk in all parts of the district. Of the non-venomous snakes the largest and far the most imposing is the python, which is found fairly frequently in the Tarai swamps and in the moist valleys of the lower hills. This snake grows to a length of thirty feet, though specimens of this size are undoubtedly rare. The python is a most handsome creature with the most gorgeous colouring; its strength is enormous and it can squeeze any living animal to a jelly. A moderately large python can swallow a fair-sized chital. Out of the eight venomous snakes three are far more common than the others; these are the cobra, karait and Russell's viper. Of these the first two are too well known to need any description; they occur in all parts of the district. Russell's viper is a reddish-brown snake that grows to about four feet six inches in length. It has three rows of blackish-brown annular ocelli surrounded by an inner white and an outer black ring down the back and sides. A broad-arrow mark on the head formed by two pale lines from the snout over the eyes to the temporal region forms another distinctive feature. There are three other vipers found in this district, but they are not common. As in all parts of India, the number of deaths attributed to snake-bite yearly is large.

The commoner birds of this tract are those which are found throughout the Himalayan range; but situated as it is, many stragglers from the surrounding regions are found among the rarer birds. This district is peculiarly rich in bird-life, as besides the hill pattis it embraces a large area of plain and forest in the Tarai and Bhabar, much of which consists of the marshes and savannahs so dear to many genera of birds. Thus with an elevation ranging from over 9,000 feet to the lowlying swamps of the Tarai there is a happy hunting-ground for the ornithologist that it would be hard to equal in any part of India. Numberless birds make their home in this district, and very many resort here as migrants during different parts of the year. About 450 species have been recorded as having been seen in this district, the greater number by far of which also breed here. A complete list is given in Oates' work, so that it would be superfluous to attempt anything in a nature of a catalogue in an article of this description. In the hills are found nearly all the Indian eagles, vultures and many of the hawks; of the first there are some twelve species and seven kinds of vultures are known. About 24 varieties represent the hawks, kites, buzzards and ospreys. Owls, woodpeckers and kingfishers abound; cuckoos are particularly noticeable for their variety; shrikes, thrushes and babblers also occur in great numbers in the hills and plains slikes. Of the smaller birds, finches, tits and warblers, it may be said that their name is legion. The sheltered Duns form an admirable abode for birds, with their abundance of water, forest, and wild climate.

The district is well supplied with game-birds of every description, from the peacock to the jack-snipe. Of the pheasants there is the magnificent munal, which descends, from the upper ranges in the cold weather to the higher parts of this district; he never comes down far below the snow-line, but prefers the wooded tops of hills, where he may frequently be seen in the open when he comes out to catch the early morning sun. The munal is rivalled by the koklas and the dungi or Himalayan argus-pheasant, which are not very uncommon in this district. More frequent are the chir and kalij pheasants, the latter especially abounding in the lower hills. Jungle-fowl are found in vast numbers in the forests of the Bhabar and Tarai. Several varieties of partridge occur: the common grey partridge and the black partridge abound in the Tarai, and that grand sporting bird, the chakor, is common in the hills. Besides these there are the two hill partridges, known as piura, which are found above 5,000 feet in small numbers. Seven species of quail belong to this district and occur in great numbers in the Tarai and Bhabar; enormous bags have been made near Haldwani when the quail come up from the plains after the cutting of the rabi crops in April. The greater and lesser florican are both found in the open grass stretches of the Tarai, the latter being more rare than its larger congener. Snipe, too, of the usual three varieties are to be found in the jhils of the Tarai in the cold weather, especially toward the end of th season, but for some reason or other the snipe of this district are not such good eating as those of the plains. Wood-cock are found in small numbers in the ravines of the hill *pattis*. Water-birds and wild-fowl are numerous in the swamps of the southern parts of the district as migrants in the winter months; all the ducks teals and pochards that are found in the plains are to be met with here too. They do not breed here, with the probable exception of the spotted-bill.

Fishes

Fish are generally used as an article of food throughout this district by all classes, with the exception perhaps of a few Brahmans and Banias. The Tharus and Bhuksas of the Tarai are great fish-eaters, as also are the Dome of the hill pattis. Hither to no sustained and systematic efforts have been made to protect fish from the reckless poaching that is the natural results of this proclivity; but the question has recently been considered, and good results may be shortly expected from the preservative measures that are being taken in hand. Already something has been effected in this direction, as the fishing in the lakes is regulatd by a system of licenses. The hillman needs no education in the way of poaching; he has learnt the use of dynamite, lime and otters, and he has no sporting instincts to hamper him in their use.

Except in the lakes fish as "forest produce" belong to the District Forest Department and therefore no fishing is allowed except to right-holders without a permit issued by the district authorities. Fishing is granted as a right in the settlement of each village, and thus an indirect hold is kept over poaching; but much more stringent measures are needed in any real good is to be effected in this direction. The mahseer, especially, needs a helping hand; this fish, so good for food and sport, commences to run up the smaller streams about the end of March or the beginning of April, and in June or July large specimens, weighing from ten to fifteen pounds, may be seen in little streams no more than a few yards wide. These are all heavy with spawn and fall easy victims to the poacher. Where the streams are narrow and run between rocks the Doms fasten a series of strings with sharp barbed hooks three inches apart to the rocks on each side, and thus secure a vast number of the larger fish. In the hills, too the practice of poisoning pools with various vegetable drugs is common. Another well-known method of poaching is by placing lumps of meal poisoned with *bhang* in the shallow bays of lakes and the backwaters of rivers. The drug renders the fish insensible and they are thus easily secured the next morning. In 1899 the operations of the Indian Fisheries Act were extended to the Naini Tal, Sat Tal, Malwa Tal, Bhim Tal and Naukuchhiya Tal lakes, as well as to certain portions of the Kosi, Baur and Gola rivers.[19] In 1992, however, the lakes were excluded from the operations of the Act. Fish are universally eaten by the casteless classes that form the bulk of the population. It is unnecessary here to enter into a description of the various species of fish found in this district. In the hills the most common is the mahseer *(Barbus tor),* and in the Tarai are found the same kind as those which occur throughout the United Provinces.

Cattle

It is very difficult to estimate the number of domestic cattle in the district, for it varies with the population, vast numbers of animals migrating with the hill people to the Bhabar from the upper pattis to the hills in the cold weather. There they remain from October to May, sheltered in temporary sheds. In the Tarai, too, the cattle temporarily increase in numbers every year by reason of the droves brought up from the plains for pasturage. Consequently the only figures available are far from accurate. The last cattle census took place in 1904. It was then ascertained that there were 114,118 bulls and bullocks in the district and 155,287 cows, as well as 76,519 young stock. To these must be added and indefinite number imported in the winter to find pasturage in the Bhabar, and an equally indefinite number which paid grazing tax in the Tarai and which came from other districts. In the hills the domestic cattle of indigenous origin are small in size and usually red or black in colour. Early every morning the village herds are driven to the ridges of the neighbouring hills for pasture, and are again collected before sunset and housed either in the lower storey of the dwelling-house or in a temporary shod erected close to the village site. As a rule the milch-cattle are not fed on grain or chaff, but are only pastured, and after the harvest are allowed to eat down the stalk remaining in the fields. Neither bullocks nor buffaloes are used for commercial transport, but they share with ponies and women the duty of carrying their owners, baggage in the annual migration to and from the Bhabar. Below the hills most of the bullocks are bred in the Bhabar itself, or else are imported from Kheri, Pilibhit and the north of Oudh. Several attempts have been made to improve the local based but without success, for the finer kinds brought from Hissar could not stand the climate and were considered too heavy for common purposes. Buffaloes are kept for milking purposes and manure. At the 1904 census male buffaloes numbered 113,435; they are chiefly confined to the Bhabar and Tarai, Cow-buffaloes amounted to 38,309—a comparatively small number, which is very greatly exceeded by Almora.

Sheep and Goats

Sheep and goats at the time of the cattle census numbered 37,257 and 36,398 respectively; in the cold weather large flocks are brought up to the Tarai from the plains about the end of October for pasture. They consist for the most part of ewes, and as soon as the lambs are sufficiently strong, they are taken again to the plains. Goat and sheeps are kept for wool, for food and for penning on the land. Goats in the hills are not milked, but are solely kept as articles of food and suppliers of manure: no man, it is said, who possesses a large flock of goats ever has poor crops. The large Tibetan sheep which are brought down as pack-animals by the Bhotiya traders are not included in the figures given, for they are merely beasts of burden and cannot be included in the agricultural stock of the district. The sheep brought up for the supply of the Naini Tal market usually comes from the

Kangra and Kulu districts of the Panjab-Himalaya, although many come from the middle Duab, and though smaller in size yield excellent mutton when fed on gram for a time. The hill sheep are small with wiry brownish-grey wool, short tails and long horns. They are not of a high quality and are chiefly valuable for their wool, out of which coarse blankets are made. Goats are sometimes imported from Tibet for food or sacrifice, but their flesh is very strong and ill-flavoured. The indigenous breed is raised in the same places and by the same people who keep the indigenous sheep.

Ponies

The number of ponies at the stock census of 1904 was, 9,054—a figure which is far in excess of the total of Almora and Garhwal together. The Tibetan or hill pony, generally known under the name of *ghunt,* are the best and often fetch high prices. They are clumsy, rough and small, but very strong and active, sagacious, docile and sure-footed. The pony, however, in more common use is the *banjara* variety, which is bred in large numbers along the foot of the hills. It is a very hardy and useful, though small, animal, and does most of the carrying work between the plains and the hill sanitaria.

Cattle Diesease

Cattle diesease appears to be endemic in the hills, the Bhabar and the Tarai. Rinderpest broke out first in 1850, and there were violent epidemics in 1864 and 1872, since which time is has been always present. Foot-and mouth disease seems to have been prevalent at all times, and dysentery or *chira* causes great havoc in the Tarai. The disease known as *surra,* too, often appears in the Bhabar, attacking cattle and horse, and its ravages have frequently been such as to disorganize the tonga servie between Kathgodam and the Brewery. It would appear from the returns that in the Tarai a damp winter causes the greatest mortality; disease is undoubtedly connected with the moist climate, and it has been suggested that one of the chief causes is the absence of salt-licks for the cattle, salt being especially necessary for health in the presence of excessive moisture. In order to combat cattle diseases and to reduce its ravages by inoculation, a verterinary assistant was posted to the district in July 1894. Since that date there has been a steady and constant decrease in the mortality. In 1893 the ravages of disease were so great that it destroyed plough-cattle to such an extent that its effects were visible in a shrinkage of the Tarai cultivation and a falling off of rents. From 1894 to 1903 the average cattle mortality was 6,971-7 deaths annually; but since 1898 it has only been 2,994. During the decade, the average mortality from rinderpest was 1,989, from foot-and-mouth disease 2,417; and from dysentery 2,575. These figures do not include deaths from other—causes. In 1898 a disease locally called phatikia appeared in the hill pattis; this is probably another name for rinderpest, which is called manrog in the submontane tracts.

Climate

The extraordinary range of elevation in the district occasions an endless variety of climate in the different parts. There is only one regular meteorological station, that at Mukhtesar, in the district, but no statistic are necessary to emphasize the difference in climate between, for example, Naini Tal, Haldwani and Kichha, all of which lie on the single highway that traverse the district from north to south. In the Tarai to the south the climate differs from that of the adjoining plains country, chiefly in the variations of temperature between the day and night, which are due to the nature of the soil and are the proximate cause of the heavy sickness which attacks the inhabitants of the tract at the commencement of the hot weather and towards the end of the rains. The large areas of jungle and forest, moreover, have a most pernicious effect on the climate, while the line of springs towards the north and the high waterlevel in all parts necessarily render the tract most unhealthy. The excessive moisture, combined with a great heat, is always productive of malaria, ague and kindred sickness. After the beginning of May the climate begins to be dangerous to Europeans, while in the rains it is positively deadly. In the hot weather and the rains a sharp attack of a peculiarly malignant type of malarial fever is the certain penalty for going out before the sun is well up or remaining out of doors after five O'clock. It is said that by exercising caution in this matter and a careful use of mosquito nets it is possible for Europeans to remain in the Tarai for a short period during the rains, but as a matter of fact few have been known to do so with complete immunity. The climate of Kashipur is very similar to that of the Tarai, although it improves greatly in the extreme southern portion. Both in Kashipur and the Tarai the clearings, and especially the older settled villages, are much more healthy than the remainder of the tract, and this is also the case in the Bhabar. In the latter portion of the district the climate on the whole is not much better than in the Tarai. Mr. C.H. Roberts writes. "The climate is at all times of the year trying, owing to the proximity of the hills the circulation of the air being much retarded; the direct and refracted sun heat makes it close, hot and muggy. In the months of August, September and

October, when forest undergrowth grows up, the climate is extremely malarious; during other portions of the year the climate, though enervating, is not so unhealthy. During most of the year at the mouth of the valleys or passes a nasty cold wind sets in after sundown, which is trying to the constitution after the heat of the day."[20] In the highly afforested tracts east of the Nandhaur, where, too, a very high spring-level exists, the climate is extremely malarious except during the cold weather months; that of the tract of country westwards has much improved since it has been opened out and cultivated; nevertheless the inhabitants suffer severely from fever, especially from July to October, and in a greater degree those who live on the southern limites of cultivation owing to their proximity to the Tarai swamps. The southern portion of Chilkia in the extreme west of the Bhabar greatly resembles the Tarai and the hillmen are quite unable to stand the climate.

In the hills an entirely different state of things prevails. At Naini Tal the thermometer seldom reads above 85 degrees at any time, while in the coldest part of the winter months it has an average of about 32 degrees, although the bright sun renders the cold little felt. Naini Tal itself is colder than the rest of the hill tracts, owing to its shut-in-position and the dampness resulting from the heavy rainfall. The meteorological readings taken at Mukhtesar show a maximum of 85° and a minimum of 25.5° in the shade for the year 1900, and this is probably about the general range of temperature in all years. At lower elevation, and especially to the north of the first range of hills the temperature rises rapidly. Almora and Ranikhet are much hotter than Naini Tal, and at the same time the humidity is very much less. Frequently during the rains the headquarters of the district are enveloped in clouds, while the sky is almost clear beyond the Gagar range. Lower down, the malaria, which produces such an effect in the Tarai, extends into the depressed rich valleys on the banks of the Kosi and other rivers, and generally into all places of low elevation. These spots, though fertile, are often very hot, and are all considered more or less unhealthy, particularly at the end of the rains. The medical aspects of the district will be dealt with the dispensaries and medical arrangements, most of which are in the hands of the District Board.

Rainfall

The variation in the climate is very largely due to the difference in the nature of the rainfall in the several parts of the district as well as to the change of altitude and the varying configuration of the surface of the ground. The greatest fall of rain occurs in the outer slopes of the hills, the southern face of the lofty Gagar range appearing to attract the rain-clouds and precipitate their mositure. It is a remarkable fact that Naini Tal itself, owing to its position on this southern, slope, receives doube the rainfall of Ranikhet, and even Mukhtesar, which stands at a great elevation has a far smaller rainfall than the district headquarters. The zone of heavy rainfall extends from the great peaks of the Gagar range to the bottom of the hills. In the Bhabar the rainfall is decidedly heavy, and further south in the Tarai the average is much greater than in the southern districts of Rohilkhand, but it rapidly decreases towards the southern border. In the hills seldom a month passes without rain in some part of the district; the rainy season begins earlier than in the plains and lasts up to the end of September. There is almost always a considerable winter fall in Naini Tal, which becomes snow on the heights and rain in the valleys; it is heaviest in the month of January. Snow generally falls every year in almost all the hill pattis, but it is seldom of long duration.

Rain-gauge Stations

Rain-gauges are maintained at Naini Tal and Mukhtesar in the hills, at Haldwani, Ramnagar and Kathgodam in the Bhabar, and at Kilpuri, Nagla, Rudarpur and Kashipur in the Tarai. Records are available for Naini Tal since 1856, and for Kashipur, Radurpur, Kilpuri and Haldwani since 1870. The rain-gauge for Ramnagar dates from 1891, that at Nagla from 1894 and Kathgodam from 1896. The average fall for Naini Tal is 97.49 inches, the greatest amount recorded in one year being 154.33 inches in 1893, and the least 67.1 inches in 1887. July and August are the wettest months, and November and December the driest. At Kathgodam the average fall is 91-27 inches: it generally varies with that of Naini Tal, but not exactly, for in 1898 for instance the rain-gauge recorded a full of over 22 inches in exceess of that of Naini Tal. Of the Bhabar stations, Haldwani has an average of 81-8 inches and Ramnagar 65.66 inches. This illustrates the general phenomenon that the rainfall is much heavier in the eastern portion of the Tarai and Bhabar than in the west. Thus Kilpuri has an average of 64.08 inches, while Rudarpur in the centre of the Tarai shows 57.97 inches, and Kashipur in the east only 46.4 inches. This feature reacts not only on the climate, but also on the agriculture, for in pargana Bilberi there is in consequence less need of irrigation works.

Source : Naini Tal District Gazetteers, Superintendent Government Printing, United Provinces, Allahabad, 1904.

REFERENCES

1. Mr. Huton's Report, p. 5
2. C.S. Middlemiss, Physical Geology of the sub-Himalaya of Garhwal and Kumaon, *Geological Survey of India*, Vol. XXIV, part 2.
3. C.S. Middlemiss, Physical Geology of Naini Tal, Rec. *Geol. Survey of India*, Vol. XXIII, part-4
4. C.S. Middlemiss, Crystalline and Metamorphic Rocks, Rec, *Geol. Survey of India*, Vol. XXIII, part. I
5. T. H. Holland's Report on Geological Structure and Stability of Hill slopes around Naini Tal.
6. *Asiatic Researches*, Vol. XVI, pp. 387-397.
7. To Board, February 5th, 1819 and From Board, February 6th, 1819.
8. From Board, June 27th. 1820. To Board, July 19th, 1820. From Board, August 4th, 1820.
9. Notification No. 407 F.C. dated the 5th September 1877.
10. Notification No. 173 F., dated the 26th February 1870.
11. Notification No. 85F / 200-77, of 6th February 1890.
12. Notification No. 510 / XIV–200–123 of 6th July 1899.
13. Notification Nos. 139/XIV—819A-93 of 27th February, 414/XIV—406-68
14. Notification No. 818F—110A-23 of 6th November, 1890.
15. Notification No. 201F / 574-36 of March 24th, 1890
16. Notification No. 818F / 110 – 23of 6th November, 1891.
17. Notification No. 551/XIV–213-125 of August 26th 1898.
18. Government Gazettee, August 19th and 11th December, 1899.
19. Notification No. 2082 / I – 483 of 17th June, 1899
20. Bhabar Assessment Report, 1890, p. 2

16

PITHORAGARH DISTRICT

Origin of Name

The district is named after its headquarters town, Pithoragarh. Tradition has it that during the reign of the Chand rajas of Kumaon, one Piru, also called Prithvi Gosain, built a fort here and named it Prithvigarh which, in course of time, got changed into Pithoragarh. According to another local legend, Pithora, a Gurkha raja, constructed a fort here and called the place Pithoragarh.

Location, Boundaries, Area and Population

Location and Boundaries

The district forms the north-eastern part of the Kumaon Division and lies between Lat. 29°27' N. and 30°40 N. and Long 79°50' E. and 81°3 E., the length from north to south, being about 151 km. at its maximum, and the breadth from east to west, reaching its maximum at about 119 km. It is bounded by Tibet on the north, Nepal on the east, district Almora on the south and the districts Almora and Chamoli on the West.

Area

According to the Central Statistical Organisation, the district had an area of 7,242 sq. km. in 1961 and in size occupied the tenth position in the state.

Population

According to the census of 1961, the population of the district was 2,63,579 (females being 1,35,287).

History of District as Administrative Unit

With a view to meet the felt needs of the residents of the northern borders of the state for comprehensive development of the area, the State government created the Uttarkhand Division comprising district Chamoli, Pithoragarh and Uttarkashi in 1960. District Pithoragarh was constituted on February 24, 1960 with 32 *pattis*-30 *pattis* from tahsil Pithoragarh and two *pattis* from tahsil Almora. In December 1968, the district was included in the Kumaon Division which was reorganised to comprise districts Naini Tal, Almora and Pithoragarh.

Sub-divisions, Tahsils and Thanas

The district has been divided into four sub-divisions: Dharchula, Didihat, Manayari and Pithoragarh, each forming a single tahsil of the same name.

Triangular in shape, Dharchula, the north-eastern tahsil of the district, is bounded on the north-east by the water-parting ridge which separates it from Tibet; on the south-east and east by the Kali river which separates it from Nepal; on the west by the Panch Chulhi range which divides it from tahsils Didihat and Mansyari. The tahsil consists of five *pattis*. Its population was 32,566 (females, 15,753).

Tahsil Didihat is bounded, on the north by tahsil Manayari, on the east by tahsil Dharchula and the river Kali which separates it from Nepal on the south and west by tahsil Pithoragarh and on the north-west by district Almora. It consists of the *pattis*. Its population was 96,518 (females, 50,452).

Manayari, the north-western tahsil of the district, is bounded by Tibet on the north, tahsil Dharchula on the east, tahsils Dharchula and Didihat on the south and districts Chamoli and Almora on the west. It consists of 3 *pattis*. Its population was 30,377 (females, 14,992)

Tahsil Pithoragarh, forming the south-western part of the district, is bounded on the north by district Almora and tahsil Didihat, on the east by the Kali river which separates it from Nepal, on the south and west by the Sarju river which divides it from district Almora. It consists of 15 *pattis*. Its population was 1,04,118 (females 54,090).

Police Station

For purpose of police administration there are four police-stations in the district, one at each tahsil headquarters. Each of the 32 *pattis* of the district is a revenue police circle.

Geology

The district lies in the Himalayas which are the youngest mountains in the world and the land mass now covered by them was occupied by the great geosynclinal Tethys sea during the Mesozoie period. The probable date of commencement of the elevation of the Himalayas is about the close of the Mesozia period.

According to geological formations of the district, it may be divided into four broad belts, viz., (1) the innermost Siwalik hill ranges, (2) the lesser and middle Himalayas (3) the inner Himalayas and (4) the thin belt bordering the Tibetan Himalayas, roughly tending east-south-east.

The belt of the innermost hill ranges of the Siwalik group lies in the southern part of the district. In the rock formations here sandstones alternate with clayey shales. The sandstones are dirty, friable and micaceous and are, therefore, unsuitable for the building, ballast and industry.

The second belt, comprising the ranges of the lesser and middle Himalayas, extends north of the Siwalik group to Dharchula. It contains sedimentary and low to medium grade metamorphic rocks such as limestone, slate, quartizite, phyllite and mica-garnet schist. Mineralization of copper, magnesite, soap-stone etc. is known to occur in the belt.

The third belt, containing higher ranges of the inner Himalayas, is wholly composed of crystalline metamorphic rocks such as mica and garnet schists, kyanite and sillimanite schists, gneisses, granulites and quartzites. This belt if very little known geologically. The belt extends from near Dharchula to Garbyang.

The fourth belt, bordering the Tibetan Himalayas has an average width of about 7 km. It contains marine sedimentry rocks such as quarzities, fossiliferous limestones and shale.

Minerals

A number of minerals are found in the district, and brief notes about them are given in the following paragraphs.

Copper

The region around the town of Pithoragarh has been one of the important centres of copper mining in the past. The remnants of old copper mines which collapsed long ago reported to have existed below Pithoragarh town where there is now a natural spring, of which the water has a metallic taste. These mines were abandoned due to the poor quality of ore and difficult mining conditions. Copper ore is found to occur as disseminations in crystalline dolomites and as segregations in quartz veins traversing the former. Chalcopyrite, tetrahedrite, cuprite and malachite are said to have been found in the mine. South of village Askot malachite is commonly found staining the country rock, which is also traversed by quartz veins bearing galens, pyrite, arsenopyrite and challcopyrite. Chalcopyrite speaks and clusters up to 4 cm. in length have been found at Bora-Agar in a band of crystalline dolomite extending for about 1,209 m. Associated minerals are cuprite, tetrahedrite and malachite. Chaleopyrite along with malachite and azurite, disseminated in quartz stringers and also in crystalline dolomite, occurs near Dewal Thal.

Magnesite

Several scattered deposits of magnestic are found in the area around Pithoragarh. They are associated with the dolomite limestone. Very little work has been done on these deposits. Extensive deposits of the minerals occur at several scattered localities in the neighbourhood at Dewal Thal. Some of the more promising ones being located at Dewal Thal, Chandag, Phadyarl and Satsilang. Other promising deposits occur at Osail, Bcvalthal, Harali, Pathrauli, Ramkot, Bunga, Chhina and Masum Bheo. Between Tong and Dhurni in Rani Agar occur two promising zones of crystalline magnesite which extend for almost a kilometre. The deposits in the northern zone are about 23 m. and in the southern about 60 m. in thickness.

Soapstone

Several small deposits of soapstone occur in association with magnesite at Dewal Thal and Chandag.

Arsenic

Orpiment deposits exist near Manayari. Both orpiment and realgar are reported to be available in scattered fragments on the moraines of the

Shunkalpa glacier. The ore had probably come down from the hill face immediately above.

Sulphur

This mineral is found in the bed of the Ramganga (eastern) and in tahsil Manayari.

Kyanite

At Girgaon (south of Malpa) there is a thin layer of blue sealy kyanite, the rocks also bearing sericite quartzite.

Graphite

Graphitoid pigmentation in schistose rocks is found near villages Sobala and Dar in the Dhauli valley and north of Sirdang in the Kali valley.

Slate

Slate quarries exist throughout the district and it is utilised locally for building purposes.

Limestone

Though vast reserves of limestone exist in the district, they are dolomite and appear to be fit only for ballast.

Climate

The elevation of the district ranges from 500 m. above sea level in the valleys in the south to over 7000 m. in the snow-bound Himalaya in the north and north-west. The climate, therefore, largely depends on altitude and varies according to aspect and elevation. Although tropical heat may be experienced in the southern valleys during the summer, the winters are severe. As most of the district is situated on the southern slopes of the Himalayas, monsoon currents penetrate through the deep valleys and rainfall is at the maximum in the monsoon season (June to September), particularly in the southern half of the district. The northern half of the district also gets considerable rain during the winter season which lasts from mid-November to March.

Rainfall

Records of rainfall in the district are available for eight rain recording stations which, however, are so located that the records are more properly representative of rainfall in the river valleys. The rainfall generally increases from the south towards the north and owing to the nature of the terrain is highly variable from place to place. Most of it occurs during the monsoon period, being between 75 per cent and 85 per cent of the annual precipitation in the south and between 50 per cent and 70 per cent in the extreme north and north-east. July and August are the rainiest months. In September depressions from the Bay of Bengal occasionally affect the weather and, in association with them, heavy rain may occur cousing floods. In the monsoon season there are a few occasions when there are spurts of heavy rain in the hills causing flood in the rivers. The rainfall decreases rapidly after September and is the lowest in November. During winter, from December to March, considerable precipitation occurs in association with the passage of western disturbances across the region, particularly in the northern parts where it is considerably higher than in the rest of the district, being about 20 per cent to 40 per cent of the annual total.

During the fairly long period between 1901 and 1960, for which rainfall data are available for five older stations, the number of years when less than 80 per cent of the annual normal precipitation occurred was 13 at Askot, 12 at Pithoragarh, 10 at Chaukori, 9 at Berinag and 2 at Dharchula. The number of spells of two consecutive years when such low precipitation was recorded was one each at Pithoragarh and Berinag and two at Chaukori; the number of spells of three such consecutive years was two at Askot, which also recorded a long spell of low precipitation losting five years from 1928 to 1932. The heaviest rainfall in 24 hours recorded was 274.3 mm. at Chaukori on June 22, 1916.

Temperature

There is no meteorological observatory in the district. The following account of the climate is based mainly on the records of the observations in the neighbouring districts where similar meteorological conditions prevail. Variations in temperature are considerable from place to place and depend upon elevation as well as aspect. As the insolation is intense at high altitudes, in summer temperatures are considerably higher in the open than in the shade. Pools of cold stagnant air in the valleys cause the diurnal range of temperature to be considerable. January is the coldest month with a mean maximum temperature of 10°C. at heights of 2,000 m. above sea-level, the mean minimum temperature being at the freezing point (0°C). cold waves in the wake of western disturbances often make winter conditions rigorous. With the onset of the monsoon towards the end of June, day temperatures fall by about 3° to 5°C. and with its withdrawal towards the third or fourth week of September, day and night temperatures begin to decrease, slowly in the beginning but more rapidly after October till January, which is the coldest month. Temperatures are much lower at higher altitudes towards the north. In association with western disturbances, precipitation at higher altitudes occurs mostly in the form of snow which accumulates considerably in the valleys.

After January, both day and night temperatures begin to rise, rapidly from March to May or June, the last two being the warmest months. The mean daily maximum temperature is about 25°C. at stations 2,000 m. above sea-level, 15° to 18°C. at 3,000 m. above sea-level and still lower at higher elevations. With the incursion of the monsoon current. temperatures fall slightly by about 3° to 5°C.

Humidity

The humidity is highest during the monsoon months and particularly so during the rainiest months of July and August. During the winter months, it increases towards the afternoon at high altitudes.

Cloudiness

Skies are heavily clouded during the monsoon months and for short spells when the region is affected by western disturbances. During the rest of the year, the skies are generally clear to lightly clouded.

Winds

Owing to the nature of the terrain, local effects are pronounced and when the general prevailing winds are not too strong to mask these effects, there is a tendency for diurnal reversal of winds which blow up the slopes during the day (Anabatic flow) and down the slopes at night (Katabatic flow). Katabatic wind can blow with considerable force.

Flora

The northern part of the district, comprising the larger portions of tahsils

Mansyari and Dharchula, where there are high mountains and ridges, is rocky, blank and covered with perpetual snow. The forests are confined to the river valleys and the southern parts of the district. In 1968, an area of about 2,80,403 hectares or 38.71 per cent of the total area of the district was covered with forests. Of the total forest area tahsil Manayari contained 1,98,493 hectares, tahsil Didihat 58,832 hectares, tahsil Dharchula 11,555 hectares and tahsil Pithoragarh 11,523 hectares.

Taking into consideration the differences in the altitudes and the climate conditions which obtain in the district, its flora may be divided into four main divisions—the sal forests, *chir* forests, oak forests and the coniferous forest. The willow and older trees are, however, common everywhere in damp situations. The deodars are introduced plants in the district but have become wild. They are found in the southern part of the district around the temples where they had been planted for many generations, their magnificent groves being seen around Gangolihat in tahsil Pithoragarh.

Sal Forests

These forests occur in the southern part of the district and the chief tree, sal, is found up to a height of about 1,220 m. and as far as north as *patti* Malla Askot. On the hills the sal does not attain the height to which it grows in the plains. Other associated trees which also grow in these forests are the haldu, sain, *kharik,* and *tun kharik,* the last two being comparatively less common. The sal logs are chiefly used for building purposes. The *bhyunl,* an extremely useful tree, growns in the valleys and lower hilly slopes and is carefully protected, for its leaves afford excellent fodder for cattle, and the fibres of its young shoots are twisted into ropes. Up to heights of about 900 m., trees common in the plains, viz., the mango, pipal, banyan and, sissoo are very frequently in evidence.

Chir Forests

The *chir* is the principal component of forests up to altitudes of about 1,800 m., growing between 500 m., when not unduly exposed to the sun, and 2,200 m. on a south aspect. Chir trees are usually found alone, for they appear to have the power of driving away all other vegetation from the tract where they are found *chir* is the staple building timber in the hills, while vast quantities of it are exported in the shape of sleepers. Torches are cut out of the living wood. Resin is also extracted from the tree. Its seeds are eaten.

Oak Forests

The principal varieties of oak found in the district are the *banj, tilonj* and the *kharsu,* each occupying a more or less distinct altitudinal zone.

Banj begins to grow at heights of 1,200 m. above sea-level but its best growth is confined between the altitudes of 1,800 m. and 2,450 m. The tree usually attains no great height. Its wood, being hard and gnarled, is used for agricultural implements and fuel. It has the capacity to establish itself on the highly unfavourable south aspect. *Banj* forests are usually dense on the north aspects but open on the south aspects. The other trees found in these forests are the rhododendron and *ringal* which occurs in clumps rising to about 4 m. to 6 m. and containing as many as one hundred shoots.

Between the altitudes of 2,150 m. and 2,450 m. *tilonj,* is the chief species of the oak forest and between the altitudes of 2,450 m. and 3,550 m. *kharsu* is the dominant tree. The main associated trees of the *tilonj* and harsu forests are the horse-chestnut and the sycamore. The *tilonj* and *kharsu*, the hardier oaks, resemble the *banj* and are used for the same purpose, but they are straighter and less knotted.

Coniferous Forests

Between the altitudes of 3,250 m. and 4,000 m. the dominant species are the conifers. The chief species is the *ragha* (Himalayan silver fir) which mainly occurs between the heights of 3,250 m. and 3,500 m. above the sea-level.

It is a tall tree which resembles the cypress at first glance, its branches being short and close. It attains a height of about 45 m. and a girth of about 4 m. The wood is considered to be equal to that of the chir but owing to its remote situation is seldom used except for roofing shingles. The blue pine *(chil),* the yew *(thaner)* and the cypress *(surain)* are also found in this region. The cypress sometimes attains an enormous size. The wood is hard, tough and durable and too heavy for flotation by itself. With these forests is found the variegated bush rhododendron with flowers of all colours, pink purple, blue and pure white. The birch grows up to heights of about 4,000 m. and its stems give the famous *bhurjapatra* or *Bhoj-patra* which in earlier times, was used as writing material before the invention of paper. Many old manuscripts written on *Bhoj-patra* are still available in the country.

Fauna

Animal

The wild animals of the district have greatly declined in number and variety during the past few decades.

Of the animals in the district, the sambur which is the most widely distributed of all the deer tribes is found up to an altitude of about 3,050 m. above sea-level. The sambur of the hills, where it is called the *jarau,* is a stouter and more massive beast than the sambar of the plains and has very heavy horns which are shed during May. The rutting season for the animal is October-November. The *kakar* or barking deer is also met with up to the same height. The musk-deer *(kastura)* is found in the upper ranges from an altitude of 2,400 m. above sea-level to above the limit of the forest but it has now become almost extinct owing to reckless shooting for its valuable perfume-bearing pod. It is about 50 cm. in height and has a brownish grey colour with harsh and brittle hair. It is generally solitary, very active and sure-footed and prefers rocky, precipitous ground. The nilgai is occasionally found at the foot of the hills and, the four-horned antelope, in the lower sal-clothed hills. The goral or Himalayan chamois is found at heights up to 3,350 m. but its usual habitat is between altitudes of 900 m. and 2,750 m. Both sexes have horns, those of the male being about 15 cm. and of the female about 10 cm. in length. They are generally found in herds of three to four animals but the largest male is usually solitary. The affect moderately steep grassy slopes not too thickly covered with pine. The goral is very tenacious of life and will often carry away a lot of load. The *thar* is found in the most precipitous parts of the upper ranges between 2,100 m. and 3,700 m. above sea-level, according to season. Both sexes have horns but those of the female animals are much slighter and shorter. The male *thar* is about a metre in height and carries horns about 40 cm. long. The *jarau,* which also belongs to the goral family, is nearly as large as the *thar.* It inhabits the precipitous rocks alothed with dense forest, and is a very shy, strange and uncouth beast. It horns are 20 cm. to 25 cm. in length. The bharal or wild blue sheep is rare in the district. It frequents the grassy slopes between the heights of 3,000 m and 5,000m.

The tiger found here is different from that found in the plains, being stouter in build and with longer and more furry hair and shorter and thicker tail. The *bagh, baghera* or panther is common throughout the district. It lives upon cattle, goats and sheep and is a bold and blood-thirsty beast. The snow leopard is rare in the tract south of the snowy range but there are generally one or two available on all hills where the bharal is found. The Himalayan black bear is common throughout the district and is generally seen during the rains. The rare red bear is found in the northern part of the district. It feeds on roots, weeds, grasses and even insects, but will also eat the flesh of animals killed by itself. It has also been known to feed on carreon. Its scent is keen but sight and hearing are dull. It hibernates from December to March and is a timid, unaggressive animal. The jackal is found up to a height of 2,150 m. and the wild pig up to that of 3,050 m. Monkeys and langurs are found throughout the district.

Birds

The district is very rich in birds. Birds of prey like eagles hawks, falcone and vultures, are very common. Among game-birds the *lungi* pheasant is found at an altitude of about 3,700 m. and the *monal* pheasant at elevations between 2,400 m. and 3,700 m. The *kokla* or *pokra* is seen between heights of 1,800 m. and 3,700 m. and the chir pheasant is found between altitudes of 1,500 m. and 2,400 m. above sea-level. The *kalij* a common pheasant, and black partridge frequent the thick forests up to a height of about 2,400 m. The *chakor* is a very common bird among partridges. The snow partridges are rare. The Himalayan snow cock is found on or near the snowline. Among pigeons,the wood-pigeon and the blue rock-pigeon are comon. Flocks of snow-pigeons are also seen in the higher ranges. Duck and teal occassionally rest on the rivers.

Reptiles

There are 34 species of snakes which are found in the district, out of which 26 varieties are non-poisonous and 8 poisonous. The cobra is found up to an elevation of 1,800 m. beyond which it is rare. The krait is very common in the low hills and grows to a length of about a metre. Its colour above is deep, lustrous, blue-black, uniform, or steaked and reticulated with white; below, it is white. The wall's krait has a glistening black colour on the back marked with milky white cross lines, formed of smallish oval or round spots. Below it is white, mottled with slate towards the tail. It resembles the common krait in appearance but is larger in size. The king cobra grows up to 2.5 m. in length. *Callaphis Mac Clellandi* is rarely seen here. The nigriventer, which occurs in the sub-tropical belt is venomous but not fatal for the human species. Russell's viper is common up to a height of about 1,800 m. and the *Ancistrodon himalayanus* is the only hill snake which is found above that of 2,500 m.

Among the non-venomous snakes the python is most notable. It grows to about 10 m. but specimens of over 7 m. are rare. Its rarity in the upper hills has invested the few specimens seen with almost supernatural terror. It is called the *charao* in the hills and superstition attributes to it an enormous size, with a flowing mane of red hair, and the habit of using a large pine tree as a walking stick when descending from the mountains. The *dhaman* which grows to about 2 m. in length is common in the district.

The blood Sucker lizard inspite of its name is perfectly harmless and grows to lengths of between 35 cm and 40 cm. The leech is particularly active during the rains and prefers oak forests. Ater a smart shower it appears in myriads, and any barefooted wayfarer is soon made uncomfortably aware of its presence. The bite of the *mora*, a small stinging fly, also causes small painful sores and intense irritation to travellers.

Fish

Fish abound in all streams of the district. Among the larger species the *mahaseer* and the *kalabans* are very common. The *gunch* or fresh water shark inhabits the deeper pools of the Sarju. The trout is rare, but the *chilwa* swarms wherever there is running water. Among the other species found in the district are the *asela, rohu* and *garra.* In the latter part of the hot weather the fish run up the stream to deposit the ova and return in the rainy season, when they are generally caught.

Game-laws

The game-laws obtaining in the district are governed by the wild Birds and Animals Protection Act (Act VIII of 1912), as amended by the Wild Birds and Animals Protection (Uttar Pradesh Amendement) Act, 1934 (Act XIII of 1934), and sub-section (1) (i) of Section 36 of the Indian Forest Act (Act XVI of 1927), as amended by the Indian Forest (Uttar Pradesh Amendment) Act, 1965.

Ancient History

The area covered by the district of Pithoragarh, which is the easternmost of the three districts of the erstwhile Uttarakhand Division and the northernmost of the three districts of the present Kumaon Division, formerly (prior to 1960) formed part of the Almora district and lies in the heart of the snow range of the central Himalayas. According to the *Manasa-khanda* section of the *Skanda purana* it would seem to lie in the

Manasa-khanda, one of the five divisions of the Himalayan region, which is said to have extended from the Kailash mountain in the north to the *Bhabhar* and *Tarai* in the south. The Manasa-Khanda also gives the route to the Mansarowar lake, which passed through this district and on which lay some of the important holy places of this area, like Patal Bhubaneshwar (tahsil Didihat)where the pilgrim should worhship Siva for three days, while observing a complete fast, Baleshwar on the Ramganga, the Paban mountain (tahsil Didihat, the Pataka or Dhaj (Dhwaj) peak (tahsil Pithoragarh), the confluence of the Gori and the Kali (near Askot) where the pilgrim should take a bath, Chaturdanushtra (tahsil Dharchula), Vyasa Ashram (tahsil Dharchula) the source of the kali, the Kerala or Chhechhala mountain where he should worship Devi, the Puloman peak (on the range dividing Byans from Darma) on the foot of which is the sacred lake Man Talab also called Byankshiti, the Taraka mountain, the confluence of the Tarani and the Sarda where he should take the sacred dip, behold the caves, worship the gods, shave his beard, keep fast and perform *shraddha* (obsequies) and lastly the Gori mountain where the pilgrim passes out of the district and goes direct to the Mansarowar lake.[1]

Kumaon, the popular name of the region in which the district lies, is said to be a corruption of Kurmachala, the name of a mountain standing to the east of Champawat in Almora district, which is said to be associated with the Kurma (tortoise) avatar of Vishnu.[2]

Among items of archaeological interest in the district may be mentioned the old and celebrated temples of Patal Bhubaneshwar Pancheshwar, Rameshwar, Koteshwar, Thalkedar and Nanda Devi, the ruins of the Katyuri capital Lakhanpur (near Ganai) and of the old town of Bagrihat near Champachal which is said to have been the first of the eight or eighty forts which gave this particular region the name Askot, the Siva temple on the Champachal hill, a large cave on the Chipula or Najurkot hill and the temple of Kali and remains of certain other old temples at Gangolihat.[3]

Parts of the district appear to have been inhabited since remote times, the early inhabitants being, perhaps, the Asuras, Nagas, etc.[4] who seem to have been superseded in course of time by the Kiratas, Khasas and Kunidas.[5]

The region has been traditionally described as the land of gods and demons and the place of penance of rishis, many legends being associated with the mountains, rivers, forests and other sites in the district close to the northern borders of which are located the holy mountain Kailash and the divine lake Mansarowar.[6] According to the Jain tradition the emperor Bharata, son of the first tirthankara Adinatha, is said to have conquered this region and to have gone on the Kailash to pay homage to his father who attained nirvana on that mountain. The Buddhists believe that the Buddha along with 500 Bodhisattvas resides there and the Hindus that it sis the permanent abode of Siva and his spouse Parvati (the daughter of Himachala or Himalaya personifed), a majority of the other members of the Hindu pantheon also being supposed to reside there.[7] The Nanda Devi mountain (on the western border of the district) is also sacred to Parvati in her form of Nanda Devi, who is the presiding deity of the district, the Nanda Kot mountain being said to represent her counch and the Trisul mountain Siva's trident.[8] A large number of the inhabitants of the district have been devotees of Siva who, it has been suggested, was probably a non-Vedic god worshipped by the aborigines of these parts orignally, Saiva shrines and legends still abounding in the district.[9]

The Asura (Datiya or Danawa) king Hiranyakaship and his successors down to Banasura are said to have ruled over these Himalayan regions in early times, the Danpur trac of the district being believed to owe its name to the Danavas.[10] These Asuras, etc., do not seem to have been confined to hills and were probably the chief enemies (referred to in Vedic literature as Dasas or Dasyus) of the early Aryans whom the latter had to encounter in their expansion in northern India. When the Aryans were firmly entrenched in the plains, some of their kings, such as Mandhatri, Yayati, Kartiavirya Arjuna, Sagara, Raghu and Bharata, appear to have attempted the conquest of the Himalayan country and, in particular, Divodasa and Sudasa, the Tritsu kings of Panchala, are said to have waged a prolonged war against its Asura king Shambara who, it seems, possessed 90 or 99 strong forts which his enemies tried repeatedly to destroy.[11]

The Pandava brothers of the Hastinapur royal family were the next important princes from the plains, who are said to have effected conquest of these parts. They passed the period of their exile here and married local Naga and Rakshasa girls, there being no dearth of legends connecting a number of sites in the district with Bhima and with Arjuna who is said to have fought with Siva disguised as a Kirata in the Darukavana, a forest located in the south-western part of the district. In the Mahabharata War, Ghatotkacha, son of Bhima by his Rakshasa wife, who was probably a Rakshasa chief of these parts, fought on the side of the Pandavas while some of the Kiratas and Hunas, probably also of this region, sided with the Kauravas. Several of the ancient rishis, such as Bhrigu, Sanatkumara, Valmiki, Kapila and Vyasa are also believed to have been associated with this district. Byanas is said to have been named after the sage Vyasa who is supposed to have resided on the Kalirong peak near Changru in this *patti,* a place being still pointed out as Vyasa Ashram (hermitage of

Vyasa), and Bhrigutunga (a peak in *patti* Bherang) is traditionally associated with the rishi Bhrigu, while the cave of Patal Bhubanesh war is believed to have the sages mentoned above.[12]

After the abdication of Yudhishthir, Parikshit, the king of Hastinapur, may have held sway over this region, but he was killed in battle by the Nagas who were for this reason driven out of the plains by Janamejaya, his son, and they strengthened their position in the entire Himalayas where they seem to have put an end to whatever authority the Hastinapur kings had been exercising there. The important Naga chiefs of the district were probably Ananta, Takshaka, the great Naga at Bastir, Berinaga, Kedar Kalinaga, Karkotaka Naga and Vasuki, the last five having their strongholds in what are now Mehar, Baraun, Pungraun, Pandegaon and Danpur respectively, where they are still worshipped as Nagar godlings.[13]

The district also seems to have been, for a time, the stronghold of the Kiratas, who gave this region the name Kiratamandala and whose surviving remnants are probably the Rajis (also known as Rajyakiratas or Rawats) of Askot, who claim to be the descendants of an aboriginal prince of these parts who had fled with his family to the jungles in order to escape destruction threatened by an usurper.[14] The Khasas had also entrenched themselves in parts of the distrct and by suppressing gradually all the former inhabitants became the most dominating people, giving the region the name Khasamandala, a number of petty Khasa chiefs probably ruling almost independently here till at least the time of the Mauryas.[15]

The Kiratas and Khasas also find mention in the *Mahabharata* where they are represented as bringing their peculiar presents to the Pandava king Yudhishthir. Four groups of the Kiratas belonging to four different regions have been described there and one of these hailed from the northern slopes of the Himalayas, wore skins and lived on tubers and fruits, which description fits in with the Kiratas of this area and it is very likely that the modern Rajis (Rajyakiratas) are the descendants of those Kiratas of old. The Khasas were a widely spread people and the lands they then inhabited seem to include the mid-Himalayas where this district lies. The adjective *ekasana* used for them has been taken to mean that they were settled as opposed to other wandering tribes, and there is little doubt that the present Khasas of the district are the descendants of those Khasas of old. The Jyohas, another tribe mentioned in the *Mahabharata*, are believed to have been suggested that the Johar tract of tahsil Mansyari of this district was from very earl times occupied by the migrating Jyohas who gave their name to it.

Parvataka and his brother and son were probably the hill chiefs of the

Kumaon-Garhwal Himalayas, who helped (Chandragupta Maurya in his coup against the last Nanda king of Magadha, about 325 B.C. the imperial Maurya army being also said to have had in it Kirata highlanders.[16] During Asoka's regin a Buddhist mission of five monks is said to have arrived in these Himalayan regions and converted the people here.[17] The Sakas, who entered India in the first century B.C. and are said to have had certain affinities with the Khasas, such as those revealed in the worship of the sun and the erection of a peculiar type of burial mounds, also appear to have reached these parts. A few coins discovered in this area and assigned to the first century A.D. bear the names of Sivadatta, Sivapalita and Heridatta,[18] who may have been the Hinduised Saka satraps of Indo-Scythian or Indo-Parthian kings of north-western India, or local chiefs probably of the Kuninda branch of the Khasas. the Kunindas, who had a republican constitution and seem to have predominated in the region in the early centuries of the Christian *era*, are probely identical with the Kulindrine tribe mentioned by the geographer Ptolemy (*circa* 150 A.D.)

About the last quarter of the first century A.D. the empire of the Kushanas, a branch of the Sakas, under Kanishka included in it the western and central Himalayas and ports of Tibet, which regions seem to have remained under the sway of his successors for the next hundred years or so,[19] the Kunindas of this region probably becoming their feudatories. Some Kushanas may also have settled down here and Buddhism gained in strength durin this period.[20]

The Kunindas are mentioned as being among those who were instrumental in bringing about the downfall of the Kushana, empire about the second quarter of the third century A.D.[21] as a result of which some more Kushanas including a few scions of the royal family are likely to have taken refuge in these parts. Among the refugees, was probably one Vasudeva (not an uncommon name among the later rulers of the Kushana dynasty)[22] who may have been identical with the traditional founder of the well-known early local dynaty, the Katsyuri, after the name of which the tract adjoining this district on the south-west came to be called the Katyur valley. The Sakas and Kushanas, who had by this time been completely Hinduised, soon mingled with the local Khasas or Kunidas and the Katyuri, dynasty, probably with a Saka (or Kushana)—Khasa (or Kuninda) origin, thus seems to have come into being about the end of the third century A.D., with its capital at Kartripura of Katyuripura, also known as Karttikeyapura, which name together with the terms Katyur being believed to have been derived from the name of the family deity Kartikeya, located near Baijnath in the Katyur valley (Almora district)[23]. It has been suggested that it was this Kartripura which figures in the list of Kingdoms conquered by the Gupta emperor Samudragupta about 350 A.D.[24] and that the Khasa raja of Karttikeyapura whom Chandragupta II killed about 375 A.D.) in order to avenge his brother's defeat and to rescue his sister-in-law from captivity (as mentioned in Rajashekhara's *Kavyamimamsa*) was none other than the ruler of this Himalayan Kingdom. It appears that the bulk of the district of Pithoragarh was under the rule of these early chiefs of the Katyur valley.

In the neighbourhood of the Katyuri kingdom there appears to have existed another kingdom founded probably by some Kshatriyas from the plains, Sukhavanta, one of its early rulers, being said to have invaded the kingdom of Rajapala of the early Garhwal dynasty.[25] One of the two copperplate grants, preserved at Taleshwar (Almora district) and assigned to the sixth century A.D. purports to have been issued in the fifth regnal year of Dyutivarman (entitled *parama-bhattaraka-maharajadhiraja*) the son of Agnivaraman, grandson of Vrishavaraman and great-grandson. of Vishnuvarman I, and the other by Vishnuvarman II (Dyutivarman's son). The family is described as descended both from the most and the sun and as the Paurava line of kings, and the kingdom as th Parvatakara Rajya (the hill kingdom). Both the characters are stated to have been issued from the city of Brahmapura (apparently the capital in Uttarkashi), in favour of the god Vireneshvara, an avatar of Ananta (probably Sheshanaga)[26] who seems to have been the family deity of these kings and may have been the same as the Berinaga of the Pithoragarh district. A small inscription (found inscribed on a rock near Almora) of about the same period records a pious deed of one Rudresha.

Growth of Population

The first estimate of the population of the region covered by the district of Pithoragarh may be said to have been made when, in 1821, Traill, the first British Commissioner of Kumaon, assessed the population of the old district of Kumaon which included the present districts of Pithoragarh, Almora and Naini Tal. It was only a rough estimate and the figure for the population of the tract covered by the first two of these districts was given as 1,35,533. As the figures, at most of the subsequent enumerations, for the tract representing the Pithoragarh district have been a little more than a quarter of those for the combined population of the districts of Pithoragarh and Almora, those for the former appear to have been in the neighbourhood of 40,000 in the first census of Traill.

Estimates, equally rough, were also made in 1848, and between 1863 and 1868 for the population of this tract, while in 1852 a census was taken. At the census of 1872, which was more systematic, the population of the region comprising the Almora and Pithoragarh districts was found to be 3,54,579, at that of 1881 it was 3,60,967 and at that of 1891, when the Almora district (including the Pithoragarh region) was for the first time consituted as a separate unit, its population was returned as 4,16,868. Presuming that the ratio between the population of the entire tract and that of its part now constituted into the Pithoragarh district remained almost unchanged the population of the latter in 1891 would be about 1,20,000. Figures for the subsequent decennial censuses with respect to these two regions separately are available.

On February 24, 1960, the district of Pithoragarh as a separate administrative unit was constituted out of the Pithoragarh tahsil plus two *pattis* (containing 164 villages) of the Almora tahsil of the erstwhile district of Almora and it was only in 1961 that the first regular census of the Pithoragarh district proper was undertaken. Its area according to the Central Statistical Organisation, was 7,243 sq. km. in 1966, and the total population in 1961 was returned as 2,63,579, the males numbering 1,28,292 and the females 1,35,287.

Source: P.C. Saxena, *Pithoragarh Gazetteer*, Superintendent Government Printing, Allahabad, 1975

REFERENCES

1. Atkinson, E.T., *The Himalayan Districts of the North-Western Provinces of India*, Vol. II, pp. 298-323
2. *Ibid.*, Vol. II, p. 506; Vol., III, pp. 162-163, 384-385
3. *District Gazetters of the United Provinces of Agra and Oudh—Supplementary Notes and Statistics*, Vol. XXXI—Almora District, C. Vol. (1925), p. 21; Atkinson, *op. cit.*, Vol. II, pp. 318—323; Vol. III, pp. 13, 232-233
4. *Ibid.*, pp. 299-300, 376
5. *Ibid.*, pp. 269, 283, 362-366, 376-382
6. *Ibid.*, Vol. II, p. 271; Vol. III, pp. 376-378
7. *Ibid.*, Vol. II, pp. 309-312
8. *Ibid.*, pp. 307, 313, 792-793
9. *Ibid.*, pp. 314, 319-323, 364, 701, 739-740, 782
10. *Ibid.*, Vol. II, pp. 277, 318, 322, 506-507; Vol. III, pp. 334-335
11. Majumdar, R.C. and Pusalkor, A.D. (Ed.), *The History and Culture of the Indian People*, Vol. I, pp. 249-250, 293-294
12. Atkinson, *op. cit.*, Vol. II, pp. 319-321
13. *Ibid.*, pp. 281, 315, 320, 321, 373-375
14. *Ibid.*, pp. 363-368

15. *Ibid.*, pp. 375-382
16. Majumdar and Pusalker, *op. cit.*, Vol. II, p. 57
17. Atkinson, *op. cit.*, Vol. II, p. 409
18. Majumdar and Pusalker, *op. cit.*, Vol. II, p. 161
19. *Ibid.*
20. Atkinson, *op. cit.*, Vol. II, p. 409
21. Majumdar and Pusalker, *op. cit.*, Vol. III, p. 54
22. *Ibid.*, Vol. II, p. 151
23. Atkinson, *op. cit.*, Vol. II, pp. 383,467-469
24. Majumdar and Pusalker, *op. cit.*, Vol. III pp. 8, 12
25. Atkinson, *op. cit.*, Vol. II, pp. 411-412
26. Majumdar and Pusalker, *op. cit.*, Vol. IV, pp. 123-124

17

UTTARKASHI DISTRICT

Origin of Name

The district is named after its headquarters town, Uttarkashi. As the name denotes, this place is the 'Kashi' of *uttara* (north) as against the 'Kashi' (Varanasi) of the plains, and is located near the Varanawat hills between the rivers Syalam Gad and Kaldi Gad, also known respectively as the Varuna and the Asi which are also the names of the rivers between which the Kashi of the plains is situated. Similarly, one of the bathing ghats on the Bhagirathi here is also known as Manikarnika and there is also a temple of Vishvanatha here. According to the *Puranas*, Siva prophesied that in the *Kaliyuga* his seat in Kashi (Varanasi) would lose its religious sanctity and that he would move to the Himalayas. The place, being the northern (uttara) seat of Siva, came to be known as Uttarkashi.

Location, Boundaries, Area and Population

Location and Boundaries

The district lies between Lat. 30° 28' and 31° 28' N. and Long. 77° 49' and 79° 25' E., its maximum length from east to west being about 154 km and maximum breadth from north to south about 109 km. The northern boundary of the district is formed by district Kinnaur and the territory of Tibet. On the east lie Tibet and the district of Chamoli. On the south it is bounded by the districts of Chamoli and Tehri Garhwal and on the west lie the districts of Mahasu and Dehra Dun.

Area

According to the Central Statistical Organisation the district has an area of 8,016 sq km and stands 4th in the State in area.

Population

According to the census of 1961, the population of the district is 1,22,836, the number of females being 60,302. The rural population of the district is 1,20,159 (females 59,390) and the urban 2,677 (females 312). The district stands 54th in the State in respect of population which is 77.5 per cent higher than what it was in 1901.

History and Administrative Unit

The district of Uttarkashi was created in 1960 out of the parganas of Rawain and Uttarkashi of the Rawain tahsil of the district of Tehri Garhwal, the princely state till its merger in the state of Uttar Pradesh in 1949.

Sub-divisions, Tahsils and Thanas

The district has been divided into three divisions Bhatwari, Dunda and Purola-each of the first two constituting a single tahsil of the same name and the thrid comprising the tahsils of Raigarhi and Purola. A tabular presentation of the composition of the district is given in Table 17.1

TABLE 17.1: Composition of Uttarkashi District

Tahsil	Sub divisions	Old parganas	No. of pattis	No. of villages Populated	Unpopulated	Total
Purola	Parola	Rawain	4	108	2	170
Rajgarhi			4	176	—	176
Dunda	Dunda	Uttarkashi	8	222	5	227
Bhatwari	Bhatwari		4	96	2	98
District total			20	662	9	671

Tahsil Bhatwari is bounded by Himachal Pradesh and Tibet on the north, the district of Chamoli on the east, the districts of Chamoli, Tehri Garhwal and tahsil Dunda on the south-west and tahsils Dunda, Rajgarhi and Purola on the west. It has a population of 21,436 (females 10,063), the rural population being 18,759 and the urban 2,677. The district headquarters, Uttarkashi, lies in this tahsil.

Tahsil Dunda, is bounded by tahsils Rajgarhi and Bhatwari on the north, the district of Tehri Garhwal on the east and south-west and tahsil Rajgarhi on the north-west. It has a population of 43,471, females numbering 23,109. The river Bhagirathi flows through this tahsil dividing it into two parts with four *pattis* on either side.

The tahsil Rajgarhi is bounded by tahsil Purola on the north, tahsils Bhatwari and Dunda on the east, the district of Tehri Garhwal on the south and the district of Dehra Dun and tahsil Purola on the west. It has a population of 29,703, females being 14,058. The sub-divisional headquarters is located at Barkot.

The tahsil Purola comprising the north-western portion of the district is bounded by Himachal Pradesh on the north, tahsils Bhatwari and Rajgarhi on the east, tahsil Rajgarhi and the district of Dehra Dun on the south and the district of Dehra Dun on the west. It has a population of 28,226, females being 13,072. The famous valley of flowers, known as Harkidun, lies in this tahsil.

Thana

There are two thanas (police stations) in the district. Tahsils Dunda and Bhatwari fall under the jurisdiction of the police station of Uttarkashi and tahsils Rajgarhi and Purola under that of Barkot.

Geology

Geologically the district may be divided into two major belts—the northern and the southern, demarcated by the river Sainj. The former is occupied mainly by higher ranges and snow covered peaks and consists entirely of high grade metamorphic rocks such as slates, quartzite, marble and various types of micaceous schists and gneisses permeated by later volcanic rocks. The southern belt comprises essentially sedimentary and low grade metamorphic rocks such as limestone, quartzite slates and sericite biotite schists.

As the district is very little known geologically, knowledge regarding the occurrence of minerals is limited to that derived from stray surveys. The more important of the minerals found in the district are given below:

Soapstone

Small scattered occurrences of soapstone are found near Dharasu.

Iron

Poor mineralisation of iron is known for the schists and the quartzite from near Bhatwari.

Copper

Copper occurs at various places in the district. Boulders of malachite stained quartzite are reported to have been noticed in the valley of the Jadh Ganga near Dasumdu. Chalcopyrite—bearing quartz veins in granite boulders have been noticed in a south-western branch of the Mana glacier. Malachite has been observed to extend over 85 m. near Uttarkashi.

Graphite

Graphite is met with in the graphitoid schists in the forest area near Harsil.

Limestone

There are wide outcrops of limestone in the district but most of them are dolomitic and hence of little industrial use.

Kyanite

Large blades of blue kyanite have been noticed in the schistose rocks near Suki.

Mica

Abundant mica schists occur between Lohari Nag and Suki, but economic exploitation of the deposits in this area is not practicable as the quality of mica is very poor.

Climate

The climate of the district varies according to aspect and elevation. Monsoon currents can penetrate through the valleys and the rainfall is at the maximum in the monsoon from June to September.

Rainfall

Short period records of precipitation in the district are available for six stations only which are situated in the valleys of the Bhagirathi and the Yamuna. Rainfall generally increases up the valleys in the southern half of the district and is highly variable spatially, depending upon elevation and aspect. About 75 per cent of the rain occurs during the monsoon season, June to September, August being the rainiest month. In September depressions from the Bay of Bengal occasionally affect the weather and in association with them heavy rain can occur causing floods. In the monsoon season there are a few occasions when there are spurts of heavy rain causing floods in the rivers. The rainfall decreases rapidly after September and is the lowest in November. About 17 per cent of the annual precipitation, mostly in the form of snow, particularly at higher elevations, occurs in association with the passage of western disturbances. The precipitation during the pre-monsoon months, about 7 per cent of the annual total, and the post-monsoon months is frequently associated with thunderstorms. During the short periods for which rainfall data are available, less than 80 per cent of the annual normal precipitation occurred only once at Jamna Chetty and Uttarkashi, twice at Rana and Dharasu and thrice at Kharsali. No two consecutive years recorded such low rainfall. The mean number of rainy days varies from 61 to 114, the lowest recorded number of rainy days being 52 in 1958, and the highest 142 in 1956. The heaviest rainfall recorded in 24 hours was 400.8 mm. at Kharsali on September 15, 1963.

Temperature

Variations of temperature from place to place are considerable and depend upon elevation and exposure to the sun. As the isolation at high altitudes is intense, temperatures in the open are considerably higher than in the shade in summer. In the valleys, pools of cold stagnant air cause the diurnal range of temperature to be considerable. Temperatures generally begin to rise rapidly from about the end of February. May and June are the warmest months when the mean maximum temperature may be about 25°C at stations located 2 km above sea-level, 15° to 18°. at those situated 3 km above sea-level and lower temperatures at higher stations. With the onset of the monsoon towards the end of June. Day temperatures fall by about 3° to 5°C and with its withdrawal, towards the third or fourth week of September, day and night temperatures begin to decrease initially at a slower rate but more rapidly after October till January, which is the coldest month, with the mean maximum and minimum temperature being about 10° C. and 0°C. (freezing point), respectively at elevations 2 km above sea-level. During the winter season, cold waves in the wake of western disturbances may cause temperature to fall appreciably. Snow accumulation in the valleys is considerable.

Humidity

Humidity is the highest, nearly 90 per cent, in the monsoon and the lowest during the pre-monsoon months when it may drop to even less than 40 per cent.

Cloudiness

Skies are heavily clouded during the rainy season and for short spells in winter when the region is affected by passing western disturbances. During the transitional months thunder clouds occasionally develop, particularly in the afternoon.

Winds

Winds are mostly light, in the wake of western disturbances and also in association with thunder-storms, they may be quite strong. Anabatic and strong katabatic winds are also experienced as local effects produced by the nature of the terrain.

Flora

The area under the forest department in the district is about 6,88,907 hectares, about 88 per cent of the total area of the district of which a major portion is rocky and barren and covered with perpetual snow.

Table 17.2 gives the tahsilwise distribution of the forest area in hectares under the forest department:

TABLE 17.2: Tehsilwise Distribution of Forest Area

Tahsil	Forests Area
Bhatwari	1,45,539
Purola	86,218
Rajgarhi	66,628
Dunda	36,744
Total	3,35,129

Taking into consideration the differences in altitude and the climatic conditions, the flora of the district may be divided into main botanical divisions—the pine forests, deodar forests, fire and spruce forests, *kharshu,* birch and juniperus forests and alpine pastures.

Pine Forests

These forests occupy almost the entire area between the altitudes of 900 m and 2,000 m. Pine trees are tapped for resin and turpentine. Their seeds also yield oil and when baked become edible. The dry leaves are utilised in manuring, the pine flowers from February to April, the seeds being shed in October next and scattered over a large area by the fast wind.

The other trees growing in the pine forests are *ayar, burans, kunis, himari, padam narka, kirmola, semal, rohini kakra* and *kail.* The chief varieties of shrubs which grow here are the *kandai, tatar* and *dhaula.* Where the growth of pine is poor the *suina, mirch-gandh, golda* and *tachla* grasses are found.

Deodar Forests

These forests are found between the altitude of 2,000 m and 3,000 m. The other trees growing in this region are *kail, leuri, burans* and *moru,* the main associated shrubs being the *kala hinser, kasmor, matoi, satpura* and *ghugtai.* The chief ground flora of the region are the *banafsha, somaiya* and *janu,* and the *kauni* and *banoi* are the chief climbers.

Fir and Spruce Forests

These forests are confined to protected sites of the northern aspects over 3,000 m in altitude their magnificent growth being found in tahsil Purola. The trees growing in these forests are the *panger, kanjar, Jamnoi, bhotia, badam, akhrot, kharik, khagsi, bhambeli* and *kathbhui* and the shrubs, the *kola kimsar, bhunra kiyoi, bhutoni* and *jamu.*

Kharshu, Birch and Juniperus Forests

These forests occur up to a height of 4,000 m. above the fir and spruce forest zone, the main associates being the *bhuj, thuner, semru* and *guia* trees and the *khandeur, chatrod* and *banchulu* shrubs. The *banafsha,* a ground plant generally found in deodar forests, is also met with in these forests.

Alpine Pastures

These are found throughout the district between elevations of 3,500 m and 4,877 m above sea-level. The land remains covered with snow from October to May but from June to September it produce rich varieties of grasses, shrubs and herbs.

Medicinal Plants

A large number of plants used in the indigenous systems of medicine grow wild in the forests of the district and can be classified into three main categories—(1) plants found in the higher altitudes, (2) those found in the submontane tracts, and (3) those found in the valleys. The medicinal plants of the higher altitudes are the *atis* or *ativisha, vatsnabh* or *bis, pati, purcha, papri, chuyn, kakriya, bhojpatra, bhatkeshi, kesar, guggal, salammisri, hathjari* or *salam panja, angu, gandrayan, faran* or *jamboo, soma, nirbishi, khurasani ajwain, bakola, jhora*, or *chichia, etgha* or *bhumi-madhin, kutki* or *kaurai, jatamansi, archa* or *dolu, bankakri, chiraita, nairpati, ugal* or *phaphra, ratanjot, gaonjaon, kooth, talis patra* or *barmi* and *ghantiyali* or *morvel.* The medicinal plants which grow in the submontiance tract are the *kaner* or *karvira, peepal, betain* or *bakayan, akhrot* or *akshotaka, chir* or *salla, gulab, aru, tejpat, kachnar, inda* or *andi, kilmora, deodar, bhangra, bruns, galla, dhatura, vasak, pari, banajsha, samco, jeishalparni, timru, jhunjhunia, puddum, aila* or *ilaichi, makol, pissumer, mamini* or *pingli, jari, pasanbheda* or *silphora, bherar* or *kaladana, hisatoo, gwalkakri, dhauanak* or *dhania, souf, heldi, ban haldi* or *ama haldi, bacha*, or *buj, brahmdandi, chota gokhroo, dudhia, sahdevi bari, isabgol, amerbel, ekthir, jhinti, ghania* or *tukhmalanga, bastuk* or *bethua, anjuwar, chalmar* or *almer, barua, bana, khinna, bichhu, rishwak* or *lahsunia, keura, gristika, kukurdara, kariua* or *satawari* or *jhiran, nagarmontha, kapoor, kachri, gilos*, or *gurcha, tooni* or *toon, bannibu, pudina, ban ajwain, kharik, hansraj, keddu, nashpati* or *bihi, durba, lijari, kahu* or *kulhba, banjwan, changeri, ainus, banbiaj* or *ghesuas, kathkonkon, jyotishmati, makagni, bajradanti, mahmeda, sajji or apamarg, dhataki* or *dhaula, priniparni, amtaki* or *amla, gindaru* or *gajiyar, manjistha, kakrasinghi* or *karkatsringhi, piobi* or *basant, muli* or *mulaka, gokhru, kukurimakuri, sahtara* or *ban tulsi, tamkakoo, chupra* and *gaunchi.* The medicinal plants of the hot valleys are the *bel* or *bilwa, kampilak* or *kamila, hariteki* or *harar, bahera* or *bair, arjuna, khubaji, palas, kanthkari, nirgunidi, amra* or *am (mango), ank, seesham, pipal, kadali* or *kela, chaksoo* and *chitrak.*

Fauna

The chief carnivora found in the district are leopard, snow leopard, Himalayan black bear and brown bear. The snow leopard is a rare species which is found in the alpine forests and preys on the *thar, bharal,* sheep and goat. The wild pig is found up to a height of 3,000 m. The leopard, which is quite common in rocky forests, preys upon sheep, goats, mules and sometimes bullocks and cows. Cases of leopard turning maneater are rare. The black bear infests deep jungles and is fairly common in the deodar zone. It attacks without provocation and lives on roots, acorns of the oak, fruits and the bark of trees. It rarely kills for flesh, but instances of its mauling human beings are not unknown. It hibernats in winter. Among the antelopes which are met with here are the Himalayan blue sheep, *thar,* goral, serow, muskdeer, barking deer and sambar. The Himalayan blue sheep (bharal) lives at an altitudes, of about 3,500 m above sea-level and prefers undulating open ground. It is shy, quick and nimble. The Himalayan *thar* prefers moist rugged mountain terrain with little cover and lies under bushes or trees. In summer it is seldom found below heights of 3,000 m but in winter it comes dowm to elevations of about 1,800 m. It is dark brown to almost black in colour, the older male being darker. The goral, a goat-like animal of a pale brown colour, which turns to almost grey in the summer, haunts the rocky hills in the middle of the forests up to an altitude of about 2,500 m. It usually lives in groups of two to six. The serow is a rare animal found between heights of 1,800 m and 2,700 m. It is similar to the goral in its eating and dwelling habits but has less inclination for the rocky precipitous hills. It is greyish brown in colour. The musk deer, which is famous for the musk-pod, frequents steep hills with cover and is usually found above heights of 2,700 m. It is becoming extinct as it has been ruthlessly killed in the past for the valuable musk which is of high therapeutic value and used in the preparation of perfumes. The *kakar* or barking deer likes deep moist forests and avoids dry rocky areas. It is found in the oak belt up to an altitude of 2,700 m. The sambar or *jarao* also is found up to a height of 2,700 m and prefers moist deep forests. The young ones are greyish brown but the older males are much darker in colour. The monkey is not seen above an altitude of 2,150 m but the langur is found at higher levels also. The *kaug,* a kind of wild dog, is found in herds of five to ten. On the approach of herds of the *haug,* other animals leave the forests in dread. However, it does not attack human beings and does not intrude into inhabited sites.

Birds

The variety of birds found in the district is amazing, in particular pheasants, pigeons and doves of various kinds abound here and are the chief game birds. Bird life has a zonal distribution here according to altitude. Among the pheasants found here are the *kalij, kakla, chir* and *monal.* The *kalij,* a common bird, is found at elevations below 2,600 m. in heavy undergrowth of forests. The male is blakish with a gloss like that of steel and has a white rump, a long white crest, scarlet patches round the eyes and a long tail. The female is of a reddish brown colour. The *kokla* is of the same size as the *kalij* but lacks the scarlet patches round the eyes and is grey, streaked with black above and chestnut below. A white patch on either side of the head is prominent. The female is mottled black, and has a conspicuously white throat. It is found in the deodar and fir zones and prefers moist woody tracts. The *monal* frequents the *kharshu,* birch and fir forest and comes down to the upper deodar forests in winter. Among partridges the most common are the *kala titar, peord* and *chakor.* The *kala titar* or black partridge is found upto heights of 1,800 m. and frequent the grass and shrub patches near cultivated land. It is found singly or in pairs, the female being drab-looking. The *peora* or hill partridge, a dweller of evergreen forests, is found between the altitudes of 1,300 m. and 2,700 m and prefers broad-leafed forests. Its colour is olive brown, mottled black, the chin and the throat are black and there is a crimson patch round the eye. The *chakor* loves barren and open hill slopes dotted with bush and grass and is found between the altitudes of 1,300 m and 3,600 m. It regularly visits cultivated fields in search of grain or tender shoots and lives in parties of six to 20 but is found in pairs in summer. The pigeons found in the district are *harial* or wedge-tailed green pigeon, malyo or blue rock pigeon and *safed malyo* or the snow pigeon, and among doves are the *ghugti* or rufous turtle dove and the *fakhta* or ringed dove. The *harial* is seen mostly in banj forests. Its colour is yellowish green with maroon markings on the middle of the back. It is found in flocks and is essentially a fruitarian bird. The *malyo* has a slaty grey colour with a metallic glisten, a purple round neck and a head washed steel blue. It lives gregariously on cliffs and precipices, large flocks regularly visiting cultivated fields in search of food. The *safed malyo* is a beutiful pigeon with a white under body, black head, a white cross bar on the tail and three white bars on grey wings and completely replaces the blue rock pigeon in the higher altitudes. In habit it closely resembles the blue rock pigeon. The *ghugti* is a large pinkish brown dove with a rust coloured scaly pattern on its upper parts and spotted patches on either side on the hind neck. It is found upto heights of 3,000 m and likes well-wooded forests and is generally seen in pairs or bigger groups. The *fakhta* is a large dove which is found upto an elevation of 2,700 m and is usually seen in the out houses of bungalows in the forests. The bird is migratory and both sexes are alike in appearance. The *shyam karka* or woodcock is also a game bird which dwells in moist fir forests and is nocturnal in habits. It looks like an outsized snipe and has dirty grey and brown markings. Its eyes are placed further back in the head than in other birds. It migrates to south India in winter.

The non-game birds generally found in the district are the magpie, jay nut, thrushes, babblers, laughing thrushes and woodpeckers. The birds found along the water courses are the brown dipper, spotted forktail, little fortktail, white-capped redstart, plumbeous redstart and various wagtails.

The other birds found in the district are the paradise fly catcher, great Himalayan barbet, grosbeak, parakeet, golden oriole, hedge sparrow, tit, sunbird, flower pecker, *niltava,* robin and minivet. Besides, a number of fly catchers, warblers, bulbuls and myna, various swifts, skylarks, bush chats, swallows and buntings are the other smaller birds which add to the rich bird life of the district.

Fish

Fish are found in almost all the rivers of the district. The rainbow trout has been introduced recently in the Deodital lake in plenty. The *mahaseer* and *kalhana* are the other fish which are found in the lower reaches of the rivers.

Game-Laws

The game-laws obtaining in the district are governed by the Wild Birds and Animals Protection Act, 1912, (Act, VIII of 1912), as amended by the Wild Birds and Animals Protection (Uttar Pradesh Amendment) Act, 1934 (Act XIII of 1934) and sub-section 1, (a) (i) of section 26 of the Indian Forest Act, 1927 (Act XVI of 1927), as amended by the Indian Forest (Uttar Pradesh Amendment) Act, 1965.

SUPPLEMENTARY INFORMATION
CENSUS 1971

Population

Total Population	1,47,805
Females	69,973
Rural population	1,41,785
Females	67,765
Urban population	6,020
Females	2,208

Sub-divisions, Tahsils and Thanas

Composition of the district

Tehsil	No. of villages		
	Populated	Un-populated	Total
Purola	177	3	180
Rajgarhi	179	4	188
Dunda	222	1	228
Bhatwari	94	3	97
District Total	672	11	683

Tahsil Bhatwari

Total Population	29,465
Females	12,719
Rural population	23,445
Urban population	6,020

Tahsil Dunda

Total population	52,300
Females	26,560
Rural population	52,300
Urban population	Nil

Tahsil Rajgarhi

Total Population	33,123
Females	15,300
Rural population	33,123
Urban population	Nil

Tahsil Purola

Total population	32.917
Females	15,394
Rural population	32,917
Urban population	Nil

HISTORY

Ancient Period

The area covered by the district of Uttarkashi lies in the north-western part of the region which is celebrated in ancient Indian literature as *Kedar Kshetra* (sacred region) and the Hindu kingdoms of Brahmapura, Kumaon and Garhwal flourished here. The Jadh Ganga river which has its origin in the northern corner of tahsil Bhatwari, derived its name according to the *Purana* from Jahun who was a descendant of Soma and fifth in descent from the Pururvas, the son of Buddha and Ila. While performing sacrifice he saw the whole place overflowing with waters of the Ganga *(yajna)* and getting angry drank up the river which by the intercession of the gods was restored as his daughter, hence the river is called Jahnavi.'

In the Rigvedic period the land of the Tritsus, one of the five principal tribes of the Aryans, lay between the Yamuna and the Parushni[1] and extended towards the north as far as the range of the Himalayas at the foot of which lies Gangotri. Divodasa, the first king of the Tritsus, was engaged in continuous warfare with Shambara, the chief of the aborigines of the same name in Garhwal.[2]

It has been suggested that it was in this region that the land of the ancient Uttara Kurus lay. In the *Aitareya Brahmana* (VIII. 141), this land is described as located beyond the Himalayas. It is believed to have been the land where the *devas* performed their sacrifices. The way of life of the Uttara Kurus and some of their customs are reflected in the life of the rural people of parts of the district. The *Kaushitaki Brahmana* mentions this place as being a land where the Vedic language was better known and better spoken than elsewhere and that people went to this region to learn speech.

In the Upayana Parva of the *Mahabharata*, hill tribes like the Kiratas, Uttara Kurus, Khasas, Tanganas, Kunindas and Paratanganas find mention. These tribes had brought wonderful presents for Yudhishthira's Rajasuya sacrifice. Scholars have tried to identify the territory inhabited by these tribes with portions of this district and neighbouring regions. The Tanganas, along with the Kiratas and the Kunindas are mentioned as inhabiting the Tarai region in the kingdom of Subahu in the mid-Himalayas. Like other hill tribes they were skilled in slinging stones. Ptolemy speaks of the domian of the Tangnoi as lying along the Ganga on its eastern side and further to the north and adds that through their land flowed the river Sarabos (Saryu). Ptolemy further places the Kunindas (Kulindrine) above the sources of the Beat, the Sutlej, the Yamuna and the Ganga. The Kiratas are mentioned as living on the northern slopes of the Himalayas from where the sun rises.[3]

During the epic period Nakuri, at a distance of about 9.6 km from Uttarkashi town, was a place of great renown.[4] Parashurama, the great rishi is said to have killed his mother, Renuka here. There is, at Nakuri a temple dedicated to her as she is worshipped in these parts.[5] The *Mahabharata* gives an account of the penances performed at Uttarkashi by Jada Bharata, sage of great spiritual attainments.[6] During that period, seven tribes of the Dasyus were residing in this region.[7] A mention of Uttarkashi and of the rivers Bhagirathi, Jahnavi and Bhillaganga is to be found in the Kedara Khanda section of the *Skanda Purana.*[8] Uttarkashi has also been referred to as the Varnavata where an attempt was made by Duryodhana to destroy the Pandava brothers by burning down their house of lac, in which he had requested them to stay.[9] According to the *Mahabharata,* North Panchala, in which this Himalayan region lay, was conquered and annexed to the Kaurava kingdom. It comprised the greater portion of the area covered by Garhwal of which the district forms a part. The Kurus continued to rule over these parts until the Kingdom was divided between the Kauravas and the Pandavas, Garhwal coming under the sway of the latter, as is evident from the *Mahabharata* which mentions that at the time of Yudhisthira's Rajasuya sacrifice the Tanganas and the Paratanganas who occupied these parts, brought presents of gold, sheep, wool, blankets,[11] etc., for him. After the Pandavas were exiled for 13 years, this region may have come under the Kauravas for some time, when Uttarkashi might have been the scene of a fierce fight between Arjuna and Siva, who appeared in the form of a Kirata warrior[12] and Arjuna's receiving the Pashupata bow from Siva. The *Mahabharata* recounts that the Pandavas perfomed certain *yajanas* (sacrifices) in this disrict on the banks of the Bhagirathi. Bhagdatta, a raja described in the *Mahabharata,* led a huge army mostly composed of the Kiratas to aid the Kauravas in the Mahabharata war, from which it may be inferred that during the period Bhagdatta exercised sway over this territory under the aegis of King Dhritarashtra of Hastinapur.[13] The Kauravas were exterminated in this war and the five Pandavas established their rule in this region also till their retirement when Parikshit, their grandson, was placed on the throne.[14] When the five Pandavas retired to the mountains to end their days, they are said to have halted for a while at Patangini (1.6 km north of Gangotri) and then to have gone to the mountain Swargarohini, the place where they are said to have died.[15]

After the Mahabharata War, the Nagas, Kulindas, Kiratas, Tanganas, probably of the Taknaur region of the district, and the Khasas came into prominence and their petty chiefs seem to have ruled over different parts of the district down to the time of the Mauryas in whose empire this region may have been included. During the early centuries of the Christian era the Kushana empire of northern India is said to have covered the western and central Himalayas as far as Tibet and it is presumable that the region covered by the district was included in it.[16]

It was also about the beginning of the Christian era that Rajapala, a descendant of Janamejaya, the Kuru King of Hastinapur, founded a kingdom in the Badrinath region of the adjoining Chamoli district. It is probable that Rajapala and his successors extended their sway as far as the Uttarkashi region.[17]

Some time after the disintegration of the Kushana empire, about the middle of the third century AD, the Katyuri kingdom was founded in the Katyuri valley in the Almora district of the Kumaon Division.[18]

As inscription of about the fifth century AD found on the famous copper trident (about 7 m high) of Shakti, standing in the courtyard of the Vishvanatha temple in the heart of the town of Barahat (Uttarkashi), consists of three stanzas in Sanskrit and is in praise of a valiant and benevolent prince named Ganeshwara who after erecting the temple retired to the forests of Mount Sumeru and whose son Guha, a handsome, brave, able, learned and pious person became the King. Guha fought, several battles and erected this trident, the last stanza of the inscription on it containing a prayer for his long life and immortality of his name and fame.[19]

The first historical notice of the Hindu kingdom prevailing in this region, covering the district of Uttarkashi was to be found in the account of the Chinese traveller Hiuen Tsang. In AD 634 he journeyed from Malawar to Mayurapura close to Hardwar and thence to Po-lo-ki-mo-pou-lo or Brahmapura. The memoirs described the kingdom of Brahmapura surrounded on all sides by mountains... for many centuries the ruler has been a woman and hence it is called the 'Kingdom of the Queens'. Brahmapura is present Barahat (Uttarkashi) and was the site of the capital of that ancient kingdom. An ancient inscribed rock trident symbol of its being the capital, still stands there.

It was some time in the seventh century AD that a branch of the Katyuris established a new kingdom with its capital at Joshimath in Chamoli district and which according to local tradition extended from the Satadra (Sutlej) to the Sarda (Kali) and from the watershed to the plains. This principality developed into a powerful empire which dominated the entire region of Kumaon and Garhwal, evidently including this district, for several centuries.[20] The descendants of Rajapala, of the Kshatriya principality of the Badrinath region, were pushed south westward where they continued to rule from Chandpurgarhi as feudatories of the Katyuris, the last raja of Rajapala's line being Bhanupratapa who occupied a pre-eminent position among the 52 chiefs or Garhpals (fort-owners) after whom this region came to be known as Garhwal.[21] He had only two daughters, one of whom was married to Kanakpal, a Paramara prince of Malwa, who had come to these parts on pilgrimage. Bhanupratapa abdicated the throne making his son-in-law, Kanakpal, his heir, the date of the latter's accession being generally accepted at Samvat 945 (AD 888)[22] This King was the virtual founder of the dynasty of the Garhwal rajas who had been ruling over this region till its merger in the Indian Union in 1949.

Kanakpal is said to have built his strong and beautiful fort on a lofty and steep mountain in pargana Chandpur of district Chamoli, which was covered with thick forests abounding in fine scenery.[23] Most of the high caste families of these parts of Garhwal also claim that their ancestors had come and settled down here with Kanakpal.[24] The country was still divided among more than fifty petty chiefs and he was only one of them, though perhaps the most important. Some of these chieftainship, particularly those of Mungragarh, Sankrigarh, Idiyagarh and Qadtangarh seem to have been located in what is now the district of Uttarkashi.[25]

Kanakpal and his successors for several generations sought to increase their power at the expense of these Garhwal chiefs on the one hand and the declining power of their overlords, the Katyuri kings of Joshimath in the north on the other. But it is not known as to what portion of the present district of Uttarkashi was under their sway.

Four versions of the genealogical list of the Garhwal rajas beginning with Kanakpal are available and barring minor discrepancies agree among themselves.[26] Nothing, except their names, is known about the first ten rulers of the line down to Bhagatipal who lived about the latter half of the 11th century. They appear to have been mere feudatories of the Katyuri kings of Joshimath, but probably their domains included parts of the district of Uttarkashi.[27] The Katyuri dynasty was succeded by the Chand dynasty of Kumaon and the Pala dynasty of Garhwal, each with a long line of kings. Subsequently, as the power of the Katyuris declined, the rajas of Kanakpal's line seem to have gained in strength. Anantpal I, the 17th raja in the line, is said to have changed his headquarters to Maluwakot, probably about the beginning of the second quarter of the 12th century. Fourth in descent from him was Vikrampal who is placed in the last quarter of that century and is also said to have shifted his seat to Amulna-kot.[29] He was probably a contemporary of Viradeva, the last

Katyuri King of Joshimath, who was a fool and a tyrant and in whose time the Joshimath line of the Katyuris came to an end, Viradeva himself with his family probably migrating to the ancestral seat in the Katyuri valley in Almora district. By this time the Garhwal rajas appear to have secured for themselves an honoured and even an enviable place among the 52 traditional fort-owners of this region.[30]

Vikrampal's successor was Vichitrapal in whose time towards the close of the twelfth century, Aneka of the Halla dynasty of Nepal conquered this area (Kadarbhumi). This is recorded on a trident at Gopeshwar in Chamoli. The ancient brass and copper trident standing in front of the Vishvanatha temple at Barahat (Uttarkashi) also bears on it some Sanskrit verses in the same script and metre as those inscribed on the iorn trident at Gopeshwar (Chamoli district) testifying to the conquests of Aneka Malla in these parts.[31] The statement contained in the Gopeshwar inscription that it is a pious act to raise up a worthy foe when he has been humbled"[32], seems to allude to the subjugation of Vichitrapal, the then ruler of these parts, who was probably allowed to retain his kingdom and kingship as a feudatory of the victor.

Medieval Period

This conquest of the district appears to have been short-lived[33] and as soon as the conqueror's back was turned, Sonpal who succeded Vichitrapal's successor, Hanspal, and is assigned to *circa* AD 1209-1216 retrieved his position. It is said that he also shifted his headquarters to some place in the valley of the Bhilangana, that a number of Khasa chief owed allegiance to him and that he held sway over all western Garhwal and commanded the pilgrim route to Gangotri[34] indicating that the greater portion of this district formed part of his kingdom. History seems to have repeated itself in the case of this raja who, like Bhanupratapa of old, is said to have had no son but only a daughter, married to Kadilpal, a Paramara prince from Dharanagar in Malwa, who had come here on pilgrimage[35] just as Kanakpal, the traditional founder of the Garhwal dynasty, had done more than 300 years before.[36] It is not known if the two traditions refer to two independent, although remarkably alike, events or are the two versions of one and the same tradition with only a change in the names of the principal persons involved. Sonpal mentioned in one genealogical list as Sohanpal and in another as Suvarnpal, is said to have given to Kadilpal, mentioned in the lists variously as Kantipal, Kantikripapal and Kanhapal, a part of pargana Chandpur as dowry and made him his heir. Kadilpal was the 25th raja in the line and is assigned to AD 1216-1221. He was suceeded by

Kamdeopal and the latter by Salakhanpol (AD 1236-1254).

Nothing, except names is known about the successors of Salakhanpal till Ajaipal who was the 10th in descent from him and the 37th in the line and whose reign is variously assigned to AD 1358-70, 1446 and AD 1500-1519, the first of these dates, however, appearing to be the most acceptable one.[38] With the accession of Ajaipal as the King, the history of the Garhwal kingdom, in which this district was included, begins to assume a firm footing. In his time the raja of Champawat, in district Almora, invaded Badhan in district Chamoli, which formed part of Ajaipal's dominion. In the first round of the battle Ajaipal suffered a heavy defeat but ultimately he succeeded in routing the enemy's forces and in driving him out of his territory.[39] It was probably on account of this invasion from the east that Ajaipal transferred his capital from Chandpur garhi to Dewalgarh.[40] He is also said to have chosen the site which later developed into the capital city of Srinagar, laid its foundation and started building a big palace there which was completed by his successors.[41] One tradition has it that Ajaipal, who was also a Paramara Rajput, entered the service of the raja of Chandpur whom he ousted and usurped the throne, which shows that he was probably not the lawful successor of the previous ruler. Originally he seems to have been a petty chief with his headquaters in the village of Chaund in pargana Chandpur, district Chamoli. He appears to have gradually subjugated his neighbouring chiefs and extended his power considerably.[42] It is said that before him almost every glen in Garhwal had a chieftain of its own and he seems to have brought together many of these chiefs into a sort of confederacy with himself at its head.[43] Thus the credit of first attempting a consolidation of the entire region from the Himalayas in the north to Chandi, near Hardwar, in the south and from the Yamuna in the west to Badhan in the east is given to him.[44] It is also believed that the region formerly known at Kedarbhumi, now began to be called by the name of Garhpal or Garhwal which has since stuck to it. He defined the boundaries of his territories, reorganised parganas and pattis, treated the subordinate chiefs generously and loved his subjects, 'Ajaipal's sthapana (settlement or administration), having become proverbial in Garhwal.[45]

Ajaipal was succeded by his son, Kalyanpal, and the latter by Sundarpal.[46] It was probably in the time of the last named raja that Timur, after having sacked Delhi and Meerut and crossed the Ganga (in AD 1398) fought several battles near Hardwar and the Chandi hill, opposite Hardwar, across the Ganga, and then invaded the country of a raja named Bahraz, which lay in a valley between the Ganga and the Yamuna. The raja put up a stiff resistance but was defeated and rich booty fell into the hands of the invader who, however, gave up the idea of penetrating further into the hills and returned to his country.[47] As the name Bahruz, mentioned in Muslim chronicles, or Brahmdatta of which Bahruz can be a possible corruption, is not found in the list of the Garhwal rajas and cannot be identified with the name of any of Ajaipal's successors for several generations, the latter's direct sway does not seem to have then extended as far south as Hardwar. Bahruz may, therefore, have been some local chief of these parts who may or may not have owed allegiance to the raja of Garhwal.[48]

Sundarpal was succeeded by Hansdevapal and the latter by Vijaipal who is said to have led an unsuccessful expedition against the King of Tibet in the north,[49] the route taken probably passing through the district of Uttarkashi. The next raja was Sahajpal who lived about AD 1425 and whose successor was Balbhadrapal.[50]

It was this raja, also known as Balbhadra Sah and Bahadur Shah, who is said to have changed the dynastic cognomen from Pal to Sah. It is said that the Sultan of Delhi, probably Buhlul Lodi (AD 1451-88), was somehow so much pleased with this raja that he sent to him a rich Khila't (robe of honour), gave him the name, Bahadur Shah, and conferred upon him the title Shah (or Sah) to be used by him and his successors. This, however, does not mean that the raja in any way lost his independence and became subordinate to the Sultan of Delhi. The Sultan's gesture and the response made by the raja appear to have been only tokens of mutual friendship.

Balbhadra Sah's successor was Man Sah who issued a grant in AD 1547, which is for the first time an authentic landmarks in the chronology of the Garhwal rajas.[54] He is said to have led raids into the plains in the south, to have invaded Tibet in the north defeating its king in a battle and to have extended the boundaries of his kingdom.[55] De Laet, a foreign traveller of the time, described the snow-capped Garhwal, with Srinagar as capital, as a 'very fertile' kingdom and wrote that its ruler 'Mansa' (Man Sah) dined in 'dishes of gold'.[56] His successor Sham Sah, is said to have been a ruthless and wilful despot who defeated the King of Tibet.[57] The next raja was Dularam Sah who issued a grant in AD 1580.[58] and was perhaps the first of his line to come into direct conflict with the rising power of the Chand rajas of Kumaon. Rudra Chand (AD 1565-97), who had become supreme in Kumaon, sought to add Badhan Garhwal. Consequently he sent an expedition against Garhwal under Parkhu, his General, but the latter was killed in an action near Gwaldom. Rudra Chand then led in person an expedition but retreated without effecting any conquest of the territory of Garhwal.[59] His son and successor, Lakshmi Chand (AD 1597-1621), continued to pursue the aggressive policy of his father and is said to have invaded Garhwal seven times but to have been repulsed each time with considerable loss by Mahipati Sah, the then reigning raja of Garhwal,[60] who had ascended the throne after Dularam Sah's death in AD 1580.[61]

Mahipati Sah, entitled Garbhabhanjana[62] was a brave man and a great ruler. It was he who finally removed the capital from Dewalgarh to Srinagar of which city he is said to have been the virtual founder. He was also the first raja of this line to consolidate effectively his rule over the whole of Garhwal,[63] the entire district of Uttarkashi evidently being under his sway. At this time Akbar, the great Mughal emperor, was ruling over the greater part of the plains of India. He reorganised the administration of his vast empire on a very sound basis. Within his subah of Delhi there figures a subdivision named the sirkar of Kumaon which comprised 21 *mahals* or parganas, the revenue assessment of as many as nine of the *mahals* has, however, not been mentioned and shown as undetermined.[64] The account given of the mineral wealth and of the birds and beasts of Kumaon, which is described as part of the northern mountains of this subah (Delhi), may as well apply to Garhwal as to Kumaon. None of the *mahals* mentioned under the sirkar of Kumaon, however, seems to have been situated in the hills and, therefore, within the territories of the raja of Garhwal.[65] There is also a story that on one occasion Akbar, being pleased with the ingenuity of the raja of Srinagar, exempted him from payment of any tribute and his territories from assessment of revenue payable into the imperial treasury.[66] It appears, therefore, that the rajas of Garhwal continued to enjoy almost full independence with the exception, perhaps of acknowledging nominally the emperor of Delhi as their overlord but paying no tribute and supplying no contingents to him.[67] Mahipati Sah continued to reign till at least AD 1625 which date figures in an inscription of his, discovered in the Kesho Rai monastery of Srinagar, and he seems to have remained on friendly terms both with Akbar and Jahangir, his contemporary Mughal emperors.

The historian Firishta, who is believed to have completed his work about AD 1623[69] writes. "The Raja of Kumaon also possesses an extensive dominion, considerable quantity of gold is procured by washing the earth mounds in his country, which also contains copper mines. His territory stretches to the north as far as Tibet and on the south reaches to Sambhal which is included in India. He retains in pay an army of 80,000 men both in cavalry and infantry and commands great respect from the emperors of Delhi. His treasures too are vast. It is a rule among the kings of Kumaon not to encroach on the hoards of their ancestors, for it is a saying amongst them that whoever applies his father's treasuers to his own use will become mean and beggarly in spirit; so that at the present day fifty-six distinct treasures exist which have been left by the Rajas of Kumaon, each of which has the owner's seal upon it. The sources of the Jamna and the Ganges are both to be found within the Kumaon territory".[70] It appears that Firishta was also confused about the distinction between Kumaon and Garhwal, his description being truer of the latter region than of the former. Garhwal has been celebrated from the earliest times for its mines of copper and lead and the gold-washings in the valleys of the Alaknanda and the Bhagirathi. The sources of both the Yamuna and the Ganga (Bhagirathi) lie in the district of Uttarkashi which has always been a part of Garhwal and never of Kumaon. Moreover, the number of rajas who had reigned till then is nearer the truth in the case of the Garhwal dynasty in which Mahipati Sah (the then ruler) was the 54th[71] whereas his contemporary Lakshmi Chand (1597-1621) of Kumaon was only the 45th raja in his own line.[72] The statement that the raja 'commands great respect from the emperors of Delhi' is also in keeping with what is otherwise known of Mahipati Sah's relations with his contemporary Mughal emperors. In 1625, Antonio Andrade, a Jesuit missionary, arrived in Srinagar and reported that although the raja paid tribute to the Mughals, yet 'no regard was paid to the rescripts from Jahangir and Asaf Khan with which they had armed themeselves.' And about August, 1631, Francis de Azevedo, coming from Agra, mentions how on the death of the raja of Srinagar sixty ladies of the *zenana* committed *sati*.[73] The raja was obviously Mahipati Sah who with his minister, Jhaliya Dham Singh Bhandari, was killed in the battle of Kakubmora, fighting against the Chand raja of Kumaon. The leaderless Garhwal army is said to have retreated to Srinagar with their raja's dead body.[74]

Mahipati Sah was succeeded by his son Prithvi Sah some time between 1625, the last known date of the former, and 1640 in which year the latter issued a grant.[75] He was a powerful ruler and is said to have extended and fixed the western boundaries of his kingdom by waging war upon the chief ruling in that direction.[76] In 1635, a dreadful famine is said to have raged in Garhwal.[77] Soon after, in 1635-36, the imperial forces, consisting of 30,000 horse and a lakh of infantry, under Mirza Shaja Najabat Khan Badakhshi invaded Garhwal. Prithvi Sah allowed this army to enter the interior of his hilly region and then beleaguered it, blocking all exits. The imperial soldiers began to starve and could save their lives and return home only after having their noses cut, to serve as trophies for the raja's men, while the imperial general, in order to escape disgrace, poisoned himself.[78] In 1647, Dara Shukoh, on behalf of the Emperor Shahjahan is said to have sent a robe of honour to Prithvi Sah who seems to have been reconciled to the Mughal court by this time.[79] Later in the reign of Shahjahan, in AD 1954-55 Khalil Ullah Khan, an imperial general, was again dispatched with 8,000 men in order to coerce the 'zamindar of Srinagar',[80] which inadequate title was obviously meant for Prithvi Sah, the raja of Garhwal. This hostile force overran the Dehra Dun region, then under the sway of the raja of Garhwal, with little resistance from the side of the raja but could not penetrate further into the hills and Khalil Ullah Khan gave up the attempt and returned to the imperial court.[81] Baz Bahadur Chand, the then raja of Kumaon, is also said to have joined the imperial forces in this unsucceeful attempts against Garhwal.[82]

A few years later, after the discomfiture of Dara Shukoh at the battle of Samugarh, in AD 1658, and his subsequent flight, his son, Sulaiman Shukoh, took refuge in Garhwal where Prithvi Sah accorded him hospitality.[83] For more than a year the raja remained firm in his promise of protecting the unfortunate prince and did not yield to Aurangzeb's threats, the invasion of the Dun by the imperial forces, the aggressions made by the rajas of Kumaon and Sirmor from the east and the west at the instance of the emperor, or to the persuasion of his own ministers and the crown prince, Medini Sah.[84] At last the force of circumstances prevailed upon the raja and he reluctantly handed over Sulaiman Shukoh to Ram Singh, the agent of Aurangzeb and a son of Raja Jai Singh of Amber.[85]

Baz Bahadur Chand of Kumaon continued his aggressive policy against Garhwal and for a time succeeded in annexing some of its border areas[86] which Prithvi Sah shortly after recovered. In his last campaign the raja of Kumaon seems to have been more successful but a peace was concluded between the two rajas.[87] The last known date of Prithvi Sah is AD 1664 which figures in an inscription of his reign discovered on the gateway of the Raghunath temple at Devaprayag.[88] Prithvi Sah is said to have lived for 76 years. The crown prince, Medini Sah, had already died in his lifetime at Delhi in 1661. And when in 1664 Prithvi Sah died, he was succeeded by his grandson, Fateh Sah, who was a minor of only seven years of ago. As soon as Fateh Sah ascended the throne Aurangzeb issued a firman, dated Saturday, January 16, 1664, in his favour. During his minority, Rani Bartwali, his mother, seems to have acted as regent.[89] The Chand rajas of Kumaon, Baz Bahadur Chand and his successor Udyot Chand (1678-98), continued to remain hostile towards Garhwal,[90] but now Aurangzeb appears to have sided with and given his moral support to the Garhwal rulers against the Chands.[91] It was, perhaps, in 1684 that Fateh Sah took the reins of government in his own hands, and he appears to have remained on friendly terms with Aurangzeb till the latter s death in AD 1707.

Modern Period

There was occasional fighting between Fateh Sah and his contemporary Chand rulers, Gyanchand (1698-1708) and Jagatchand (1708-1720) of Kumaon, the Garhwalis wresting back a portion of the Kumaon territory which had been under the control of their rajas for a considerable period.[92] Fateh Sah is credited with extending his sway over parts of Tibet, and it was, perhaps, he who made a memorable raid in 1692 from Dehra Dun into Saharanpur from where he could be expelled with difficulty by Sayyid Ali, the Mughal General.[93] This raja is known to have issued grants in 1685, 1706, 1710 and 1716.

Fateh Sah died in 1716 and was succeeded by his son, Dilip Sah, who ruled only for a few months and made way for Upendra Sah. The latter also did not stay long on the throne and after ruling for about nine months was succeeded by his nephew, Pradip Sah,[94] who ruled over Garhwal for over half a century and was notably successful in one of the encounters which he had with the rajas of Kumaon .

In 1745, the territory of Kalyan Chand, the then ruler of Kumaon, was invaded by the Rohillas under the command of Hafiz Rahmat Khan who occupied Almora.[95] The Kumaonis invoked the assistance of Pradip Sah who after some hesitation agreed to fight against the Rohillas. But the combined forces of Pradip Sah and Kalyan Chand suffered defeat and the Rohillas even threatened Srinagar, the capital of Garhwal. The raja of Garhwal was forced to pay three lakhs of rupees on behalf of Kalyan Chand, in consideration of which payment the Rohillas agreed to go back.[96] The peace that followed inaugurated an era of exceptional prosperity in Garhwal for some time which attracted the notice of the Rohillas who under Najib Khan once again invaded and devastated Garhwal in 1757.

A few years later Pradip Sah again intervened in the affairs of Kumaon and claimed suzerainty over the territory up to the river Ram-ganga but his demand was refused.

Pradip Sah was succeeded in 1772 by his son, Lalit Sah, who took advantage of the internal strife in Kumaon and led an army against the raja of that kingdom, gaining a complete victory at Bagwali Pokhar in 1779.[97] He installed his younger son, Pradyuman Sah, on the throne of Kumaon under the title of Pradyuman Chand. The elder son Jayakrit Sah, succeeded his father on the throne of Garhwal after the latter's death.

Soon after, differences arose between the two brothers, Pradyuman Sah and Jayakrit Sah, the latter demanding acknowledgement of his seniority by right of birth which the former refused to concede on the ground that Kumaon had never accepted the supremacy of Garhwal.[98] Jayakrit Sah began to intrigue with the influential Mohan Chand, a pretender to the throne of Kumaon, who had been exiled and was on inimical terms with Pradyuman sah. Harsh Dev Joshi, the Prime Minister of Kumaon, proceeded to Garhwal and sought an interview with the raja in the hope of ariving at a settlement on behalf of his King. Pradyuman Sah. Jayakrit Sah, however, did not react favourably to the overture and attacked Harsh Dev Joshi. He was, however, defeated and obliged to seek safety in flight during which he died,[99] the Kumaonis occupying Garhwal up to Srinagar. Parakram Sah, another brother of Jayakrit Sah, proclaimed himself raja of Garhwal, but Pradyuman Sah came over from Almora, assumed the crown of Garhwal[100] and transferred his own throne of Kumaon to his younger brother, Parakram Sah. As Parakram Sah did not prove a strong ruler, Mohan Chand made good his re-entry into Kumaon in 1786 and ousted Parakram Sah. Thus the Garhwal domination in Kumaon came to an end. Mohan Chand now became supreme in Kumaon, but only for a short period. In 1788, he was killed by Harsh Dev Joshi, who invited its former King, Pradyuman Sah, to the throne of Kumaon but the offer was declined.[101]

Nepali troops over-ran Kumaon in 1790 and Garhwal in 1805 which included the area covered by the present district of Uttarkashi, but while they were busy making arrangements for a more determind attack, the news of a Chinese invasion of Nepal caused the withdrawal of their troops for the defence of their own country.[102] This show of the Gurkha power so impressed Pradyuman Sah that he agreed to pay a yearly tribute of Rs. 25,000 to the Nepalese government and sent an agent to the court of Kathmandu. This agreement lasted for twelve years and preserved some appearance of amity between the two governments.[103]

About the beginning of 1803, a severe earthquate occurred in the whole of Garhwal including Uttarkashi, which destroyed many houses and killed many human beings and heads of cattle. Soon after, the Gurkha leaders, Amar Singh Thapa, Hastidal Chautariya and others, once again invaded Garhwal with a large and powerful army. No resistance was offered to them. Scarcely had the Gurklhas approached Srinagar when Pradyuman Sah with his family fled by way of Barahat (Uttarkashi) to Dehra Dun where with most of his followers he was killed in 1804.[105] The fourth brother, Pritam Sah, was taken prisoner and sent in custody to Nepal, Pradyuman Sah's son, Sudarshan Sah, and Parakram Sah having also escaped, the former into British territory.[106] The Nepal government appointed Amar Singh Thapa, governor of this region. With the advent of the Gurkha raj many "old families were destroyed, persons of rank and importanace were either banished or killed and their villages burnt and desolated and a great number of inhabitants were sold as slaves.[107] Gurkha officers were severe and their manners as conquerors rough. Rapine was of common occurrence and the Gurkha soldiery forcibly married many Garhwal women.

The Gurkhas now came into contact with the British power as by 1814 their frontier in Garhwal had become conterminous with that of the British.[108] The border districts of the British territory suffered terribly from the incessant inroads of the Gurkhas. Lord Hastings, the Governor General, now resolved to settle once for all these border disputes.[109]

General Gillespie was instructed to enter Garhwal by way of Dehra Dun with 3,500 men and to dislodge Amar singh Thapa from Srinagar. The General himself brought up the reserves but was killed.[110]

In April, 1815, the Kumaon and Garhwal regions were again invaded by the British who defeated the Gurkhas. The Nepalese government made the treaty of Sigauli whereby the Gurkhas agreed to withdraw all their troops east of the Kali river and gave to the British all Nepalese territory from Kumaon to the Sutlej. Kumaon and Garhwal were annexed as British districts. Garhwal to the west of the Alaknanda excepting the Dun and the pargana of Rawain lying between the Alaknanda and the Bhagirathi was handed over to the Raja of Garhwal and came to be known as Tehri Garhwal State. The Garhwalis now retaliated by killing large numbers of Gurkhas, isolated bands being massacred or driven away to die of exposure and starvation in the mountains.

On its annexation by the British, Garhwal was divided into eastern Garhwal and western Garhwal.[111] The former was kept by the British government under its own authority, and the latter was made over to Sudarshan Sah, the eldest son of Pradyuman Sah, to form the State of Tehri Garhwal. In 1815, the British handed over to the raja the portion of Garhwal situated to the west of the Alaknanda with the express reservation of the Dun and the pargana of Rawain (now district Uttarkashi) lying between the Alaknanda and the Bhagirathi.[112] Pargana Rawain comprised comparatively barren and rocky country and the inhabitants too were turbulent, accustomed to plunder and disinclined to work.[113]

In 1816, Traill, the Assistant Commissioner of Kumaon, brought to the notice of the British government the difficulty that might arise if the boundary between British Garhwal and Tehri Garhwal were not more precisely defined. Although pargana Nagpur, now in the Chamoli district, was clearly intended to be included in the territory retained by the British, the loose mention, in the negotiations, of the Alaknanda and Mandakini as marking the boundary could be construed as depriving the

British of some valuable portions of that pargana, including *pattis* Bamsu and Maikhanda and the mines near Dhamoli, which lay to the west of those rivers. In 1823, the raja laid claim to the villages lying to the west of the Mandakini but it was held that the term Nagpur as used in the negotiations included all the subdivisions which fell within its established limits.[114]

In 1818, Traill complained of the disorderly state of the pargana of Rawain, the inhabitants of which being relieved from the fear of both the Gurkhas and the British had taken to their old occupation of plundering the pilgrims visiting Gangotri and Kedarnath. The raja of Tehri Garhwal did not prove equal to the task of establishing peace in the area. The boundaries were then laid down as they now exist, and pargana Rawalin was formally annexed to the Raja's State in 1824.[115]

Raja Sudarshan sah, however, was a ruler of an amiable disposition. He soon re-established his power over his subjects. During the freedom struggle of 1857, Sudarshan Sah rendered valuable assistance to the British government.[116] He died in 1859 without any male issue, and the State lapsed to the British government. However, in consideration of the services of Sudarshan Sah, a near male relative, Bhawani Sah, was allowed to succeed. He subsequently received a *sanad* giving him the right of adoption. Bhawani Sah died in 1872 and was succeeded by his son, Pratap Sah, who died in 1887.[117] At the time of his death, his son Krit Sah, was a minor and the administration of the State was carried on by his mother, Rani Guleri, till his attaining the age of majority in 1892.[118] He married a grand-daughter of Maharaja Jang Bahadur of Nepal. Kirti Sah was an enlightened and educated prince who completed the reforms initiated by his father and introduced some of his own in the State. He died in 1913[119] leaving behind his minor son, Narendra Sah, the administration being carried on by a British political agent. Raja Narendra Sah was installed on the throne in 1916, his son Manvendra Sah succeeding him during his lifetime in 1948.

During the rule of Narendra sah a spontaneous public movement, known as Rawain Kand, took place in 1930 against forest settlement. People were dissatisfied with the attitude of the forest authorities, and the Maharaja invited their representatives for negotiations to Rajgarhi, but got them put under arrest. This aroused great resentment and people resorted to violent measures to get back their leaders. They succeeded and captured Surendradutt, the Sub-Divisional Magistrate, while Padmadutta Raturi, the forest officer, made his escape to Narendra Nagar. The Maharaja sent about 300 soldiers under the State Diwan, Chakradhar, to suppress the movement. The soldiers opened fire at the public and arrested about a hundred person of whom sixty-five were sentenced to various terms of imprisonment for sedition.

India became independent on August 15, 1947, and the State of Tehri Garhwal was merged with the State of Uttar Pradesh in 1949 and the area covered by the present distrilct of Uttarkashi formed part of the district of Tehri Garhwal till February 24, 1960, when this district was constituted as a separate administrative unit.

Growth of Population

At the census of 1951, the total population of the Rawain tehsil which was converted into the district of Uttarkashi in 1960, was found to be 1,06,058, the number of females being 52,844. The first census of the district as it is now, was taken in 1961, when its population had risen to 1,22,836, the number of females being 60,302.

The figures of the population of the area covered by the present district from 1901 to 1961 are given in Table 17.3.

TABLE 17.3: Population 1901 to 1961

Year	Persons	Male	Female
1901	69,209	34,343	34,866
1911	77,429	38,213	39,216
1921	81,958	40,282	41,676
1931	89,978	44,611	45,367
1941	1,02,280	51,758	50,522
1951	1,06,058	53,214	52,844
1961	1,22,836	62,534	60,302

The decennial growth of the population from 1901 to 1961 is shown in Table 17.4.

TABLE 17.4: Decennial growth of population, 1901 to 1961

Census Year	Population	Total	Rural	Urban
1901	69,209	—	—	—
1911	77,429	+11.9	+11.9	—
1921	81.958	+5.9	+5.9	—
1931	89,978	+9.8	+9.8	—
1941	1,02,280	+13.7	+13.7	—
1951	1,06,058	+3.7	+3.7	—
1961	1,22,836	+15.8	+14.6	+122.2

The district occupies the fourth place among the districts of the State of Uttar Pradesh with respect to area and the last position with regard to population.

Source: Uttarkashi Gazetteer, Government Press, Allahabad

REFERENCES

1. Macdonell, A. A. and Keith, A. B., *Vedic Index of Names and Subjects*, (reprint 1958), p. 321
2. Bahadur, Rai, P. R., *Garhwal, Ancient and Modern*, (Simla, 1916). pp. 171-172
3. Chandra, Moti: 'Studies in the Mahabharata'—*Journal of the U.P. Historical Society*, Vol. XVII, Part I, pp. 32-40.
4. Nautiyal, G.P., *Call of Badrinath*, p. 20; Painuli, P.N.: *The Valley of Gods*, p. 41
5. Painuli, *op. cit.*, pp. 35-36; Vaishnava, *Saligram: Shri Kedar Khanda Rahasya*, p. 221.
6. Datar, B.N, *Himalayan Pilgrimage*, (1961), p. 34
7. Atkinson, E.T., *The Himalayan Districts of the North-Western Provinces of India*, Vol. II, p. 279
8. Dabral, S.P., *Uttarakhand ka Itihasa*, pp. 96-99.
9. Nautiyal, G.P., *op. cit.*, p. 20
10. Bahadur, Rai, P.R. *op. cit.*, pp. 173-174
11. *Ibid.*, p. 174
12. Painuli, P.M., *op. cit.*, p. 41
13. Bahadur, Rai, P. R., *op. cit.*, pp. 174-175
14. Bahadur, Rai, P. R., *op. cit.*, pp. 175
15. Raturi, H.K.: *Garhwal ka Itihasa*, p. 81: Vaishnava, Saligraom, *op. cit.*, p. 226
16. Majumdar, R.C. and Pusalker, A.D. (Ed.) *The History and Culture of the Indian People*. Vol. II, p. 161: Bahadur, Rai, P.R., *op. cit.*, p. 177
17. Raturi, *op. cit.*, pp. 338-339
18. Atkinson, *op. cit.*, Vol. II, pp. 467-468
19. Dabral, S.P., *op. cit.*, pp. 520-521
20. Sankratvayan, Rahul: *Kumaon*, pp. 37, 39
21. Raturi, H.K. *op. cit.*, pp. 337-389
22. *Ibid.*, pp. 351-354
23. Bahadur, Rai, P. R. *op. cit.*, p. 185
24. Walton, H.G., *British Garhwal: A Gazetteer* (Allahabad 1910), p. 61
25. Raturi, H.K., *op. cit.*, pp. 323-330
26. Atkinson, E.T., *op. cit.*, Vol. II, pp. 445-447
27. *Ibid.*, p. 446
28. *Ibid.*
29. *Ibid.*
30. Bahadur, Rai, P.R., *op. cit.*, pp. 220-221
31. Dabral, *op. cit.*, pp. 397-398; Sankratyayana, *op. cit.*, pp. 61-63; Atkinson, *op. cit.*, Vol. II, pp. 511-514, 523
32. *Ibid.*, p. 514
33. *Ibid.*
34. *Ibid.*, p. 446
35. *Ibid.*,
36. Zila Uttarkashi ki Settlement Report, 1963-64 (Allahabad, 1956). p. 1
37. Bahadur, *op. cit.*, p. 208.
38. Atkinson, *op. cit.*, Vol. II, p. 526
39. Raturi, *op. cit.*, pp. 364-365
40. Ibid., pp. 365-366: Dabral, *op. cit.*, p. 283
41. Raturi, *op. cit.*, pp. 366.367: Bahadur, *op. cit.*, p. 186
42. *Journal of the U.P. Historical Society*, Vol. XVI. Part I (July, 1943), pp. 74-76
43. Atkinson, *op. cit.*, Vol. II. p. 527

44. Bahadur, *op. cit.*, p. 187
45. Raturi, *op. cit.*, pp. 367-368
46. *Ibid.*, p. 369
47. Elliot, H.M. and Dowson, J., *The History of India as told by its own Historians,* Vol. III (London). pp. 461, 513: Atkinson, op. cit., Vol. II, pp. 524-526; Bahadur, *op. cit.*, p. 190
48. Atkinson, *op. cit.,* Vol. II, pp. 526, 527
49. Raturi, *op. cit.,* p. 370
50. Genl. (R)-1979-3
51. Walton, *op. cit.* pp. 114-115
52 Saletore, G.N., "The Mughals and Garhwal Rulers (1624-1664)'—*Proceedings of the Indian Historical Records Commission,* Mysore Session, 1955; Vol. XXXI, p. 17, foot note 2; Raturi, *op. cit.*, pp. 371-373
53. *Ibid.* pp. 371-375
54. Atkinson, *op. cit.,* Vol. II, p. 526
55. Raturi, *op. cit.*, pp. 375-376
56. De Lael, *Empire of the Great Moghal,* (ed. Hoyland and Banerji), p. 60; Saletore, *op. cit.*, Vol. XXXI, p. 17, foot note 2
57. Raturi, *op. cit.*, pp. 376-377
58. Atkinson, *op. cit.*, Vol. II, pp. 447, 527
59. *Ibid.*, pp. 553-554., Sankratyayana, *op. cit.*, pp. 84-85
60. *Ibid.*, p. 85: Atkinson, *op. cit.*, pp. 556-557
61. *Ibid.*, p. 527
62. *Ibid.*, p. 543
63. Atkinson, *op. cit.*, Vol. II, pp. 527, 543: Walton, *op. cit.*, p. 116
64. *Ain-i-Akbari of Abul Fazal-i-Allami,* tr. by II, S. Jarret and annotated by J.N. Sarkar, Vol. II, (2nd ed., Calcutta, 1949), p. 294
65. *Ibid.*, p. 285
66. Atkinson, *op. cit.*, Vol. II, p. 549; Walton *op. cit.*, pp. 116-117
67. Bahadur, *op. cit.*, p. 192
68. Atkinson, *op. cit.*, Vol. II, p. 447
69. *Ibid.*, p. 543: Elliot and Dowson, *op. cit.*, Vol. VI (London, 1866-77). p. 209
70. Briggs, Col. J., *Tarikh-i-Firishta* (Eng. trans). Vol. IV, (London, 1829), pp. 547, 549: Atkinson, *op. cit.*, Vol. II, pp. 542-543
71. *Ibid.*,
72. *Ibid.*, pp. 501-555
73 Mac Lagan, Jesuits and the Great Mogal, pp. 343, 350: Saletore, *op. cit.*, p. 17
74 *Ibid.*,
75. Atkinson, *op. cit.*, Vol. II, p. 563
76. Raturi, *op. cit.*, pp. 382-383
77. Saletore, *op. cit.*, pp. 17-18
78. *Ibid.*, p. 18
79. *Ibid.*,
80. Elliot and Dowson, op. cit., Vol. VII, (Allahabad, 1964), p. 105 (Extract from Ineyat Khan's *Shahjahan-Nama)*
81. Elliot and Dowson, *op. cit.*, Vol. VII., pp. 105-107; Burn, R. (Ed.): *The Cambridge History of India,* Vol. IV, p. 207
82. Elliot and Dowson, *op. cit.*, Vol. VII, p. 107
83. *Ibid.*, pp. 229-230, 263 (extract from Khali Khan's *Muntakhabu-i-Lubab*)
84. Raturi, *op. cit.*, pp. 382-390
85. *Ibid.*, pp. 387-388l Elliot and Dowson, op. cit., Vol. VII, p. 263: Atkinson, *op. cit.*, Vol. II, pp. 563-+565: Saletore, *op. cit.*, p. 19

86. *Ibid.*, pp. 567-568; Sankratyayana, *op. cit.*, p. 86
87. *Ibid.*, p. 88
88. Raturi, *op. cit.*, p. 391
89. Saletore, *op. cit.*, pp. 19-20
90. Atkinson, *op. cit.*, Vol. II, p. 570
91. Saletore, *op. cit.*, p. 20
92. Atkinson, *op. cit.*, p. 573
93. *Ibid.*,
94. Walton H.G., *British Garhwal: A Gazetteer*, (1910), p. 118
95. Haimilton, Francis, An Account of the Kingdom of Nepal, and of the Territory annexed to this Dominion by the House of Gorkhas, pp. 294-295
96. Bahadur, P. R., *Garhwal: Ancient and Modern*, p. 191
97. Sankratyayana, Rahul, *Kumaon*, pp. 92-93; Raturi, H.K., *Garhwal ka Itihas* p. 401
98. Atkinson, *op. cit.*, p. 577
99. Sankratyayana, *op. cit.*, pp. 95-96
100. *Ibid.*, pp. 96-97
101. Pande, Badridutt, *Kumaon ka Itihas*, pp. 361-362.
102. Sankratyayan, *op. cit.*, pp. 96-97: Hamilton, *op. cit.*, pp. 295-296
103. Sanwal, B.D., *Nepal and the East India Company*, (Bombay), pp. 62-63: Sankratyayana, *op. cit.*, pp. 114-115
104. Bahadur, P. R., *op. cit.*, p. 194
105. Raturi, *op. cit.*, pp. 418-419
106. Bahadur, *op. cit.*, p. 199
107. Hamilton, *op. cit.*, pp. 300-301: Raturi, *op. cit.*, p. 437
108. Lahadur, *op. cit.*, p. 204
109. Dodwell, H.H. (Ed.) *The Cambridge History of India*, Vol. V. p. 378
110. Hamilton, *The Marquess of Hastings*, pp. 63-64: Dodwell, *op. cit.*, Vol. V. p. 348
111. *Ibid.*,
112. *Ibid.*, pp. 378-379
113. Bahadur, *op. cit.*, p. 21
114. Atkinson, E.T., *The Himalayan District of the North-Western Provinces of India*, Vol. p. 680
115. *Ibid.*, p. 681
116. *Ibid.*, p. 600
117. Raturi, *op. cit.*, p. 465
118. *Ibid.*, pp. 476-477
119. *Ibid.*, pp. 478-480
120. *Ibid.*, p. 484

18

PLACES OF CULTURAL IMPORTANCE AND TOURIST INTEREST

Almora in Kumao Hills is an enchanting town, ringed by picturesque hills crowned by temples. Kathgodam is the gateway to Almora as well as the entire Kumaon area. From Almora, as one goes to the Pindari Glaciers for trecking, one passes through moments of unforgettable communion with nature.

Kalinath Kesar Devi Temple and Brigton Corner are the other important places.

Badrinath is the most ancient *Teertha* (place of pilgrimage) in India. The area is said to have been sanctified by 'Nar and Narayan' in the 'Satyayuga', by Lord Dattatreya in the Tretayuga, by Ved Vyas in 'Dwaparyuga' and by Shankaracharya in 'Kaliyuga'. It is situated on the right bank of the graceful river Alaknanda. The majestic Narayan Parvat overlooks it.

Badrinarayan is a form of Vishnu seated in a meditative pose. On his forehead dazzles a huge diamond. His body is covered by a variety of jewels. On his head hangs a cannopy of gold.

Shri Adi Shankaracharya discovered the importance of this place and got the ancient idol installed in the temple.

During the winters, the doors of the temple are kept closed and are reopened with the coming of summer. During the winters deity is worshipped at Joshimath, a place near Badrinath.

Carbett National Park, named after the naturalist Jim Corbett, a renowed hunter of man-eaters and a fine author of Indian forest life, is located along the borders of Nainital and Garhwal districts. This park at the foothills of the Himalayas runs along the bank of the river Ramganga.

The park is 225.8 sq km in area. It has been famous for its tigers and hog deer. A variety of animals are found here.

Dehradun, was originally called, Dehra Drona, the legend is that Drona, the *guru* of the Pandavas and the Kauravas princes had founded a school here to impart education and the art of warfare to princes.

On the outskirts of the town are the Forest Research Institute, Tapkeshwar, an ancient temple of Lord Shiva, and Raipur Springs, a fine picnic spot. Dehradun is also the headquarters of the Surveyor General of India.

Gangotri and Yamunotri are the sources of Ganga and Yamuna rivers respectively. The traditional belief of the Hindus is that these places wash away the sins of the sinners.

The Gangotri mountain is at a height of 23,327 feet above sea level. It is always covered with snow as it receives snow-fall all round the year. Glaciers are all round. The Gangotri glacier provides a perennial supply of pure water to river Ganga, Shankaracharya, founded the main temple which has a beautiful idol of mother Ganga. Close to it are Suryakund, Brahmakund and Bhagirath Shila.

It was at Gangotri that Bhagiratha, a great prince of the past, had made the Ganga, descend on earth.

The sacred mountain top of Yamnotri is similar to that of Gangotri. The place has a number of ponds of hot water. The water of some of these ponds is so hot that one can boil potatoes and rice by immersing them for some time in the water. Close by is Kalindgiri, the melting snow of which supplies Yamuna with water. Therefore, Yamuna is also called Kalindi.

Kedarnath temple is at an elevation of about 11,735 feet above sea level. Kedarnath Jyotirlinga also known as Kedareshwara is situated on the Kedar mountain in the beautiful Himalayas. Here Upmanyu offered worship to Lord Shiva in Satyayuga. The Pandavas did penance at this place in the 'Dwaparyuga'. Nar-Narayana also prayed to Lord Shiva at Kedarnath. Pleased by their prayers, Lord Shiva granted a boon to Nara-Narayana for His remaining there for the welfare of the people. Thereafter, Lord Shiva remained here in the form of a Jyotirlinga. There is also a reference to the Kedar region in the *Skand Purana.* The Hindus believe that merit, is earned by bathing and offering *Dan* (Charity) here.

It is believed that it was here that Arjuna did his penance for getting divine weapons as a boon.

The river Mandakini originates nearby Kedarnath and it meets Alaknanda at Rudra Prayag. Alaknanda meets Bhagirathi to form Patitpawani Ganga. Gauri Kund where Parvati took bath, and Agnikund with burning flames are situated in Kedarkhand.

Pilgrims often visit Yamunotri and Gangotri—the sources of the Yamuna and Ganga to collect their holy waters for offering to Kedarnath.

Mussoorie often referred to as the Queen of Hill Stations offers bewitching sights of the snow-clad Himalayan peaks on the one hand and the Doon Valley on the other. At night the twinkling lights of Dehradun below look like a patch of starry sky that had fallen down.

Mussoorie is a young hill station that probably began with an army officer, Captain Young, building a house in 1827.

Lal Bahadur Shastri Academy, the highest institution for imparting training to Indian Administrative and Allied Service Trainee Officers, is located here.

Among the important places of tourist interest are: Gun Hill, Mosi Falls, Bhatta Falls, and Kemti Falls.

Lal Tibba, the highest peak of the Mussoorie Hills, gives wonderful opportunity for observing several Himalayan abodes, including Kedarnath and Badrinath.

Nainital, one of the best hill stations in India, derives its name from goddess Naina Devi whose temple stands at the edge of the lake around which it is built. The town is surrounded by towering peaks. The lake provides yatching facilities. It was in the 1840's that the place began to grow as a summer resort.

Cheena Peak, Bhim-Tal Lake, Bhowali (a smaller hill resort), Jeilikate (famous for bee-keeping) and Kilbury (a picnic spot) are some of the peaceful as well as charming spots around.

Ranikhet, the centre of the Kumaon region is a small town nestled amidst oak, cedar, cypress, commanding a wide view of the central Himalayan Range. Ranikhet has to be crossed on the way to Badri Nath.

Bhalu Dam about 13 km away is the refreshing sight of the artificial lake, considered as an 'angler's paradise.

Other nearby places are: ***Kalika*** having an ancient temple didicated to goddess Kalika and a modern forest nursary; ***Upat*** famous for a five golf course and known for pine trees.

Pilgrims often visit Yamunotri and Gangotri — the sources of the Yamuna and Ganga [illegible] by trekking to [illegible].

Mussoorie often referred to as the Queen of Hill Stations, offers breathtaking views of the snow-clad [illegible] peaks on the one side and the Doon Valley on the other. At night, the sparkling lights of Dehradun below look like [illegible].

[illegible] came into being [illegible] built a [illegible] house in 1827.

[illegible] Lal Bahadur Shastri [illegible] Academy of Administration [illegible] training to Indian Administrative and Allied Services [illegible] Officers [illegible].

Among the important places of tourist interest are: Gun Hill, Mossy Falls, Bhatta Falls, and Kempty Falls.

Lal Tibba, the highest point of the Mussoorie hills, gives wonderful [illegible] of the surrounding [illegible] including Badrinath and Kedarnath.

Nainital, the [illegible] hill station [illegible], derives its name from goddess Naina Devi whose temple stands at the edge of the lake around [illegible]. The lake is surrounded by towering peaks. The [illegible]. It was in the 1840 that the place began to grow as a hill resort.

Naina Peak, Tiffin Top, [illegible] offers [illegible] of the snow-clad [illegible] as well as charming spots around.

Ranikhet, the [illegible] of the Kumaon region is a small [illegible] with [illegible], commanding a wide view of the central Himalayan Range. Ranikhet has [illegible].

[illegible] Chaubatia about 10 km away [illegible] orchards [illegible] products.

Other [illegible] places are [illegible] temple [illegible] golf course and [illegible] pine trees.

SECTION V

CONTEMPORARY REACTIONS AND RESPONSES WITH CHRONOLOGLY OF SIGNIFICANT EVENTS

19

AND WHY NOT UTTARAKHAND/ UTTARANCHAL

ANIL BHATT

The hilly terrain of Uttar Pradesh in the north-west consisting of the eight districts of Almoraha, Nainital, Pauri, Pithoragarh, Chamoli, Tehri, Uttarkashi and Dehradun forming a part of Central Himalayas is the symbol of the aspirations of a people struggling to find their identity. They are reacting against the long and unpardonable neglect they had to suffer ever since the Treaty of Sugoli in 1814. The natural and anthropogenic assets of the region are immense and mostly unexplored, yet by virtue of its topography it is perhaps the most frequently visited place in the country by the foreign tourists.

To a common Indian, Uttarakhand is the seat of the Holy Trinity, i.e., Brahma, Vishnu and Mahesh who alongwith Lord Ganesh and Durga Ma, are known as the 'Panch Parmeshwar'. The sacred Hemkunt Saheb in the back-drop of the 'Valley of the Flowers', has been the most ideal place for Sikh scholars to meditate on and interpret the verses of the Holy *Granth Saheb*. The region in question is also punctuated with medieval Mosques scattered in all the districts as also various Gurudwaras and a few Churches. Thus Uttarakhad has become synonymous national pilgrimage centre. It is the custodian of the Badrikadham, the birth place of the Ganga—the holiest river in the world and practically the seat of solace and continuity for a common Indian as well as to a complex non-conformist *Tantrik*. The region also provides very conducive academic atmosphere. No wonder the most prestigious public schools are housed here. It is not

---

Note : The writer is a senior Reader in the English Department of Rajdhani College of Delhi University. He belongs to the hills and is quite familiar with the aspirations of the natives. His father Shri B.D.Bhatt, the former Director of Education in Delhi, was the founder Vice-Chancellor of Garwhal University.

only the breeding bed of formative minds but also provides tranguil atmosphere to the brains which are to look after the administration and defence of the country . The young man and girls selected for the Indian Administrative Service (IAS) and Indian Foreign Service (IFS) are trained here, so are the cadets of the Indian Military Academy and the Forest Research Institute of India. Is it not thus pathetically ironic that the region which is the Headquarter of the Surveyor General of India, should be searching for its own recognition?

The region also happens to be the resource reservoire for the 200 million people of the northern plains. It provides the eroded soil for the Gangetic range. Many other rivers also originate in this area which carry water for irrigation and domestic use. Like a benevolent deity it gifts the country with timber, medicinal herbs and fruits, etc. What is more important is that its variable climate ranging from the hot equatorial to the polar cold provides bio-diversity and genetic material of remarkable value. Uttarakhand can certainly claim that it is the Himalayan range which has saved the north and central India from becoming a vast desert.

This region has given to Uttar Pradesh three Chief Ministers, one of them highly valued as a great Parliamentarian and visionary, the other

MAP 19.1: Himalaya: Survey and Political Borders

for his extraordinary drive and dynamism and the third for his poise and reserve. The region has also given the country literature of very high quality, to wit , Sumitra Nandan Pant, Ila Chand Joshi, Shivani, etc. Apart from these many poets country-wide drew inspirations from these very hills. Besides, there is a distinct school of painting now recognised as 'Gharwal school of Painting' by well known critics. As for the Uttarakhand highlanders, Walton in his invaluable gazettee fittingly stated "He has more self-respect, is less wont to cringe, is a fine faithfull friend, and a more open enemy than his neighbours of the plains". Hill people from Scotland to the Himalayas are more individualistic and tend to keep to themselves unless provoked or pleased. No doubt, that the women folk of the hills are extremely hardworking. They, on an average, have a working day of 12 to 14 hours. None, who has not seen the rigorous work schedule of these women can imagine the extent of tortuous work schedule of these women, can imagine the extent of tortuous work involved in walking with loads of fire wood, fodder and often water too in this tough terrain. The men are observant, though not very vocal but their reserve makes them very hardworking and honest to a fault in as much as they trust others to be like themselves and are thus easily defrauded. If any regiments can claim to have risen phoenix-like from their ashes, they are Gharwal and Kumaon Infantries. It was incidently, a soldier-son ot this soil—Chandra Singh 'Gharwali' who refused to shoot his countrymen.

The terrain is so tough and arable land so scarce that the youngsters are left with no choice but to give up schooling and seek employment in the plains far and wide from Saharanpur to Kanyakumari. The fact that they have to maintain two householdes compels them to contribute only meagre amounts to the family kitty for whose very sake they had originally gone into exile. It is both a tragic irony and startling paradox that the area, which they leave behind and perhaps will never go back to, not only has numerous untapped natural resources in minerals, renewable hydel power, tourism and cottage industry but also is the richest reservoir of medicinal herbs in the world! What Juvenal observed centuries back holds good for the hill people today, "The misfortunes of poverty carry with them nothing harder to bear than that it exposes men to ridicule". Such exactly is the case of the poor people of Uttaranchal. They are poor, no doubt, but any pilgrim to Badri or Kedar must have noticed that they insist that the pious visitor has a cup of tea "on the house". These very pilgrims laugh at their vaivete and the common epithet for a Gharwali is "Mundu"—literally 'a dumb dodo'.

Even a great-visionary and modernite like, Jawaharlal Nehru, whose last wish was for his ashes to be immersed in the Ganges, could not or, as is generally believed by the literate population of the hills, was deliberately kept in ignorance of the potentiality of the region and its people. Ironically again the Frost lines from Nehurvian desk come to mind:

> "the hills are lovely, dark and deep
> And I have miles to go before I sleep".

though Ralph Hodgson is more direct and impersonal:

> "I stood upon that silent hill
> And stared at the sky until
> My eyes were blind with stars still."

The Ganga is by no means the largest river in the world but to the Hindu psyche it is a 'mother' symbol. Nehru was by no means or stretch of imagination a religious man but his emotional attachment to the holiest river in the world are evident:

> "the Ganga is beloved of her people round which are intertwined her racial memories, her hopes and fears, her songs of triumphs, her victories, and her defeats. She has been a symbol of India's age-long culture and civilization; ever charming, ever flowing and yet ever the same. She reminds me of the snow-covered peaks and the deep valleys of the Himalayas which I have loved so much and of the rich and vast plains below it."

For an eye opener the shocking injustice and the poverty of perhaps the richest region in the country is on the records. Whereas the per capita income of India is $ 330 Uttar Pradesh is poorer still with its per capita income of $120. Uttarakhand region is poorest amongst the poor with a per capita income of $80!

If this is the concept of social justice than even God's wrath will not be able to save the State or Central Government's boasting of the conept of social welfare. The hollow talk of the state Government being 'concerned' has become a joke in village Panchayats. Nobody thinks of the Gharwali farmer who has a private consumption of only Rs. 26 to 21 per month when the national poverty line is fixed at Rs. 85 per capita. These are sordid and unpalatable facts and most of them emanate from and pertain to the deliberate neglect of the area by the authorities. The sons of Himalayas, I am more than convinced, can any day put up a better show in a couple of years than any State Government with its indifferent and unwieldy bureaucracy. The fault therefore lies with the system. Uttar Pradesh in itself is a very unwieldy State. It is well nigh impossible for the Chief Minister or his team to visit the hills except during the pre-election period. The people of Uttarakhand are peace-loving and humble. The deforestation, the dam-dispute and the tourism trade exploitation, as well as the rape of the hills has been tolerated for a long time. They are not asking for the moon. All they demand is to manage the affairs of their region themselves. They have not asked for a separate state—though the Central Government should not hesitate to create one. For a gesture they must be given autonomy in the social, economic and political fields. Uttarakhand is simmering with discontent—more so everyday when the State Government takes away their revenue dues and the Central Government promptly creates States like Gorkhaland. The discontent of the highlanders from Dehradun to Nainital will soon erupt into angry violence (some signs are already visible). There is a popular saying amongst the hill folks that when you get angry dont break the head of your bullock but break the closest hillock. Once, and I strongly reiterate that, the Central Government take the initiative and shows wisdom in time. The current situation will be easily diffused. Otherwise the highlanders who know how to die laughingly for their country, will not hesitate to die for a better future for their children.

The Central Government has got a golden opportunity to evolve a model in which the smaller units would not be totally isolated from the main national stream and the developed industrial, financial, socio-economic and socio-cultural streams in accordance with their needs and traditions. Minority cultures are being encouraged to forge unbreakable linkages with the main stream of national aspirations and this should apply more to the depressed areas—particularly those which have suffered through neglect over a long span of time.

The Prime Minister Rao is a sensitive scholar. He takes his time but prefers to take decisions before the situation gets out of hand. If he moves in the right direction *vis-a-vis* Uttarakhand he will be adored by not only the folks of that area but the entire Uttar Pradesh.

Let him be aware of the dangerous pitfalls of 'masterly inactivity'. After all silence is not the mother tongue of the highlanders. It is about time when package deals are being doled to successionists and separarists that the silent serving ones should at least be given their due. Uttarakhand will be, unlike many States, a miniscule India. It will be an ideal amalgamation of all faiths, castes and creeds. We all are sitting on the crater of a volcano. The sooner the Central Government takes the initiative the better it will be for all concerned. Let us hope good sense prevails.

20

CONTEMPORARY REACTIONS AND RESPONSES FROM CROSS-SECTION OF SOCIETY

20.1 Uttarakhand: For Justice

"We want justice" cry the hill school-kids but the lessons of the past 30 years is that they will have to take it preferably by constructive sacrifice-since it will not be given easily.

The answer to the cry of "elitism" is that development flows from where the spenders go. Only with an environmentally conscious tourist industry can funds be raised to carry the war against want in the villages. Prophets of doom predict that an Uttarakhand State will be unviable, and it certainly would be if the past 30 years mood of fatalism were allowed to continue. The movement for an Uttarakhand hill State has been bandied amongst politicians but never took off owing to the extreme postures of its fractious leadership.

What the current reservation folly has fanned is the flame of pahari self-respect. Now overnight every-one in the hills—including those not born there feel they could do better on their own; that they have a stake in preserving their area's chief asset—its natural beauty.

Judging by public opinion there is enormous outrage that the Centre and the State Governments have used the hill environment for every-one's advantage except that of the locals. Whether it is schoolboys deprived of a job by Government policy, long-suffering local stone masons unemployed while outsiders build huge hotels, or retired infantrymen who gave the best years of their lives to uphold the honour of their nation, the feeling is different from the euphoria of 1963.

Its no use when you are poor clinging to old thought patterns. Instead of the traditional *neta* leadership the hills need managerial talents in marketing. Uttarakhand that seemed to have been served the *joker* in the pack (with an impossibly intimidating terrain for the easy removal of its poverty) overnight, thanks to the new consciousness, now seems to hold an ace.

Source: Bill Atiken, *Hindustan Times* (New Delhi), September 18, 1994

20.2 Politics and Uttarakhand's Underdevelopment

Will the creation of Uttarakhand State help remove the age-old poverty of this hilly region of the country? Leaving aside the job reservation politics about which much has been written, nobody has analysed the broad parameters of the economic development and the impediments thereof.

The Upper Ganga and the Jamuna spring from the mountains of Uttarakhand, a land rich in beauty and legends evocative of faith. This idyllic picture masks the sorrow of Uttarakhand: human impoverishment, decades of neglect, faulty land use patterns and inappropriate technologies that have ravaged the forests and soil to set in motion a process of erosion and destructive landslides, drying up of springs and the loss of fertility, income and employment, resulting in the migration of able-bodied men to the plains while their women-folk are condemned to a life of increasing privation and drudgery, trapped as they are in a vicious circle of economic deterioration and environment degradation.

Source : B.G. Verghese, *Deccen Chronicle*, September 31, 1994

20.3 The Uttarakhand Question

Is Separation Necessary?

The entire Himalayan region stretching from Arunachal to Kashmir comprises either State—Arunachal, Sikkim, Himachal and Kashmir—or autonomous regions like Gorkhaland, or nations such as Bhutan and Nepal. There is one exception—the eight mountain districts of Kumaon and Garhwal which are part of the huge State of Uttar Pradesh. The upsurge for Statehood in this area is as much part of the relentless logic of the political economy of such regions as of their cultural and ethnic exclusivity. What marks out Uttarakhand is not just its geography but its history, culture and social anthropology. It is not surprising, therefore, to find that the pattern of caste distribution turns out to be very different from that of the plains.....

The Best Course

Many arguments for Uttarakhand have had the element of sentimentalism, but the mountain people must examine their options in a dispassionate fashion and see what is the best for them as a community as a whole—upper castes, backward castes or dalits.....

Wider Implications

Mr. Narasimha Rao and his colleagues in New Delhi could not be bothered about the problems of a region that provides just five members to the Lok Sabha. Their worries, again quite short-term, relate to the coming elections in Andhra Pradesh and Karnataka. Their compulsion is to oppose any measure which can make them appear to be backing upper castes against the backwards or dalits. Even in the medium term, no Central Government can afford to look at the problem from the point of view of one region alone. Any decision with regard to the hill district of U.P. has implications for ongoing agitations in Bodoland and Jharkhand, not to speak of a dozen other regions where separatist feeling simmer below the surface.

In these circumstances the decks seem to be stacked against the Constitution of an Uttarakhand State at this juncture. It would be best perhaps if the Central leadership took the initiative and negotiated the formation of an autonomous hill council through an ordinance which could also incorporate a provision nullifying the clauses relating to the Mandal reservation in the hill districts.

There is little doubt that with an area of about 50,000 sq km and a population of 5.5 million, the region can be a viable State. But the issue of Statehood requires closer examination, given the specific political economy of the region. Protecting the political and cultural autonomy of the hill regions is only one aspect of the solution. Arguably the more important one is the ability of this unit to flourish and meet not just the emotional needs of its people, but their practical ones as well.

Source : Manoj Joshi, *Times of India* (New Delhi) September 20, 1994

20.4 Uttarakhand/Uttaranchal: In National Interest

Dr. Murli Manohar Joshi, former president of Bharatiya Janata Party and a Rajya Sabha M.P. from Uttar Pradesh visited hill areas in September

1994 and made the following observations in an interview with *organiser*:

"We are of the opinion that not less than 35 people have been killed (in police firing during Uttarakhand agitation in September, 1994)

The Mulayam Singh Government is falsely implicating BJP leaders. One BJP legislator, Shri Rajendra Singh Shah is facing trial under Section 302, while actually he was 6 km away from the scene of the incident, where the police had detained him

The Centre as well as the Mulayam Singh Government in U.P. are to blame. This situation has arisen because there is a clash of interests between the Centre and the U.P. Government. The Central Government is unwilling to create a separate State and the State Government does not want to stop the implementation of the 27 per cent reservation order in Uttarakhand. If the Centre agrees in principle to the creation of Uttaranchal State and Mulayam Singh holds the reservation order in obeyance till the creation of a separate State, the issue can be easily resolved.

The Central Government is afraid that if a separate State is created, the Congress will have no influence there. As the demand for a separate State was first made by the BJP when they were in power in U.P.; they had passed a resolution of a separate State. Even earlier the Janata Government had appointed a Cabinet Minister, who was from Jana Sangh , for the hill regions. If any work has been undertaken for the development of the hill areas, it is the Jana Sangh and the BJP who had done. Therefore, the Central Government fear that their party will be wiped out from the separate State, when it is formed.

This is not a new demand We, have been demanding it for many years. We consider this necessary for the development of the region and the security of the country. Uttaranchal region is contiguous with our international borders with Nepal and China. And this Himalayan region is no longer secure as it used to be. Moreover, the migration of youth from the region, if it continues, will leave only elderly people, women and children in Uttaranchal and the region will become sensitive from the security point of view.

Secondly, the region is important also from the economic angle. It is rich in natural resources, hydel potential and talent. The region needs special attention, given which it can progress economically. Therefore, the need for a separate State. The demand for the State is not based on language, caste or community but purely on national interest

Today, the region is being administered without taking into account its topography. *Gramsabhas* have been formed for every 1000 population, while in the hills 1000 people may be spread over 20 sq kms. For the most trivial things the people have to go to Lucknow or even Delhi to get official approval. This severely hampers developmental activity and as a result there is stark poverty and an alarming number of educated unemployed.

This region continues to be neglected as it is considered politically insignificant. Of the 425 seats in the U.P. Assembly, Uttaranchal is represented by just 19. But in spite of this, the people of the region have always been part of the national mainstream.

It is not correct that Uttaranchal will not be able to support it financially. The Himalayas have contributed to our culture and philosophy, our land is watered by the rivers rising from the Himalayas. We have exploited these resources but have not put back anything. It is the duty of the nation to preserve the Himalayas. In the initial stages, the State may need Central aid but the region is rich in natural resources and through the development of tourism and the pilgrim centres, the region can certainly support itself financially.

Just as there are Himachal and Arunachal, we have named it Uttaranchal. Then of course, the word *anchal,* is suggestive of material protection and security, whereas *Khand* is just a cut piece.

When there is a lot of resentment among the people, some elements always try to canalise it to their own purpose; but it has little impact.

This is the first instance where a resolution has been passed twice in an Assembly. The Centre now has no excuse for not accepting the resolution.

The agitation will continue, till Uttranchal is created.

If Mulayam Singh agrees to a separate State, he should leave the decision on reservation quotas to the new State. Every State forms its own reservation policy.

If they (the Congress) don't withdraw their support to the U.P. Government, the agitation will continue. Today only women, children and the aged remain in the villages, while the youth are migrating in search of jobs. When developmental activities are undertaken and jobs are created, this will stop, and with more habitation, security of the area will also grow. Besides, there are a large number of ex-servicemen there and the locals are brave, and patriotic people. That is why we want that proper conditions are created to encourage these people to stay on in the hills which will boost the security of that border region."

Source : Organiser (New Delhi), September 18, 1994

20.5 Uttarakhand: For Economic Reconstruction

B.K. Joshi, Director Giri Institute of Development Studies, Lucknow analyses the problem in the context of the 'retarded development' of

Uttarakhand.

"While more money for development is always welcome, no one—neither the Central Government (and the Planning Commission which allocates plan funds) nor the State Government, and nor indeed the people's representatives—has ever bothered to ask what happens to the money, and what is being achieved in regard to the living conditions of the ordinary people and the State of the regional economy.

The honest answer to such questions is indeed very simple but too stark and disturbing for the 'system' to contemplate: very little.

Indeed one could go a step further and claim that money has become a part of the problem rather than a part of the solution in Uttarakhand today. With so much money floating around, a few people have found an easy way of making a quick buck, what with the government system leaking like a sieve!

Money can solve problems only if some thought is given to drawing up an integrated plan of development based on (i) an understanding of the existing situation at the ground level especially the constraints, obstacles and opportunities for development, nature of the regional economy and society and their linkages with wider national economy, and (ii) on a vision of the future with clearly articulated goals and a set of strategies and programmes following from the goals in a logical manner.

Unfortunately the development plans for Uttarakhand fall short of these requirement" ....

The basic economic infirmity from which Uttarakhand suffers is structural in nature. Over 90 per cent of the population in six districts which are exclusively hilly (i.e., excluding Dehradun and Nainital), is rural. Over 80 per cent of the total population in these districts is dependent on agriculture for its sustenance and livelihood.

The secondary sector is virually non-existent in much of the region except in certain favourably located and well endowed area like the Nainital Terai and the Doon Valley. Agriculture, outside of these latter areas, is largely a subsistence activity.

It has been estimated that less than two per cent of the cultivating households sell any part of their foodgrain production in the market. A vast majority cannot produce enough for their own needs. Hence they have to purchase the rest.

Thus most of the rural households need a secondary occupation and source of income.

Money Order Economy

Various survival mechanisms have been adopted by the people over the years. One of the most widely used is migration by one or a few members of the household to the plains in search of employment and remittance of money back home. This has led to the application of 'money order economy', being applied to the hilly economy.....

The approach to planning and development adopted so far in Uttarakhand has not addressed itself in any meaningful sense to these issues, especially overcoming or transcending the basic structural weakness of the regional economy.

The expenditure of large sums of money in such a situation has a number of consequences, most of them undesirable.

For one, the productive sectors of the economy—agriculture and allied activities and industry, especially manufacturing—remain weak and undeveloped. The tertiary sector grows out of proportion to the growth of the productive sector.

Two, the economy produces very little for reinvestment in productive activities so the process of deepening of the economic base hardly takes places. The little investment that does take place goes either into unproductive areas (real estate) or into the service sector (especially) passenger transportation.

Three, while the productive base of the economy stagnates, the consumer economy fuelled by import of goods from outside the region flourishes.

Four, more than four-fifth of the people, who are locked into the subsistence economy do not derive any tangible benefits.

Source: Hindustan Times, (New Delhi), September 19, 1994

20.6 Viability of the Hill State

The reservation issue inflames passions, but the viability of a hill State remains doubtful.

Whether Uttarakhand will work as a State is anybody's guess. A new State must have bankable resources. And the hill districts, lacking industrialisation or even arable land, have only forests and tourism as sources of revenue. While forests have limited potential for revenue generation, tourism generates finance only for the local populace. Also, tourism is a sector where any kind of cess is determental. Besides the hill State will have to meet the costs of establishing a separate State.

For now, tensions can be defused by creating a separate administrative hill council for Uttarakhand. The council could also study the delimination of the hill constituencies for better representation in the Vidhan Sabha. But past experience, as in Darjeeling, is that hill councils can be controversial. Indeed, that has forced the Centre to think twice before awarding similar status to Jharkhand. Finally, the idea of splitting bigger States on the basis of caste, religion or even economic criteria could open a Pandora's box in the rest of the country."

Source : Charu Lata Joshi and Dilip Awasthi, *India Today*, September 30, 1994

20.7 Mulayam Singh's Stakes

The month-long agitation in Uttarakhand is reminiscent of the anti-Mandal agitation during V.P. Singh's regime. The stir that originated in the hills has now spread to nearly 20 of the State's 65 districts and threatens to engulf the whole of Uttar Pradesh. And like the former Prime Minister, Mulayam is showing a hidebound cussedness and gearing up for a long drawn-out battle.

Not surprising, since Mulayam's every move is made with an eye on the next elections, which, as the head of a minority government, he knows could come any day. In a State in which the OBCs account for 37 per cent of the population—half of the Yadavs—Mulayam knows it will pay to woo a wider audience than he did in 1991 when his 'Maulana Mulayam' image saw the BJP ride to power on a Hindu wave. That explains his search for a new and larger combination that seeks the support of the OBCs and Muslims and the backing of a reasonable number of the State's 22 per cent Dalit voters that his alliance partner Kanshi Ram brought alone with him last time.

And Uttarakhand has since turned out to be the ideal testing ground for the new strategy for the simple reason that Mulayam has no stakes in the region. His SP won just one of the 19 seats in the region where the OBC and Muslim presence is minimal with the rest going to the Congress (I) and the BJP. As such Mulayam knows he need fear no backlash there. By doing this, Mulayam has thrown the ball right back into his opponents' court, putting the Congress (I) and the BJP in a position where both have to prove their ability to check the Mulaym juggernaut.

Source : Dilip Awasthi and Zafer Agha, *India Today*, September 30, 1994

20.8 Mulayam Singh's Strategy

U.P. Chief Minister Mulayam Singh Yadav today (September 21, 1994) took one more step to consolidate his position among the powerful Jats of Western U.P. by conceding a series of demands of the Bharatiya Kisan Union (BKU), headed by its enigmatic leader Mahendra Singh Tikait.

Mr. Yadav, who had a two-hour meeting with Mr Tikait heading a six-member BKU delegation, announced that his Government would withdraw all criminal cases pending in various courts against the farmers and BKU leaders in connection with BKU agitations. Orders to this effect would be issued to all the district magistrates to move the appropriate courts for the withdrawal of criminal cases.

After his pro-reservation statewide bandh on September 13, 1994, which was an attempt to consolidate the OBC vote bank, Mr. Yadav addressed a mammoth farmers' rally, sponsored by the BKU and Mr. Tikait at Sisauli in Muzaffarnagar district on September 14, 1994. Mr. Tikait had described Mr. Yadav at that meeting as the true successor of the late Chaudhary Charan Singh, whose Jat support helped him to become the Prime Minister, though for a short spell.

Referring to the demand of rebate on the electricity bills for tubewells for one year from April 1, 1987 to March 31, 1988, the Chief Minister announced that all the farmers would be given this rebate not only on the electricity bills but the farmers would also be given rebate on surcharge of electricity bills even though six years have elapsed.

The Chief Minister said that all those farmers who had not been given the rebate on electricity bills with surcharge subject to a maximum concession of Rs. 10,000 for a period of 20 months from April 1, 1988 to November 30, 1989, would be extended this concession afresh. The step is unprecedented as the concession of Rs. 10,000 to defaulters is being offered with retrospective effect.

Mr. Yadav conceded another demand relating to waiving off of electricity surcharge on the farmers for the period of February 1, 1991 to November 20, 1993 (a total of two years and 10 months).

He also offered another concession in the form of extending the period of payment of arrears of electricity bills for this period. The arrears of two years and 10 months were to be paid by the farmers till September 30, 1994, which Mr. Yadav has now extended to January 31, 1995.

Source: Hindustan Times (New Delhi), September 22, 1994.

20.9 Bandh, Agitation and Condemnation of Police Firing

It is alleged that several protestors against the policy of 27 per cent reservation in the hill areas, were killed and hundreds infured in police firings and *lathi charges* in Khatima (Nainital) Mussori and Puri Districts. Thousands of protestors are said to have been rounded up, *Curfew* was imposed in various hill areas and all educational institutions remained closed for several days. Several Organisation supporting the Uttarakhand movement have condemned the police firing on anti-reservationists.

20.10 Rights Violation Probe

Kashi Singh Aeri of the Uttarakhand Kranti Dal, which is spear heading the movement in U.P. hills stated on September 21, 1994 that the National Human Rights Commission has conceded their demand for a probe into complaints of human rights violation in the hill districts.

Source: Hindustan Times (New Delhi), September 22, 1994.

20.11 CBI Report into Violence at Allahabad High Court

Central Bureau of Investigation (CBI) Chief K. Vijay Rama who led a 15 member team to probe incidence of violence in the Allahabad High Court premises on September 13, submitted his report to the Supreme Court on September 22, 1994. Mr. Rama Rao was appointed as an independent commissioner on the Court's behalf. Pro-reservationists had gone on a rampage during the September 13, *bandh,* stormed into the High Court premises and vandalised the Chamber of Justice S.S.Sodhi.

Several advocates and members of the High Court Staff were injured in the violence and the subsequent police lathi-charge and firing.

Justice Sodhi summoned the Army when State police failed to protect members of the bench and the bar.

In a complaint to Chief Justice of India M.N. Venkatachaliah, Justice Sodhi said police had connived with the vandals.

The Supreme Court, taking a serious view of the matter, treated it as an assault on the judiciary.

While directing the CBI chief to personally investigate the September 13, incidents and submit his report in a sealed cover within a week, the Supreme Court had fixed September 22, for further hearing in the matter.

CBI team had recorded the Statements of at least 275 people, including judges, politicians, journalists, lawyers, police, administration officers and other eyewitnesses.

The CBI team also collected photos and other material of evidentiary value.

The investigators also visited the officers of local newspapers and collected copies of newspapers dated September 13 and 14 and the negatives of photographs of the incidents.

CBI Additional Director Arun Bhagat, who also accompanied the CBI chief, talked to the Uttar Pradesh Chief Secretary on telephone regarding the incidents in the Allahabad High Court premises.

The CBI stored all the information collected in computers specially taken to Allahabad for the purpose.

The Supreme Court indicated that the purpose of inquiry into the ugly happenings at the Allahabad High Court premises on September 13 was not to destablise the Mulayam Singh Government but to prevent recurrences of such incidents in future and punish officials for their lapses. The judges of the Supreme Court appreciated the work done by the CBI Director and his team of officers and said "we place on record our deep sense of appreciation at the prompt and efficient execution of its function". The court appointed the Solicitor-General Mr. Deepankar Gupta, to assist the court to come to a decision as to whether, a *prima facie,* contempt had been made out against any of the police officials and also to act as the prosecutor.

Source : Hindustan Times (New Delhi), September 20, 22, and 23, 1994.

20.12 Union Territories Status of Uttarakhand

Though the spirit of the Mandal Commission cannot be questioned, this movement highlights the discrepancies and flaws in the existing reservation policy. It, therefore, provides scope for re-examination. If necessary, special clauses may be incorporated for the hills.

So far, the Centre has not played a very positive role and has shown total apathy towards this movement. Is the Centre waiting for some more killings to take place? It is high time it acted and stopped weighing the political gains and possibilities.

It is a question of the future of the people of Uttarakhand. The schools, colleges and universities have remained closed for the last one month. All social activities have come to a standstill. People are feeling ignored by the Centre's numbness.

Though an independent State cannot be formed today itself the Centre can at least provide a solution by providing Union Territory status. Union Territory status would not only be able to bail out Mulayam Singh Yadav but also save the energy of the youth of this area and restore their lost faith.

Source: Hindustan Times (New Delhi), September 12, 1994

20.13 Uttarakhand Movement may Continue

The Uttarakhand issue has taken the shape of a people's movement and it will continue till the formation of a separate hill State.

In an informal talk with newsmen Bharatiya Janata Party member of Parliament, Major General Bhuvan Chandra Khanduri, after his release from the Central Jail, said the people were themselves coming out of their homes and actively participating in the movement.

He said in the 48 years of country's independence there had been no development of hill districts while other States of Himalaya have made tremendous progress. There were natural resources in the eight hill districts of Uttar Pradesh and after formation of a separate State we would exploit them which would help development.

He said there were a large number of army personnel in these districts and they had shed blood for the nation. They were patriotic as the people of other districts in the country.

Mr. Khanduri warned that if the repression by the State Government continued, they would be forced to take up arms which would be most unfortunate for the country. He alleged that to crush the Uttarakhand movement, the police had opened fire on the peaceful people and even women were not spared.

Criticising Uttar Pradesh Chief Minister Mulayam Singh Yadav's role in this movement, Mr. Khanduri said that his actions were shameful for a cultured society. He said that our movement was not against reservation but for the formation of separate hill State. He also alleged that the Central Government was also extending support to the anti people State government in U.P..

Source: The Pioneer (Lucknow), September 19, 1994

20.11 Caste Loyalties

Politicians, who are used to playing the cards of casteism to strengthen their vote bank, are unaware of the psyche of the people of the area and want to crush the movement through force. Mulayam Singh has provoked the peaceful and non-violent movement. The senseless killings of innocent people at Khatima and Mussoorie show the callous attitude of the administration. If the administration does not change its attitude, many more precious lives could be sacrificed. If we analyse the events, it clearly points to a plan of the administration to crush the movement by any means.....

Though the spirit of the Mandal Commission cannot be questioned, this movement highlights the discrepancies and flaws in the existing reservation policy. It, therefore, provides scope for re-examination. If necessary, special clauses should be incorporated for the hills. So far, the Centre has not played a very positive role and has shown total apathy towards the movement. It is a question of the future of the people of Uttarakhand. The schools, colleges and universities have remained closed for the last one month. All social activities have come to a standstill. People are feeling ignored by the Centre's numbness. As it is, the politics of reservations has accelerated and intensified caste confrontations in North India. During the last 47 years, multiple social constituencies have been mobilised on the basis of primordial loyalties. However, the new phase of caste politics is fundamentally different from the early post-Independence political process in India. First, the Congress evolved a coalition of high caste Hindus, Scheduled Castes and Scheduled Tribes to win elections. The Congress system of a "patron and client" caste coalition did not target castes outside its coalitional politics.

The champions of reservations have mobilised the upwardly mobile backward peasant castes by targeting the upper caste domination which is presented as a historical fact of Indian society. The "new caste politics" is confrontational because it is situated in the philosophy of "undoing the cruelties of history" whose present representatives and custodians are upper caste Hindus, irrespective of their economic status. Such a mobilisation of caste in politics has been built around "hatred" and the manageable levels of social violence. This has been happening during the last four years of caste politics and is a definite break from the earlier phase of Indian politics. Second, the Congress system, while winning the elections on the basis of a "caste coalition", did not govern the country on the basis of mere caste factors. A political party mediates and harmonises conflicting and competing social interests after winning elections because the government stands for the whole society.

It is true that such neutral governance is a "pure model" but a ruling party by definition is "relatively autonomous" of its specific social support structure. The Janata Dals or the Samajwadi Party on the other hand are not political formations of an autonomous character. They are mere instruments in the hands of the elite of their castes. This is a casteisation of politics where the upwardly mobile backward peasant castes and the elite of the other Dalit castes are not mere voters; they are the rulers. The only yardstick of governmental performance in Uttar Pradesh and Bihar is the successful promotion and protection of specific caste interests. Laloo Prasad Yadav and Mulayam Singh have to show to their caste supporters that their governments are openly practising policies of discrimination against the so-called upper castes.

Those who believe in the progressive potential of backward castes in democratic politics in India can be traced to Ram Manohar Lohia's "Asian model". Many caste reform movements have been in existence in India and they have exercised great influence over social change in various regions of the country. But caste mobilisation for elections to change peasant India for egalitarianism was Ram Manohar Lohia's contribution. It is not without reason that Mulayam Singh claims legitimacy from Ram Manohar Lohia in spite of the lact that so-called socialists like Sharad Yadav, Ram Vilas Paswan, or Laloo Prasad have caricatured Ram Manohar Lohia by ignoring his complex social philosophy. And that too without answering some important questions about the serious limitations of the Lohia model.

First, Ram Manohar Lohia was extremely marginal in Indian politics because the Congress's caste coalition was more successful in gradually changing Indian society. Second, many progressive socialist contemporaries of Ram Manohar Lohia did not accept his diagnosis or analysis as relevant for India. His claim that the backward peasant castes have the potential of causing progressive change in India was a non-starter even when he was alive. Charan Singh, the most conscious caste and class leader of the upwardly mobile peasants, never practised caste exclusivism. The current caste leaders cannot appropriate even the politics of Charan Singh because he imbibed some values of the national movement and dissociated himself from Ram Manohar Lohia.

Ethnic politics in India has the same dangers as caste politics. Leaders strengthen ethnicism and casteism because their universe is limited and only confrontations can bring political dividents. In the process, neither is caste weakened nor can it be used for social harmony and governance.

Source: Fazal Mehmood, *Amrit Bazar Patrika* (Calcutta), September 21, 1994.

20.15 Beijing is nearer to us than Delhi, say Uttarakhandis

The situation in Uttarakhand is worsening day by day and people of the hills are finding it difficult to survive because of exorbitant hike in the prices of essential commodities including the wheat flour.

The new slogan coined by the protagonists of the Uttarakhand State *Beijing nazdeek hai aur Dilli door hai* (Beijing is nearer to us than Delhi). The slogan rented the air on the Himalayan top towns during the last several days.

The report reaching suggest that the situation is going out of hands of the local administration and the people are hell bent to fight for their rights once and for all. The wheat flour is being sold for over Rs. 16 per kg in the Kumaon hills. The situation is the same in the districts of

Garhwal division.

The transport system has been affected with the result that essential commodities are not being made available in the hill towns. The people of the plains living in the hills have already started feeling insecure. Government employees working in different projects in the hill districts have started seeking transfers back to the plains.....

The students agitation hints that there might be no session this year as the possibility of the reopening of schools appears bleak because of the surcharged atmosphere.

The agitation by the anti-reservationists in the hills is not getting any support by people living in the Terai and the foothills of the proposed Uttarakhand State. The population in these areas consist mostly of Muslims, Sikhs, Dalits and backwards. A sizable chunk of the population is for reservation and also against the carving out of separate State.

These people feel that if a separate State is created, the law and order situation will worsen and there is the danger of the region being used as a safe haven by foreign powers for disruptive activities.

The people in the Terai are seriously considering of forming a separate organisation to counter the move of the hill people for the creation of a separate State. They strongly believe that the entire agitation in the hill districts has been fuelled by foreign powers who are interested in the division of the country by creating anarchy.

A huge amount of cannabis that is grown in the Himalayan range is smuggled to the West through these borders and this is how the economy of the hill people gets going, a report from the directorate of revenue intelligence suggests.

Source : Asian Age (New Delhi), September 21, 1994

20.16 Uttarakhand Movement Hogs Political Limelight

The Uttarakhand movement has suddenly brought Uttar Pradesh, the most populous State of the country, to the centre-stage of the Indian political scene. The movement for a separate hill State in the picturesque hill districts on the northern border has become a political focal point, all the more because of inter-wining of the movement for a separate hill State with that for anti-OBC reservation.

A word about Uttarakhand. An attraction for tourists worldwide, the northern part of U.P. comprising districts of Pithoragarh, Almora, Nainital, Dehradun, Uttarakashi, Chamoli, Tehri and Pauri, is known for its socio-economic backwardness despite being rich in natural resources. These districts mostly provided domestic servants, class IV employees to homes and offices in plains in Uttar Pradesh as well as beyond its borders, and, of course recruits for the Army...

Politically speaking, the area used to be a stronghold of the Congress but the scene has changed in the nineties. All the four Lok Sabha seats from the eight hill districts have gone to the BJP and out of the total 19 MLAs, 10 are shared by the BJP, six by the Congress and one each by the ruling SP and local UKD while one is Independent.

It was the political complexion of the hill districts that made many feel that Chief Minister Mulayam Singh Yadav's circular to enforce 27 per cent reservation in educational institutions was a calculated move with partisan political objectives in mind. He promptly got the U.P. Assembly to adopt a resolution unanimously favouring formation of Uttarakhand and thus passed the buck on the Union Government and deftly delinked the Uttarakhand demand from the reservation issue which SP-BSP would like to keep in focus.

Mulayam Singh, with this approach, has nothing to lose in the hill districts whereas it enables him to consolidate his socio-political base in the area where he has political stakes. Moreover, the Ayodhya issue has been relegated into the background, and the SP-BSP clash, which has been a demoralising element for the Chief Minister, too has gone out of focus...

Views are sharply divided on this issue in the Congress with U.P. Congress Chief N.D. Tewari wanting the High Command to allow the State party to forthwith withdraw its support to the Mulayam Singh Government. A section of the High Command, not very vocally, is lending support to the UPCC resolution in this regard. They seem to project that U.P. political scene has undergone transformation after Mr. Tewari's takeover as UPCC chief and that the State policy has already been polarised as between Mr. Mulayam Singh Yadav and Mr. N.D. Tewari.

The other opinion in the Congress would not like to take a narrow view of the developments in Uttar Pradesh whether pertaining to reservation or even the Allahabad High Court episode. However, it would not like to take any step which may further alienate the party from the backwards, scheduled castes and even the minorities, not only in U.P. but more so beyond its borders.

What is more significant is that to register its point emphatically, the supporters of "delinking" line are trying to project that the Congress President was ignoring the party organisation in the northern States in order to keep the challengers (N.D. Tewari being one of them) at bay...

The U.P. Congress under the leadership of former Chief Minister Narain Datt Tewari unanimously decided to withdraw Congress support to the Mulayam Government, which seemed to put the State Government under Mulayam Singh in jeopardy. But the Congress High Command has still not responded favourably to the U.P. Congress resolution and understandably so. The Congres central leadership is still undecided though its tilt favours the Mulayam Government.

For one thing, the Congress High Command cannot be oblivious of the fact that Mulayam Government as of today can manage the needed 212 votes in the State Assembly on its own in a House of 425 (SP-BSP together command 198, while 3 seats are vacant) and will be able to survive even if the Congress withdraws support.

But, in reality, the Congress High Command is more worried about the likely implications of the issues involved in the U.P. scene of today for other States, and the fallout for the national scene. Having worked strenuously not to appear to be anti-reservations in so far as other backward castes are concerned, can it now allow itself to be considered against reservation for the OBCs? It can ill-afford to ignore the likely implications thereof in the Assembly elections scheduled in December this year and again in February next year. Hence the Centre's vacillations...

For the BJP in U.P., Uttarakhand may appear to be a blessing in disguise but it too faces an uphill task. The Ram Janmabhoomi wave does not exist any more. And, the Uttarakhand coupled with anti-reservation stir can drive OBCs away from it, the BJP would like to avoid such a pitfall. Like the Congress, the BJP too has to weigh the implications of the developments in U.P., for other States slated for election sooner or later

Source: Narendra Sharma, *Patriot* (New Delhi), September 22, 1996

20.17 Call to Boycott Elections in Hills

Sixty three local action committees from the Alaknanda Valley converged on to the banks of the river to mark the beginning of a new phase of the separate State movement, even as the popular support to the movement continues unabated.

In terms of number, the participation in today's (September 21, 1994) rally was relatively low as compared to the Pauri rally of September 2, but it was well organized with a systematic declaration of a long-term and short-term programme of agitation.

"The conveners declared a boycott of all elections in the hills, starting with the forthcoming panchayat and nagarpalika elections. The people of Uttarakhand have no use for legislators," the spokesman of the reorganizing committee said. Elected representatives, who have allegedly failed to live up to the expectations of the people are being called upon to resign *en masse*.

Dr. S.P. Sati outgoing convener handed over a memorandum to the district administration to be forwarded to the Centre. Besides, the primary demand for a separate State, the memorandum demands release of all those arrested in connexion with the agitation and compensations of Rs. 5 lakhs and Rs. 1 lakh respectively to the families of those killed and injured at Khatima and Mussoorie...

It is by now amply clear that students continue to play decisive role in the agitation although the separate State movement has taken primacy over the quota stir.

The indefinite strike sponsored by the Parvateeya Karmachari Sangathan demanding a separate hill State, continued for the second day in the entire hill districts.

Rallies and protest demonstrations were held to press for the demand of a separate hill State. All Government institutions barring the Jal Sansthan, hospitals, and some other emergency services remained paralyzed...

Mr. Kanshi Singh Aeri, President of the Uttarakhand Kranti Dal and convener of the recently formed Uttrakhand Joint Action Committee, told a Press conference that the people of the hill districts will also boycott the panchayati polls in the State.

To ensure complete success of the boycott, a total bandh would be observed in the hills during the period of nominations. Delimitation of the Panchayat on the basis of area instead of population was not acceptable to the hill people.

Mr. Aeri hoped that the Uttarakhand agitation will soon develop a central leadership, which will have representation of all political parties and other organizations supporting the agitation. He said all political parties including the Congress and Samajwadi Party were represented in the newly formed Uttarakhand Joint Action Committee, adding that only the BJP had chosen to keep out.

Source : The Statesman, (New Delhi), September 22, 1994

20.18 A Mass Upsurge

Never before have the hills of western U.P. reverberated in such unison with the peoples' voice as they are now. From the picturesque vales of Dehra Dun to the inhospitable upper reaches of the Garhwal hills, the cry for fulfilment of just aspirations has taken the form of a demand for a separate State.

It is a virtual mass movement on a scale, perhaps unparalleled in the recent past. From young boys, barely in their teens to old men and women, from the educated youth in the towns and cities to remote village folk, from State Government employees and teachers to long forgotten ex-servicemen, everybody has joined hands in a vociferous reaction to what they feel has been long years of deliberate marginalisation...

What initially began as a student stir against the reservation policy has now turned into a full-fledged movement for a separate State of Uttarakhand within which the former issue has been submerged...

The rapidity with which the movement spread from Pauri to the entire region encompassing the Garhwal and Kumaon Divisions is a manifestation of the high levels of alienation with the rulers in Lucknow, latent within the hill people. In a region known for its backwardness and dubbed as the 'money-order' economy because of its dependence on remittances of the menfolk working outside, the announcement of the reservation policy was the last straw that broke the camel's back.

Admits District Magistrate Pauri, Mr. Bhupendra Singh, "The agitation has gradually turned into a mass movement and not a day passes here without a procession or a rally in support of a separate State." According to another official in Pauri, the rally held here on September 2, saw the participation of over a lakh people from different parts of the region, the biggest ever in the town...

Says Shanti Devi Nautiyal, a member of the Uttarakhand Joint Action Council in Rishikesh, "Most menfok are away working in various jobs outside the region and many students have been picked up by the administration, leaving the women the task of carrying the movement forward."

"Women here have traditionally been very active and participated willingly in earlier movements in the region such as the Chipko movement of the early 70s and the movement for prohibition later and this is a much more sensitive issue which involves the future of the coming generations", she adds.

What is ominous is the increasing restlessness among the ex-servicemen in the area who comprise a sizeable chunk of the population—around four lakh, according to one estimate. The last one month has witnessed an unprecedented mobilisation of these retired soldiers.

Both officers and soldiers have joined the movement for Uttarakhand and the police firings on agitators in Khatima and Mussoorie recently has left put them in a belligerent mood. Says Colonel U.S. Negi, who retired from the services recently, "So far the movement has been conducted in a peaceful manner but if repression goes on, then the ex-servicemen here who have served the country loyally could be forced to take hard decisions."

Source : Sanjiv Sinha, *Indian Express* (New Delhi), September 22, 1994

20.19 Uttarakhandis should Accept HDC as First Step: Ghising

The Uttarakhandis should not renege from their demand for a separate State and must turn their agitation into a 'do-or-die' movement in order tó ensure that they are no longer exploited by people from the plains.

Stating this to the *Economic Times* Mr. Subhas Ghising, President of the GNLF and Chairman of Darjeeling Gorkha Hill Development Council, expressed his party's 'complete solidarity' with the Uttarakhand movement.

> "We support their demand for a separate State and are prepared to extend all cooperation towards realisation of the demand," Mr. Ghising said.

Cautioning the "brothers of Garhwal and Kumaon" against accepting the offer of a Hill Development Council, on the lines of DGHDC, Mr. Ghising said, "The Hill Development Council (HDC) offer is nothing but an escape route which the Union Government adopts in order to suppress the real aspirations of the region."

The Gorkha leader was of the view that the HDC formula makes a joke of the peoples' demand for autonomy. "I have been heading the DGHDC for over five years now, but we have to still listen to the dictates of the State Government," he said, while complaining against development funds for the Hill Development Council being routed through the State government.

Besides, Mr Ghising felt that real autonomy cannot be achieved unless the Home Department is also transferred to the Hill Development Council.

Asked what should the Uttarakhandis do if their demand for a separate State is not accepted by the Central Government, Mr Ghising said, "Like us, they should then adopt the strategy of accepting the Hill Development Council as a first step towards realisation of the ultimate goal of Statehood."

Mr. Ghising wants the people of Uttarakhand to accept the HDC formula only if the Central Government agrees to constitute two separate Hill Development Council— "one for the Garhwal region and the other for Kumaon."

"This would ensure de-centralisation of power in the vast hill tracts as well as creation of more jobs for the hill people", he said, wondering "why shouldn't thier demand be conceded when every hill region of the Himalaya range enjoys autonomy?"...

He hoped the Samajwadi Party—Bahujan Samaj Party government will not make the mistake which the Left Front government made in West Bengal while dealing with the Gorkhaland movement.

Source: Kamaljeet Rattan, *Economic Times* (New Delhi), September 22, 1994.

20.20 Uttarakhand Becoming Irresistible

If the creation of Uttarakhand as a separate State comprising the existing eight districts of Garhwal and Kumaon helps to end the present economic exploitation by outsiders, the current agitation would seem to be justified. But there is more to the agitation in favour of Uttarakhand than economies alone. There is a substantial element of politics behind the demand for separate Statehood which, seen in purely economic terms, has been fanned recently by the proposed imposition of 'reservations' and 'quotas'. But we should not ignore the ambitions of local politicians or those who would like to get into the highly profitable sport of politics in the future.

Just think of what a separate State of 59 lakh people would mean to those who see no chance of becoming political leaders in a vast and highly competitive ocean of humanity called Uttar Pradesh. To start with, there would be a separate Vidhan Sabha of, say, even 30 or 40 members, and the power, perks and status that go with such membership. Take, then, the advantages of a separate government, howsoever small in size, and the joys and benefits of becoming a Minister. A separate government secretariat and other offices would also provide more jobs for local educated boys and girls.

Uttarakhand would then be squarely on the map of India as a regional entity with a name and place of its own. The word 'pahari', often used with a trace of contempt by people in the plains for the denizens of the hills, would cease to have its present lowly status, and the Garhwalis and Kumaonis would come into their own as worthy of respect and recognistion. These are no small considerations for people who—the Garhwalis more than the Kumaonis—have come to be known in the plains of the northern parts of the country mostly as domestic servants and chowkidars.

It is strange (isn't it?) that we in the plains seldom think of the Garhwalis and the Kumaonis for their martial qualities, with special regiments of their own and regimental centre, respectively, at Lansdowne and Ranikhet. The two fighting groups have produced some fine soldiers both in the officer and other ranks. And let us remember, too, that the present Chief of Army Staff is a Kumaoni named B.C. Joshi with the rank of a four-star general...

Nor have the political leaders of the proposed Uttarakhand done too badly for themselves in the past. Between them, Garhwal and Kumaon have already provided three Chief Ministers of U.P., and all three also held important positions at the Centre in their time. Govind Ballabh Pant was Cheif Minister of his home State and Home Minister in the Union Cabinet, although his high status was not limited to ministerial office alone H.N. Bahuguna was Chief Minister of U.P. as also a Cabinet Minister at the centre. So was N.D. Tiwari whose portfolios in Delhi included Finance, External Affairs, Industry and Planning.

We must not forget K.C. Pant either. Now Chairman of the Finance Commission, he has held several ministerial posts in Delhi before this. Among other important politicians from Kumaon who made good was the late P.C. Joshi, the Communist Leader, whose contribution to the growth of his own party is now a matter of history. Incidentally, did you know that Begum Liaquat Ali Khan, wife of the first Prime Minister of Pakistan, was also a Pant, although a member of the Christian Community? Our Pakistani neighbours may not wish to recall this fact, but it is worth putting on record even as a piece of gossip....

Outside the realm of politics the Uttarakhand region has produced quite a few civil servants with meritorius records as administrators. The Pants and Pandes head that list and there have also been several Joshis in positions of importance both within and outside U.P. It must be admitted though that Kumaon has enjoyed a clear edge over Garhwal in the area of government service in the past. In both Kumaon and Garhwal, however, the high jobs have gone to the upper castes which is probably one of the pointers to the existing social structure of the region.

Is there really an Uttarakhand in the making in the currently oversized U.P.? Going by the strength and passion behind the present agitation, the move to carve out a separate State is becoming irresistible by the day. Although the Congress has not yet taken a categorical stand in the matter, the BJP is strongly in favour of Uttaranchal (which is its own title for Uttarakhand) and Mulayam Singh, whose coalition government enjoys little support from the region, does not seem to care.

Talk about the danger of 'balkanising' India if new States are created out of the present geographical map of India should not be dismissed as unwarranted fear. We already have a potential Jharkhand on our hands, and both Vidarbha and Marathwada are waiting for a chance to acquire formal recognition as separate units. Certain other parts of the country could also conceivably start thinking on the same lines in due course. There is, however, no reason to panic. But our political leaders must show the necessary sagacity to deal effectively with regional grievances and aspirations and not allow these to be turned into controversies for short-term electrical gains.

Source : Prem Bhatia, *Tribune* (Chandigarh), September 23, 1994

20.21 Mulayam's Belligerence

Mr. Mulayam Singh Yadav's handling of the anti-reservation agitation in the Uttar Pradesh hills, especially his call for a retaliatory State-wide bandh... suggests a reversion to the belligerence that characterised his earlier stint as Chief Minister. After his exit in 1991 following a rather costly stand-off with the champions of the temple movement, it was widely believed that he had realised the dangers of arousing passions beyond a point...

... Mr. Yadav appears to have forgotten that he is fighting not just his political rivals, but a section of his own people. It is, indeed, even possible that what appears convenient to him now as a political ploy will turn in the long run into an endemic problem, an eventuality no Chief Minister, however committed he is to his special group of supporters, can afford. Mr Yadav's opponents, for their part, must realise that no State Government can be compelled to be selective in its enforcement of policies. In the circumstances, the only solution to the contentious question lies perhaps in carving out a separate hill state. In the years since the States Reorganisation Committee submitted its report, Haryana has separated from Punjab and Assam has split. But U.P. has always resisted such attempts, despite its unwieldy size and huge population, although those advocating its division included such men as K.M. Panniker and Charan Singh. The main reason for this was the fierce opposition to the idea from the Congress which recognised the clout that an undivided U.P. commanded. In recent years with simultaneous campaigns for separate States picking up, the party's stand has understandably hardened. On the other hand, the peculiarities of the U.P. hill, with 60 per cent of its villages without water or electricity and less than 15 per cent of the land suitable for cultivation, dictate that the region be treated with considerable sensitiveness, a requirement only a separate State can fulfil.

Source: Times of India (New Delhi), September 10, 1994, editorial

20.22 The New State

The perception in the plains, especially in Lucknow, the State capital, is that the agitation is being stoked by the BJP. In reality, however, the movement cuts across party lines assuming the character of a mass upsurge with students forming the core. Rallying behind them are government employees, teachers, lawyers and even local businessmen, who are united in their struggle for a separate State and rejection of the OBC quota.

"We are agitating under the banner of the Uttarakhand Samyukta Sangharsh Samiti (USSS) which brings together diverse pro-Uttarakhand forces," says S.P. Sati, a geologist and the movement's chief coordinator in the Garhwal region. USSS activists deny any political affiliation and insist that parties are free to join the front only if they lend unconditional support to the USSS' twin demands: withdrawal of the OBC quota and creation of a hill state...

The agitators are not keen to let the national parties steal the initiative. "They have too many interests to look after and tend to compromise easily," says Yogendra Singh Negi, ex-president of Garhwal University in Srinagar (Pauri Garhwal)....

But how serious is the situation in the hills? While Chief Minister Mulayam Singh would like to dismiss the unrest as a BJP-engineered stir to nettle his government, officials in the hills concede that the agitation, which begin spontaneously, is spreading like wildfire. "It's alarming," said Pauri's Superintendent of Police Devendra Singh Chauhan, who confessed that the administration just didn't have enough force to contain the stir.

That the Uttarakhand issue has at last struck the right chord after several false starts, was evident when women came out in large numbers. In Musoorie, they led a pro-Uttarakhand demonstration on 2 September and three of them were killed when police opened fire. The next day, women squatted on roads in several places, blocking vehicular traffic in protest against the killings....

Interestingly, the USSS is not against reservation as such. Indeed the agitationists say they do not mind the 23 per cent quota for the SC/STs. "But what's the point of a 27 per cent reservation for OBCs when their number doesn't exceed two per cent of the population?" asked a teacher. "The quota structure must take into account a region's demographic pattern and should not be determined by political exigencies", he said. Of the 60 lakh people in Uttarakhand, 80 per cent belong to two upper castes as against the national average of 13.

Although the hill region has produced three Chief Ministers — G.B. Pant, H.N. Bahuguna and N.D. Tiwari — over time, the people harbour a deep sense of neglect...

Ironically, Kashmiri militants had tried to prevent devotees from going on their annual pilgrimage to Amarnath, in Kashmir, this July; now devout Garhwali Hindus have shut off the Kedarnath shrine.

Yet, Mulayam Singh Yadav remains blind to the writing on the wall. He and the Bahujan Samaj Party leader, Mayawati, have been blowing hot and, till the time of going to press, were disinclined to consider the demands. Instead, for the first time in U.P.'s history, they called a State-sponsored bandh on 13 September to counter the pro-Uttarakhand agitation.

In the last Assembly session, Mulayam hurriedly got a resolution passed giving a green signal to the creation of a Uttarakhand State. He thus lobbed the ball into the Center's court.

But the ploy failed. "If Mulayam is really sincere about Uttarakhand, why doesn't he concede our basic demand of declaring each of the hill districts backward?", asked Kashi Singh Aeri, a UKD leader and MLA who resigned from the House, protesting the reservation policy...

It is clear that Mulayam Singh is playing to the galleries in the plains, where the OBCs have got a 27 per cent quota system. Mayawati has dared the Congress to withdraw support to the SP-BSP government in the belief that the backward vote-bank will remain with them.

At least Mulayam is being honest. The hills don't matter to him politically. Even if the pro-Uttarakhand stir intensifies and a new State is formed, he would be happy to hang on as the Chief Minister of a truncated U.P.. But there is always that outside chance that if a quick solution is not found, the country may be saddled with another intractable problem. And that will be Himalayan blunder, yet again.

Source: Anish Gupta and Sharat Chandra, *Sunday*, September 18-24, 1994.

20.23 Making Sense of Uttarakhand

The turmoil which has engulfed the hill districts of Uttar Pradesh had, like that of the Indian elephant, a prolonged gestation. It is grounded on many years of oppression, exploitation and neglect. But it is one thing for a people to feel oppressed and another for it to go into battle. The people of the eight hill districts of U.P.—Uttarkashi, Tehri Garhwal, Pauri Garhwal, Chamoli, Dehra Dun, Nainital, Almora and Pithoragarh — in the last few weeks have made this transition from perception to action.

The trigger has been the utter thoughtlessness of the Chief Minister of U.P., Mulayam Singh Yadav. Mulayam has been somewhat cornered politically since Kanshi Ram and Mayawati came into the limelight...

This policy which reckoned without the enormous demographic and economic variations within the sprawling and unwieldy State of U.P. caught a Tartar in the hill districts of the State. To the hill people this policy of reservation seemed like the proverbial last straw on top of many years of neglect and discrimination. Only 2 per cent of the population of the hill districts belong to the OBCs. There is therefore some justification in the view of the hill people that the reservation policy is entirely out of tune with the needs and requirements of their region...

The Kumaon-Garhwal region is not a homogeneous entity in terms of religion, language or in terms of the ethnic origin of the people. Their identity is based on their common proximity to the mountains and their feeling of distinctness from the plains. The area is rich in natural and mineral resources. As a result it has been quarried indiscriminately by people and organisations from the plains. This has destroyed the area's ecological balance and denuded it of its forest resources.

Because of the backwardness of the region, jobs, grade and business were controlled and dominated by people who migrated into the region from the plains. But in the last decade or so with the growth of literacy and education, there has emerged a vocal and aspirant middle class. Avenues of employment are already clogged by non-*paharis*; Mulayam's reservation policy further blocks them. Reserved jobs will be filled by OBCs from the plains. Natives of the hills, most of whom belong to the upper castes, will fall way behind in the race...

Mulayam has been brazen enough to admit that he has no personal stake in the hills and does not care what happens to them. For personal stake read electoral stakes. His lack of concern for the hills is related to two things. One, the hills are largely upper caste and therefore unlikely to vote for a champion of the OBCs. And second, the statement expressed the contempt of the plains politician for the people of the hills. It hardly becomes a responsible Chief Minister.

Mulayam's irresponsibility is manifest in his pitting of the lower castes against the upper castes. It might bring to him electoral rewards but the long-term implication are bloody and disastrous. Like most politicians in India, Mulayam cares for little more than his narrow self-interest. So long as he remains in power, no matter through what means, nothing else matters.

Not only is the Chief Minister pushing U.P. towards a prolonged and horrible caste war, he is also creating a political space for the BJP to pose as great protectors and upholders of the interests and grievances of the hill people. Vicious caste politics is feeding the evil of communalism.

In this vortex of politicking the genuine problems of Kumaon and Garhwal are receding into the background. A spontaneous protest born out of grievances suffered for many years is running the wrist now of becoming a handy tool for political parties and their electoral ambitions. Of such stuff is separatism spawned.

Source: Rudrangshu Mukherjee, *Sunday*, September 18-24, 1994

20.24 Narayan Dutt Tiwari and Uttarakhand

State Congress President Narayan Dutt Tiwari... came out strongly against the creation of an Uttarakhand State saying that he was opposed to the bifurcation of U.P..

Talking to media-persons, Mr Tiwari... said that he had been consistently advocating, since 1952, that Uttar Pradesh should not be divided into smaller States.

He pointed out that once the demand for Uttarakhand was accepted, there would be demands for the formation of smaller States within U.P..

Mr. Tiwari referred to a 1974 judgment of the Supreme Court and said that the entire Uttarakhand should be declared a backward region.

Source: Hindustan Times (New Delhi), September 25, 1994

20.25 U.P. Congress (I) Support to Mulayam Government?

Ajit Singh, Congress leader, feels that the Uttar Pradesh Congress Committee's resolution on withdrawal of support to the Mulayam Singh's government is very well justified because for all practical purposes there is no government in the State: The administration is working only for two persons — Mulayam Singh and Mayawati. For instance, Singh's State sponsored bandh the other day was to endorse his reservation policy and show his strength in the State. At many places, the authorities force shop owners to down shutters.The bandh was marked by large scale violence. In fact, the bandh was uncalled for because on the reservation issue, some 11 parties have already reached an agreement. Prime Minister Narasimha Rao has already initiated the process of implementation of the Mandal Commission recommendatiom... the *bandh* was an attempt to provoke caste conflagration by Mulayam Singh Yadav. It might help him electorally.

The *bandh* is not an isolated incident — there are many others like violence in Muzaffargarh, the recent shameful scenes at Allahabad High Court, etc. The police are working in the interest of the ruling Samajwadi

Party and its ally Bahujan Samajwadi Party. There have been a number of land grabbing cases.

Therefore, reservation is not the only issue at stake. There is a serious law and order problem, graft cases involving sale of sugar mills to the so called socialists, over a 1000 cholera deaths, non-availability of medical facilities, and, of course, increasing criminalisation of politics.

It is in this context that the UPCC had passed a unanimous resolution and conveyed to the central leadership its decision to withdraw support to the Mulayam Singh government.

I do not believe that withdrawal would mean that the Congress Party is against the official reservation policy. It will neither help the BJP to consolidate its position nor would it help project Mulayam Singh Yadav as a secular messiah. Those Congressmen who oppose our withdrawal of support to the U.P. government should leave the final decision to the UPCC chief N.D. Tiwari and the party's central leadership.

Shuja-u-Bin Sajid, Delhi Samajwadi Party president, disapproves withdrawal of Congress-I's support to reservation and other such issues. He calls the Uttar Pradesh Congress Committee a defunct body: The withdrawal demand was raised out of the internal confusion created by some Congressmen of the hilly region.

If the Congress Legislature Party (CLP) really meant business, it would have gone to the Uttar Pradesh Governor and demanded the dismissal of the Mulayam Singh government. But very soon it realised that it might have to apologise before the public for its wrong decision and hence did not go in for such a move. In fact, the CLP is almost a defunct body which is not in a position to take any drastic decision and act on it. It is evident from its graded response to the whole situation. It has the will to harm, yet is afraid to strike. Actually, the withdrawal issue was raised by a section of upper caste leaders in the party which has never been in favour of uplifted and development of backward classes of society.

The withdrawal on the reservation issue will have unimaginable implications for the Congress-I itself. It will expose the internal resentment towards reservation and, of course, the party inclination to protect the interests of upper caste and ignoring backward caste.

With this, the party's vote bank of backward and scheduled castes will definitely get diluted. In a way, it will push the Congress-I closer to the BJP in terms of political agenda. In a recent statement, the BJP leader, L.K. Advani even suggested to the Congress central leadership to accept the unanimous resolution of the UPCC for withdrawal.

It is a very strange statement. What could be the motivation of the BJP leader in issuing such a statement? But so far, the High-Command has been positive in its attitude to the Mulayam Singh government. I don't think it is likely that they will withdraw support to Mulayam Singh government under this pretext. But, at the same time, if the Congress-I really wants to deal with the Uttarakhand issue, it should move a resolution and call for a special session of Parliament for discussion.

Source: The Independent (Bombay), September 25, 1994

20.26 Uttarakhand and the Centre

Uttar Pradesh Chief Minister Mulayam Singh Yadav said... the question of granting autonomy to the hill region for creating a separate State now rested with the Centre.

Talking to newsmen at the Calcutta airport, Mr Yadav said the State Assembly had already passed a unanimous resolution on granting special status to the hill region. However, he declined to comment on whether the State Government was prepared to give any immediate concession to the hill people to assuage their feelings following the Uttarakhand agitation.

Source: Patriot (New Delhi), September 26, 1994

20.27 Samajwadi Party and Uttarakhand

The Samajwadi Party national secretary, Mr. Binod Barthwai... urged the Prime Minister to clarify his stand on the Uttarakhand issue to resolve the crisis prevailing in the hill districts of Uttar Pradesh.

Addressing a press conference, Mr. Barthwal regretted that the large amount of money allotted for the development of the hill regions in the State was lying unutilised as life there had come to a standstill following the agitation...

He said the party had fulfilled its election promise of having a resolution on Uttarakhand passed in the State Assembly. The Chief Minister, Mr. Mulayam Singh Yadav would soon request the Prime Minister, Mr. P.V. Narasimha Rao to accept the proposal.In case, the Centre rejected the proposal, the party would chalk out its future strategy on the issue.

"We have requested Mr. Yadav to initiate an enquiry into the Khatima and Mussoorie firing incidents and provide compensation to the family members of the victims," he said.

He said a sum of Rs. 613 crores had to be spent on the development of the hill region before March-end next falling which it would lapse. Out of this sum, Rs. 51 crores were meant for resolving the acute water crisis in the remote areas of Garhwal and Kumaon.

It was said ... that the agitation which had at its heart the welfare of the hill people, was also responsible for delaying developmental works in the hills.

He alleged that Congress(I) and Bharatiya Janata Party MLAs from the region were misleading the agitationists as these two parties had "no clear stand" on the Uttarakhand issue.

Source: The Hindu (New Delhi), September 27, 1994

20.28 Lt. General (Retd.) S.K.Sinha on Uttarakhand

Disconcerting

The grave situation in U.P. over 27 per cent reservation for OBCs in Uttarakhand region is very disconcerting. Apart from it being a statistically bizarre proposal, it ignores the ethnic and economic compulsions, affecting the hill people. Article 370 of the Constitution protects the interests of the local people of Kashmir, the Inner Line restriction does so for the indigenous people of the North-Eastern States and there are special provisions for the tribal areas in Bihar, Orissa and Madhya Pradesh. The Mandal formula has not been made applicable to States like Nagaland, Mizoram, Manipur, Sikkim and Arunachal Pradesh where there are no OBCs. Keeping all these aspects in view, if the U.P. Government was sincere about the unanimous resolution for creation of Uttarakhand State passed in the Assembly, it could at least have held the implementation of the Mandal formula in abeyance for this region, pending decision on the creation of Uttarakhand State.

Mr. Mulayam Singh Yadav, who surrendered so abjectly before the supremo of his coalition partner, appears to have chosen to declare war on the people of Uttarakhand and has already fired the first few shots. He has stated that he is not dependent on support of this region. State repression has been let loose and trigger-happy policemen have been shooting down people at Khatima and Mussoorie. Judicial inquiry has been denied into these police killings. Even though reservation is not an issue in the plains region as the Mandal formula stands accepted by all, he called for a pro-resevation *bandh* on September 13, 1994. The aim was to show his strength and terroise his opponents, particularly the people in the hill districts. The absurd situation of the State committing an act of illegality was sought to be justified on the basis of the Cummunists having adopted such tactics in West Bengal. While he sought Central intervention to resolve the issue, he was adamant that there could be no compromise on the reservation issue and the *bandh* of September 13 could not be called off. He flouted the advice of the Prime Minister about the *bandh*. There was inevitable violence leading to several deaths and injuries while the police remained mute spectators. The pro-reservationist hoodlums entered the Allahabad High Court, beat up advocates and damaged the chamber of the Chief Justice. The police was in attendance of these hoodlums, abetting in their crime. The Chief Justice had to summon the Army which responded promptly and the situation was brought under control. Never in the history of democracy has such vandalism been committed in a high temple of justice nor had ever a Chief Justice summoned Army's help for protection. September 13 will be remembered as a black day in the history of Indian democracy. No amount of expressing of regret or shedding of crocodile tears can absolve Mr Mulayam Singh Yadav from his responsibility for this outrage.

Irrational

While Kumaon and Garhwal have been burning, Mr Mulayam Singh Yadav has been fiddling with his political antics in Lucknow. Thousands of ex-servicemen with their war medals have come out to protest on the streets of Uttarakhand, against the Government's irrational fiat. The services rendered to the nation by these gallant men and the sacrifices made by them far outweigh those of the self-seeking politicians in Lucknow. Yet some of the latter who launched a tirade against the Father of the Nation, have dubbed these gallant and patriotic ex-servicemen as traitors. The rulers both at Delhi and Lucknow are oblivious of the threat that may arise to our national security. The State's repressive measures are alienating the people of the hills and may sow the seeds of insurgency and secessionism in a moutainous terrain, suited for guerilla warfare, which borders on China. Despite the unanimous recommendation of the UPCC, the flouting of the Prime Minister's advice and the black deeds of September 13, the Prime Minister continues to follow the policy of indecision and inaction. Petty party interests and the fear of losing the elections in U.P. to the BJP are taking precedence over national interests.

Alienation

The rulers at Delhi have not learnt the lesson from their earlier misguided policy in propping up Bhinderwale in Punjab and political manipulations which contributed to the alienation of the people of Kashmir, with disastrous results in these two States. After more than a decade of suffering the situation in Punjab was retrieved but in the process, some 30,000 innocent people were killed. Kashmir's agony continues to be in flames. The risk of Uttarakhand going the same way as Punjab and Kashmir, is ever present if the present irrational policy continues...

Source: S.K. Sinha, India's Bane: Social Harmony's, *Hindustan Times* (New Delhi), September 27, 1994

20.29 Scholars and the Demand for Uttarakhand

The people of Uttarakhand, not unlike their brethren in other parts of the Himalayan ranges, have for decades been paying a heavy price for their uncorrupted simplicity. It was only inevitable that their reservoir of resilience would give way one day and their woes would express themselves as an unbridled outcry to secure a place under the sun.

The outburst that snowballed into a full-scale agitation, unfolded like a bundle of pent-up emotions. Understandably so, it appeared disoriented, incoherent and incomprehensible at first. Caste passions, baser instincts, political manoeuverings and dithering leaderships have indeed plagued the upheval, but it is only the spirit of mass sentiment that promises to throw up possibilities of better articulation.

As the dust raised by the initial storm settles, spokes-persons and organizers are emerging from the chaos to give the movement purpose and shape...

Source: Prashant Rahi, *The Statesman* (New Delhi), September 27, 1994

20.30 Tehri Project

The Uttarakhand agitation and the non-release of funds by the Uttar Pradesh Government have put paid to the first stage of the Tehri Hydro-electric Project to be commissioned by 1988-89. After a recent review of the works completed on the ambitious but controversial scheme, the commissioning of the first stage of the Tehri project was staggered to the first two years of the Ninth Five Year Plan (1997-2002) with two units of 250 mw each to be commissioned in 1997-98 and the remaining two of 250 mw each in 1998-89.

The first stage includes the construction of the Tehri dam with a capacity of generating 1,000 mw of hydro-electricity. It also includes the construction of pump storage plant at the Tehri and Koteshwar hydro-electric project.

While the agitation in Uttarakhand is a recent phenomenon, the project has been feeling the resource crunch eversince the construction works were transferred to the Tehri Hydro Development Corporation

(THDC) by the State Government in June 1989. Though the Government had assured to make available the total Plan Outlay of Rs. 1,303 crore in the Eighth Five Year Plan, since June 1989 the Uttar Pradesh Government has not released any fund.

Amidst reports of work coming to a standstill in the wake of the agitation, coupled by the non-availability of resources, the completion of the first stage of the project might be delayed even further. Which means it would not be before the first decade of the next century that the Tehri dam will become a reality.

Cost escallation has been the bane of the power project since its inception. Earlier, the works suffered on account of a movement against the construction of the Tehri project as it was feared it would cause environmental degradation. Besides, it was feared that the rock-filled dam would trigger off a wave of seismic activity since the entire area was situated in a seismic zone.

The Tehri project was granted investment clearance by the Planning Commission in June 1972 as a State-sector project for implementation by the U.P. Government with an installed capacity of 600 MW at the then estimated cost of Rs 192.92 crore. Four units of 150 MW each were proposed to be set up.

The electricity generating capacity of the Tehri project was subsequently revised to 1,000 MW in 1983 for peaking purposes keeping the height of the dam unchanged. The scope of the project was again revised to include four components with installed capacity of 2,400 MW.

Construction work commenced in 1978. However, in view of the resource constraint of the State Goverment, and keeping in view the benefits from the project, it was decided in November 1986 to hand over the project to the THDC, a joint venture of the Union Government and the State Government with financial participation in the ratio of 75:25 respectively. This arrangement was for the power component; the irrigation part was to be funded entirely by the State Government.

Of the total estimated cost of Rs 5,538 crore an amount of Rs 873.08 crore has already been spent till March this year on the various components of the mammoth project.

However, in view of the resource constraint, the Central Government on March 15, 1994 approved implementation of the first stage of the project only, involving a total cost of Rs 2,963.66 crore.

Source: Atiq Khan, *The Observer* (New Delhi), September 27, 1994

20.31 Capital City Delhi and Uttarakhand

Nothing which happens in Uttarakhand leaves Delhi untouched because of the presence of about 10 lakh of them in the Capital. Though they live scattered, they do form a vote bank capable of influencing polling results in many areas. It is not without reason that political parties in the Capital compete with each other for addressing the Uttarakhand samities fromed in various colonies.

The hill people here have maintained a cymbiotic relationship with their relatives back home. In fact, most families in Uttarakhand depend upon the money orders sent to them by their relatives in the Capital. Thus, the opinion of the hill people residing in Delhi assumes significance even among the policy-makers.

It is not that the hill people are unanimous in their demand for satehood. Nonetheless all agree that the hill region has been given step-brotherly treatment by the Government in Lucknow irrespective of the party in power...

Before it is too late, the decision-makers must act or else the feeling of frustration may lead to dangerous consequences. The hill people are aware that they have one of the highest number of ex-servicemen and if the agitation takes a seccessionist turn, it woud became difficult to control it.

Surely, no one wants another problem area in the country.

Source: Renu Kaul, *The Hindustan Times* (New Delhi), September 28, 1994

20.32 Patriot Garhwalis

... The two districts of Garhwal and Kumaon are two major recruiting areas and provide nearly 20 per cent of the personnel for the armed and paramilitary forces. They have a glorious histroy and an outstanding battle record. They are known for their gentle behaviour throughout the Indian Army. Their present agitation against reservation involving even women shows to what desperation they have been driven to.

It was the Garhwali battalian which had refused to fire at the *Khudai Khidmatgars* of the Frontier Gandhi, Khan Abdul Gaffar Khan, in Peshawar in 1930. No other unit can claim such patriotism during the British Raj.

Source: Col. S.R.Nanda (Retd.), *The Hindustan Times* (New Delhi), September 28, 1994, letter to the editor.

20.33 Uttarakhand's Story of Statehood

... The movement in the hills of Uttar Pradesh for a separate State of Uttarakhand is the biggest movement in the history of the region, even bigger than the famous Tilari agitation, which was launched in 1930 in the *riyasat* of Tehri Garhwal for people's rights over forests and forest-produce.....

The demand for a separate State of Uttarakhand and creation of local political outfits like the Uttarakhand Kranti Dal, the Uttarakhand Jan Sangharsh Vahini, the Uttarakhand Mukti Morcha, the Uttarakhand Party, the Uttarakhand Jan Morcha, the Uttarakhand Raksha Manch, the Uttarakhand Shanti Vahini and dozens of action Committees is the expression fo the demands of a neglected people.

The genesis of the ongoing agitation is remarkable in many ways. It took off as a protest against the implementatin of reservation for OBCs. Eventually, it resulted first in the demand for including the entire Uttarakhand region in the list of the OBCs and then in the demand for a separate hill State...

The question of Uttarakhand State is directly associated with the issue of the management of the Himalayan region. Failure in managing the Himalayan eco-system will lead to a catastrophe. An expert group of the Planning Commission recommended strongly creation of an apex body such as the Himalayan Development Authority (HDA) to address the major issues and to evolve a policy framework for effective management. The formation of a separate State of Uttarakhand will be a step in the direction of proper management of the Himalayas.

The Uttarakhand movement needs to be seen in the light of the historically independent identity of the region. The region was able to maintain its political, economic, and cultural identity from the earliest times to the late eighteenth century. The Malla occupation and Rohila invasioon did not have a lasting impression on the life of its people and these incidents were merely possing phases of local history...

Today, socio-economic problems, large scale unemployment, and the disillusionment with the State and Central Governments have given a new dimension to the question of Uttarakhandi identity...

The people of Garhwal and Kumaon have also realised that they do not have different political ends to pursue or for that matter different identities to adopt, since they are a single people in all respects. The rise of Garhwal and Kumaon as two independent principalities has become irrelevant for them and a thing of the past. The only salvation, if there is one, lies in this identity.

One canot ignore the fact that a new kind of socio-political alignment has emerged in the ongoing movement. Even during earlier times, such alignments emerged after every major political event, be it the Rohila war, the Gorkha occupation, or British rule. After each of these events, history was re-invented to legitimise the newly acquired socio-political status of certain people who emerged dominant in the changed political circumstances. This will also happen in the near future when a separate State is formed. But, this time, it wil be the turn of the common man. And, the same current is flowing throughout Uttarakhand as the whole region is united in a cultural bond. Otherwise, the reaction to the brutal massacres in Khatima and Mussoorie would not have been equally intense throughout the region...

Uttarakhand's story since Independence has been one of persistent exploitation of its forests and mineral wealth and neglect of its people. The neglect of regional aspirations led to the emergence of this movement as early as 1952 when P. C. Joshi of the undivided Communist Party of India raised this demand. Even Pandit Nehru envisaged division of UP, with complete statehood for Uttarakhand. But G. B. Pant, who hailed from the same region, opposed the idea and that was the end of the matter as far as the national polity was concerned. Nehru, at the Srinagar Congress Session, advocated the idea of a seperate administrative set up for the region...

The attitude of the Cenral Governjment is about to lead to the situation going out of control. The people are convinced that the Government is not at all serious about their demand. The sentiments of the local people need to be addressed properly, otherwise, the Government would have to face a very piquant situation.

The region has more than three lakh ex-soldiers and ex-paramilitary personnel. Most women of the region know how to handle rifles. The Government got a taste of what might be in the offing when ex-soldiers took out well-attended rallies in the region wearing their uniforms.

Source: Suresh Nautiyal, *The Obeserver* (New Delhi), September 29, 1994.

20.34 U.P. Government's Financial Sanction for Hills

The Uttar Pradesh Government has sanctioned Rs 1.10 crore for strengthening medical services in urban and rural areas of Uttarakhand and providing better facilities to the people.

Giving this information, Uttarakhand development secretary Indu Kumar Pande said at present 405 allopathic, 369 ayurvedic and 55 homeopathic hospitals with 8,676 beds were catering to medical and health needs of the people in Uttarakhand. Besides, 233 primary health centres and 1438 family welfare centres were also working in the region.

Mr. Pande said during the current year five primary health centres, two community health centres, two homeopathic and two ayurvedic dispensaries would be set up. Buildings for five primary health centres, 20 sub-centres and 4 community health centres would also be constructed. Under the medical services extension programme, the facility of 30 beds in the hospitals of urban area and 52 beds in the rural areas would be provided during the current financial year.

In another significant development the State Government has directed that all those officers and employees who have been transferred to the Uttarakhand should take their charge immediately.

In a Government order... it has been stated that the officers and employees who will not join their duties immediately, their increament will be stopped and they will be deprived from promotion for next two years.

It has also been clarified that the officers and employees should be positively posted for at least two years in the regions.

The decision was taken by the government in view of the complaints received from various sources that the officers and employees transferred to the hill areas were not joining their duties and trying to get their transfer orders concelled.

Meanwhile, tranquil life in the region has been shattered in the wake of the unprecedented agitation by all sections of the people demanding a separate hill State and opposing the State Government's reservation policy.

The vibrant region, also called the valley of gods and a favourite destination for pilgrims and nature-lovers, today echoes with slogans like "Uttarakhand *hamara hai* and "give us Uttarakhand and scrap the reservation for OBCs".

Source: The Observer (New Delhi), September 29, 1994.

20.35 Uttarakhand Delegations: Negotiation with Minister of State for Home Affairs

Minister of State for Home Rajesh Pilot... extended an open invitation to the leaders of the Uttarakhand movement tocome to the negotiating table to defuse tension in the hill areas of Uttar Pradesh.

He told a delegation of senior Congress leaders including MLAs from the hill districts... that the on-going movement was a matter of concern to all including the Centre. The meeting between the minister and the delegation led by Seva Dal Chief Harish Rawat and T. S. Negi lasted about two hours.

The meeting was significance as it was the first time that interaction between the agitationists and the Centre took place after the movement took a violent turn in the hills recently. The delegation included Shoorbeer Singh Sajwan, MLA from Tehri and four other State legislators.

The delegation complained about the atrocities allegedly committed by the State police on innocent citizens who were participating peacefully in the Uttarakhand agitation. The members demanded a judicial inquiry into such incidents of abuse of authority, and payment of compensation "who sacrificed their lives" for the cause.

The delegation which included a large number of student leaders, ex-servicemen and mahila organisations representatives voiced concern at the lack of employment opportunities for them.

They cited a Supreme Court judgement which upheld reservation in medical colleges for the people of hill areas on the ground that they were socially and educationally backward people.

At one stage, the delegation pointed out that the people were reconciled to the constituton of the Government.

The delegation, therefore, suggested that the Centre convene a meeting without further delay to resove the issue. Pilot readily agreed to the suggestion.

Pilot assured the delegation that he would take up the matter with the Uttar Pradesh Chief Minister regarding the demand for a judicial inquiry and payment of compensation to the deceased.

Source: Business Standard (New Delhi), September 30, 1994, News Item

20.36 Uttarakhand : The Fire Next Time

There is a good deal of talk of changing its present peaceful course. A good number of young people feel that wrecking of communication lines and government property may become necessary to put pressure on the rulers. Look at Nagaland, Mizoram, Meghalaya, or even Andhra Pradesh or Maharashtra earlier. None of them came into being by peaceful means, they argue. The Government was compelled into creating them when the people took the law into their own hands.

On the day of the total Uttarakhand *bandh*, on August 23, a number of communication lines were in fact damaged and a Police Station pelted with stones in the Kedarnath valley. Some others, still in minority are of the opinion that armed action may be necessary.

Where would you get arms, I asked some of them at one point? There is a big bazar of illicit arms in the country now, they said. All the leftover American weapons from Indo-China and Afghan wars are pouring into India from both east and west. If others in the country can get them, so can we, they argued. But you need money, big money to buy them, I said. For that, we could, for instance, rob bank, treasuries, or other institutions, they said.

Then there is China, with a wide open border , just a few kilometres away. Thousands of ex-servicemen live in these hills. They could fire the first shot, or, at least train the young in wielding weapons, they said. Like others, we too will learn by practising the art of fighting.

These may be fringe people. But then in an armed struggle it is never the majority which takes up weapons. On September 14 a Police Station in Rishikesh was in fact set on fire by armed men.

The news of Mussoorie firing came late, when most of the groups were already on their way home, a day's drive away. Otherwise, there surely would have been a massacre in Pauri. One should have seen the spirit of those that were prepared to fight!

Source: Harish Chandola, *The Hindustan Times* (New Delhi), September 30, 1994.

20.37 Uttarakhand Will Do Well

The Congress leader Mr. Ajit Singh is absolutely right, 'Ajit in favour of separate western U.P. State' (Sept. 23), when he demands the States Reorganisation Commission. This is the right time to constitute the SRC when the demands of small States from Uttarakhand, Western U.P., Bundelkhand, Poorvanchal, Vananchal, Vidharbha, Telangana and so on have been gearing up.

We should not forget the words of Mr K.M. Pannikker of the SRC that India should have at least 58 States. India is virtually being run by God, otherwise it is a nation of disparities where a State, Mizoram or Nagaland or Meghalaya has a population of less than 10 lacs while in the same country U.P. has 15 crores.

This is our country where all the Himalayan regions have been declared as separate States but for Uttarakhand, having similar geographical conditions, has not yet been given the same treatment...

This hill region has enough economic viabilities as the area is full of water and other natural resources.

Only the three major rivers of Uttarakhand can earn more than Rs. 1000 crore per annum while the entire territory has dolomite, magnesite, cement, lime stone and many other minerals. Besides forest products, orchards, tourism and other resources. Uttarakhand will not be a dependent state like the North Eastern states.

Source: Indian Express (New Delhi), September 30, 1994, letter to the editor.

20.38 Heed the Cry for Uttarakhand

... The demand for a separate Uttarakhand is more than four decades old. Although many important leaders came from that region—supplying as many as three distinguished Chief Minister for Uttar Pradesh—the question of a separate Uttarakhand was all the time put aside on the shelf. Uttarakhand has had an impressive tradition of participation in the freedom struggle, having been an active political base of the Congress without any regional insularity. Despite all this—or perhaps, because of this—Uttarakhand has so long been denied its due recognition of having a distinct identy of its own on the map of India. It is only now that the question of Uttarakhand has become a very live issue, thanks to the provocative posture of the present Government in U.P., particularly of its Chief Minister...

As it always happens in such cases, the movement which began with the students rapidly spread to other sections of the people, and today it has the character of a veritable mass upheaval in which all classes and castes are participating. The intelligentsia which is of considerable eminence in Garhwal and Kumaon, are extraordinarily active.

Inflamed Public Opinion

The entire administration has been affected, with total no-work campaign in the Government offices in Garhwal spreading over a week at the time of writing. More serious is the impact within the armed forces, as the Kumaon and Garhwal jawans and officers are bound to be affected by the tension at home. It is of no mean significance that General Joshi, Chief of the Indian Army, met the Uttar Pradesh Chief Minister at the very beginning of this movement and urged him to expedite a settlement warning him about its snowballing effect.

There are critics opposing any separation of Uttarakhand from U.P., who say that the region connot be economically viable. However, the more responsible section in the Government concede that when the Himachal Pradesh was made into a separate State in 1971, there is no earthy reason why Uttarakhand should be withheld. The area of Himachal Pradesh covers 55,675 sq. km, while the area of the proposed Uttarakhand, including the foothills, would easily come to over 55,000 sq km. The population of Himachal is 51,11,079, while that of Uttarakhand is about 60 lakhs. Himachal has made striking progress in the sphere of economic development after it was made into a separate State. Uttarakhand is at the moment a very neglected area—its horticulture, fruit potential and tourist attractions can easily surpass those of Himachal Pradesh...

Justness Denied of the Demand

Leaving aside these hard-headed calculations of political party leaders, one has to acknowledge the justness of the demand for Uttarakhand, with which is interwoven many traditions of our entire country. Any procrastination on this score may lead a section of our restless youth into the path of militancy.

Source: Nikhil Chakravartty, *The Pioneer* (New Delhi), September 30, 1994.

20.39 Locals and Uttarakhand Demand

'One Two, One Two, Mulayan Singh Khantu (toothless)'— chant a group of illiterate women sitting on *dharna* seeking the creation of separate Uttarakhand State in a small place called Nand Prayag...

The fact that the movement is leaderless is acknowledged by the agitationists themselves. "We do not have any leaders. But we don't want any *neta* to takeover the movement from us. Whoever joins us must resign his position as MLA or MP and then only we will accept him," says Rahul, a young student of Rudra Prayag...

A glimpse of the real state of affairs is experienced by us only when we reach Srinagar. The neat sign boards welcoming the tourists put up by the Garhwal Mandal Vikas Nigam means nothing as the rest houses run by the Nigam have not been allowed to function since August...

Mr Manish Gupta, who runs the canteen attached to the Tourist Home... informs us that his business had come down almost by one fourth— mainly on account of the dwindling tourist traffic... A number of ordinary people, whom we talk to on the way, give their sharp reactions about the state of affairs in the hilly regions.

One of them goes to the extent saying, "We will have to have a separate State. If the Prime Minister does not wake up, we wil have to go to China, we are almost on the Chinese border and we may have to think of going there".

Talking to a group of shepherds sitting near the spot where Jim Corbett shot a maneater, near Rudra Prayag I find that they are quite hopeful that Uttarakhand would get them employment and development...

At Karna Prayag, as we stop for tea, I talk to a group getting ready to leave for Delhi to join the rally. I ask them who is footing their bill; they promptly say they are spending it from their pockets and are also carrying their own food for the next two days. "When we get Uttarakhand State we will have our own Chief Minister" he proudly declares. When I ask him who would be the Chief Minister, he promptly declares "How does it matter. It could be anyone. All are same".

Mr Rawat, a young teacher working in Srinagar explains that people in the area have imposed curfew on themselves and are not allowing any Government office to function. All the schools remained closed. Uthkarsh, an eight year old boy, who joined our group from Rishikesh is very happy that since August they have had no classes and schools may reopen only after Diwali.

Mr Rawat explains that only essential services are exempted. For three days the banks, post offices and hospitals are allowed to open — on Monday, Tuesday and Wednesdays. Other days they remain closed...

The rest house officer points out that the response to the Uttarakhand demand is quite spontaneous. He directs us to a nearby *pandal* where a group of illiterate women sat in *dharna*. These women say they take turns and sit there from eight in the morning to six in the evening. "Are you with us or with Mulayam Singh? Do you know Mayawati?" they ask. One of them suggested that I give them a lecture and promptly directs me towards a mike kept on a table. After a few minutes, they themselves start chanting slogans against Mulayam Singh and inform us that they are planning to tattoo those who were not for Uttarakhand. An old woman predicted that if we went back there next year we would then be living in UK(Uttarakhand).

Source: Kalyani Shankar, *The Hindustan Times* (New Delhi), October 5, 1994.

20.40 Centre and Union Government's Views on Uttarakhand

The Union Government virtualy rejected the demand for separate statehood for the hill areas of Uttar Pradesh, but hinted at an autonomous status for the region through an institutional arrangement.

At a meeting he convened..., Union Home Minister, S.B. Chavan, reiterated what the Prime Minister P.V. Narasimha Rao, had told an opposition delegation on October 3, that granting full statehood for U.P.'s hill region would open the Pandora's Box and lead to similar demands elsewhere in the country.

The demand for statehood was supported by all parties present at the meeting, except the CPI-M, which is known to be for autonomy on the lines of Darjeeling. However, Mr. Chavan responded by saying that the Centre had in mind an arrangement in U.P. that would be "something short of statehood."

The repressive measures resorted to by the Mulayam Singh Yadav Government were criticised by the Opposition leaders present, but they warned against the State Government's dismissal. Such a measure would only escalate the tension and worsen the situation, which needed to be tackled politically.

The Home Minister's response, according to some of the leaders present at the meeting, was that the Centre had no such plans "at present."

A tangible result of the meeting was the agreement that the cases of alleged molestation of women protesters at Muzaffarnagar would be delinked from the judicial inquiry into the firing incidents and probed separately, possibly by the CBI.

Mr. Chavan agreed to this demand after Major General (Rtd.) B.C. Khanduri, the BJP member of the Lok Sabha from Garhwal, made an emotional reference to the humiliation of women agitationists and alleged atrocities committed by the U.P. Police.

Elaborating the Centre's approach, Mr Chavan said that the Centre would not do anything to reverse the reservation policy of the U.P. Government. The response of Mr. J.P. Mathur (BJP) was that the Home Minister was shutting the doors on all future discussions.

Mr. Chaturanan Mishra (CPI), reacting to the idea of autonomy, said this could not be discussed in a vacuum and the opposition could not be expected to make suggestions on it when it was for full statehood. It was for the Centre to come up with specific proposals as the starting point of any furture debate. The opposition would like to know whether the Centre had a set up in mind like the ones in Darjeeling, Telengana or the Chhota Nagpur area.

Mr. Chandrajit Yadav (JD-G) said the Uttarakhand demand of the hill people was a long-standing one and the Centre should not drag its feet. Already, the region had suffered economically and now it was acquiring emotional dimensions.

Mr. Yadav also pointed out that two Governments and two legislatures in U.P. had passed resolutions and the Centre should not reject these outright.

At the end of the 90-minute dialogue, it became clear that Centre is not ready for statehood and may be working out an arrangement for autonomy to meet the aspirations of the hill people.

Meanwhile, former Defence Minister and the Tenth Finance Commission, Chairman K.C. Pant, met both Mr. Rao and Mr. Chavan during the day to emphasise the point that the Yadav Government in U.P., which had resorted to harsh measures instead of providing " a healing touch" to the agitators, had "forfeited its moral aim to remain in office".

Mr. Pant expressed shock at the treatment meted out to students, women and ex-servicemen by the U.P. Government, which had shown a total lack of awareness to the "dangers stocking the fires of lawlessness in this sensitive, peace-loving, patriotic border area.

The Home Minister, when contacted, declined to give details of the discussions. There was no indication of another round of discussions, if any, in future.

The hastily called meeting was attended by Mr. J.P.Mathur, Maj. Gen. (Rtd.) Khunduri (both BJP), Mr Saifuddin Choudhury (CPI-M), Mr. Anant Ram Jaiswal, (Samajwadi Janata Party), Mr. Chandrajeet Yadav and Mr Mohammed Yunus Saleem (JD-G) Mr Krishna Marandi (Jharkhand Mukti Morcha). The Home Minister was assisted by Mrs Margaret Alva, Minister of State for Personnel.

While there was no representative from Samajwadi Party that rules U.P., its coalition partner, Bahujan Samaj Party was represented by its general secretary, Ms Mayawati. There was no representative from Janata Dal (Bommai).

***Source:** The Hindustan Times* (New Delhi), October 5, 1994.

20.41 Congress Working Committee and Uttarakhand

I. The Congress Working Committe (CWC)... appealed to the people of Uttar Pradesh, and Congressmen in particular, to maintain peace, discipline and adhere to legal and constitutional methods in finding a lasting solution to the complex question of the creation of separate State of Uttarakhand comprising of eight hill districts of the State.

"Such questions have been solved elsewhere in the past and the CWC is convinced that given patience and goodwill on the part of the concerned, this can be done in the present context as well," a statement issued at the end of the meeting said.

"The CWC expressed its deep anguish, sorrow and concern at the recent happenings in the hill areas of the State. It strongly condemned the police firing and incidents of violence and loss of lives at Muzaffarnagar on the 2nd of this month *October*. The meeting also conveyed its condolences to the bereaved families.

"The CWC is aware of the glorious role of the men and women of the hill areas in the freedom struggle and in various spheres of activity, including defence, and in building the country. Their sacrifice and dedication in the service of the motherland are truely exemplary," the statement said.

The CWC called upon the government and the party at the central and State level to take necessary steps to cool the emotions of the people and see to it that their reasonable demands were acceded to. It also asserted that any incident of high-handedness or brutality should not go unpunished.

The All-India Congress Committee (AICC) spokesmen Mr. V.N. Gadgil, told newsmen that the party would pay Rs. 50,000 each to the families of victims who died in police firing in Uttar Pradesh.

Source : Deccan Chronicle (Hyderabad), October 6, 1994

II. The Congress Working Committee has authorised the Congress President P.V. Narasimha Rao to look in the affairs of Uttar Pradesh including the withdrawal of support to the Mulayam Singh Yadav Government.

According to sources, Rao was asked to deal with the matter when the issue came up for discussion. Union Welfare Minister Sitaram Kesri, who opposed the resolution of the UPCC asking for withdrawal of support, asked the Congress President to reject the demand. However, the other Central Ministers Balram Jakhar, A.K. Antony, and R.K.Dhawan stated that in the absence of Tiwari, the matter should not be discussed and the decision should be left to the Congress President. All of the members agreed to the suggestion and the next agenda for discussion was taken up.

Chief Minister Sharad Pawar stated that the impression was given in the country as if the Congress and the BJP were working jointly to dislodge the Mulayam Singh Yadav Government, he was of the view that this notion should be removed since the prospects of the party were bound to suffer in the elections to the ten States to be held within six months.

Source: Free Press Journal (Bombay), October 6, 1994

20.42 U.P. Hills Surcharged Emotions

"Pahar ka swabhav hai chup rehna; nadiyon ka bahte rehna; jis din lagegi unke swabhiman par chot, pani main paida hogi aag; pathar-pather ban jayega bam". (The mountains are inherently tranquil; the rivers flow quietly; the day their inherent nature is hurt, there will be fire in the rivers and the Himalayas will burst like a bomb.) This couplet from

Charu Chand Chandola, a local poet, was recalled by a student activist when he was asked to react to the prevailing situation.

The people are more agitated over the incidents at Muzaffarnagr than the police firing at Mussoorie itself on September 2 in which six persons were killed. When reminded that there were seven casualties in that incident, a senior citizen intervened to say that one of the killed persons was a Deputy Superintendent of Police who was on the side of 'demons', and any demon killed in action could not be conferred the status of a martyr...

They are not ready to accept the argument that cops cannot rape women in open fields, and that too in the presence of public and senior police officers.

Kunwar Singh, a young man from Saingi village on Kempty Road, recalled the incident and said that he himself saw a semi-neeked young woman running for cover. He held Mr Mulayam Singh Yadav, the Chief Minister of Uttar Pradesh, directly responsible for hurting the sentiments of hill people. He added that the PAC jawans, mostly hailing from backward communities, not only abused women rallyists verbally, but also dared to molest them...

It is believed in the villages around Mussoorie that the police pushed away the driver of a bus carrying women rallyists and took the same to the Police Lines. The question posed by villagers is: "What did the police do with those women?" The eyes of a young man brimmed with tears when he described the Muzaffarnagar incident as one of shame not only for the hills, but for the entire country. He cautioned that meekness of the people in the hills should not be construed as their weakness.

Source. Anil Maheshwari, *The Hindustan Times* (New Delhi), October 6, 1994

20.43 Uttarakhand and Social Justice

... Even if an expansive reclassification of OBCs in the U.P. hills is undertaken, that category cannot, scientifically speaking, increase from some 2-3 per cent to more than 8-9 per cent, The benefit of reservations in this area, will therefore, overwhelmingly go to the plains-people. Since the hill people are already alienated, is it surprising that the U.P. hills are burning?

But this surely is not the road to real social justice. Politicians will continue to take the easy way out. But the citizenry must not allow this. Pseudo-socialist rhetoric coupled with pro-rich policies must not be allowed to masquerade as social justice, particularly by those, who like this columnist, suport reservations. And in the specific case of U.P. the message must be unequivocal. Uttarakhand is not for burning!

Source: Kamal A. Mitra Chinoy, *The Independent* (Bombay), October 6, 1994.

20.44 Repercussions of Union Government Stand

The catergorical refusal of Union Home Minister S.B. Chavan to accede to the dual demand of creation of a separate hill, State and to keep the hill districts of Uttar Pradesh beyond the purview of 27 per cent reservation for backward classes, as reproted prominently in the reginal vernacular Press, has further fuelled the agitation mood in the Garhwal hills.

Meanwhile, sporadic incidents of violence in the remote and inaccessible areas of the Garhwal hills continued unabatted. More than half-a-dozen towns are reeling under the curfew restrictions for the last several days without any relaxaton. The schools and colleges are already closed for an indefinite period. The civil life has come to a standstill throughout the Garhwal division.

The residents of the Garhwal hills blame the Central Government's lukewarm attitude in addressing this issue and thus transforming a peaceful movement into a violent one.

Ganesh Shelly, a noted writer, said that the statement of the Union Home Minister had further dampened the hopes of already affected Garhwalis. He alleged that the Chief Minister of U.P. and the Union Home Minister seemed to be working in tandem to jeopardise the interest the hill residents. He recalled that a few weeks ago. Mulayam Singh Yadav had also described the residents of the hills as "traitors." He blamed Mr Mulayam Singh Yadav for creating hatred within the society by treading on his favourite theme of playing one caste against another — an almost a new feature for the hill districts which all along had not witnessed caste distinction.

Riyaz Punjabi, a visiting teacher at JNU Delhi, who was here to take back his son from a boarding school, said that all the developments pointed out that the U.P. hills were on way to become another Kashmir.

Source: Anil Maheshwari, *Hindustan Times* (New Delhi), October 7, 1994.

20.45 Abode of Gods Going to Devil?

Blood stains mark the route to the hill districts of Uttar Pradesh — the curfew-bound "abode of the Gods" Repeated police firings, an official death toll of 25, which keeps mounting, allegations of gang-rape and mass-rape of women by the constabulary, and marauding policemen arresting people at random mark the restoration of "law and order".

It is almost as if a primordial *manthan* (churning of the oceans) has taken place in the normally placid mountain sides. Nobody shouts slogans anymore...only the eyes reflect the dark abyss of determined fury...

Ex-servicemen, including those who have retired from the police and paramilitary forces, have refused to surrender their licensed weapons. "Where are our boys?..." the old soldiers have begun asking, determined to transform the unruly students into disciplined soldiers of a new self assertion.

"From what I see and hear... I just can't understand why the administration is doing this..." Prof. I. Punjabi of the Jawaharlal Nehru University and a member of the Indian delegation to the UN Commission on Human Rights said in bewilderment.. "In Kashmir, one can still find excuses... insurgency the foreign hand ..but here ...?"

The hills were just sputtering back to normalcy when the "Massacre at Muzafarnagar" broke the shattered calm with blood-strewn streets and bullet-ridden bodies..

"This shouldn't have happened," a Station Officer posted in one of the Dehra Dun Police Stations confided. "I still don't understand the reason for the firing. I personally sent the message asking whether the buses carrying demonstrators to Delhi should be stopped, and was told to let them proceed after searching them for possible arms. I personally stoped and checked 46 buses. We faced the usual routine barrage of abuses... we searched all the buses and let them go since there was nothing which could be remotely used as an instrument...I asked for instructions once again and was told to let the buses proceed...."

... At the foothills near Muzaffarnagar, the State Government had prepared a reception commitee; late in the night trucks plying on the highway were summarily requisitioned to block the tri-junction and buses from all over the Garhwal hills trapped in a police prepared funnel—one hundred buses at the minimum-were surrounded by hundreds of armed PAC men...

As the news of the massacre spread into the hills, angry groups stormed Police Stations and came out onto the streets... with reports of missing women and girls streaming ineven the old and the infirm wanted to know: Why....?

Almost spontaneously, the local constabulary in the hills stood apart from the new recruits sent to "teach the Paharis a lesson", and shops downed their shutters waiting for the echoes of anger.

The administration had to impose curfew and call in Central help, and the Rapid Action Force was deployed since the traditional police forces did not act on the one sentence command: *Bhoon do*... (finish them) which came over loud and clear over the wireless sets...

Tension within the police forces were also apparent. The Central Reservce Police Force has reportedly told the PAC platoons to remain within their own parameters and senior army officers are worried about the possible repurcussions on the Garhwal and Kumaon regiments. No leave is being granted to soldiers from these regiments so that they do not go to their charged homes.

In Uttarakhand, there is no debate any longer. Uttarakhand IS...

"The Himalayas were formed by a tumultous upheaval... Siva's *tandav nritya* started here... " and the wizened old Chand Singh Dondiyal looked away from the plains and towards the peak.

Source: Chand Joshi, *Hindustan Times* (New Delhi), October 7, 1994

20.46 Nominated Uttarakhand Council: Union Government's Formula

Having rejected the Opposition demand for according full-fledged statehcod to Uttarakhand, the Centre is busy working out a formula that will include an economic package to meet the aspirations of the people.

The formula is, of course, subject to changes and consultations with political parties and others concerned. At the meeting convened this week, Home Minister S.B. Chavan was told by Opposition parties that it was for the Government to come up with specific proposals.

Sources say the issue has a number of aspects that need to be viewed in a holistic manner. First, it is not the Government's policy to create more States. Second, it is pointed out that whatever the intensity and justification of statehood, the past experience has been that any division of the politically crucial State of Uttar Pardesh has been ruled out. The demand is as old as 1952, when the first memorandum was submitted to Mr. Jawaharlal Nehru. The leadership of the day, and subsequent ones, have merely scoffed at the demand.

Third, the yardstick of the North-East or even Jharkhand region is not being applied to U.P.. The tribal factor is absent here. Moreover, even the North-East is sought to be integrated more and more. And granting statehood to Uttarakhand would send wrong signals to the border areas and the tribals.

The Centre is also worried about the security aspects, what with a 'live' border with Nepal and Tibet in the north and the Terai region in the south, where settlers from undivided Punjab have had a role to play in aiding militancy both in the region and Punjab during the entire period of the turmoil in Punjab. The situation is still under close watch.

As things stand now, the autonomy package would comprise a nominated body institutionalised through legislation. The provision of some people being elected is being ruled out for the moment. The rationale is that an elected member of the autonomous council, or whatever its name and nomenclature, is bound to come into conflict with the elected MPs and MLAs. If the Government is not about to create a separate State, it also does not want an elected legislature.

The economic package, as per the initial thinking, could include industrial projects that are capital and labour intensive, but environment friendly. The idea is to provide as many jobs to the youth and wean then away from the plains and large cities...

A possible way out, according to sources, is that the reservation quota may be made applicable to the entire hill region in the name of reservation for the hill people... An omnibus reservation for the hill people may obviate such a possibility...

Source : Mahendra Ved, *Hindustan Times* (New Delhi), October 7, 1994

20.47 Peoples Union of Civil Liberties (PUCL) Views on Firing

The unprovoked and unjustified firing by the U.P. police, resulting in a score of deaths, on Uttarakhand supporters is most condemnable. The firing on processionists, who were peacefully proceeding to Delhi, shows that the claim of the U.P. Government to be sensitive to the demand of the poor people is hollow and false. The Government has denied the people the right to exercise their fundamental rights to freedom of speech. Coming in the wake of the U.P. Government's involvement in the Allahabad High Court incident, the latest police killings call seriously into question, the credentials of the U.P. Government.

The PUCL demands a judicial enquiry by a High Court Judge and payment of compensation to the next of kin of the dead and the injured.

Source: Rajinder Sachar, President (PUCL), *Hindustan Times* (New Delhi), October 7,1994, letter to the editor.

20.48 Muzaffarnagar Firing Equals Jallianwala Bagh Massacre: Chipko Movement Leaders Views

Leader of the famous 'Chipko Movement' in U.P. hills and Magsaysay Award winner Chandi Prasad Bhatt... expressed shock and deep anguish at the recent incident in Muzaffarnagar, where over a dozen Uttarakhand activists were killed in police firing and several women molested by the PAC personnel while they were on their way to attend a rally in the Capital.

On his return... from a two-day fact-finding visit to the site of the gruesome incident and nearby villages with a team of Gandhi Peace Foundation members, Mr Bhatt stated it was clear from eyewitness accounts of the villagers that the local police and administration had, in a calculated move, unleashed a savage attack on thousands of unarmed men and women protectors of Uttarakhand.

Comparing the police action with the infamous Jallianwala Bagh massacre during British rule, the Gandhain leader charged U.P. Chief Minister Mulayam Singh Yadav with having deliberately engineered the violent incident to terrorise the peaceful hill people of the State.

The Central Government also shared responsibility for the despicable incident as it continued to support the Mulayam Singh Yadav Government...

At a Press Conference... they narrated their findings about the sequence of events on the fateful night of October 1 and early morning of October 2, as gleaned from the accounts of the villagers and rallyists present on the spot.

They recalled that the 5 km stretch of road near Rampur Ka Tiraha was littered with tell-tale signs of police brutality, like broken glass and bloodstains, even two days after the incident. This despite frantic measures by the administration to cover them up. Mr Bhatt stressed that it was "a matter of great shame and sorrow" that such "barbaric violence" had been perpetrated and women dishonoured on the 125th birth anniversary of Mahatma Gandhi.

He was, however, all praise for the helpful and deeply sympathetic attitude of the Hindu and Muslim residents of the five nearby villages who provided shelter, food and protection to the shattered hill people. These 'saviours' included Hindus, Muslims and even Dalits and hailed from villages Sisona, Bangaunwali, Medhpur, Budhedi and Rampur.

A *bhandara* (kitchen) was hurriedly set up by the villagers to feed about 15,000 rallyists, who were also given clothes and treatment.

Source : Hindustan Times (New Delhi), October 7, 1994

20.49 V.P. Singh and Uttarakhand

The former Prime Minister V.P. Singh, described the present situation as "most ideal" for formation of a separate Uttarakhand State and demanded "special attention" of the Centre for the backward and remote northeastern region.

Addressing a series of meetings and a press conference during his day-long visit, Singh described the demand for Uttarakhand as 'unique'. For the first time since Independence, the entire population of a particular region were demanding a separate State and all major political parties backing it. Two resolutions had also been passed supporting the demand, he said.

Reiterating the Janata Dal's stand for smaller States and a restructuring of the Centre State relationship, Singh said a formula should be evolved whereby the north, eastern and other backward States would get more financial aid...

Source : *Amrit Bazar Patrika* (Calcutta), October 7, 1994

20.50 National Human Rights Commission (NHRC) Team's Visit to U.P. Hill Areas

The Chairman of the National Human Rights Commission, Justice R. N. Mishra, assured delegations of the Uttarakhand Sanskritik Sangathan and All India Uttarakhand Lawyers Association, who called on him.. that a team would be sent to the affected areas to get a first-hand account...

Source : The Hindu (New Delhi), October 9, 1994

20.51 Janata Dal and Uttarakhand

I. Mr. Chandrajit Yadav, Lok Sabha Member from the Janata Dal (George), has appealed to the Uttarakhand movement agitators to withdraw their movement as it is 'getting out of hand."

Mr. Yadav said in a statement that it had become clear that the movement for a separate Uttarakhand has achieved its end as "almost all the opposition parties except the CPI-M have supported the demand for a separate Uttarakhand in the meeting convened by the Home Minister recently."

Moreover, he said, two governments of Uttar Pradesh, one formerly led by Mr. Kalyan Singh and the other Mr. Mulayam Singh, have supported the demand. In fact, about three months ago the Uttar Pradesh Assembly passed a unanimous resolution supporting the demand. The lone opposition was from the CPI-M.

Mr. Yadav said under these circumstances the agitators should withdraw their movement because, if it turns violent now, they would lose the sympathy of everyone and it would harm the cause of Uttarakhand.

He has also appealed to Prime Minister P. V. Narasimha Rao to have a direct meeting with the leaders of the movement to solve the problem since the entire Opposition has supported this.

Source : Evening News (New Delhi), October 7, 1994

II. The Janata Dal (George) has taken a soft line on the Uttarakhand issue by appealing to hill people to suspend their movement and asking the Prime Minister, Mr. P. V. Narasimha Rao, to invite them for negotiations.

The party also supports Mr. Rao's line that the Uttar Pradesh government should not be dismissed. "This will further complicate the problem and provoke statewide unrest," the leader of the JD(G) Parliamentary Party, Mr. Chandrajit Yadav, said.

Source : Asian Age (New Delhi), October 8, 1994

20.52 Uttarakhand Activists' Views on Firing

Two women who were witness to the molestation of the women supporters of Uttarakhand and the assult on men by police in Muzaffarnagar on the night of October 1, have claimed that the police firing was pre-planned by the "Centre and State-Government".

The women—Mrs Kaushalaya Debral and Mrs. Sushila Dhayani were part of the contingent of Uttarakhand supporters from Chamoli and Dehra Dun, on there way to the rally in Delhi. They arrived at the spot, five hours after the outbreak of violence at 9. p.m. which continued for the next nine hours.

Addressing media persons the women lambasted the PAC and the local administration which had denied all reports of rape, molestation, and the killing of supporters that fateful night on a desolate highway bordered by sugarcane fields and a canal.

Refuting reports of the male supporters being armed, Mr. H.P. Bhatt, president of the H.N. Bahuguna, University, Srinagar Teachers' Association, said that there was no incident of policemen or Government officials getting injured.

The women recounted the incident: "As our buses reached the area, we found the road blocked by trucks loaded with coal. There was no space for us to squeeze past. The PAC broke the headlights of our buses so we could not see. Interestingly, by 5 a.m. water tankers had reached the spot to clean the road of the blood stains." The women maintained that the violence was unprovoked.

The account given by Mrs. Dabral and Mrs Dhyani was reinforced by Mrs. Neeru Vohra, a lecturer of Delhi University, who recently visited the spot on behalf of the Gandhi Peace Foundation. "There are no contradictions in the account given by the residents of all five neighbouring villages who gave shelter to the men and women who fled police atrocites

Source : Indian Express (New Delhi), October 9, 1994

20.53 Trampled Tranquility of the Somnolent Hills

The sleepy villages of the Uttar Pradesh hills will never be the same again. The simple, peace-loving village folks now speak of vengeance, of *azadi* from the *raj* of Mulayam Singh. And the hills resound with a call to arms.

"The Muzaffarnagar massacre has proved that arms is the only option for self-defence and to safeguard the dignity of our women," says Madan Singh Panwar of villge Badiyar Gargh, Tehri. The villagers need no CBI report to convince them that their women folks were raped.

The mood is militant, defiant, Slogans like *Ikayavan-bavan-trepan-chauvan, humko de do AK47* have started reverberating in the vales and gorges of the hills.

The whole of Uttarakhand is an angry shade of red. The people are not in a mood to accept anything short of a separate State. The hills echo and re-echo the aggressive slogans *Jisko hamase pyar nahin, woh apani sarkar nahin*. The villagers alienation need no better demonstration.

Even tiny tots from primary school are setting up barricades. They know not what the movement is really for. But still cry: *Uttarakhand ki thani hai, har bacha senani hai*.

The peaceful land has metamorphised into a military camp, guarded as it were, by the RAF, the PAC—the might of the State trampling upon the flowers of innocence.

The Uttarakhandis are preparing for a long-drawn battle, But, the Centre and State politicians are busy with their games. The slaughter of innocents and the gang-rape by the police is shrugged off as "part of politics"...

Source : Manoj Gairola and Suresh Nautiyal, *The Observer* (New Delhi), October 8, 1994

20.54 Repercussions of Brutalities

The sorrow-swept land of Uttarakhand, especially its Garhwal division, is now out of Government control. Massive stone and tree barriers have come up along all its main roads, which one would only cross at one's own peril. It has once again become a land of fortifications, (*garh* means fortifications, and wal, land)...

Source : Harish Chandola, *The Pioneer* (New Delhi), October 8, 1994

20.55 Uttarakhand Another Punjab

Following the increasing incidents of violence in the hill districts of Uttar

Pradesh, political observers... fear the region may become another hotbed of militancy unless an early solution is found to the Uttarakhand problem.

A Nainital-based Uttarakhand activist told *The Sunday Observer* after the police firing on rallyists at Muzaffarnagar... in which 10 persons were killed. "The government is testing our patience by not allowing us to even voice our protest through democractic means. They are forcing us to think of more militant means."

Sure enough, the first disturbing signs of change are noticeable. In Dehra Dun on October 3, a group of angry youths stormed a police outpost and decamped with three rifles and ammunition. And Uttarakhand supporters see enough justification for such acts. "What would you do if your brethren were nowed down or sisters were raped by policemen?" asked an Uttarakhand activist.

The presence of a large number of retired military personnel and the region's proximity to China, Tibet and Nepal further render it vulnerable to millitant activity.

Source: Polly Wilson, *The Sunday Observer* (New Delhi), October 9, 1994

20.56 Agitation in Hill Areas

While the police appear to have gained the upper hand in Dehra Dun and Pauri Garhwal districts, the agitation is still on in Tehri Garhwal, Uttarkashi and Chamoli in the Garhwal division. There are also reports of protest marches in curfew-bound Haldwani, Nainital, Almora and Pithoragarh districts of Kumaon division.

Most leaders of the Samajwadi Party in Garhwal have, meanwhile, severed ties with their party although the Barthwal-Dhasmana faction of Dehra Dun remain loyal to the Chief Minister. Among those who deserted the SP are Mr. Barpia Lal Juantha, legislator from Uttarkashi, Mr. Narendra Singh Bhandari, Garhwal party chief from Pauri, Mr. Mantri Prasad Naithani, district chief from Tehri Garhwal, Mr. Harish Pujari, district chief from Chamoli and Mr. Subhash Sharma, State executive member from Dehra Dun. From the Congress camp, former Mussoorie legislator, Mr. Kishori Lal Saklani has resigned alongwith his followers from primary membership of his party...

Source : Statesman (New Delhi), October 8, 1994

20.57 Uttarakhand Mahila Sabha (UMS), Views

The Uttarakhand Mahila Sabha (UMS) in a memorandum to President

Shankar Dayal Sharma urged him to take over the administration of Uttarakhand in the best interests of the region.

They also asked him to expedite the creation of a separate Uttarakhand State which has become a raging issue.

In a statement, UMS leaders Chandravati Negi and Uma Joshi said that demands have also been made for immediate dismissal of the Mulayam Singh Government in U.P. for allowing mass rape and killing of peaceful demostrators.

Further they have called upon the President to terminate without delay the services of the officers responsible for administration in the region—the DIG Meerut Range, the DM and the SP of Muzafarnagar.

Source : Indian Express (New Delhi), October 10, 1994

20.58 Union Minister of State Home Affairs Views on Political Crisis in U.P.

Minister of State for Home Rajesh Pilot... said there was no political crisis in Uttar Pradesh over the question of withdrawal of support to the Mulayam Singh Yadav Government.

Mr. Pilot told newspersons that everything at the party-level would be sorted out very soon. Stating that both Prime Minister P. V. Narasimha Rao and UPCC chief Narain Dutt Tiwari were very senior leaders; he said "I hope both will discuss and sort out the problem very soon."

On his meeting with Mr. Tiwari during the day, Mr. Pilot said the meeting was long and could be fruitful. "It is our internal matter. We will definitely take a decision on the question of withdrawal of support to the Samajvadi Party-Bahaujan Samaj Party (SP-BSP) Government in the State. The problem will be resolved soon," he said.

Asked to comment on the Muzaffarnagar police firing and the alleged molestation of some women by the police, Mr. Pilot said molestation of women was a very a shameful act and a serious issue and strict action should be taken against the culprits if the allegations were found correct by the enquiring authority.

Stating that the Centre was ready to play its role in finding out a solution to the Uttarakhand problem, Mr. Pilot said the issue could be discussed by the affected parties as soon as peace was restored in the Uttarakhand region; "let the situation be normalise". he added.

Source : National Herald (New Delhi), October 10, 1994

20.59 Parliamentary Delegation's Visit to Hill Areas

An all-party Parliamentary Delegation on Sunday (October 9) visited three villages of the district for an on-the-spot study of the incident in which some Uttarakhand activists were killed in police firing while on their way to attend a rally in Delhi.

The 14-member delegation, comprising Congress, CPI (M), CPI, Janata Dal, BJP, Janata Dal (S), Samajwadi Party and BSP, talked to the villagers, who sheltered a large number of rallyists after they fled the scene of action.

Though most of the villagers had said their menfolk rescued several "terrified" women activists hiding in sugarcane fields with their clothes torn and tattered, the villages were not sure of whether the women rallists were subjected to rape allegely by the PAC personnel.

The members travelled through the bumpy roads and trekked in dusty and slushy bylanes in Rampur, Sisauna and Medhpur villages listening to a large number of villagers to ascertain the facts of the incident which was described by some of the members as "black Sunday"...

Source : The Observer (New Delhi), October 10, 1994

20.60 Reign of Terror in Uttarakhand

It seems that an undeclared emergency has been imposed in the Uttarakhand region and brutal forces like PAC and the forces from other States have been deployed to crush the people and terrorise them.

In curfew-bound areas people are forced not to even peep out of the houses. The activists are being taken away to undisclosed places with the use of force. They are being denied their democratic and basic rights.

All tools of terror and repression are being used freely to crush the mass movement.

The government has turned indifferent completely instead of providing a healing touch to the wounds after the Muzaffarnagar incident. In such a situation, tendencies of alienation are sure to occur. It would not be surprising if some outfits with militant out-look come into existence in the near future.

The people believe that there is no point in holding the U.P. state together at the cost of bloodshed at a time when they have already seceded from the State mentally and emotionally.

There is no point in denying the people their basic right simply because Congress has to fight elections in some States in the near future and if it dismisses the U.P. government it will loose the elections...

The aggression on these people in the form of State terrorism has once again reminded them of the Gorkha aggression, which was equally brutal. Today, the whole Uttarakhand is vibrating with aggressive slogans. The participation of women and students is unprecedented and overwhelming...

Source : The Observer (New Delhi), October 10, 1994.

20.61 Muzaffarnagar DM Anant Kumar Singh's Views on Firing and Rape

Muzaffarnagar District Magistrate Anant Kumar Singh was compared to General Dyer of the Jallianwalan Bagh after he gave orders to shoot Uttarakhand activists at Rampur Tiraha on October 2. Several agitators were reported killed in the firing. Talking to Raman Kirpal, he justified his action and proferred arguments in his support. Stating that no person was killed in the firing at Rampur Tiraha, he alleged that the reports of the killings were part of a deep-rooted consipiracy to malign him and his Administration.

R K : Villagers say there was no provocation for you to order firing on the Uttarakhand activists?

AKS : This is not right. I used all other methods first to control a 12,000-strong mob. I tried to convince them to allow the police to check their vehicles after which they could proceed to Delhi. But they did not agree. On the contrary, they started stoning us. I first ordered a lathicharge and then teargassing. Unfortunately, the teargassing affected us more because the wind direction was towards our side. The agitators closed in on us and indulged in heavy brick batting. Only 200 policemen were fighting against such a strong mob and there was every chance of us being lynched. Thus, I gave shoot orders.

R K : Is stone-pelting reason enough for shoot orders?

AKS : If you had gone to the spot, you must have seen lots of bricks lying on the roadside. They had showered brick after brick at the police and marched towards us. The fear that a leaderless crowed can kill all of us forced me to order fire. Someone has to take action at a given point of time. Two years ago at Ayodhya, the disputed structure was demolished by miscreants, because the District Administration did not take any action. This act had brought shame on the entire country. And I did not want it to be repeated at Delhi, as most of the agitators were carrying firearms as per my information.

R.K.: The main cause of the Muzaffarnagar incident was that you wanted to search their buses, but the agitators did not allow you to do so and the situation deteriorated. Did you get anything during the search?

AKS: We had a written order from Intelligence Bureau to check their buses thoroughly before giving them passage to Delhi. In the order, the IB had expressed fear that several ex-servicemen accompanying the agitators were carrying firearms. Later we seized. 12 bore revolvers, cans of petrol and several bottles of liquor.

RK: Can you be specific about how many of them you seized?

AKS: We seized several revolvers, but I cannot tell you the exact number of items seized at the moment. These items are lying at the office of SP. City.

RK: Were you on the spot during the entire operation?

AKS.: Yes.

RK: Did the agitators use firearms against you and did any of the wounded policemen receive bullet injuries?

AKS: The agitators threw only bricks on us and no policemen received bullet injury.

RK: Villagers say the police fired twice on the agitators, once on the night of October 1 and then in the wee hours of October 2?

AKS: This is rubbish. The firing took place only once at Rampur Tiraha in the wee hours on October 2. A total number of 34 bullets were fired. On the night of October 1, we used only lathicharge to disperse the mob.

RK: How many persons were killed in the firing?

AKS: I want to make a categorical statement here that no person died in the firing at Rampur Tiraha. When the mob was dispersed after the firing, I saw four persons lying on the road. All of them were alive and had shot wounds below the waist. We immediately took them to the Government Hospital of Muzaffarnagar where they are getting proper medical treatment and are out of danger.

RK: But records at the Roorkee hospital confirm that five bodies were brought to the hospital from Rampur Tiraha?

AKS: The bodies were brought to the Roorkee hospital, but not from Rampur. Another firing had taken place 43 km. away at Narsen in Haridwar District. See, there seems to be something wrong somewhere. Let me tell you what happened. At 11.30 a.m. on October 2, I received a call from the Haridwar District Magistrate, saying that five bodies were brought from Rampur to Roorkee. I immediately made my enquiries and found that it was just not possible. If the bodies were taken from Rampur to Roorkee, there should have been entries at two police check points at

Chappar and Purkaji, which are on the way. However, the entries were made only at Purkaji, which is close to Narsen where the Haridwar Administration had ordered a firing. It is possible that the bodies were taken from Narsen and the buck was passed on me to malign the Muzaffarnagar Administration.

RK: Have you told your senior officials about this?

AKS: On October 3, I sent a report about the incident to the Chief Secretary and he has sought a judicial enquiry to determine where the bodies came from. I have also sent a spot map indicating four persons were found injured after the firing at Rampur and no person was killed.

RK: Several eyewitnesses have confirmed that the women accompanying the agitators were raped and molested.

AKS: I do not deny it completely. But I want to draw your attention to a fact that women hid themselves in the sugarcane fields when the brick-batting was going on. Whether the policemen or the agitators themselves raped them, I can tell you only after conducting investigations. You see, it is human tendency. When a woman is seen at a lonely place in the jungle, any man will be inclined to rape her. In this particular case. I will certainly hold investigation.

AK: Finally, did you have orders from the State Government for not letting the Uttarakhand agitators reach Delhi for the rally?

RKS: I had orders not to let agitators go to Delhi from Rampur Tiraha point till the police made a thorough search of their buses. Had the agitators allowed us to check, I would have allowed them to proceed.

Source : The Pioneer (New Delhi), October 10, 1994

20.62 Sit-in Staged by Uttarakhand Women

A women's group from Uttarakhand protested against police firing on a peaceful demostration in Muzaffarnagar on Gandhi Jayanti by holding a sit-in at Rajghat.

The Uttarakhand Mahila Sabha alleged the Union Government with the U.P. government, has used repression, including rape to suppress the Uttarakhand movement.

The State Government has lost the moral right to rule, said Sabha convenor Uma Joshi. The President must intervene, create an Uttarakhand State, dismiss the U.P. Government, sack top police and administration officials for their role in firing, have Punjab and Delhi police withdrawn from the region and generally halt repressive policies, the Sabha demanded.

Source: Times of India (New Delhi), October 10, 1994

20.63 MP's Team Confirms Molestation of Uttarakhandis

Most members of the all-party fact-finding team, barring BSP general secretary Mayawati, agreed that the police firing on the Uttarakhand agitators on October 2 could have been avoided.

Members of the team, which comprised 14 M.P.s told reporters that circumstantial evidence gathered from a cross section of people from Rampur, Madhpur and Sisona villages indicated that the authorities could have resorted to some alternative means to tackle the situation.

Describing the firing as unjustified and unwarranted, most members felt that the authorities concerned had acted at the behest of the SP-BSP coalition Government. They added that the Intelligence Bureau's routine report about the possibility of some agitators carrying arms appears to have been used as a pretext to open fire on the agitators. However, not a single weapon was recovered from the agitators who were mostly ex-servicemen and youths.

Speaking to reporters on behalf of the six Congress MPs in the delegation, Girja Vyas, who is also President of the Mahila Congress Committee said circumstantial evidence indicated that several women were molested while a 22 year-old girl from Chamoli district was criminally assulted.

Ms. Vyas said many villagers told them that some women activists were stripped. chased and humiliated by the police. Their discussion with the authorities revealed that tenstion had begun to build up soon after the police put up blockades or the Muzaffarnagar-Rourkee national highway in Hardwar district...

Source : Times of India (New Delhi), October 10, 1994

20.64 Uttarakhand: Nemesis of Indian Colonial Mindset

Like it or not but people of India in general and of Uttar Pradesh in particular have always treated the mountain areas of Kumaon and Garhwal as their colonies. And this is the genesis of the present-day Uttarakhand movement for creation of a separate State. Uttarakhand is the indigenous answer of some very indigenous policy of colonialism followed by mindless Indian rulers for long. And this despite the fact that some very bright sparks of leaders have come from this very area of Uttarakhand. Our relationship with the mountains of Uttar Pradesh has been very colonial—benign but exploitative. From the time some enterprising Sikhs started buying Tarai lands for a pittance to the present day this exploitation continues. Notwithstanding the fact that some manipulative builders actually own a whole lot of hilltops, the hill areas of Garhwal and Kumaon interest the rest of Indian only as places of seasonal tourism or where the *baba log* attend some residential school in the protected and insulated environs of some very English sub-culture.

The "reservation policy" announced by Mulayam Singh Yadav may have proved to be an igniting spark or the proximate cause but the problem was brewing for far too long. It is not the absolute deprivation *per se* which has brought all the Uttarakhandis together but it is the perceived policy of deliberate deprivation of a whole people from the mainstream of job opportunities. The people from hill areas of U.P. have descended to the plains in search of jobs ending up as school teachers, *chhota babus, mundus* in the Dhabas and, in some stray cases, as sharers of power at the Centre making it a money-order economy or sorts. But, by and large, unemployment and perpetual poverty has been the fate of the people in Garhwal and Kumaon areas. Exploitative colonialism does not have an unending life anywhere on the earth. The Garhwalis and Kumaonis have come to perceive themselves as the "wretched of the earth" in their own homeland which, for all practical purposes and intents, is a place behind the beyond for the people from plains who see these places as some kind of punishment postings. Naturally, the people posted in the hills from the plains are not motivated for any meaningful development of the area. Some bureaucrat sitting in distant Lucknow can hardly have the expertise or sensitiveness to see the growth potentials of an area even as a tourist resort much less as a motor to further the economic growth...

But, then, as long as Uttarakhand remains part of the larger tract of land called Uttar Pradesh it will have to remain subservient to the colonial masters even if they happen to be Indians from the plains. It is this realization that has led to the present-day movement for a separate State of Uttarakhand and there is really no reason for the country to resist this perfectly natural demand of a people to manage their own affairs without separating from the country. Autonomy is not a concession. It is a right. Uttarakhand region thus has a case for statehood. A new State Reorganisation Commission, like the one of 1953 yore, should be also considered to carve out Indian States afresh. This should also serve to create separate states like western U.P. which is only logical. The important thing is that the country should remain together. Personal egos of the ministers and leaders can wait.

Source: University Today (New Delhi), October 10, 1994, editorial.

21

SURVEY FINDINGS ON THE DEMAND FOR UTTARAKHAND STATE

Following specific points were selected for the purpose of finding the general public opinion on the various issues involved in the demand for the Uttarakhand State. The sample consisted of 1,030 individuals, belonging to different age groups and residing in Kumaon region.

1. Development process through separate hill State.
2. Resource availability in the separate hill State.
3. Solution of regional problems
4. Vested political interests
5. Mass support
6. Participation readiness
7. Attitude towards leadership
8. Possibility of conflict over the capital of the separate hill State
9. Rivalry between Kumaon and Garhwal
10. Perceived influence of the demand on General Elections.
11. Fulfilment of regional needs and its influence on the demand for a hill State.
12. Attitude towards alternatives to the demand for a separate hill State
13. Demand as a separatist tendency.

Findings

1. About 50 per cent respondents expressed that a separate hill State would facilitate the process of development. About 25 per cent

were neutral and the rest had a negative attitude.

2. Thirty-nine per cent respondents expressed positive attitude towards availability of sufficient resources in the State. About 30 per cent were neutral and 31 per cent expressed a negative attitude.
3. About 47 per cent respondents viewed that different regional problems could be solved through a separate hill State, about 27 per cent were neutral and the rest had negative views.
4. Approximately 32 per cent respondents perceived interplay of vested political interests in the demand for a separate hill State. About 41 per cent respondents were of the view that there were no vested political interests in the demand for a separate hill State and rest remained neutral.
5. The percentage of the opponents of the demand for a separate State was about 22. About 51 per cent felt that there was a mass support to the demand for a separate hill State.
6. About 47 per cent expressed participation readiness in the movements for a hill State, 26 per cent were undecided and 27 per cent respondents were found to be not ready to participate.
7. About 25 per cent respondents felt satisfied with regional leadership in the context of the demand for a separate hill State. About 24 per cent expressed neutrality on this aspect. About 52 per cent expressed dissatisfaction with leadership.
8. About 33 per cent felt that the problem of the selection of the capital of the hill State would be solved amicably. About 31 per cent did not express any opinion. About 36 per cent felt there was a possibility of conflict on this issue.
9. About 43 per cent of the respondentss felt that the rivalry between Kumaon and Garhwal would not hinder the creation of a hill State 30 per cent were neutral and 27 per cent felt that rivalry will create difficulties.
10. About 45 per cent respondents felt that the demand for a separate hill State tended to influence general election, about 28 per cent were neutral and about 27 per cent felt no influence.
11. About 38 per cent respondents tended to State that if development needs of the hill region were fulfilled, the demand would subside. About 34 per cent respondents negated any such influence. Approximately 28 per cent respondents tended to the neutral on this issue.
12. About 36 per cent respondents were favourably inclined to the suggestion of declaring U.P. hill areas as centrally administered

1955, May 22	Delhi Sammelan of the workers of the hill districts passes resolution of a hill State.
1957	Tehri Naresh Manvendra, B J S M.P., raises the issue of a hill State
1965	Formation of All Party Council by P.C. Joshi and demand for a separate hill State
1968, June 24-25	Ram Nagar Sammelan and the demand for a hill State
	Demonstration at Boat Club in New Delhi.
1973	Publication of a book on a separate hill State
	Uttarakhand State Parishad formed in Delhi
1978	Sammelan at Boat Club in New Delhi.
1979	Formation of Uttarakhand Rajya Parishad by the Janata Government
	Rally in New Delhi and demand for Uttaranchal State
	Publication of a book in Hindi: *Why Uttarakhand Kranti Dal.*
1981	Memorandum for Uttarakhand State to Smt. Indira Gandhi the then Prime Minister of India on her visit to Nainital.
1985	Kashi Singh Aeri of Uttarakhand Kranti Dal (UKD) elected to the Vidhan Sabha.
1986	Kashi Singh Aeri becomes the President of UKD.
1987	Publication of a book in Hindi on the State of Uttarakhand
	Rally for Statehood.
1988 Feb. 23	Demonstrations in support of a hill State at district headquarters.
Sept. 12-13	Uttarakhand bandh.
Dec. 15-31	Uttarakhand Kranti March.
1990, April 10	'Delhi Chalo' slogan by Uttaranchal Sangharsh Samiti
1991	Founding of Uttarakhand Mahasabha
1991 August 12	BJP Government in U.P. adopts a resolution for the creation of Uttaranchal State and sends it to the Government of India
Sept. 23	Founding of Uttarakhand Jan Parishad
1994, Aug.2,	Major demonstration at Pauri
Aug.8,	Firing and Lathi Charge in Pauri
Aug.10,	Setting up of a Joint Action Committee at a meeting

	at Srinagar (Garhwal)
August 23	Bandh in Uttarakhand
September 1,	Police firing in Khatima
September 2,	Demonstration at Pauri
September 6,	Demonstration at Joshimath
September 7	Demonstration at Uttarkashi
September 8,9	Markets closed in Uttarkhand
September 11	Uttar Pradesh Congress Committee dicides to withdraw support to Mulayam Singh Government in U.P.
September 13	Pro-reservation band sponsered by the ruling SP-BSP Party,
	Ugly incidents at the premises of Allahabad High Court.
	Allahabad High Court refers the matter to Supreme Court. Supreme Court orders for a CBI enquiry.
September 14	No lamplit.
	Hundred of Pradhans resign
	Lathi charge and firing on the people in Pauri,Uknimath, Khatima and Mussori
September 14	Supreme Court Summons top U.P. Officials including Chief Secretary on Allahabad High Court issue.
September 30	Supreme Court for action against some U.P. Officials
October 2	At least ten Uttarakhand supporters are said to have been killed in police firing at Muzaffarnagar and over hundred injured. The supporters were coming to Delhi for the rally.
	More than 30 vallyists from Uttarakhand region injured during police lathi charge in Delhi.
	Speakers at the rally reiterate their demand for a hill State, abolition of 27 per cent reservation for backward classes in the hills and judicial inquires into the firing at Khatima (Nainital) and Mussori during the Uttarakhand stir in September 1994.
October 3	Three persons were killed and several injured in hill towns of Uttarakhand in protests against the police firing in Muzaffarnagar.
	Curfew imposed in Pauri, Srinagar, Dehradun, Rishi Kesh and Kotdwar. Government property

unification of Karnataka, the co-operation of Mysore State is essential and that it may require some time for preparation. In Kerala there is a general recognition that, without the merger of Cochin and Travancore States, a separate province cannot exist; and the demand there is weakest and is rightly conditional upto the formation of any other linguistic province out of Madras, and the people are prepared to wait till a United Kerala comes into existence. Maharashtra is a late-comer in the field of agitation for lingusitic provinces, and it is still a divided house comprising three cross-divisions of Konkan, Desh and Mahavidarbha, none of whom has suffered in any way in the struggle for political power.

The main ground put forward for the demand for lingustic provinces is that these are essential for the working of democracy, as also for the working of the Constitution, and a linguistic province is the best form of a homogeneous province, which the existing circumstances in India permit to be formed. It is said that the working of democracy is impeded in the field of education, Legislature and Administration by a multiplicity of languages spoken in a province. It is further said that autonomous provinces are embodied in our Federal Constitution and autonomous provinces imply autonomous States. And as the larger linguistic groups now existing in India claim historically to have formed sub-nations, they contend that the appropriate place for these sub-nations is in a linguistic State, just as, for the same reason, the correct principle upon which autonomous provinces should be formed is the lingustic principle.

Linguistic homogencity in the formation of new provinces is certainly attainable within certain limits but only at the cost of creating a fresh minority problem. More than half the Malayalam and Kannada speaking people are living in Indian States, and only a little less than half of the Telugu and Marathi-speaking people are living either in Indian States or in Union Provinces from which they cannot be transferred to new linguistic provinces either for want of geographical contiguity or want of thir consent to be so transferred. These must remain, at least for many years to come, outside the sphere of a linguistic province. Even in the limited areas of the Union, which can be made homogeneous linguistically, border districts on each side and the capital cities of Bombay and Madras will remain bilingual or multi-lingual. And, as has been explained before, nowhere will it be possible to form a linguistic province of more than 70 to 80% of the people speaking the same language, thus leaving in each province a minority of at least 20% of people speaking other languages. And considering the evidence, which has come before us in regard to the Telugus, who were transferred to Orissa from Madras at the time of the formation of the Orissa Province, and the Tamils, who live in Southern

Travancore, it is easy to foresee that similar minority problems on a much more extensive scale will arise all over the linguistic provinces.

As for persons speaking the same language forming a sub-nation, whatever may have been their condition in the past, now for 200 years these people have got separated and scattered over different areas in British-made Provinces or Indian States and have become assimilated with them, so much so that the Rayalaseema districts are not at present eager to throw in their lot with the coastal districts; Cochin and Travancore would not easily coalesee with Malabar; and there are difficulties in the way of Mysore merging in Coorg and Karanataka districts; and Mahavidarbha is not keen on joining Bombay (Maharashtra). Each of these differing elements now has its own special needs and problems, which require individual treatment and which prevent these elements from easily coming together in one homogenous province contemplated by the Constitution unless special provisions be made for them.

It may, therefore, be safely assumed that linguistic groups as sub-nations do not exist anywhere at present. But if the intention were to bring sub-nations into existence, there could not be a better way of doing it than by putting together these differing elements in a lingustic province. An authonomous linguistic province in other words, means an autonomous linguistic State and an autonomous linguistic State means, in the words of one of its exponents, that its territories are inviolate. And if in a linguistic province the majority language group comes to regard the territory of the entire provinces as exclusively its own, the time cannot be far distant when it will come to regard the minority living in that province and people living outside it as not their own. And once that stage is reached it will only be a question of time for that sub-nation to consider itself a full nation.

The strength of the demand for linguistic provinces lies in the fact that there is some advantage in imparting education, in the working legislature and in administration if a large majority of the people speak the same language and in the fact that these linguistic groups do not seem to live happily in the existing provinces and are anxious to separate. The demand receives added force from the fact that several of the existing provinces more or less possess linguistic homogeneity. That one part of the country is linguistically homogeneous, including the small Province of Orissa, which has to be maintained by subvention from the Centre, is a source of constant irritation to linguistically heterogenous provinces. It certainly does not lie in the mouth of those who are living in a linguistically heterogenous provinces. It certainly does not lie in the mouth of those who are living in a linguistically homogenous province to point out its evils to those living in a heterogenous province. Moreover the formation of linguistic provinces has been an article of faith in the current political thought of the country during the last 30 years and has received the support of the Congress and the blessings of Mahatama Gandhi.

The weakness of the demand lies in the fact that it involves the recognition of the principle of Government of a province by a linguistic group, which is basically wrong. Further it paves the way for the recognition of other group Governments for which there may exist a tendency in the country, for example, Government by Southerners in the south of India, Government by Sikhs and Jats in the north of India, and even Government by the non-Brahmins in certain areas of this country. It leads to the breaking up or deterioration of vital organisms like capital cities and border district where, for generations, a bilingual or multi-lingual life has flourished happily. It would further create minority problems and State problems of a kind which did not exit before. And, above all, it would bring into existence provinces with a subnational bias at a time when nationalism is yet in its infancy and is not in a position to bear any strain. And, lastly, the motive behind the demand is open to serious challenge. It is not the ostensible ground of making democracy run smoother, but the fact that these several communities living in the province cannot get on together, that is behind the proposal to separate and form Governments of their own.

The existing Indian Provinces are administrative units of British imperialism. They came into existence in a somewhat haphazard way, and were not designed to work as democratic institutions; they are certainly susceptible of more scientific and rational planning. But they have taken root and are now living vital organisms and have served the useful purpose of bringing together people, who might otherwise have remained separated. And though they may be somewhat disadvantageous in working modern democracy, they are not bad instruments for submerging a subnational consciousness and moudling a nation.

In any rational and scientific planning that may take place in regard to the provinces of India in the future, homogeneity of language alone cannot be a decisive or even an important factor. Administrative convenience, history, geography, economy, culture, and many other matters will also have to be given due weight. It may be that the provinces thus formed will also show homogencity of language and, in a way, might resemble linguistic provinces. But, in forming the provinces, the emphasis should be primarily on administrative convenience, and homogeneity of language will enter into consideration ony as a matter of administrative convenience and not by its own independent force.

But this is certainly not the time for embarking upon the enterprise of re-drawing the map of the whole of southern India, including the Deccan, Bombay, and the Central Provinces. India is yet to become a nation, and Indian States are yet to be integrated. The problem of regrouping the provinces would become simpler when the future of the remaining States is definitely known. Again, India can ill spare at this moment and for some time to come the money, material, or administrative talent, which will be required for setting up half a dozen new Governments and new Capitals. It cannot afford to add to its anxieties the heat, controversy and bitterness, which the demarcation of boundaries and allotment of the capital cities of Bombay and Madras will involve. And lastly by splitting three existing provinces into half a dozen the economy of almost half the country will be so seriously upset that it should not be attempted without a great deal of study, preparation and planning. However urgent the problem of redistribution of provinces may be, it is not more urgent than the defence problem, the inflation problem, the refugee, problem, the food problem, the production problem, and many other problems with which India is burdened today. All these must get priority and the redistribution of provinces must wait till India has become a nation and has been fully integrated. If India lives, all her problems will be solved; if India does not survive, nothing will be gained by solving her linguistic provinces problem alone.

In order to secure this stability and integration, India should have a strong centre and a national language. Indian nationalism is deeply wedded to its regional languages; Indian patriotism is aggressively attached to its provincial frontiers. If India is to survive, Indian nationalism and patriotism will have to sacrifice some of its cherished sentiments in the larger interests of the country. India has chosen for herself the destiny of a Federal Republic. In the Constitution, which is now being forged for her, a framework may be set up, which would enable her to find her destiny. Provide, if you will, for authonomous provinces and for adult franchise; but also recognize that there will be a period of transition, a period of trial and error, during which India will have to prepare for its destiny and during which the Centre must possess large, overriding powers of control and direction-powers which may be kept in reserve and may be sparingly used and finally abandoned, but which must be available for effective use if and when occasion arises.

Till nationalism has acquired sufficient strength to permit the formation of authonomous provinces, the true nature and function of a province under our Constitution should be that of an administrative unit functioning under delegated authority from the Centre and subject to the

Centre's overriding powers in regard to its territory, its existence, and its functions. These powers are required to form new provinces and to mitigate the rigour of Government by linguistic majorities, to prevent a breakdown of the administration on account of disputes amongst linguistic groups, to check fissiparous tendencies and strengthen national feeling, and above all to build up an Indian nation.

An immediate solution has, however, to be found for the desire for separation which exists among the Telugus, Malayalees, Kannadigas, and Maharashtrians, These linguistic groups are entitled to their legitimate share in the administration, Government and development of their provinces. Two of these linguistic groups, namely Malayalees and Kannadigas, are situated at the tail-end of their provinces and represented by ineffectal minorities in their Legislatures. Two others, namely, the Telugus and the Maharashtrians in C.P. and Berar, are represented by large, virile, and group-conscious minorities; but they are faced with equally group-concious majorities and the two refuse to coalesce and produce a harmonious Government. The clash and conflict, which exists between them, has brought the administration in Madras to a breaking point, and C.P. and Berar are also showing signs of going the same way. No particular grievance would seem to exist in the case of the Bombay Maharashtra group.

A number of constitutional safeguards were suggested to us to prevent such a breakdown. One commonly-favoured suggestion was that the Governor should always come from another province and should be selected by the Centre for his character and ability and armed with powers to prevent injustice to minorities, and charged with this duty in his Instrument of Instructions. Another suggestion was that Provincial Subjects should be reduced and Joint Subjects enlarged, and the Centre given residuary and overriding powers. The third was that the Goverment in these provinces should be run by turns by linguistic groups, or be divided into administrative regions, and that the Centre should impose conventions in regard to these matters under which the administration might be carried on. We have not considered in detail these and other siilar suggestions made to us as it is not strictly within our province to do so. They all, however, lead to the inference that the Centre must be armed with overriding powers and must assume rsponsibility to guide democracy till Indian nationalism has been sufficiently strengthened and democracy is able to stand on its own legs.

The only good that we can see in a linguistic province is the possible advantage it has in working the legislature in the regional language. But this is more than counter-balanced by the obstruction the linguistic

Sira	Baleshwar Thal	Vrish solstice	Shiva
	Bhagling	Nag Panchami	Bhagling
	Devchula		Local deity
		Anant Chaturdashi	
Kali Kumaun	Narsing Temple, Faraka	Vijaya Dashmi Narsingh	
	Chamdeval, Gumdesh	Chamde and Dashami	Local deity
		10th day of April-May	
	Garhmukteshwar	Full moon of Oct.-Nov.	Shiva
	Khilpati	Full moon of June-July	Akhil Tarini Devi
	Risheshwar Mahadev Lohaghat	Mahashtami	Shiva
	Devidhura	Full moon of July-August	Varahi Devi
Danpur	Bageshwar	Uttarayani	Shiva
	Ranchula Kot	Nandasthami	Nanda
Pali Pachchaun	Somnath Givar	Som Nath	Shiva
	Vibhandeshwar, Dora	Vishvat Sankranti	Shiva
	Boorha Kedar	Full moon of Oct.-Nov.	Shiva
	Neeleshwar, Bhikiyasain (Nauleshwar)	Shiv Ratri	Shiva
	Mamla Devi	Vishvat Sankranti	Shiva
	Kapileshwar Mahadev Malla Kaklasaun	Shiv Ratri	Shiva

(2) DISTRICT NAINITAL

Chhakhata	Nainital	Dol	Shri Krishna
	Nainital	Nandashtami	Nanda Devi
	Ranibagh	Uttaryani	Mahadev

	Chitrashula		
	Chitrashula	Shiv Ratri	Shiva
Dhyani Rau	Kailash	Dark half 14 of Oct.-Nov.	Shiva and Jwala Devi
Kota Pahar	Teerath	Shiv Ratri	Shiva
	Seeta Vani	Amavasya of Januray-February	Seeta
Chhakhata Bhatar	Haldwani	Dussehra	Shri Ram Chandra
	"	Janmashtami	Shri Krishna
Kota Bhabar	Kaladhungi	Dussehra	Shri Ram Chandra
Chilkia	Ramnagar	Dusshera	Shri Ram Chandra
Kashipur	Kashipur	Chaiti	Bal Sundari Devi
	Kashipur	Bhadon(Aug.-Sept.)	Zahar Aulia Peer
	Kashipur	Gudasi(12th of light) Aug.-Sept.	Burha Baba
	Kashipur	Dussehra	Shri Ram Chandra
Khasipur	Jaspur	Janmashtami	Shri Krishna
Gadarpur	Gadarpur		
		Shiv Ratri	Mahadev
Bazpur	Alapur	Dussehra	Shri Ram Chandra
"	Jharkhandi	Shiv Ratri	Mahadev
Rudrapur	Rudrapur	Shiv Ratri	Mahadev
	Kichcha	Janmashtami	Shri Krishna
Kilpuri	Kilpuri	Shiv Ratri	Mahadev
	Sitaganj	Dussehra	Shri Ram Chandra
Nanakmata	Nanakmata	Deepawali	Nanak Shah
Bilari	Chakrapura	Shiv Ratri	Mahadev

Appendix-7

THE GARHWALI SOLDIER

The Garhwali Soldier leapt into fame in the battle of Neuve Chapelle during first World War.

The Allied Spring Offensive opened in France on March 10, 1915, when Sir Johan French, commanding the British Expeditionary Force, struck a heavy blow for the recovery of the fortified village of Neuve Chapelle, for whose possession there had been hard fighting in the last week of October 1914. The British trenches lay a few hundred yards to the west of the village, behind which was the Aubers Ridge and the wide plain of Lille and Turcoing. The Fourth Army Corps and the Indian Corps led the assault on the village, while the Second Army in the north and the First Army Corps in the neighbourhood of Givenchy demostrated in order to distract the attention of the Germans from the focal point of attack.

Two division

The 8th Division on the left and the Meerut Division on the right—were deployed for the attack on a half-mile front. The story revolves round the exploit of the 1st and 2nd Battalions of the 39th Garhwal Rifles, forming part of the Garhwal Brigade of the Meerut Division. The Garhwal Brigade led the attack, the Dehra Dun Brigade was in support, and the Bareilly Brigade played the holding role. The offensive was launched with 2/3 Gorkha Rifles and the 2nd Leicesters in the centre and the Garhwalis on the flanks (the 1st Battalion on the right and the 2nd Battalion on the left).

It was the Garhwalis' first major action, and they acquitted themselves nobly on the battlefield. The obstacle before them was a most serious one, for the German front was seamed with trenches, girdled with wire, and fringed with machine-guns. At half-past seven in the morning the British

Barron, n.d., *Wanderings in the Himmala by a Pilgrim*
Basak, R.G., 1919-20, The Five Damodarpur Copper Plate Inscriptions of the Gupta Period, *E.I.*, XV, p113-145
Bashiruddin Ahmad, ed, 1981, *Garhwal Bye-Election: Report of the Fact Finding Committee,* Citizens for Demoeracy, New Delhi, 88p
Basu, B.D., 1914, *Sacred Books of the Hindus*, Calcutta, vol 16
Batton, n.d., *Reports on Kumaon*
Beal, Samuel, 1881, *Buddhist Records of the Western World*, Trubner's Oriental Series, London, 2 vols
Beni Prasad, 1928, *The State in Ancient India,* Allahabad
Bernier, Francois, 1901, *Berniers Voyage to the East Indies*, reprinted for the Resuscitation of Indian Literature by H.C. Dass, Calcutta
Bernier, Francois, 1972, *Travels in the Mogul Empire*, tr by Archibald Constable, originally published 1891
Berreman, G.D., 1963, *Hindus of Himalayas*, Bombay
Beveridge, Henry, ed, 1968, *The Tuzuk-i-Jahangiri or Memoris of Jahangir*, New Delhi, originally published 1909
Bhagat Laxman Singh, 1909, *Guru Gobind Singh*, Lahore
Bhagawan Lal Indraji, 1881, An Inscription at Gaya; *Ind. Ant.*, X, p347-357
Bhagawan Lal Indraji, 1885, *Twenty-Three Inscriptions from Nepal*, Bombay
Bhandarkar, R.G., 1913, *The Vaisnavism, Saivism and Minor Religious Systems*, Karl J. Trubner, Strassburg
Bhandarkar, D.R., 1904-07, An Ekling Ji Stone Inscription and the Origin and History of the Lakulisa Sect, *J.B.B., R.A.S.*, p151-165
Bhandarkar, D.R., 1925, *Asoka*, Calcutta
Bhandarkar, D.R., 1931, Mathura Pillar Inscription of Chandragupta II G.E. 61, *E.I.*, XXI, p1-9
Bhat, S.D. and Pane, R.K., eds, 1991, *Ecology of Mountain Waters*, Ashish Pub House, New Delhi, p149-173, 306-320
Bhattacharya, B.C., 1939, *The Jaina Iconography,* Lahore
Bhattasali, N.K., 1929, *Iconography of Buddhist and Brahmanical Sculptures in the Dacca Museum*, Dacca
Blunt, 1931, *Caste System of Northern India*
Briggs, G.W., 1938, *Gorakhanatha and the Kanaphata Yogis*, Calcutta
Briggs, John, 1910, *History of the Rise of the Mahomedan Power in India till the Year 1612*, tr from the original text of Mohamed Kasim Farishta, vol 2 and vol 4
Brown, Percy, 1956, *Indian Architecture: Buddhist and Hindu,* voll
Bruce, Charles Granville, 1910, *Twenty Years in Himalayas*

Bühler, G., 1892, The Prasasti of the Temple of Lakhamandal, *E.I.*, I, p10-15

Bühler, G., 1959, *Indian Palaeography*, Calcutta

Burn, R., ed, 1957, *The Cambridge History of India*, Delhi, vol 4

Bury, J.B., 1900, *History of Greece to the Death of Alexander the Great*, London

Carnac, H. Rivett, 1877, Rough Notes on some Ancient Sculpturing on Rocks in Kumaon similar to those Found in Monoliths and Rocks in Europe, *J.A.S.B.*, XLV, pt I, p1-15

Chakrabortty, S.K., 1935-36, The Tribal Coins of Northern India, *J.R.A.S.*, p31-98, Numismatic Supplement, XLVI

Chhabra, B. Ch., 1944, Lakhamandal Fragmentary Inscription of the Gupta Period, *J.U.P.H.S.*, XVII, p80-82

Chhabra, B. Ch., 1953, Devaprayag Brahmi Inscriptions, *E.I.*, XXX, p133-135

Chhabra, B. Ch., 1961, *Diplomatic Sanskrit Copper Plate Grants*, Delhi

Clay, J.M., nd., *Nainital*

Cole, H.H. and Magnor, R, 1947, *Animal Agriculture*, W.H. and Co, San Francisco

Coomaraswamy, Ananda K., n.d., *The Dances of Siva*, Bombay

Commaraswamy, Ananda K., 1926, *Catalogue of the Indian Collections in the Museum of Fine Arts*, Boston, Part V: *Rajput Painting*, Part VI: *Mughal Painting*, Boston, reprint 1981, Varanasi

Coomaraswamy, Anand K., 1927, *A History of Indian and Indonesian Art*, London

Commariswamy, Ananda K., 1931, *The Yakshas*

Cousens, H., 1926, *Chalukyan Architecture*, Calcutta

Crocker, H.E., 1930, A Trip to Lakhamandal, *J.U.P.H.S.*, IV, pt II, p26-31

Crooke, W., n.d., *The Tribes and Castes in the N.W.P.*

Crooke, W., 1896, *Religion and Folklore of Northern India*, Calcutta

Cunningham, A., 1862-63, *Archaeological Survey of India*, vol I, p248-251

Cunningham, A, 1870, *Ancient Geography of India*, reprint, 1979, Varanasi

Cunningham, A., 1871-72, *Archaeological Survey of India*, vol III, p13-45

Cunningham, A., 1878-79, *Archaeological Survey of India*, vol XIV, p 125-135

Cunningham, A., 1891, *Coins of Ancient India*, London

Dabral, Shiv Prasad, 1961, *Uttarakhand*, Dogadda, Garhwal

Dasgupta, S.N., 1955, *A History of Indian Philosophy*, Cambridge

Datar, B.N., 1961, *Himalayan Pilgrimage*, Publications Division, Government of India, Delhi

Dewar, Deuglas, n.d., *A Hand Book to the English Pre-Mutiny Records in the Government Records Room of the United Provinces of Agra and Oudh*, Allahabad

Dey, Nundo Lal, 1927, *Geographical Dictionary of Ancient and Mediaeval India*, London

Dhaky, M.A., 1961, The Chronology of the Solanki Temples of Gujarat, *J.M.I.P.*, no 3

Dhoundiyal, N.C., et al, 1993, *The Separate Hill State*, Shree Almora Book Depot, Almora, vol 2: (English), 190p

Diskalkar, D.B., 1932, Some Brahmanical Sculptures in the Mathura Museum, *J.U.P.H.S.*, V, pt I, p18-57

Dikshitar, T.A.V., 1945, The Vedic Sacrifices and Temple Worship, *B.V.*, V, p62-70

Dikshitar, V.R.R., 1932, *The Mauryan Polity*, Madras

Dodwell, H.H., ed, 1958, The *Cambridge History of India*, Delhi, vol 5

Duff, C. Mabel, 1899, *The Chronology of India from the Earliest Times to the Beginning of the 16th Century*, White Hall Gardens

Elliot and Dowson, 1867-69, *History of India as Told by Its Own Historians*, London, vol 1, vol 2 and vol 8

Evatt, J., 1924, *Hand Book on Garhwalis*, Calcutta

Farishta, Mohamed Kasim, n.d., *Tarikh-i-Farishta*, tr by John Briggs, London

Fasiuddin, M., n.d., *Land Revenue Settlements in U.P.*

Fergusson, J., n.d., *Tree and Serpent Worship*

Fergusson, J., 1910, *History of Indian and Eastern Architecture*, London, vol I

Fleet, J.F., 1888, Inscriptions of Early Gupta Kings and Their Successors, *C.I.I.*, III

Foster, Williams, ed, 1968, *Early Travels in India, 1583-1619*, S. Chand, Delhi, 351p, illustrations, map, originally published, 1921, London

Francke, A.H., 1914, *Antiquities of Indian Tibet*, Calcutta, pt I

Führer, A., 1891, The Monumental Antiquities and Inscriptions of the North-West and Oudh, *Archaelogical Survey of India*, Allahabad

Gairola, T.D., 1934, *Himalayan Folklore*, Allahabad

Gairola, T.D., 1943, Early History of Garhwal Rajas (AD 634-1325), *U.U.P.H.S.*, XVI, pt I, p72-82

Getty, A., 1936, *Ganesa*, Oxford

Ghurye, G.S., 1953, *Indian Sadhus*, Bombay

Gill, A.R., 1952, *Valley of the Doon*, Dehradun

Goetz, H., 1945-46, The Role of Gujarat in Indian Art History, *B.B.M.*, III, p1-10

Goetz, H., 1951, The Chronology of the Chand Dynasty and the Mediaeval Monuments, *J.I.H.*, XXIX, p33-52

Goetz, H., 1955, *The Early Wooden Temples of Chamba*, Leiden

Goetz, H., 1961, The Art of Chamba in the Islamic Period, *J.O.I.*, XI, pt II, p135-144

Goetz, H., 1962, The Art of Chamba in the Islamic Period, *J.O.I.* XI, pt III, p217-236

Gokhale, S., 1960, *Studies in the Historical and Cultural Geography and Ethnography of Madhya Pradesh*, Poona University, Pune, Phd Thesis

Gordon, n.d., *The Khasis*

Grierson, G.A., 1927, *Linguistic Survey of India*, Calcutta, vol 1, vol 3, vol 9, part I

Gupte, Y.R., 1915-16, Two Talesvar Copper Plate Grants, *E.I.*, XIII, p109-121

Gyani, R.G., 1950-51, Identification of the So-called Surya and Indra Figures in Cave no 20 of the Bhaja Group, *B.P.W.M.*, 1, p19-21

Hamilton, 1812-28, *East India Gazetteer*

Hamilton, Frances (Buchanan), 1819, *An Account of the Kingdom of Nepal, and the Territories Annexed to This Dominion by the House of Gorkhas*, Edinburgh

Hari Datt, 1953, Gurukula Museum Hardwar, *J.I.M.*, XXII, p109-121

Havel, E.B., 1908, *Indian Sculpture and Painting*, London

Henwood, W.J., n.d., Notice of the Rock Basons Deo (Devi) Dhoora near Almora in Upper India, *E.N.J.P., N.I.*, IV, p204-206

Hodgson, 1870, *The Language, Literature and Religion of Nepal and Tibet*, London

Hultzsch, E., 1925, Inscriptions of Asoka, *C.I.I.*, 1, Calcutta

Hunter, W.W., 1893, *The Marquess of Hastings*, Oxford

Jackson, M.G., 1983, A *Strategy for Improving the Productivity of Livestock in the Hills of Uttar Pradesh : Proceedings of the Seminar on Environmental Regeneration in the Himalays*, Concept and Strategies (CHEA), Nainital

Johar, Srinder Singh, 1967, *Guru Gobind Singh : A Biography*, Jullundur

Joshi, B.M., 1987, Infrastructure and Regional Imbalances in UP: An Inter-District Analysis, *Indian Journal of Regional Science* 19(2)

Joshi, Dharna Nand, n.d. *Notes on the Garhwal District*

Joshi, Laxmi Datt, 1929, *Khasa Family Law*

Joshi, Lokmani, n.d., *Almora*

Joshi, Lokmani, n.d., *Report on the Industrial Survey of the Nainital District*

Joshi, P., ed, 1988, *Uttrakhand*, Himalaya Publishing House, Bombay, vol 2, p145-157

Joshi, S.D., 1929, *Report on Preliminary Agricultural Survey of the Almora District*, Government Press, Lucknow

Kala, S.C., 1935, Further Light on the Territory of the Kunindas *J.U.P.H.S.*, VIII, pt I, p36-37

Kala, S.C., 1953, Some Interesting Coins of the Yaudheyas, *J.N.S.I.*, XVIII, pt I, p46-48

Kane, P.V., 1938, Naming a Child or Person, *I.H.Q.*, XIV, p224-244

Kane, P.V., 1946, *History of Dharmasastra*, Bhandarkar Oriental Research Institute, Poona, vol 3

Keith and Macdonell, 1912, *Vedic Index*, John Murry, London

Kelkar, D.G., 1962, *Lamps of India*, Delhi

Khan, Shah Nawaz, 1946, *My Memoirs of I.N.A. and Its Netaji*, Delhi

Khanka, S.S., n.d., *Industrial Development of Kumaun Division in Uttar Pradesh : Problems and Prospects*, New Delhi, ICSSR Research Project

Khanka, S.S., 1990, Lopsided Industrialisation of Kumaun Division : A Study, *Yojana* 34(8) May 1-15

Khanka, S.S. and Best, N.S., 1977-78, Opportunity Conditions Influencing Entrepreneurship in the Kumaun Hills (Uttar Pradesh), *P.U. Management Review*, 10-11

Khosla, Prem Nath, 1941, *Working Plan for the Tehri Forest Division, 1939-40 to 1969-70*, Tehri Garhwal State

Kielhorn, F., 1896, Pandukesvar Plate of Lalitasura Deva, *I.A.*, XXV, p177-84

Kielhorn, F., 1902-3, Inscriptions of Southern India, *E.I.*, VII, p1-170

Kirkpatrick, n.d., *The Account of Kingdom of Nepal*, London

Kramrisch, Stella, 1933, *Indian Sculpture*, Calcutta

Kramrisch, Stella, 1946, *The Hindu Temple*, Calcutta, 2 vols

Kramrisch, Stella, 1946, The Image of Mahadeva in the Cave-Temple of Elephanta Island, *A.I.*, 2, p4-8

Krishna Deva, 1959, The Temples of Khajuraho in Central India, *A.I.*, 15, p43-65

Krishnan, M.B., 1960, *Geology of India and Burma*, Madras

Longhurst, A.H., 1936, *The Story of Stupa*, Colombo

Maclagan, Edward, 1932, *The Jesuits and the Great Mogul*, London

Majumdar, D.N., 1958, *Races and Cultures of India*, Bombay

Majumdar, R.C., 1960, *The Classical Accounts of India*, Calcutta

Majumdar, R.C. and Pusalkar, A.D., eds, 1953, *The History and Culture of the Indian Prople*, vol 2: *The Age of Imperial Unity*, 2nd edn, Bombay

Mc Crindle, n.d., *Ancient India*

Mehta, N.C., 1926, *Studies in Indian Painting*, Bombay

Misra, N.N., 1935, Ancient Historical Monuments of Baijnath and Dwarahat, *J.U.P.H.S.*, VIII, p71-82

Misra, N.N., 1936, A Note on the Dhikuli and Ujhin Ruins, *J.U.P.H.S.*, IX, pt II, p45-48

Mitter, R.L. n.d., *The Tribes and Castes in the N.W.P.*

Mohan, I, ed, 1989, *Environmental Issues and Programmes*, Ashish Pub House, New Delhi, vol 2, p87-93

Moorcraft, William and Trebeck, 1837, *Travels in the Himalayan Provinces of Hindustan and Punjab*, London, reprint, 1971, New Delhi

Moreland, W.H., 1911, *The Revenue Administration of the N.W. Provinces*, Allahabad

Moti Chandra, 1945, *Geographical and Economic Studies in Aupayanaparva of Mahabharata*, Bombay

Mukandi Lal, 1968, *Garhwal Painting*, Delhi, 1968

Mulay, S., 1959, *Studies in the Hisotrical and Cultural Geography and Ethnography of Deccan*, Poona University, Pune, Phd Thesis

Munshi, K.M., 1955, *The Glory That Was Gujjar Desh*, Bombay, pt 1

Murphy, C.W., n.d., *Nainital and Kumaun*

Nagar, M.M., 1945, A Visnu Image from Aligarh, *J.U.P.H.S.*, XVIII, p98-100

Naik, A.V., 1947 *Archaeology of the Deccan*, Poona University, Pune Phd Thesis

Narain, A.K., 1957, *The Indo-Greeks*, Oxford

Narvane, V.S., 1959, Ancient Monuments of Kumaon, *I.W.*, August, p28-29

Nautiyal, G.P., 1962, *Call of Badrinath*, 4th edn, Badrinath

Nautiyal, J.C. and Babor, P.S., 1985, Forestry in the Himalaya, *Interdisciplinacy Science Review*, 10, p27

Nautiyal, K.P., 1961, The Numismatic History of Kumaon, *J.N.S.I.*, XXIII, p375-386

Nautiyal, K.P., 1962, An Iconographical Survey of Kumaon with Special

Reference to a Few Unique Images, *East and West*, (Rome) New Series 15(3-4) September-December 1965
Nautiyal, K.P., 1962, An Interesting Visnu Image from Baijnath (Almora), *B.D.C.R.I.*, XXII, p170-174
Nautiyal, K.P., 1962, Three Kushana Gold Coins from Kashipur, *J.N.S.I.* XXIV, pts I & II, p 181-182
Nautiyal, K.P., 1962, Two Lakulisa Representations from Kumaon, *J.O.I.*, XIII, no 1, p54-58
Nautiyal, Kanti Prasad, 1969, *The Archaeology of Kumaon*, Chowkhamba Sanskrit Series Office, Varanasi
Negi, Jodh Singh, n.d., *Himalayan Travels*
Neoille, 1904, *Nainital Gazetteer*
Nestfield, n.d., *Castes and Tribes in U.P.*
Newell, D.J.F. 1882, *The Highlands of India*, London, 2 vols
Oakely, E.S., n.d., *Holy Himalaya*
Oakley, E.S., 1917, The Folklore of Kumaon with Reference to Folklore in General, *J.U.P.H.S.*, I, pt I, p34-59
Painuli, P.N., n.d., *A Tourist's View of the Valley of Gods*, Tehri
Pande, B.D., 1993, *History of Kumaon*, tr in English by C.M. Agrawal, Shri Almora Book Dept, Almora, 2 vols
Pandey, R.B., 1952, *Indian Palaeography*, Banaras, pt I
Panigrahi, K.C., 1960, Sculptural Representations of Lakulisa and Other Pasupata Teachers, *J.I.H.*, XXXVIII, pt III, p635-43
Panigrahi, K.C., 1961, *Archaeological Remains at Bhubanesvara*, Calcutta
Panna Lal, 1931, *Kumaon Local Customs*, Allahabad
Pant, D., n.d., *Commercial Policy of Mogals*
Pant, Govind Ballabh, n.d., *The Forest Problem in Kumaon*
Pant, K.P., 1948, *Working Plan for the Tons Forest Division, 1945-46 to 1964-65*, Tehri Garhwal State
Pant, M.C., et al, 1983, Fish Productivity in Lake Nainital, *Current Science* 52(17), p828-829
Pargitar, F.E., 1922, *Ancient Indian Historical Tradition*, London
Pati Ram Rai, 1992, *Garhwal: Ancient and Modern*, Vintage Books, first printed, 1916, Pati Ram Parmar, Shimla
Parmar, Pati Ram, 1916, *Garhwal: Ancient and Modern*, Simla
Pearse, Hugh, 1905, *Five Generations of an Anglo Indian Family*, London
Pillai, L.D.S., 1922, *Indian Ephemeries*, Madras, vol 1
Powell, Price, 1930, Some Notes on the Early History of Kumaon, *J.U.P.H.S.*, IV, pt II, p5-14

Powell, Price, 1945, Kunindas and Katyuras, *J. U.P.H.S.*, XVIII, p214-18

Powell, Price, 1955, *A History of India*, New York

Prater, S.H., 1965, *The Book of Indian Animals*, Bombay

Prayag Dayal, 1937, A New Hoard of Yaudheya Coins from Dehra Dun, *J.N.S.I.*, II, p109-112

Rajashekhara, 1934, *Kavyamimamsa*, ed by C.D. Dalal, Baroda

Ram Gopal, 1964, *India-China-Tibet Triangle*, Lucknow

Ram Rahul, 1970, *The Himalayan Borderland*, Delhi

Ramakant, 1978, *Indo Napalese Relations (1816-1877)*, Delhi

Ramchandran, T.N., 1953, Asvamedha Site near Kalsi, *J.O.R.M.*, XXXI, pts I-IV, p1-31

Rao Gopinath, T.A., 1914-16, *Elements of Hundu Iconography*, Madras, vol I, pts I and II, 1914; vol II, pts I and II, 1916

Rapson, E.J, 1899, *Indian Coins*, Oxford

Rapson, E.J., ed, 1955, *Cambridge History of India*, Delhi, vol I, reprint

Raturi, Padma Dutt, 1938, *Working Plan for the Uttarkashi Forest Division*, Tehri Garhwal State

Rawat, A.S., n.d., *History of Garwal 1358-1947*, Indus Publishing Company, New Delhi

Rawat, Ajay Singh, 1983, *Garhwal Himalayas : A Historical Survey*, Delhi

Regmi, D.R., 1960, *Ancient Nepal*, Calcutta

Rice, L., 1882, *Appendix to the Report of Indian Education Commission of* 1882

Rizvi, Saiyid Ali Akhtar, 1979, *Chamoli District Gazetteer*, Government of India Press, Lucknow

Rowland, B., 1953, *The Art and Architecture of India : Buddhist, Hindu and Jaina*, London

Saklani, Indra Dutt, 1940, *Tehri Garhwal Raiya Forest Manual*, Tehri Garhwal State

Saletore, R.N., 1943, *Life in the Gupta Age*, Bombay

Salim Ali, 1964, *The Book of Indian Birds*, Bombay

Sankalia, H.D., 1939, Rare Figures of Visnu from Gujarat, *J.U.B.*, VII, pt IV, p3-7

Sankalia, H.D., 1939, Six Different Types of Ganesa Figures, *J.I.H.*, XVIII, pt II, p188-194

Sankalia, H.D., 1941, *The Archaeology of Gujarat (including Kathiawar)*, Bombay

Sankalia, H.D., 1944, *Studies in the Historical and Cultural Geography and Ethnography of Gujarat*, Deccan College Monograph Series,

Puna

Sanwal, B.D., 1965, *Nepal and the East India Company*, Bombay

Sarkar, Jadunath, n.d., *Aurangzeb*, 5 vols

Schrader, F. Otto, 1916, *Introduction to Pancaratras*, Madras

Semple, E.C., 1947, *Influences of Geographic Environment*, New York

Sen Gupta, R., 1962, The Panels of Kalyanasundarmurti at Ellora, *Lalit Kula*, 7, p7-12

Sewak, 1963, *Fascinating Uttarakhand*, Information Department, Government of Uttar Pradesh, Lucknow

Shafer, Robert, 1954, *Ethnography of Ancient India*

Shah, Priyabala, 1958, *Visnudharmottara Purann*, Gaikwad Oriental Series, CXXX, III, Baroda

Shah, U.P., 1953, Gupta Sculpture from Idar State Gujarat, *J.I.M.*, IX, p 90-103

Shah, U.P., 1955, *Studies in Jaina Art*, Bombay

Sharma, R.C., 1990, Hill Area Development, *Employment News* December, 1-7

Sherring, Charles A., n.d. *Western Tibet and Kumaon Boundary*

Sherring, Charles A., 1906, *Western Tibet and the British Borderland*, London

Shukla, D.N., 1958, *Vastu Sastra*, Lucknow, vol 2

Singh, J.S., et al, eds, 1980, *Science and Rural Development in Mountains*, Gyanodaya Prakashan, Nainital, p437-448

Singh, O.P., ed, 1983, *The Himalaya: Nature, Man and Culture*, New Delhi

Sircar, D. C., 1951, Some Ancient Kings of Kumaon and Garhwal, *B. V.*, XII, p149-152

Sircar, D.C., 1955-56, Three Plates from Pandukesvar, *E.I.*, XXXI, p277-298

Sircar, D.C., 1960, *Studies in the Grography of Ancient and Mediaeval India*, Banaras

Sircar, D.C., 1962, Some Inscriptions from U.P., *E.I.*, XXXIV, pt V, p 243-254

Sirkar, D.C., 1973, *The Saka Pithas*, Delhi

Sirkar, D.C., 1983, *Select Inscriptions*, Delhi, vol 2

Sivaramamurti, C., 1950, Geographical and Chronological Factors in Indian Iconography, *A.I.*, 6, p21-63

Sivaramamurti, C., 1961, *Indian Sculpture*, New Delhi

Smith, n.d., *Ancient History*

Smith, George, n.d., *Twelve Indian Statesmen*

Srivastava, K.P., ed, 1974, *Mughal Farmans 1540-1706* AD, Lucknow,

vol 1
Srivastava, Madhuri, ed, 1971, *Gazetteer of India: Uttar Pradesh : Tehri Garhwal*, Lucknow
Srivastava, S.S. and Yadav, R.A., 1986, *Management and Monitoring of Industrial Sickness*, Concept Publishing Company, New Delhi
Sten, Konow, 1917, The Ara Inscription of Kanishka II in the Year 41, *E.I.*, XIV, p130-143
Stowell, V.A., 1907, *A Manual of the Land Tenures of Kumaon Division*, Allahabad, 1907
Tendulkar, D.G., 1967, *Abdul Gaffar Khan*, Gandhi Peace Foundation, New Delhi
Tewari, D.D., n.d., *Historical and Political Notes on Kumaon*
Thapar, Romila, 1961, *Asoka and the Decline of the Mauryas*, Oxford
Tod, James, 1899, *Annals and Antiquities of Rajasthan*, Yorkplace, Portsman Square, vol 2
Toye, Hughe, 1959, *The Springing Tiger*, London
Tripathi, R.S., 1937, *History of Kanauj*, Banaras
Tucci, G., 1956 *Preliminary Report on Two Scientific Expeditions in Nepal*, Roma
Upreti, Ganga Datt, n.d., *Martial Castes of Almora District*
Upreti, Ganga Datt, n.d., *Proverbs and Folklore of Kumaon and Garhwal*
Valdiya, K.S., 1980, *Geology of the Kumaon Lasser Himalaya*, Wadia Insitute of Himalayan Geology, Dehradun
Valdiya, K.S., ed, 1988, *Kumaon: Land and People*, Gyanodaya Prakashan, Nainital
Varem, Dangli Prasad, 1979, *Dehradun District Gazetteer*, Government of India Press, Lucknow
Vats, M.S., 1926-27, Mediaeval Saiva Sculptures from Jagatsukh and Jagesvar, *A.S.I., A.R.*, p234-36
Vats, M.S., 1950-52, Sculptures in the Main Temple at Baijnath, *P.I.H.C.*, XII, p100-106
Vats, M.S., 1952, Gupta Temple at Deogarh, *A.S.I. Mem.*, 70
Vats, M.S. and Agrawala, V.S., n.d., A Note on the Sculptures from Lakhamandal, *J.U.P.H.S.*, XVII, pt I, p87-89
Vogel, J. Ph., 1926, *Indian Serpent Lore*, London
Vogel, J.Ph., 1927, *Antiquities of the Chamba State*, Calcutta
Waddell, L.A, 1939, *The Buddhism of Tibet*, Cambridge
Wadia, D.N., 1944, *Geology of India*, London
Walton, H.G., 1911, *Almora Gazetteer*
Walton, H.G., ed, 1910, *British Garhwal : A Gazetteer*, Allahabad,

District Gazetteers of the United Provinces of Agra and Oudh, vol 36

Watters, Thomas, 1961, *On Yuan Chwangs Travels in India*, Ist Indian edn, New Delhi

Whalley, P., 1921, Place Names in United Provinces of Agra and Oudh, *J.U.P.H.S.*, II, p1-58

Whalley, P., 1923, Place Names in United Provinces of Agra and Oudh, *J.U.P.H.S.*, III, pt I, p47-48

Whalley, P., 1928, Place Names in the United Provinces of Agra and Oudh, *J.U.P.H.S.*, IV, pt I, p91-129

Wheeler, Mortimer, 1959, *Early India and Pakistan*, London

Whitehead, R.B., 1914, *Catalogue of Coins in the Panjab Museum*, Clarendon Press, Lahore

Williams, G.R.C., 1961, *Historical and Statistical Memoirs of Dehradun*, Roorkee

Wilson, H.H., 1864-66, *Visnu Purana*, London

Woodyatt, Nigel G., 1929, *The Regimental History of the 3rd Queen Alexandra's Own Gurkhas Rifles (1815-1927)*, London

Wright, Daniel, 1877, *History of Nepal*, Cambridge

Young-Husband, Francis Edward, 1977, *Wonders of the Himalayas*, Indian reprint, Chandigarh, 1st edn, 1924, London

Zoya, Hasan, 1989, *The State, Polilical Process and Indentity*, Sage

*Some Primary Sources**

1. Inscription of Raja Sahaj Pal of the Year AD 1548 on the Stone Door of the Temple of Kshetra Pal at Deoprayag
2. Inscription of the Year AD 1561 of Raja Sahaj Pal on a Bell in the Temple of Raghunath ji at Deoprayag. (The bell is supposed to be dedicated to the temple by Sahaj Pal.)
3. Inscription of Raja Man Shah on the Door of the Temple of Kshetra Pal at Deoprayag, Dated AD 1608
4. Inscription of Man Shah in the Temple of Raghunath ji at Deoprayag of the Year AD 1610
5. Cooper Plate Inscription of the Year AD 1640 Issued by Maharani Karnavati on behalf of Her Son Maharaja Prithvi Pat Shah
6. Inscription of Maharaja Prithvi Pat Shah in the Monastery of Madho Dass in Laxmi Narayan Temple of the Year AD 1642 at the Village Bhaktiana Which is Adjacent to Srinagar. (The inscription is in the outer portion of the main temple wall.)

* Source : *History of Garhwal*

7. Farman of Aurangzeb of the Year AD 1662 Sent to the Raja of Garhwal
8. Inscription of Maharaja Prithvi Pat Shah on the Southern Door of the Temple of Raghunath ji in Deoprayag, Dated AD 1664
9. Inscription on the Western Doorway of the Temple of Raghunath ji in Deoprayag of the Year AD 1664
10. Farman of Aurangzeb of the Year AD 1665 Sent to the Raja of Garhwal
11. Copper Plate Inscription of the Year AD 1667 of Maharaja Fateh Shah Which Bears the Seal of Maharaja Prithvi Pat Shah
12. Copper Plate Inscription of the Year AD 1700 of Raja Fateh Shah
13. Copper Plate Inscription of the Year AD 1706 of Raja Fateh Shah
14. Copper Plate Inscription of the Year AD 1716 of Raja Fateh Shah
15. Copper Plate Inscription of the Year AD 1716 of Raja Pradip Shah
16. Two Coins of Raja Pradip Shah Which Are Available in the State Museum, Lucknow
17. Two Coins of the Reign of Raja Lalit Shah Which Are Available in the State Museum, Lucknow
18. Copper Plate Inscription of the Year AD 1788 of Raja Pradyumna Shah
19. Inscription on a Stone Slate Affixed to the Wall of the Temple of Parshuram at Uttarkashi Which Bears the Names of the Kings from Pradip Shah to Sudarshan Shah
20. Inscription in the Temple of Vishwanath at Uttarkashi in Which the List of the Kings from Pradip Shah to Sudarshan Shah Has been Given

Original Manuscripts

1. Sanwari Granth of the Reign of Raja Ajay Pal. (It is a *tantrik* Manuscript.)
2. Sanwari Granth of the Period of Maharani Karnawati. (It is a *Tantrik* Manuscript.)
3. Fateh Shah Karna Granth by Jatadhar
4. Fateh Prakash by Ratan Kavi
5. Vrit Kaumudi by Mati Ram
6. Sabha Sar by Raja Sudarhan Shah
7. Garh Rajya Vansha Kavya by Mola Ram

National Archives, New Delhi

1. Foreign Department, Political, Box No. 57, Sunud, Dated December 10, 1824
2. Foreign Department, File No. 86, Political Proceedings, 16-30, August 1833
3. Foreign Department, Political Proceedings, 19-27, September 1833, Letters Nos. 7 and 8
4. Foreign Department, Political 1848, File No. 62, Letter No. 611
5. Foreign Department, Political 1848, File No. 63, Letter No. 612
6. Home Depertment, Political, File No. 393/30
7. Tehri Garhwal State Records, File No. 220/1905
8. Tehri Garhwal State Records, File No. 42/1907
9. Tehri Garhwal State Records, File No. 281/1913
10. Tehri Garhwal State Records (Political Agent for Tehri State, File No. G-30-8/Tehri
11. Tehri Garhwal State Records, File No. 55/1923
12. Tehri Garhwal State Records, Extracts from the Fortnightly D.O's of Commissioner Kumaon, Letter Dated 1st December 1923
13. Tehri Garhwal State Records, Copy of the Confidential Note on Annual Administration for 1922-23, Letter Dated 15th July/1923/ Tehri
14. Home Department, 1930, Political, File No. 174
15. Home Department, 1930, Political, File No. 174, Letter No. 57915/28/G
16. Tehri Garhwal State Records, File No. 247/1930
17. Tehri Garhwal State Records (Political Agent for Tehri), Letter No. 6/125-IV A
18. G.B. Pant Papers, File No. 4/2, Letter Dated 11th July/1934
19. G.B. Pant Papers, File No. 4/3, Item No. 22, Letter Dated 17th July/1945

State Archives U.P., Lucknow

1. Settlement Letters Issued, Vol. I, 1837-39, Letter No. 8
2. Settlement Letters Issued, Vol. II, 1839-42, Letter No. 56
3. Report on the Administration of N.W. Provinces for the Year 1875-76, Allahabad, 1878
4. Pauw, E.K., *Report on the Tenth Settlement of the Garhwal District*, Allahabad, 1896
5. Burh, R., *Census of India, 1901*, Vol XVI, Part I: *N.W.P. and*

Oudh, Allahabad, 1902

6. Report of the Working of the Garhwal Central Scarcity Committee, from April 30, 1918 to February 28, 1920, Dehradun, 1920
7. Brahmawar, R.N., *Working Plan for the Garhwal Forest Division, 1930-31 to 1939-40*, Allahabad, 1932

Garhwal State Records: Dynastic Collection, Thakur Shoor Beer Singh, Purana Durbar, Tehri

1. Annual Administrative Report of Tehri Garhwal State for the Year 1907-1908, Dated May 26, 1908, Tehri
2. Annual Administrative Report of Tehri Garhwal State for the Year 1909-10, Dated May 26, 1910, Tehri
3. Sir Kirti Shah Ka Sankshipt Jeewan Charit, Dehradun, 1913
4. Annual Administrative Report of Tehri Garhwal State for the Year 1918-19, Dated May 26, 1919, Tehri
5. Narendra Hindu Law, Tehri Garhwal State, 1919
6. Doval, Ram Prasad, Revenue Settlement Report, Tehri Garhwal State, Babat, 1924
7. Niyam Prabhu Seva va Coolie Utar, Tehri Garhwal State, 1930
8. Prant Panchayat Vidhan, Tehri Garhwal State, 1930
9. Niyam Vasooli Bura, Tehri Garhwal State, 1930
10. Tehri Garhwal Rajya, Nagar tatha Pur Panchayat Vidhan, Tehri Garhwal State, 1932
11. The Tehri Garhwal State Naturalization Act No. 1, of Samvat, 1992, State Press, Narendra Nagar
12. Tehri Garhwal Rajya ka Dund Sanghra, Tehri Garhwal State, 1937
13. Tehri Garhwal Rajya, Prant Panchayat Manual, Dehradun, 1938
14. Tehri Garhwal Rajya ka Kusht Vidhan Bill, Samvat 1996. Dehra Times Press, Dehradun
15. Niyam Babat Marne Machli va Shikar, Tehri Garhwal State, 1940
16. Tehri Garhwal Rajya ke Bhumi Sambandhi Adhikar Niyam tatha Vidhan, Dehradun, 1941
17. Parganna Pratap Nagar, Jila Tehri Garhwal ki Assessment Report, Lucknow, 1965
18. Letter No. 560/C, Dated 23rd May, 1927 and Endorsement No. 1839/50/26-27, Dated 13th June 1927, from Tehri Garhwal State to Dhar State
19. Report of the History Officer of Dhar State Contained in letter No. 17, Dated 22nd July 1927 and D.O. No. 1004, Dated 10th December, 1927 from Dhar Durbar to Tehri Garhwal State

Journals and Proceedings Scanned

Hindustan Times, June 21, 1992; September 11, 1992; July 23, 1992
Journal of the U.P. Historical Society, XVI, part I, July, 1943
Proceedings of the Indian Historical Records Commission, (Mysore Session, vol 31, 1995)
Yojana (Publications Division, Government of India), March 16, 1988

Abbreviations of Journals and Composit Books used in the Bibliography

A.I.	Ancient India
A.S.I., A.R.	Archaeological Survey of India Annual Reports
A.S.I. Mem.	Archaeological Survey of India Memoirs
A.P.R., N.C.	Annual Progress Report Northern Circle
B.B.M.	Bulletin of Baroda Museum
B.V.	Bharatiya Vidya
B.D.C.R.I.	Bulletin of Deccan College Post Graduate and Research Institute
B.P.W.M.	Bulletin of Prince of Wales Museum
C.I.I.	Corpus Inscriptionum Indicarum
E.I.	Epigraphia Indica
E.N.P.J.N.S.	Edinborough New Philosophical Jurnal, New Series
I.A.	Indian Antiquary
I.G.I.	Imperial Gazetteer of India
I.H.Q.	Imperial Historical Quarterly
I.W.	Illustrated Weekly of India
I.A.R.	Indian Archaeology : A Review
J.U.P.H.S.	Journal of U.P. Historical Society
J.O.I.	Journal of Oriental Institute, Baroda
J.O.R.M.	Journal of Oriental Research, Madras
J.I.M.	Journal of Indian Museum
J.I.S.O.A.	Journal of Indian Society of Oriental Art
J.B.B.R.A.S.	Journal of Bombay Branch of Roayl Asiatic Society
J.A.S.B.	Journal of Asiatic Society of Bengal
J.N.S.I.	Journal of the Numismatic Society of India
J.R.A.S.	Journal of Royal Asiatic Society
J.M.I.P.	Journal of Madhya Pradesh Itihas Parishad
J.U.B.	Journal of University of Bombay
P.I.H.C.	Proceedings of Indian History Congress
S.B.E.	Sacred Book of the East

fied under 1500 Descriptors 1886-1990
S.P. Agrawal and **Rajeev Kumar Sharma** Rs. 600

CICIL-34 Communication Informatics and Librarianship in India : An Introductory Guide to Publications Based on a Survey of Libraries in Capital City of India
S.P. Agrawal and **Pushpa Rani Sharma** Rs. 720

CICIL-35 Problems of Collection Development in Special Libraries
M.S. Sridhar Rs. 225

CICIL-36 National Information Resources for Social Sciences in India : Mobilisation, Dispersal and International Enhancement
S.P. Agrawal Rs. 225

CICIL-37 Modern History of Punjab : A Look Back into Ancient Peaceful Punjab Focusing Confrontation and Failures Leadingto Present Punjab Problem, and a Peep Ahead : Relevant Select Documents
J.C. Aggarwal and **S.P. Agrawal** Rs. 400

CICIL-38 India Information Sources : Economics and Business
Kyllikki Ruokonen and Manohar Lal Rs.

CICIL-39 Educational Planning in India : With a Slant to Educational Financing and Administration, Vol. 1, Reports of Committees and Commissions, Five Year Plans, Statistical Tables
J.C. Aggarwal and **S.P. Agrawal** Rs. 650

CICIL-40 Integrated Library System : Two Case Studies : Latin America and India
Maria Luiza Rigo Pasquarelli, Rosaly Favero Krzyanowski, Ines Maria M. Imperatriz and **S.P. Agrawal** Rs. 160

CICIL-41 Social Science Information in India: Effort towards Bibliographical Control
S.D. Vyas Rs. 300

CICIL-42 Higher Education in India Since Independence: U.G.C. and Its Approach
O.P. Gupta Rs. 360

CICIL-43 Government and Politics in India: A Bibliographical Study of Contemporary Scenario Chronicling Rajiv Gandhi Era
S.P. Agrawal and **Rajeev Kumar Sharma** Rs. 500

CICIL-44 Second Handbook of Psychological and Social Instruments
D.M. Pestonjee Rs. 300

CICIL-45 Development/Digression Diary of India; 3D Companion Volume to Information India: 1990-91
S.P. Agrawal Rs. 200

CICIL-46 Development/Digression Diary of India; 3D Companion Volume to Information India: 1991-92
S.P. Agrawal Rs. 300

CICIL-47 Information India 1991-92: Global View
S.P. Agrawal and **J.C. Aggarwal** Rs. 500

CICIL-48 Committees and Commissions in India 1974, A Concept's Project, Compiled by a team of professionals guided by Virender

Kumar (Vol. 12) Rs. 450

CICIL-49 Committees and Commissions in India 1975, A Concept's Project, Compiledby a team of professionals guided by Virender Kumar (Vol. 13) Rs. 450

CICIL-50 Committees and Commissions in India 1976, A Concept's Project, Compiled by a team of professionals guided Virender Kumar (Vol. 14) Rs. 450

CICIL-51 Committees and Commissions in India 1977, A Concept's Project, Compiledby a team of professionals guided by Virender Kumar (Vol. 15) (in four parts) Rs. 450 each

CICIL-52 Committees and Commissions in India 1978, A Concept's Project, Compiledby a team of professionals guided by Virender Kumar (Vol. 16) (in two parts) Rs. 450 each

CICIL-53 Subject Guide to Communication, Informatics and Librarianship in India (Based on a Survey of Library Holdings in Capital City of India)
S.P. Agrawal and **Pushpa Rani Sharma** Rs. 400

CICIL-54 Restructurring of Library and Information Science Curriculum
A. Tejomurty Rs. 250

CICIL-55 Committees and Commissions in India 1979, A Concept's Project, Compiledby a team of professionals guided by Virender Kumar (Vol. 17) (in two parts) Rs. 450 each

CICIL-56 Committees and Commissions in India 1980, A Concept's Project, Compiledby a team of professionals guided by Virender Kumar (Vol. 18) (in two parts) Rs. 450 each

CICIL-57 Third Historical Survey of Educational Development in India
S.P. Agrawal and **J.C. Aggarwal** Rs. 700

CICIL-58 Model Library Legislation
Velaga Venkatappaiah Rs. 400

CICIL-59 Indian Library and Information Science Literature (1990-91)
Sewa Singh Rs. 525

CICIL-60 Librarianship and Library Science in India
Mohamed Taher and **Donald Gordon Davis, Jr.** Rs. 350

CICIL-61 Comprehensive Glossary for Library & Information Science by
O.P. Gupta Rs.300

CICIL-62 Information India 1992-93:
S.P. Agrawal and **J. C. Aggarwal** Rs. 500

CICIL-63 Automation of Libraries and Information Science
R.K. Shukla Rs. 250

CICIL-64 Modern History of Jammu and Kashmir
J.C. Aggarwal and **S.P. Agrawal** Rs. 1500 (per set of 2 vols.)

CICIL-65 Library and Information Science: Emerging Trends:
Sister M. Esperanza, A. C. Rs. 250

CICIL-66 Mental Retardation in India (A Bibliography)
S. Venkatesan and **V.G.D. Vepuri** Rs. 275

CICIL-67 Information Management in Health Science Libraries in India
R.P. Dixit (*Foreword* **Dr. Uton Muchtar Rafei**) Rs. 550

CICIL-68 Information Behaviour of Scientists and Engineers:
M.S. Sridhar Rs. 500